THE BIBLICAL
FOUNDATIONS
FOR MISSION

THE BIBLICAL
FOUNDATIONS
FOR MISSION

Donald Senior, C.P.
Carroll Stuhlmueller, C.P.

ORBIS BOOKS
Maryknoll, New York 10545

Sixth Printing, November 1995

The Catholic Foreign Mission Society of America (Maryknoll) recruits and trains people for overseas missionary service. Through Orbis Books Maryknoll aims to foster the international dialogue that is essential to mission. The books published, however, reflect the opinions of their authors and are not meant to represent the official position of the society.

Copyright © 1983 by Carroll Stuhlmueller, C.P., and Donald Senior, C.P.

Published by Orbis Books, Maryknoll, NY 10545

Manufactured in the United States of America
All rights reserved

Manuscript editor: Lisa McGaw

Library of Congress Cataloging in Publication Data

Senior, Donald.
  The Biblical foundations for mission.

  Includes bibliographical references and index.
  1. Missions—Biblical teaching. 2. Bible—
Criticism, interpretation, etc. I. Stuhlmueller,
Carroll. II. Title.
BV2073.S45 1983   266'.001   82-22430
ISBN 0-88344-046-6
ISBN 0-88344-047-4 (pbk.)

Table of Contents

Foreword   *xi*

Introduction   *1*

PART I
THE FOUNDATIONS FOR MISSION IN THE OLD TESTAMENT
Carroll Stuhlmueller, C.P.

1 From Secular Liberation to Salvation History and World Mission   *9*

A Theology of Election and Signals of Universalism   9
From the Secular to the Sacred   11
Secular Origins and Religious Motivation   13
Historical Moments for Israel—Symbols for World
     Mission   15
   The Patriarchal Age (1850–1550 B.C.E.)   16
   The Mosaic Period (1240–1200 B.C.E.)   18
   The Initial Stages of the Covenant Religion
     (1200–921 B.C.E.)   21
   The Disintegration of Politics and the Prophetic Challenge
     (921–585 B.C.E.)   23
   Exile and a Call to Re-creation (587–539 B.C.E.)   26
   Reconstruction and Apocalyptic Expectations
     (539–7 B.C.E.)   28
Conclusion   31

2 The Biblical Process of Acculturation   *36*

God as Savior and as Creator   36
Struggle—Indigenization—Challenge   38
Violence or Struggle in the Old Testament   40
Indigenization   44
Conclusion   50

3 Humanization Prophetically Challenged   *55*

Prophecy: Its Origin and Characteristics   56
Prophetic Challenge to Culture   63

v

Prophetic Challenge to Politics   69
    The Political Circle   69
    Religious and Social Abuses   72
    An Insight of Faith   75
Conclusion   79

4   Israel's Election and World Salvation   *83*

Election: Its Basis and Its Dangers   83
Israel's Reactions toward the Nations   89
    In the Patriarchal Era   89
    In Egyptian Bondage   90
    Foreign Influences   90
    After the Exile   92
    Israel and the Gentile World   93
The Development of Israel's Sense of Election   94
From Election toward Universal Salvation   98
Conclusion   105

5   Israel's Prayer and Universal Mission   *110*

Hymns of Praise   111
    Spontaneous and Persistent Praise   112
    Psalm 29   114
    Psalm 95   118
    Psalm 46   122
Prayers of Supplication   124
Conclusion   134

PART II
THE FOUNDATIONS FOR MISSION IN THE NEW TESTAMENT
Donald Senior, C.P.

6   Jesus and the Church's Mission   *141*

Jesus and the Gentiles   142
Jesus and the Kingdom of God: Starting Point and Context for
    Mission   144
Jesus' ''Definition'' of the Kingdom   145
    Jesus' Extraordinary Piety   146
    Jesus' Ministry of Compassion to Peripheral
      People   147
    Jesus' Interpretation of Law   148

Jesus' Teaching on Reconciliation and Forgiveness   *148*
Jesus' Ministry of Healings and Exorcisms   *149*
The Universal Implications of Jesus' Kingdom Ministry   151
  An Expansive Image of God   *151*
  An Inclusive View of God's People   *152*
  A Positive View of Human Destiny   *155*
Conclusion: The Mission of Jesus and the Mission of the
    Church   157

7 The Mission Theology of Paul   *161*

Posing the Questions   161
The Sources   162
Influences on Paul   163
  Judaism   *163*
  Early Christian Tradition   *164*
  Hellenism   *164*
The Starting Point: Paul's Conversion   165
  Galatians 1:11–17   *165*
  1 Corinthians 15:8–11   *166*
  1 Corinthians 9:1–2   *166*
The Theological Foundations of Paul's Mission   171
Paul's View of History, of Law, and of Israel   177
  History   *177*
  The Law   *178*
  Israel   *179*
Paul's Compulsion to Preach   181
The Strategy and Content of Paul's Mission   182
  Paul's Strategy   *182*
  The Content of Paul's Preaching   *185*
Conclusion   187

**8 The Cosmic Scope of the Church's Mission in Colossians
and Ephesians**   *191*

The Relation of Colossians and Ephesians to Paul   191
New Dimensions: Preparation for Cosmic Missiology in the
    Letter to the Colossians   193
  Paul's Mission to the Gentiles   *193*
  Cosmic Christology   *195*
Cosmic Lord and Cosmic Mission: The Message of
    Ephesians   199
  God's Universal Plan of Salvation (Eph. 1:3–23)   *199*

The Reconciliation of Jew and Gentile as Sign of God's
    Redemptive Work (Eph. 2:11–22; 3:3–6)   203
Responsibility of a Missioned Church (Eph. 3:10, 14–20;
    chaps. 4–6)   204
Paul: Model of the Missionary Apostolate of the
    Church   206
Conclusion   207

9 **The Mission Theology of Mark**   *211*

Introduction: The Gospels and the Mission Question   211
The Background of Mark   212
Handing on the Tradition: The Kingdom Ministry of Jesus in the
    Gospel of Mark   213
Interpreting the Tradition: The Message of Mark and the
    Mission of the Church   214
    The Choice of a Story Genre   214
    The Signs of a Universal Mission   217
    Discipleship: Following a Crucified Jesus   225
    Jesus as Revelation of God   228
Conclusion   229

10 **The Mission Theology of Matthew**   *233*

The Context of Matthew's Community   233
Elements of Matthew's Mission Theology   235
    Matthew's Debt to Mark   235
    Salvation History in Matthew   238
    Response as a Universal Principle   247
The Missionary and Matthew's Church   249
    The Mission Discourse of Matthew 10   250
    The Final Commission, Matthew 28:16–20   251
Conclusion   252

11 **The Mission Perspective of Luke-Acts**   *255*

The Link between the Story of Jesus and the Story of the
    Church: The Keynote of Luke's Mission
    Theology   256
The Gospel of Luke: Jesus and the Universal Mission   260
    The Universal Scope of the Mission   260
    Continuity with the History of Israel   261
    A Mission of Salvation   262
    The Formation of Community   264
    Persevering Witnesses   265
    The Power of the Spirit   267

The Acts of the Apostles: The Community's Universal
      Mission   269
      The Structure of Acts   *269*
      The Mission Message of Acts   *271*
Conclusion   276

12   *The Johannine Theology of Mission*   *280*

The Environment of the Gospel and the Mission Perspective of
      the Johannine Church   280
Christology and Mission   283
The Paraclete and the Mission   286
The Community and Its Mission   288
Conclusion   292

**13   *Witness and Mission: The Remaining Books of the New
      Testament***   *297*

1 Peter: The Witness of Hope   297
The Book of Revelation: Prophetic Witness   302
The Pastoral Letters: 1 and 2 Timothy, Titus   305
Hebrews, James, Jude, 2 Peter   309
Conclusion   310

**PART III
CONCLUSION
Donald Senior, C.P.
Carroll Stuhlmueller, C.P.**

14   *The Biblical Foundations for Mission*   *315*

Synthesis   315
      The Old Testament   *315*
      The New Testament   *318*
Biblical Foundations   321
      *1. The Sovereignty of God and His Will to Save
        Humanity*   *321*
      2. History as Sacred and Revealing   *323*
      *3. The Created World: Arena of Revelation and
        Salvation*   *326*
      4. Religious Experience: Catalyst to Mission   *329*

The Modalities of Mission   332
    Direct Proclamation   333
    Prophetic Challenge in Word and Sign   334
    "Witness" on behalf of the Gospel   335
    Mission as Personal and Social Transformation   338
The Bible and Contemporary Mission   339
    A Universal God   339
    A Progressive Eschatology   340
    A Dialectic between Outreach and Identity   340
    The Role of Religious Leadership   341
    The Value of Religious Experience   342
    The Scriptures as Source of Vision and Strategy   343
    Pluralism as a Value   344
    The Unanswered Questions   344

Index of Scriptural References   *349*

Index of Authors   *363*

Index of Subjects   *366*

Foreword

Christians have always turned to the Bible as the charter document for their missionary activity. In so doing they have mined those rich resources in many ways, and for a variety of reasons. Sometimes they have been guided for personal reasons, seeking inspiration to rekindle and guide their missionary motivation. At other times the reasons have been practical or apologetic, to address specific problems or to underwrite certain strategies. In still other instances they have looked to the Scriptures for blueprints of missionary action or criteria for the establishment of the Christian community.

Yet there has always been a lingering suspicion that reading the Scriptures with such singleness of purpose could become myopic and even self-serving. To read only Luke-Acts to discover procedures and criteria for planting churches ignores other New Testament witnesses. To concentrate solely on the classical prophets as a means for buttressing strategies of social transformation and liberation precludes the complex witness of Jesus in the synoptic gospels. And to direct one's motivation wholly to the Great Commission of Matthew 28 without looking into the complexity of experience attested to by Paul in Romans 9–11 makes for superficial missionary activity. A sensitive reading of both Testaments makes it clear that Scriptural testimony to the mission of salvation is not a solo voice, but a chorus from the many communities and persons which made up the Hebrew and Christian communities.

Donald Senior and Carroll Stuhlmueller have labored to capture the multiplicity and the harmony of that testimony for us in this book. They focus on the relation of Israel and Church to the Gentiles, that point of contact where an awareness of universalism and election, of judgment and justice, of promise and fulfillment takes place. As the reader will see, they lead us into our being caught up in the contrapuntal variations on experience and witness that mark the rich biblical traditions. They touch upon the spirituality and motivation for mission, the relation of secular and sacred in the development of the divine plan, the meaning of God's activity in history and our destiny within it, and the intertwining of justice and salvation as biblical themes.

In short, they have provided us with the biblical *foundations* of mission in the best sense of that word—a fundament which, in dialogue with the concrete situations and exigencies of our world, can lead to the building up of the body of Christ, the Church. They are not satisfied with superficial readings or with the amassing of critical reflections. They try to probe the spirit of the texts, and, to my mind, succeed admirably in doing so.

xi

No comprehensive and critical study of the biblical bases for mission has been written in twenty years. Donald Senior and Carroll Stuhlmueller's book will, I believe, ably fill that gap. They examine the range of current critical scholarship on the Bible to draw out for us the images and energies for Christian mission. This book should serve well both to ground and inspire the work of those called into Christian mission, and to aid those reflecting on the theological problems that face contemporary missiology in a world Church. The scholarship and the spirituality evident in this book will be sound and much-needed partners in the continuing mission enterprise of the Church.

Robert J. Schreiter, C.PP.S.,
Dean, Catholic Theological Union at Chicago

Introduction

Every now and then someone puts a finger squarely on the pulse of the church. Such seems to be the case with an address delivered by Karl Rahner in April 1979 entitled, "Towards a Fundamental Theological Interpretation of Vatican II."[1] Rahner's goal was to pinpoint the basic issue that throbbed beneath the multiple concerns and debates of that momentous council. His conclusion: Vatican II is the first major official event in which the church experienced itself as a *world* church.[2] For the first time the leadership of the church began to glimpse and actually to experience the implications of a gospel that was not merely European or North American but truly universal.

Rahner attempts to put this into perspective by considering church history from a theological standpoint. He suggests that viewed theologically rather than merely chronologically, the church's history can be divided into three major phases. The first was that of Jewish Christianity. Jesus' own mission was in and to Israel. The first disciples in the apostolic community at Jerusalem were thoroughly Jewish in custom and outlook. But this initial Jewish phase of the church's history soon underwent profound transformation. Missionary expansion and the resulting influx of Gentile converts moved the church into the second major phase, that of "Hellenistic," or "European," Christianity. This shift from a predominantly Jewish Christianity to a predominantly Hellenistic, or European, Christianity caused radical changes in almost every aspect of the church's life: cultural identity, language, seat of authority (eventually shifting from Jerusalem to Rome), styles of worship, patterns of morality, and so on.

It is important to realize, Rahner contends, that the church remained in this Hellenistic, or second, period of its history from the third quarter of the first century until our own day. Obviously, Western culture itself underwent enormous development and change, but Christianity remained fixed within a basically Greco-Roman, or "Western," cultural framework. Even though extensive missionary activity was undertaken and the gospel spread around the globe, these new areas of the church were, for the most part, thoroughly Westernized and their indigenous cultures made little impact on the self-consciousness of the church as a whole.

The political and historical explosions of the post-World War II period brought momentous consequences for the world and the church. The colonial period came to an abrupt halt and a new awareness of cultural and national identity swept through the globe like a brush fire. These developments signaled a moment of profound transition in the church's own history: from a long period in which the gospel was embedded almost exclusively in a Western, European context to a period when, perhaps for the first time in its history, the church would begin to glimpse the true meaning of universality and pluralism.

Rahner concludes his reflections with a challenge: Can we expect that the shift from the second to the third period of the church's history will be any less thorough and traumatic than the change from the first to the second? In other words, if the shift from the narrow confines of Jewish Christianity into the broader arena of the Roman empire meant profound changes in every aspect of the church's life, can we expect the shift from a Western-dominated church to a genuinely universal church to be any less revolutionary? Should not we, too, expect bold transformations in liturgy, moral values, church government, and patterns of theology, as the church crosses the boundaries of race, culture, and gender?

The question of universalism is no mere academic question; it has staggering consequences for the pastoral life of the church. Neither is it an issue that the church can simply tolerate or even avoid. To be universal, capable of embracing and being expressed by all cultures and all peoples, is essential to the gospel. The God-given mission of the church is to go to "all nations."

The biblical foundations for that universal mission are the subject of this book. If, as Rahner suggests, the epochs of church history give needed perspective for our current experience, so does the Bible. Other disciplines such as theology and the social sciences must be brought into the picture. Vital, too, is the guidance of legitimate church authority. Yet from the perspective of faith, the Bible as the inspired Word of God stands as a unique source of the church's reflection. The Bible expresses the rich experience of a people who were convinced that in historical events and great leaders God was shaping their destiny.

The explicit mandate to bring the message of salvation to the "end of the earth" is, of course, found only in the New Testament. But the roots of the church's mission go deeper, even beyond the history of Jesus and the early church. The taproot of the church's universal mission can be traced within the Old Testament. The sovereign and compassionate God who calls together a disparate group of slaves and unclassified people and forms them into a "chosen people" and a "royal priesthood" is ultimately the same God who will push his people to distant coasts beyond the frontiers of the Promised Land. One of the basic principles of this study, therefore, is that the biblical foundations for mission span the entirety of God's Word.

Given the crucial importance of the issue of universalism in the church today, it is somewhat surprising that relatively little exegetical work has been done on the question of Bible and mission, especially in mainline churches.[3] The problem may be the connotations of "mission" for many theologians and church leaders. For some "mission" conjures up images of feverish and often insensitive proselytizing. And even for those who may have a more sophisticated notion of mission, there can still be hesitation about this dimension of the church's life. The missionary effort of the church has undergone profound crisis in the mid-twentieth century. The rejection of colonialism, newfound respect for non-Christian religions, changing models of the church—these and other contemporary experiences caused the bottom to drop out of the missionary enterprise in the post-Vatican II era. Only in the 1980s do we find a sense of perspective being restored.

The agenda of theology and exegesis is set, at least in part, by the experiences and preferences of those who take up these studies. It is not surprising, therefore, that such domestic issues as the evolution of church structures and ministries, or more speculative questions such as Christology, dominate the present agenda. These, in fact, are the issues that many professional exegetes and theologians find more palatable.[4]

But the contemporary life of the church and the nature of the biblical data demand that more prominence be given to the question of the church's universal mission. The church's call to be universal touches the very issues that seem to perplex the church today: the impact of liberation theology, the urgent challenge of global justice and peace, debates over pluralism in dogma and praxis, dialogue with Judaism and non-Christian religions, church government, the emergence of new forms of ministry, the role of women. Having to struggle with such issues is a necessary consequence of belief in a universal gospel. For by definition that gospel cannot be bottled up in one culture, one social class, one gender, or one power group. The Bible itself would raise these issues even if contemporary Christian life did not. The pages of the Scriptures—both Old and New Testaments—are filled with the struggles of God's people to be faithful to his covenant, to bring justice and salvation to the poor and defenseless, to reach beyond the boundaries of Judea and Samaria, to find identity as God's people in new times and in new places. The mission question is intrinsic to the Bible.

Today no one should be doomed to think of "mission" in purely propagandistic terms. Missionary activity involves much more than "making converts," as most missionaries can testify. By "mission" in this book we mean the God-given call to appreciate and share one's religious experience and insights, first within one's own community and tradition, and then with people and communities of other cultural, social, and religious traditions. In so doing Christians attempt to fulfill the divine mandate given to the church that humanity reflect God's own life as one people drawn together in love and respect. Such a notion means that mission is two-way: faith is shared but not imposed, and the missionary will be instructed and enriched by discovering God's salvation already at work in the people and culture to whom he or she is sent. This dialectical pattern rules out any imperious forcing of a religious system on individuals or communities. The gospel comes in the person and message of the missionary as a free and respectful invitation. The gospel-bearer must be aware that he or she is not the proprietor of all truth but bears a gift of God's salvation that, in many ways, the non-Christian has already experienced.

Our purpose is not to study the entire biblical message of salvation; such a task would involve a theological reflection on practically every facet of the Bible. Our task is more limited but, we hope, still vital. We want to search out those traditions and dynamics that shaped Israel's consciousness of its destiny in relation to Gentiles, and that ultimately led Christians to proclaim the gospel to Gentiles. In other words, we are concerned with how the universal mission became an accepted part of the Christian scriptural perspective.

To do this we shall range over the entire Bible. Because a universal mission is not an explicit part of Israel's consciousness and because of the vast historical and literary scope of the Bible, our approach to the Old Testament must be different from that to the New Testament. In the first major section of the book (part I), Carroll Stuhlmueller will take a more thematic approach, kneading together those theological traditions in the Old Testament that have significant consequences for the mission issue. The dominating presence of mission in the New Testament and the brief historical scope of the early church enable us to give detailed attention to individual New Testament books in part II. After an initial chapter on Jesus, Donald Senior turns to the mission theologies of Paul and other New Testament authors. A concluding major section (part III) summarizes our results and considers some possible implications of this study for contemporary theology and church life.

The idea for this book began in a seminar on Bible and Mission that we conducted for several years at Catholic Theological Union. We were blessed that the participants in that class were themselves a microcosm of the universal church. We had students from Europe, Africa, Asia, Latin and North America, Australia, and New Zealand. Not a few were veteran missionaries who had spent the best years of their lives in places far from home. We also had young men and women who were preparing for missionary work in cultures and lands not their own. Many others were there simply because they were concerned about questions of justice and ministry, and wanted to know what the Scriptures might have to say.

That course convinced us that the mission question is vital, not just as a pastoral issue but as a biblical issue. We discovered that approaching the Bible from the vantage point of mission led to the center of its message. This book attempts to capture some of that discovery.

We have tried to make our results as understandable as possible for as many people as possible, including those who may not have a professional background in exegesis but whose experience and interests make them alert to the mission question. For this reason we have, wherever possible, sought to eliminate or explain technical jargon. The notes have been kept to a minimum and we have tried to offer a variety of references so that the notes may be useful to the serious scholar and the serious beginner.

Above all we hope that our study breathes a sense of respect for those heroic men and women whose lives of incredible generosity testify that our God is a God of compassion and justice—and the God of everyone. They are all over the globe: in the Serengeti Plain, among the minority tribes of Mindanao, with the peasants of El Salvador, in the urban hells of Manila and Chicago, in the de-Christianized areas of Charleroi, Belgium, in the impenetrable technological façade of Tokyo, in the teeming refugee camps of Hong Kong, with the migrants in Salinas, California, and among the hard faces of children in Belfast. The biblical story we have attempted to trace continues in them.

A special word of thanks is due Robert Schreiter, C.PP.S., dean of Catholic Theological Union, for his encouragement in this project and for the inspiration of his own scholarship in the area of mission. We are honored that he was willing to contribute the foreword to the volume. And we surely cannot thank enough Kay Sheskaitis, I.H.M., for her efficient, cheerful, and long-suffering work in typing the several versions of the manuscript and Ann Maloney, O.P., for graciously helping with the many chores necessary in getting a book to the publisher. We also gratefully acknowledge the generosity and expertise of Kenneth O'Malley, C.P., Director of the library at Catholic Theological Union, who prepared the indexes for this volume.

Donald Senior offers a special word of gratitude to Maryknoll's Center for Mission Studies. The awarding of a James A. Walsh–Thomas F. Price Fellowship for Mission Study and Research in the spring of 1979 made this entire project possible. That generous fellowship enabled him to fund a sabbatical leave in order to give full attention to the design of this project, to do the basic editorial work, and even to test out some of its contents on missionaries and local churches in Asia and Africa. Funds from the grant also provided the necessary secretarial help. For all of that, both authors are more than grateful and hope that this book itself might be a worthy sign of appreciation for Maryknoll's courageous ministry, both in the field and in print.

DONALD SENIOR, C.P.
CARROLL STUHLMUELLER, C.P.

NOTES

1. K. Rahner, "Towards a Fundamental Theological Interpretation of Vatican II," *Theological Studies* 40 (1979): 716–27.

2. In Rahner's words the council was "the church's first official self-actualization as *world* church" ("Towards a Fundamental Theological Interpretation of Vatican II," p. 717). He points to such things as the significant presence of indigenous hierarchies in third-world countries, the movement for the vernacular in liturgy, the trend to discuss ecumenism and relationships with non-Christian religions, etc.

3. Major biblical studies of mission from a critical perspective are rare: cf. J. Blauw, *The Missionary Nature of the Church* (Grand Rapids, Mich.: Wm. B. Eerdmans, 1962), and F. Hahn, *Mission in the New Testament*, Studies in Biblical Theology 47 (Naperville, Ill.: Allenson, 1965). Blauw's study originated as a working paper commissioned jointly by the World Council of Churches and the International Missionary Council in 1961. Hahn's important study was first published in German in 1963 and concentrates solely on the New Testament. Note that throughout this study we use the commonly accepted terms "Old Testament" and "New Testament." We acknowledge that this nomenclature reflects a strictly Christian viewpoint; Judaism would not consider its sacred books the "Old" Testament. However no adequate replacement for the terms "Old Testament" and "New Testament"

has yet been developed. Designations such as "Hebrew Scriptures," while more ecumenically sensitive, have other liabilities; for example, not all of the books in the Roman Catholic "Old Testament" are written in Hebrew (e.g., the Book of Wisdom was written in Greek), and to designate these as "Hebrew" Scriptures might also give the impression that they are not really intrinsic to the Christian Bible. As the whole spirit of our study suggests, in using the designation "Old Testament" we do not mean that these sacred writings are rendered obsolete by the *New* Testament. "Old" in this context means "First" and, therefore, revered.

4. "Exegetical inquiry often depends upon the theological and cultural presuppositions with which it approaches its texts. Historical scholarship therefore judges the past from the perspective of its own concepts and values. Since for various reasons religious propaganda, mission, and apologetics are not very fashionable topics in the contemporary theological scene, these issues have also been widely neglected in New Testament scholarship. Many exegetes do not presently perceive the history of early Christianity as the history of a propagandistic-missionary endeavor. Instead they consider the New Testament writings primarily as documents of an inner-Christian doctrinal struggle and they understand early Christian history mainly as a 'confessional' history, as a struggle between different Christian parties and theologians" (E. Fiorenza, *Aspects of Religious Propaganda in Judaism and Early Christianity* [South Bend, Ind.: University of Notre Dame Press, 1976], p. 1; cf. also her article, " 'For the Sake of Our Salvation. . . . ' Biblical Interpretation as Theological Task," in *Sin, Salvation and the Spirit*, ed. D. Durken [Collegeville, Minn.: Liturgical Press, 1979], p. 30).

PART I

THE FOUNDATIONS FOR MISSION
IN THE OLD TESTAMENT

Carroll Stuhlmueller, C.P.

1

From Secular Liberation to Salvation History and World Mission

I will make of you a great nation, . . . so that you will be a blessing . . . [to] all the families of the earth [Gen. 12:2–3].

The question is serious and we must face it straightforwardly at the very start of our inquiry. What contribution to world mission could ever come from a people like Israel whose history separated them more and more from all other neighboring nations and whose sacred books developed an ethnocentric theology of being exclusively God's chosen ones? As a matter of fact, to this day Israel possesses no significant missionary program to proselytize non-Jews and so is uniquely different from Christianity and Islam.[1] This centripetal momentum came initially from the patriarchal traditions and was strengthened with the Mosaic legislation; it moved Israel rather firmly away from the Gentiles and centered upon the *bᵉnê yiśrā'ēl* as a single elect people. Israel never felt the need to include the salvation of the nonelect within a theological synthesis of its major doctrines.[2]

A THEOLOGY OF ELECTION AND SIGNALS OF UNIVERSALISM

A key sentence, immediately before the revelation on Mount Sinai, articulates eloquently Israel's separatism:

> Thus you shall say to the house of Jacob, and tell the people of Israel: You have seen what I did to the Egyptians, and how I bore you on eagles' wings and brought you to myself. Now therefore, if you will obey my voice and keep my covenant, you shall be my own possession among all peoples; for all the earth is mine, and you shall be to me a kingdom of priests and a holy nation [Exod. 19:3–6].

These lines within the second book of Moses are generally attributed to the same tradition that produced the book of Deuteronomy. In this latter book, the fifth

9

within the Torah, still stronger statements are found, even an endorsement of the holy war against Gentile nations.

The chapter of Deuteronomy, in fact, that expresses most tenderly the Lord's love for Israel also summons Israel to the *herem*, or holy war. The following sentences are juxtaposed in Deuteronomy, chapter 7:

> When the Lord your God brings you into the land which you are entering to take possession of it, and clears away many nations before you, . . . you must utterly destroy them; you shall make no covenant with them, and show no mercy to them [7:1–2].

> For you are a people holy to the Lord your God; the Lord your God has chosen you to be a people for his own possession, out of all peoples that are on the face of the earth. It was not because you were more in number than any other people that the Lord set his love upon you and chose you, for you were the fewest of all peoples; but it is because the Lord loves you, and is keeping the oath which he swore to your fathers [7:6–8].[3]

How, we ask, can a policy of mission be detected within these lines of ardent exclusivism and even of violent repudiation of the foreigner? Not only here in Deuteronomy but in almost every book of the Old Testament, Israel is considered the elect people and all other nations remain the nonelect. If these foreign nations, as Bruce Vawter writes, "were fairly remote from the life, the geography, and the history of the people of Israel,"[4] and so were reduced (practically speaking) to harmless nonexistence, or if they entered into friendly and favorable treaties with Israelites, then they were grouped in the category of "the descendants of Japheth" in the table of nations of Genesis 9–10 and a partial blessing was invoked over them. If, on the contrary, the foreign nations were drawn into close, competitive contact with Israel, they were classified under the "descendants of Ham" and a curse was leveled against them:

> Cursed be Canaan;
>   a slave of slaves shall he be to his brothers.
> . . . Blessed by the Lord my God be Shem;
>   and let Canaan be his slave.
> God enlarge Japheth,
>   and let him dwell in the tents of Shem;
> and let Canaan be his slave [Gen. 9:25–27].

The centripetal thrust of these passages is evident. Yet here as so often in the Hebrew Scriptures, a careful reader will detect signals or flashes of a contrary movement. An opposite, or centrifugal, radiation away from Israel toward the Gentile nations is stirring beneath the surface. In Genesis 10 the ancestors of Israel were not separated from other people; in fact they were indistinguishable in what seems to most modern readers to be a welter of unpronounceable foreign names: "Elam, Asshur, Arpachshad, Lud, and Aram . . . Uz, Hul, Gether, and Mash . . . Almodad, Sheleph, Hazarmaveth, Jerah, Hadoram . . ." (Gen. 10:22–27). Yet as we follow the biblical text from Genesis 10 into 11, we find that within the lineage of Arpachshad appears the name of "Terah . . . the father of Abram." In origin, according to its own sacred Scriptures, Israel was no different from any other Gentile people (cf. Ezek.16:3). Israel has no particular, supernatural status by birth and early history. Gerhard von Rad makes an important observation for this study:

> . . . the saving action which began in Israel was divested of all mythological character by means of the insertion of the Table of Nations [in Genesis 10]. The biblical primeval history, which has as its climax the world of the nations, gives Israel the same creaturely status as the nations, and excludes any mythological primacy assigned to her primeval times. Her future experience of God will be in the realm of secular history and, indeed, according to Genesis 10 *in the realm of universal secular history.*[5]

Within this biblical passage, according to Gerhard von Rad, a signal of universal salvation is being flashed to us. If Arpachshad can be the progenitor of a chosen people, why could God not choose Sheleph or Hazarmaveth, Greece or Rome, Tanzania or Papua, New Guinea at some later time to provide the historical background, the political and cultural setting for revelation and worship? If Israel's salvation is to be accomplished "in the realm of universal secular history," then the nations of the world will have something positive to contribute to Israel's understanding of God's will and even to the rich symbolism of its liturgy. G. von Rad's words on another occasion corroborate this intuition: "What Israel learns and experiences of Yahweh occurs exclusively within the realm of history."[6] As in the use of Arpachshad and Shelah, God can raise up a new chosen people from other, least likely candidates in the days of John the Baptist . . . "from these [seemingly lifeless] stones" (Lk. 3:8).

FROM THE SECULAR TO THE SACRED

Israel's election and salvation "in the realm of universal secular history" draw attention to another important observation. Here we touch upon the way by which secular events evolve into religious symbols. We also meet another instance by which the events, which separated Israel from all other nations, at the same time contained a hidden potential to attract these same foreign people to the God of Israel. Israel's history somehow became symbolic of world salvation, for it spoke a message that was understandable and meaningful for people everywhere.

Scholars have seriously nuanced the meaning and scope of a term like "salvation history."[7] If a pivotal or key position of Israel's religion, such as the exodus out of Egypt or the acquisition of the Promised Land, left no trace in the archives of Egyptian or Canaanite nations, can we honestly characterize these events as "historical"? To be called "historical," much more is required than the simple fact that something happened on planet earth. Most of life's real episodes never qualify as history. No one, perhaps, realized this humble and often discouraging fact of nonhistory more poignantly than Ecclesiastes:

> What has been is what will be, . . .
> And there is nothing new under the sun. . . .
> There is no remembrance of former things,
> nor will there be any remembrance
> of later things yet to happen . . . [Eccles.1:9,11].

Other countries, like Egypt and Mesopotamia, have left us historical monuments of breathtaking magnitude, such as the pyramids and the ziggurats far more magnificent than anything unearthed by archeologists in Israel. Volumes of sacred and profane literature from the archeological sites of these neighboring countries tell us more about their everyday life, their court protocol, and their empire building than we can ever salvage from Israel's past. As J. J. M. Roberts has reminded us, Mesopotamian historiography must not be underestimated.[8] As in Israel, it attempted to recognize continuity from one period to another, human freedom for influencing events, and a modulating or evolving theological explanation of great moments in the past. In fact, if we judge by the bulk of material, Egyptian and Mesopotamian peoples were more historical-minded than Israel, and like Israel developed a synthesis that combined human achievement, divine endorsement or condemnation, and a cultic way of celebrating significant events. We must conclude that Israel's religion was not distinguished from other religions by any extraordinary insight into "salvation history." Yet, as we shall discuss later, there was a unique and persistent quality about Israel's religious interpretation of its history that differentiated it from other ancient religions.

We are one step on our way in this discussion of Israel's special brand of historiography by admitting how insignificant and nonhistorical were the earliest episodes in Israel's origins: the migration of the patriarchs and the escape from Egypt. Yet these events, which left no mark on world monuments or archives, continue to fashion lives and direct the consciences of millions of men and women today. Moses, who remained unmentioned on Egyptian hieroglyphics, is still making history. Jews are still living under the impact of his genius, an impact that affects the formation of the state of Israel, the oil crisis, and world economics. A godless state as in the Soviet Union cannot ignore the "salvation history" of Israel.

Israel's religion turned insignificant happenings into historical events. It is crucial for our method of investigating the mission statement of the Old Testament to take note that religion not only develops out of the ingredients of secular events but also leaves a definite mark upon the course of secular history. Biblical religion is sandwiched between the secular; Israel's worship of God and its sacred literature were intertwined within "the realm of universal secular history." While religion championed that aspect of Israel's origins that drew it aside and separated it from the nations, the secular origins and the continued secular impact upon

Israel's religious expression were subtly yet unrelentingly summoning Israel to the outside world.

SECULAR ORIGINS AND RELIGIOUS MOTIVATION

Three vital stages mark the transition from the secular to the sacred in Israel's religion.[9] The first two stages appear secular in purpose yet contain (what we shall place in parentheses below) a religious motivation on the part of a few key persons. The third period brings this religious motivation out into the open to be shared with everyone. It should be evident by now that "secular" implies nothing derogatory or irreligious; it refers to events and circumstances that are plainly visible and require no special religious insight or any divine revelation to recognize or explain. In fact an economic, political, or military specialist may understand them better than a saint who relies solely on prayer and mystic intuition. We shall first quickly enumerate the three stages and then explain them more fully by way of example.

a. Secular events, often of insignificant proportion, liberate a people in time of crisis. (It is possible that the leader who undertook the task would be motivated by religious faith and would consider himself or herself to be summoned by God for this task.)

b. Secular celebrations are held once this liberation is achieved. (Yet at least a few people among the crowd would be moved by religious wonder and gratitude to God.)

c. Liturgical ceremonies reorchestrate the earlier events and initial celebrations in such a way as to bring to center stage what had been peripheral, invisible, or parenthetical—the divine call and faith of the leader as well as the religious feelings of a core group. Liturgy kept the memory of Israel's origins from being lost in the sands.

These three stages in the formation of the Bible enable us to review our earlier statements about salvation history. The liturgy of the sanctuaries and of tribal gatherings supplied very many if not most of the details to be recorded in the Bible and in the process replaced many "historical" details in the biblical account of what actually took place.[10] In an almost contradictory way, that which replaced historical *details* enabled the basic historical *fact* to be remembered. Salvation history derives its "history" as well as its "salvation" from the sanctuary. Liturgy furnished the context or popular setting by which an event like the flight from Egypt was not forgotten but was celebrated, narrated, acted out, and transformed into a symbol meaningful for future generations. Thomas L. Thompson put it forcefully: "Salvation history did not happen; it is a literary form which has its own historical context."[11] This historical context in most cases turned out to be the sanctuary. The "literary development" of the Bible was often centered in evolving forms of worship, songs, and sacred narratives. The liturgical actions modulated as *new* secular needs or crises were met and introduced as points of prayer and worship.

An example from the Old Testament may clarify this concept of "history" and "salvation" within the Bible and at this time direct us in our method of clarifying a statement about world mission in the Old Testament.

The exodus of the Israelites out of Egypt seems to have consisted of a series of many escapes over a century or more. This is what we would expect of harshly treated slaves anytime, anywhere. Even the Bible combines at least two of these departures under the name of Moses: in one series of passages, the people flee from Egypt against the pharaoh's wish (Exod. 10:27-29; 14:5a); in another series they are deliberately expelled by the pharaoh (Exod. 6:1b; 11:1; 12:39).[12] These intermittent and at times elusive flights toward freedom in no way seriously affected Egyptian politics or economy, no more than the bits and pieces of expulsion, escapes, or more legal types of departures from the Soviet Union modify Russia's policies or lifestyle. Such escapes were given the same silent treatment in Egypt as they are in the Soviet press today. Yet one of these departures was destined to impress its name upon world religions and international politics. It was undertaken by a leader of overwhelming faith in God and of irresistible courage in the face of opposition. His name was Moses; his achievement, the exodus. This secular event of liberation from slavery is to be attributed to a nonsecular, thoroughly faith-dominated person, Moses.

Liberation under Moses was bound to be celebrated by songs of gratitude to God (Exod. 15:20-21), but most of the people were caught up in the revelry of eating, drinking, and dancing. The excesses and the grumbling of the populace drew a stern and bewildered warning (Exod. 15:22-17:7). The classic text of murmuring in the desert occurs in the book of Numbers:

> Now the rabble that was among them had a strong craving; and the people of Israel also wept again, and said, "O that we had meat to eat! We remember the fish we ate in Egypt for nothing, the cucumbers, the melons, the leeks, the onions, and the garlic; but now our strength is dried up, and there is nothing at all but this manna to look at" [Num. 11:4-6].

After witnessing and actually taking part in the exodus out of Egypt, the people grumbled about leeks and garlic! For this reason among others, it is difficult to accept as historical data all the pomp and circumstance in chapter 14 of the book of Exodus. Could the people, only three days later, have forgotten the *mirabilia Dei* and with no trace of these wonders in their memory have murmured about the taste of the water (Exod.15:24)? The passage of Numbers, quoted just above, distinguishes the "rabble" or "riffraff" [13] (called more politely "a mixed multitude" in Exod.12:38), from the true, fervent Israelite. Even though religious people could be corrupted, they still remained the nucleus of faith and devotion. Their perseverance in faith enabled Israel to survive for forty years in "that great and terrible wilderness" (Deut.1:19) stretching between Egypt and the Promised Land. Again the less visible, more fragile attitudes of faith and religious feeling among the "true" Israelites prevented a secular act from disappearing in the sandy stretches and rocky wadis of Sinai.

After the initial secular acts of liberation and festivity, we come to the third and crucial moment, that of liturgical celebration. What had remained mostly invisible, or at least submerged beneath secular excitement, now moved to center stage. The faith of Israel's leaders at the moment of liberation as well as the religious feelings of the group in the midst of secular festivities—what we placed within parenthesis in the earlier outline—are now made visible through liturgical actions, words, and personnel. Henceforth the Scriptures will speak of a religious procession instead of an escape or expulsion from Egypt, of priests and levites instead of military commanders, and of inspired words for remembering the past instead of recitations around the family campfire. The Song of Moses in Exod. 15: 1–8, the Canticle of Deborah in Judg. 5:2–31, and somewhat later the thanksgiving songs in Psalms 18 and 68 all represent some of the earliest poetry in the Bible, probably retaining a more primitive shape than the prose narratives of similar length elsewhere in the Torah of Moses.[14]

Actions like the exodus, people such as Moses and Miriam, and stories about the departure from Egypt have now become sacred symbols, so that the invisible elements of faith in people's lives may become apparent and direct their entire existence. This system of symbols enabled continuing generations to recall their actions and to form their decisions by the heroic norms of earlier generations, and to contribute their own new insights to the evolving form of the symbol. Liturgy enabled the full potential of earlier actions like the escape from Egypt and the desert wandering to grow and bloom. By highlighting God's compassionate action for the lonely and the overwhelming power of his grace within the weak bodies and discouraged hearts of the people, liturgy turned an insignificant event into a key historical moment for Israel. Perhaps we can appreciate better the earlier statement: liturgy that replaced earlier historical *details* with sanctuary ritual and sacred narratives, thereby enabled the basic historical *fact* to be remembered.

While the first two stages of secular liberation and secular celebration were centripetal, drawing Israel away from the nation of Egypt to seek new life for itself in its own land, the third stage of liturgical celebration contained a centrifugal reaction, enabling Israel to find in these same events a pattern of God's care for the oppressed, whoever these people may be. This insight into Israel's history could cut across national and ethnic boundaries. In no way does one have to be an Israelite in Egypt to be classified as oppressed or poor. This development whereby the liturgy invested secular events with symbolic value for an ever increasing number of people and at the same time stressed the need of caring for and freeing the poor will prove to be a biblical model very important for the world mission of the church. Church leaders will be asked to look for new examples of secular liberation that can be linked with the biblical exodus and be celebrated liturgically, so that God's compassion for the poor will continue to be recognized through the ages.

HISTORICAL MOMENTS FOR ISRAEL— SYMBOLS FOR WORLD MISSION

By here reviewing the major periods of Israel's history, we shall acquire not only a clearer focus upon the long, complicated history from Abraham to Jesus but also a basic methodology for reading the Old Testament within the world mission of the church. Most of all, we shall draw attention to the relationship between the secular and the sacred and to those signals of world concern within a history otherwise restricted to a single elect people, Israel.

The history of Israel can be divided into six major periods, not always equal in time span and documentation but each an essential ingredient in the formation not only of the people Israel but also of our answer to God's will for universal salvation.

1850–1550 B.C.E.*	The Patriarchal Age
1240–1200 B.C.E.	The Mosaic Period
1200–921 B.C.E.	The Initial Stages of the Covenant Religion, first under charismatic leadership, then under Davidic dynasty
921–587 B.C.E.	The Disintegration of Politics and the Prophetic Challenge
587–539 B.C.E.	Exile and a Call to Re-creation
539–7 B.C.E.	Reconstruction and Apocalyptic Expectations

*Before the Common Era.

The Patriarchal Age (1850–1550 B.C.E.)

The patriarchal age is extremely difficult to reconstruct historically,[15] yet a few facts of solid credibility and of serious consequence for our discussion emerge by way of comparison with the Mosaic age and any later period of Israel's existence. For one thing, despite the fact that Israel's later evaluation of its ancestors was mixed, partly favorable and partly unfavorable,[16] the people remembered them for their key role in the development and later in the reformation of the covenantal religion. Biblical texts as significant as Exod. 3:6 identify Yahweh first as "the God of your ancestors, the God of Abraham, the God of Isaac, and the God of Jacob." The remembrance of a patriarchal or ancestral intuition of God laid a basis for theological development and refinement. Patriarchal traditions emerged prominently during the two most international periods of Israel's history—when David established an empire of vassal and covenantal states and when Israel was absorbed within the Babylonian empire. During the Babylonian exile (587–537 B.C.E.) this era was recalled by someone like Second Isaiah, in order to re-create and revitalize a religion in shambles:

> Look to Abraham your father
> and to Sarah who bore you;
> for when he was but one I called him,
> and I blessed him and made him many.
> For the Lord will comfort Zion:
> he will comfort all her waste places,
> and will make her wilderness like Eden [Isa. 51:2–3].

This same prophet formed a synthesis of ancestral traditions with many aspects of Babylonian life and religion.

Israel's ancestors, the patriarchs, willingly accepted and interacted with Canaanite forms of worship and lifestyle. The patriarchs are seen to worship at traditional Canaanite shrines like "the sacred place at Shechem" (Gen. 12:6), Bethel (Gen. 12:8), Hebron (Gen. 13:18), and Beersheba (Gen. 21:33). Although Abraham built altars to his family god (Gen.12:8; 13:4), he never instituted a separate priesthood. In fact he accepted a blessing from the non-Israelite priest Melchizedek and offered him tithes in return (Gen. 14:18–20). Biblical references to the shrine-city of Shechem are particularly helpful, and as Bruce Vawter points out, "in Israel's early days Israelites (who worshiped Yahweh) and Canaanites (who worshiped Baal) lived together in Shechem side by side."[17] The texts of the Bible can slip back and forth and speak indiscriminately of the Canaanite god as El-berith and Baal-berith (berith = "covenant"); for example, see Judg. 8:33; 9:4, 46. Eventually "El" remained an acceptable title for Israel's God, "Baal" was repudiated and ever more frequently was replaced by the Hebrew word for shame, *bosheth*.[18] Yet each was a common Semitic name, "El" signifying a deity, "Baal" meaning lord or master.

If the syncretism of culture and religion between the Israelites and the Canaanites, between the worshipers of Baal and the worshipers of Yahweh, was still a significant factor after the Mosaic period, this process would have been more active in the patriarchal period. At this early period there were no religious authorities or creedal statements, such as later were inherited from Moses, to direct the people. M. J. Mulder writes in the *Theological Dictionary of the Old Testament*:

> The important differences between the worshippers of Yahweh who immigrated from the wilderness and the settled agricultural worshippers of Baal could not prevent Israel from borrowing from the very first both secular and religious customs and practices, which were assimilated rather quickly from the settled population in Canaan. This led to a struggle between Yahweh and Baal. . . .[19]

We note therefore a double movement, of absorption and of rejection. The patriarchs, as well as the early Israelites after their installation in the land with Joshua, breathed in the Canaanite culture and were hardly distinguishable in language, architecture, farming, legal system, and values. Yet, the other movement of rejection, or at least of discrete selectivity, is also evident. "Baal," as we mentioned, was eventually rejected.

The Bible records an experience of a new call, which it interprets as a radical breakthrough: "Now the Lord said to Abram, 'Go from your country and your kindred and your father's house to the land that I will show you. And I will make you a great nation, and I will bless you, and make your name great, so that you will be a blessing' " (Gen. 12:1–2). Even while God was calling the patriarchs away "from your country and your kindred" (Gen. 12:1) to be the parents of a unique, elect people, it was being done in such a way as to show the *positive* contribution from secular environment and preexisting "pagan" religions. A message is being flashed to us that religion is never a pure creation by God but a synthesis of the best under a new inspiration from God. Secular movements, like the extraordinary migration of people across the fertile crescent of the ancient Near East during the twentieth and nineteenth centuries B.C.E., were to become key religious symbols because of the faith of Abraham.

Several conclusions significant for our study of world mission can be drawn from the bibical remembrance of the patriarchs. A new religious experience took place without the creation of a new religion. Abraham remained within the Canaanite religious system. Despite this system's proclivity to sexual excess in the Baal worship, Abraham recognized a dignity and genuineness about it, and through its instrumentality he acquired his own religious language, style of worship, and system of moral values. In fact the "God of the Ancestors" appeared to Abraham at Canaanite holy places. Religious practices and even the perception of God's special presence evolved *within* the geography and politics of a local area. Only by first accepting the worth and authenticity of preexistent religions were biblical people able to purify, challenge, and develop them. Divine inspiration operated under local conditions. The prehistory antedating Abraham (Genesis 9–11) as well as the patriarchal narratives themselves (Genesis 12–50) recognize the world bonds of Israel's religious origins. Understandably enough, later religious leaders like David, Second Isaiah, and Paul of Tarsus will make a special appeal to the patriarchs if they are emphasizing a more universal aspect within Israelite life or religions. Nonetheless, even after we grant the environmental influence upon biblical religion, the Bible always recognized a very special, even miraculous intervention by God. This quality is brought to our attention not only by the accounts about the special call of the patriarchs (Gen. 12:1–3; 28:13–15), but also by the stories about a sterile couple who wondrously conceived the promised child, or those about God's mighty protection amid colossal world powers like Egypt.

The Mosaic Period (1240–1200 B.C.E.)

The Mosaic Period marks the formal inauguration of a new religion with its own distinct priesthood, ritual, and creed. Through the creative and divinely inspired genius of Moses, Israel gradually acquired: (*a*) a sacred object, the ark of the covenant (Exod. 25:1–31:18; 35:1–40:38) and/or a tent for meeting (Exod. 33:7–10; Lev. 1:1; 6:26,30), for drawing near to God in the Sinai wilderness; (*b*) sacred ministers, the Levitical priests (Num.1:47–54; chaps. 3–4; Lev. 8; Deut. 31:9, 24–28); and (*c*) a "creed," or formal statement of faith (Exod. 15; Deut. 26:5–10; Josh. 24).

It is difficult to decide how many and which of the liturgical and legislative details in the books of Exodus through Deuteronomy originated with Moses. Yet, it is equally hazardous to deny the "historical and religious importance" of this leader who "was not only a guide enabling his compatriots to escape from Egypt, but was also a chief who united them into a single people, author of their faith, legislator and religious initiator.''[20] Roland de Vaux, who wrote the preceding statement, confirmed it in his final work, *The Early History of Israel.* De Vaux, moreover, qualified his position with words that will assist us in relating the Mosaic age to the themes of world mission:

> Moses played an essential part in the origins of the religion of Israel. . . . But . . . it is still doubtful whether the title of ''founder'' is a correct one. The whole person of Moses exceeds the rather narrow categories within which authors, past and present, have tried to enclose him. He was not a thaumaturge, nor was he a judge, a priest or a prophet. He was all these and he was more than all these. He was the man who received Yahweh's revelation of himself and who communicated that revelation to the people. He was the mediator of the covenant between Yahweh and his people and the leading charismatic figure of the people of Yahweh. He did not, in other words, ''found'' a religion in the sense of establishing its institutions and its teaching. What he did is nothing compared with what God did. He was no more than the instrument used by God and, what is more, he was the instrument used by God only in the first stages of the history of Israel's salvation. At the time of Moses' death, before the people of Israel had entered the Promised Land, Yahwism was still the religion of a small group of seminomadic people. It was *only in the course of a long process of development that it became a world religion*, other men of God and God himself playing a part in this development. Moses, however, was *at the beginning of this movement.* It was he who planted the seed which proved to be extremely fertile. He was the first of Yahweh's ''servants'' (Exod. 14:31) and it is with all this in mind that it is possible to speak of a religion of Moses.[21]

Because of Moses, the people would no longer feel comfortable to act as the earlier patriarchs, merging with the Canaanites at their sanctuaries, blessed by Canaanite priests, praying to God under Canaanite titles. Israel no doubt continued to absorb Canaanite styles, yet Israel now possessed its own religious structures for judging and assimilating these influences. Despite Moses' intimacy with God (Exod. 33:11; 34:29–35; Num. 12:8; Deut. 34:10), the human, environmental influences continued. This extraordinary person, Moses, still had to consider all the earthly details within a decision and adapt his judgment not just to divine ideals but equally to human possibilities. He himself was subject to tiredness, even exhaustion, as his father-in-law pointed out: ''What you are doing is not good. You and the people with you will wear yourselves out, for the thing is too heavy for you; you are not able to perform it alone . . . Choose able men . . . and they will bear the burden with you'' (Exod. 18:17–22).

Moses adapted his decisions to the circumstances of the Sinai wilderness. He chose as sacred objects, around which the people could assemble to pray and to receive God's inspiration, only what was suitable to the wilderness where material resources were limited and where people must be ready to break camp and move onward. A ''tent of meeting'' was collapsible; it was rolled up and carried to the next oasis. The "ark of the covenant" was designed precisely for transporting from one place to another: "You shall make poles of acacia wood, and overlay them with gold. And you shall put the poles into the rings on the sides of the ark, to carry the ark by them" (Exod. 25:13-14). This text combines the ancient Mosaic tradition with the "golden," or elegant, style of King Solomon. Exodus 25-31 may reflect a liturgical revision of Mosaic practices from the Solomonic and later periods.[22] Even when the ark was no longer carried about, the sacred "poles" remained as a remembrance of the early days and as a symbol of life's journey under God's direction.

These examples may seem incidental to Israel's religion yet they clearly manifest a religion that could combine extraordinary charismatic power with delicate concern for the immediate human situation. We are also alerted to the possiblility of major developments. One day in the future the ark would no longer migrate with the people but would rest permanently within the Holy of Holies behind a solid stone wall and a heavy brocaded curtain (1 Kings 6:7; Exod. 26:31-34). That innovation, too radical even for David to execute (2 Sam. 7:1-7), resulted from a series of secular achievements: the military conquest of Jerusalem, the political mandate of centralized authority, and the massive building program of Solomon.

From the Mosaic period, the creative moment when religious experiences were transformed and directed in the way of a new religion, several conclusions can be drawn, crucial for the world mission of the church today. Styles of worship were being imported from foreign cultures at crucial moments of development. Moses conformed to wilderness needs and migration practices; Solomon adapted Mosaic regulation to new wealth and city customs. In Mosaic days religion did not dare dictate to the desert but learned from its rules and exigencies.

The charismatic element does not consist in brand-new revelations about liturgy or in striking clashes with local cultures, but in the heroic way by which people are led to overcome political oppression, to sustain hopes for land and freedom, and to be transformed by their faith in "The Lord, the Lord, a God merciful and gracious, slow to anger, and abounding in steadfast love and faithfulness, keeping steadfast love for thousands [of generations], forgiving iniquity and transgression and sin" (Exod. 34:6-7).

With its conception in the patriarchal age and its birthpangs in the Mosaic period, biblical religion will always be characterized by its spirit of "migration." Its greatest peril consists in a false peace at having "arrived" at the full and final expression of its doctrine, worship, and exhortation. The epistle to the Hebrews, despite its insistence upon the cleavage between the "old" and "obsolete" covenant of Moses and the "new" covenant in Jesus' death and resurrection (Heb.8:13), still maintains the Mosaic insistence upon "exodus" and reaching onward:

> Therefore, since we are surrounded by so great a cloud of witnesses [within the Mosaic covenant], let us also lay aside every weight, and sin which clings so closely, and let us run with perseverance the race that is set before us, looking to Jesus the pioneer and perfecter of our faith, who for the joy that

was set before him endured the cross . . . and is seated at the right hand of
the throne of God [Heb. 12:1–2; cf. Phil. 3:12–14].

The Initial Stages of the Covenant Religion (1200–921 B.C.E.)

Mosaic religion emerged out of an interaction between economics, politics, and
culture, on the one hand, and the presence of a God-Savior, on the other hand,
who challenged, purified, and transformed human institutions. As a result, the
evolving circumstances of human life set the agenda for Israel's religion and the
basic context of its insight into God's presence. Yet the religious intuitions as well
as the moral expectations far exceeded what seemed humanly possible. People
grumbled, so that "murmuring" became a key motif of the wilderness traditions.[23] Yahweh did not relent but responded with charismatic might in the person
of such leaders as Moses and Joshua. Here then are two fundamental aspects of
biblical religion, very visible in the initial stages of the covenant and still present
today as religion continues to migrate from one culture to another.

First let us take note of the biblical insistence on an orderly, divinely willed
transition from Moses to Joshua. The final editor(s) of the books of Deuteronomy, Joshua, Judges, Samuel, and Kings were very conscious of the relationship. Deuteronomy ends and Joshua opens with reference to the death of
Moses and the succession of Joshua (Deut. 34; Josh. 1:1–9).[24] The same repetition, this time verbatim, occurs in reporting the death of Joshua in Josh. 24:28–29
and in Judg. 2:6–9. In this way we are kept aware of the transmission of the
charismatic spirit from Moses to Joshua, and from Joshua to various judges. We
note the line of continuity and the role of the spirit:

> And Joshua the son of Nun was full of the spirit of wisdom, for Moses had
> laid his hands upon him [Deut. 34:9].

> And the people served the Lord all the days of Joshua, and all the days of
> the elders who outlived Joshua, who had seen all the great work which the
> Lord had done for Israel [Judg. 2:7].

> The spirit of the Lord came upon him [the judge Ehud] and he judged Israel
> [Judg. 3:10].

> But the spirit of the Lord took possession of [the judge] Gideon [Judg.
> 6:34].

The transition from the judges to royalty is attested in the story of the last and
possibly the greatest of the judges, Samuel. Samuel's birth was announced ahead
of time at the sanctuary of Shiloh where the ark of the covenant was enshrined (1
Sam. 1:17–20), thus assuring a link with Moses. Samuel was able to guide Israel
from the early charismatic leadership of Moses, Joshua, and the Judges to the
more stable institution of monarchy. He announced the presence of the spirit as a
sign of the first king's choice. The same spirit that came upon a charismatic judge

(Judg. 3:10), enveloped Gideon (Judg. 6:34), and stirred Samson (Judg. 13:25) was to "come mightily upon" Saul and turn him "into another man" (1 Sam. 10:6). Because of disobedience (1 Sam. 13:13–14; chap. 15), "the spirit of the Lord departed from Saul, and an evil spirit from the Lord tormented him" (1 Sam. 16:14). In the meanwhile "the Spirit of the Lord came mightily upon David from that day forward" (1 Sam. 16:13).

The key phrase, linking Moses with David, turns out to be "the spirit of the Lord," the divine force by which extraordinary acts were accomplished. This *charismatic spirit*, by which God broke into human life, formed a key element of Mosaic religion. It inspired and sustained God's extraordinary hopes among the people Israel. The other key element was *human life* with emphasis upon its weak, evolving, and compromising character. The biblical tradition joined Moses with David by the bonds of human flesh. This earthly link could be weak and fallible (Num. 20:2–13), painful and purifying (Judg. 2:10–23), humorously sarcastic (Judg. 3:12–20), free and indifferent (Judg. 21:25), as sensuous and intriguing as any Byzantine court (2 Sam. 6–21; 1 Kings 1–2).

Num. 20:2–13. Moses and Aaron, because of their impatience with the Israelites, "a stiff-necked people" (Exod. 34:9), were prevented by God from leading the people into the Promised Land.

Judg. 2:10–23. Judges were raised up to deliver Israel from a bondage that had been brought on by abandoning the Lord. The Lord left the oppressor-nations in the Promised Land to test Israel.

Judg. 3:12–30. A key moment in the drama of the judge Ehud is described with barracks humor, when the servants of the Moabite king fail to intervene in his behalf because "they thought, 'He is only relieving himself in the [water] closet.' "[25]

Judg. 21:25. A transition to royalty was more and more necessary because "everyone did what was right in their own eyes."

1 Sam.8:5. The people insist that the traditional leadership of charismatic judges be dropped in favor of royalty, because "you are old and your sons do not walk in your ways." Moreover, they wanted Samuel to "appoint for us a king to govern us like all the nations." It was not divine revelation nor any other spiritual motive but emulation of foreigners that called for the new and radical institution of royalty.

2 Sam. 6–21; 1 Kings 1–2. The long succession narrative about the perpetual right to royalty within the family of David and the choice of Solomon among David's many sons is marked by jealousy, disdain, incest, adultery, fratricide, and ambition—the worst of court intrigue and family sins.

Nonetheless, the psalmist can see beneath this all-too-human situation and declare not only the achievement of God's providential plans for his chosen people but also the transfer of God's fidelity and family love to the Davidic dynasty.

Divine qualities, which are the determining factor of continuity for David, reach back to Moses on Mount Sinai: "The Lord, the Lord, a God merciful and gracious . . . abounding in steadfast love and faithfulness" (Exod. 34:6). These divine epithets are repeated in Psalm 89 and granted to David and his successors:

> I will sing of thy steadfast love,
>   O Lord, forever;
> with my mouth I will proclaim thy
>   faithfulness to all generations. . . .
> Thou hast said, "I have made a covenant
>   with my chosen one, . . .
> . . . David my servant:
> I will establish your descendants for ever. . . ."
> My *faithfulness* and my *steadfast love*
>   shall be with him [Ps. 89:1, 3, 24].[26]

Many applications to mission can be drawn from these two initial stages of covenant religion. In a later chapter we shall consider some of the parallels, for example, the biblical involvement in military violence, radical changes in styles of religious and civil government, acceptance of new moral and cultural values and the mitigation of earlier Mosaic values. At this point we underline the way by which the biblical authors were convinced of a strong continuity with Moses even if the secular world was controlling the external forms by which the Sinaitic Covenant would be reexpressed. What seemed to be happening principally through secular impulse turns out later to be attributed to the Spirit of the Lord and to be seen in direct continuity with Moses.

In the period immediately after Moses we have found two almost contrary movements: one, a full acceptance of radically new forms from the surrounding culture; the other, an explosive countermovement of the Spirit. With the same stern and practical good judgment by which Moses dealt with the desert wilderness and forged "Israel" out of murmuring ex-slaves and other riffraff, later Israelite leaders in Canaan tackled the new problems of agriculture, political treaties, and new forms of government, and formed a new "Israel" from desert invaders, identured servants, and other wandering *'apiru*.[27] There was always an immediate, human motivation for each change. Yet serious spiritual challenges were also directed against the new culture and these were linked with the charismatic challenge of the Mosaic days. It was the ability of faith to detect this dynamic presence of the Mosaic spirit within Israel's existence in Canaan that enabled Israel to strike deep roots in Canaan and at the same time develop a distinctively new religion.

The Disintegration of Politics and the Prophetic Challenge (921–587 B.C.E.)[28]

At the death of Solomon the united monarchy of north and south fell apart. Although religious leaders, notably the prophets, spearheaded and sanctioned the revolution against Jerusalem by the northern, Mosaic tribes (1 Kings 11:29–39; 12:22–24), still, as Walter Brueggemann wrote: ". . . the split did not happen over a theological dispute, but it was triggered by a concrete issue of political oppression and social liberation."[29]

The northern tribes would not accept King Rehoboam's ultimatum: "My father [Solomon] made your yoke heavy, but I will add to your yoke; my father chastised you with whips, but I will chastise you with scorpions" (1 Kings 12:14). The north's angry rejection of the Jerusalem royalty in 922 would echo about two centuries later in the fiery invectives of the prophet Jeremiah against King Jehoiakim at Jerusalem (609–597 B.C.E.). Jeremiah contrasted this wily Machiavellian prince with King Josiah:

> Woe to him who builds his house by unrighteousness,
> > and his upper rooms by injustice;
> who makes his neighbor serve him for nothing
> > and does not give him his wages;
> who says, "I will build myself a great house
> > with spacious upper rooms,"
> and cuts out windows for it,
> > paneling it with cedar
> > and painting it with vermilion.
> Do you think you are king
> > because you compete in cedar?
> Did not your father [King Josiah] eat and drink
> > and do justice and righteousness? . . .
> He judged the cause of the poor and needy;
> > then it was well. . . .
> But you have eyes and heart
> > only for your dishonest gain,
> for shedding innocent blood,
> > and for practicing oppression and violence [Jer. 22:13–17].

Although these words of Jeremiah, a blend of outrage and sarcasm, centered upon social injustices, the prophet did not speak as a social reformer or from a political economic base. The prophet felt compelled to speak by a special commission from the Lord and in the name of a God who is "merciful and gracious, . . . abounding in steadfast love and faithfulness" (Exod. 34:6). A divine call sent the prophets on this mission, as is clear in their story. For example:

Amos 7:15. The Lord took me from following the flock, and the Lord said to me, "Go prophesy to my people Israel."[30]

Jer. 1:7. But the Lord said to me, "Do not say, 'I am only a youth'; for to all to whom I send you, you shall go, and whatever I command you, you shall speak."

The occasion that stirred the prophets to a new appreciation of Yahweh came in the cry of the poor and the oppressed; the attitude or temperament that enabled them to hear the cry was formed by the ancient Mosaic tradition; the prophets' language was forged from ancient texts in the heart of contemporary controversy.

The achievements of Moses and Joshua, liberating slaves and other victimized peoples from the Egyptian pharaohs and the Canaanite petty kings, had been reversed. A whole new multitude of poor and defenseless people appeared, this time brother and sister Israelites, oppressed by a royalty that considered itself the heir and protector of the Mosaic religion. Yet, kings had profaned and contradicted the message of Moses by their disregard for family rights, by their luxurious lives and heavy taxation, and by their control of religious symbols to justify themselves. Several examples will illustrate the almost impossible task of the prophets to condemn kings, priests, and fellow prophets, all correctly anointed and validly installed in office.

Amos 7:13. The prophet was ordered by the high priest Amaziah, in the name of King Jeroboam: "Never again prophesy at Bethel, for it is the king's sanctuary, and it is a temple of the kingdom.'"

Jer. 7:4. The prophet shouted that the sacred phrase, "This is the temple of the Lord," is deceptive, no matter how often it is invoked. Jeremiah repeats it three times. Therefore, "thus says the Lord, '. . . I will make this house like Shiloh [where the ark was once enshrined], and I will make this city [of Jerusalem] a curse for all the nations of the earth' " (Jer. 26:4,6).

1 Kings 21. Within the context of fasting and prayers, King Ahab and Queen Jezebel contrived to seize the ancestral property of Naboth. Ancient traditions, protecting the rights of families and clans (Lev. 25) were brushed aside in favor of royal privileges.[32]

It was the prophets who summoned princes and priests to accountability. People without official status and institutional ordination were thus passing judgment upon the country's valid leaders, religious and civil. Prophets reached back to the ancient covenant. Because the agony of the poor was heard with such a new and urgent demand for action, the prophets called this covenant "new" and thought of it as spoken for the first time.[33] As in the days of pharaoh and Canaanite petty kings, God would sweep away—rather, he would summon foreign nations to destroy—temple, city, and dynasty in order to justify his promise of compassion toward the poor.

Strangely enough, biblical religion would survive only if centralized in the holy city of Jerusalem, and it would be justified in its goals of uniting people with a compassionate God only if the holy city were destroyed. Biblical religion found survival within its institutional leaders and centers; it was worthy of survival only by its anti-establishment leaders, the prophets.

The principal message for the mission enterprise of the church from this period, beginning with the death of Solomon and climaxing in the demise of Jerusalem (922–587 B.C.E.), lies in the recognition of prophets who cry out in the name of the oppressed and the role of foreign nations in vindicating that cry.

Exile and a Call to Re-creation (587–539 B.C.E.)

With the destruction of Jerusalem in 587 B.C.E. and the deportation of the people into a foreign land, Israel was driven back to the days before Moses:

> The Lord has brought to an end in Zion
>   appointed feast and sabbath,
> and in his fierce indignation has spurned
>   king and priest.
> The Lord has scorned his altar,
>   disowned his sanctuary;
> he has delivered into the hand of the enemy
>   the walls of her palaces;
> a clamor was raised in the house of the Lord
>   as on the day of an appointed feast. . . .
> her king and princes are among the nations;
>   the law is no more,
> and her prophets obtain
>   no vision from the Lord. . . .
> My eyes are spent with weeping;
>   my soul is in tumult;
> my heart is poured out in grief
>   because of the destruction of the daughter of my people
>   [Lam. 2:6–11].

These sorrowful lines were composed in the devastated Promised Land by one of the few Israelites left behind by the Babylonian conquerors.[34] Because this lament turned to the ancient covenant creed and called upon "The Lord, the Lord, a God merciful and gracious, slow to anger, and abounding in steadfast love and faithfulness" (Exod. 34:6), sorrow recognized a glimmer of hope:

> The steadfast love of the Lord never ceases,
>   his mercies never come to an end;
> they are new every morning;
>   great is thy faithfulness. . . .
> For the Lord will not
>   cast off for ever [Lam. 3:22, 31].

The future, however, was not to be entrusted to the remnant left behind in the former kingdom of Judah, nor to the people who had fled from the Promised

Land into Egypt, dragging the prophet Jeremiah with them against his will (Jer. 43:1-7). The exiles in Babylon would claim the title of the Lord's "true remnant," the stock from which the new people of God would develop (Jer. 24; Ezek. 11:14-21; Ezra 4:1-3).[35]

A serious sectarianism, therefore, carried over from the earlier period into the exile and after the exile into the final five hundred years before Christianity.[36] In some cases the differences that would separate the Jewish diaspora from the homeland widened into an unbridgeable gap, as happened with the Jews at Elephantine in Egypt. At other times the diaspora was no further away than Samaria, just thirty miles north of Jerusalem, yet the rift turned into an insurpassable canyon, religiously and psychologically. Even among the "true remnant" in Mesopotamia, two rival groups were taking shape. Two leaders were preaching a message, each compatible enough with the other to be included within the one Bible. Yet their message of comfort and new life tended to emphasize different values in the blueprint of a repatriated Israel.

The prophet Ezekiel, who preached before and after the fall of Jerusalem (chaps. 4-24 before 587 B.C.E.; chaps. 33-39, 40-48 afterward), became the spokesperson for the southern tradition of Jerusalem; the other prophet, called Second or Deutero-Isaiah, whose words in chapters 40-55 were attached to the scroll of Isaiah by a later editor, echoed the northern tradition of Deuteronomy, Hosea, and Jeremiah.[37] Points of comparison and contrast are summarized here:

Ezekiel	*Second Isaiah*
Stresses the cultic or liturgical acts in Israel's reconstruction (36:16-38)	Deemphasizes sacred language and liturgical function (Isa. 43:22-28)
Centers life within Jerusalem and the temple (chaps. 40-48)	Speaks symbolically about Jerusalem and never mentions the temple, unless in the controversial passage of 44:28b
Strengthens the role of the Zadokites or Jerusalem priesthood against other Levites (40:46; 43:19; 44:15-31)	Ignores the priesthood, even in passages like 52:11-12 (in Deut. 18:1-8 the privileges of the non-Zadokite Levites are defended)
Recognizes a role for the Davidic king, now called "prince" (46:2).	Returns royal privileges to the common people (55:3-5).
Identifies the moment of return by the appearance of the Lord's glory in the temple (43:1-9)	Calls the pagan foreigner Cyrus the Lord's "anointed" (45:1), like a new Moses to lead the people to freedom (45:1-7; 41:25-29)
Ends in the rejection of the nations (chaps. 38-39).	Concludes to the salvation of the Gentiles (49:6).

These points of comparison and contrast between Ezekiel and Second Isaiah could be developed at much greater length. We shall return to these key prophets in later chapters of this study. For the moment several conclusions can be reached, important for the overview of the Old Testament and helpful for the discussion of the church's mission to the world. We first summarize the biblical issues:

a. At a crucial moment like the exile when Israel was at the crossroads and faced a serious decision about future directions, no single, all-inclusive answer was available. The differences between Ezekiel and Second Isaiah were theological in that they involved priesthood, temple, and the criterion for membership within the elect people. Yet it was political and economic factors that forced Israel to rethink its theology. For instance, the question was raised whether or not the nations could be the Lord's instrument, not only to punish Israel but also to contribute positively to its salvation. Could God deign to choose a pagan foreigner, the Persian King Cyrus, to be another Moses in liberating the people? Could Israel's Babylonian experience of worshiping without a temple and without key roles for Zadokite priests indicate God's will for religious leadership and styles of prayer into the future? Could the norms of the Jerusalem temple be relaxed (Second Isaiah) or should they be tightened (Ezekiel)?

b. The two main prophets appealed to tradition to support their divergent conclusions: Ezekiel to the southern, or Jerusalem, customs and centers; Second Isaiah to the northern kingdom of Israel. While Ezekiel's case may have seemed more traditional because it had endured almost unbroken for the past half-millennium, Second Isaiah's roots reached behind the Jerusalem "innovation" of David and Solomon to the simpler forms of worship with Moses and the judges.

c. Ezekiel's theology dominated the next five hundred years of the postexilic period. Nonetheless, the response of the Second Isaiah exerted minor influences and so kept alive a religious ideal that Jesus was to evoke in his ministry and prayer.[38] While Ezekiel's successors sustained a clear and ever more rigid line of theological continuity, which almost amounted to a type of voluntary ghetto existence at Jerusalem, especially after the rules enacted by Ezra were enforced (cf. Ezra 10), Second Isaiah's traditions permitted flashes of universal salvation and the Lord's cosmic kingdom to light up even the temple ritual. Second Isaiah's influences were strongly felt by the composers of Psalms 96–99. Therefore, while the temple rules inherited from Ezekiel were very restrictive, temple symbols that came from Second Isaiah reached freely across the universe.

Reconstruction and Apocalyptic Expectations (539–7 B.C.E.)[39]

The five hundred years after the exile, which led up to the manifestation of Jesus to Israel, turn out to be the most difficult to re-create historically.[40] While many details about government and international relations or about religious parties and feasts remain shrouded in historical mists, one fact about the religious scene seems quite certain. It is verified by the bits and pieces of documentation available to us as well as by the final outcome of the postexilic period. Strenuous efforts were made to preserve the purity of the elect people. The exclusivism resulted in a serious dispute, not only between the two rival groups in exile that centered either around Ezekiel or around Second Isaiah, but even more dramatically in the seemingly innocent question: Who constitutes the true remnant of Israel? Those who returned from Babylonian exile claimed that title and rejected the stragglers left behind in the Promised Land. The struggle lasted over a century and was definitely settled by Ezra around 428 B.C.E. He demanded that all "foreign" wives and their children be dismissed (Ezra 10). At this point the split between "Jerusalem" and "Samaria" turned into irrevocable hostility.

"Samaritan" then is the name given to a people who emerged from intermarriage between the "remnants" (left behind in the destruction and deportation of the northern kingdom in 721 and the southern in 587) and foreigners who were brought in or who came spontaneously into the land. The Samaritans restricted their sacred books to the Hexateuch (the six books of Genesis, Exodus, Leviticus, Numbers, Deuteronomy, and Joshua) and so claimed close ties with Moses the lawgiver and Joshua the conqueror. The "Jews" at Jerusalem, on the contrary, emphasized a different part of their history. This other slant is seen in the two books of Chronicles, plus the books of Ezra and Nehemiah. Here the history begins with Adam and reaches to Jacob, then a quick leap to David, his dynasty, and the sacred city of Jerusalem. The period of Moses and the covenant are bypassed. These four books of 1 and 2 Chronicles, Ezra, and Nehemiah, moreover, transfer royal prerogatives to temple priests and personnel. A strict relationship is thus defended theologically among the pure Israelites, the land, the Zadokite priesthood, and the God who dwells in their temple.[41]

"A second characteristic feature of [postexilic] Judaism," to quote Werner Foerster, ". . . is the irrational fact that prophecy gradually died out."[42] The disappearance is not totally irrational. It can be explained, at least partially. Classical prophecy, as we observe it in Amos, Micah, Isaiah, or Jeremiah, presumed a situation in which politics and economics could impact upon priests and theologians and force them to new symbols and styles of worship as well as to new moral expectations. Postexilic Judaism, on the contrary, combined religion and politics so exclusively in the control of the priests that the healthy tension between these forces disappeared. Judaism, moreover, became so tiny in its geographical lines that world politics could pass it by until the very late period of the Maccabees and Hasmoneans (167–63 B.C.E.). Within its "ghetto" it tended to ignore the world and concentrate upon its ritual and ethnic purity. The natural setting for prophecy no longer existed. Prophets could not draw upon an independent, secular life to challenge and purify the religious establishment.

Yet Judaism was far more than this exclusively controlled theocracy. We can spot islands of loyal opposition among the inheritors of tradition from Jeremiah and Second Isaiah. These were an open-minded yet agonizing group of people responsible for chapters 56–66 in Isaiah as well as for books like Jonah and Ruth. These "religious rebels" challenged Judaism to reach outward:

> Let not the foreigner who has joined himself to the Lord say,
> "The Lord will surely separate me from his people";
> and let not the eunuch say,
> "Behold, I am a dry tree."

For thus says the Lord:
". . . These I will bring to my holy mountain,
   and make them joyful in my house of prayer;
their burnt offerings and their sacrifices
   will be accepted on my altar;
for my house shall be called a house of prayer
   for all peoples.
Thus says the Lord God,
   who gathers the outcasts of Israel,
I will gather yet others to him
   besides those already gathered" [Isa. 56: 3-4, 7-8].

Other "loyal opposition" groups could be found at Jerusalem. The descendants of the early sages, once close to the royalty at Jerusalem, now tended to keep their distance. Neither did they trust nor admire the earlier prophets. These sages were moderate people, financially well off, religious but by no means fanatic in their liturgical piety. The Book of Proverbs, for instance, seldom if ever mentions covenant, temple, or sacrifice; its nine-chapter introduction, composed last during the post-exilic age, draws upon royal and prophetic traditions only to attribute such benefits to wisdom.[43]

Finally, at Jerusalem the apocalyptic movement emerged out of many influences, some quite dramatic. This movement reached its most intense expression in Daniel 7-12. Weird symbols reflect the horrendous times, when the "Abomination of Desolation" was set up in the temple and the law was annulled (Dan. 9:27; 1 Macc. 2:57). The apocalyptists announced the destruction of the persecutors and the coming of God's kingdom. Yet the answer turned out differently. The kingdom of God did not drop down from heaven; rather, the Hasmonean dynasty seized political and religious power. Reactions in Judea took various forms. Different and at times hostile religious groups or sects emerged, like the Sadducees, the Pharisees, the Zealots, and the Essenes.[44] The history is long and complicated. The Romans occupied Judea in 63 B.C.E. In 37 B.C.E. the Hasmonean dynasty was totally swept aside and the last of its heirs, Antigonous, was beheaded by the Romans, who installed Herod the Great as king.

This scan of the postexilic age is not complete without calling attention more explicitly to the Pharisees, a lay religious group who became very active in winning converts to Judaism. Their missionary activity was encouraged and furthered by the large number of Jews already living abroad in the diaspora. The most successful convert work seems to have been in Asia Minor and northern Africa. Strong and influential groups of Jews also lived in Egypt and the eastern area that once was Babylon. It is no accident that out of the diaspora should come the great apostle of the Gentiles, Paul of Tarsus.

From this long postexilic period we draw two observations significant for discussing church mission. First, serious tensions emerged for the Jews when religion tended to be narrowly conservative at its home base yet simultaneously taking firm root in many distant parts of the world. The differences even amounted to a larger canon of sacred books at Alexandria, Egypt, than was normally used at Jerusalem. While Gentiles were forbidden under pain of death to go beyond the larger outer court of the Jerusalem temple, they could be admitted into the synagogues of the diaspora under the category of "God-fearers." These people believed in Yahweh yet did not submit to circumcision or follow other dietary/ceremonial rules. The diaspora was forced to question some of the traditional rules and demands of the Jerusalem priesthood.

Second, economics and politics were responsible for the spread of Jews into the Gentile world, and here the major religious leaders were lay persons, scribes and rabbis, rather than men of the Zadokite priestly line.

CONCLUSION

In drawing this chapter to a close, we shall attend to some important aspects of Israel's long history that can be important later in developing a theology of mission. The parallels can be striking and can contribute important norms or solid wisdom for the mission apostolate. We shall quickly alert the reader to some of these.

In many instances we have seen that biblical religion did not develop simply because religious leaders drew upon their own theological resources and decided to act differently. The impact of economics and politics forced priests and princes to deal with completely new situations. Wars fought by Assyria or Babylon against Egypt and its petty satellite states, as well as the entry of Greece and Rome upon the Israelite scene, scattered the Israelites and produced the diaspora. The tensions once observable between the northern and southern kingdoms of Israel and Judah were stretched to international proportions. These secular facts behind the religious changes informed Israel that it had no complete control over its agenda and development. The church, like Israel, must react to a scene oftentimes forced upon it politically.

Israel had to learn to react positively. In other words the foreign nations and the secular world of the Israelites survived and are remembered today because of the tenacity of Israel's religious tradition, but this sacred tradition was enormously enriched by the nations and by secular concerns. Escape from Egypt under Moses or the conquest of the Jebusite city by David evolved into key religious symbols of "exodus" and "holy city Zion." The church must ask what are the central events and tensions of today that can become key religious symbols to manifest the gospel message.

As Israel transformed secular events into religious types or images, religion purified and granted new life to the secular phenomena. Sometimes those secular acts were rather insignificant and never would have made history. Liturgy imparted an enduring existence by making them the rallying point for future generations and the messengers of God's secret hopes and goals for his people. The church today should never underestimate its power to reach outward and to remake those secular movements that may carry some harmful or degrading features yet are nonetheless capable of communicating the mysterious presence of the Creator.

The secular, or peripheral, world was always giving signals or flashes of great importance to Israel. The visible world preserved the memory and the presence of its invisible Maker, which Israel could turn into a word of God's personal love. Very often those incidental intuitions were as important as the main body of Israel's doctrine and life; the former summoned Israel to interact vigorously and so to fulfill its mission.

We shall proceed now according to the basic methodology of this first chapter: (1) from secular events, at times insignificant, to world history by means of liturgical celebrations and religious symbol; (2) from signals about God's universal concern for all his people to the enrichment and expansion of Israel's doctrine and life.

NOTES

1. J. R. Rosenbloom, *Conversion to Judaism from the Biblical Period to the Present, 1978* (New York: Ktav, 1978), supports the reform position that Judaism should adopt a more positive attitude toward actively seeking proselytes. The special issue of *Face to Face*, Anti-Defamation League of B'Nai B'rith (Fall–Winter 1977), devoted to "Christian Mission and Jewish Witness," is almost exclusively concerned with the legitimacy of a Christian mission toward Jews, and very little with conversions to the Jewish faith.

2. S. Sandmel, *The Several Israels* (New York: Ktav, 1971), faces the serious problem of the nonelect in a religion that emphasizes election.

3. The importance of this verse is shown by its strong echo in Isa. 43:1–7 and by the reflections upon it in 1 Pet. 2:5,9. It will be investigated in chap. 4, below.

4. B. Vawter, *On Genesis: A New Reading* (Garden City, N. Y.: Doubleday, 1977), p. 144.

5. G. von Rad, *Old Testament Theology*, 2 vols. (New York: Harper & Row, 1965), 2:342. Italics added.

6. G. von Rad, *Genesis* (Philadelphia: Westminster Press, 1972), p. 145.

7. J. Barr, "Story and History in Biblical Theology," *Journal of Religion* 56 (1976): 1–17, has rightly questioned whether biblical events like the exodus can be called "history" unless we stretch that term to a meaning quite different from secular history. Writers like Bertil Albrektson, *History and the Gods: An Essay on the Idea of Historical Events as Divine Manifestations in the Ancient Near East and in Israel* (Lund, Sweden: Gleerup, 1967), has shown decisively that the Old Testament idea of historical events is not a distinctive quality of biblical religion. In fact it "must be counted among the similarities, not among the distinctive traits; it is part of the common theology of the ancient Near East" (p.114).

8. J. J. M. Roberts, "Myth *versus* History," *Catholic Biblical Quarterly* 38 (January 1976): 1–13, argues forcefully that Israel and other ancient Near Eastern people combined both myth and history in their formulation of religious documents.

9. Cf. C. Stuhlmueller, "History as the Revelation of God in the Pentateuch," *Chicago Studies* 17 (Spring 1978): 29–44.

10. J. Barr, "Story and History," admits that "story," his preferred word in place of history, can be a source of fairly reliable bits of historical evidence and contains segments very close to actual history writing. Yet the overall purpose and context is not to report the original event but its ongoing impact, its divine causes, its relation to instruction and worship.

11. T. L. Thompson, *The Historicity of the Patriarchal Narratives*, Beihefte zur Zeitschrift für die Alttestamentliche Wissenschoft 133 (Berlin, 1974): 328. He writes further, on p. 329: "The faith of Israel is not an historical faith, in the sense of a faith based on historical event; it is rather a faith within history. . . . Its justification . . . is not in the evidence of past events . . . but in the assertion of a future promise."

12. Cf. R. de Vaux, *The Early History of Israel* (Philadelphia: Westminster Press, 1978), pp. 370-73.

13. Both English words "riffraff" and "rabble" catch not only the pejorative slur but also the word structure of the Hebrew, *hā'sapsup*. Even the Hebrew word in Exod.12:38, *'ereb rab*, by repeating key consonants, gives the impression by sight and sound of "a mixed multitude" or shall we say, "a mixed-up multitude."

14. F. R. Cross and D. N. Freedman have devoted lengthy investigation to Israel's earliest poetry: see Cross, *Canaanite Myth and Hebrew Epic* (Cambridge: Harvard University Press, 1973); see also their combined work, *Studies in Ancient Yahwistic Poetry*, Society of Biblical Literature Dissertation Series, 3 (Missoula, Mont.: Scholars Press, 1975, written in 1950), and their article, "The Song of Miriam," *Journal of Near Eastern Studies* 14 (1955): 237-50. See also D. A. Robertson, *Linguistic Evidence in Dating Early Hebrew Poetry*, Society of Biblical Literature, Dissertation Series, 3 (Missoula, Mont.: Scholars Press, 1972). Still another example of the way by which early events have been subsumed within later liturgical action is to be found in Joshua 1-6; see J. A. Wilcoxen, "Narrative Structure and Cult Legend: A Study of Joshua 1-6," *Transitions in Biblical Scholarship* (Chicago: University of Chicago Press, 1968), 6:43-70, and J. N. M. Wijngaards, *The Dramatization of Salvific History in the Deuteronomic School*, Oudtestamentische Studiën, 16 (Leiden: E. J. Brill, 1969).

15. For an excellent popular summary of the classic solution of the Pentateuchal question along the lines of the four traditions—J (Yahwist), E (Elohist), D (Deuteronomic), P (Priestly)—and their intertwining with Israelite history and worship, see W. Brueggemann and H. W. Wolff, *The Vitality of Old Testament Tradition*, 2nd ed., (Atlanta: John Knox Press, 1982). One of the most serious challenges has come from T. L. Thompson, *The Historicity of the Patriarchal Narratives*. See *Journal for the Study of the Old Testament* 2 (April 1977) and 3 (July 1977), for the patriarchal narratives and the Yahwist tradition.

16. While Genesis 10-50 is generally favorable to the patriarchs and recognizes a divine plan in their lives (opening statement in Gen. 12:1-4 and closing statements in Gen. 45:5; 50:20), other cautious or unfavorable judgments appear; about Judah in Genesis 38; about Simeon and Levi in Genesis 34; 49:5-7; and about Terah in Josh. 24:27.

17. B. Vawter, *On Genesis*, p. 355.

18. Hos. 2:16-17 (18-19) orders the people no longer to address Yahweh as "My Baal." Jer. 11:13 already substituted the word *bosheth* for *ba'al*: "altars you have set up to shame" (RSV). At times a late book like Chronicles, composed long after the religious threat of *ba'al* was over, will preserve the original form of *ba'al* with proper names: *'eshba'al* in 1 Chron. 8:33; 9:39; *Meribba'al* in 1 Chron. 8:34; 9:40; the earlier

book of Samuel, composed during the religious battle against *ba'al* syncretism with Yahweh worship will read *'ish-bosheth* (2 Sam. 2:8) or *Mephiboseth* (2 Sam. 4:4).

19. M. H. Mulder, *"Ba'al," Theological Dictionary of the Old Testament* (Grand Rapids, Mich.: Wm. B. Eerdmans, 1974–), 2: 200.

20. R. de Vaux, "Israël, " *Dictionnaire de la Bible Supplément* (Paris: Letouzey & Ané, 1928–), 4:736.

21. R. de Vaux, *The Early History of Israel*, pp. 453–54. Italics added.

22. Cf. B. S. Childs, *The Book of Exodus* (Philadelphia: Westminster Press, 1974), pp. 529–37. He concludes, on p. 537: "We recovered a level of ancient tradition which preceded the Priestly source, but which then was carefuly adjusted to the Priestly theology, in spite of signs of continuing friction between the levels."

23. Cf. G. W. Coats, *Rebellion in the Wilderness: The Murmuring Motif in the Wilderness Traditions of the Old Testament* (Nashville: Abingdon, 1968).

24. The early chapters in the book of Joshua are particularly conscious of this modeling of Joshua upon the image of Moses: cf. Josh. 3:7; 4:14; 5:13–15.

25. Along with low humor this account of the judge Ehud is written in a brilliant ballad style with catchy rhythm, play on words, skillful repetition, and all the suspense of a detective story: i.e., Ehud, a left-handed individual from the tribe of Benjamin (*Ben-jemini* in Hebrew means "Son of my right hand") was commissioned to bring a tribute of grain to the foreign oppressor. He really "gives it," however, when with his left hand he forces another kind of tribute upon the Moabite king—a sword "into his belly," which was so obese that "the fat closed over the blade."

26. The parallels between the Mosaic covenant and the Davidic covenant, between Yahweh's royal power and that of the Davidic kings are developed by J.-B. Dumortier, "Un rituel d' intronisation: Le Ps. LXXXIX 2–38," *Vetus Testamentum* 22 (1972): 176–96.

27. The history and even the meaning and spelling of *'apiru* are involved questions. We refer to the extensive review by R. de Vaux, *The Early History of Israel*, p. 861, historical index. On p. 214 he summarizes the two principal characteristics that "could certainly be applied to the ancestors of the Israelites": (1) strangers not fully integrated into the population where they lived; (2) mobile and ubiquitous. Their presence in the Bible will be discussed more fully in chap. 2, below.

28. The final planning of this chapter was completed before my reading of W. Brueggemann, "Trajectories in Old Testament Literature and the Sociology of Ancient Israel," *Journal of Biblical Literature* 98 (1979): 161–85. However, I am indebted to Brueggemann, not only for confirmation of some ideas but also for many excellent new insights.

29. W. Brueggeman, "Trajectories," p. 172.

30. In the episode in Amos 7:10–17, a confrontation between Amos and the high priest Amaziah (vv. 10–13) prepares for two significant oracles by Amos; the first concerns his call by Yahweh (vv.14–15), the second God's judgment against Amaziah; cf. H. W. Wolff, *Joel and Amos* (Philadelphia: Fortress Press, 1977), p. 308. Amos' call is modeled upon the extraordinary way that God "took [David] from the pasture and from the care of the flock to be commander of my people Israel" (2 Sam. 7:8). Amos' stress upon Yahweh's initiative in his prophetic call is evident again in 3:8, a text that "suggests the authority of the one who must speak out in no uncertain terms . . . just as surely as Yahweh placed his awesome demand upon him" (Wolff, p. 187).

31. The prophetic author of this section makes a brilliant play on Hebrew words: "never again prophesy at Bethel [the Hebrew reads "house of God] for it is . . . a

temple of the kingdom [the Hebrew reads *beth-mamlākâ*]." The high priest of Bethel repudiates the words that came from God and certainly belong in the "house of God" (*beth-'el*) because he claims that Bethel really is the house of royalty (*beth-mamlākâ*).

32. Cf. W. Brueggemann, "Trajectories," p. 172.

33. Such is the way that Jer. 31:31–34 reinterprets Deut. 6:4–9. Cf. J. Swetnam, "Why Was Jeremiah's New Covenant New?" *Studies on Prophecies, Supplement to Vetus Testamentum 26* (Leiden: E.J. Brill, 1974): 111–15.

34. Cf. D. R. Hillers, *Lamentations* (Garden City, N.Y.: Doubleday, 1972), p. xxiii.

35. D. E. Gowan, *Bridge between the Testaments* (Pittsburgh: Pickwick Press, 1976), pp. 36–38, "Tensions between the Returnees and the 'People of the Land.' "

36. This sectarianism became ever more pronounced, particularly after Ezra hardened the conditions for belonging to "Judaism." See M. Stone, *Scriptures, Sects and Visions: A Profile of Judaism from Ezra to the Jewish Revolts* (Philadelphia: Fortress Press, 1980); W. S. McCullough, *The History and Literature of the Palestinian Jews from Cyrus to Herod* (Toronto: University of Toronto Press, 1975). P. D. Hanson, *The Dawn of Apocalyptic*, 2nd ed. (Philadelphia: Fortress Press, 1979), explains and documents the struggle, principally between the "realistic," or "pragmatic," element and the "visionary" element. The latter won out, so that preexilic prophecy was silenced and an apocalyptic movement developed gradually in its place. Resistance to this development is evident in books like Isaiah 56–66.

37. The similarities between Ezekiel and Second Isaiah were overstressed by D. Baltzer, *Ezechiel und Deuterojesaja* (New York: Walter de Gruyter, 1971), yet this book indicates the close interaction of thought and the possibility of a workable synthesis. See my review in *Biblical Theology Bulletin* 3 (1973): 100–102.

38. Cf. P. D. Hanson, *The Dawn of Apocalyptic*, chap. 2; and, below, chap. 6.

39. The date 7 B.C.E. represents the birth of Jesus. It is difficult to decide on the real, pivotal moment when the disciples of Jesus moved away from their parent, Judaism: cf. below, chap. 6.

40. Cf. J. Bright, *A History of Israel*, 2nd ed. (Philadelphia: Westminster Press, 1972), p. 343: "To write the history of Israel in this period is difficult in the extreme. Our Biblical sources are at best inadequate. . . . dismaying lacunae and baffling problems remain."

41. Cf. S. Japhet, "Conquest and Settlement in Chronicles," *Journal of Biblical Literature* 98 (1979): 205–18.

42. W. Foerster, *From the Exile to Christ* (Philadelphia: Fortress Press, 1964), p. 4. Cf. Ps. 74:9; 1 Macc. 4:46; 9:27; 14:41.

43. The most adequate treatment of the sapiential movement has been written by G. von Rad, *Wisdom in Israel* (Nashville: Abingdon, 1972). The interaction of *Wisdom and Cult* is the title of a book by L. G. Perdue (Missoula, Mont.: Scholars Press, 1977) where the sages' reaction is not seen to be overly negative and is carefully nuanced. E. E. Urbach, *The Sages: Their Concepts and Beliefs* (Jerusalem: Magnes Press, 1975), pp. 551–54, takes up the topic of "election and proselytization" in Judaism after the fall of the temple and later in the Roman empire. Urbach points out the ambiguity among the Jewish rabbis and sages, whether or not to encourage or discourage converts, and how difficult to make the conditions. R. Gordis, *Poets, Prophets and Sages* (Bloomington: Indiana University Press, 1970), pp. 160–97, discusses "The Social Background of Wisdom Literature."

44. See references cited in n. 36, above.

2

The Biblical Process of Acculturation

Your origin and your birth are of the land of the Canaanites; your father was an Amorite, and your mother a Hittite [Ezek. 16:3].

God did not begin biblical religion by creating Israel out of nothing at the first dawn of life on planet earth. God chose Israel after the world and the human race had already existed for thousands and perhaps millions of years. Consequently the earliest appreciation or understanding of God within the Bible did not center upon God as maker of the universe or as creator of the human race but as *savior* of the chosen people Israel. In this chapter we pursue some of the consequences of this divine decision to intervene primarily as savior rather than as creator. World mission, too, never begins ex nihilo but within a preexisting culture.

GOD AS SAVIOR AND AS CREATOR

Chronologically, of course, creation came first, but salvation is to be given first place theologically. The Bible does open with a dramatic narrative about "the generations of the heavens and the earth when they were created" (Gen. 2:4), yet the first eleven chapters of Genesis were gathered together at a late period of Israelite history, solemnly to introduce God's law of salvation in the Torah (the five books from Genesis through Deuteronomy). These chapters of Genesis are best interpreted as a theological commentary upon God's way of saving his people Israel.[1] The organization of these chapters was first undertaken during the reigns of David and Solomon (1004–921 B.C.E.) and revised during the exile (587–539 B.C.E.). Each time the new revision served a religious purpose: for David and Solomon, the framework for their empire and the support of their dynasty; during the exile, the hope of re-creating their lives in the Promised Land; after the exile, the faith in God's final kingdom on earth.

It is important for the theology of mission that we pursue further this distinction between "creation" and "salvation."[2] If biblical religion were based upon God's act of creation, then we would conclude *(a)* that God normally acts alone in solitary divine splendor, as he must have done in making the world out of nothing; *(b)* that God achieves at once whatever he decides and is known most of all for his omnipotence; *(c)* that God acts within a perfect situation, for he can produce nothing unworthy and so the refrain rings out: "And God saw that it was good" (Gen. 1:4,10,12,18,21,25,31); *(d)* that the details of God's creative action throughout the universe can be measured by scientific instruments; and *(e)* that God's first creative act is unique and can never be repeated.

If, on the contrary, biblical religion is not inaugurated at the moment of first creation but within the course of human history, then there is a radical shift in emphasis. By contrast with the creation-based model of religion just described, we now see *(a)* that God does not act alone but within an elaborate human network of politics, economics, and social customs; *(b)* that God does not impress us so much with his power as with his mercy and tolerance toward human weakness, ignorance, and even deliberate sin; *(c)* that the setting of God's action is no longer the unimpeded, open arena of nothingness as at first creation, but the muddy water and polluted atmosphere of human life; *(d)* that God's action turns out to be immeasurable, for no one can determine the height and depth of his motivating love (Eph. 3:18); and *(e)* that God's great redemptive acts (the *mirabilia Dei*) could, in fact must, be repeated over and over again.

According to this new schema, biblical religion rests upon God's willingness to deal with the complicated situation of human life, not only as formed according to its culture and values, but also as deformed by its sin, weakness, and prejudice. Religion results from God's initiative within a preexisting pattern of human existence. This process by which God draws upon a people's lifestyle, purifies and redirects it, and so enables this community to fashion under divine providence a pattern of worship, morality, and hopes—this process within religion we are calling "acculturation." One biblical text in particular articulates this mysterious, immanent way of Immanuel, or God-with-us:

> Seek the Lord while he may be found,
>   call upon him while he is near;
> let the wicked forsake his way,
>   and the unrighteous man his thoughts;
> let him return to the Lord that he may have mercy on him,
>   and to our God, for he will abundantly pardon.
> For my thoughts are not your thoughts,
>   neither are your ways my ways, says the Lord.
> For as the heavens are higher than the earth,
>   so are my ways higher than your ways
>   and my thoughts than your thoughts.
> For as the rain and the snow come down from heaven,
>   and return not thither but water the earth,
> making it bring forth and sprout,
>   giving seed to the sower and bread to the eater,
> so shall my word be that goes forth from my mouth;
>   it shall not return to me empty,
> but it shall accomplish that which I purpose,
>   and prosper in the thing for which I sent it [Isa.55:6–11].

The importance of these lines for guiding our appreciation of Old Testament theology and for directing our pastoral application to mission cannot be overestimated. We call attention to the sequence of action within this poem: *(a)* though wicked and unrighteous, we can still call upon the Lord "while he is near" us; *(b)* we are expected to make a clean decision: "Call upon him . . . let the wicked forsake their way"; even if we cannot foresee all the consequences, we must act resolutely and trustfully; *(c)* continuing the attitude of confident surrender to God, we are reminded of the Lord's mysterious plan of salvation for us; God's thoughts are higher than ours "as the heavens are higher than the earth"; *(d)* yet God does not remain transcendentally aloof, nor are his thoughts suspended like majestic clouds in the sky. Rather, God's Word falls gently, "as the rain and the snow come down," soaking the ground, and gradually "it shall . . . return to me," says God, not empty but in the earthy form of trees, bushes, and grain.

The divine Word reaches back toward God in human forms—in ancient languages and psychological patterns, even within the compromising situations of human prejudice, ambition, and ignorance. No matter how embarrassingly human the setting and form of God's message may be, it still throbs with an impulse or élan toward heaven. Like plants and bushes, God's Word reaches spontaneously toward the sun. At the heart of our human existence, individually and socially, an effective and mysterious core of life prompts us to live "divinely," with hopes, decisions, and actions that are heroic, beyond a merely human explanation.

The cycle of life with which Second Isaiah described God's way of dealing with his human family catches the spirit and the tension of this chapter and the following one. Here in chapter 2 we discuss the process of acculturation by which God's Word was absorbed and then communicated within human language and culture. In chapter 3 we face up to the challenges that come to our earthly existence as God's hopes draw our human way above earth toward heaven. Neither chapter can be adequately understood without the other.

According to Isa. 55:6–11, God's will and plan preexist from all eternity. Nonetheless they are not known until, like rain and snow, they soak the earth and emerge out of the earth in new forms of life. God's mysterious Word, once as transcendentally above us as sky and clouds, is now manifest within the context and relationship of human life. Having accepted this human form of God's will within our society, almost at once we are impelled to protest prophetically against our inadequate and biased understanding of God's Word. Yet, as mentioned above, the sequence is crucial and must be respected. Not until we accept the human form can we ever begin to intuit the divine impulse *within it* and from this insight the prophetic challenge erupts.

STRUGGLE—INDIGENIZATION—CHALLENGE

A second introductory question must be faced. The acculturation process, by which revelation rises to the surface and directs human life according to God's will, generally follows a three-stage procedure.[3] Put as succinctly as possible, it reads: *(a)* a new people or a new idea at first generates some type of violence or struggle; *(b)* a long process of indigenization follows by which the new people or the new idea adapts itself and becomes fully at home in its surroundings; *(c)* after this sinking of roots and adaptation to the environment, a prophetic challenge emerges on the home front. The first two stages will be investigated in this chapter. The third stage of prophetic confrontation will be examined in chapter 3.

This threefold method is foundational to our study of the Old Testament and its application to mission. Actually it is repeated over and over again in public as well as in private areas of human life. Israel in its history went through this cycle of initial violence, long indigenization, and prophetic challenge quite often. For example:

1. *In the patriarchal narratives.* After Abraham was uprooted from Ur of the Chaldeans (Gen. 11:31), he eventually made his home in Canaan, and resided briefly in Egypt. In each instance he was a *gēr,* or resident alien (Gen. 15:13; 23:4).⁴ Never completely accepted, Abraham must have felt in his life and in his family circle some of the struggle associated with stage *(a).* Nonetheless he followed local customs (Gen. 16:1–6), worshiped at Canaanite shrines (Gen. 12:6,8), purchased a burial plot (Gen. 23), and so settled into stage *(b),* indigenization. Yet there are also signs of the stage *(c),* of prophetic challenge, when Abraham eventually differed with Canaanite sexual practices (Gen. 20) and with child sacrifice (Gen. 22).

2. *In the settlement of the land.* No matter how peaceful or how turbulent was Israel's taking possession of Canaan, the initial beachhead after crossing the Jordan had violent repercussions. It precipitated revolts among the slaves of Canaan and other migrant people like the *'apiru.* This initial stage was followed by Israel's energetic endeavor to control the land, to adapt to its needs and possibilities, and to become Canaanite in most external ways, stage *(b).* The serious prophetic threat of stage *(c)* came only much later, close to five hundred years after Joshua and the start of stage *(b).*

3. *In exile.* During this time the three-stage principle is established in reverse. Despite the initial stage of violence when Jerusalem was destroyed in 587 B.C.E. and the majority of the people dragged into exile, Israel refused to adapt itself to Babylonian ways and instead, through its leadership, dreamed of and planned a return to the Promised Land. Therefore, so far as the biblical account is concerned, a prophetic challenge to Israel's adoption of Babylonian customs never came to pass (the later history of the diaspora and of the Babylonian Talmud is another question, outside our present scope of study). Therefore, unless a long period of settling in takes place, the classical prophetic response does not occur.

4. *After the exile.* Despite the long periods of silence in the postexilic period (539 B.C.E. onward), we can still detect the repetition of the three-stage principle. The first returnees encountered many difficulties, not only because of their small numbers, their inertia, and their poverty (cf. Haggai), but also because of the local inhabitants (Ezra 4; Neh. 3:33–4:16; chap. 6). During the early years of the postexilic period Israel's style of settling in was spectacularly different from the period of Joshua, Judges, and the preexilic monarchy. The returnees lived within

a small country only ten miles square and refused all contact with the local inhabitants. The people of Judah developed a self-contained theocracy, small enough to be called a ghetto. For this reason, as mentioned in chapter 1, above, the prophetic challenge of stage *(c)* never eventuated in the postexilic period, unless it be in such scattered attempts as Jonah, Job, or Ruth, where a more universal outreach questioned the prevailing, narrow view of the ruling class at Jerusalem, or in the anthology of prophetic preaching in Isaiah 56–66.[5]

Both stages *(a)* and *(b),* which we shall now consider, offer a good biblical model for the missionary apostolate. So often the first appearance of Christianity came either with conquering armies or at least with the shock waves of its Western forms of worship and its separate scale of values. Since the close of World War II, and for the Roman Catholic church particularly since Vatican II, the long period of indigenization has set in.

VIOLENCE OR STRUGGLE IN THE OLD TESTAMENT

According to the schema we are following, many periods of biblical history began with some type of violence or struggle: the appearance of the patriarchs in the Promised Land; the beachhead of the invading Israelites under Joshua; the thrust into exile; the reestablishment in the land after the exile. Violence also shook the history of Israel at many other times, particularly in the wars fought by Israel in the days of David or waged against Israel in answer to prophetic threat. The fact of violence in the Old Testament is recognized by everyone. As Peter C. Craigie wrote: "Our role is more to explain than to defend the warlike material of the Old Testament. We need to explain its theological richness, its implications for our understanding of God, and its relevance to Christian living."[6] We shall first define violence and then in the light of this definition indicate its many different forms in the Old Testament. We shall then proceed with two sets of consequences, helpful for the mission apostolate.

Violence intrudes upon us on many different levels of human existence and cannot be reduced simply to physical force. Within our present century we have heard of many sophisticated kinds of psychological injury or injustice, like brainwashing, massive propaganda, vilification, threats, and high-pressure advertising. Psychological violence may be necessary and beneficial. It is obligatory to report the death of a loved one, even though it induces a flood of emotional agony and deprives that person of rational speech. Physical violence is practiced continuously in hospitals, for example, when people are anesthetized and driven into unconsciousness; or when arms or legs or other bodily organs are removed. Even if the purpose is to prolong life or at least to curtail pain, nonetheless the means that are used represent a severe and at times irreversible intrusion upon the normal process of life.

When violence is viewed across this wide span of human activity, physical or psychological, volitional or nonrational, for good as well as for evil motives, our definition of it has to be morally neutral and descriptively far-reaching. *Violence then is here understood as any strong initiative or forceful action that reaches*

*beyond normal dialogue, infringes upon the freedom of the other(s), and imposes
a solution or a situation upon others, at times against their desires.*

In order to understand better this definition for future discussion about mission, we indicate some types of violence in the Old Testament.

Physical violence occurs frequently enough in the biblical narrative, from the
murder of Abel in the first book of the Bible (Gen. 4:8) to the destruction of
Jerusalem in the final chapter of the second book of Chronicles, the last book in
the Hebrew arrangement of the Bible. In the last chapter of 2 Maccabees (2 Macc.
15:35), the book that closes the Vulgate arrangement of the Old Testament, we
read about the impalement of "Nicanor's head on the wall of the citadel." The
Old Testament sanctioned [7] war, even the *herem*, or "holy" war (1 Sam. 15)[8];
Peter C. Craigie wrote:

> . . . in expressing a particular understanding of the realities of political
> existence (and of the necessary implications of statehood), I am suggesting
> that the existence of the ancient state of Israel *necessarily* involved an asso-
> ciation between that state and violence (especially war) at every point in its
> existence.[9]

The Hebrew Bible also legislated for capital punishment by stoning (Deut. 17:5),
by burning (Lev. 20:14), and by the sword (Deut. 13:15).[10]

Psychological violence shows up in many forms. We cite the trauma of Sarai
whom Abram instructed: "Say you are my sister, that it may go well with me
because of you"(Gen. 12:13). Abram was paid handsomely. On another occasion
psychological violence swirled around Abraham himself when God ordered him:
"Take your son, your only son Isaac, whom you love, and go to the land of
Moriah, and offer him there as a burnt offering" (Gen. 22:2).

Ascetical violence is demanded of the high priests who "shall not go in to any
dead body, nor defile himself, even [to be present at the death or to mourn] for his
father or for his mother" (Lev. 21:11). Jeremiah was ordered by the Lord "not
[to] take a wife, nor [to] have sons or daughters in this place" (Jer. 16:2). Ezekiel,
likewise, was forbidden any normal public acts of mourning at the death of his
wife, "the delight of your eyes" (Ezek. 24:16–18). Usually redundant and wordy,
Ezekiel at this point remarked with sturdy self-control: "I did as I had been commanded." These examples symbolize severe crises and painful losses, by which
God purified and transformed his people.

Liturgical violence is reflected in the many sacred ceremonies that commemorated the Lord's victory over hostile powers. In fact, one of the earliest yet most continuously used titles for Yahweh was *gibbor* (warrior).[11] The
prophet Isaiah firmly established another title in biblical tradition, *yahweh
ṣba'ôth,* the Lord of armies or hosts. These and other similar titles were
drawn from the military. When applied to Yahweh, these terms signified (as Israel confessed) that "with us is the Lord our God, to help us and *to fight our
battles"* (1 Chron. 32:8). The Lord was also described battling superhuman
forces:

Thou didst crush Rahab like a carcass
thou didst scatter the enemies with thy mighty arm [Ps. 89:10].

Liturgy was reflecting battles of cosmic proportions between mammoth forces of goodness and evil, which somehow affected the daily lives of Israelite people.

Prophetic violence is seen not only in the role of prophets to anoint kings and to topple dynasties but also in such dramatic contests as that between Elijah and the 450 prophets of Baal. This latter episode ended when Elijah ordered them to be seized, so that "not one of them [might] escape." The prophet then "brought them down to the brook Kishon, and there [translating the Hebrew literally] he slaughtered them by slitting their throats" (1 Kings 18:40).

God inspired particularly the prophets to act energetically in the name of justice and to defend the poor and the helpless. We read that "Elisha the prophet called one of the sons of the prophets: and sent him to anoint Jehu king over Israel. After pouring the oil on his head, he declared:

Thus says the Lord the God of Israel, I anoint you king over the people of the Lord, over Israel. And you shall strike down the house of Ahab your master, that I may avenge on Jezebel the blood of my servants and prophets and the blood of all the servants of the Lord [2 Kings 9:6–7].[12]

In this way God fiercely vindicated the rights of many innocent sufferers, including Naboth whose vineyard had been confiscated and whose life had been taken by decree of King Ahab and Queen Jezebel (1 Kings 21).

In the prophetic literature we detect an important development in the topic of violence: from the earlier "charismatic" prophets like Samuel, Elijah, and Elisha, to the later "classical" prophets like Amos and Isaiah, and finally to the apocalyptic movement within prophecy. The charismatic prophets summoned Israel to war against the foreigners, as in the case of Samuel (1 Sam. 15), or they precipitated a palace revolt to wipe out a dynasty, as in the case of Elisha (2 Kings 9). A radical new turn came "with the appearance of [the classical] prophets who stood holy war on its head by audaciously declaring that in the wars at hand Yahweh fought [with the foreign nations] against Israel."[13] In these wars, according to the prophet Isaiah, the Gentiles had a positive role in forming the religious history of Israel.[14] Prophetic evolvement continued into the later, apocalytic literature like Daniel 7–12, in which Yahweh no longer depended upon any earthly power but battled directly against gigantic forces to establish the promised kingdom. At this juncture no human being participates in the holy war, only God, the angels, and the demons; men and women have been reduced to absolute helplessness.

After defining violence and surveying some of its manifestations in the Old Testament, we now attempt to isolate two aspects of this topic that may be helpful for future application to the mission apostolate.

First of all, violence cannot be dismissed or excised from the Old Testament without mutilating the basic structure of the Scriptures, or at least without seriously interrupting the development of thought or action in key books. The many forms and the almost continuous presence of violence in the Old Testament mean that violence is closely intertwined with the question of biblical inspiration. We cannot deny inspiration to the "violent passages" and still uphold the overall inspiration of the Old Testament. Nor can we relegate the statements about war and struggle to a few isolated and minimally inspired passages. They are not confined to appendices like 2 Samuel 21–22.

Violence ought to be considered a charism or gift put to the service of God's people and God's providential plan, just as truly as any other quality, like pacifism or prayer.[15] Some persons have the knack of going straight for the jugular vein of any issue. Like the prophet Jeremiah they are called

> to pluck up and to break down,
> to destroy and to overthrow,

before they are summoned

> to build and to plant [Jer. 1:10].[16]

These persons reduce major questions to a plain Yea or Nay (Mt. 5:37) so that sides are quickly taken and the battle lines drawn.

A second parallel between the presence of violence in the Old Testament and the missionary effort of the church can be seen in the heroic demands made upon the human agent. For these "chosen" people there is simply no easy and certainly no normal way of acting. Marriage was denied Jeremiah; he had to face many other deprivations. Ascetical violence was the only effective way to proceed.

Jeremiah's celibacy was understood symbolically, uniting the prophet with "the sons and daughters who are born in this place, and [with] the mothers who bore them and [with] the fathers who begot them in this land" (Jer. 16:3). These parents would be deprived of their children who "shall die of deadly diseases. . . . They shall perish by the sword and by famine" (Jer. 16:4). The book of Jeremiah does not develop the theological consequences, yet this asceticism was an important aspect of the prophet's spiritual development and an equally essential element in his message, a message that was ultimately directed "to build and to plant."

The heroic quality and personal dedication within biblical asceticism remind us that violence blindly dedicated to destruction is as wrong as passive refusal ever to inflict suffering or death. M. Douglas Meeks pointed out the misdirection and mistakes that are possible on either side, when he wrote that "power without suffering is a-historical and self-destructive, just as suffering totally bereft of power would be a state of non-being or an illusion."[17] This statement leads to serious difficulty when we remember that in the Bible God fulfilled his plans by various forms of violence, and by divine inspiration God sanctioned the positive infliction of pain, as our previous examples have indicated.

At this point we are drawn into the mystery of pain, which the long and masterful book of Job could not unravel. Again we quote from Meeks' study:

> God is most problematic and "dangerous" for us (theologically speaking) when he is *in passion:* angry, cursing, in rage, crying, broken hearted over his creatures, and suffering to free them. These are the unbecoming aspects of God which we had not expected to encounter. But should we not take seriously the *theologia crucis?*[18]

If "it is obscene to say that oppressed people should suffer for their salvation,"[19] then those who fight for their liberation must be "the pure of heart" who can restore and again see the face of God upon these his beloved (cf. Mt. 5:8).

This section on violence and struggle was investigated under the rubric of a three-stage plan of acculturation and salvation that is repeated in many important cycles of biblical religion. At first a new idea or a new people generates some type of violence or struggle; they upset the old order. Such violence must be followed by a long period of indigenization if the new idea or new people is to take root, adapt itself, and prosper. Much later a prophetic challenge calls into question the false forms of adaptation that compromise the basic insights of biblical religion. It has been our position that the first stage—violence in its many forms—makes a positive contribution and is directly willed by God. We have delayed over this stage because violence is such a prevalent phenomenon in many mission countries and in cross-cultural ministries. We now turn to the second stage by which God's message of salvation is lived and expressed—the prolonged process of indigenization.

INDIGENIZATION

We find ourselves within the context of Israel's settlement in the land of Canaan after the death of Moses (Deut. 34). While military expeditions were undertaken against the local population by Joshua and the later judges, the studies of Norman Gottwald and George E. Mendenhall have shifted attention away from "the frequency, scope, and degree" of these wars.[20] The sociopolitical base of events is turning out to be far more complex than what scholars earlier imagined.[21] This complicated intertwining of faith with politics, economics, and war demonstrates how thoroughly Israel's leaders were willing to accept the consequences of indigenization for their religion.

Two aspects of this second stage combined in such a way as to maintain continuity with the earlier Mosaic period and at the same time to transform the Mosaic religion. In this healthy tension we detect the principle of growth.

The first aspect summoned Israel in the spirit of the Mosaic age to liberate slaves and care for defenseless and needy people. What began in Egypt and continued in the Sinai peninsula was right at home in the heart of Canaan, where many people had been reduced to severe economic conditions and political helplessness by the petty kings within the land. These people were on the verge of revolt when the Israelites crossed the river Jordan and acquired a beachhead near the ancient city of Jericho.

The other aspect, this time of discontinuity with the Mosaic spirit, is seen in a constant temptation for the "Israelites" to get control, to establish royal dynasties and to subjugate foreign people as slaves. From Moses came the spirit of liberation and migration; from Canaanite city-states came the desire for power and stability.

The first aspect. The Israelites who fled Egypt under Moses and were led across the river Jordan by Joshua easily recognized a special bond of kinship with two types of people in the land of Canaan. One group consisted of the farmers in the countryside who had lost most of their independence to the petty kings who ruled the city-states. Another group was made up of foreigners who had been forced to migrate into Canaan by the upheavals in northern Syria and the Mesopotamian area. This latter group would hire themselves out as mercenaries to the petty kings and yet could easily be tempted to side with the farmers or with rival vassals.

The unsettled conditions of Canaan at this time and even earlier are revealed in a series of diplomatic letters written by the kings and by Egyptian officials in Canaan and Syria to the Egyptian pharaohs Amenophis III and Amenophis IV (the latter is the famous "monotheist," also called Akhenaten). Some of these letters, called the Amarna tablets, refer to a rebel group of people as the *'apiru*.[22]

The word *'apiru*, or *'abiru*, comes from the same Semitic root from which our word "Hebrew" was derived. Each has the same set of consonants. The basic root was *hbr*, or *'hr*, which meant "to cross" (Gen. 31:21) or "to pass on" or "to pass through" (Gen. 12:6; Judg. 11:29). Mendenhall writes:

> . . . the term "Hebrew," *Hab/piru, 'Apiru* . . . recurs in many sources from 2000 B.C. to its last occurrences in the Hebrew Bible about the time of David, who was himself a Hebrew in this sense when he was fleeing from King Saul—not through choice, but through necessity of self-preservation. . . . If the early Israelites were called "Hebrews," they could be termed so only from the point of view of some existing, legitimate political society from which they had withdrawn. In other words, no one could be born a "Hebrew"; he became so only by his own action, whether of necessity or by the inability any longer to tolerate the irrationalities of the society in which he was born.[23]

Joshua united the dissident groups in Canaan with his own followers—at times by treaty (Josh. 8:30–35) and at other times militarily (Josh. 10:28–11:23). Together they formed a federation that in the days of David and Solomon eventually became the twelve tribes of Israel. At the very center of these treaties and conquests there abided an intuition of Yahweh as compassionate toward the lowly, as firmly loyal to his elect people, as sternly just in securing the rights of the dispossessed. Israel's religion found its origin and continuity in God's concern for the lowly, the deprived, and the helpless. This religion was rooted in a historical-sociological process, and yet it ran independently of national or urban power-centers and therefore in this latter sense it was not part of what normally constituted the fiber of the historical-sociological process.

This new birth of national life came from a most unlikely source of weakness and sterility. As a result biblical tradition could speak of a miraculous source of power and of charismatic leadership. From Abraham and especially from Moses onward, people arose with sudden bursts of energy. Israelite history followed most unpredictable ways. At the heart was God's compassionate love and powerful determination to make the poor and lowly the center of his concern, and their liberation the goal of his intervention.

The second aspect. This aspect of Israelite religion was a countermovement that strove for stability, control, and success. It drew Israel back into "the same sort of power-centered, status-centered society as that which they had escaped."[24] It took shape, first, in absorbing various modes or styles of Canaanite culture and, second, in establishing the institution of monarchy. Despite the seeming betrayal of Mosaic ideals, this development must not be judged too harshly. It was necessary if Israel was to survive in the new land of Canaan, the "Promised Land." Through the Davidic dynasty came the city and temple, and through the Jerusalem temple Israel found a lifeline that extended across the long postexilic period into the common era with Christianity.[25]

We have observed that the earliest facets of Israel's faith—its inspired intuition of God as compassionate toward the poor and its own identification as God's "migrant" or "exodus" people—were mediated through the sociological-political situation of escape from Egypt and journey through the Sinai desert. Likewise Israel's new forms of life and worship in the Promised Land a fortiori would have been derived from human sources, principally from the Canaanites but also from the larger Near Eastern environment. Even if this human shape of Israel's life received a solemn, divine endorsement as God's Word in the Holy Scriptures, it is important to note that the external forms were not immediately revealed by God. The implications of this fact will be crucial for any discussion of the acculturation process in the missionary work of the church.

In ancient Israel—and for that matter, today—the acculturation process could turn out to be very threatening to what many consider to be the divine and therefore the immutable truths of religion. For Israel the spirit of the "exodus" was an essential aspect of Mosaic religion. Symbolically this exodus motif demanded that the ark of the covenant must always move with the people, and therefore it was not to be hidden away in a grandiose temple and to be visible only to high priest or king. This concern for the ancient, mobile symbol of the ark was linked with a fear of many aspects of Canaanite worship: its sensuality, its pompous ceremonial, its wealth, and its class-consciousness. When David wanted to build a temple, God sent this negative reply through the prophet Nathan:

> Would you build me a house to dwell in? I have not dwelt in a house since the day that I brought up the people of Israel from Egypt to this day, but I have been moving about in a tent for my dwelling. In all places where I have

moved with all the people of Israel, did I speak a word with any of the judges of Israel, whom I commanded to shepherd my people Israel, saying, "Why have you not built me a house of cedar?" [2 Sam. 7:5-7].

Later when Solomon was finally able to construct a temple along Canaanite lines, the symbol of the exodus still remained. The long sticks or poles by which the ark was once carried about were preserved—even though the ark was never again to be taken anywhere. We read in the dedication ceremony of the new temple:

Then the priests brought the ark of the covenant of the Lord to its place, in the inner sanctuary of the house, in the most holy place, underneath the wings of the cherubim. For the cherubim spread out their wings over the place of the ark, so that the cherubim made a covering above the ark and its poles. And the poles were so long that the ends of the poles were seen from the holy place before the inner sanctuary; but they could not be seen from outside; and they are there to this day [1 Kings 8:6-8].

These developments toward an even more elaborate temple ritual (as we shall see in chap. 3) eventually stirred the prophets into dramatic defiance. Yet the evolution in religious practice and symbolism at the Jerusalem temple turned out to be a life-preserver for Israel and its religion. We shall now investigate two examples of radical religious change, one in the area of leadership and the other in sociological patterns of living, as major examples of indigenization in ancient Israel.

The first example relates to the area of government and is drawn from chapter 18 in the book of Exodus. Here we are informed about the origin of "elders," an institution whose significance shows up at once by noting the evolution of the Hebrew word for elder: zāgēn, ("men with full beard") was translated into the Greek presbyteros, and thence into the English "priest."[26] The editor of the Torah deliberately placed the incident before chapter 19 and therefore before the wondrous theophany and the divine revelation on Mount Sinai; thus the human origins and family setting of the episode were accentuated.

The story begins when Moses' father-in-law, Jethro, a priest of Midian, "heard all that God had done for Moses and for Israel his people" and came to him "in the wilderness where he was encamped at the mountain of God." He brought with him Moses' wife, Zipporah, and their two sons, Gershom and Eliezer. The narrative continues:

When Moses' father-in-law saw all that [Moses] was doing for the people, he said, "What is this that you are doing for the people? Why do you sit alone, and all the people stand about you from morning till evening? . . . What you are doing is not good. You and the people with you will wear yourselves out, for the thing is too heavy for you; you are not able to perform it alone. Listen now to my voice; I will give you counsel, and God be with you! . . . Choose able men from all the people, such as fear God, men who are trustworthy and who hate a bribe; and place such men over the people as rulers of thousands, of hundreds, of fifties, and of tens . . . [Exod. 18:13-21].

To determine the seismic impact of this episode, we must remember *(a)* the sacrosanct and unique position of Moses in Israel's later traditions, where we are told that there was "none like him for all the signs and wonders which the Lord sent him to do" (Deut. 34:11); *(b)* the pagan background of Jethro, his Midianite father-in-law, from a people not always in good favor with Israel (cf. Num. 22:4,7; 25:6–9); *(c)* the friendly yet forceful correction given to the overly eager son-in-law, and the implication that divine wisdom is not exclusively channeled through the highest religious authority and may even be distorted to the people's harm by Moses' inability to delegate and share authority.

Before drawing any conclusions, let us turn to chapter 11 in the book of Numbers. Again Moses was beset with trouble, this time with the grumbling stirred up by "the rabble [or riffraff] that was among" the Israelites. The biblical text continues:

And the Lord said to Moses, "Gather for me seventy of the elders of Israel, whom you know to be the elders of the people and officers over them; and bring them to the tent of meeting, and let them take their stand there with you. And I will come down and talk with you there; and I will take some of the spirit which is upon you and put it upon them; and they shall bear the burden of the people with you, that you may not bear it yourself alone" [Num. 11:16–17].

Comparing this passage with Exodus 18, we observe some glaring differences: *(a)* the unique and complete competency of Moses was recognized—he was endowed with the fullness of the spirit; even if the elders "prophesied," they "did so [this one time and] no more" (Num. 11:25); *(b)* the pagan priest Jethro has disappeared from the scene, along with his rebuke, or paternal warning, to Moses; *(c)* wisdom and authority came directly from the Lord to Moses, and through Moses they were shared with others. Even while helping others, Moses lost nothing but instead maintained his full possession of the spirit.

These two passages from Exodus 28 and Numbers 11 illustrate the origin and development of religious authority. What arose from secular wisdom—and in this case from a Midianite priest—was later accepted as exclusively divine in its origin. While Israel benefited greatly by this theological endorsement of worldly prudence, Israel was to be harmed at a later time when the priests and prophets at the temple refused to be corrected by Jeremiah. Jerusalem and religious leadership in the city had acquired such a firm place in Israel's sacred tradition that to threaten the temple or to differ from the priests and prophets would be interpreted as denying God and apostasizing from religion (Jer. 7:26). This religious aberration, as the classical prophets announced, would be rectified by politics and foreign armies. Again the religion of Israel developed, was purified, and reached new insights into God's will through the human process. We call it indigenization.

While the office of elders can be traced back to Mosaic times, that of kingship appeared as a challenge and even a distortion of the Mosaic spirit. Moses did not bequeath a strong governmental structure, certainly not a royal dynasty centered in a city and temple. The ark moved with the people. The Canaanite groups, moreover, which aligned themselves with the invading Israelites, would not possess a congenial attitude toward royalty and centralization. They were either mercenary forces *('apiru)* or former slaves, all hostile or at least potentially traitorous toward the petty Canaanite kings.

During the period of the judges (1200–1050 B.C.E.) some Israelites succumbed to the temptation of having a king. They accepted an offer from Abimelech, son of the judge Gideon by a concubine at Shechem. The story erupted in fury: the slaughter of Abimelech's seventy brothers, the burning alive of a thousand men and women in the citadel at Shechem, and finally Abimelech's own death after a millstone was cast upon his skull (Judges 9).

The Philistine threat proved too powerful for the divided and jealous tribes of Israel. Again the people wanted a king! The elders came to Samuel at Ramah and said to him. "Behold, you are old and your sons do not walk in your ways; now appoint for us a king to govern us like all the nations" (1 Sam. 8:15). The words "like all the nations" are crucial for our discussion. The Davidic royalty, which was to save Israel from the Philistines and secure its own important place in biblical theology, was not directly revealed.[27] It resulted from a threat to Israel's political existence and from the accumulated wisdom of the surrounding nations. Still more significantly, it clashed with one of the dominant attitudes of Israelite religion: the Lord's compassionate concern for the poor against royal despots. Little wonder that "the thing displeased Samuel when they said, 'Give us a king to govern us.' " Theologically we can understand the Lord's reply to Samuel: "They have not rejected you, but they have rejected me from being king over them" (1 Sam. 8:6–7).

If styles of religious government came directly from God, rarely could the divine institution be substantively modified or reversed. Israel could never be permitted to change the divinely ordained form of charismatic judge to the institution of royal dynasty, from loose confederation to strong centralization. Religious authority, as it follows the acculturation process, will not only evolve with the times, but will also be forced to radical changes. The determining factor is to be located in politics and international forces; these secular elements set the agenda for theological development and also the main lines of a solution.

The acculturation process included not only the evolving form of government but also the structure of the tribes. One of the most characteristic features of Israelite society is located in the "blood relationship" or "blood bond." The Hebrew word was gō'ēl.[28] Several features of this phenomenon touch closely upon our discussion of the way by which divine revelation developed from a societal custom. This time we are involved in the serious moral question of polygamy.

The interrelationships of *gō'ēl* extended across the clan and were meant to maintain the strength and integrity of the people's life. The *gō'ēl*, or "nearest of kin," must regain family property and keep the patrimony intact (Lev. 25:23–34), must execute anyone who murdered a relative lest the sign of life within the family or clan be endangered and the equilibrium or wholeness of tribal relationships be upset (Num. 35:9–29). The extent to which the *gō'ēl* obligation included the levirate marriage is not clear, but there are sufficient reasons for including it here.[29] The closest-of-kin of the male sex was obliged to marry a widow who had borne no son and to beget a son who would receive the name of the deceased husband and inherit the latter's property. This closest-of-kin would normally be married—it could even include the dead husband's father (Gen. 38)—and so the custom sanctioned polygamy.

The obligations of *gō'ēl* were based on blood and made great demands of generosity and concern. The secular institution became an ideal image for God's love and fidelity toward Israel. Second Isaiah developed it fully when he declared that the Lord, as Israel's *gō'ēl*, would bring back his sons and daughters from slavery (Isa. 43:1–7) and would even perform the levirate marriage toward the barren spouse (Isa. 54:1–10).[30]

When we observe the acculturation process by which social institutions became a means of formulating theology, we realize the full extent that God worked within and through the human forms of society to reveal himself. We also see from the *gō'ēl* setting that sexual morality is not determined exclusively by the physical form of male or female, nor is it weighted heavily toward emotional compatibility but, rather, is regulated by the peace and strength of the clan or family. Within such a healthy social setting husbands, wives, and children were to find the greatest resources, over the longest period of time, for a happy marriage. Polygamy is to be judged, then, not so much by a static ideal, nor by the demands of pleasure or power, but by overall security and serenity within society.

Several further comments may help our discussion here. First, polygamy was seldom the normal pattern of marriage. Almost as soon as the patriarchal age ended, so did polygamy. The practice of having more than one wife survived only with the royal harem, a symbol of the king's fertility and therefore of the whole country's productivity. The intrigues and jealousies of the royal harem provide their own condemnation of polygamy. In the case of the levirate marriages, polygamy was the exception to the rule. In the Bible marriage by its very nature tended toward the monogamous form. Yet the existence of the levirate marriage within the larger family, or *gō'ēl*, relationship points out how moral laws ought to be based primarily upon the societal setting, its stability and peaceful evolution. To rule polgamy as immoral without discussion can cause great harm and have disastrous effects in sexuality.[31]

CONCLUSION

In this chapter we have considered the consequences of the biblical conviction that God is to be known and worshiped as savior; only in the course of redeeming his people did God manifest himself as creator, or better, as re-creator of his destitute people. God as savior works through the human, earthly details of Israel's existence. We call this process "acculturation" and recognize the three important stages of violence, indigenization, and challenge. We confined ourselves to the first two stages: *(a)* the initial "beachhead," when a new people or a new idea upsets the old order and precipitates some kind of violent change; *(b)* the long process of indigenization when the new idea or a new people takes root and reexpresses their religious beliefs and practices according to local conditions. Although there would have been signals and warnings ahead of time, the first stage usually broke loose suddenly and violently—like Israel's exodus out of Egypt, the conquest-settlement in Canaan, and the construction of the Jerusalem temple. Some of these changes came through military expeditions. The violence of war is too frequent in the Scriptures and too central to the development of Israel's main theological themes for us not to accept some forms of violence as divinely inspired and as numbered among God's charisms. In our definition the meaning of violence was extended to any strong initiative or forceful action that infringed upon the freedom of others and imposed a solution or a situation upon others, at times against their will. Within the Bible secular powers imposed many *faits accomplis* upon Israel, or Israel itself or one of its religious leaders acted with a finality that left little or no room for liberty. Often enough the violence was provoked by the sight of social injustices.

After the initial, violent beachhead, Israel usually settled down to a long stretch of indigenization. We observed how the invading Israelites congenially joined forces and made treaties with the foreign *'apiru* and the disenfranchised peasants against the petty kings throughout the land of Canaan. These alliances were fully in accord with the Mosaic spirit of liberating captives in the name of a compassionate God. While Israel was the energetic catalyst to unite all these groups, it was the poor and indigenous people of Canaan as well as other groups in the Near East that provided many cultural and economic factors: architecture, agriculture, government or family structures. At times, especially when Israel turned to a royal dynasty "like the other nations," these human institutions even clashed with the spirit and norms of the Mosaic tradition. Israel's secular and religious structures then were not directly revealed by God—even though they were later called the revealed Word of God in the Bible—but were mediated through the tried and visible forms of human existence.

If changes took place, as they certainly did from a loose confederation to centralized power, from a more agricultural lifestyle to a predominantly urban culture, these modifications did not contradict earlier "revealed" truths but indicated a shift in values. The importance of "exodus" and tribal freedom gave way to the new value of security and unity in walled city and permanent dynasty.

Biblical religion safeguarded the major priorities within a culture and, in the name of a compassionate God, it dedicated the values to a heroic concern for the poor. Mosaic religion purified and strengthened a culture, even challenged and corrected its abuses. How this happened will be the subject of the next chapter. As was stated already, this present chapter cannot be adequately understood or applied to the mission apostolate without keeping in mind all three stages of the interaction between religion and culture: the first stage of violence, always generated by abrupt new ideas or people; the second stage of indigenization, long and involved; the final stage of prophetic challenge that transforms both culture and religion. The first stage makes the beachhead, the second secures its roots and influences its external form, and the third makes survival worthy of God's hopes.

We opened this chapter citing a text from Ezekiel about Israel's human origins from the Canaanites, Amorites, and Hittites. We close with two readings from Deuteronomy, which witness to God's continuous way of fulfilling his plans for Israel through a combination of the "divine" and the "human"—of "signs and wonders" and of "wars, cities, and vineyards":

> Or has any god ever attempted to go and take a nation for himself from the midst of another nation, by trials, by signs, by wonders, and by war, by a mighty and an outstretched arm . . . [Deut 4:34].

> And when the Lord your God brings you into the land which he swore to your [ancestors] to give you, with great and goodly cities, which you did not build, and houses full of all good things, which you did not fill, . . . and vineyards and olive trees, which you did not plant, and when you eat and are full, then take heed lest you forget the Lord, who brought you out of the land of Egypt, out of the house of bondage [Deut. 6:10–12].

NOTES

1. Cf. H. W. Wolff, "The Kerygma of the Yahwist," in *The Vitality of Old Testament Traditions,* ed. W. Brueggemann and H. W. Wolff, 2nd ed. (Atlanta: John Knox Press, 1982), pp. 29–40; reprinted from *Interpretation* 20 (1966): 131–58.

2. Cf. B. W. Anderson, *Creation versus Chaos: The Reinterpretation of Mythical Symbolism in the Bible* (New York: Association Press, 1967); J. Reumann, *Creation and New Creation: The Past, Present, and Future of God's Creative Activity* (Minneapolis: Augsburg Publishing House, 1973); C. Westermann, *Beginning and End in the Bible* (Philadelphia: Fortress Press, Facet Books, 1972).

3. For a more involved sequence of interaction, cf. W. Dietrich, *Israel und Kanaan* (Stuttgart: Verlag Katholisches Bibelwerk, 1979).

4. D. Kellermann, *"gûr," Theological Dictionary of the Old Testament* (Grand Rapids, Mich.: Wm. B. Eerdmans, 1974–), 2:439, offers the basic meaning of "tarry as a sojourner," and favors the root *"gwr* II = subordinate form of *grh,* 'to attack, strive,' [and therefore] 'to be foreign' and 'to be hostile' can be simply two different observations about the same person."

5. The decline of prophecy, its reduction to an ever smaller group on the fringe, and its evolution into apocalypticism in the postexilic age are developed by R. P. Carroll, *When Prophecy Failed: Cognitive Dissonance in the Prophetic Traditions of the Old Testament* (New York: Seabury Press, 1979), and P. D. Hanson, *The Dawn of Apocalyptic,* 2nd ed. (Philadelphia: Fortress Press, 1979). R. P. Carroll's position is

summarized in the article, "Twilight of Prophecy or Dawn of Apocalyptic," *Journal for the Study of the Old Testament* 14 (1979): 3–35.

6. P. C. Craigie, *The Problem of War in the Old Testament* (Grand Rapids, Mich.: Wm. B. Eerdmans, 1978), p. 103.

7. The Hebrew phrase *qaddēšû milḥamâ*, literally "sanctify a war," occurs in Jer. 6:4; Joel 3:9; Mic. 3:5; and a similar phrase occurs in Jer. 22:7; 51:27–28. The word *ḥerem* "actually means 'consecrate' (cf. common Semitic *ḥrm*, 'be separate, sacred'), and to put under the ban was to devote to Yahweh," P. K. McCarter, Jr., *I Samuel*, Anchor Bible (Garden City, N.Y.: Doubleday, 1980), p. 265. Chapter 15 in 1 Samuel presents the most serious problem, for here Saul is rejected as king precisely for not carrying out the extermination warfare against the Amalekites. According to Deut. 25:19, Israel "shall blot out the remembrance of Amalek from under heaven."

8. Various writers point out that a preferable term to "holy war" would be "Yahweh war"; cf. Craigie, *The Problem of War*, p. 49.

9. Craigie, *The Problem of War*, p. 52.

10. Cf. M. Greenberg, "Crimes," *Interpreter's Dictionary of the Bible* (Nashville: Abingdon, 1962), 1: 741.

11. Cf. F. M. Cross, "The Divine Warrior," *Canaanite Myth and Hebrew Epic* (Cambridge: Harvard University Press, 1973), pp. 91–111. See Deut. 10:17; Isa. 9:5; 10:21; Jer. 20:11; 32:18; Zeph. 3:17; Neh. 9:32; Pss. 19:6; 24:8; 78:65; Job 16:14.

12. Cf. R. R. Wilson, *Prophecy and Society in Ancient Israel* (Philadelphia: Fortress Press, 1980), pp. 204–5. The abrupt and a-rational action of the prophet in anointing Jehu in 2 Kings 9 causes the latter's companions to refer to the prophet as a madman *(mĕšuggāʿ).* "However, in this case the commanders take the prophet's message seriously. They proclaim Jehu king, and he sets about reforming the political and religious establishments along the lines demanded by Elisha and his support group."

13. N. Gottwald, "War, Holy," *Interpreter's Dictionary of the Bible, Supplement* (Nashville: Abingdon, 1976) p. 944.

14. Such is one of the principal theses, argued convincingly by F. Huber, *Jahwe, Juda und die Andern Völker Beim Propheten Jesaja* (New York: Walter de Gruyter, 1976). See Stuhlmueller's review in *Catholic Biblical Quarterly* 39 (1977): 420–22.

15. Cf. C. Stuhlmueller, "Does the Bible Preach Hate?" *The Bible Today* 46 (February 1970): 3190–96; for a good summary of viewpoints, see C. Barth, *Introduction to the Psalms* (New York: Scribners, 1966), pp. 43–48.

16. These lines of Jeremiah occur elsewhere in the prose sections: 12:14–17; 18:7–9; 24:6; 31:26, 40; 42:10; 45:4. The prophet was to proclaim oracles about the overthrow of nations, including Judah, as well as to announce their restoration. But as is noted by J. A. Thompson, *The Book of Jeremiah* (Grand Rapids, Mich.: Wm. B. Eerdmans, 1980), p. 151, Jeremiah "did comparatively little of this constructive preaching and a great deal of the destructive kind."

17. M. D. Meek, "God's Suffering Power and Liberation," *Journal of Religious Thought* 33 (1976): 52.

18. Ibid.

19. Ibid.

20. The citation is from N. Gottwald, "War, Holy," p. 942. See also his major book, *The Tribes of Yahweh: A Sociology of the Religion of Liberated Israel, 1250–1050 B.C.* (Maryknoll, N.Y.: Orbis Books, 1979), and G. E. Mendenhall, *The Tenth Generation: The Origins of the Biblical Tradition* (Baltimore: Johns Hopkins Press, 1973).

21. For a bibliographical survey, see N. K. Gottwald and F. S. Frick, "The Social World of Ancient Israel: An Orientation Paper for Consultation," *Seminar Papers, Society of Biblical Literature* 1 (1975): 165-78.

22. Cf. E. F. Campbell, Jr., "The Amarna Letters and the Amarna Period," *The Biblical Archaeologist Reader* (Garden City, N. Y.: Doubleday, Anchor Books, 1970), 3:67-78, reprinted from *Biblical Archaeologist* 23 (February 1960): 2-22.

23. G. E. Mendenhall, "The Hebrew Conquest of Palestine," *The Biblical Archaeologist Reader*, 3:105-6. The article is reprinted from *Biblical Archaeologist* 25 (September 1962):66-87.

24. Mendenhall, "The Hebrew Conquest of Palestine," p. 111.

25. One of the fullest studies of the impact of city culture upon biblical life and religion is F. S. Frick, *The City in Ancient Israel* (Missoula, Mont.: Scholars Press, 1977). Jerusalem as a melting pot of traditions and people is described by S. Yeivin, "Social, Religious and Cultural Trends in Jerusalem under the Davidic Dynasty," *Vetus Testamentum* 3 (1953):149-66. For the more religious implications of Jerusalem, see *The Bible Today* 97 (October 1978) and *Le Monde de la Bible*, 1 (November-December 1977). For further comparative study of Jerusalem with Athens and Rome, see M. M. Eisman, "A Tale of Three Cities," *Biblical Archaeologist* 41 (June 1978): 47-60.

26. For a fuller investigation of the origins and early evolution of priesthood from the Old Testament into the early church fathers, see the articles by C. Stuhlmueller, R. J. Karris, and C. Osiek in *Women and Priesthood* (Collegeville, Minn.: Liturgical Press, 1978), pp. 23-68.

27. The origins of the Davidic dynasty in premonarchical Israel as well as in other parts of the ancient Near East are carefully nuanced by K. W. Whitelam, *The Just King: Monarchical Judicial Authority in Ancient Israel* (Sheffield, England: University of Sheffield Press, 1979).

28. Cf. H. Ringgren, "*gā'al,*" *Theological Dictionary of the Old Testament* (Grand Rapids, Mich.: Wm. B. Eerdmans, 1974–), 2:350-55; F. Holmgren, *The Concept of Yahweh as Gō'el in Second Isaiah* (Ann Arbor, Mich.: University Microfilms, 1963); C. Stuhlmueller, *Creative Redemption in Deutero-Isaiah* (Rome: Biblical Institute Press, 1970), chap. 5, "Yahweh-gō'el, Israel's Creative Redeemer."

29. H. Ringgren, "*gā'al,*" p. 352, does not include the levirate marriage under the *gō'el* obligation. R. De Vaux, *Ancient Israel* (New York: McGraw-Hill, 1965; reprint of 1961 ed.), 1:21-22, would do so.

30. Cf. Stuhlmueller, *Creative Redemption*, pp. 110-15, for Yahweh's redeeming his children from slavery; pp. 115-22, for performing the levirate marriage for Israel in chap. 54.

31. Cf. E. Hillman, *Polygamy Reconsidered* (Maryknoll, N.Y.: Orbis Books, 1975), chaps. 2-4. J. Omoregbe, "Polygamy and Christianity," *African Ecclesiastical Review* 21 (December 1979): 363-72, concludes that "there is no valid reason for excluding polygamists from the Christian religion." M. C. Kirwen, *African Widows* (Maryknoll, N.Y.: Orbis Books, 1979), seldom refers to the Bible but presents careful parallels to biblical culture.

3

Humanization Prophetically Challenged

From the day that your ancestors came out of the land of Egypt to this day,
I have persistently sent all my servants the prophets to them, day after day
[Jer. 7:25].

From a consideration of the human environment for God's way of salvation in
the Hebrew Bible, we turn now to the spirit and goals by which God induced Israel
to think and to act beyond its natural strength and limited hopes. This challenge
did not come principally through visions and miracles, not even through charismatic heroes like the early judges, who were remembered for their extraordinary
exploits, nor through a transcendent, spiritual attitude, suspicious of the flesh
and earthly concerns. It will seem strange at first, but Israel's religion was su-
pernaturally corrected, punished, and restored, so that God's glory once again
dwelt with the people (Ezek. 43:1–5), from a basis of common sense, severe
honesty, and an elementary concern for social justice. God's instruments for
purifying and reinvigorating Israel's religious attitudes were the classical
prophets. These individuals emerged in the person of someone as salty and earthy
as Amos, whom "the Lord took from following the flock" (Amos 7:15), or as
timid as the young Jeremiah, who belonged to the discredited "priest . . . in
Anathoth" (Jer.1:1; 1 Kings 2:26).

These individuals to whom Israelite tradition was to give the name of
"prophet" spoke indeed in the name of God:

> The lion has roared;
> who will not fear?
> The Lord God has spoken;
> who can but prophesy? [Amos 3:8].

But these prophets spoke as well in the name of the poor whose basic human
rights had been violated:

> How the faithful city [Jerusalem]
>   has become a harlot . . . !
> Your princes are rebels
>   and companions of thieves.
> Every one loves a bribe
>   and runs after gifts.
> They do not defend the fatherless
>   and the widow's cause does not come to them [Isa. 1:21,23].

These two passages combine the human and divine elements within prophecy. With a burning concern over social injustices, prophets resonated God's call to Moses to bring slaves out of bondage. Prophets spoke for "the Lord, a God compassionate and gracious . . . abounding in steadfast love and faithfulness" (Exod. 34:6).

We cannot delay here over the long history of prophecy or the diversified forms of prophetic discourse. Here we seek the origins of classical prophecy, first in the creative, pioneering days of Moses and Joshua, and then more specifically in Elohist and Deuteronomic traditions of the Pentateuch and in the Deuteronomic books of Joshua, Judges, Samuel, and Kings. Then a definition of classical prophecy will be proposed as a setting in which to discuss the prophetic challenge to Israelite culture and politics.

PROPHECY: ITS ORIGIN AND CHARACTERISTICS

We have already drawn upon the sociological studies of scholars like George Mendenhall, Norman K. Gottwald, Frank S. Frick, and Walter Brueggemann for new insights into Israel's early history. We now summarize these results to trace roots of prophecy. In fact, prophets often reached behind such later developments as royalty, city, and temple and appealed to the pure, simple perceptions and expectations of the Mosaic period. For their insights and authority prophets in some ways reverted to the "prereligion period" before the secure establishment of such institutions as Levitical priesthood and warrior-judges or before the emergence of a national identity as Israelites distinct from all other peoples or nations. Prophets gathered their convictions and spoke their minds within a context of liberating oppressed people and believing in a God who is compassionate and faithful.

The word "Israelite" puts us in touch with these prophetic origins. It has various meanings in the Bible, but originally it stood somewhat vaguely for a blending of various peoples whose only common bond consisted in their status (or lack of status) as refugees, resident aliens, and dispossessed people uprooted from their original homeland and frequently at the mercy of the local residents or landlords. The patriarchs are classed as sojourners, or newcomers, in the land without secure protection and yet always free for this reason to pack up and move onward, as Jacob and his family did by going into Egypt. The Hebrew word for this class of people was *gēr*, which the prophets will use for defenseless persons or even of God, whose presence seems uncertain:

> Let the outcasts of Moab
> *sojourn* among you [Isa.16:4].
> O thou hope of Israel,
> its savior in time of trouble,
> why should thou be like *a stranger* in the land,
> like a wayfarer who turns aside to tarry [only] for the night?
> [Jer.14:8].

In Egypt "Israelites"are a mixture of *'apiru* (outlaws or refugees) and *shosu* (marauders from the area of Edom). In the exodus narratives the Bible describes "Israelites" with such uncomplimentary terms as *'ēreb rab* ("a mixed multitude"; Exod. 12:38) and *hā'sapsup* (the "riffraff" of Num. 11:4). Once established in Canaan, the word "Israelite" referred to a conglomerate as diversified as former Egyptian slaves who slipped out of Egypt over the years or who were led out by Moses and entered Canaan under Joshua's leadership, peasant farmers who were once indentured servants of Canaanite petty kings, and others who were classifed as *gēr*. Only under David and Solomon was this fragmented group organized as the twelve tribes of "Israel."

When the prophets attacked kings for manipulating to steal a family's ancestral land (1 Kings 21; Mic. 2:2), they were championing the rights of defenseless people in early Canaan and reliving the days of Joshua. When Amos struck fiercely against the pride of Israel for feeling "better than thou" toward foreigners, the prophet recalled how Israel itself once consisted of many types of landless refugees, newcomers in the land:

> "Are you not like the Ethiopians to me,
> O people of Israel?" says the Lord.
> "Did I not bring up Israel from the land of Egypt,
> and the Philistines from Caphtor and the Syrians from Kir?"
> [Amos 9:7].

Political developments after Moses and Joshua were to receive God's blessing. The prophet Nathan sanctioned the Davidic dynasty in 2 Samuel 7, and Jersualem was honored in Psalm 48 as Yahweh's "holy mountain . . . the city of the great King [where] God has shown himself a sure defense." Prophetic memory, nonetheless, could reach behind such institutionalization and confidently declare that Jerusalem shall be destroyed "like Shiloh" (Jer. 26:6) and the dynasty be reduced to a stump or to roots hidden beneath the earth (Isa. 11:1).

In the humanization process, as described in chapter 2 of this book, the early heroic or charismatic forms of leadership were institutionalized, for instance, as Levites or Nazirites. Levites, who possessed no landed inheritance, symbolized

Israel's wandering, propertyless days under Moses (Num. 18:20). Nazirites followed the stern rules of the desert, drinking no liquor, allowing their hair to grow uncut and untrimmed, never mourning the dead (Num. 6:1–21). When the prophets condemned later Israelites for their corrupt, sensuous ways, they recalled the early, almost prereligious stage of Israel's existence, as in the words of Amos:

> "And I raised up some of your sons for prophets,
>   and some of your young men for Nazirites.
> Is it not indeed so, O people of Israel?"
>   says the Lord.
> "But you made the Nazirites drink wine,
>   and commanded the prophets saying,
>   'You shall not prophesy' " [Amos 2:11–12].

Prophets, therefore, recalled those early days often as a threat, at other times as an idyllic period of peace and love (as in Jer. 2:1–3):

> I remember the devotion of your youth,
>   your love as a bride,
> how you followed me in the wilderness,
>   in a land not sown,
> Israel was holy to the Lord,
>   the first fruits of his harvest.
> All who ate of it became guilty;
>   evil came upon them,
>   says the Lord [Jer. 2:1–3].

Prophecy, we can say, sought to reform Israel's religious and civil institutions by reverting to the free, uncomplicated, and heroic times of Moses and Joshua and to the moment when Israel was acting more immediately under God's leadership. Those were the days when the impact of God's will was felt directly within Israel's secular, daily life. The desert evoked heroic responses spontaneously from persons strong and brave; in desert life there was very little red tape to cut through and an urgent need to act swiftly. Likewise in the days of the prophets, people like Amos and Jeremiah were summoned directly by the Lord to a heroic career in defense of the poor, who stood in need of homes, honest work, authentic religion, and political protection.

When returning to the prereligion stages of Israel's existence, Isaiah, Micah, and other classical prophets were never attempting to found a new religion but to reform the old by suffusing new life into it. They did so by appealing to religious practices and worship *(a)* that were more closely aligned with the popular piety of the poor than with the more stylized shape of city or temple worship; *(b)* whose symbols were drawn from wilderness wandering, from early struggles for justice and security, and from agricultural or pastoral pursuits; *(c)* that had no strong ties to political institutions; and *(d)* that encouraged a spirit more willing to risk for the future than to stabilize the ancient form.

We can appreciate the contribution of prophecy for church mission, not only from its remembrance and utilization of key aspects of early Israelite life under Moses and Joshua, which we have just rehearsed, but also from manifestations of prophecy within Israelite history as described in the Elohist and Deuteronomic traditions.[1]

The Elohist tradition viewed the prophet *(a)* as intercessor with God, *(b)* as a source of blessing, *(c)* as a wise person or elder in deciding practical questions, and *(d)* above all as someone true to the Mosaic heritage. The Elohist texts are neither plentiful nor continuous, yet they are significant enough to reach the general conclusions of the preceding sentence, as we shall see by examining the passages now.

During the incident at Gerar in Genesis 20 when Abimelech had sent for Sarah to be absorbed within his royal harem, God warned the king in a dream not to touch another man's wife. The Elohist tradition added that Abraham "is a prophet [*nabî*] and he will pray for you, and you shall live" (Gen. 20:7). Prophecy enters this episode to defend the purity of marriage and the dignity of the woman Sarah. This Elohist narrative is significantly more elevated in its moral tone than the companion piece of the Yahwist tradition in Gen. 12:10–20. The power of prayer or intercession is also to be noted.

In Numbers 22–24 the somewhat ubiquitous and certainly mysterious figure of Balaam is summoned from "Pethor . . . near the river [Euphrates] in the land of Amaw" (Num. 22:5).[2] We follow the study of Robert R. Wilson, in which the more positive side of Balaam as a "seer" and as a professional agent of blessing and curses is associated with the negative image of a "diviner," who for a proper fee sets up altars and conducts sacrifices to discover God's will. The Elohist tradition, therefore, is carefully passing judgment upon those later Israelite priests, who are like Balaam:

> [They] cry "Peace"
>> when they have something to eat,
> but declare war against him
>> who puts nothing into their mouths [Mic. 3:5].

In another Elohist passage, in Numbers 11, the elders have already become a fixed institution. Their office is securely within the Sinaitic covenant and is carefully associated with Moses and with the gift of the spirit: "The Lord came down in the cloud and spoke to him [Moses] and took some of the spirit that was upon him and put it upon the seventy elders, and when the spirit rested upon them, they prophesied" (Num. 11:25). Textually, however, the Elohist tradition has surrounded this spirit-anointing of the elders with some negative or at least some qualifying episodes: the story of the people's grumbling, the Lord's sending of fire, the renewed complaints of the riffraff (*hā'sapsup*) about their craving for leeks and onions, and another incident where Joshua is jealous about two other persons receiving the spirit and prophesying. It seems that the editor is warning against jealousy and personal aggrandizement in the exercise of sacred offices, a deterioration that can happen when religious or civil leaders separate themselves from the humble and popular Moses (cf. Numbers 12).

The Deuteronomic tradition, not only in the book of Deuteronomy but also as it continues in the Deuteronomistic books of Joshua, Judges, Samuel, and Kings, portrays prophets in a central role of administration, at least at first, but we also discern a momentum that relegates prophecy more and more to the periphery.

Deut. 16:18–18:22 clearly associates prophecy with the other standard offices of judge, king, and priest. Each has its allotted space in a section that immediately follows the rules for celebrating major feasts. Moses is telling the people: "The Lord your God will raise up for you a prophet like me from among you, from your brethren" (Deut. 18:15). Those prophets, moreover, must beware of divining and soothsaying, whereby they were tempted to deal with hidden information, proper only to the divine realm, thereby to control life in a superstitious way. Prophecy, therefore, was subject to the Mosaic traditions and to the people's common sense. It was open to the people's evaluation, for it had no hidden, private source of information. In this case it comes close to the Elohist idea of "elders" in Numbers 11.

The office of prophet reaches into many other areas of activity in the Deuteronomistic tradition. We think of "Deborah, a prophetess, the wife of Lappidoth, [who] was judging Israel at that time" (Judg. 4:4). Not only did she "sit under the palm of Deborah between Ramah and Bethel [so that] the people of Israel came up to her for judgment" (4:5), but she also summoned Barak to war against the invading army of the king of Hazor and afterward sang the magnificent canticle of victory. Her authority must have depended upon clear perception, unimpeachable honesty, and strong character.

In the Deuteronomistic tradition Samuel the prophet wore many hats; he was judge, leader of worship, and anointer of kings.[3] In fact, it was his mammoth authority that secured a firm place in Israel for the new and very innovative order of kings. Samuel first anointed Saul (1 Sam. 10:1) and then David (16:13). This tradition of anointing and removing kings continued with the prophets Elijah and Elisha (2 Kings 9:1–3), prophets who also defended the common people against royal injustices (1 Kings 21).

We cite one final passage from the Deuteronomistic tradition. In the incident of the prophet Micaiah (1 Kings 22), we see the serious deterioration of prophetic authority.[4] They quarreled among themselves and except for Micaiah curried the royal favor with lying prophecies (1 Kings 22). Prophets have become creatures of the king. One of the last "prophets" in the Deuteronomistic books is Isaiah, who appears authentically as an intercessor. He did not occupy an *office* as prophet, but appeared only as needed (2 Kings 18–20).

From this quick summary of prophecy in ancient Israel, especially within the Elohist and Deuteronomic traditions, these features emerge: *(a)* fidelity to the spirit of Moses; *(b)* avoidance of secret or lucrative means of probing hidden information; *(c)* religious office of intercessor; *(d)* civil office of elder and judge in deciding practical cases; *(e)* popularity with the common people; *(f)* at times clustered in religious communities, as at Ramah or Jericho. We also note a tendency for prophecy to deteriorate and to be swept to the periphery. Robert R. Wilson concludes:

> The social functions of Ephraimite prophecy [as seen within the Elohist and Deuteronomistic traditions] seem to have changed over the course of Israelite history. . . . After the rise of the monarchy, Ephraimite prophets seem to have functioned primarily on the periphery of society. . . . They apparently ceased to play a role in the central cult and had no voice in governmental affairs.[5]

This serious decline of early prophecy was due to internal disputes, to jealous jockeying for power and prestige, to living off former popularity, and to selfish and superstitious ways of determining an oracle of the Lord. Prophecy remained, but was shifted to the outer circle of the power base, where its presence becomes a confusing factor in the people's lives. These "professional prophets" also precipitated trial and suffering for the new set of "classical prophets," individuals who seldom at first considered themselves to be prophets—only honest, perceptive persons, compelled by God to speak out. Yet these later "prophets" drew their inspiration and guidance from the earlier history of prophecy within the Elohist and Deuteronomic traditions. We need to define more clearly this new series of religious leaders to whom Jewish tradition gradually gave the name "prophet" and whom modern scholars classify as the "classical prophets."[6]

The initial problem in defining "prophecy" as applicable to such individuals as Amos, Hosea, and Isaiah—prophets with books bearing their names—is that these persons seldom, and in some cases never, used the noun *nābî'*, or "prophet," of themselves. Rolf Rendtorff states:

> *nabi'* can on occasion be used for the writing prophets. In the older prophetic books [beginning with Amos] this use is rare, though it increases later. Amos rejects the title, 7:14. Hosea, however, uses it of himself in 9:7f. It is not used in this sense in Isaiah, though 8:3 refers to the *nebî'āh*, obviously Isaiah's wife. Jeremiah is called to be a *nābî' lāgôyim* 1:5. In the narrative sections (the Baruch narrative) he is always called a *nābî'*. Ezekiel is emphatically called a *nābî'* in the vision at his calling and then indirectly in 14:4.[7]

Amos, the first of the writing, or classical, prophets, rejected the noun, or the title, but he applied the verb "to prophesy" to himself: "I am no prophet, nor a prophet's son, but a herdsman, and a dresser of sycamore trees, and the Lord took me from following the flock, and the Lord said to me, 'Go, prophesy to my people Israel' '' (Amos 7:14–15). We can visualize Amos spitting back his vitriolic reply to the high priest Amaziah, who had patronizingly grouped Amos with the now decadent and corrupt prophetic bands. Amos said: "Do not insult me by calling me a prophet. I work for a living, and in the midst of my honest employment, the Lord took me and said: 'Speak a new kind of prophecy!' ''

Israel needed prophecy, for the people would always be helped by a strong, clear voice that spoke authentically of God's concern for the poor and, indeed, of God's presence in their midst as once in Egypt, the Sinai wilderness, and Canaan. Even Amos, in the same breath that he condemned the entire religious scene in Israel, enunciated the frightening situation of an Israel without prophecy:

> "Behold, the days are coming," says the Lord God,
> "When I will send a famine on the land;
> not a famine of bread, nor a thirst for water,
> but of hearing the words of the Lord.
> They shall wander from sea to sea,
> and from north to east;
> they shall run to and fro, to seek the word of the Lord,
> but they shall not find it" [Amos 8:11–12].

The new series of prophets appears, not only because of the serious lacuna in Israel's religious life, not only because Israel's roots in the Mosaic covenant still bore the germinal life and basic inspiration of religious intercessors and honest judges, but also because a popular literacy arose in Israel, coupled with renewed international correspondence. From the religious vacuum and the secular advance in written documents arose the "writing prophets."[8]

The following definition of the "classical" or "writing" prophet is offered as a summary of our discussion here and as a guide for the remainder of this chapter:

> Classical prophets are those persons, (a) so consistently and fully a member of their community and in touch with its traditions and (b) so perceptive and articulate (c) that as a result they can bring the internal challenge of the community's conscience, its divinely inspired hopes and ideals, to bear upon the external form of the community's life style and work.[9]

As integral members of their community, prophets were willing to suffer in their own persons the consequences of their prophecy against Israel and Judah. In this regard Jeremiah is the prime example. Even when "Nebuchadnezzar, king of Babylon, gave command concerning Jeremiah . . . : 'Take him, look after him well and do him no harm' '' (Jer. 38:11–12), Jeremiah did not opt for preferential treatment in Babylon but remained with the remnant left behind in Judah—only to be mistreated again by them. By remaining this close with the common folk, prophets were in touch with the practical and serious needs of daily life. They thus kept alive the Mosaic traditions of concern for the poor and in their very capable way of speaking and writing they challenged the community conscience.[10]

PROPHETIC CHALLENGE TO CULTURE

Hosea ben Beeri, one of the first of the classical prophets, interacted vigorously both with tradition and with culture. The setting for his book is to be found in the agony and torture of his marriage. He was outraged by his wife's infidelities. She probably slipped back into Canaanite fertility rites at the local sanctuary. Yet Hosea was able to find in this painful affair a symbol of God's agony over Israel's infidelities. Despite his intense suffering from the excesses of Canaanite sensuality, Hosea was still able to draw from Canaanite religion and its fertility rites one of the Bible's most effective symbols of divine love. By challenging rather than destroying the culture, by purifying rather than condemning it outright, Hosea not only plumbed new depths in appreciating the Mosaic covenant but also rose to new heights in his expectations of marriage. Because the interacting of religion and culture, of acceptance and challenge, is complex in the prophecy of Hosea, we need to look more carefully at the facts.

So well did Hosea know the religious history of his people that he might easily have been a Levitical priest; he certainly kept in close contact with religious groups who inspired, supported, and educated him. "Knowledge of God" in Hosea means far more than factual data or theoretical reasoning; especially in its Hebrew form, *da'at 'elohim* denotes an intimate or experiential knowledge.[11] A value or relationship has become so much second nature that one is firmly convinced of its truth without being able to explain or define it. Yet Hosea also knew the objective facts. It is helpful to see how he combined the objective data and subjective experiences of his people's history.

Hosea moved at ease through a millennium of Israelite history. His references reached back a thousand years to the patriarch Jacob (Hos. 12:2–4,12). He was at home with the principal tenets of the Mosaic tradition. He neatly wove together his own experiences with the deliverance from Egypt (2:15; 11:1; 12:13–13:4), the wandering in the wilderness (2:3, 14–15; 9:10; 13:5), and the occupation or conquest of the Promised Land (2:8,15; 9:10; 10:9–12; chap. 11; 13:5–6). He refers to the atrocious crime at Gilead in the days of the judges (9:9; 10:9), to the kingship of Saul (13:10–11), to a massive military defeat at Betharbel (an incident not recorded elsewhere in the Bible), and to the bloody coup d'état, sanctioned by the prophet Elisha, which inaugurated the dynasty of Jehu (2 Kings 9–10; Hos. 1:4–5). The incumbent king, Jeroboam II, was the fourth and greatest in this line, and the next to the last. His son Zechariah was assassinated after a six-month reign (2 Kings 15:8–12).

Not only did Hosea have Israelite history at his fingertips, but he had thoroughly absorbed every aspect of life in the northern kingdom of Israel. Robert R. Wilson comments: "Most of the [geographical] places that Hosea refers to in his speeches are located in the north: Samaria . . . Bethel . . . Gilgal . . . the Valley of Achor . . . Adam . . . Ramah, Gibeah . . . and Gilead."[12] Wilson then proceeds from geography to literary details: "The similarities between the language of the Deuteronomic History [as found in Deuteronomy, Joshua, Judges, and the books of Samuel and Kings] have long been noted."[13] Both employ similar or identical phrases to condemn worship on the high places, the folly of worshiping idols, and the violation of the covenant. "Hosea seems to have accepted the Deuteronomic notion that in each generation [cf. Deut. 18:15-18] Yahweh raised up a Mosaic prophet to lead the people."[14] Hosea wrote:

> By a prophet the Lord brought Israel up from Egypt,
>   and by a prophet he [Israel] was preserved
>   [Hos.12:13; cf. Exod. 14:21-22].

> I spoke to the prophets;
>   it was I who multiplied visions,
>   and through the prophets gave parables [Hos. 12:10].

Hosea's prophecy, as already mentioned, witnesses to a person thoroughly at home in the prophetic tradition of the northern kingdom. Unlike the prophet Amos whose stark and rugged imagery came mostly from the Judean wilderness of the south, Hosea is continually moving through the warm farmlands and fertile vineyards of the northern kingdom. He also shows up in severe contrast with Amos in his outreach for friends. Amos was the loner and Hosea the lover, and so the son of Beeri colored his prophetic speeches with continual references to marriage, children, and the home.

Another feature of life within the northern kingdom, prevalent in the prophecy of Hosea, is the strong, pervading presence of Canaanite fertility rites. Men and women consorted with male and female temple prostitutes in order to be incorporated mystically into the lives of gods and goddesses and thereby to obtain from them a rich fertility at springtime in their farmlands, their livestock, and their own families. Wolff concluded: "Hosea's theology develops openly in dialogue with the [Canaanite] *mythology* of his day in a remarkable process of adaptation of and polemic against this mythology."[15]

Sanctuary worship and its heavy use of symbols and myths also induced in Hosea a way of viewing the past events as happening *now*. Once again he appears in sharp contrast with Amos. Even in the tragic story of his marriage, Hosea follows a literary style, called *memorabile* by H. W. Wolff,[16] in which details are carefully selected, so that each item evokes a reaction in the listener or reader of what is happening in the present moment. This effect is achieved, not by comparing the present with the past but, rather, by actualizing now an important feature of what happened then.[17] The reliving never happened by literal imitation but by feeling the full impact of the past in a new set of circumstances.

It is important for our discussion of mission to examine more closely how the past was actualized in the present moment. Normally the earlier event could stand on its own for what it achieved in its own age. The exodus out of Egypt and the occupation of the land of Canaan were both important enough acts of God within Israel's history to be finalized at once within the lifetime of Moses and Joshua. Yet these acts, important for Israel although insignificant for the rest of the world, took on a symbolic, religious form in the liturgy by which new generations felt themselves to be coming out of Egypt and newly acquiring the land. The exodus thus became symbolic of a passage from sin to grace, from hardship to joy, from fear to tranquility.

Under these circumstances people would be attracted to think about the symbols when they were caught in trials and sorrow. The amazing accomplishment of the prophet Hosea lies in his ability to unite two seemingly opposite sets of symbols, one from ancient Israelite times and the other from Canaanite lifestyle, and thereby to challenge, enrich, and purify each one. Here is the model by which missionaries challenge and enrich the national or ethnic culture(s) to which they are sent as well as the religion under whose commission they are sent. We shall look at a larger pattern within the prophecy of Hosea of activating ancient religious symbols, and then study in more detail the steps by which Hosea openly dialogued "with the [Canaanite] mythology of his day in a remarkable process of adaptation of and polemic against this mythology."[18]

Hosea, as pointed out already, frequently availed himself of the ancient Mosaic traditions of exodus, desert wandering, and possession of promised land. The contemporary crisis of his own marriage and of the country's infidelity to the covenant not only induced Hosea to turn to the ancestral traditions for guidance and strength, but also provided the setting for speaking about the Mosaic heritage.

The long, divine speech in 2:2–15 [2:4–17, New American Bible] presupposes "a thriving economic situation in Israel [along with] . . . the undisturbed organization of religious festivals in Palestine."[19] Within this passage we glimpse various attempts at reconciliation between Hosea and his wife, Gomer, and see also the bountiful agricultural produce of the northern kingdom.[20] At the climactic moment of reuniting husband and wife, Yahweh and Israel, Hosea offers a portrait of people about to leave the deserts of Sinai or Transjordan, to cross the river Jordan and, like Joshua, to penetrate the interior of the Promised Land by the Valley of Achor.[21] This passage of idyllic joy and endearment reads:

> Therefore, behold, I will allure her,
>   and bring her into the wilderness,
>   and speak tenderly to her.
> And there I will give her her vineyards,
>   and make the Valley of Achor a door of hope.
> And there she shall answer as in the days of her youth,
>   as at the time when she came out of the land of Egypt [Hos. 2:14–15].

Another lengthy development, folding the exodus motif into the contemporary moment, occurs in chapter 11, certainly one of the most precious gems of the Bible. It reads in part:

> When Israel was a child, I loved him,
>   and out of Egypt I called my son.

> The more I called them,
>   the more they went from me,
> they kept sacrificing to the Baals,
>   and burning incense to idols.
> Yet it was I who taught Ephraim to walk
>   I took them up in my arms;
>   but they did not know that I healed them. . . .
> They shall return to the land of Egypt,
>   and Assyria shall be their king,
>   because they have refused to return to me. . . .
> How can I give you up, O Ephraim!
>   How can I hand you over, O Israel! . . .
>   my compassion grows warm and tender. . . .
> they shall come trembling like birds from Egypt
>   and like doves from the land of Assyria;
>   and I will return them to their homes,
>   says the Lord [Hos. 11:1–3, 5, 8, 11].

The Exodus theme is introduced more quickly in a series of other passages (7:16; 8:13; 9:3,6; 12:8; 13:4). In all of these lines Egypt is viewed, as it was in the days of Moses, as a hostile land of oppression and exile. Sin meant the return to Egypt in punishment and guilt. As a matter of fact, however, Egypt at the time of Hosea was an ally of Israel and a land of refuge from the military invasions of Assyria. Hosea thus combined the ancient traditions about Egypt as a "house of bondage" (Exod. 20:2) with the contemporary religious situation in which Israel was under the bondage of sin, guilt, and punishment.

We now approach the heart of this discussion of the prophecy of Hosea: his dialogue with Canaanite mythology, accepting and adapting it while simultaneously arguing vigorously against it. First, however, Hosea dialogued with his own hopes and emotions, with his passion to love and to be loved. Hosea approached his marriage with Gomer with excitement and ideals—he shows himself just that type of person throughout the prophecy but especially in chapters 1 and 2, with great highs and tragic lows, with intense involvement and with crisscrossing anger and forgiveness, hope and frustration, tenderness and sarcasm, expectation and rejection. As a man of intense passion, Hosea must have seemed the ideal bridegroom: romantic, dependable, delicately sensitive, capable of loving and desirous of being loved, affectionate and playful toward children (cf. Hosea 11). For the sake of this discussion let us call this moment the hour of three on the face of a clock.

As the hand of the clock descended toward the hour of six, Hosea's suspicions were aroused by what was being ground out in the gossip mill. Very soon his wife's infidelities became public knowledge. She openly sought and paid her lovers, even with gifts once showered on her by Hosea. She did more then return occasionally to the sensually attractive but morally degrading fertility rites at the sanctuary. She cohabited with her paramour (Hos. 3:1), and Hosea would not accept the paternity of the second and third children.[22] Even though the northern law code permitted divorce for "some indecency," far less offensive than adultery (Deut. 24:1)—in fact, adultery was punishable by death (Deut. 22:22)—Hosea could never follow through with the divorce proceedings (Hos. 2:2). He accepted Gomer back more than once. Each time he ran the danger of reopening and extending old wounds and agonizing more acutely over a new desertion. And again Gomer wandered into a stranger's embrace! The hour of six plunged Hosea into an abyss of tragic darkness.

Hosea persevered in obeying the Lord's command: "Go again, love a woman who is beloved of a paramour and is an adulteress" (Hos. 3:la). Now the hand of the clock begins to reach upward toward the hour of nine: Hosea continued to contemplate the ancient traditions about the exodus and the desert wandering. His own wife made him recall how the ancient Israelites had drifted away from the Lord, had had their fill of good food and intoxicant drinks, had proudly lifted up their hearts and had forgotten the Lord (cf. Hos. 13:6). They were enticed into the fertility rites at Baal-peor and, as Hosea wrote, they "became detestable like the thing they loved" (Hos. 9:10). Yet the Lord could not destroy Israel and make a covenant with another people. From the darkness of his own heart Hosea heard the Lord cry out in desperate agony:

> How can I give you up, O Ephraim!
> How can I hand you over, O Israel!
> How can I make you like Admah!
> How can I treat you like Zeboiim!
> My heart recoils within me,
> my compassion grows warm and tender.
> I will not execute my fierce anger,
> I will not again destroy Ephraim;
> for I am God and not man or woman,
> the Holy One in your midst,
> and I will not come to destroy [Hos.11:8–9].

By continually keeping in touch with the ancient traditions Hosea gradually realized why he could never divorce Gomer. He stated it clearly: "Even as the Lord loves the people of Israel, though they turn to other gods" (Hos. 3:1b). Just as Yahweh could not desert Israel, neither could Hosea reject Gomer.

What Hosea learned between the hours of six and nine about the passionate, loyal love of Yahweh, he always knew. He acquired no new information. His "knowledge of the Lord," however, turned from being a theoretical or statistical series of facts about Israel's origins into a practical, life-giving experience of Yahweh's ancient forgiving love in his own life. This new appreciation was not nearly so clear as his former knowledge of revealed truths; in fact it was caught up in the mystery of God's transcendent goodness:

> I will not execute my fierce anger, . . .
> for *I am God and not man or woman*,
> the Holy One in your midst . . . [Hos.11:9; italics added].

Sublimely the hands of the clock reach upward to the peak hour of twelve. Here Hosea can formulate ideals and expectations far exceeding those of his youth at the hour of three. These are supernatural hopes, beyond the power of human comprehension; they are accepted or rejected, partially or entirely, depending upon the depth of one's own mystical experience of the Lord's love. This experience is rooted in ancient tradition, nourished by the secular and cultural environment, and matured by long contemplation and God's mystical graces. These hopes have become so genuinely embedded in the heart of the believer that to deny them is to destroy oneself.

Under the impact of these mystical perceptions, Hosea reaffirmed the covenant traditions of his ancestors and reacted strongly against the moral depravity of Canaanite fertility rites, honoring the male deity Baal and the female Anath. The prophet announced: "And in that day, says the Lord, you will call me, 'My husband,' and no longer will you call me, 'My Baal.' For I will remove the names of the Baals from her mouth, and they shall be mentioned by name no more" (Hos. 2:16–17).

In this condemnation of Baal-Anath worship, Hosea employed a terminology and imagery indigenous to Canaanite culture and religion. Yahweh is to be called *'ishî* ("my husband"). Fertility language is formally and affirmatively incorporated into Israel's worship and theology. The earlier covenantal language of Lord and vassal is now modulated to read husband and wife. The reference to the land's mourning and the people's languishing also echoes Baal ritual as reenacted during the long, hot, dry season of the year. The most explicit statement of fertility language occurs in a collection of sayings (2:16–23) that display a greater depth of theological reflection and application than the more spontaneous outbursts in 2:2–15. It may be that the redactor of the book assembled here some of Hosea's later and calmer considerations. If such is the case, then the prophet and Israelite tradition are reaffirming all the more consciously this reinterpretation of the Mosaic covenant in Canaanite terms: "And I will betroth you to me for ever; I will betroth you to me in righteousness and in justice, in steadfast love, and in mercy. I will betroth you to me in faithfulness; and you shall know the Lord" (Hos. 2:19–20).

In conclusion we see that Hosea so challenged Canaanite culture that its finest perceptions are salvaged and purified, and then they are given a new life within the Mosaic covenantal tradition. The sensuous laxity of the Canaanites was fiercely counteracted by Israel's remembrance of the Sinai desert and its strong homespun morality. At the same time Canaanite culture had its own impact upon the covenantal theology by enabling Israel to speak of God's love in terms of marital union and its mystical depths.

This prophetic challenge upon Canaanite morals and the Canaanite revitalization of the Mosaic covenant took *time.* This serious onslaught by Hosea upon the fertility rites came after several centuries of Israel's indigenization within the land of Canaan. For many years Israel had been absorbing important elements of Canaan's culture and worship. Israel, therefore, did not immediately exterminate the lifestyle and moral structure of the local inhabitants. Hosea too required time.

Even after taking back his wayward wife, he stipulated (as translated in the New American Bible):

> Many days you shall wait for me; . . .
> I in turn will wait for you (Hos. 3:3).

Hosea was far too serious and far too delicate to revive full marital status at once. He obeyed the Lord and his conscience; he immediately purchased his wife from her paramour and reintroduced her into his home. But the full reunion and its meaning would take both of them more time to complete and accept.

PROPHETIC CHALLENGE TO POLITICS

Just as Hosea ben Berri has enabled us to observe closely the interaction between prophecy and culture, another and different model is provided for us in Isaiah ben Amoz, the prophet responsible for the first major part of the Isaiah scroll (chaps. 1–39).

Isaiah's prophecy enables us *(a)* to investigate the way by which a major religious leader on his or her own religious terms can swivel in and out of the complicated circle of politics; *(b)* to observe the role of a lay religious leader in seeking to reform temple and palace from common-sense laws of right and wrong; and *(c)* to conclude that a religious leader's base for correcting political or social abuses consists in an insight of faith.

The Political Circle

Isaiah remained independent enough of political parties and religious institutions to question any of their programs or plans, yet he was also close enough to be on target with his evaluation. Not only his wisdom and eloquence but also his political connections assured him immediate attention. Isaiah appears strong in the conviction that if God calls a lay person like himself, such a person must obediently speak God's Word against priest and temple, against king and royal court. Prophets established the foundation of their critique in the secular origins of religion. Isaiah, then, acted most of all from a perspective of faith—a conviction beyond proof that Yahweh was always *Immanuel*, God-with-us in all areas of life, secular as well as religious. From a secular base God can challenge every other area of his presence, even if it be as sacred as temple or royal dynasty.

In contrast with the prophets Amos, Hosea, and Micah, Isaiah moved easily in the highest levels of society and government. An incident in Isaiah 7 establishes Isaiah's easy access to royalty; it combines charm, composure, and competence. In the midst of family relaxation the prophet turned to serious government business. Isaiah was strolling along with his young son, who had been given a symbolic Hebrew name, Shearjashub, "a remnant will return." They met no less a person than the king, who was inspecting the sufficiency of Jerusalem's water supply in case of siege. The encounter happened "at the end of the conduit of the

upper pool on the highway to the Fuller's Field'' (Isa. 7:3). Without formal introduction—almost on a first-name basis—Isaiah proceeded to speak with the king.
The Hebrew style bears the typical Isaian hallmarks of high quality; we note the
skillful contrasts, the intriguing depths of insight, the economy of words, the
clarity of being on target, the non-negotiable elements of religious faith, and the
good common sense of a wise person. We shall tarry over these aspects of Isaiah's
style in order to show how divine faith was aided by human expertise. We note,
for instance:

1. *Stylistic excellence and skillful contrasts*: two positive and two negative
verbs: "take heed and be quiet; do not fear and do not let your heart be faint"
(7:4a); we also hear the haunting, rhythmic cadence of v. 9b:

> *'im lō' tǎ' amînû*
> *kî lō' tē' āmēnû*
>
> If you will not hold firm,
> surely you shall not be held firm.[23]

2. *Intriguing depths*: by doing nothing, Isaiah implies that everything will be
done right. No morally acceptable course of action was available; to fight the
invading armies of Israel and Syria was doomed to failure; to turn to the superpower, Assyria, would betray Judah's independence and wreck the people's
morale.

3. *Non-negotiable faith*: not only is Yahweh present among the people of Judah, but he will be true to his promises of an eternal covenant with David's successors on the royal throne (2 Sam. 7:16) and of his "dwelling [in the temple]
forever" (1 Kings 8:13).

4. *Common sense and political insight*: King Ahaz's military forces could not
equal the strength of the invaders, nor would distant Assyria come to Judah's
defense and march against the invaders until Assyria was ready to do so for its
own interests. Ahaz, in panic, was bartering national independence to prop up his
throne and to salvage his personal career.

These qualities of Isaiah's style must have come from family breeding, from
long exposure at court, from the opportunities of wealth and education, from
unswerving loyalty to Jerusalem and the crown, and from a strong piety and
tested faith in God. For these reasons Isaiah attracted immediate attention in
"the city's central social structure."[24] Yet Isaiah's insights were too strong and
daring, his style too clear and exacting, his conscience too pure and his faith in
God too absolute for him to be tolerated for long within the key decision-making
group around the king. In order to appreciate how Isaiah forced politics to a
prophetical stance of Yea or Nay to God's demand, we need to scan the important
moments of his career.

According to chapter 6, Isaiah began his long prophetic pursuit of justice and
faith within politics "in the year that King Uzziah died [740 B.C.E.]" (Isa. 6:1).
During the extended, prosperous reign of this king success had degenerated into
sensuous luxury and insensitivity toward the poor. The bloated culture and cal-
lused injustice toward the impoverished continued during King Jothan's short

reign (740–736 B.C.E.). A natural antipathy must have set in, separating Isaiah from government officials and court functionaries. Most probably he was invited less and less for official consultation and social entertainment. Isaiah felt the hopelessness of reforming the royal court. God's words in the prophetic call may well reflect the situation:

> Go, and say to this people:
> "hear and hear, but do not understand;
> see and see, but do not perceive."
> Make the heart of this people fat,
> and their ears heavy,
> and shut their eyes;
> lest they see with their eyes,
> and hear with their ears,
> and understand with their hearts,
> and turn and be healed [Isa. 6:9–10].

The reaction toward Isaiah soured into sarcasm during King Ahaz's reign (736–716 B.C.E.). This crucial period for the nation's history was unfortunately pockmarked by open apostasy from Yahweh. Ahaz could even defend his religious indifference by quoting sacred traditions against Isaiah. The prophet had told him to "ask a sign of the Lord your God," to which the king replied with bogus piety: "I will not ask, nor will I put the Lord to the test" (Isa. 7:11–12). Ahaz' answer pompously paraphrases a prohibition in Deut. 6:16, "You shall not put the Lord your God to the test!" Ahaz's successor, King Hezekiah (716–687 B.C.E.), instituted a vigorous religious reform (2 Kings 18–19; 2 Chronicles 29–32) and Isaiah moved back into the center of Jerusalemite society. In the eyes of the prophet, Hezekiah was born with a golden spoon in his mouth, yet in the end the king acted against Isaiah's advice and revolted against Assyria. This action led to a parting of the ways. According to a late Jewish tradition, Isaiah was martyred during the reign of the next king, Manasseh (687–642 B.C.E.). We are told that "Manasseh shed very much innocent blood, till he had filled Jerusalem from one end to another" (2 Kings 21:16).

From this review of Isaiah's character and career it is difficult to discern any consistent political policy. He belonged to no political party and advocated no single program. He could seem anti-Assyrian when he urged Ahaz not to form an alliance with that superpower, pro-Assyrian when he argued against revolt at Hezekiah's court, and once again anti-Assyrian if he was martyred by order of Manasseh, one of Assyria's most loyal vassals. Another variable in Isaiah's preaching is seen in his unswerving loyalty to the Davidic dynasty. Yet his final solution that only a stump or root was to remain of this royal tree (Isa. 11:1), turned out to be so radical that anyone who remembered the initial promises made several centuries earlier to David (2 Sam. 7:8–17) would hardly have recognized any positive continuity with Isaiah's words.[25]

With this background in mind about Isaiah's "inconsistency" in addressing problems within politics and religion, we turn to his two major consistent policies. First, he firmly believed in God's presence in secular, everyday life, and from this faith he was able to bring a strong, practical response to abuses in religion and politics. Second, he acted on the conviction that God was directing, mysteriously yet firmly, the future of the holy city of Jerusalem and of the royal house of David. The prophetic call of Isaiah, recorded in chapter 6, and the summary of his preaching in chapter 1 turn out to be excellent examples of the way by which he launched a vigorous challenge, in God's name, against the religious-political establishment, from a secular base.

Religious and Social Abuses

The autobiographical account of Isaiah's call to be a prophet manifests strong ties with Israel's sacred traditions. From this ancient base, which antedated religion or at least lay outside it, he was able to judge and condemn his own contemporary world of religion and politics.

Chapter 6 is rich in literary contrasts that support Isaiah's attack against religious and social abuses:

1. *In the year that King Uzziah died, I saw the Lord sitting upon a throne*: Uzziah of the royal Davidic line was afflicted with leprosy and "dwelt in a separate house," unable to fulfill any royal functions (2 Kings 15:5). Isaiah quickly dismissed the achievements of his long and prosperous reign. The true king was God. Isaiah reached back to the days before David and Saul when God ruled more immediately by charismatic leaders (cf. 1 Sam. 8:7).

2. *I saw the Lord [in] the temple*: Isaiah, a layperson, peered into the Holy of Holies. Usually only priests, and on rare occasions kings, entered this most sacred part of the sanctuary. No anointed king or sacred priest received the commission to preach immediately in God's name and to judge and redirect the scope of God's promises.

3. *Holy, holy, holy is the Lord of hosts; the whole earth is full of his glory*: The transcendent wonder of God, like the ark where it appeared, belonged exclusively to Israel. The phrase, "The Lord of hosts," is associated with the earlier period of the "holy wars" and Israel's military measures against foreigners. Isaiah sees this glory to extend from the Holy of Holies across "the whole earth," so that the world is transformed into a divine throne room.

4. *And I said: "Woe is me! For I am lost . . . for my eyes have seen the King, the Lord of Hosts!"* These words echo a long tradition, repeated as they were by Jacob (Gen. 32:30), Moses (Exod. 33:20), Gideon (Judg. 6:22–23), Manoah and his wife (Judg. 13:22), and Micaiah ben Imlah (1 Kings 22:17). Isaiah, therefore, is found in a line of people outside the official worship or cult: some, like Jacob and Moses, antedating Israel's religion; others, like Gideon or Manoah and his wife, Samson's parents, living at a distance, geographically and socially, from Israel's sanctuaries; or still others, like Micaiah, opposing the anointed kings and their court prophets.

Subtly yet effectively, Isaiah, the lay person, claimed his right to challenge Israel's sacred institutions and ultimately condemn them to destruction, despite their long list of divine credentials and promises.

Chapter 6, as a matter of fact, appears to be every bit as much a divine judgment against the city of Jerusalem and the kingdom of Judah as it is an account of Isaiah's call to prophecy.[26] In this regard Isaiah was being called by God, less to do something and more to accept and announce what is divinely ordained and irreversible, the destruction of the southern kingdom. Here we encounter the paradox of Isaiah. He was summoned to put his extraordinary human talents to work, announcing that nothing human, but God alone, will save the people, a fact to be proved by the collapse of all of Israel's human institutions. The inability of the people to "turn and be healed" (Isa. 6:10) and therefore the inevitability of destruction were clearly announced to Isaiah:

> "Go, and say to this people:
>   'Hear and hear, but do not understand;
>   see and see, but do not perceive' . . ."
> Then I said, "How long, O Lord?"
> And he said:
>   "Until cities lie waste without inhabitant, . . .
>   and the land is utterly desolate . . ." [Isa. 6:9–11].

Even though Isaiah received this divine call while at prayer in the temple courtyard and proceeded to date the event by the reigning (and dying) king, nonetheless his credentials to challenge temple priests and anointed kings came independently of these "divine" institutions. He was called *immediately by God*, like Jacob, Moses, and Micaiah. He stood directly before God and therefore did not approach the Lord through liturgical symbols and ceremonial actions. From the "throne" over the ark, within the Holy of Holies (cf. Lev. 25:22), Yahweh spoke to Isaiah with a directness and urgency seldom heard by priest or Levite. While remaining a lay person, Isaiah was placed in judgment over priests and kings. Rolf Knierim explains the paradox of this prophet as "a man deeply rooted in the cultic traditions of the temple in Jerusalem. . . . He had a vision corresponding to a traditional cultic pattern but directed [his account and later preaching] against the traditional contents of cultic experience."[27]

This reform of the "sacred" from "secular" wisdom was a question of survival or destruction. Isaiah 1, which seems to be the entire book in miniature, clearly summarizes the prophet's well-informed and loyal attitude toward worship as well as his pressing demand for its reform. Not only is the chapter to be separated from the following chapter 2, where a new introduction is provided in verse 1, but the sections are clearly organized to reinforce the necessity of secular areas of life. We shall first summarize the contents of chapter 1 and then draw some conclusions:

Isa. 1:2–3,10–20, a judgment speech.[28] Jerusalem is found guilty, yet instead of sentencing the people to harsh punishment, a second chance is provided "if you are willing and obedient" (v.19)

vv. 2–3	calling the court witnesses to attention
v.10	summoning the defendant
vv. 11–12	interrogation of the defendant and first accusation
vv. 13–15b	indictment
v. 15c	verdict of guilt: "Your hands are full of blood"
vv. 16–20	sentence of leniency, pardon and a new chance.

Isa. 1:4–9, a lament over the widespread destruction of the kingdom of Judah after Sennacherib's invasion in 701 B.C.E. (cf. Isa. 36–37); because Judah did not listen and obey, the country is "desolate" and only "a few survivors" remain; future generations must take the prophet's warning much more seriously than their ancestors did.

Isa. 1:21–26, a combination of lament in the third person (vv. 21–23) and a judgment speech or sentencing in the second person (vv. 24–26); Jerusalem will be revived "as at the first," to manifest God's "righteousness" and "faithfulness," but only after severe, purifying sorrow at the hands of foreign nations.

Isa. 1:27–28, 29, 30, 31, an appendix of four "one-liners," continuing the theme of Zion-Jerusalem.[29]

The setting of chapter 1 is obviously the holy city of Zion-Jerusalem. (Zion refers to the elevated place and temple courtyard at the northeast corner of the city.) It was not only the place of worship (vv. 11–15b) but also the symbol of God's "faithfulness" to his promises and thereby of his "righteousness." These promises, definitely to be fulfilled, were nonetheless conditioned by the people's obedient response to the Lord. Obedience was not to be gauged by ritual correctness or docile cooperation with divinely consecrated leaders, the priests and king. The norm was to be found in secular life. The theme of social justice occurs in key lines:

> defend the fatherless,
>   plead for the widow [v. 17].
>   . . . murderers [v.21].
>
>   . . . companions of thieves.
>   Every one loves a bribe . . .
> They do not defend the fatherless,
>   and the widow's cause . . . [v. 23].

The witnesses are summoned across heaven and earth, even from the animal kingdom of oxen and asses. The example of Sodom and Gomorrah is drawn from pre-Israelite, pre-Mosaic days (vv. 9–10; cf. Gen. 19:24). Israel's morality is to be judged by a basic pattern of the natural order.[30] Israel cannot wait for the juridical procedure or for the liturgical process of contacting God through priests, elders, and kings. Rather, God's will is manifested with an insightful immediacy, too obvious to be debated, too ingrained in human nature to be denied, yet too overwhelming in its expectations to be desirable and acceptable.

A supernatural purity and grandeur were imparted to a human, or natural, goodness. The latter was seen by Isaiah, however, within the context of the Mosaic covenant and the ancient patriarchal traditions. These imparted a "righteousness" and a "faithfulness," mirrored in God's fidelity to Israel over the centuries and in the Lord's anxious concern for defenseless slaves in Egypt and for harassed peasants in Canaan. Covenantal-liturgical traditions, then, contributed the vision of faith and the expectations of supernatural holiness; secular life and natural relationships within the family and other human bonds imparted the challenge and judgment to live up to these religious hopes. Covenantal religion, the context of prophetic activity, bestowed continuity and survival. Yet innate goodness and secular common sense made that survival worthwhile. These were the prophetic norms for judging goodness and evil and for gradually changing Israel's comprehension of prophecy and its fulfillment.

An Insight of Faith

A major piece of Isaiah's preaching was collected into the book of Immanuel, chapters 7 to 12. We cannot spend time over the long, complex process of editing these chapters. Our purpose, instead, is to appreciate better Isaiah's conviction that the Lord was truly Immanuel, "God-with-us," not only as we have just seen in the secular arena of life, but also in that part of secular existence seemingly antagonistic to "a God merciful and gracious" (Exod. 34:6) and even contrary to Isaiah's faith in the absolute continuity of Jerusalem and the Davidic dynasty. Isaiah will confess that Immanuel is present with the invading military machine of foreign powers. We have already been prepared by 1:4–9 and 1:21–26 for Isaiah's final solution: the nations will perform a positive role in purifying Jerusalem and the Davidic dynasty and in redirecting their future.

The book of Immanuel (Isa. 7–12) is snarled in numerous problems of interpretation. The difficulties begin with its key verse, 7:14: "Therefore the Lord himself will give you a sign. Behold, a young woman shall conceive and bear a son, and shall call his name Immanuel." What G. Hölscher wrote in 1914 about this prophetic statement is still true: "So viel Köpfe, so viel Meinungen!" ("As many heads, so many opinions").[31] J. Steinmann fully agreed: "On the sense of each line of this celebrated text, the grandest confusion reigns among critics."[32] There is a wide divergence of interpretation as to the identity and symbolic meaning of Immanuel and of Isaiah's two sons, Shearjashub (Isa. 7:3—"a remnant will return") and Maher-shalal-hash-baz (Isa. 8:1—"quick spoils; speedy plunder"). Yet from the fact that these names are woven in and out of the literary fabric of chapters 7–11, some important conclusions can be drawn for our discussion: *(a)* God was present within the catastrophic events to which these chapters refer; and *(b)* God was achieving positive effects through them for the salvation of Israel. In fact, the great design of God for Israel's salvation through the Davidic dynasty becomes ever more clear as these chapters progress.[33]

One of the historical events thundering within the lines of these chapters was the horrendous destruction of the northern kingdom of Israel. Invaded twice, its northern area became a land of gloom, anguish, and contempt in 732 B.C.E. (cf. Isa. 9:1) and a few years later, in 721 B.C.E., the capital city of Samaria was captured after a long siege and its population deported. Out of this dark collapse Isaiah foresaw a new era of light and victory and was able to write his euphoric coronation hymn:

> For to us a child is born,
>   to us a son is given;
> and the government will be upon his shoulder,
>   and his name will be called
> "Wonderful Counselor, Mighty God,
>   Everlasting Father, Prince of Peace."
> Of the increase of his government and of peace
>   there will be no end,
> upon the throne of David, and over his kingdom
>   to establish it, and to uphold it
> with justice and with righteousness
>   from this time forth and for evermore.
> The zeal of the Lord of hosts will do this [Isa. 9:6–7].

Isaiah's famous lines about the silent waters of Shiloah in chapter 8 anticipate the Assyrian invasion of the southern kingdom of Judah. The waters of Shiloah were "sent" (which is the meaning of the Hebrew root *shalah*) to it by a conduit from the spring of Gihon. This was the water system that King Ahaz was inspecting in 7:3. Gihon was famous not only for being the life support of Jerusalem but also as a place of worship. Here Solomon was anointed king (1 Kings 1:33–34, 38–40). These waters flowed so gently that they hardly seemed to the naked eye to move at all, yet anyone standing within the stream could feel the cool, steady rhythm of this water upon their legs. It was an ideal image of God's silent, constant, life-giving presence among his people. If Israel rejected these waters—this Immanuel—at the threat of military action from the kingdoms of Israel and Syria and sought salvation by intrigue and other immoral means, then the people would bring destruction roaring down upon themselves, the hordes of the Assyrian army. Yet even in these raging waters Israel could still find Immanuel, a divine saving presence of God. Isaiah wrote:

Because this people have refused the waters of Shiloah that flow gently, and melt in fear before [the kings of Syria and Israel], Rezin and the son of Remaliah; therefore, behold, the Lord is bringing up against them the waters of the River, mighty and many, the king of Assyria and all his glory; and it will rise over all its banks; and it will sweep on into Judah, it will overflow and pass on, reaching even to the neck; and its outspread wings will fill the breadth of your land, O Immanuel [Isa. 8:6–8].

Assyria did invade the kingdom of Judah and left the entire country devastated. Jerusalem alone escaped the scorched-earth policy of brutal Assyria. Yet the days of mighty Assyria were also numbered. About ninety years later, in 612 B.C.E., it disintegrated from dissension among its generals and from the battering armies of Babylon and the Medes, thirsting for blood and revenge. After Assyria collapsed, an inspired commentator reflected upon God's continual protection of his people Israel through the *Sturm und Drang* of international politics. The earlier section about the waters of Shiloah was reinterpreted. "Immanuel" no longer designated God's presence among the invading Assyrians but, rather, his powerful determination to overcome all the foreign peoples hostile to his chosen nation, Israel. The inspired editor of Isaiah's oracles added these lines:

> Be broken, you peoples, and be dismayed;
> give ear, all you far countries;
> gird yourselves and be dismayed;
> gird yourselves and be dismayed.
> Take counsel together, but it will come to nought;
> speak a word, but it will not stand,
> for God is with us [Hebrew: Immanuel] [Isa. 8:9–10].

God was confessed to live among his people as savior through all these secular acts of violence whether these were directed against Israel or against a foreign nation.

In another text (10:5ff.) Isaiah became still more explicit about the positive role of the non-Israelite nations in the story of salvation. No longer, as in the earlier traditions found in the books of Joshua and Judges, are the nations simply hostile forces that stand in Israel's way and are to be conquered. Nor are the nations, as in the "colonial" days of David and Solomon, to be absorbed militarily into the kingdom of Judah and Israel, and forced to worship Yahweh (2 Sam. 8; Psalm 87). According to Isaiah's insight, the nations are explicitly chosen by Yahweh to punish and purify his people, to reduce Israel to a remnant that will return humbly to the Lord, chastened and renewed. Isaiah could go no further with the idea. He had no world plan that includes the nations in the saving work of God. In fact, once Assyria began to boast against the Lord and to set up a world empire that clashed with Yahweh's hopes for Israel, this foreign nation was dismissed. Nonetheless, the limitations to Isaiah's vision for the nations must not blind us to his real advance over earlier traditions.

The key passage in Isaiah is 10:5–27, a section that William L. Holladay considers to be "perhaps the most important passage of all [in particular, 10:5–15] in setting forth Isaiah's view of the place of Assyria in God's scheme of things."[34] The original unit may have consisted of 10:5–7a, 13b–15a, 20–22; other verses were probably added in the course of adapting the passage to later pastoral settings, until the book of Isaiah acquired its present canonical form.

> Ah, Assyria, the rod of my anger,
> the staff of my fury![35]
> Against a godless nation I send him
> and against the people of my wrath I command him,
> to take spoil and seize plunder,
> and to tread them down like the mire of the streets [Isa.10:5-6].

In these verses Isaiah states clearly the positive intentions of Yahweh in his plans for Judah. Yet when Assyria decided to react against those plans for its own world kingdom, Isaiah declared on God's part:

> But he [Assyria] does not so intend,
> and his mind does not so think.
> For he says: . . .
> I have removed the boundaries of peoples,
> and have plundered their treasures;
> like a bull I have brought down those who sat on thrones.
> My hand has found like a nest
> the wealth of the peoples;
> and as men gather eggs that have been forsaken
> so I have gathered all the earth. . . .
> [Then the Lord replies:]
> Shall the axe vaunt itself over him who hews with it,
> or the saw magnify itself against him who wields it?
> [Isa.10:7-15].

With Assyria's rejection by the Lord, full attention is once again given to Israel:

> In that day the remnant of Israel and the survivors of the house of Jacob will no more lean upon him that smote them, but will lean upon the Lord, the Holy One of Israel, in truth. A remnant will return, the remnant of Jacob, to the mighty God [Isa. 10:20-21].

These lines not only reveal the development of Isaiah's mind toward the end of his career, but also echo some of his earliest moments. They modulate upon the names given to his two sons, born most probably in his early twenties, before 740 B.C.E. The Assyrians swept into Judah in 701 B.C.E. The Hebrew form of Isaiah's words in 10:6, *lē-shĕlōl shālāl wĕ-lā-bōz baz*, adapts the name of the second son: *Maher-shalal-hash-baz* (8:1); the third and fourth syllables, *shalal* (spoil) and the last syllable, *bas* (prey), become part of Isaiah's message to Israel through the instrumentality of the Assyrians. Verse 20 and especially verse 21 reflect the name of Isaiah's elder son, *shearyashub* (6:3), when they speak about the remnant of Israel (in Hebrew, *shear yiśrā'ēl*) and about the remnant that will return (in Hebrew, *shear yāshûb*).

This contact with Isaiah's youth indicates that along with the many shifts and changes in his career, there was also a steady continuity. His positions on politics would seem to be inconsistent and unreliable. The prophet, however, was guided by a strong, pure morality that would have been unusually wise even from a political evaluation. This morality was based not only on respect for people's natural rights and the national welfare, but also on a firm conviction that God was *always present*, as Immanuel, throughout all the political fluctuations. Even, and in a way especially, was God present in the turmoil of war and deportations.

CONCLUSION

This investigation into the prophetic response to culture and politics has been long and complicated. Although there is no simple way to outline the steps and the method, a few simple and important facts emerge. These can be capsulized in that symbolic Hebrew name, *Immanu-el, with us-God*. God is with us, not only in the call of Abraham and Moses and in the establishment of Israel's religion, not only in the acquisition of the Promised Land and in the promises to the Davidic dynasty at Jerusalem, but also in the secular moments that preceded the religion of Israel, in the advanced yet corrupt culture of the Canaanites, and in the international politics and military expeditions of foreign nations. Prophets insisted ever more clearly that these secular, or non-Israelite, forces contributed positive insights into the meaning of the Mosaic covenant.

Hosea was able to reformulate the Sinaitic Covenant in terms of a sacred marriage between Yahweh and Israel. He derived this insight from Canaanite fertility cults, the very cause of his wife's infidelity and the children's doubtful paternity. Isaiah was more determined in seeing the foreign nations as God's instruments in purifying and transforming Israel and its sacred institutions.

Prophecy, moreover, derived its authority directly from God. It was not commissioned by priest or king. It represents a "lay" religious movement. As lay, it was most closely in touch with Israel's secular origins of impoverished slaves in Israel or migrant disfranchised *'apiru* in Canaan or indentured servants of petty Canaanite kings. As "lay missionaries," prophets were able to summon Israel's priests and kings to the primitive rule of life that worshiped "a God merciful and gracious, . . . abounding in steadfast love and faithfulness" (Exod. 34:6).

Prophets were called directly by God, but the catalyst that directed their preaching came from social injustice. They did not condemn Israel for its bad theology or invalid liturgies. The liturgies were sumptuously correct, and the theology carefully repeated the ancient traditions and firm promises as derived from Moses, David, and other consecrated leaders. Yet when religion no longer adequately defended the rights of widows and orphans and sanctioned overbearing and proud displays of religious authority, the prophetic conscience could no longer remain silent. Religion was reformed from secular, nonreligious sources.

Prophets worked within the religious system. God called Hosea within a setting of the covenant, and the glory of the Lord appeared to Isaiah from the Holy of Holies. Prophets never organized a new, rival religion. They worked to reform what existed. The line of continuity came from the religious structure; yet the power to make that survival worthwhile came from secular sources.

If prophets challenged religion, they equally stood up against false cultural inroads that corrupted religion. By their insights of faith, they perceived what was precious and godly in world culture; by their common-sense goodness they used secular resources to deepen Israel's appreciation of religion.

Israel's religion emerged out of international politics and military interventions (slavery in Egypt and peasant revolts in Canaan), and prophets were keenly aware that through the politics and wars of their own day religion would revive some of its finest moments and regain its purest insights into "a God merciful and gracious."

Prophets received their call within Israel's religion, yet independent of Israel's priests and kings; they perceived God's interventions within international politics, yet in ways never perceived by foreign Kings. Prophets were never totally committed to any theological system or political program. Isaiah threatened the traditional theology of the Jerusalem temple; Hosea reformulated the theology of the Mosaic covenant. Each could be pro-Assyrian and anti-Assyrian in politics. Prophetic consistency came from their basic commitment to Yahweh, who summons life into existence, within a bond of loving compassion, for a goal beyond this earth's dimensions. Faith in Yahweh's concern for the poor, and a conviction that Yahweh will be present as Immanuel to lead the pilgrimage to exalted glory: here is where the prophets found the wisdom and strength to challenge the humanization process of Israel's religion.

NOTES

1. The following summary is indebted to R. R. Wilson, *Prophecy and Society in Ancient Israel* (Philadelphia: Fortress Press, 1980), especially chap. 4.

2. Cf. Wilson, *Prophecy and Society*, pp. 132–33, 147–50. Balaam is mentioned in an Aramaic inscription discovered at Deir 'Alla in modern Jordan and dated around 700 B.C.E. (J. Hoftijzer and C. van der Kooij, *Aramaic Texts from Deir 'Alla* [Leiden: E.J. Brill, 1976])

3. Wilson, *Prophecy and Society*, p. 169: Samuel "exercised priestly, prophetic, judicial, and governmental functions." Cf. 1 Sam.1:1–25:1.

4. The weakening of prophetic authority, due to the prophets' quarreling among themselves, is the principal thesis of S. J. DeVries, *Prophet against Prophet* (Grand Rapids, Mich.: Wm. B. Eerdmans, 1978).

5. Wilson, *Prophecy and Society*, p. 252.

6. The title "classical prophecy" became an accepted term through the publications of scholars like W. Eichrodt, *Theology of the Old Testament* (Philadelphia: Westminster Press, 1961–), 1:338–91.

7. R. Rendtorff, *"nabi'* in the Old Testament," *Theological Dictionary of the New Testament* (Grand Rapids, Mich.: Wm. B. Eerdmans, 1964–), 6:804.

8. Cf. H. P. Scanlin, "The Emergence of the Writing Prophets in Israel in the

Mid-Eighth Century," *Journal of the Evangelical Theological Society* 21 (1978): 305–13.

9. C. Stuhlmueller, *Thirsting for the Lord* (Staten Island, N. Y.: Alba House, 1977), pp. 19–20; 2nd ed. (Garden City, N.Y.: Doubleday, 1979), p. 36.

10. This term derives from the title of B. Vawter, *The Conscience of Israel* (New York: Sheed & Ward, 1961).

11. Cf. H. W. Wolff, *Hosea* (Philadelphia: Fortress Press, 1974), p. 67.

12. Wilson, *Prophecy and Society*, p. 227. Samaria (Hos. 7:1; 8:5–6; 10:5, 7; 13:16); Bethel or Beth-aven (Hos. 4:15; 5:8; 10:5; 12:4); Gilgal (Hos. 4:15; 9:15; 12:11); the Valley of Achor (Hos. 2:15); Adam (Hos. 6:7); Ramah, Gibeah (Hos. 5:8); and Gilead (Hos. 6:8; 12:11).

13. Wilson, *Prophecy and Society*, p. 227.

14. Ibid., p. 228.

15. Wolff, *Hosea*, p. xxvi.

16. Ibid., pp. 57–58.

17. Cf. C. Stuhlmueller, *Creative Redemption in Deutero-Isaiah* (Rome: Biblical Institute Press,1970), pp. 60–66.

18. Wolff, *Hosea*, p. xxvi.

19. Ibid., p. 33.

20. Ibid., p. xxiv: "In principle he omits no sphere of life [in his rich and versatile symbolism]; but the imagery drawn from the vegetable and animal world and from family life clearly predominates."

21. The Valley of Achor is difficult to identify. Wolff, *Hosea*, pp. 42–43, argues for "the water-supplying [broad-sweeping] *Wadi en Nuwe'ime*, northwest of *Tell es-Sultan*." M. Noth, *Josua*, 2nd ed. (Tübingen: Mohr 1953), p. 88, and others, prefer to identify it with *Wadi en-Nar*, southeast of Jerusalem. I suggest that Hosea deliberately chose this phrase to symbolize Israel's quick settlement in the heart of the country between north and south.

22. Only in the case of the first child (Hos. 1:3) does the text say explicitly that "she conceived and bore *him* a son." In 1:6 and 1:8 the text reads "she conceived and bore a daughter . . . a son," omitting the word *him,* in Hebrew *lô.*

23. The translation is from F. James, *Personalities of the Old Testament* (New York: Scribners, 1939), p. 252.

24. Wilson, *Prophecy and Society,* p. 271.

25. Cf. R. P. Carroll, "Inner Tradition Shifts in Meaning in Isaiah 1–11," *Expository Times* 89 (1978): 301–4.

26. Cf. B. O. Long, "Prophetic Authority as Social Reality," in *Canon and Authority*, ed. G. W. Coats and B. O. Long (Philadelphia: Fortress Press, 1977), p. 12.

27. R. Knierim, "The Vocation of Isaiah," *Vetus Testamentum* 18 (1968): 67.

28. J. Harvey, *Le Plaidoyer Prophétique Contre Israël Après La Rupture de L'Alliance* (Montreal: Les Éditions Bellarmin, 1967), pp. 36–42.

29. W. L. Holladay, *Isaiah Scroll of a Prophetic Heritage* (Grand Rapids, Mich.: Wm. B. Eerdmans, 1978), p. 8, shows the effective use of key words to link material in the book of Isaiah, even within this appendix.

30. Cf. J. Barton, "Understanding Old Testament Ethics," *Journal for the Study of the Old Testament* 9 (1978): 44–64.

31. G. Hölscher, *Die Profeten* (Leipzig, 1914), p. 229.

32. J. Steinmann, *Le Prophète Isaïe* (Paris: Editions du Cerf, 1950), p. 88, fn. 11. Cf. Stuhlmueller, "The Mother of Emmanuel," *Marian Studies* 12 (1961): 165–66.

33. J. Jensen, "The Age of Immanuel," *Catholic Biblical Quarterly* 41 (April 1979): 232–34, concludes from strong arguments that the Immanuel is not simply one of Davidic descent through whom the dynasty and its promises will be continued, "but a special individual through whom the dynasty will be restored and its promises realized, . . . a messianic king to rule in the new order . . . much different from the present one, . . . a judge who would establish justice (Isa.11:4; Jer. 23:5)."

34. W. L. Holladay, *Isaiah Scroll*, p. 79.

35. This line can be translated more adequately, according to Holladay, ibid., "a staff is he in the hand of my fury."

4

Israel's Election and World Salvation

> *For the sake of my servant Jacob*
> *and Israel my chosen,*
> *I call you by your name,*
> *I surname you, though you do not know me [Isa. 45:4].*

The understanding of Israel as God's chosen people puts a major stumbling block before our attempt to formulate a mission statement for the "un-chosen." One key passage in the Old Testament reads: "For you are a people holy to the Lord your God, the Lord your God has chosen you to be a people for his own possession, out of all the peoples that are on the face of the earth" (Deut. 7:6). Election at once raises a serious question about the nonelect. This problem twists and turns into an ever more complicated conundrum, first of all because election is not a peripheral idea, scattered here or there throughout the Old Testament. Not only is this doctrine at the center but, according to the "acculturation process," election is intertwined within Israel's unique history, geography, and culture.

Israel's election was frequently caught in the tension of world mission. Even Abraham's separation from all other nations included a clause about being a "blessing [to] all the families of the earth" (Gen. 12:3). And according to the passage from Isa. 45:4, quoted at the beginning of this chapter, Cyrus the Persian king was called by name, "though you do not know me," "for the sake of . . . Israel my chosen." We will gradually separate the warp and woof of this tension—election and world mission—by, presenting first, the basis and the dangers of election; second, Israel's various reactions to the nations; third, the development of Israel's sense of election, out of which, fourth, came an outreach toward universal salvation.

ELECTION: ITS BASIS AND ITS DANGERS

For the elect people, God did not choose angels, free of earthly attachments, but a human family with a distinctive, though evolving culture; men and women were created out of their peculiar setting of earth, sky, and ancestral background: "The Lord God formed *'ādām* of dust from the *'ădāmāh''* (Gen. 2:7). Just as humankind *('Ādām)* came from planet earth *('ădāmāh)*, Israel was formed out of its specific corner of the earth. Mission, however, sends people to every part and corner of the earth and cannot be limited to any single piece of property or tied to any individual culture or history. Admittedly, two major obstacles to any missionary's work are the restrictions imposed by the ethnic boundaries of culture and language and a foreign country's suspicion of migrant aliens. Each country guards its "promised land" and its "elect status" against intruders, be they missionaries, soldiers, journalists, or business people. The Old Testament doctrine of a "chosen people" develops out of this common, secular phenomenon and seems to sanction governmental or ethnic constraints upon the outsider.

The doctrine of a chosen people can be traced to the remote origins of Israel's religion. Even in Israel's prehistory, as recounted in Genesis 1-11, a process of differentiation and separation was continuously at work: God chose Abel and then Seth instead of Cain (Gen. 4:4, 25-26), Shem instead of Noah's other sons, Ham and Japheth (Gen. 9:25-27), Abram instead of Nahor, Haran, and Lot (Gen. 11:27). This prolonged way of singling one person out of many others is summarized in Gen. 12:1:

> Now the Lord said to Abram, "Go from your country and your kindred and your father's house to the land that I will show you. And I will make of you a great nation . . . and make your name great so that you will be a blessing [to] all the families of the earth [Gen. 12:1-3].

The religion of Israel formally began a couple centuries after the patriarchs with God's bringing Israel out of Egypt and revealing a special covenant to Moses on Mount Sinai. The initial statement of this contract is so important that it has become the first of the Ten Commandments for Jewish people: "I am the Lord your God, who brought you out of the land of Egypt, out of the house of bondage" (Exod. 20:2). The theological urgency of being the Lord's "own possession out of all the peoples that are on the face of the earth" (Deut. 14:2) caused one of the final editors of the Bible to insert at the beginning of the account of the Sinai covenant:

> You have seen . . . how I bore you on eagles' wings and brought you to myself. Now therefore, if you will obey my voice and keep my covenant, you shall be my own possesssion among all peoples, for all the earth is mine, and you shall be to me a kingdom of priests and a holy nation [Exod. 19:4-6].

Paul-Eugène Dion calls this passage the "document capital" on election.[1]

Samuel Sandmel, a highly respected Jewish scholar and beloved ecumenist who died in 1980, agrees with Dion: "Much that is the Pentateuch is only indirectly related to this theme of election, but all of it in some way exists only in the light of the supposition."[2] Sandmel honestly recognized the serious question raised by

Israel's status not only of being God's special "possession" (Deut. 14:2) but also of possessing thereby a right to a promised land. He expressed the difficulty in no uncertain terms: "It is clear that the promised land had once belonged to others, who were not the elect, . . . yet they were to lose the land and the Hebrews to gain it. Is there not a certain uneasiness reflected in some of the overtones of Scripture about one people's taking a land which had not been theirs?"³ A little later in his book this sincere and open-minded Jewish writer added: "I am not suggesting that we should condemn, but only that we should recognize that along with the gratifying Bibical doctrine of the elect there has been a tacit but implied doctrine of the un-elect."⁴

By discussing and, we hope, unraveling this Gordian knot we may be able to recognize a distinctive quality about biblical election that paradoxically prepared for the universal outreach of the New Testament. It should be stated, however, that the Israelites were no different from their neighbors in thinking of themselves as specially chosen by a deity. At the heart of this conformity with other ancient Near Eastern peoples, however, a crucial difference shows up. These two steps— of conformity (or acculturation) and of difference (or prophetic challenge)—correspond to the method followed in chapters 2 and 3 of this book.

Not only was a sense of election felt by other countries of the ancient Near East, but other aspects of Israel's special choice by God are also manifest among them. In Egyptian documentation starting with the Middle Kingdom (twenty-first to eighteenth centuries B.C.E.), the king was chosen for a special work and was said to be "loved by God more than all others are loved by him."⁵ As in Israel, one of the royal titles "from the eighteenth dynasty on was *stp n*, 'chosen by' the deity."⁶ These two traits, election for a purpose and election because of divine favoritism, are just as apparent in Mesopotamian literature. Here the king is designated as "the one chosen by the faithful heart of God"; he is "the one to whom the eyes of the gods have been directed." In the case of Hammurabi, the king is chosen in view of special duties, "in order to be shepherd of the land" and "in order to preserve righteousness and justice."⁷

When we look more closely into the reasons for God's choice of Israel and compare them with Egyptian and Mesopotamian documents, some subtle yet important differences appear. Divine choice in the case of other nations was usually associated with their historical origins, that is, with the original foundation of their city and temple and the establishment of their dynasty. For these other countries, religion moreover turned into a means of stabilizing and continuing what the gods were thought to have done at the beginning in choosing them and their king. Election therefore secured their wealth and possessions, so much so that riches, power, and fertility were considered a proof of true election. It was not the same with Yahweh's people Israel.

Israel's election was connected with its Promised Land, but other circumstances of its choice by God set it apart ideologically and religiously from other nations. Israel's call, or choice, by Yahweh did not take place at the moment of its emergence as a separate nation, nor did it happen at the time of its first possession of the Promised Land. God called, or chose, Israel at a low point of its existence, not as in the case of Egypt or Babylon at the exalted moment of establishing a capital city and a brilliant empire. When God entered Israel's history, it was a moment hardly worthy of being called historical and written down in world archives. "Israel" as such did not exist, only a conglomerate group of dispossessed people, marred and confused by revolutions, migrations, and wars. "Israel" was a refugee from Egypt, a temporary sojourner in desert oases and at times a seminomad. Such was the situation when the main lines of the Mosaic covenant were struck. Even the principal religious object of Israel, the ark of the covenant, was made in the form of a box with rings on the side and with poles inserted in those, in order to be transported from one place to another (cf. Exod. 25:13–14). It maintained these mobile features even when placed permanently in the Holy of Holies (1 Kings 8:8).

Israel's settlement in the Promised Land therefore bore a challenging and almost contradictory message. Because Israel was chosen by Yahweh in the desert, land appeared at once as a fulfillment of divine promises and as a threat to those promises. In the desert, people are chosen to move onward, not to stay put. Yet desert people are always attracted by the fertile green land that surrounds their dry thirsty sand. Israel was not intended by God to remain in the desert, but at the same time land was to be held in trust according to its obedience to a desert morality (cf. Lev. 25:23). Walter Brueggemann has caught the serious tension of land that the Bible considers simultaneously a gift, a temptation, a task, and a threat. He wrote: "The land, source of life, has within it seductive power. It invites Israel to enter life apart from covenant, to reduce covenant place with all its demands and possibilities to serene space apart from history, without contingency, without demand, without mystery."[8] Brueggemann also pointed out that to possess land responsibly as God's covenanted people, the land

> becomes a meeting between giants and grasshoppers, between powerful agents of force and hopeless victims incapable of resistance or assertion. It is the new land that creates the contrast and creates in Israel a sense of fear and hopelessness. It is the very land of promise, the purpose of the whole journey of faith, which causes the failure of nerve. . . . The land is precisely for those and only for those who sense their precariousness and act in their vulnerability.[9]

For Israel, therefore, divine choice was not linked with ancient privileges and landed property. Covenant, moreover, as it provided promises of land and fertility, was always demanding an attitude of humble sharing. Israel's election was not based upon a memory of national or ethnic rights and privileges; it did not place Israel at the center of the universe. Rather, as H. Seebass pointed out toward the end of his article on "Election":

> The nation of Israel always saw the necessity of viewing the greatness of the nation in light of the greatness of her God. This viewpoint is clearly expressed in this passage [Deut. 7:7–8]. Israel is smaller than all peoples; her God is not that of national power, and the viewpoint of her election is not determined by the number of people that occupy the land. [The words in

Deut.] 7:7 f. also speak quite positively of the undemonstrable mystery of the love of God for his people. . . . It is crucial that the choice of Israel is to be understood not in terms of national might, but of the love with which Yahweh loves his people.[10]

The condition of a god's love is shared with Egyptian and Mesopotamian documents, but the added quality of God's love for a poor and dispossessed people is unique to Israel.

Israel's election is to be considered under these terms: a choice by a personal God, in favor of a helpless people, with promises and gifts to be held as loaned and borrowed, never as possessed and owned, as signs of love rather than indicators of power, as goods to be shared instead of riches to be hoarded and defended. Because election promised so much, yet on such demanding terms, God's choice of Israel ran repeated risks and at times collapsed with very little hope of revival. Strangely enough, colossal losses reduced Israel to the very condition necessary in God's eyes for election and covenant: a helpless, enslaved people. This conditional nature of the election—a threat to lose one's possessions if they were ever held with pride and sensuality—led to that absolute condition of helplessness that assured divine compassion and choice.

The risks, as already mentioned, are great. Some of these risks are in the area of systematic or speculative theology, while others center in the moral weakness of our common human nature. As to the theological hazards, we draw attention to the desire of all religions to possess eternal security for itself and to provide everlasting truths for its adherents. This problem arose for Israel from the way election led to divine promises, divine promises to partial fulfillment, partial fulfillment to the expectation of a never-changing status quo. In other words, the fulfillment that has come from God must be divine; and if it is divine it must be unchangeable. As an example: if Israel's possession of the Promised Land or the Davidic family's right to the throne resulted from God's promises and action, then no offense on Israel's part can change this pattern. Each is God's elect.

Certain biblical passages seem to have fallen into this theological trap. Even the prophet Hosea, despite his strong denunciations and summoning of death (Hos. 13:9,14), could not accept the ultimate destruction of the northern kingdom. Hosea heard God cry out in an agony of divine passion:

> How can I give you up, O Ephraim! . . .
> My heart recoils within me,
>   my compassion grows warm and tender.
> I will not execute my fierce anger,
>   I will not again destroy Ephraim;
> for I am God and not man [or woman] . . . [Hos. 11:8–9].

Yet God did give up the northern kingdom. Its people disappeared from recorded history after the destruction of their capital city in 721 B.C.E. and their dispersion within the Assyrian empire.

The sense of false security shows up again in the southern kingdom. Jerusalem and the Davidic dynasty considered themselves indestructible. After all, God had promised to David:

> When your days are fulfilled and you lie down with your fathers, I will raise up your offspring after you. . . . I will not take my steadfast love from him. . . . Your house and your kingdom shall be made sure for ever before me; your throne shall be established for ever [2 Sam. 7:12,15–16].

This promise is repeated again within one of the psalms addressed to David and his successors:

> My steadfast love I will keep for him for ever,
>   and my covenant will stand firm for him.
> I will establish his line forever
>   and his throne as the days of the heavens. . . .
> His line will endure for ever [Ps. 89:28–29, 36].

Yet the Davidic throne was smashed to pieces and the line disappeared from several centuries of documented history. In the wars of independence during the days of the Maccabees, the Davidic family never appeared. One of the Maccabees, of a priestly family within the tribe of Levi, and therefore not of the royal family of David (1 Macc. 2:1) declared himself king under the name of Judas Aristobulus I (105–104 B.C.E.). Earlier, at the time of the collapse of the Davidic line, the author of Psalm 89 broke out in lament. Contrasting his words with the Lord's eternal promises, he revealed the trauma of faith:

> But now thou hast cast off and rejected,
>   thou art full of wrath against thy anointed.
> Thou hast renounced the covenant with thy servant;
>   thou hast defiled his crown in the dust. . . .
> How long, O Lord: Wilt thou hide thyself for ever? . . .
> Lord, where is thy steadfast love of old,
> which by thy faithfulness thou didst swear to David?
>   [Ps. 89:38, 46, 49].

The psalmist felt that by quoting to God earlier promises and reminding God of his ancient choice, God was obliged to renew the Davidic dynasty as it had always been. Theology normally functions that way, quoting Scripture as the ultimate answer. Yet we sense something wrong about this process.

Election not only brings us to the outer edge of false confidence and self-righteous stubbornness; it can also cause people to swing to the other extreme of a vague, soft pantheism. God, in this view, has created and chosen the entire universe. All its forces and therefore every impulse and manifestation of life are very good. Challenge and tension disappear—at least for a while. People lose a sense of a personal God who struggles passionately against evil. The agony of a Jeremiah is muffled beneath blankets of rose petals. The dirty smell of prison and death is wafted away by an artificial fragrance and false peace. The Bible, however, has a different story of election and fulfillment. In the Scriptures, election, like the Promised Land—again in the words of Walter Brueggemann—remains a gift, a temptation, a task, and a threat.

Risks and questions emerge from the biblical doctrine of election. We shall now turn to a more careful study of the biblical text, to trace the dramatic breakthrough from election to world mission.

ISRAEL'S REACTIONS TOWARD THE NATIONS

Because election and universalism immediately involve Israel's relation with the nonelect outsiders, it will be helpful to review the many different attitudes in the Old Testament toward foreigners. It is difficult to find the right English word: outsider, foreigner, nations, Gentile, non-Israelite; there are various Hebrew designations, each with a different nuance. The word "Israelite," for instance, evolved in its meaning and can apply *(a)* to escapees and "riffraff" in the Sinai desert; *(b)* to a mixture of people under Joshua crossing the Jordan and entering Canaan from the desert, the indentured servants of Canaanite petty kings, the hired mercenary, or *'apirû*, and others in alliance with Joshua; *(c)* to the twelve-tribe system under David and Solomon. Likewise, the word "Gentile" applies to an evolving cross-section of people, always considered "outsiders" in relation to "Israel." At one point in the Bible a particular group like the Hittites would be considered foreigners subject to the *herem* war (Deut. 7:1) or to slavery (1 Kings 9:20–21) and at another time they would be called ancestors of Israel (Ezek. 16:3). The word *gôyim*, or nations, "stresses political and social rather than kinship bonds." [11]

To complicate the scene still more, "Gentile" can refer to crypto-Israelites who as apostates attempted to live and act like the non-Israelites, yet at heart remained attached to the Mosaic covenant. These distinctions should be kept in mind as we follow the major historical moments of Israel's relationship with the outsider. [12] In any case Israel's frame of mind and policies were dictated by geographical proximity and international politics. From this secular context developed a theology of election and nonelection.

In the Patriarchal Era

During the patriarchal period we sense a very cordial relationship with the Gentiles. Abraham settled among them as *ger*, or resident alien (Gen. 15:13; 23:4; Deut. 26:5), and purchased a burial lot in their midst (Gen. 23). Abraham anticipated a long existence for his descendants in this land. Although the patriarchs were careful not to intermarry with the Canaanites, nonetheless Abraham accepted two secondary wives, Hagar (Gen. 16:1–4) and Keturah (Gen. 25:1), from the local people who were "foreigners" or "outsiders" from a biblical viewpoint. The Canaanite Tamar bore one of the ancestors of King David to the patriarch

Judah (Gen. 38:12–19, 27–30; Ruth 4:18–22; Mt.1:3). Politically and economically the patriarchs could not have survived in any other way but by friendly cooperation with the "foreigners."

In Egyptian Bondage

The attitude soured into hatred during the Egyptian bondage. This memory of hardship also haunted the minds of many of the indentured servants in the land of Canaan who joined Joshua in taking control of the land. Hatred or at best confrontation dominated the biblical traditions toward "foreigners" from Moses through the age of Joshua until the royal period of David. From a position of power David conquered the neighboring Moabites (2 Sam. 8:2) and from a position of mutual help he entered into treaty arrangements with Tyre, as also did his son Solomon (2 Sam. 5:11; 1 Kings 5:26).

Once again the foreign nations are judged biblically from the viewpoint of Israel's benefit. Joshua saw a partial fulfillment of promises in setting up a series of independent, federated "tribes" in Canaan (Joshua 24). David seemed to extend those promises and their fulfillment by establishing a large empire in which foreign people marched with booty to pay tribute to David or Solomon and worship Yahweh in the temple. One such ceremony seems to be recorded in Psalm 87:

> On the holy mount stands the city he founded;
>   the Lord loves the gates of Zion [temple]
>   more than all the dwelling places of Jacob. . . .
> Among those who know me I mention Rahab and Babylon;
>   behold, Philistia and Tyre, with Ethiopia—
>   "This one was born there," they say.
> And of Zion it shall be said,
>   "This one and that one were born in her";
>   for the Most High himself will establish her.
> The Lord records as he registers the peoples,
>   "This one was born there."
> Singers and dancers alike say,
>   "All my springs are in you."

In this psalm politics seemed to have spilled over into the area of theology. Military conquest and international treaties provided the means of religious development. The kingdom of David had to pass through several more stages before it provided a good symbol for God's messianic kingdom.

Foreign Influences

A new situation erupted when Israel's pristine morals and religious customs were infiltrated and corrupted by foreign sensuality. Politically too the scene had changed drastically. Because of Israel's sins, according to the theology of the

Deuteronomic books (Judg. 2:6–3:6), God summoned the nations against his people Israel. Jeremiah felt the walls of his heart collapsing under the tumultuous beat of the roaring army (Jer. 4:19), yet he could not silence God's call to arms against the once holy city:

> Prepare war against her [in Hebrew, sanctify a war], . . .
> Thus says the Lord:
> "Behold a people is coming from the north country,
>   a great nation is stirring from the farthest parts of the earth.
> They lay hold on bow and spear,
>   they are cruel and have no mercy,
>   the sound of them is like the roaring sea . . ." [Jer. 6:4, 22–23].

Prophets had earlier announced the destruction of Samaria (2 Kings 17) and now they predicted Jerusalem's demise (Jer. 7:25). They also pronounced solemn oracles against the nations; foreign peoples in their arrogance and brutality sought to control God's plans for his chosen people Israel (Isa. 10:13–14). These special sections in the prophetic books, called the "Oracles against the Nations," first appeared with Amos (1:3–2:16) and became a pattern with almost all the prophets.

After the destruction of Jerusalem in 587 B.C.E. cries of pain and anger, vengeance and frustration produced what Paul-Eugène Dion has rightly called a "dossier of hate" against foreigners.[13] It included such unforgettable lines of distorted theology as,

> Happy shall he be who takes your little ones
> and dashes them against the rock! [Ps.137:9].

A more repentant attitude shows up in Psalm 79, begging God

> Do not remember against us the iniquities of our forefathers;
> let thy compassion come speedily to meet us,
> for we are brought very low [Ps. 69:8].

Anger mingles with piety in later lines of this same psalm:

> Let the groans of the prisoners come before thee;
>   according to thy great power preserve those doomed to die!
> Return sevenfold into the bosom of our neighbors
>   the taunts with which they have taunted thee, O Lord! [Ps. 79:11–12]

Israel confesses with faith that what was done to her was experienced by God: "The taunts [with which they have ridiculed us are those] with which they have taunted thee, O Lord!"

Second Isaiah, one of the prophets at this time, also began his career with hatred and rejection of the foreigners, especially the Babylonians. We shall discuss below how his words modulated into a message of salvation for Gentiles. In any case the religious view claimed equal prominence with political and economic reasons in the prophet's judgment of the nations. This was a definite advance over the earlier period.

After the Exile

After the exile Israel's reactions toward the Gentiles took on different forms, dependent upon their geographical location in the Near East. At Jerusalem the Jews tended to be locked into a small ghetto. The dominant theology there rejected all outside contact, repudiated and even dissolved mixed marriages (Ezra 9–10), and dreamed of the final battle and victory over the nations in the valley of Jehoshaphat (Joel 3:9–21). The prophet Joel reread and reversed the meaning of some important earlier prophecies of peace. Radically he revised the vision of peace within the books of Isaiah and Micah (Isa. 2:1–5; Mic. 4:1–4) into an oracle of war:

> Beat your plowshares into swords
> and your pruning hooks into spears [Joel 3:10].

While Ezra repudiated even the Jews who had been left behind in Judah at the time of the Babylonian exile and who tended to intermarry with foreigners, Third Isaiah (chaps. 56–66) argued on behalf of these same people and other foreigners:[14]

> And the foreigners who join themselves to the Lord,
>   to minister to him, to love the name of the Lord,
>   and to be his servants,
> every one who keeps the sabbath, and does not profane it,
>   and holds fast my covenant—
> these I will bring to my holy mountain,
>   and make them joyful in my house of prayer; . . .
> for my house shall be called a house of prayer
>   for all peoples.
> Thus says the Lord God,
>   who gathers the outcasts of Israel,
> I will gather yet others to him
>   besides those already gathered [Isa. 56:6–8].

Therefore, while the dominant attitude at Jerusalem during this particular period was not a favorable one toward the Gentiles, a few more tolerant spirits proclaimed a new hope for a wide expanse of Judaism.

Hatred for the foreigner burned with white heat in the apocalyptic literature, which had its origins in such passages as Ezekiel 38–39 and reached an apex in 1 and 2 Maccabees and Daniel 7–12. Yet the first six chapters in the book of Daniel foresaw the possibility of the conversion of heathen kings, and a book like the Wisdom of Solomon, composed in Egypt around 50 B.C.E., attempted to dialogue with pagan philosophy. There was no consistent policy toward the foreigners; there was no central, generally accepted theology of universal salvation. In the end Israel did not know exactly how to deal with its own special election over against the multitude of the nonelect.

Israel and the Gentile World

Before looking more closely at the doctrine of election and at one biblical writer's adaptation of it to universal salvation, we shall quickly itemize the various ways Israel viewed the Gentile world:

1. A friendly need of cooperation was required of the partriarchs.
2. Legitimacy, as Mendénhall points out, is required of Israel. The people must be able to trace their origin back to their first ancestors, whom the Lord chose and blessed. To be the children of the patriarchs, however, is not determined simply by blood descent but by the way that the present generation could join ranks with the refugees whom Moses led out of Egypt and with the dispossessed people of Canaan who allied themselves with the liberating army of Joshua and the early judges. All these found their unity in worshiping "a God merciful and gracious, slow to anger, and abounding in steadfast love and faithfulness." Israel is chosen "because the Lord loves you, and is keeping the oath which he swore to your fathers."
3. Military victories and international treaties led to a respectable empire under David and Solomon; this achievement eventually became a symbol of God's final kingdom. In a few cases, as in Psalm 87, the Gentiles are said to worship at the Jerusalem temple.
4. Growing hostility and then violent hatred toward the nations dominated biblical thought after the destruction of Jerusalem in 587 B.C.E. and during the Babylonian exile.
5. The postexilic period shows a variety of reactions—separatism, friendliness, suspicion, anger—depending on the opportunity of a ghetto existence at Jerusalem, a need for cooperation in Egypt, Mesopotamia, and elsewhere in the diaspora, and once more an experience of invasion and persecution.

We can locate all these responses of an elect people toward the nonelect foreigners within Israel's literature. For the sake of completion we also call attention to three more aspects:

6. Biblical writers speak of conversion, but we must ask on what terms. For instance, in Isa. 45:14 Egyptians, Ethiopians, and Sabeans worship Yahweh, yet "they come over in chains."
7. Biblical writers are capable of exaggeration, as in Psalm 117: "Praise the Lord, all nations." If this psalm is read carefully, we find that Yahweh is to be

praised "for great is his steadfast love *toward us* [i.e., toward the people of Israel]."

8. Biblical writers addressed only Israelites. The exceptions merely prove the rule. There was no direct ministry to foreigners. Gentiles might be summoned to worship Yahweh by way of exaggeration, as in Psalm 117 or the "coastlands" or the "end of the earth" might be named, actually referring to crypto-Israelites[15] who were still believers at heart but had adopted Gentile patterns externally (Isa. 42:1).

If the most basic position within Israel's religion consisted in a personal and community dialogue with and about Yahweh who had chosen them, then Israelites must respect their traditions and never compromise the intense family relationship with their Lord and God. Election, which expressed and safeguarded the unique doctrine of a personal, compassionate God, must not be abandoned but should be enriched and extended. This task of uniting "election" with "universal salvation" required the entire length of the Old Testament as a preparatory stage, the struggles of Jesus and New Testament writers as a firm base for theological expression, and the missionary endeavors of the church for these past two millennia as only a partial fulfillment. If "election" is essential to secure what will be shared in mission, then we need to investigate the term still more carefully.

THE DEVELOPMENT OF ISRAEL'S SENSE OF ELECTION

The Hebrew word for election, *bāḥar*, became a technical word, so important in Israel's tradition that no series of synonyms ever substituted for it.[16] From its many occurrences in the Old Testament (the verb alone, 164 times) two essential characteristics emerge: *(a) bāḥar* "means *a careful choice* occasioned by actual needs, and thus a very conscious choice and one that can be examined in light of certain criteria";[17] important among these norms would be "an act of an especially intimate relationship"; *(b) bāḥar* implies a *special purpose or mission*, especially when people are involved. When a person is chosen "out of a group," such a "one discharges a function in relationship to the group."[18] In this regard H. Seebass reaches a conclusion more advanced than the position of most scholars:

> The horizon of the election of the people of Israel is the peoples of the world, in relationship to which as a whole the "individual" Israel was chosen. [The Hebrew word *bāḥar*] as a technical term for the election of the people of Israel stands under the symbol of universalism.[19]

This synthesis of election and universalism emerges at least in the prophecy of Second Isaiah (chaps. 40–55). Later we shall follow the main steps in that development.

The theology of Israel's election can be traced back to earlier secular moments of Israel's history. First the Hebrew word *bāḥar* occurs in a number of nonreligious settings, yet always with a sense of "a careful choice . . . [and] actual needs";

for example, *Gen. 13:11:* Lot chose the Jordan Valley after a careful scrutiny of its "well-watered" condition. *Josh. 8:3:* "Joshua chose thirty thousand mighty men of valor [to] lie in ambush against the city" and be ready for the crucial moment of the battle. *1 Sam 17:40:* As David prepared to battle with Goliath, he "chose five smooth stones from the brook" for his sling.[20]

Second, other economic or political moves on the part of Israel's ancestors prepared for the religious meaning of *bāḥar.* The actual word may not always appear, but the idea of carefully separating one person or one group from a wider assembly of people and the sense of a mission or at least of a future are prominent characteristics. These two ingredients of separation and mission were the essential elements in our earlier explanation of election. We find them quite visible in the following key examples:

Gen. 12:1-3. Abraham is told to "go from your country and your kindred and your father's house to the land that I will show you." This severance of a person from the immediate surroundings or this preference for one person over other members of the same family becomes a pattern of life in the book of Genesis. It occurs at major transitions. God singled out Seth instead of Cain (Gen. 4:4, 25-26), Noah's family, who alone "found favor in the eyes of the Lord" (Gen. 6:8), Shem over Noah's two other sons (Gen. 9:25-27), Isaac rather than Ishmael (Gen. 21:1-21), Jacob rather than Esau (Gen. 25:23).[21]

Exod. 3:8. "I [the Lord] have come down to deliver them [my people Israel] out of the hand of the Egyptians, and to bring them . . . to a land flowing with milk and honey."

Judg. 2:18. "The Lord raised up judges . . . and saved them [the Israelites] from the hand of their enemies."

Although God's action is highlighted in the biblical account of these incidents, the setting of special need and the style of deliverance belong to the secular sphere of life. The context of God's choice gradually became more sacred as secular features were absorbed within the sanctuary and within Israel's styles of worship: the Levites, politically the least significant of the tribes, were picked to be priests (Gen. 49:5-7; Deut. 33:8-11); Samuel, who radically changed Israel's political system, was born after a promise at the sanctuary of Shiloh (1 Sam. 1:17); David, the youngest of Jesse's sons, was selected over all his older brothers and anointed king (1 Sam. 16:11-13). Once we arrive at royalty a new chapter begins in the history of "election." The special word *bāḥar* begins to appear with prominence and frequency.

This Hebrew word quickly became a technical term for a special act of God, singling out one person, place, or people (the king, the sanctuary, the people Israel) from all the rest for a special purpose. The criteria for this choice rested first with human need, perhaps destitution, and second with God's hopes and plans for Israel. *Bāḥar* took sole possession of this secular and now sacred area of action. As George Mendenhall wrote:

There is no word in Hebrew which can be regarded as a synonym [for *bāhar*.] In the N[ew] T[estament] similarly, the verb *eklegomai*, "choose," and derived forms . . . are without true synonyms. The conclusion seems justified, that in both languages the terminology of "choice" with "God" as subject has become technical usage with a specific meaning not communicated by any other word.[22]

Mendenhall also declared: "The very rapid acceptance and popularity of the term can certainly be attributed to the fact that it gave clear expression to very old religious convictions precisely at a time when it was most needed as an assurance of the value of the religious faith and the community."[23]

Deuteronomy is the biblical book that established the use of *bāhar* in Israel's religious vocabulary. This fifth book of the Torah, on superficial reading, seems to breathe the fresh, tranquil air of late spring; it is noted for its compassionate and prayerful spirit. Deuteronomy, however, is also a crisis book. Its preachers/writers were willing to adapt the Mosaic covenant to later needs, but they adamantly held the line on crucial issues. They urgently demanded a decision "this day," a phrase deeply rooted in the book of Deuteronomy (4:40; 5:3; 6:6; 7:11; etc.). They argued how Israel must resist the superstitious practices of the nations (Deut. 4:37; 7:6–7; 10:14–15; 14:2). Israelites were to remain faithful to the Lord, their God, and to love the Lord alone with all their strength (Deut. 6:4–9). The book of Deuteronomy was redacted, or reedited, during several periods of fervent, almost feverish religious reform. These efforts to purify and restore the ancient religion were undertaken during the reign of King Hezekiah (2 Kings 18–20; 2 Chron. 29–32) and most energetically by King Josiah (2 Kings 22:1–23:30; 2 Chron. 34–35).

Let us examine the classic text, chapter 7 of Deuteronomy. This passage combines the *herem*, or extermination warfare against foreigners, in verses 1–5 and 16–26 along with the most delicate expression of divine love for Israel, the chosen people, in verses 6–15. These latter verses were reedited on different occasions, a tribute to their long-continued use. The Hebrew text, especially verses 6–9, reveals a modulation between the second person singular and the second person plural. Unfortunately English, unlike many other languages, does not distinguish between the singular "you" and the plural "you." When speaking in the plural, the homilist or preacher is making an explicit application to *all* Israelites. The earlier account in the singular tends to be more speculative or theological and repeats the standard phraseology of the Mosaic covenant. The combination of the singular and plural texts may have been done by the same hand that was responsible for the collection of the "Deuteronomic books" of Joshua–Judges–Samuel–Kings.

v. 6 (in the singular): For you are a people holy to the Lord your God; the Lord your God has chosen you to be a people for his own possession, out of all the peoples that are on the face of the earth.

v. 7 (in the plural): It was not because you were more in number than any other people that the Lord set his love upon you and chose you, for you were the fewest of all peoples;

v. 8a (in the plural): but it is because the Lord loves you, and is keeping the oath which he swore to your father, that the Lord has brought you out with a mighty hand

v. 8b (in the singular): and redeemed you from the house of bondage, from the hand of Pharaoh king of Egypt.

v. 9 (in the singular): Know therefore that the Lord your God is God, the faithful God who keeps covenant and steadfast love with those who love him and keep his commandments, to a thousand generations.

Deut.7:6-9 ought to be studied in close connection with other election texts in Deuteronomy like 4:37; 10:15; 14:1-2; 26:18-19. From these passages we draw the following conclusions.

a. Israel belongs to Yahweh in a very special way, not because of its own worth or achievements but simply because of the Lord's unique goodness and graciousness. "It is because the Lord loves you."

b. Legitimacy, as Mendenhall points out, is required of Israel. The people must be able to trace their origin back to their first ancestors whom the Lord chose and blessed. To be the children of the patriarchs, however, is not determined simply by blood descent but by the way that the present generation joined ranks with the refugees whom Moses led out of Egypt and with the dispossessed people of Canaan who allied themselves with the liberating army of Joshua and the early judges. All these found their unity in worshiping "a God merciful and gracious, slow to anger, and abounding in steadfast love and faithfulness" (Exod. 34:7). Israel is chosen "because the Lord loves you, and is keeping the oath which he swore to your fathers. . . ."

c. Another sign of election is found in Israel's obedience to "the commandments, and the statutes, and the ordinances, which I command you this day" (Deut. 7:11). Yet this compliance with the law is not the condition of Israel's choice by the Lord, but the consequence. Yahweh has bestowed life upon Israel, and this life to be true to itself expresses itself in a well-ordered, peaceful, kindly way of action. Law would be the necessary setting so that life could reflect these noble hopes of God for his family.

d. Election also leads to renewal of life. Deuteronomy declares: "The Lord your God . . . will love you, bless you, and multiply you; he will also bless the fruit of your body and the fruit of your ground, your grain and your wine and your soil, the increase of your cattle and the young of your flock, in the land which he swore to your fathers to give you. You shall be blessed above all peoples . . ." (Deut. 7:12-14). The results of God's election and Israel's obedient response extended even to "your basket and your kneading-trough" (Deut. 28:5)—

to everything that enhances the fullness and dignity of life. These blessings reach out to the heavens and across the earth; they take on a cosmic scope. They are closely associated with God's act of creating and renewing the universe. As such, Israel's election began to reach outward and to embrace the whole world.

  e. Election also required a firm and total rejection of foreigners. These people had been partly responsible for Israel's moral corruption. Deuteronomy sanctions the *ḥerem* or extermination warfare against outsiders.[24] The book of Deuteronomy, however, is not a tirade against non-Israelites. It reflects a long history, so that at times it responds compassionately toward the nations and treats female captives with courteous consideration (21:10–14). It admits third-generation offspring of Edomites and Egyptians into "the assembly of the Lord" (23:8). Deuteronomy can also be caught up in furious nationalistic rage against foreigners. Such martial language introduces and concludes a chapter where the middle section contemplates the Lord's gracious love for his chosen people Israel. Yet it is not unusual that tender, parental love will suddenly turn savage in protecting its offspring.

  This seemingly contradictory mingling of compassion and cruelty, of acceptance and rejection, represents one of the serious risks of election. These risks were not always mastered in the Bible, nor are they always avoided in the church's missionary apostolate. At times concern for life and one's own values is coupled with harsh condemnation of another people's scale of moral and cultural values. We turn now to Second Isaiah for a further development of election and universal salvation; this prophet will provide directions to avoid the risks of misdirected zeal on the part of "elect" people.

FROM ELECTION TOWARD UNIVERSAL SALVATION

  Before investigating the process, at times quite painful, by which Second Isaiah expanded the doctrine of Israel's election to include universal salvation, we shall glance at some earlier biblical passages in which some type of universalism is implied or mentioned in passing. Second Isaiah did not create a new doctrine but lifted an obscure one into prominence.

  One series of texts clusters around the Davidic dynasty at Jerusalem and the empire that it controlled. This fact has already been mentioned in quoting Psalm 87. Here people from Philistia, Tyre, and Ethiopia bring tribute to the Jerusalem king and worship the king's God at the temple. Other psalms support the dynasty and see in Yahweh's covenant with David and presence in the temple a power to maintain security and to overcome hostile forces across the universe. Psalm 89 closely associated Yahweh's "steadfast love" (v. 2) with David's "throne [built] for all generations" (v. 4); it identifies Yahweh's mighty arm and right hand, to "rule the raging of the seas . . . the world and all that is in it" (vv. 9,11,13) with David's "right hand [set] on the sea" (v. 25). Psalm 89 implies God's intention to extend this covenantal assurance of steadfast love to the entire world.[25]

  Psalm 29 orchestrates a world symphony with the conductor at the Jerusalem temple:

Ascribe to the Lord, O heavenly beings,
ascribe to the Lord glory and strength.
Ascribe to the Lord the glory of his name;
worship the Lord in holy array.
The voice of the Lord is upon the waters;
the God of glory thunders,
The Lord, upon many waters. . . .
The voice of the Lord breaks the cedars. . . .
The voice of the Lord flashes forth flames of fire. . . .
The voice of the Lord makes the oaks to whirl. . . .
and in his temple all cry, "Glory!"
The Lord sits enthroned over the flood;
the Lord sits enthroned as king for ever.
May the Lord give strength to his people!

While there is no statement about God's intent to save the world, the psalm associates Jerusalem's peace with a worldwide scenario and with an extraordinary blending of Canaanite phrases and images.

Similar hymnic fragments show up in the prophecy of Amos.[26] The eyes of this seer are sweeping across mountains and sailing with the wind to distant places:

For lo, he who forms the mountains, and creates the wind,
and declares to us what is our thought;
who makes the morning darkness,
and treads on the heights of the earth—
the Lord, the God of hosts, is his name! [Amos 4:13].

Amos was forced into another type of world vision different from that in the preceding hymn, while arguing against the smug sense of satisfaction within Israel. The people felt ultra-holy and super-safe because they were the children of the exodus and the covenant. From the covenant Amos concluded to God's verdict: "Therefore I will punish you for all your iniquities" (Amos 3:2). Orthodox theology would put it differently: "Therefore I will bless you because of the covenant." The exodus, Amos said with classic put-down, may not be any different from the migrations of other peoples:

"Are you not like the Ethiopians to me,
O people of Israel?" says the Lord.
"Did I not bring up Israel from the land of Egypt,
and the Philistines from Caphtor and the Syrians from Kir?"
(Amos 9:7).

One could reason that God could have transformed the migrations of the Philistines or the Syrians into a sacred exodus, just as he had done for Israel. Amos, however, never drew that conclusion.

The creation stories in Genesis 1-3 and the table of the nations in Genesis 10 represent still other traditions, closely associated with Jerusalem, where intuitions of universal salvation flash between the lines. These sections may have been placed here in the Bible only at a late date, yet they circulated for centuries and found a home among the traditions and ceremonies of the Jerusalem temple and the Davidic dynasty.

A healthy tension existed at Jerusalem. While a more persistent theology of election and separatism was developing, the people—at least on the occasion of great festivals—would sight a world vista and see the Lord enthroned over the universe. This situation neatly parallels the relation of missionaries today to their home churches. Missionaries act upon the intuitions of those who send them forth and sustain the faith and vision of their family and original congregation. Without the missionaries these dreams would be lost or suppressed. Many persons on the home front are not so much interested in world salvation as they are in election, even in a selfish and rigid grasp of their own privileges, culture, and moral values. Missionaries, therefore, tend to be on the outer edge of those who send them forth and of those to whom they are sent.

The prophet who broke the impasse between election and universalism turned out to be Second Isaiah, the author of chapters 40-45 in the larger book of Isaiah.[27]

The brilliance of Second Isaiah's poetry at once puts us on the alert for profound tensions. Genius is always created by the mighty opposites which are held together long enough that wondrous, new relationships can be glimpsed. The major tension in Second Isaiah is produced by his twin concern for: a) the *particularism* of Israel's elect status and call *out of* the nations; and b) the *universal* panorama against which this divine *particularism* towards Israel is achieved. The breakthrough, vaguely or perhaps only subconsciously anticipated by Deuteronomy, Hosea and Jeremiah, occurred when Second Isaiah finally heard the divine proclamation:

> It is too light a thing that you be my servant
> [simply] to raise up the tribes of Jacob
> and to restore the preserved of Israel;
> I will give you as a light to the nations
> [Isa. 49:6].[28]

In his early preaching Isaiah was totally preoccupied with the new exodus.[29] The elect people would return from Babylonian exile to their own promised land. In ecstatic vision he sees Yahweh enthroned amid his heavenly court. He hears the Lord calling out to his celestial ministers: "Comfort, comfort my people." Second Isaiah then records the answer from one member of the Lord's court:

> A voice cries:
> "In the wilderness prepare the way of the Lord,
>   make straight in the desert a highway for our God.

Every valley shall be lifted up,
   and every mountain and hill be made low;
the uneven ground shall become level,
   and the rough places a plain.
And the glory of the Lord shall be revealed,
   and all flesh shall see it together,
      for the mouth of the Lord has spoken [Isa. 40:3–5].

Even though Second Isaiah is preoccupied exclusively with Israel's salvation, we can detect important signals of a wider concern. We shall look more closely at these intuitions of universalism, found here and elsewhere in what is often called the Book of Consolation (Isa. 40–55).

a. The prophet sees the new exodus within a large international setting. Unlike the straggly group of *'apirû* and *shosu* whom Moses led in stealthy retreat from Egypt, this new undertaking will immediately attract world attention. In the days of Moses, Egypt, its pharaoh and empire remained thoroughly intact; in Second Isaiah's vision Babylon will collapse (chap. 46) under the rapid and skillful campaign of Cyrus the Great (42:1–5). Second Isaiah honors this Persian conqueror as the Lord's "anointed," called "by your name" for a special task "for the sake of my servant Jacob and Israel my chosen" (Isa. 45:1,4). The tension between a chosen people and a world concern is clearly evident.

b. Another signal of the prophet's universal vision appears in his willingness to recognize the glory of the Lord in what even Amos called "an unclean land" (7:17). Normally the glory of the Lord, as we saw already in Psalm 29, rested in the Jerusalem temple. Anyone who traveled in foreign lands was considered "impure" and so barred from temple worship. This glory, moreover, does not throw Second Isaiah against the ground as it did the prophet Ezekiel (Ezek. 1:28). In fact, "all flesh [that is, all humankind, even in its weakness and trials] shall see it together." As a cautionary note, however, Second Isaiah did not announce the conversion of the Gentiles to Yahweh, only their admiration for the way that Yahweh was bringing his elect people out of their midst. There is even a bit of exaggeration here; *all* flesh did not see Israel's return. Yet exaggeration, like humor, always hides an important bit of sober truth. What some foreigners are seeing and admiring might become for them, as for Israel, a source of salvation. If *some* outsiders can be converted, then the way is open for a world mission to "all flesh."

c. Second Isaiah frequently employed the Hebrew word *'eretz,* and for him it always meant "earth." Ezekiel too used the word very often—198 times—and by it he meant "land" of Israel. While Second Isaiah widened his vista, Ezekiel more and more restricted his.[30]

d. Second Isaiah made the new exodus the principal setting for his poems, yet he did not refer explicitly to the Mosaic covenant. He mentioned three other covenants: those of God with Noah (54:7–10), with Abraham (51:1–3), and with David (55:3–5). Second Isaiah decentralized the Davidic covenant and in democratic style returned its privileges and obligations to all the people. The two other covenants lead to a wonderful garden "like Eden," where the parents of the whole human race once lived at peace with God, or to "the mountains . . . and the hills," where Yahweh's universal "covenant of peace" shall abide forever. In all these cases, it must be admitted, Second Isaiah was addressing himself to Israel and exclusively to their salvation. Yet ever more persistently he saw the *world implications* of what Yahweh would be doing for his chosen people.

These intuitions forced their way into an open declaration of world salvation in the Songs of the Suffering Servant. We shall sketch this transition as best we understand it.[31]

Isaiah, chapters 41–48,[32] represent the prophet's confident spirit and exalted style as he anticipated the fall of Babylon and even the possible conversion of Cyrus the Great to Israel's religion. These poems of exceptional beauty and rich theology integrate major religious doctrines: a new *exodus* (41:17-20; 43:16-21); by Yahweh's *elect* people (41:8-10; 43:8-13; 43:19-21; 44:1-5); through Yahweh's *fulfillment of prophecy* (many poems on "First and Last," especially 48:1-13); and through fidelity to his role of being Israel's *go'el* or close blood relative (43:1-7). All other gods, to whom some Israelites may have transferred their loyalty, are "a delusion . . . empty wind" (41:29).

Because of the importance of the theme of election in our investigation now, we shall pause over 44:1-5.

> But now hear, O Jacob, my servant,
> Israel whom I have chosen!
> Thus says the Lord who made you,
> who formed you from the womb and will help you:
> Fear not, O Jacob my servant,
> Jeshurun whom I have chosen.
> For I will pour water on the thirsty land,
> and streams on the dry ground;
> I will pour my Spirit upon your descendants,
> and my blessing on your offspring.
> They shall spring up like grass amid waters,
> like willows by flowing streams;
> This one will say, "I am the Lord's,"
> another will call himself by the name of Jacob,
> And another will write on his hand, "The Lord's,"
> and surname himself by the name of Israel.

Grammatically, only one word, twice repeated, *behartî* ("I have chosen"), is found in the completed, or *qaṭal*, tense: all other verbs in this poem are in some other tense or form. For this reason the action within the other lines is thought to be "incomplete" or "ongoing" and as such dependent upon that complete or definitive act by which God had chosen Israel. Because of this choice Israel's whole life will be re-created by the Spirit into a new paradise of "flowing streams." Yahweh's love will not only run lavishly like "flowing streams" in the rainy season but will reach deeply into the spring of life and carefully form each person "from the womb." Such divine love anticipates and shapes the life of each chosen person even before his or her birth. Such persons have no prior claims upon God; he freely chooses and creates. Second Isaiah seems to have been addressing apostate or crypto-Israelites—or possibly scattered foreigners—who would call themselves "by the name of Israel."[33] If choice or election is not merited, then it can be bestowed freely by God upon anyone, including apostates and foreigners.

Isaiah, chapters 49–55, were written more quickly than the preceding section, some time after the fall of Babylon in 539 B.C.E. Cyrus did not convert to Yahweh; the new exodus turned out to be small, dismal, and disheartening. The prophet was rejected by many of his own people (49:5-13), principally because he had cast the foreigner Cyrus in the role of a new Moses leading the people home (44:24-45:7). The tone of the writing turns sober and sorrowful, with a greater use of the dirge, or lament. We quote some of the sad lines:

49:14   But Zion said, "The Lord has forsaken me,
            my Lord has forgotten me."

49:19   . . . your waste and your desolate places
            and your devastated land.

49:20   The children born in the times of your bereavement.

50:1   Where is your mother's bill of divorce,
            with which I put her away?

51:17   Rouse yourself, rouse yourself,
            stand up, O Jerusalem,
         you who have drunk at the hand of the Lord
            the cup of his wrath.

Second Isaiah would not let go of his dreams, even if they brought an avalanche of ridicule, frustration, and gloom. The sorrow shall bear its fruit, in a spiritual way through a renewed dedication within the heart of Second Isaiah and in a literary way through the composition of the Suffering Servant Songs. Within these religious classics he moved from frustration to faith.

The Servant Songs, we believe, were written in two stages and then inserted within the context of the other poems by the later editor. They are now found in Isa. 42:1-4; 49:1-4, 5c; 50:4-9a; 52:13-53:12. Before composing these major servant songs, Second Isaiah was reaching for words to express and sustain his sorrow; he began to write down these initial attempts, or first intuitions. The final editor of the book gathered together these and other isolated lines and placed them before or, usually, after the principal Servant Songs. These fragments include 42:5-7; 48:22 (misplaced here from 57:21); 49:5a, b, 6, 8, 9a; 49:7; 50:10-11 (exhortations from the editor); and 51:4-6 (a very late addition to the book). To clarify what is inevitably a complex situation due to the condition of the Hebrew text, the following outline is provided. The first column indicates how a good, continuous reading existed before the insertion of the Servant Songs and fragments. The second and third columns isolate the Servant Songs and other scattered passages.

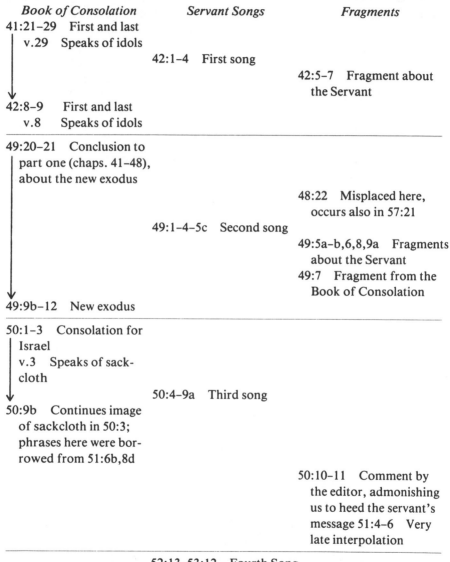

Book of Consolation	*Servant Songs*	*Fragments*
41:21–29 First and last v.29 Speaks of idols		
	42:1–4 First song	
		42:5–7 Fragment about the Servant
42:8–9 First and last v.8 Speaks of idols		
49:20–21 Conclusion to part one (chaps. 41–48), about the new exodus		
		48:22 Misplaced here, occurs also in 57:21
	49:1–4–5c Second song	

		49:5a–b,6,8,9a Fragments
		    about the Servant
		49:7 Fragment from the
		    Book of Consolation

49:9b–12 New exodus		
50:1–3 Consolation for Israel v.3 Speaks of sack- cloth		
	50:4–9a Third song	
50:9b Continues image of sackcloth in 50:3; phrases here were bor- rowed from 51:6b,8d		

		50:10–11 Comment by
		    the editor, admonishing
		    us to heed the servant's
		    message 51:4–6 Very
		    late interpolation

	52:13–53:12 Fourth Song	

The major Servant Songs portray the prophet drawn ever more forcefully into the realm of God's mysterious presence. To sustain himself with faith, Second Isaiah turned principally to the prophet Jeremiah, but also to a larger repertoire of traditions. The new exodus has led him into the interior of God's heart. The tears wrung by sorrow from his own broken heart suddenly change, as can happen in the case of delicate temperaments, into tears of joy and victory. The Fourth Song concludes in a serene vision of rebirth. The servant is wrapped in silence while others are contemplating his mission:[34]

> so shall he startle many nations;
>   kings shall shut their mouths because of him;
>   for that which had not been told them they shall see
>   and that which they have not heard they shall understand.
>   the will of the Lord shall prosper in his hand;
>   he shall see the fruit of the travail of his soul and be satisfied
>   [Isa. 52:15;53:10–11].

The key transitional lines that led Second Isaiah from a strong focus upon the chosen people Israel to this glimpse of world salvation are in one of the fragmentary verses:

> It is too light a thing that you should be my servant
>   [simply] to raise up the tribes of Jacob. . . .
> I will give you as a light to the nations [Isa.49:6].

This verse not only captured and expressed the intuitions and signals of Second Isaiah's early preaching, but also enabled him to endure the suffering of being rejected by his own people.[35] It became the catalyst for transforming ancient traditions into the contemplative visions of the four major Servant Songs. It extended Israel's election to the world, and so fulfilled the mission in Israel's being chosen in the first place.

CONCLUSION

This study of election has taken us on a long, tortuous route through the Old Testament. Yet it could not be a simple task for the Israelites to maintain—or for us to understand—that a people could claim a special status while mingling in the world at large. Serious theological problems would naturally confront Israel as it attempted to hold onto a unique revelation from God and all the while be expected to learn from others about its fuller meaning, from others who did not share these divine truths and who at times worked against them.

Because of its central role in biblical religion, election ran the risk of being manipulated for political and other selfish purposes. After all, no one could ever rise to power in Israel and ignore what was essential to the existence of Israel. Election consequently could and did become one of the main "idols" by which Israelites superstitiously basked in divine favors, which they claimed were due to them because of God's promises: my very own "possession, [carefully chosen] out of all the peoples that are on the face of the earth" (Deut. 14:2). At the same time election not only remained one of the most important means for Israelites to identify God as a personal, loving Lord (not simply as world creator and omnipotent power) and to look upon themselves as God's "special possession," but also turned out to be the way by which Israel would eventually bring this mystery of a personal savior God to the universe.

Election reached back into the earliest traditions. Particularly at crucial, transitional moments God was portrayed as calling and separating his chosen one(s) from the larger human family: Abraham from the other wandering Arameans of the mid-nineteenth century B.C.E.; the Israelite slaves from the Egyptians, Moabites, Ammonites, and other neighboring peoples; the dispossessed servants of Canaan from the petty kings and other important people of that land; David instead of his elder brothers.

This divine style of manifesting personal love for Israel finally found expression in the Hebrew word *bahar* ("he chose"). This technical word resisted all synonyms and sustained itself through the long centuries of the Old Testament era. It first appeared, however, in a secular context and denoted a careful choice because of special needs. We can still picture the youth David, leaning over and shrewdly eyeing the stones in a brook before selecting the proper ones for his slingshot and the coming duel with Goliath. *Bahar*, therefore, presumed a set of reasons or criteria for making a suitable choice, with a purpose or mission in mind.

The transition from the secular to the sacred sense of *bahar* took place when the word was applied to kings who represented the people before God, then to the sanctuary built or embellished by kings so that the people could assemble for worship; finally *bahar* qualified the Israelite people themselves as God's special possession. The use of *bahar* with royalty and sanctuary tended to move the idea of election toward grandeur and privilege and away from the origins of Israel's religion when God chose the migrant Abraham, or the slave people Israel, or the dispossessed Canaanite servants. Under a strong prophetic influence the book of Deuteronomy stressed the poverty and unworthiness of Israel, and in this way the people were in a position to be loved, protected, and cared for by the Lord, their God, who chose them. Protection, for Deuteronomy, also led to harsh rejection of foreigners, even to the *herem*, or extermination war against them.

Deuteronomy extended election explicitly to all Israel but at the same time eliminated all foreigners. The prophet Second Isaiah picked up the main themes of Deuteronomy, along with ideas from Jeremiah and Hosea. All these traditions stressed God's personal love. At first Second Isaiah applied them to Israel, now in Babylonian exile, as he called for a new exodus away from the Gentiles and back to its own Promised Land. Yet the perspectives were panoramic: heaven and earth, world politics, a new creation, covenants like those with Noah and Abraham, which reached to all humankind. Second Isaiah involved the larger secular world intimately in Israel's salvation, even claiming that the Persian Cyrus, who did not know Yahweh, would fill the role of Moses in the new exodus. Second Isaiah declared:

> For the sake of my servant Jacob,
> and Israel my chosen,
> I call you by your name,
> I surname you, though you do not know me [Isa. 45:4].

This political acculturation was too much for the majority of the Israelites and they argued against him, finally repudiating the prophet (Isa. 45:9–13). Second Isaiah's thoughts then took a radical leap. In the Songs of the Suffering Servant, actually in initial fragmentary attempts at them, he heard God's surprising declaration:

> It is too light a thing that you should be my servant
> [simply] to raise up the tribes of Jacob. . . .
> I will give you a light to the nations [Isa. 49:6].

How right it was that election, which began in suffering and destitution for Israel, should be extended to the world by a Suffering Servant.

When the purpose of Israel's election by God reached this full and clear expression by Second Isaiah, the prophet was not making an entirely new revelation. All through the Old Testament there had been indicators that pointed beyond Israel to the nations. These religious perceptions never extended into a theological synthesis, nor were they integrated with other important religious positions in Israel. Only later would Paul the Apostle achieve that work, at great cost to himself and to the early church.

NOTES

1. P. E. Dion, *Dieu Universel et Peuple Élu* (Paris: Les Éditions du Cerf, 1975), p. 67.

2. S. Sandmel, *The Several Israels* (New York: Ktav, 1971), p. 2.

3. Ibid., p. 8.

4. Ibid., p. 12.

5. J. Bergman, H. Ringgren, "*bāchar*, I. In the Ancient Near East," *Theological Dictionary of the Old Testament* (Grand Rapids, Mich.: Wm. B. Eerdmans, 1974–), 2:73.

6. Ibid.; cf. 11 Kings 1:34; Hag. 2:23.

7. Ibid., p. 74, relying upon J. M. Seux, *Epithètes Royales Akkadiennes et Sumériennes* (Paris: Letouvzey et Ané, 1968), pp. 121–22, 434–35.

8. W. Brueggemann, *The Land* (Philadelphia: Fortress Press, 1977), p. 53.

9. Ibid., pp. 68–69.

10. H. Seebass, "Bāchar, II–III," *Theological Dictionary of the Old Testament* (Grand Rapids, Mich: Wm. B. Eerdmans, 1974–), 2:84.

11. E. J. Hamlin, "Nations," *Interpreter's Dictionary of the Bible* (Nashville: Abingdon, 1962), 3:555.

12. W. Vogels, *God's Universal Covenant* (Ottawa: University of Ottawa Press, 1979), traces this relationship but with less attention to the historical process than is the case with the present study. This different approach in no way compromises his conclusions.

13. Dion, *Dieu Universel*, p. 61.

14. Such is the thesis argued convincingly by P. D. Hanson, *The Dawn of Apocalyptic*, 2nd ed. (Philadelphia: Fortress Press, 1979).

15. Cf. D. E. Hollenberg, "Nationalism and 'The Nations' in Isaiah XL–LV, " *Vetus Testamentum* 19 (1969): 23–36.

16. G. Mendenhall, "Election," *Interpreter's Dictionary of the Bible* (Nashville: Abingdon, 1962), 2:76.

17. Seebass, "Bāchar, II–III," p. 74. Italics added.

18. Ibid., pp. 82–83.

19. Ibid., p. 83.

20. Ibid., p. 75. Mendenhall, "Election," p. 77, lists still more examples.

21. B. E. Shafer, "The Root *bḥr* and Pre-Exilic Concepts of Chosenness in the Hebrew Bible," *Zeitschrift für Alttestamentliche Wissenschaft* 89 (1977):20–42, traces the origin of election theology to the patriarchal traditions.

22. Mendenhall, "Election," 2:76.

23. Ibid.

24. Seebass, "Bāchar, II–III," thinks that *herem* war was essentially linked with election, especially in the choice of kings.

25. The transfer of divine epithets and qualities to the Davidic king in Psalm 89 is carefully presented by J.-B. Dumortier, "Un Rituel d' Intronisation: Le Ps. LXXXIX 2–38," *Vetus Testamentum* 22 (April 1972):176–96.

26. We leave aside the question whether or not the three hymnic fragments in Amos were composed originally by the prophet, although they probably were not; cf. J. L. Crenshaw, *Hymnic Affirmation of Divine Justice*, SBL Dissertation Series 24 (Missoula, Mont.: Scholars Press, 1975). Because of the very early redaction of the book, these passages deserve attention in any consideration of Amos' preaching. The dating of the book by the earthquake of 760 B.C.E., (Amos 1:1) rather than by other, more shattering events like the fall of Samaria in 721 B.C.E.,indicates an "early [first] redaction" (H. W. Wolff, *Joel and Amos* [Philadelphia: Fortress Press, 1977], p. 108. Wolff, moreover, associates the doxologies with the liturgy of Bethel, another indication of early presence in Amos. W. Brueggemann, "Amos IV 4–13 and Israel's Covenant Worship," *Vetus Testamentum* 15 (1965): 1–15, even argues that v. 13 is an integral part of the entire poem and liturgy in vv. 4–13.

27. The role of election in Israel's life and particularly in the theology of Second Isaiah is developed in an article by Stuhlmueller, "God in the Witness of Israel's Election," in *God in Contemporary Thought,* ed. S. A. Matczak (Louvain: Nauwelaerts, 1977), pp. 349–78.

28. C. Stuhlmueller, "Self-Determination as a Biblical Theme: Prophetic Vision on Particularism Versus Universalism," in *Christian Spirituality in the United States: Independence and Interdependence*, ed. F. A. Eigo (Villanova, Pa.: Villanova University Press, 1978), p. 107.

29. N. H. Snaith, "Isaiah 40–66," *Studies on the Second Part of the Book of Isaiah* (Leiden: E. J. Brill, 1967), p. 147. The exodus "is not merely one of the themes. . . . It is the prophet's dominant theme . . . [his] ONE theme, and all else is subservient to it."

30. E. J. Hamlin, *God and the World of Nations* (Association of Theological Schools in South East Asia, 1972), pp. 35–36, writes: "The word *erets* appears no less than 40 times in Isa. 40–55. This frequency itself indicates an intensity of interest. What is more remarkable is that in none of these instances does the word refer unequivocally to the land of Palestine."

31. The final section of this chapter summarizes a longer article by Stuhlmueller, "Deutero-Isaiah: Major Transitions in the Prophet's Theology and in Contemporary Scholarship," *Catholic Biblical Quarterly* 42 (January 1980): 1–29.

32. Isaiah 40 is considered a formal introduction, drawn from the preaching of Deutero-Isaiah by the prophet or the editor and placed here as an ensemble of the prophet's major themes.

33. Hollenberg, "Nationalism and 'The Nations.' "

34. Cf. D. A. Clines, *I, He, We, & They. A Literary Approach to Isaiah 53* (Sheffield, England: University of Sheffield Press, 1976), p. 43: "What is significant about Isa. 53 from this point of view is the *absence* of speech. No communication occurs. No verbal message is conveyed from one *persona* to another. . . . The absence of speech as a formal element of the poem is also made concrete in the explicit depiction of silence of the servant: 'he did not open his mouth' (*twice* in 53:7). . . . Throughout, silence is kept, speech is avoided. The kings are speechless before the servant (52:15). The servant is not addressed by God, withdraws from the society of men . . . and at the moment when some word of protest may have been expected to be uttered—the moment of the unjust judgment passed upon the servant—silence again rises to the surface of the poem: 'who complained or mused aloud on, spoke of . . . his fate?' "

35. The theme of bearing the burden of one's hopes and, through suffering, of bringing them to fulfillment, is developed by Stuhlmueller in the article, "The Painful Cost of Great Hopes; The Witness of Isaiah 40–55," in *Sin, Salvation and the Spirit,* ed. D. Durken (Collegeville, Minn.: Liturgical Press, 1979), pp. 146–62.

5

Israel's Prayer and Universal Mission

O come, let us worship and bow down,
  let us kneel before the Lord, our Maker!
For he is our God,
  and we are the people of his pasture [Ps.95:6–7].

My God, my God, why hast thou forsaken me? [Ps.22:1].

In the preceding chapter on election, we observed that Israel as God's chosen people was normally seen as a people separated from the other nations. We also noticed that intuitions of world salvation would sporadically leap to the surface. These flashes of universalism converged within the mystic experience of the Suffering Servant in Isaiah, chapters 40–55. We have an opportunity to explore further these two closely related religious phenomena of intuitions and mysticism now that we turn to the psalms.[1]

It may seem at first that a tension similar to that which stretched a taut line between election and universalism will appear here also. Intuitions and mysticism can turn a person inward upon the self rather than outward toward others. However, just as the friction between election and universalism turned out to be a healthy situation, productive of a new appreciation of world salvation, a similar good result may happen here.

This study of the psalms will benefit us in still other ways. We are given an opportunity to observe evolving tradition of prayer within Israel. "It has long been recognized," writes Brevard S. Childs, "that the present shape of the Psalter reflects a long history of development in both its oral and literary stages, . . . a complex history of literary redaction."[2] Like Israel's worship, psalms often had to be adapted anew. As an example, Psalm 51 originally represented a meditation on earlier prophetic texts and did not emphasize the need for ritual acts:

For thou hast no delight in sacrifice;
  were I to give a burnt offering, thou wouldst not be pleased [Ps. 51:16].

110

A later editor, as inspired as the original psalmist, nuanced this negative attitude. Looking forward to the rebuilding of the city walls and the temple structure, the psalmist-editor added two new verses. One of them reads:

> Then wilt thou delight in right sacrifice,
>   in burnt offerings and whole burnt offerings;
>   then bulls will be offered on thy altars [Ps. 51:19].

The identical Hebrew word, *ḥapeṣ* ("to take delight"), is used in each instance, first in the negative sense of disregarding sacrifice (v. 16), and in the next sentence in the positive way of encouraging sacrifice (v. 19). The Bible is not contradicting itself but, rather, is mirroring two different, historical moments or at least two ways of viewing temple liturgy. According to one way, the liturgy was being condemned for its formal, meaningless rubrics; in the other view, the importance of public, traditional prayer and worship was being acknowledged.

The preservation and adaptation of the psalms can instruct us in the development of doctrine in Israel and enable us to recognize how earlier texts absorbed later intuitions and grew with the religious evolution of Israel. We would be closer to the truth to speak of an inspired tradition in which the Bible was prayed and celebrated rather than simply of the inspired, written text of the Bible. We are reminded of our earlier study in this volume about theological development under the impact of secular events. This principle, now to be exemplified in the prayer and worship of Israel, is basic to contemporary mission theology.

We shall investigate the two principal types of psalms, the hymns of praise and the prayers of supplication, but we shall restrict ourselves to individual psalms within these categories so as to observe more carefully the interaction of the secular and the sacred, as well as the continuous evolution of this interchange, within a context of prayer and worship. Those factors will be isolated that seem pertinent to the issue of mission.

HYMNS OF PRAISE

This type of psalm extends across the entire history of Israel, from Psalm 29, which still seems more than half Canaanite, to Psalm 95 with its ambivalence between polytheism and prophetic threat, to Psalms 146 through 150, a full orchestration of praise at the end of the psalter where each psalm begins and ends with *Hallelu-Yah* ("Praise Yah[weh]"). Praise constituted the most persistent trait of biblical religion.

Praise is also the most essential or inherent reaction to life in the psalms as well as among people throughout the world. People of every race and locale celebrate birthdays and anniversaries; weddings with their promise of new life always resound with music, dancing, and laughter. In the Old Testament the hymns of praise drew abundantly and profoundly from human nature. At least indirectly in their spontaneity and exuberance the hymns sound a universal ring. This and other aspects of the hymns of praise will link up with the mission apostolate.

Spontaneous and Persistent Praise

"Praise" we define as "a wondrous acclamation of God's redemptive acts as these continue among his people." Praise is a wondrous, even ecstatic acclamation. Praise is not a reflective response after a scientific investigation of the universe, so overwhelmingly great and meticulously perfect; nor does praise result from studying the Bible with its narrative of divine compassion and wonder. Praise begins with God's action, not with the activity of the human mind or heart. God first surrounded Israel with glorious deeds, bringing his people out of Egypt, caring for them in the desert, entering into covenant with them on Sinai, leading them into "a land flowing with milk and honey" (Deut. 6:3).

As such, praise gives nothing to God that God did not already possess or had not already achieved. Praise honestly and enthusiastically recognizes life *as it is* in its fullness. Praise does not demean God or ourselves, as though God were seated on a celestial throne, waiting to be amused or placated by our songs. Praise enables us to be absorbed in a cycle of life, coming energetically from God and through our joy returning enthusiastically to its creator. Praise resonates a full life, teaming with mysterious hopes from our ancestors, leading into a future beyond imagination, lived to the utmost at the present moment. This cycle from heaven to earth and back again toward heaven reminds us of an important text in Second Isaiah, to which chapter 2 of this book gave close attention.

> For as the rain and the snow come down from heaven,
>   and return not thither but water the earth,
> making it bring forth and sprout,
>   giving seed to the sower and bread to the eater,
> so shall my word be that goes forth from my mouth;
>   it shall not return to me empty,
> but it shall accomplish that which I purpose,
>   and prosper in the thing for which I sent it [Isa. 55:10–11].

Praise is part of the cyclic energy of life, coming upon us like soothing rain and gentle snow, and reaching upward again toward the heavens.

Praise reveals a God of life. For this reason, as we shall discuss later in this chapter, sickness, suffering, and death defied Old Testament theology for an adequate explanation. Priests were rendered impure even if they accidentally touched a corpse. The high priest could not be in the presence of death and dying, "nor defile himself, even for his father and for his mother" (Lev. 21:11). Strangely enough, for most people today, sorrow draws them toward God, while joy distracts them and can even become an occasion of sin. It was just the opposite in the case of biblical people. This preoccupation with life led to its own excesses, like the fertility cults in the temple, yet theology is on the side of the Bible. We worship a living God who promises life.

Praise, we noted, celebrates God's "redemptive acts as these continue among his people." In the Bible life centered in the *contemporary* action. The past was remembered for the way its wisdom and hopes guided and inspired the present moment. As to life after death, Israel for the longest stretch of its history had no clear belief in personal immortality (Pss. 6:5; 88:4–7; 94:17; 143:3). Praise proclaimed what God was doing *now*. It involved the worshiping community totally with processing, singing, clapping, shouting, prostrating, dancing, playing musical instruments, calling out to one another. The hymns of praise make great use of the Hebrew participle, which is as timeless as the actions in the preceding sentence.

Praise, again, is to be recognized as "wondrous acclamation of God [celebrated] among his people." We are speaking of *communal* celebration in which many people join together, generally at one of the sanctuaries. The orchestration of singing and musical instruments, the movement of procession and dance, the interchange between choral groups—all required careful planning and artistic skill. There was need therefore of a trained "clergy," the Levites, who handed down their cultic wisdom and expertise from parent to child. Some of these Levites were specifically "put in charge of the service of song in the house of the Lord" (1 Chron. 6:31). A study of the hymns of praise will disclose an intricate interlacing of words and actions, a momentum of excitement through the repetition of key words in an ever more elaborate form. This skillful and harmonious structure encouraged the largest number of people to join in the celebration. Praise thereby revealed the depth, strength, and genuineness of this people's happiness before God.

To celebrate with dignity and grandeur, the Israelites were forced to turn to the Canaanites. The Israelites, crossing the river Jordan after years of wandering in the wilderness and after centuries of enslavement in Egypt, were liturgically impoverished. As they gradually took possession of ancient shrines in Canaan, they had to learn liturgical style from the artistically and culturally advanced Canaanites. The "military conquerors" were culturally conquered by the vanquished. Granted that the "conquest" was far more complicated and extended than this last sentence implies, we can still arrive at two important results concerning the biblical hymns of praise: *(a)* the earliest hymns manifest the strongest Canaanite influence; and *(b)* the Canaanite direction and coloration continued over a long period of time. In fact Israel had absorbed so much of Canaanite style, liturgically and politically, that it is difficult to disentangle Israel from Canaan in these two areas.

Among the hymns of praise, strong Canaanite or foreign influences are evident in such early songs about creation or nature as Psalms 19a and 29, or again in psalms celebrating the Davidic dynasty, such as Psalm 89:9–18, or in still others solemnizing the Jerusalem temple, such as Psalms 46–48. More detailed study of these psalms will follow, but at this time we register an unusual phenomenon about the hymns of praise. Most of these psalms, though first in time, do not emphasize and in fact hardly allude to the earliest formative factors in biblical religion: namely, the exodus out of Egypt, the sojourn in the wilderness, the covenant on Mount Sinai. The hymns of praise manifest important differences topically from other very early poetry in the Bible, like the song of Deborah in Judges 5 or that of Moses in Exodus 15. The Torah (Genesis through Deuteronomy) centers upon "salvation history," while the first hymns celebrate creation.

One possible explanation for this serious difference at the origins of biblical worship states that Israel quickly accepted Canaanite hymns or hymn writers; another possibility, which does not exclude but complements the latter, suggests that Israel's earliest hymns mirror popular forms of piety in distinction to the more official or more orthodox forms in the Torah. In this case the Bible embraces several kinds of "spirituality": not simply in terms of a northern or more Mosaic type and a southern type with a more Jerusalem influence—both strands belonging to the central, orthodox or official positions; but also in terms of popular piety, prophetic threat, and sapiential influence, which tended to be more peripheral, enriching, or challenging. The early hymns of praise gravitate toward the popular piety, with more visible mythological allusions and with an emphasis on God as creator rather than God as savior (see chap. 2, above, for this latter distinction). We suggest that a recognition of these various forms of religious manifestation as well as a proper attention to popular piety will offer valuable directives in all forms of cross-cultural mission.

Psalm 29

We turn first to Psalm 29 as an example of Israel's acceptance of Canaanite culture and hymnology. "This Psalm," concludes A. A. Anderson, "is one of the oldest in the whole psalter, and in recent years it has been customary to stress the similarities between this poem and the Ugaritic [or ancient northwest Semitic] literature."[3] It is generally held that "an ancient Canaanite hymn to Baal . . . was adapted to Israelite worship" or at least provided "the pattern and metaphors."[4] Psalm 29 reads:

<table>
<tr><td></td><td colspan="2" align="center">I</td></tr>
<tr><td>*Call to*</td><td>1</td><td>Ascribe to the Lord, O heavenly beings</td></tr>
<tr><td>*Praise*</td><td></td><td>ascribe to the Lord glory and strength.</td></tr>
<tr><td></td><td>2</td><td>Ascribe to the Lord the glory of his name;</td></tr>
<tr><td></td><td></td><td>worship the Lord in holy array.</td></tr>
<tr><td></td><td colspan="2" align="center">II</td></tr>
<tr><td>*Motivation*</td><td>3</td><td>The voice of the Lord is upon the waters;</td></tr>
<tr><td>*and*</td><td></td><td>the God of glory thunders,</td></tr>
<tr><td>*Theophany*</td><td></td><td>the Lord, upon many waters.</td></tr>
<tr><td></td><td>4</td><td>The voice of the Lord is powerful,</td></tr>
<tr><td></td><td></td><td>the voice of the Lord is full of majesty.</td></tr>
</table>

5 The voice of the Lord breaks the cedars,
   the Lord breaks the cedars of Lebanon.
6 He makes Lebanon to skip like a calf,
   and Sirion like a young wild ox.
7 The voice of the Lord flashes forth flames of fire.
8 The voice of the Lord shakes the wilderness,
   the Lord shakes the wilderness of Kadesh.
9 The voice of the Lord makes the oaks to whirl,
   and strips the forest bare;
   and in his temple all cry, "Glory!"

III

Conclusion 10 The Lord sits enthroned over the flood;
      The Lord sits enthroned as king for ever.
     11 May the Lord give strength to his people!
      May the Lord bless his people with peace!

The poet makes an exceptionally effective use of phrases as quick and sudden as lightning; he incorporates participles like breaking and flashing, which hit us with the massive, rolling sound of thunder. The whole world seems to be falling apart. Cedars are split down the center, mountains are trembling, desert wadis become roaring torrents. By maintaining the Canaanite mythology, now transferred to Yahweh, the universe has become a tumultuous temple where "all cry, 'Glory!' " (v. 9).

Another ingenious transfer of Canaanite imagery to Yahweh occurs in verse 8. Originally it read (with the key word in italics):

> The thunder of the Lord!
> Making the wilderness convulse [like a woman in childbirth];
> The lord makes the *sacred* wilderness convulse!

This line belongs to the description of the furious winter storms that an angry Mediterranean Sea let loose against the mainland. These tempests lashed against the Lebanese and Anti-Lebanese mountain ranges, then spent themselves in the eastern desert wilderness. Because the angry gods seemed to disappear with the storm in the desert, the desert was considered "sacred" or awesome, the abode of gods and devils.[5]

The Israelites maintained this fear of the desert. Yet in this psalm they stopped translating the word as "*sacred*" and read it as a proper noun, "Kadesh." Kadesh was the name of a lush oasis, south of the Promised Land on the edge of the Sinai.[6] This change from "sacred wilderness" to "the wilderness of Kadesh" shifted the direction of the storm, so that after its initial onslaught from the Mediterranean against the Lebanese coast, north of Israel, and its penetration of the eastern desert, it turned southward, circled the Holy Land and ended at Kadesh.[7] Violent storms thundered all around the Holy Land, yet this land remained at peace and the people secure in the Lord's temple at Jerusalem. Here they all assembled to shout "Glory" (v. 9). This acclamation echoed from the distant mountains and repeated the "Glory" ascribed to Yahweh by the heavenly beings in verse 1.

No matter how excellent the translation of this psalm, inevitably *tradutorri traditori* ("translators are traitors"), for the English version fails to communicate adequately its strength and beauty. We cannot delay over the brilliant literary form of the Hebrew text, except to draw one obvious yet important conclusion. The "primitive" theology of this early Canaanite poem is communicated in an exceptionally artistic way. The poet evidently possessed a rich heritage of tradition and culture and could claim the right to instruct the Israelites whose origins lay with Moses and Joshua. Israel, in fact, gladly accepted the superior culture of the Canaanites as a means to appreciate and express its own superior intuition of a personal, compassionate God.

The polytheistic reference in verse 1 is obvious. The phrase "heavenly beings" (in Hebrew *běnê 'ēlîm)* corresponds almost verbatim to the tutelary or subordinate deities who formed a heavenly court around the principal god, Baal. A number of other loan words or phrases from Canaanite religion occur in Psalm 29. By tolerating this veiled polytheism, Israelite religion kept the universe charged with divine wonder, and Israelites closely associated the victory of goodness over evil in their own personal lives with this battle of the gods. Yahweh was triumphant within all the forces of the universe, for the wonder of his own people and thereby for his own glory.

What is translated "the voice of the Lord" (in Hebrew, *qôl Yahweh*) refers to the thunder that roars from clouds and echoes from mountains. This "psalm of the seven thunders"[8] must have been accompanied with trumpet blasts, tambourines, and cymbals:[9]

> The thunder of the Lord!
>   Roaring across the water!
> The thunder of the Lord!
>   Mightily!
> The thunder of the Lord!
>   Majestically!
> The thunder of the Lord!
>   Breaking the cedars!
> The thunder of the Lord!
>   Flashing flames of fire!
> The thunder of the Lord!
>   Convulsing the wilderness!
> The thunder of the Lord!
>   Inducing hinds to calf!

Israel's peace descended from the strong, protecting presence of the Lord, which kept the storm at bay. It was a magnificent peace. It was also a perilous peace, for the storm could shift directions again and lash its fury against Israel. Yet, so long as Israel assembled before the Lord, they would be blessed:

> The Lord sits enthroned over the flood; . . .
> The Lord gives strength to his people!
> May the Lord bless his people with peace!

The strength that the lesser gods were ascribing to Yahweh in verse 1 is now a living part of the people's lives, the Lord's gift to them. *They* are lesser gods, they assemble in the Lord's court, they live excitedly in his presence.

When Israel accepted this Canaanite psalm with only light emendation, substituting Yahweh for the god Baal and reading Kadesh as a place name south of their country, Israel not only garnered a brilliant hymn into the temple repertoire, but Canaanites must have felt at home and understood the presence of Yahweh at the Israelite sanctuary. Yahweh possessed more gloriously and more powerfully the wonder and strength that Canaanites had found in their gods. Israel could live with faith and security amid the excitement and healthy fear of the universe. Israel could plunge into the hopes and risks of life without controlling the outcome, and yet trust happily in the Lord. Israel realized an integral wholeness between itself and the world of nature, all centered in Yahweh. Yet this harmony was achieved through a combination of Canaanite and Mosaic influence, the former being much stronger than the latter. Canaanites gave Israel the language to bring the whole cycle of winter storms and spring fertility into the worship of Yahweh.

Mosaic background identified the supreme God as Yahweh and prepared the way for further liturgical development. A late addition to the psalm, found only in the introductory title of the Greek Septuagint, assigned this hymn to the last day of the Feast of Tabernacles. This feast celebrated not only a long temple tradition but also rejoiced in the final harvesting of the year, that of olives and grapes. Quite naturally Tabernacles began to symbolize the abundant and rich messianic kingdom (Zech. 14:16–21), and with the singing of Psalm 29 Israel was reminded of the eschatological battle between overwhelming forces of goodness and evil before God's final reign would be ushered in. Once more, as in the earliest period of its singing, Israelites drew upon Canaanite language to appreciate the depth and force of their own religion.

This battle motif, however, is more than a stylistic flourish; it shows an insight into a theological theme that continues through the Scriptures, the battle that not only locks world forces of goodness and evil in mortal struggle but also implicates each individual person from the moment of conception and birth.[10] We can trace the development of this religious motif according to an earlier rubric in this book: *(a)* an initial secular act by which a religious-minded Moses freed the people from Egyptian slavery; *(b)* the first secular celebrations over the newly achieved freedom by a small number of people; and *(c)* the liturgical celebration, which emphasized what was mostly overlooked earlier by the majority of people: Yahweh's compassionate and all-powerful love as intuited by Moses. No group more than the Canaanites enabled Israel's liturgical form to evolve, and in this development an ever larger number of people relived the first redemptive act of God with Moses. With the passage of time an ever larger scope of redemptive acts and religious hopes were commemorated, even the announcement of the messianic reign of God. Through this long history of Psalm 29 we glimpse the importance of cross-cultural influence, local adaptation, and popular piety in liturgy and theology.

We have alluded off and on to Israel's popular piety. The term (then as now) is difficult to explain, just as the phenomenon is hard to isolate from liturgical piety. This style of popular religious fervor could be found in scattered sanctuaries where Mosaic discipline was not as sternly enforced, as for instance at Bethel;[11] or it could move to center stage in the more official places of worship at Shechem and even at Jerusalem. In all these cases popular piety would often degenerate and get out of hand, and then the prophetic threat would be leveled against it. In a few cases, as in the ceremony of the goat for Azazel at the Yom Kippur ceremony, popular piety even in this somewhat bizarre form was tolerated and legislated in the Torah (Leviticus 16). Popular piety, however, thrived best in informal settings like the home, the evening campfire, and other natural gatherings. It must be admitted that in Israel popular piety is much more difficult to distinguish than the more formal liturgical piety, simply because the secular and the sacred, the popular and the official, the home and the temple, the recreational and the religious were closely intertwined. These distinctions, in fact, are modern, not biblical. Yet traces of them are clear enough in poetry like Psalm 29, and the implications are important enough in cross-cultural mission that attention be drawn to them.

Psalm 95

Another hymn of praise, Psalm 95, adapted Canaanite mythology much more cautiously than Psalm 29. Unlike Psalm 29, it would not represent popular piety as explained in the preceding section but belonged to the ritual of the Jerusalem temple. Psalm 95 enables us to trace the integration of Canaanite motifs into the formal liturgy at Jerusalem, and it opens up new ways of re-reading ancient religious texts, whether these come from the Bible or from cross-cultural sources. Psalm 95 reads:

I–A

Call to	1	O come, let us sing to the Lord;
Praise		let us make a joyful noise to the rock of our salvation!
	2	Let us come into his presence with thanksgiving;
		let us make a joyful noise to him with songs of praise!
Motivation	3	For the Lord is a great God,
		and a great King above all gods.
	4	In his hand are the depths of the earth;
		and the heights of the mountains are his also.

5 The sea is his, for he made it;
   for his hands formed the dry land.

I–B

Second Call 6 O come, let us worship and bow down,
to Praise   let us kneel before the Lord, our Maker!
Motivation 7 For he is our God,
               and we are the people of his pasture,
               and the sheep of his hand.

II

Prophetic   O that today you would hearken to his voice!
Threat   8 Harden not your hearts, as at Meribah,
               as on the day at Massah in the wilderness,
             9 where your fathers tested me,
               and put me to the proof, though they had seen my work.
            10 For forty years I loathed that generation
               and said, "They are a people who err in heart,
               and they do not regard my ways."
            11 Therefore I swore in my anger
               that they should not enter my rest.

We will first reconstruct the liturgical setting of Psalm 95 and then indicate the various religious motifs, some Canaanite, others Mosaic, absorbed within its lines.

Only hypothetically can we name the feast when Psalm 95 was sung in ancient Israel, yet we can confidently identify the different actions of the religious assembly. The literary form of the psalm modulates according to several liturgical movements.[12] The psalm opens with a double hymn, the first section of which is to be sung while the people are processing along the Kidron Valley, advancing up its slope to the temple mount (vv. 1–5), and the second section is to be sung while they are kneeling and prostrating themselves within the main sanctuary courtyard (vv. 6–7c). Each of these hymns is composed of a summons to praise God sung by the entire congregation (vv. 1,2,6) and of the motivation for praise sung by a special choir (vv. 3–5, 7 a,b,c). The psalm may have been interrupted after v. 7c for a scriptural reading and sermon. Afterward the psalm was completed (vv. 7d–11) as a prophetic warning to obey God's word. Looking at Psalm 95 still more closely we find:

vv. 1–2: The entire assembly began to process toward the Jerusalem temple: "Let us come into his presence! Let us make a joyful noise to the rock of our salvation." The massive rock, or esplanade, where the temple and its courtyards were constructed and where God was powerfully present with his people, has become a title for God. Psalm 95 combines this Jerusalem practice with an ancient Mosaic tradition about "the rock that yielded water in the desert, according to Exod. xvii lff."[13] This Jerusalem style of addressing God as "rock" seems more

Canaanite than Mosaic, because the divine epithet is not found in Psalm 81, the "northern" version of this psalm. Verses 1–2 would be sung over and over as a continuous invitation. It is possible that the procession began at the spring Gihon, Jerusalem's closest source of water in the Kidron Valley. Gihon itself was a sacred place.[14] Water may have been carried ceremonially in procession from the spring to the temple.

vv. 3–5: A small group of cantors motivated the people for praising the Lord during the procession. The refrain of verses 1–2 could have been sung after each line of verses 3–5 or even continuously as "background music."

v. 6: The entire assembly began a new refrain now that they had climbed up from the Kidron Valley and had gathered in one of the inner courts to bow, kneel, and prostrate themselves in adoration before God.

v. 7 a,b,c: The cantors adapted their part to the people's profound respect and overpowering wonder before God. At this point one of the temple Levites recited a passage from Scripture and preached, much in the style of the great sermons in the book of Deuteronomy.

vv. 7d–11: The cantors concluded the service with a standard exhortation to take to heart and to put into practice the biblical reading and homily. These lines draw upon Mosaic traditions of desert wandering, complaints, and punishments.

Many important religious traditions have been blended together in this psalm. It seems that the entire history of Israel is relived in singing this psalm and in processing to the temple.

The context of the psalm is one of moving onward. The people, once on their way from Egypt to Canaan (vv. 7d–11), are now proceeding from the spring Gihon to the Jerusalem temple (vv. 1–5). Here they fall to the ground in adoration and symbolically take possession of the land (vv. 6–7 a,b,c). Despite this larger setting of walking and other body movements, the psalm sets forth the goal of nonaction, or of entering into the Lord's rest. This tension between seeking and resting is one of the many excellent stylistic devices in the psalm, and beneath the style a theological stress, or anxiety, is noticeable.

We shall look more closely at the various processions, real and symbolical, that are reflected here. This inquiry will enable us to review one of the major principles of biblical interpretation for re-reading the Scriptures in terms of mission today. In chapter 1 of this book we explained the process whereby insignificant secular events are transformed into "salvation history" by being celebrated liturgically. We shall follow the modulation from the secular to the sacred, and from the external to the interior.

a. Israel's "secular" march through the desert in search of freedom from Egyptian slavery and of a dignified, joyful existence in their own land. Psalm 95 refers to incidents at Meribah and Massah during the Sinai wilderness period.
b. Israel's "sacred" procession from the Gihon sanctuary to the Jerusalem temple, reliving the exodus and entering once again upon the promises of the Lord and receiving the land as a gift from Yahweh (cf. Deut. 6:10–15).
c. Israel's "interior" exodus from being a group of grumbling or moral wanderers to becoming an obedient "flock" who "regard my ways."

The New Testament continues the adaptation to still other journeys. The letter to the Hebrews, chapters 3 and 4, intensifies this larger motif of a "journey" that extends throughout this masterly literary piece by quoting liberally from Psalm 95 and freely adapting some of its key lines.

d. The Christian journey in faith, "hold[ing] our first confidence firm to the end" (Heb. 3:14).
e. The Christian's way follows the path of Jesus, "a great high priest who has [lived and died on earth and so has] passed through the heavens [to be seated on] the throne of grace" (Heb. 4:14,16).
f. The Christian enters into the rest of paradise where "God rested on the seventh day from all his works" (Heb. 4:5; Gen. 2:2).

Whereas the letter to the Hebrews moves the context more explicitly from a liturgical procession to an interior journey of faith, later Christian prayer once again emphasized the ritual setting. This psalm is still sung at the opening of the monastic office, now called the Prayer of Christians, with a refrain drawn from the feast of the day or from the season of the church year. After each stanza of Psalm 95, the congregation sings:

Advent:	"Christ is close at hand; come, let us worship him."
Christmas:	"Christ is born for us; come, let us adore him."
Epiphany:	"Christ has appeared to us; come, let us adore him."
Lent:	"Come, let us worship Christ the Lord, who for our sake endured temptation and suffering."
Easter:	"The Lord is risen, alleluia."
Feasts of Mary:	"Come, let us sing to the Lord as we celebrate the feast of the Blessed Virgin Mary."
Feasts of Bishops:	"Come, let us worship Christ, chief shepherd of the flock."

Another piece of Canaanite theology appears in the line: "The Lord is . . . a great King above all gods." Israelite religion took Canaanite mythology seriously, placing Yahweh supreme in the pantheon. At times Yahweh is portrayed struggling against those other deities (Ps. 89:5–10), and in this battle the Israelite people have a pledge of their ultimate victory over the world forces of evil. Yet this war would not be decided superstitiously or magically, as in many Canaanite shrines, but by a moral determination on the part of Israel: do not "err in heart [lest you] should not enter my rest" (Ps. 95:10–11).

Psalm 95 has had a long, continuous use in Israel, in the Christian Scriptures, and in the church because it was always open to new processions, whether these be physical or moral. This long history of adaptation began when the Mosaic exodus and the migrating ark of the covenant were dramatically adapted to Canaanite styles of worship. The ark would no longer move with the people; the people would come in pilgrimage to the ark. Israel would not cluster around a sacred object, the ark, but would gather in a sacred place, the temple. The very form of this sacred place became a title for Yahweh, the "Rock of Our Salvation."

The final result was not a "paganization" of Mosaic inspiration but an acculturation of it. This process extended the scope of biblical religion. "The divinity," write A. Maillot and A. Lelièvre, "which the Phoenicians [or Canaanites] adore without their knowing it is the Lord [Yahweh]."[15]

Psalm 46

We turn to a final group of hymns of praise, the Jerusalem, or Zion, Psalms. We shall limit our observations to Psalm 46 and to the way by which mythology and politics were absorbed within a religious setting. The parallel seems clear and urgent for the mission apostolate where indigenous religious practices and local politics play such an important part. Psalm 46 reads:

I

Motivation	1	God is our refuge and strength,
for Praise		a very present help in trouble.
	2	Therefore we will not fear though the earth should change
		though the mountains shake in the heart of the sea;
	3	though its waters roar and foam,
		though the mountains tremble with its tumult.
Congregational		[The Lord of hosts is with us;
Response		the God of Jacob is our refuge.][16]

II

Motivation	4	There is a river whose streams make glad the city of God,
for Praise		the holy habitation of the Most High.
	5	God is in the midst of her, she shall not be moved;
		God will help her right early.
	6	The nations rage, the kingdoms totter;
		he utters his voice, the earth melts.
Congregational	7	The Lord of hosts is with us;
Response		the God of Jacob is our refuge.

III

Motivation	8	Come, behold the works of the Lord,
for Praise		how he has wrought desolations in the earth.
	9	He makes wars cease to the end of the earth;
		he breaks the bow, and shatters the spear,
		he burns the chariots with fire!

> 10   "Be still, and know that I am God.
>   I am exalted among the nations,
>   I am exalted in the earth!"

Congregational   11   The Lord of hosts is with us;
Response   the God of Jacob is our refuge.

These brief comments are made particularly with world mission in mind. The sequence of the three strophes flows from *(a)* the unashamed *mythological* references in verses 1–3 about primeval chaos with the trembling of the mountains and the foaming of the angry sea, to *(b)* a combination of mythology and liturgy in verses 4–6 about the river that flows from the altar of sacrifice,[17] to *(c)* the confession of God's desires for universal peace and for Israel's exaltation among the nations. Mythology enabled the psalmist and the entire congregation to express and thereby to realize in communal faith the dynamic presence of Yahweh at the temple. "The holy habitation of the Most High" induced a vision of universal peace, so that earlier military ventures could be silenced in favor of an ever more confident trust in Yahweh. This faith is vital today in many troubled areas of the mission apostolate. Casting Yahweh in the image of a warrior, did not mean that God sanctioned or encouraged new wars on the part of his people, but on the contrary an all-powerful God allowed Israel to "be still and know that I am God."

Psalm 46 resonates several important phrases of the prophet Isaiah, and there is also a particular clustering of allusions to the vision of peace and universal salvation in Isa. 2:1–4. The epithet "God of Jacob" occurs nine times in the book of Psalms, but in Isaiah it is found only in chapter 2, verse 3. Another phrase, which is more Isaian, is "House of Jacob" (Isa. 2:5,6; 8:17; 9:8; 10:20; 14:1; 27:6,9; etc.). It derives from the ancient northern shrines of Bethel and Shiloh.[18] At Jerusalem, according to Louis Jacquet, it indicates an outreach to include both Israel and Judah.[19] Another title for God in Psalm 46, "The Lord of Hosts," was the cultic name for Yahweh, first at the ancient sanctuary at Shiloh (1 Sam. 1:3, 11; 4:4), then (because of the transfer of the ark to Jerusalem) also at the Jerusalem temple. This epithet, moreover, occurs forty-one times in Isaiah 1–39. Psalm 46 thus seems to join with Isaiah in glimpsing an important role of the nations in acclaiming the glory of Yahweh, Lord of Hosts, at Jerusalem; the momentum is from international war to the Lord's presiding over universal peace.

> He makes wars to cease to the end of the earth. . . .
> "Be still, . . .
>   I am exalted among the nations."

The phrases in verse 8 about "desolation" ought to be understood as a liturgical reference to God's wonders seen in an awesome vision across the earth.[20] "Be still" catches the attitude of faith typical of Isaiah (Isa. 7:4; 22:1–14; 30:15–17) when Israel politically could do nothing but wait confidently upon the Lord.

Psalm 46 indicates a blend of mythology, liturgy, and politics, and through the indirect influence of Isaiah whose prophecies frequently cluster around the Jerusalem temple and the Davidic dynasty, this psalm reaches toward a vision of universal peace. When liturgy applies to Yahweh the military language of politics and war and enhances this style by mythological references, religion is able to suffuse its appreciation of the compassionate and faithful God into the divine epithets and so bring an end magnificently to war and misery. This movement from war to peace was achieved in Psalm 46 through Israel's international outlook, the memory of David's wars and of the ancient military ventures associated with Shiloh and Bethel, and the language of Canaanite mythology. All these forces led to one of the finest visions of world peace and world mission in the Old Testament.

PRAYERS OF SUPPLICATION

The next type of psalm, the prayers of supplication, actually the most numerous in the psalter, shares with the hymns of praise an attitude of persistent and spontaneous faith. Because hymns offered praise to God over the wonders of life, they developed quickly and positively. They immediately drew upon poets, literary styles, and liturgical forms of Canaanite background. Prayers of supplication, on the contrary, reacted to God's absence and therefore required a much longer time to appear. When they began to be composed somewhat frequently, close to the time of exile, Israel's theology had evolved through various religious reforms under King Hezekiah (715–687/6 B.C.E.) and King Josiah (640–609 B.C.E.); most mythological elements had been washed out of the religious scene.

Sigmund Mowinckel[21] points out a series of important differences between the biblical prayer of supplication and that of the Babylonian psalms of lamentation: *(a)* biblical prayers involve the individual sufferer more fully, give less attention to the king or high priest, and so are "more 'democratic' "; *(b)* biblical prayers are less repetitious and so do not deal with "magical phrases" to placate the gods, nor are these psalms top-heavy with praise to flatter the gods; *(c)* biblical prayers are more "ethically oriented," more specific in regard to sin or innocence, so that Yahweh never appears arbitrary; *(d)* biblical prayers are addressed personally to Yahweh, not just "to any god whatsoever" and never do these prayers turn into lamentations over the dead god. These serious differences between Israelite and Babylonian prayers of supplication show that Israel did not easily adapt itself to the way in which their neighbors dealt with suffering and death. Cross-cultural assimilation did not sweep along blindly but proceeded with discernment and decision.

As mentioned in the introduction to the hymns of praise, suffering and death had no place in the Israelite temple and liturgy. The exceptions are rare: Josh. 7:6–9; Judg. 20:23–26; 21:2; 1 Sam. 7:6. Other texts like 1 Kings 8:33–36, favor C. Westermann's position that prayers of supplication ought to be classified under the category of praise.[22] For our part we consider the incidents in the books of Joshua and Judges of fasting, mourning, weeping, and confessing sin to be more along the style of popular piety as described earlier in this chapter. In the official liturgy, at least as described in the Torah, acts such as these were not ordained for the sanctuary or temple liturgy. In the book of Leviticus, moreover, the killing of a sacrificial animal was never done by the priest or Levite but by the lay person (Lev. 1:3-9). Technically a holocaust did not symbolize death but the total union of life with Yahweh. Israel's sin offerings were always for inadvertent offenses, and as Jacob Milgrom points out from texts like Num. 5:6-8, sorrow for one's misdeed, the admission of one's guilt, and "full restitution . . . adding a fifth to it" were necessary to reduce an intentional sin to one of inadvertence, thus rendering the misdeed eligible for sacrificial expiation.[23] Secular acts of humble, honest reparation must precede the religious, liturgical functions.

These qualities of Israel's liturgy as to sin, suffering, and death clearly manifest the need to respect life and to rectify any misdeeds before approaching the Lord in worship. No cult could be used to obtain a quick release from guilt. People had to come to just terms in the secular realm before approaching God in the sanctuary. This provision then requires religion to respect the normal, honest provisions of a culture or society before attempting to construct a liturgy of repentance. The fact that Israel expanded its official liturgy for mourning as the exile approached, under the impact particularly of the prophet Jeremiah, again alerts us to another way that religion remained keenly conscious of local and international politics. Only from excessive suffering and ever more conscious guilt in the secular sphere was Israel prompted to give more attention to its liturgy and theology of atonement.

This respect for the secular area of life in the formulation of liturgy is important enough for the church's missionary apostolate that we shall pursue the question of atonement further. Expressed as succinctly as possible, the biblical doctrine of atonement states that people are redeemed from their sins by union, not by substitution. No good person can suffer as a substitute for the guilty in order to win forgiveness for their sins. The prophet Ezekiel put this principle of personal responsibility in a way that may even seem to rule out atonement:

> If a man is righteous and does what is lawful and right . . . he shall surely live, says the Lord God.
> If he begets a son who is a robber, a shedder of blood . . . [that son] shall not live . . . he shall surely die; his blood shall be upon himself.
> But if this man begets a son who sees all the sins which his father has done, and fears, and does not do likewise . . . [but] walks in my statutes, he shall not die for his father's iniquity; he shall surely live. . . .
> The soul that sins shall die. The son shall not suffer for the iniquity of the father, nor the father suffer for the iniquity of the son; the righteousness of the righteous shall be upon himself, and the wickedness of the wicked shall be upon himself [Ezek. 18:5-20].

No one is saved by the virtue of another person. This truth will startle us, especially as applied to Jesus: Jesus did not suffer or die for us—that is, as a substitute for us. Otherwise, why do we still suffer and eventually die? Jesus' suffering and death indeed do have a redemptive power in our lives because by suffering and dying Jesus united himself with our suffering and dying, and in that most intimate bond, his obedience to the Father's will surges through us, and we rise to a newness of life in his resurrection (cf. Rom. 6:1–14). This example from New Testament theology has a clear parallel in the person of Moses. The sin or offense of Moses in Num. 20:6–13, was insignificant: to be angry with the people, to hesitate for a moment and then to strike the rock twice. Yet Moses was doomed to die with the people in the wilderness and "not bring this assembly into the land that I have given them." As we trace the evolution of Moses' punishment we find, especially in the book of Deuteronomy, an emphasis on Moses' union with the people in *their* sin and so Moses' instrumental role in their forgiveness:

Deut. 1:37. "The Lord was angry with me also," Moses is quoted as saying to the people, "*on your account*, and said [to me], 'You shall not go in there' " (cf. Deut. 3:16; 4:21–22).

Deut. 9:18. Moses explained: "Then I lay prostrate before the Lord as before, forty days and forty nights; I neither ate bread nor drank water *because of all the sins which you had committed. . . .* "

Deut. 34:4–5. And the Lord said to [Moses], "This is the land which I swore to Abraham, to Isaac, and to Jacob, 'I will give it to your descendants.' I have let you see it with your eyes, but you shall not go over there." So Moses *the servant of the Lord* died there in the land of Moab.

These Deuteronomic passages reflect a theology whose impact upon Second Isaiah would evolve into the Songs of the Suffering Servant. In these songs, as was explained in chapter 4, above, the Old Testament reached its clearest expression of universal salvation.

This same theology underlies the idea of atonement in the prayers of supplication. Only by intense union between the guilty and the healthy in all areas of life, but particularly in the secular realm, do people become conscious of guilt, suffer from it, and are compelled to seek reconciliation. Because Moses remained with the guilty Israelites in the wilderness—instead of racing ahead of them into the Promised Land—they were able to find their way to the river Jordan and in the person of their children cross over to a new life.

This theology of atonement, thoroughly rooted in secular life, can be explained through the example of the human body. If poison infiltrates the human body, a violent reaction causes vomiting, diarrhea, spasms, fever, boils, and other forms of rejection. All this happens provided the person is young and healthy, with a good liver, heart, lungs, and so forth. But in the case of the elderly or those with impaired or malfunctioning vital organs, there is very little if any violence or pain. The person slips into a coma and quietly passes away.

We shall apply these remarks about "atonement through union rather than substitution'' to the prayers of supplication: first to a collective lament (Psalm 44) and then to a lament from an individual person (Psalm 22). The text of Psalm 44 reads:

I

Hymnic   1 We have heard with our ears, O God,
Introduction   our fathers have told us,
          what deeds thou didst perform in their days,
             in the days of old;
   2 thou with thy own hand didst drive out the nations,
          but them thou didst plant;
      thou didst afflict the peoples,
          but them thou didst set free;
   3 for not by their own sword did they win the land,
          nor did their own arm give them victory;
      but thy right hand, and thy arm,
          and the light of thy countenance;
          for thou didst delight in them.
   4 Thou art my King and my God,
          who ordainest victories for Jacob.
   5 Through thee we push down our foes;
          through thy name we tread down our assailants.
   6 For not in my bow do I trust,
          nor can my sword save me.
   7 But thou hast saved us from our foes,
          and hast put to confusion those who hate us.
   8 In God we have boasted continually,
          and we will give thanks to thy name forever.

II

Community   9 Yet thou has cast us off and abased us,
Lament   and hast not gone out with our armies.
  10 Thou hast made us turn back from the foe;
          and our enemies have gotten spoil.
  11 Thou hast made us like sheep for slaughter,
          and hast scattered us among the nations.
  12 Thou hast sold thy people for a trifle,
          demanding no high price for them.
  13 Thou hast made us the taunt of our neighbors,
          the derision and scorn of those about us.
  14 Thou hast made us a byword among the nations,
          a laughingstock among the peoples.
  15 All day long my disgrace is before me,
          and shame has covered my face,
  16 at the words of the taunters and revilers,
          at the sight of the enemy and the avenger.

III

Reflection upon   17 All this has come upon us,
Suffering   though we have not forgotten thee,
                         or been false to thy covenant.
                   18 Our heart has not turned back,
                         nor have our steps departed from thy way,
                   19 that thou shouldst have broken us in the place of jackals,
                         and covered us with deep darkness.
                   20 If we had forgotten the name of our God,
                         or spread forth our hands to a strange god,
                   21 would not God discover this?
                         For he knows the secrets of the heart.
                   22 Nay, for thy sake we are slain all the day long,
                         and accounted as sheep for the slaughter.

IV

Prayer for   23 Rouse thyself! Why sleepest thou, O Lord?
Help   Awake! Do not cast us off for ever!
                   24 Why dost thou hide thy face?
                         Why dost thou forget our affliction and oppression?
                   25 For our soul is bowed down to the dust;
                         our body cleaves to the ground.
                   26 Rise up, come to our help!
                         Deliver us for the sake of thy steadfast love!

In this psalm we first call attention to several stylistic features that sustain a strong bond of unity and sharing between each individual and the entire congregation. The theology of "atonement by union" can be noticed in the grammatical interchange, for instance, of the "singular" with the dominant "plural." While the group usually speaks in the plural: "*We* have heard with *our* ears . . .," a cantor will step forward in verses 4, 6, and 15 to represent each of the worshipers individually:

> Thou art *my* King and *my* God. . . .
> For not in *my* bow do *I* trust. . . .
> All the day long *my* disgrace is before *me*. . . .

Within the third stanza the psalmist speaks *to God* directly in verses 17–19, *about God* to the congregation at prayer in verses 20–21, and again *to God* in verse 22. As though God never heard, the writer then shouts to God at the beginning of the fourth and last stanza (v.23): "Rouse thyself! Why sleepest thou, O Lord?"

Another type of interaction happens in verse 2, this time presupposing a body motion or at least a directional signal from the hand or arm: Pointing away from the congregation, a group of singers praises God by exclaiming: "Thou with thy own hand didst drive out the nations." Pointing toward the congregation, the singers continue: "but them thou didst plant." Pointing away: "thou didst afflict the peoples." Pointing inward: "but them thou didst set free." In other words, the third person plural—they or them—is applied to both Israelites and non-Israelites. Bodily motions, not words, must differentiate. The psalms presume intense involvement.

Psychological and physical investment in the chanting of this psalm was demanding. Everyone was to share their pain and to wrestle with the tantalizing theological issues. The theology of election is taken seriously. The hymnic introduction (vv. 1–8) could stand by itself as a traditional confession of faith:

> We have heard with our ears, O God,
>> our fathers have told us,
> what deeds thou didst perform . . . [v. 1].

This faith included especially the gift of the Promised Land and the special status of God's chosen people:

> for not by their own sword did they win the land . . .
> but [by] thy right hand, and thy arm,
>> and the light of thy countenance;
>> for thou didst delight in them [v. 3].

Israel's understanding of this election faith could not tolerate a serious military defeat. This national elegy may be one of the many traumatic reactions to the destruction of Jerusalem in 587 B.C.E.[24] The psalmist refuses the easy explanation that everybody sinned and therefore everyone deserved the punishment:

> All this has come upon us,
>> though we have not forgotten thee,
>> or been false to thy covenant [v. 27].

Theologically "election" had arrived at an impasse. Even if the Israelites had sinned, what difference would it make? They had not acquired the land in the first place by their virtue or "by their own sword" (v. 3), but by God's free gift of love. At the end the psalmist returns to the heart of the covenant: "thy steadfast love" (v. 16). The foreign nations thus forced Israel to the ultimate basis of their faith, the Lord's personal love. This free gift, we add for the sake of the larger topic of this book, can be freely given to anyone, even to Gentiles. The psalm, however, never followed through to that conclusion. In fact, it was praying for an opposite resolution: the renewal of Israel's special election and the return of the people to a safe promised land away from the Gentiles. Yet it is important that such a universal conclusion could have been reached. As we saw in chapter 4, that step was taken during the Babylonian exile by Second Isaiah.

In Psalm 44 people are plagued with the silence of God, and shout, "Rouse thyself!" (v. 23). If God gave no answer, could they possibly trust his promises and their elect status? From the background of the prophets, particularly Jeremiah and Second Isaiah, we find a partial answer. Although all good desires are from God, not all of them are given to be fulfilled. Hope at times serves another, strange purpose—to lead people beyond themselves to a mysterious fulfillment that seems at first to contradict the hope. How can the sharing of Israel's election with the nations ever satisfy the true meaning of election? Wasn't Israel chosen out of the nations because it was dearer to God than all other peoples? What is special about election if *all* are called?

Psalm 44 enabled people to wait upon the Lord, to allow hopes and even faith to receive a new form, and to share their best with everyone so that no one was better than another! The psalm ends with a confession, not like the opening creed that the Lord did "drive out the nations," but similar to the basis of the covenant, the Lord's "steadfast love" (cf. Exod. 34:6). This love that flows from God's choice of Israel is a gift that God freely bestowed. The bonds of union between the virtuous and the guilty, which produced Psalm 44, arrived at a concept of God's gratuitous "steadfast love" that can unite Israel with all nations. Such at-one-ment is God's accomplishment but achieved through the intimate bonds among people, as evidenced in Psalm 44.

A different type of response under sorrow and tension is seen in Psalm 22, a lament this time from an individual sufferer. The clanging sound of the military in Psalm 44 is silenced; the stern and almost self-righteous questioning of God is also absent. An extraordinary peace pervades the lines, despite the shameful humiliation of the psalmist. Is that the reason the ultimate step could be taken and salvation be extended to "all the families of the nations"? Psalm 22 reads:

I

Call For Help

1 My God, my God, why hast thou forsaken me?
    Why art thou so far from helping me,
    from the words of my groaning?

2 O my God, I cry by day, but thou dost not answer;
    and by night, but find no rest.

Motive of Faith

3 Yet thou art holy,
    enthroned on the praises of Israel.

4 In thee our fathers trusted,
    they trusted, and thou didst deliver them.

5 To thee they cried, and were saved;
    in thee they trusted, and were not disappointed.

Lament

6 But I am a worm, and no man;
    scorned by men, and despised by the people.

7 All who see me mock at me,
    they make mouths at me, they wag their heads;

8 "He committed his cause to the Lord; let him deliver him,
    let him rescue him, for he delights in him!"

Prayer of *Confidence*	9	Yet thou art he who took me from the womb; thou didst keep me safe upon my mother's breasts.
	10	Upon thee was I cast from my birth, and since my mother bore me thou hast been my God.

Prayer for
Help
	11	Be not far from me,
		    for trouble is near
		    and there is none to help.

Lament	12	Many bulls encompass me, strong bulls of Bashan surround me;
	13	they open wide their mouths at me, like a ravening and roaring lion.

	14	I am poured out like water
		    and all my bones are out of joint;
		my heart is like wax,
		    it is melted within my breast;

	15	my strength is dried up like a potsherd,
		    and my tongue cleaves to my jaws;
		    thou dost lay me in the dust of death.

	16	Yea, dogs are round about me;
		    a company of evildoers encircle me;
		    they have pierced my hands and feet—

	17	I can count all my bones— they stare and gloat over me;
	18	they divide my garments among them, and for my raiment they cast lots.
Prayer for *Help*	19	But thou, O Lord, be not far off! O thou my help, hasten to my aid!
	20	Deliver my soul from the sword, my life from the power of the dog!
	21	Save me from the mouth of the lion, from the horns of the wild oxen! Thou hast heard me!

II

Song of *Thanksgiving*	22	I will tell of thy name to my brethren; in the midst of the congregation I will praise thee;

	23	You who fear the Lord, praise him!
		    all you sons of Jacob, glorify him,
		    and stand in awe of him, all you sons of Israel!

	24	For he has not despised or abhorred
		    the affliction of the afflicted;
		and he has not hid his face from him,
		    but has heard, when he cried to him.

	25	From thee comes my praise in the great congregation; my vows I will pay before those who fear him.

26 The afflicted shall eat and be satisfied;
        those who seek him shall praise the Lord!
        May your hearts live for ever!

III

Second Song 27 All the ends of the earth shall remember
of   and turn to the Lord;
Thanksgiving   and all the families of the nations
                        shall worship before him.
28 For dominion belongs to the Lord,
        and he rules over the nations.
29 Yea, to him shall all the proud of the earth bow down;
        before him shall bow all who go down to the dust,
        and he who cannot keep himself alive.
30 Posterity shall serve him;
        men shall tell of the Lord to the coming generation,
31 and proclaim his deliverance to a people yet unborn,
        that he has wrought it.

Psalm 22 was forged in the suffering heart of one of God's most faithful servants. Despite the intense pain of spiritual abandonment and physical persecution, despite the swift transitions from lament, to confidence, to prayer, to
lament, again to prayer, and finally to thanksgiving, nonetheless tranquillity pervades this poem. The psalmist is never bitter, never revengeful, never without
faith. A contemplative spirit keeps the psalmist in the presence of a God who is
seemingly at a distance, yet still *"my* God!" The author, perhaps unjustly imprisoned and physically debilitated from the confinement, has been meditating long
upon the Bible, especially upon the confessions of Jeremiah,[25] the Songs of the
Suffering Servant in Second Isaiah, penitential prayers like the Miserere (Psalm
51), and the memoirs of Nehemiah. During the long imprisonment the psalmist
thus preserved his faith and his sanity, his strength and his human dignity. If the
psalmist put questions to God, he is not necessarily expecting an explanation for
his suffering, only an opportunity to pour out the anxieties of the soul before
God. This psalm combines extreme earthiness ("I am a worm, nothing human"),
complete openness ("Why hast thou forsaken me?"), and desperate need (the
thrice repeated, "Be not far from me" in vv. 1,11,19).
    The turning point of the psalm is found in the final word of verse 21. In the
Hebrew it reads *'ănîthānî*—"You have heard [or, answered] me." Many transla-
tions, including the Revised Standard Version, follow the Greek version, which
either corrected the original or depended upon a different Hebrew word,
'ănniyyāthî—"my afflicted soul," very similar in sound but quite different in
sense from the original Hebrew reading. The value of the Hebrew text is twofold.
First, it links up with the same Hebrew root in verse 2 where the psalmist complained to God, "You do not hear [or, answer] me." In this way the Hebrew root
'ānāh ("to hear" or "to answer") encloses the first major section with a problem

and its solution. Second, faith remains the pivotal attitude, the interior conviction that God has heard the psalmist's words. We have a simple yet powerful phrase in the English language. To a closed-minded, prejudiced, or ignorant person we say with exasperation: "You do not hear me," meaning that you *refuse* to listen to me. The whole situation is turned around if this same person is later told, "You really hear me!" Now there is mutual faith, common interest, compassionate understanding. The psalmist is satisfied. God may not have released him from prison, but God understands and sympathizes. With this turn of events, the psalmist can wait and in the meanwhile prepare to thank God in the midst of the congregation.

These qualities enabled the psalmist to reach out to all the lowly, forsaken people of this world. The first song of thanksgiving (vv. 22–26), it is true, seems to remain within the confines of the Israelite congregation. It is, however, an assembly of the *'aniwim*, the poor, the afflicted, and the outcasts (vv. 24, 26). It would be only a matter of time, and the psalmist as a person of faith was willing to wait, until the *'aniwim* expanded their family circle.

A later redactor added the second song of thanksgiving (vv. 27–31) and here included Gentiles, the deceased, and the unborn among the *'aniwim*. This invitation to foreigners and the dead violated temple rules; each was considered unclean and prohibited entry into the sacred precincts. The psalmist quietly but firmly broke through these taboos by an instinctual understanding of the *'aniwim*. Because the *'aniwim* were the true worshipers of Yahweh, Gentiles and the dead qualified best of all for this assembly of "outcasts."

In order to appreciate this outreach to all God's *'aniwim*, it is helpful to review the major stages in the compositon and interpretation of this psalm. Here we rely principally upon the publications of Albert Gelin.[26]

First Stage: Sometime after the exile a sick, unjustly persecuted prisoner composed Psalm 22, verses 1–26.

Second Stage: By its sheer beauty, it forced its way into sanctuary worship to express or to bolster the faith of many afflicted or poor people. A "community" of *'aniwim* informally takes shape.

Third Stage: Psalm 22 absorbs new theological developments in Israel, that of personal survival after death and even that of explicit salvation for the Gentiles. Because both ideas, but particularly the second about the Gentiles, were never officially accepted within the central theology of the Jerusalem priests, Psalm 22 must have circulated among "outcasts" or been recited in times of popular devotion.

This evolution of Psalm 22 extended into the New Testament where it occupies an important theological place in the Passion narrative. From this application to Jesus, the crucified outcast, the psalm not only acquired a new depth of meaning but eventully found its way into church liturgy and meditative prayer. This cycle from Jesus the imprisoned, innocent sufferer on the cross to liturgical assembly corresponds well with the first stages of the psalm in the Old Testament.

This psalm also reflects the secular origins of Israel as slaves in a foreign land or as indentured servants of petty kings in Canaan. It expresses the anguish of the prophet Jeremiah who was repudiated by religious authorities (Jer. 26:11,16), beaten and thrown in prison (Jer. 37:15) and sustained only by the intense prayer of his confessions (i.e., Jer. 12:1–5; 15:10–21). In the confessions Jeremiah became an outcast from Israel's standard theology that the guilty suffer and the innocent are blessed. In Israel's and Jeremiah's history faith in God's promises clashed with secular struggles. Yet there remained an underlying confidence in the Lord's listening ear and compassionate heart. These factors combine to produce Psalm 22 and enable it to impart a pertinent message for ministering to foreigners and to the outcasts.

CONCLUSION

As we glance back over Part I, we find that Israel's friendliest, most cooperative, and "ecumenical" relations with foreign nations emerged in the pioneering days of the patriarchs (1850–1700 B.C.E.), in the creative period of Moses and Joshua (1240–1150 B.C.E.), in the empire of David and Solomon (1000–922 B.C.E.), in the moral challenge of the prophets, especially by Second Isaiah during the exile (550–537 B.C.E.), and in the prayer of Israel, particularly the hymns of praise.

During the patriarchal period there was no option but friendly cooperation. "Virtue" was an absolute necessity for survival. The patriarch Abraham, as he had to admit in requesting the right to purchase a burial lot for his wife, Sarah, was "a stranger and a sojourner" among the Canaanites. Without a formal religion of their own, the patriarchs worshiped their God at Canaanite shrines and under Canaanite titles or names.

True, the main tenets of the Mosaic religion separated "Israel" from the nations. Moses began the organization of priesthood, liturgy, governmental structures, and law code; he centered the new religion under the symbols of "exodus" out of Egypt in search of land and "covenant" with Yahweh, who elected Israelites his chosen people. Nonetheless, the "Israel" whom God called was not an ethnic group with a single, dignified historical background, but a mixture of Egyptian slaves, impoverished servants of petty Canaanite kings, migrant aliens from the East, and in the all-inclusive phrase of Num. 11:4, "the rabble." While theology or religion tended to be separatist and anti-Gentile, the redemptive acts of God toward the "mixture" and the "rabble" that became Israel were expansionist and universal. The one absolute quality was neither pedigree nor dogma but a humble faith in God's steadfast love.

Religion had to develop lest the memory of Yahweh's steadfast love and gracious acts fade away and be lost. Without liturgy and priesthood, religious symbols would never have been created as a way for Israel to adapt and relive the exodus out of Egypt and the Sinaitic covenant in later periods of its history. Without religion Israel would never have developed a steady tradition of prayer and worship toward its God and savior. The formal tenets of religion clearly separated Israel from all other nations, but religion itself degenerated into external ritual and false security.

Before this moral collapse of religion took place, David established a world empire, the most prestigious at that time when Egypt, Syria, and Mesopotamia were in decline. The glory of David's reign, made visible by the grandiose building program of his son and successor, Solomon, seemed to fulfill all previous hopes. Yet it was principally an external kingdom with little place for "humble faith in a loving God."

The false ritualism of degenerate religion, the proud security of empire building as well as the free and cosy acceptance of Canaanite excesses led to the great prophetic movement. God must sweep away the entire visible structure of religion, city, and dynasty so that Israel once again might become "a people humble and lowly" (Zeph. 3:12), "the remnant . . . [that] will lean upon the Lord, . . . a remnant [that] will return" (Isa. 10:20-21). Out of the prophetic attention to the poor and the lowly came "the light to the nations" (Isa. 49:6), yet at the cost of immense personal suffering to Second Isaiah.

The prayer of Israel reached outward to the nations principally in the hymns of praise. The hymns can be traced to the wondrous excitement of acquiring the land and forming alliances with other dispossessed people in Canaan. Strong mythological influences flowed into hymns like Psalm 29, thereby projecting the victorious battle over sin and injustice across a cosmic panorama and enabling new Canaanite converts to be at home in the Mosaic religion. They were even contributing important symbols, which communicated new depths of meaning in the origins of Israel's religion.

Prayers of supplication continued the intuitive mystic thrust of the hymns, but now with a focus upon the mystery of pain and defeat. These psalms spring principally from prophetic influence, especially that of Jeremiah and Second Isaiah. They manifest earthiness and bluntness. They question orthodox theology, not by their mythology or polytheism as in the case of the hymns, but by their raw questions: Is God sleeping? Why doesn't God recognize the justice of a cause? These psalms reach their climax in Psalm 22 when the innocent, persecuted sufferer calls an assembly of the afflicted, to which the later editor could easily invite "the families of the nations" and the most afflicted of all, the deceased.

Many other qualities of Israel's prayer that reach toward universal salvation could be mentioned in this summary. Hymns of praise draw us spontaneously and excitedly to the outer edge of theology; those hymns with mythological allusions generally belonged to popular piety or at least resided outside the central Mosaic liturgy.

Hymns abound with body action: singing, clapping, dancing, processing, playing musical instruments, bowing, prostrating, answering one another in melodic dialogue, signaling or pointing out one group or another. Hymns quickly adopted the Canaanite religious structure of a temple and radically affected the older Mosaic symbols, like the ark of the covenant, which no longer would lead the people forward but would be enshrined as a place of popular pilgrimage.

Prayers of supplication, for their part, relied upon a theology of atonement, whereby guilt was removed and innocence reborn, not by one person or group substituting for another, but by a common bond of faith in God who is "merciful and gracious, . . . abounding in steadfast love and faithfulness" (Exod. 34:6). "Atonement by union" meant that reconciliation and restitution must be undertaken in the secular areas of life before any ritual acts of forgiveness could take place. What happens in the secular sphere must respect the local customs and norms of justice. The mission country and the home, or mission-sending, church each possesses its unique virtues and its special weaknesses. Each, so united to the other through faith in Jesus, can act as an atoning agent to the other. It is the missionary's task to enable the new church to embrace the ancient Christian faith with a humble sense of need and with a dignified posture of gifts and insights.

Some of the prayers of supplication, like Psalm 44, manifest the inability of a religion based on divine promise and special election to cope with its own disasters and defeats. As a result, ancient theological formulas and strict legal prescriptions must submit to radical reformation if they are to survive. This reappraisal is done in the context of tradition and creed, as is the case with the introductory stanza of Psalm 44. The psalm arrived at conclusions in continuity with the past that were never anticipated ahead of time. In Psalm 44 military defeat brought Israel to a new awareness that life and election rested on God's steadfast love, a basis for all people to become God's chosen ones.

One of the strongest outreaches to universal mission appears in the mystic silent prayer of Psalm 22. When the human answer found only abandonment and helplessness and survived only by serenely contemplating the prophetic tradition, out of the mystic agony, which no accumulation of images could adequately communicate and which left the prisoner stripped naked in body and soul, came the one answer that elicited a hymn of thanksgiving: "You have heard me, O Lord."

When we realize that God hears the groans of distant people, as once he was attentive to the tears and stress of the psalmist and of slaves in faraway Egypt, then the strongest faith and the most creative wisdom will produce a religion faithful to its origin and responsive to its loving God.

> He has showed you, O man [and woman], what is good;
>   and what does the Lord require of you
> but to do justice, and to love kindness,
>   and to walk humbly with your God? [Mic. 6:8].

Meditating upon a prophetic injunction like this, the psalmist announced a universal message:

> The afflicted shall eat and be satisfied;
>   those who seek him shall praise the Lord!
> May your hearts live for ever [Ps. 22:26].

NOTES

1. A longer exposition of this approach to the psalms is to be found in Stuhlmueller, *Thirsting for the Lord* (Staten Island, N.Y.: Alba House, 1977; 2nd ed., Garden City, New York: Doubleday Image Books 1979), chaps. 11–12.

2. B. S. Childs, *Introduction to the Old Testament as Scripture* (Philadelphia: Fortress Press, 1979), p. 511.

3. A. A. Anderson, *The Book of Psalms* (Grand Rapids, Mich.: Wm. B. Eerdmans, 1972), 1:233.

4. Ibid.

5. Cf. Lev. 16:21–22 (goat for Azazel driven into the desert); Tob. 8:3 (devil, expelled from Sarah, "fled into [the desert of] Upper Egypt"); Mt. 4:1 (Jesus is tempted by Satan in the desert).

6. Kadesh-Barnea, location of three springs with a plentiful supply of water. Here Israel is said to have remained for many days; in fact, the Israelites arrived here in Num. 13:26 and are still here in Deut. 1:2.

7. Cf. H. Cazelles, "Une Relecture du Psaume XXIX?" *À La Rencontre de Dieu* (Paris: Xavier Mappus 1961), pp. 119–28, who shows how the psalm historicizes the holy wilderness or desert of Ugaritic literature and associates it with the exodus.

8. This is the title given to Psalm 29 by F. Delitzsh, *Biblical Commentary on the Psalms* (London: Hodder and Stoughton, 1887), p. 445.

9. Cf. O. Keel, *The Symbolism of the Biblical World: Ancient Near Eastern Iconography and the Book of Psalms* (New York: Seabury Press, 1978), pp. 339–41.

10. This sense of world struggle between good and evil is one of the ways of presenting what came to be called "original sin" in Christian theology. Cf. B. Malina, "Some Observations on the Origin of Sin in Judaism and St. Paul," *Catholic Biblical Quarterly* 31 (1969): 18–34.

11. Bethel moved in and out of the circle of Israelite worship. Here Jacob had his vision of the ladder between heaven and earth (Gen. 35:1–15), and in the early period of the judges the ark was located at Bethel (Judg. 20:18–28). This city, along with Gilgal and Mizpah, features in the activity of Samuel (1 Sam. 7:16). Yet when Jeroboam I separated the northern tribes from Jerusalem, declared Bethel and Dan to be the main sanctuaries of the north, and established a non-Levitical priesthood at these places, the Levitical priests were repudiated and, as a result, found themselves on the periphery of religious worship, certainly in the north and most probably in the eyes of Jerusalem's religious authorities. Later prophets like Amos and Hosea condemned Bethel as a house of shame, yet the sanctuary remained a popular place for the people at large. From this brief account of Bethel, the notion of "official" and "private" piety remains vague and ambiguous; so much depends on one's estimate of legitimate and illegitimate worship. Our idea of "popular" would contain elements of excessive, uncontrolled, and even superstitious activity, such as at Dan and Bethel after Jeroboam I; the term would also apply to religious communities at Bethel that gravitated around such charismatic figures as Samuel and Elijah/Elisha. The former moved too freely away from Mosaic tradition, the latter were thoroughly within the Mosaic tradition yet free of the centralized authority at Jerusalem.

12. Cf. G. G. Davies, "Psalm 95," *Zeitschrift für Alttestamentliche Wissenschaft* 85 (1973):183–95, describes the cultic activity from various indications within the

psalm. He pauses over the origin of the divine title, "Rock," as derived from "that great rock, formerly beneath either the Holy of Holies or the altar of burnt offering" (pp. 189–90).

13. M. Dahood, *Psalms II* (Garden City, N. Y.: Doubleday, 1968), p.353.

14. Here Solomon was anointed king (1 Kings 1:45).

15. A. Maillot and A. Lelièvre, *Les Psaumes* (Geneva: Éditions Labor et Fides, 1966), 2:270.

16. This refrain is missing at the end of the first strophe of the Hebrew text but is generally added by commentators (cf. New American Bible).

17. The psalm combines the river of God's gentle presence in Isa. 8:6–7, the rivers of paradise in Gen. 2:10–14, and the life-giving river as represented in such later passages as Ezekiel 47; Joel 3:18; Zech. 14:8.

18. Cf. H.-J. Kraus, *Psalmen*, 5th ed. (Neukirchen-Vluyn: Neukirchener Verlag, 1978), 1:498, who quotes from A. Alt, "Der Gott der Väter," *Kleine Schriften* (Munich: C.H. Beck'sche Verlag, 1959), 1:1-78.

19. L. Jacquet, *Les Psaumes et le coeur de l'homme* (Gembloux: Duculot, 1977), 2:73.

20. In the Hebrew v. 9 includes the word *ḥăzû* ("behold"), a technical word for vision, just as the noun *ḥōzeh* means "seer." Hebrew *šmm* ("desolation") denotes a deserted place, but it can also connote awe or fear over God's actions, and in Psalm 46 it parallels such a word, *mip'ălôth*.

21. S. Mowinckel, *Psalms in Israel's Worship* (Nashville: Abingdon, 1967), 2:182–85. Cf. C. Westermann, *The Praise of God in the Psalms* (Richmond, Va.: John Knox Press, 1965), part 2, "The Structure of the Babylonian Psalms."

22. Westermann, *Praise of God*, part 3.

23. J. Milgrom, *Cult and Conscience* (Leiden: E. J. Brill, 1976), p. 117. Cf. C. Stuhlmueller, *Thirsting for the Lord* (Garden City, N.Y.: Doubleday, Image Books, 1979), pp. 188–89; Stuhlmueller, "Proclaiming the Death of the Lord," *Proceedings of the Catholic Theological Society of America* 18 (Yonkers, N. Y. : St. Joseph Seminary, 1964): 47–76; R. J. Daly, *The Origins of the Christian Doctrine of Sacrifice* (Philadelphia: Fortress Press, 1978), pp. 25–35 ("Sin, Offering and Atonement"); E. Lipinski, *La Liturgie Penitentielle dans la Bible* (Paris: Les Éditions du Cerf, 1969).

24. Jacquet, *Les Psaumes*, 2:25–26.

25. Cf. P. E. Bonnard, *Le Psautier selon Jérémie* (Paris: Les Éditions de Cerf, 1960).

26. A. Gelin, "Les quatre lectures du Ps 22," *La Bible et Vie Chrétienne* 1 (1953): 31–39; also his book, *The Poor of Yahweh* (Collegeville, Minn.: Liturgical Press, 1964).

PART II

THE FOUNDATIONS FOR MISSION IN THE NEW TESTAMENT

Donald Senior, C.P.

6

Jesus and the Church's Mission

My mission is to the lost sheep of the house of Israel [Mt. 15:24]

A review of the Old Testament has demonstrated that the issue of mission, in its broadest sense, is not absent. Israel was born among the nations; it freely borrowed and adapted its language, cult and culture from the surrounding nations. Among the many traditions woven into the Old Testament there was concern for Israel's role as witness to surrounding peoples of God's living presence. And even in the ethnocentric concentration that dominated postexilic Judaism there were attempts to check too exclusive a claim on God's favor.

In the period contemporary with Jesus, Judaism enjoyed a rich and sometimes conflicting diversity. Sectarian groups such as the Essenes took a decisively exclusive stance against those Jews considered lawless and against Gentiles. Other Jewish groups who were more at home with Greek culture, such as diaspora Jews living in the cities of the empire outside of Palestine or even more cosmopolitan Palestinian Jews such as the Sadducees and Pharisees, took a more favorable attitude to the Gentiles. The Alexandrian Jew Philo attempted to explain Judaism to his non-Jewish contemporaries in their own philosophical and cultural categories. Some Jews carried on active proselytizing among Gentiles, drawing such ''God-fearers'' into the embrace of Judaism (the Gospel of Matthew takes a dim view of such activity, cf. Mt. 23:15).

However, first century Judaism never experienced a call to mission among Gentiles equivalent to that which swept through early Christianity. While there are deep currents of continuity between Old and New Testaments on the issue of mission (as in so much else), there is also striking development. What previously had been prophetic intuitions of God's favor toward and presence among the nations would now become an explicit and dominant concern of the New Testament communities. It is to this new consciousness we now turn.

The catalyst that triggered the missionary consciousness of the early church and shaped its basic message was the person and ministry of Jesus. In him the

141

centrifugal forces we have detected in the Old Testament reach their point of explosion; in him the worldwide perspective of early Christianity finds its source. But a careful look at the biblical data reveals that this missionary impulse did not come from Jesus of Nazareth in the form of an explicit, clean-cut, and immediate missionary program. Jesus, in effect, was *not* the first missionary to the Gentiles. As we shall document, the connection between the ministry of Jesus and the post-Easter missionary activity of the church is more subtle, more developmental, more rooted in the dynamics of history.

The connection between the mission of Jesus and the worldwide mission of the church forms the backdrop for almost all of the New Testament sections of this study. In this chapter we want to consider two significant aspects of this broader question: (1) What are the characteristics of Jesus' person and mission that led to the universal gospel proclaimed by the post-Easter community? (2) What is the nature of the connection between the pre-Easter Jesus and the post-Easter church? This latter question will also be discussed in subsequent chapters on the Gospels and the other New Testament traditions.

JESUS AND THE GENTILES

The most significant link between Jesus of Nazareth and the worldwide mission of the early church was not an explicit universal missionary program launched by him. Before considering some key dimensions of Jesus' ministry, it is important to clarify this point. After all, there are incidents in the Gospels where Jesus encounters Gentiles such as the Syro-Phoenician woman (Mk. 7:24–30) and the centurion (Mt. 8:5–13). And there are dramatic injunctions to proclaim the gospel to the whole world, as in Mt. 28:19 and Lk. 24:47.

These materials need to be considered in conjunction with other significant gospel evidence. Reports of Jesus' encounters with Gentiles are relatively rare, and there is strong evidence that he concentrated his mission first and foremost on the community of Israel. Mt. 10:5 and 15:24 present Jesus as explicitly rejecting activity among the Gentiles, and he is highly critical of the proselytizing activity of the Pharisees (cf. Mt. 23:15). These texts may be the formulation of Matthew but they do catch the spirit of Jesus' Jewish-oriented ministry.[1] The few Gentiles who play a role in the Gospel story always approach Jesus; never the reverse. There is very little evidence that Jesus set out on a conscious program of preaching to Gentiles, even though such evidence would have been highly useful for the later evangelists who were writing to an increasingly Gentile church.

Almost all of Jesus' universal mission commissions found in the Gospels are presented in *post*-Easter contexts. Texts such as Mt. 28:16–20, Mk. 16:14–20, Lk. 24:47, and Jn. 20:21 are all in resurrection–appearance stories. Mk. 13:10 and Mt. 24:14 and 26:13 refer to the post-Easter activity of the community. Thus the Gospels do not offer strong evidence that during his lifetime Jesus of Nazareth engaged in an explicitly universal mission, nor did he so commission his disciples. The gradual and often painful evolution of the church's global consciousness as documented in Acts and in the Pauline correspondence backs up this picture.[2] If Jesus had started a mission to the Gentiles and so instructed his disciples, then the reluctance of the early Palestinian community to follow through on this is perplexing.

Scholars have been divided on how to assess this evidence and, particularly, how to relate it to the post-Easter mission of the community. F. Hahn offers a convenient statement of the question by delineating four attempted solutions.[3] The first solution maintains that Jesus was, in fact, a full-fledged misssionary to the Gentiles. The reports of his movement through Gentile territory, his open attitude to Gentiles, and the universal missionary summons to the apostles support this. But as we have already suggested above, this viewpoint, while correctly noting Jesus' openness to Gentiles, overlooks the negative side of the evidence and fails to take into account the post-Easter nature of the mission texts.

A second, more subtle position maintains that Jesus did not inaugurate a Gentile mission during his lifetime but that he did have such a program in mind and, after his resurrection, so instructed his disciples. This solution gives proper deference to the post-Easter nature of the mission texts but makes some debatable assumptions about the historical consciousness of Jesus. To conceive of Jesus of Nazareth—in his human consciousness—envisioning the later full-blown Gentile mission of the church may not take seriously enough the humanity of Jesus and the role of history in the development of the church's own identity. It also runs aground on the obvious hesitation of the early church concerning the inclusion of Gentiles.

A third position, championed by A. Harnack and other nineteenth-century liberal Protestant theologians, considered the Gentile mission to be a product of the early church's reflection on the universal dimensions of Jesus' teachings. Jesus himself did not undertake such a mission but the early church recognized the implications of his message. This viewpoint does respect the evidence of the church's dawning consciousness but, as with much of nineteenth-century liberal Protestantism, it tends to overlook another important factor about Jesus and the early church. Both Jesus and the early community were conscious of "time" and believed that the final age of history had begun. The mission, then, is not reducible to universal theological principles inherent in Jesus' teaching—as important as they may be—for it also flows from his declaration that the moment of God's salvation is *now*.

A fourth position is found in Joachim Jeremias's book *Jesus' Promise to the Nations*, where Jeremias has given full stress to the factor of "time" in the advent of the Christian mission.[4] He argues that Jesus himself did not inaugurate a Gentile mission, nor did the church merely deduce it from aspects of his teaching. Rather, Jesus' resurrection from the dead convinced the early community that the final age of salvation had dawned. One of the events expected at the end-time was the pilgrimage of the nations to Zion. This conviction triggered missionary activity on the part of the church. Jeremias' solution certainly gives the eschatological element its proper due, but, as a number of critics have pointed out, it fails to explain the dynamism of the mission. In other words, if God is bringing the Gentiles to Zion why would the Christians be compelled to go out and proclaim? Such a solution offers little reflection on the inner relationship between the message of Jesus and the message of the church's missionary proclamation.

The juxtaposition of these four solutions—each with some value and each with evident liabilities—helps to clarify the multiple connection points to be observed in relating the history of Jesus to the missionary efforts of the early church. We have to respect the inner connection between the message of Jesus as proclaimed to the mainly Jewish audience of his day and the message that the early church ultimately proclaimed to Jew and Gentile. We must also respect the connection between Jesus' vision of the decisive historical moment inaugurated by his kingdom ministry and the early church's conviction that the final age had dawned. And, finally, we cannot lose sight of the essential link between the person of Jesus of Nazareth and his impact on his disciples and the person of the risen Jesus as Lord and animator of his missionary church.

We are now in a position to examine some of the features of Jesus' person and ministry that eventually would nourish the early church's sense of mission.

JESUS AND THE KINGDOM OF GOD:
STARTING POINT AND CONTEXT FOR MISSION

The central motif of Jesus' ministry was the "coming of the Kingdom of God" (cf. Mk. 1:14–15).[5] This rich biblical symbol helped Jesus to understand and to articulate the nature of his own mission to Israel. The notion of God's coming rule and its impact on the life of God's people was a motif forged over a long period of Israel's history. Although the metaphor was current at the time of Jesus it was by no means a dominant note of Jewish theology.[6] Jesus seems to have deliberately chosen this theme as most appropriate for expressing the meaning of his mission. Because this symbol of God's rule, or kingdom, was fluid, capable of a variety of nuances and interpretations, it is important that we respect the particular meaning given to it by Jesus' own statements and actions.

The motif of the kingdom of God had broad traditional meaning in the consciousness of Israel. The ultimate source of the kingdom metaphor at its deepest level was the saving relationship between Yahweh and his people. Israel experienced its God as a saving God who rescued it from slavery in Egypt, forged a covenant, and brought his people to a land of promise. This same God was recognized as the "one God" who ruled the universe and all peoples.[7]

Thus one of the great paradoxes of Israel's creed is that the Lord God without peer had linked his will and life with the historical fortunes of Israel. From this covenant bond between Israel and Yahweh sprang the reservoir of hope that characterizes so much of the Old Testament. Despite, and to an extent because of, the failure of human institutions such as monarchy and priesthood, Israel looked increasingly to the future vindication of its hopes by God's might alone. A new and perfect temple would be established; a worthy anointed servant would lead the people; God would come to establish *his* rule. In other words, from Israel's conviction that God had ultimate authority over the life of his people and was intent on rescuing his people from all evil developed the metaphor of the "coming of the kingdom of God."

Walter Kasper has conveniently tagged three basic dimensions of this motif, dimensions that provide a sound orientation to Jesus' own interpretation of the kingdom of God.[8]

First, the kingdom of God has an eschatological character. That is, it deals with the hopes of Israel concerning its ultimate destiny, "with the certainty of the belief that at the end God will reveal himself as the absolute Lord of all the world."[9] For this reason, Jesus' choice of the kingdom metaphor immediately plunges his mission into the question of history. To use the coming of the kingdom of God as his keynote must have meant that Jesus of Nazareth was convinced a decisive moment in Israel's history had arrived and that his own mission was bound up with this *kairos*.

A second dimension of the kingdom motif is its theological character. "In the tradition of the Old Testament and of Judaism the coming of the Kingdom of God means the coming of God."[10] For this reason, the term *basileus* is translated by some as "rule" or "reign" rather than kingdom. It is God's very presence—a saving and transforming presence—that Israel longed for. This is a crucial insight into the nature of the kingdom motif and is the justification for relating Jesus' teaching on the nature of God to his kingdom ministry.

Third, the kingdom of God metaphor has a soteriological, or saving, character. The God who is coming to rule Israel is a God committed to saving his people, a God intent on destroying pain, sickness, evil, death.[11] The notion of ruler or king obviously implies the exercise of power, the establishment of order. Because the rule of God will transform Israel, there is some justification for speaking of the *kingdom*, and not just "rule" or "reign." God's active saving presence will forge a renewed people and a peaceful land. Here is the foundation for relating Jesus' acts of power and healing to the kingdom motif.

The comprehensiveness and the fluidity of the kingdom symbol may be some of the reasons Jesus himself chose to adopt it as the keynote of his ministry. The shape of the motif may also offer one lead toward reconciling the restrictive nature of Jesus' mission with the universal scope of the church's mission. The kingdom of God motif was thoroughly Jewish, evolving from its staunch monotheism, its tortured political experience, and its tenacious hope. The Lord King will come to rescue his people Israel. But, at the same time, the cosmic dimension of Israel's hopes gave this very nationalistic motif a universal dimension. The God of the kingdom is also the Lord of the universe who rules all peoples. The moment of his intervention is the decisive moment, the climax of all history, Israel's and the nations'. And his saving action is definitive, the ultimate defeat of evil and death. As we shall note, these universal proportions erupt in almost every facet of Jesus' own proclamation of the kingdom of God.

JESUS' "DEFINITION" OF THE KINGDOM

At no point in the Gospels or in the New Testament as a whole does Jesus offer his definition of the kingdom of God. The phrase is explicitly cited in some of the important summaries of his ministry in the Synoptic Gospels (cf., for example, Mk. 1:14-15 and parallels) and is a refrain for many of his parables and sayings (cf., for example, Mk. 4:26,30; Mt. 13:44,45,47), but its meaning is not spelled out. What Jesus meant by this metaphor must be deduced from the overall message of his preaching, his lifestyle, his commitments. That is why we have to keep in mind the comprehensive scope of the kingdom theme. Jesus' parables about a gracious God, his fellowship with outcasts and women, his healing and exorcisms, his conflicts over interpretation of law—all of these become a cumulative definition of what the kingdom of God meant.

Jesus' Extraordinary Piety

There is a strong consensus among New Testament scholars that one of the characteristic features of Jesus of Nazareth was his remarkably free and intimate relationship with God.[12] As is now well known, the affectionate term *abba*—an Aramaic diminutive for "father" used by both children and adults in addressing their fathers—may have been Jesus' habitual way of addressing God in prayer (cf. Mk. 14:36).[13] Such an address for God in prayer is practically without analogy in Jewish piety and contrasts with the reverential formality and elaborate address typical of intertestamental Jewish piety. Jesus' own example of prayer in Lk. 11:2-4 smacks of the same extraordinary freedom and directness implicit in the *abba* address.

Jesus' intimacy with his Father should be linked with another feature of the Gospel tradition, Jesus' emphasis on the mercy and compassion of God. The reason Jesus is free to address the awesome God of Israel as *abba* is because he had experienced his God as gracious, loving, and compassionate. The God Jesus knows is powerful yet immediately responsive to the needs of his people.

This experience of God is revealed in several of Jesus' most brilliant parables. The three mercy parables of Luke 15—the lost sheep, the lost coin, the lost son— portray God as generous to a fault in his compassion for a single lost Israelite. The parable of the householder who hires day laborers for the vineyard (cf. Mt. 20:1-16) and whose generosity to the last hired offends the other workers seems to make a similar point: "Do you begrudge my generosity?" Mt. 5:43-48 couples Jesus' call for unlimited reconciliation—"love your enemy"—to the boundless compassion of the Father who "makes the sun rise on the evil and the good and sends rain on the just and the unjust."

This latter text in which God's way becomes the pattern for human response ("So that you may be sons of your Father who is in heaven," Mt. 5:45) illustrates another significant aspect of Jesus' piety. The experience of God as overwhelmingly compassionate calls for a response on the part of those who experience it.[14] The call for conversion is an intrinsic part of the kingdom motif: "The Kingdom of God is at hand; repent; and believe in the good news" (Mk. 1:15). God's overwhelming compassion is not cheap grace but transforming grace. On this foundation will be built much of Jesus' teaching on reconciliation and his interpretation of law—points we shall take up below.

Jesus' Ministry of Compassion to Peripheral People

Closely related to Jesus' image of God as gratuitously compassionate is another characteristic feature of his kingdom ministry. The Gospels present Jesus as provocatively associating with those members of Jewish society considered outside the law and, therefore, excluded from participation in the religious and social community of Israel.[15] The evidence is found throughout the Gospel tradition, predominantly but not exclusively in the Synoptics.

Jesus shares table fellowship with outcast public "sinners" and tax or toll collectors (cf., for example, Mt. 9:10; 11:19; Mk. 2:15-17; Lk. 7:31-35). His statements about the "poor" betray an obvious sympathy for the defenseless and place Jesus thoroughly within the prophetic tradition, which sided with the oppressed against the exploiters (cf. Lk. 6:20-26).[16] He shows an open attitude to the despised Samaritan (cf., for example, Lk. 10:10-37; 17:11-19; John 4). He freely associates with women, including them in his community of disciples, openly conversing with them, and publicly accepting their signs of affection and loyalty—actions taboo for a public religious teacher in the patriarchal society of Jesus' day (cf., for example, Lk. 7:36-50; 8:1-3; Jn. 4:27, etc.).[17] Even though Jesus does not inaugurate a systematic mission to the Gentiles there are several incidents in the Gospels that illustrate a basically open attitude toward the foreigner, who was feared and avoided by most of Jesus' contemporaries (cf. Mt. 8:5-13; Mk. 7:24-30; and Jesus' favorable comments regarding the Gentile towns in Mt. 11:20-24). Jesus seems able to detect goodness in those people his society presumed to be bankrupt.

These provocative associations of Jesus are not incidental to his ministry. The extension of compassion, loyalty, and friendship across well-defined boundaries of exclusion was a parable in action, a way of vividly communicating Jesus' understanding of God and of the quality of his rule.[18] The setting Luke gives for the mercy parables of chapter 15 makes this point: Jesus defends his friendship and table fellowship with the "tax collectors and sinners" (15:1-2) by telling three parables on God's own scandalous mercy. Both Jesus' association and his parables are challenging statements about the nature of the God who is coming to rule a transformed Israel.

The compelling mercy of the God of the kingdom pushes over any arbitrarily erected boundaries. This current of thought is detectable in a number of key Gospel passages. In Mt. 11:16-30 the evangelist couples Jesus' hymn with the altercation over his ministry to outcasts. Similarly the text of Hos. 6:6 about God's desire for mercy rebuts the murmuring of Jesus' opponents about his table fellowship with sinners (cf. Mt. 9:10-13; 12:7).

Thus the provocative style of Jesus' ministry must ultimately be linked with his piety. Not unlike the classical prophets, Jesus of Nazareth had experienced, and then made the heart of his mission, a renewed appreciation of the free and gracious nature of the God of Israel, this God who could not be controlled or limited by Israel's own carefully constructed boundaries. This prophetic insight of Jesus will not only explain many of the features of his ministry in Israel but becomes a crucial link to the ultimately universal mission of the church itself.

Jesus' Interpretation of Law

Although later controversies between the early church and the synagogue have left their mark on the many conflict stories of the Gospels, there is little doubt that Jesus of Nazareth differed with some of his contemporaries over interpretation of the law.[19] And here again a direct link can be made between the overall thrust of Jesus' Kingdom ministry and his attitude to the law.

While Jesus himself was undoubtedly a strict Jew, there are examples where he summons up his own authority and his own experience to place the values of compassion and inner integrity in direct confrontation with his opponents' interpretation of the law. In Mk. 2:23-28, for example, one of a string of conflict stories introduced early in Jesus' ministry, the command against reaping on the Sabbath is subordinated to the disciples' need for food. In Mk. 3:1-6 Jesus' cure of a man with a withered hand is done as a direct challenge to the prohibition against healing on the Sabbath. In Mk. 7:1-23 (cf. Mt. 15:1-20) the purification rituals are relativized in favor of inner cleanliness and integrity. In Mt. 23:23 the tithing laws are subordinated to the "weightier matters . . . justice and mercy and faith." The subordination of all law to the love command accurately captures the spirit of Jesus' teaching (cf. Mt. 22:40; cf. also Mk. 12:31; Lk. 10:25-37).

Conflicts over the law can be seen as another note of Jesus' kingdom proclamation. The God who is coming to rule Israel is a God of overwhelming compassion, one attentive to human pain and need. From this springs the will of the Father for humanity; this was the true intent of the law in Jesus' eyes. Therefore he challenges any interpretation of law that seems to run counter to this fundamental will of God to save and nourish human life. Therefore all human response and all human structures within the family of Israel must be transformed in the light of this pressing reality. As Bornkamm notes: "The ground of his [Jesus'] command to love is simple because it is what God wills and what God does."[20]

Jesus' Teaching on Reconciliation and Forgiveness

Another prevailing theme in the authentic Jesus material of the Gospels is an emphasis on reconciliation and forgiveness at the expense of judgment or retribution. Here again is a facet of Jesus' teaching that directly relates to his experience of God as merciful and to the transforming response that flows from this. The God of the coming kingdom is a God who forgives gratuitously; therefore the one who accepts this God must transform his or her life accordingly.

This kind of direct logic underlies a number of Gospel texts on reconciliation. Both versions of the Lord's prayer (Lk. 11:4; Mt. 6:12) link God's forgiveness and human reconciliation. As already noted, the call to love even the enemy (Lk. 6:35; Mt. 5:44)—a saying highly characteristic of Jesus—is directly related to the indiscriminate love of the Father toward all. The antithetical statement found in Mt. 5:23-24 calling for reconciliation before offering the gift at the altar echoes the prophetic injunctions on authentic worship (cf. Isa.1:10) and also binds together the experience of God and human reconciliation.

Mt. 18:21-35 is, perhaps, the most extended illustration of this facet of Jesus' teaching.[21] Peter's question about the limits of forgiveness (Mt. 18:21) is answered by Jesus' call for limitless reconciliation ("seventy times seven times"). The parable of the merciless official (Mt. 18:23-35) becomes a thinly veiled allegory on the experience of the God of the kingdom (cf. 18:23) as gratuitously forgiving ("and out of pity for him the Lord of that servant released him and forgave him the debt," 18:27). The servant's response is incongruous because he ignores what his Lord has done for him and immediately treats his fellow servant without mercy. The conclusion to the parable reiterates the petition of the Lord's prayer (18:35).

Here again we see the kingdom ministry of Jesus dissolving alienation and breaking down walls of hostility or exclusion. This momentum toward an increasingly wider scope of community takes its place in the cumulative list of themes intrinsic to Jesus' ministry that ultimately lays a basis for a universal mission.

Jesus' Ministry of Healings and Exorcisms

Another constitutive part of Jesus' ministry that helps define the meaning of the kingdom of God is his powerful acts of healing and exorcisms. Contrary to more rationalist tendencies of a few decades ago, contemporary scholarship recognizes that the miracle tradition belongs to the earliest layer of the Gospel material, even though this material has obviously been influenced by the Easter reflection of the church.[22]

All of the Gospels portray Jesus as a person possessing extraordinary personal authority and charism, one who in his encounters with the sick had the ability to heal. He heals physical ailments such as fevers (Mk. 1:30-31), gives sight to the blind (Mk. 8:22-26), restores paralyzed and withered limbs (Mk. 3:1-6), cleanses skin diseases (Lk. 5:12-16). He releases victims from a large spectrum of psychological afflictions (cf. the summary of Mt. 4:23-25). In the Synoptics (especially in Mark) Jesus also performs a large number of exorcisms, liberating people from the mysterious grip of "evil spirits."

Our task here cannot be to review critically the miracle stories or to launch a discussion of their metaphysical implications. Rather, we want to consider how this action-dimension of Jesus' ministry relates to his notion of the kingdom of God, a relationship apparently made by Jesus himself and further amplified in the evolution of the Gospel tradition.

In Lk. 11:20 (and a similar text in Mt. 12:28) Jesus explicitly relates his healing and exorcism activity to the kingdom of God: "But if it is by the finger of God that I cast out demons, then the kingdom of God has come upon you." This saying climaxes a controversy with Jesus' opponents (cf. Lk. 12:14-23; Mt. 12:22-30; and a similar incident in Mk. 3:22-27) who interpret his acts of power as evidence that he is in league with Satan. The *fact* that Jesus performs cures is not at issue, only the significance of such power. Jesus himself in this saying (and in the curious parable of the housebreaker, which immediately follows, cf. Mk. 3:27; Mt. 12:29; Lk. 11:21–22) states that his actions are linked to the saving intent of God himself. It is on this level that the entire miracle and exorcism tradition can be joined to Jesus' interpretation of the kingdom. The God of the kingdom is coming as the ultimate end of sickness, death, evil. Therefore Jesus' liberating power reveals the nature of this God and even initiates his rule. As Schillebeeckx notes:

> The gospels make it clear that a salvation that does not manifest itself here and now, in respect of concrete, individual human beings, can have nothing in the way of "glad tidings" about it. The dawning of God's rule becomes visible on this earth, within our history, through victory over the "powers of evil." This it is that the miracles of Jesus exemplify. In the struggle with evil Jesus is totally on the side of God. Jesus is a power of goodness that conquers Satan.[23]

Recalling the scope of the kingdom symbol sketched above, we can see the reasons for the incorporation of the powerful acts of Jesus under this heading. Jesus' healing activity directly confronts the evil that grips humanity: sickness, pain, death. The exorcisms honor the fact that evil is experienced as a transcendent mysterious force that goes beyond the perversity of human choice. Thus the commitment of Jesus' ministry to human liberation vividly illustrates the soteriological nature of the kingdom. And because Jesus acts in the name of God, as one who is convinced that he is obedient to God's call and to the power of God's Spirit within him, his liberating acts of healing and exorcism reveal the very nature of the God of the kingdom and are, therefore, theological in the strict sense. The God of the kingdom is disclosed as compassionate, merciful, life-giving, transforming.

The healing, and particularly the exorcisms, are also given an eschatological significance in the Gospel tradition. The overthrow of Satan and the definitive defeat of evil and death were characteristic themes of Jewish apocalyptic. When Jesus of Nazareth pursued a healing ministry in the name of God's coming rule, he gave to his activity an acutely eschatological significance. The definitive fulfillment of Israel's hopes, the ultimate transformation expected at the end-time, was already breaking into history through Jesus' liberating action on God's behalf.

These broad dimensions of the powerful acts of Jesus are a further impulse for the universal implications of Jesus' mission. Even though most of Jesus' healing and exorcism activity seems to have been on behalf of Jews, the nature of the struggle illustrated in these encounters is universal and cosmic. As Boff observes:

> The kingdom of God that Christ announces is not a liberation from this or that evil, from the political oppression of the Romans, from the economic difficulties of the people, or from sin alone. The kingdom of God cannot be

narrowed down to any particular aspect. It embraces all: the world, the human person, and society; the totality of reality is to be transformed by God.[24]

Jesus' healing activity demonstrated that the saving grace of God extends not only to personal guilt and broken relationships but to human bodies, to societal structures, to mysterious forces that hold creation itself in check. Problems of pain, of death, of the nature of the material universe are inherently universal questions. The deutero-Pauline literature, especially Colossians and Ephesians, will develop this aspect of the tradition and relate it to the church's own cosmic mission. Because the risen Christ is Lord of all the world and of all powers, the church also has the same universal scope for its responsibility (cf. chap. 8, below). One can sense the direct line leading from Jesus' ministry of healing and exorcisms through the risen Christ's exaltation to the cosmic mission of the church itself.

The sum total of these various dimensions of Jesus' ministry defines what he meant by the "kingdom of God." Through his experiential image of God, his teaching and interpretation of law, by his associations and commitments, by his powerful acts of healing and exorcism, Jesus of Nazareth gave substance and bite to a potentially abstract symbol. The coming kingdom was the effective, transforming rule of an overwhelmingly compassionate God.

THE UNIVERSAL IMPLICATIONS OF JESUS' KINGDOM MINISTRY

With this basic description of Jesus' kingdom ministry we can now concentrate on its implicit universal dimensions. As we noted at the outset, Jesus did not inaugurate a programmatic universal mission, but his own person, his teaching, and his actions would become an irrepressible catalyst for and shaper of the church's sense of mission.

An Expansive Image of God

From the Gospel tradition we can surmise Jesus of Nazareth did not speak speculatively about the nature of God. He drew on his great Jewish heritage. Over centuries of tested faith Israelites had come to assume their God was Lord of the universe and creator of all things. The world and its history were God's own sphere of action and Israel was a special but not exclusive concern of his love.

None of the content in Jesus' image of God is an addition to his Jewish heritage. What does have unique force are particular emphases in his teaching about God. One such emphasis would be the stress in Jesus' life and teaching on the intimate relationship possible between God and the believer, God's availability, as it were. We have already noted this extraordinary piety in Jesus himself. Although the Gospels also suggest that Jesus' own relationship was singular and unrepeatable, there is still emphasis on the nearness of God to his creatures. The disciples are not to be anxious, because God cares for them more than for the lilies of the field and the birds of the air (Mt. 6:26–30). His nourishing love outstrips the care of human parenthood (Lk. 11:10–13). Thus one of the characteristic themes of Jesus' instructions on prayer is confidence: the disciples are to pray repeatedly and without hesitation (Lk. 11:5–10), to be sure of being heard. The disciples are, in fact, invited to address God as "Father" (Lk. 11:2; Matt. 23:9), one of the key metaphors of the historical Jesus in speaking of God.[25]

Thus a specific thrust of the Jesus tradition is to proclaim God as near, as accessible, as inviting human relationship. Although Jesus proclaims this offer of God as gratuitous and unconditional, the very reality of such an offer invites and even demands response. Jesus' teaching, therefore, also focuses on the typical theme of "obeying the will of my Father" (cf. Matt. 7:21), of "leaving all" for the sake of the kingdom (Mk. 10:28–31), of "forgiving as you are forgiven" (cf. Matt. 6:12, 14–15). The failure to respond is ultimately destructive of human life; it invites judgment. But what must not be lost sight of is the emphasis in Jesus' entire proclamation on the fact that the initial experience of God is not judgment or exclusion, but invitation, compassion, forgiveness. Judgment texts and reconciliation texts are not on the same level in the Gospel tradition. The first impulse of God proclaimed by Jesus is acceptance, expansion, inclusion—he touches insider and outsider, righteous and sinner.

As already noted, this dominant note of love and compassion leads to a provocative boundary-breaking tendency in Jesus' own ministry. It is also a significant element in the later mission theologies of the New Testament. Paul is working with a similar experience of God—directly related to the Jesus tradition—when he proclaims God as "rescuer of the ungodly," as "impartial," as freely offering salvation to Jew and Gentile. Luke-Acts also highlights the theme of God's benevolent "impartiality" and directly relates it to Jesus' own boundary-breaking ministry. Matthew stresses the theme of the responsive outsiders, such as the Magi (Mt. 2:1–12), Gentiles such as the centurion (Mt. 8:5–13) or the Canaanite woman (Mt. 15:21–28), and the "sheep" at the last judgment (Mt. 25:31–46). These respond to the favor of God freely shown them. Johannine tradition speaks on a cosmic level of God's love for the world and Jesus as revealer of that inclusive love (Jn. 3:16–17). Thus while Jesus himself does not draw full-blown mission implications from his teaching on God, the kinds of qualities prophetically singled out cannot be made restrictive and, in fact, nourish the universalism already inherent in the Jewish notion of God as Lord of all nations.

An Inclusive View of God's People

The thrust of Jesus' kingdom ministry moves away from a too rigidly defined notion of Israel as an elect people toward a potentially inclusive view of God's people. Jesus exercised his ministry with Jews and on behalf of Israel. However, through the cumulative impact of his message, his use of theological motifs and symbols, and his prophetic critique of the institutions of Israel,

Jesus tended to relativize an emphasis on "identity" for the sake of a higher set of priorities.

Some specific examples can illustrate this point. Jesus' choice of the Twelve suggests that his favored image for the destiny of Israel was not that of the remnant but of the fully restored "people of God." In Jesus' own day the remnant motif—the expectation that only a choice portion of Israel would remain faithful and be saved—was much in vogue.[26] This itself was part of a pervasive sectarian atmosphere caused by the threat of the Roman occupation and the debilitating compromise of ruling groups in Israel. In the century before Jesus a number of reform groups had sprung up, such as the Qumran Essenes and the Pharisees, who considered themselves as an elect remnant, faithfully keeping the tradition of Israel over against a faithless majority.[27]

The choice of the title "Twelve" obviously refers to the twelve tribes of Israel and indicates that Jesus interpreted his own mission as working toward the restoration of God's people. His disciples are given a share in that eschatological vision. The community that Jesus begins to form is symbolic of a fully restored Israel, which the God of the kingdom will effect.[28] Jesus returns to the more traditional notion of "people of God." This metaphor is obviously related to Israel and its identity, but it is a symbol much more open than the sectarian symbol of remnant. And, in fact, one of the key issues reflected in the later Gospel tradition and in Paul is precisely the question of who belongs to God's people.

Another more inclusive symbolization is Jesus' apparent preference for the messianic banquet theme as corrective to the motif of the eschatological pilgrimage of the nations to Zion. Mt. 8:11 (cf. the parallel in Lk. 13:28–29) concludes the incident of the centurion's marvelous faith with Jesus' words: "I tell you, many will come from east and west and sit at table with Abraham, Isaac, and Jacob in the Kingdom of heaven, while the sons of the Kingdom will be thrown into the outer darkness; there men will weep and gnash their teeth." This statement, which appears to be an authentic saying, places the Gentiles on equal footing with the Israelites in the messianic age. They come to Zion not in subjugation (a basic part of the traditional pilgrimage motif) but to share fully in the joy of the kingdom. This participation is due to their admirable response, the point of the centurion incident in Mt. 8:5–13.

The banquet theme and the favorable reactions of Gentiles are echoed in a number of Gospel texts. The messianic feast is one of Jesus' favored eschatological images (cf., for example, Mt. 22:1–14; 25:1–13; Lk. 14:1 15–24; 15:6,9,22–24; 22:16). A recurring motif is the opening of the banquet to all who are willing to respond to the invitation (cf. Lk. 14:21–24). The criterion of response, as we shall note, results in judgment on the invited guests who balk (Israel) and praise for the outcasts who are willing to come. A similar set of texts is found in Mt. 11:20–24, where the rejection Jesus experiences from the Galilean cities is contrasted with acceptance in the Gentile regions of Tyre and Sidon and even the perennial badlands of Sodom (cf. also Mt. 10:15).

The expansive potential of Jesus' message about the people of God is reinforced by two other characteristics of his preaching. Jesus seems to have avoided the motif of vengeance on the nations while, at the same time, giving strong emphasis to right response to God's grace as the basic criterion for inclusion in his people. The motif of eschatological vengeance, or retribution, on the lawless Jews and the Gentiles was a strong motif of Jewish literature in the time period parallel to that of Jesus and the early church.[29] Some Jews had compromised their faith and were disobedient to the law, thus sapping the strength of Israel. Gentiles, particularly the Romans, had persecuted the people and corrupted their lives. Thus many law-abiding Jews became convinced that God would avenge these wrongs in the Day of Judgment. That day would be a day of wrath for the Gentile and the lawless.

This theme is conspicuously absent from Jesus' preaching. Instead there is a consistent emphasis on the response of faith and obedience to God as the critical criterion for judgment, a criterion that relativizes race and status. Examples of this motif abound. In addition to the stories of the centurion (cf. Mt. 8:5–13) and the Syro-Phoenician woman (Mk. 7:24–30), a number of sayings illustrate this theme (cf. especially, Mt. 7:15–27; 10:15; 11:22; 21:28–32; 25:31–46).

An allied motif is that of sincerity. A large portion of Jesus' sayings puncture inauthentic piety (cf. Mt. 6:1–18) or the performing of works "for people to see" (Mt. 6:1). Jesus' emphasis on integrity and authenticity as the touchstones of genuine religion is, of course, not foreign to Judaism itself; it is a consistent theme of the prophetic tradition (cf., for example, Isa. 1:1–17). But the intensity that Jesus brings to this message and the coupling of an emphasis on authentic response to the other open symbols of his preaching and ministry provide a powerful stimulus to the universal mission of the church. As we shall note in subsequent chapters, these themes are amplified in the Gospel tradition and—although more obliquely—by Paul to justify the inclusion of Gentiles in the people of God on equal footing with Jews.

The prophetic qualities of Jesus' ministry disclose another dimension of his mission with which we can conclude our discussion of his expansive concept of God's people.[30] We have already observed a number of such prophetic challenges in Jesus' mission under other rubrics (for example, his association with outcasts, his interpretation of law, his openness to Gentiles who were responsive to God's grace). An overall view of the ministry of the historical Jesus shows a consistent challenge to attitudes, practices, and structures that tended arbitrarily to restrict or exclude potential members of the Israelite community. Most of the "outsiders" Jesus defended were Jews: (for example, Jewish women, Jewish tax and toll collectors, public sinners, Jewish sick and infirm) but they also included Samaritans (cf. Lk. 9:55; 10:33) and more rarely Gentiles (Mk. 7:24–30; Mt. 8:5–13).

His prophetic challenge confronted the root causes of such exclusion by reinterpreting the law in the direction of mercy and compassion (cf. the Sabbath controversies), by risking condemnation under the law by direct association with outcasts (for example, table fellowship, recruitment of outcasts as disciples), or by action taken on their behalf (statements in Simon's house, tours on the Sabbath, etc.), probably including the inflammatory prophetic gesture of cleansing the temple.

In the context of Jesus' day such a course of action ran directly counter to the legitimate concern for identity and cohesion that the leaders of the Jewish community must have experienced under the threat of Roman occupation. For Jesus, an influential teacher, to have relativized some of the strictly defined boundaries of membership in the faithful community of Israel must have been perceived as a dangerous threat to stability. A close examination of the Gospel materials leaves little doubt that this issue—Jesus' prophetic challenge to boundaries—was a prime cause of the hostility directed against him and a major reason for the reluctant cooperation of Jewish leaders and Roman officials in his execution.[31] It is this prophetic thrust of Jesus' mission—reinterpreted in the light of his resurrection and filtered through the theological perspective of the various authors of the New Testament—that will ultimately emerge as an authentic characteristic of early Christianity in its movement toward the Gentiles and in its radical relativizing of the law.

A Positive View of Human Destiny

Jesus' kingdom ministry includes one other aspect that will have significant consequences for the New Testament understanding of mission: a sense of history. One of the difficulties concerning the kingdom of God motif as proclaimed by Jesus is deciphering his statements about its "timing." While some of his statements and parables seem to say that the kingdom is imminent, "at hand" (Mk. 1:14–15), others imply that the kingdom's advent is still future and that a significant interval is to be expected (Mt. 13:24–30).

These apparently conflicting statements may, in part, be due to possible ambiguity concerning the kingdom's timetable on the part of Jesus (cf. Mk. 13:32) and the early church. But, more importantly, they also derive from the very nature of the kingdom experience. The coming kingdom of God is not reducible to some localized set of circumstances or events, and thus definable for this particular moment of history. The kingdom is, even more radically, an experience of God's rule; it is a metaphor describing a *quality* of life and not just a reference to the climax (or termination) of history. Only because it is such could Jesus have connected the experience of the kingdom with such things as his exorcisms (Lk. 11:28) or with reconciliation (Mt. 18:25–35). In these present experiences of God's power, one encountered God's definitive rule. The consummation of that rule—its full consequences on a cosmic and historical level—remain future, but its presence is already breaking into human history. In both instances—present and future—the kingdom is a result of God's saving initiative. It is not neatly evolutionary. The Lord of the kingdom is already making his presence felt in the present and orienting his people and his world toward their full destiny.

This conviction about God's relationship to human history as expressed in

Jesus' own teaching and ministry had subtle yet substantial implications for the early Christian sense of mission. We might attempt to synthesize Jesus' convictions about history in the following fashion:

1. Jesus' teaching—particularly his parables—manifest a decidedly "optimistic," or hopeful, view of history. That is, despite turmoil and trial, the ultimate victory of God's rule is assured. The parables of growth (cf., for example, the seed parables of Mk. 4:3–9, 26–29, 30–32) make this point: although the seeds appear insignificant and vulnerable and the condition of the soil appears inhospitable, the harvest is inevitable and abundant. As Conzelmann points out, these kinds of parables do not comment on the developmental nature of the kingdom but on the final triumph of God's power.[32] Other types of sayings move in the same direction. Of particular importance are Jesus' words associated with the Last Supper (cf. Mk. 14:25; Lk. 22:16,18). His declaration in the face of imminent and violent death—"I will drink [the fruit of the vine] new in the kingdom of God"—is a powerful testimony to Jesus' triumphant view of human destiny.[33] His statement about the triumph of his prophetic ministry breathes the same spirit: even though he may be experiencing rejection and death, he "will be raised up on the third day," a traditional expression of apocalyptic hopes.[34]

2. Jesus was also convinced that the coming of the kingdom would mean victory over evil and death. In this Jesus shares a decidedly apocalyptic view of history. His exorcisms are previews of Satan's final defeat (cf. Lk. 10:17). A number of his parables speak of a final reckoning in which the good and bad will be separated, the latter for destruction (cf. Mt. 13:14–43, 49–50). The apocalyptic discourses, although obviously influenced by later Christian experience, build on authentic Jesus material that envisions an epic struggle with evil and death but ultimate triumph over these forces (cf. Mk. 13:7–27).

3. These two interrelated dimensions of the kingdom motif—the assured future triumph of God's Lordship and the ultimate defeat of death—converge on the present. Repeatedly, Jesus' eschatological vision becomes part of his present ministry. In view of the assured victory he counsels "alertness" (Mk. 13:33–37) and fearless confidence (cf. Mt.10:16–31; Mk.13:11,13). He himself faces rejection and even death (Lk. 13:33; Mk. 14:26; Mt. 26:18) in the same fashion. The victory and its implied defeat of evil animate Jesus' own ministry of healing, exorcism, and prophetic challenge. Values that will be the ultimate criteria for human life—justice, compassion, peace—become the operative norms for victory now in the present (cf. Mt. 25:31–46 and the Beatitudes). This same reasoning seems to reinforce Jesus' openness to Gentiles and outcasts. Even though the influx of the nations is part of the final scenario of the reign of God, the approach of responsive Gentiles is welcomed and praised (Mt. 8:11) because that inclusive vision of redemption is inbreaking now.

There is little doubt that this eschatological tone of Jesus' kingdom ministry had enormous impact on the early church, including its motivation for mission. The experience of resurrection validated and intensified the historical perspective that Jesus communicated to his followers. As we shall point out in discussing Paul and the Gospel literature, this conviction about the advent of the kingdom became an integral part of the church's mission theology.

CONCLUSION: THE MISSION OF JESUS
AND THE MISSION OF THE CHURCH

These reflections on the kingdom ministry of Jesus and its relationship to the mission perspective of the early church might be synthesized as follows: Jesus and his mission are ultimately decisive for the *character*, the *scope*, the *urgency*, and the *authority* of the early church's Christian mission.

The character: The post-Easter perspective of the early church and the particular circumstances of the New Testament writers and their communities would substantially reinterpret the historical tradition rooted in Jesus. But there is little doubt that, taken in global fashion, the mission theologies of the early church are stamped with the character of Jesus' own ministry. The New Testament stress on God's initiative in salvation, the centrality of the love command, the emphasis on reconciliation and community, the overture to the marginal and the needy, the church's sense of confidence in God and its ecstatic piety —all these essential features of early Christian proclamation find their initial and decisive impulse in Jesus' own message.

The scope: As our survey of the New Testament literature will illustrate, the question of "boundaries" remained a central concern of the early church, as it had been for Jesus himself. The struggle of the early church to move beyond the confines of Israel, to be open to the Gentiles, was a major theme of the Pauline letters and of much of the Gospel tradition. The interaction of the church with the uncharted religious waters of the Hellenistic world, as found in the letters of Peter, echo a similar thrust. The letter to the Colossians and the deutero-Pauline tradition of Ephesians move the question of boundaries to a cosmic scale in declaring the Lordship of the exalted Christ—and therefore the responsibility of the church's mission—to be boundless. This centrifugal movement of the early community prevented it from ever becoming purely sectarian, and this spirit, too, finds its origin in the shape of Jesus' own perspective.

The urgency: The early community had a full-blown eschatological atmosphere. It eagerly awaited the end-time and was convinced (particularly clear in Luke and Paul) that it was living in the expected age of the Spirit. It had an evident hope of future triumph (clear not only in the apocalyptic features of the Gospels and Revelation but also in Paul, the deutero-Pauline letters, and other New Testament traditions). All these characteristics of early Christian proclamation continued and developed Jesus' own sense of history. There is little doubt that this historical consciousness, although not the sole reason for the church's overture to the Gentiles, was a primal motivation of the early Christian mission.

The authority: A careful evaluation of the link between Jesus and the early church's mission might correctly conclude that it was not ultimately *what* Jesus said or did but *who* he was that made the difference. The crucifixion both historically and theologically could be interpreted as a radical question mark placed alongside the person and ministry of Jesus. This was, in fact, the conviction of Paul and it is echoed in the Synoptic passion narratives. Jesus' entire ministry—his privileged sense of piety, his interpretation of the law, his association with the lawless, and the source of his healing power—was put in question by public crucifixion at the hands of the Romans and with the consent of the religious authorities of his own people.[35] More than just a repudiation of a man's actions, this death blow struck at the very claims of his person.

Thus resurrection is rightly interpreted by much of early Christian theology as the vindication of Jesus (cf. Acts 2:36: "God has made him both Lord and Christ, this Jesus whom you crucified"). Through God's saving power not only is Jesus' mission in all its facets validated, but his very person is disclosed as exalted, chosen, transcendent. The resurrection event reveals to the early community the awesome identity of Jesus as the Christ, as Son of God, as Son of man, as Lord of the universe. The Christological authority implicit in the graceful words and actions of Jesus of Nazareth was now explicitly revealed as the authority and mission of God's Son. This dynamic gives birth to the mission theology, properly so called, of the New Testament.

NOTES

1. The question of Jewish proselytizing at the time of Jesus has not yet been adequately explored. There does seem to have been considerable "missionary," or apologetic, activity among Gentiles on the part of Jews, and many rabbinic sayings (some of which may be dated from the first century) speak positively of Gentiles. But such activity seems to have remained basically ethnocentric in perspective; some Jews were open to Gentile converts but these were to be grafted onto the Jewish nation. On this question, cf. W. Braude, *Jewish Proselytizing in the First Five Centuries of the Common Era* (Providence, R. I.: Brown University Press, 1940); *Aspects of Religious Propaganda in Judaism and Early Christianity*, ed. E. Fiorenza (Notre Dame: University of Notre Dame Press, 1976), pp. 2–3; F. Hahn, *Mission in the New Testament*, Studies in Biblical Theology 47 (Naperville: Allenson, 1965), pp. 21–25.

2. On Acts, cf. below, chap. 11 pp. 269–76. Paul's account of his confrontation with Peter over this issue in Gal. 2:1–14 corroborates the basic picture of a struggle for universalism as presented in the early chapters of Acts.

3. F. Hahn, *Mission in the New Testament*, pp. 26–41. Cf. also, J. Jeremias, *Jesus' Promise to the Nations*, Studies in Biblical Theology 24 (Naperville: Allenson, 1958).

4. J. Jeremias, *Jesus' Promise to the Nations*, especially pp. 55–73.

5. This is affirmed by virtually every New Testament scholar. Cf., for example, the remarks in N. Perrin, *Rediscovering the Teaching of Jesus* (New York: Harper & Row, 1967), p. 54; J. Sobrino, *Christology at the Crossroads* (Maryknoll, N.Y. : Orbis Books, 1978), p. 41; W. Kasper, *Jesus the Christ* (New York: Paulist Press, 1976), p. 72.

6. Cf. G. Klein, "The Biblical Understanding of 'The Kingdom of God,' " *Interpretation* 26 (1972):387–418.

7. J. Bright, *The Kingdom of God* (Nashville: Abingdon, 1953), pp. 24–26.

8. W. Kasper, *Jesus the Christ*, pp. 72–88.

9. Ibid., p. 75.

10. Ibid., p. 78.

11. On this point, cf. particularly E. Schillebeeckx, *Jesus: An Experiment in Christology* (New York: Seabury Press, 1979), pp. 141–43.

12. E. Schillebeeckx, *Jesus*, pp. 256–71; J. Dunn, *Jesus and the Spirit* (Philadelphia: Westminster Press, 1975), pp. 11–40.

13. On the import of this form of address for God in the context of Jewish piety, cf. J. Jeremias, *The Prayers of Jesus*, Studies in Biblical Theology 6 (London: SCM Press, 1967), pp. 11–65. The Aramaic term appears in the Gospels only in Mk. 14:36; the other evangelists provide the Greek equivalent (cf., e.g., Matthew's *pater mou*, "my father," in 26:39). The Aramaic expression is also found in Rom. 8:15 and Gal. 4:6.

14. The "love your enemy" text has been described as the most characteristic saying of Jesus, one without direct parallel in Judaism. On this remarkable text, cf. V. Furnish, *The Love Command in the New Testament* (Nashville: Abingdon, 1972), pp. 45–59; J. Piper, *'Love Your Enemies'*, Society for New Testament Studies Monograph Series (New York. Cambridge University Press, 1979); L. Schottroff, "Non-Violence and the Love of One's Enemies," in *Essays on the Love Commandment*, ed. R. Fuller (Philadelphia: Fortress Press, 1978), pp. 9–39.

15. On this aspect of Jesus' ministry, cf. N. Perrin, *Rediscovering*, pp. 102–8. J. Jeremias discusses the background of this motif in the Palestinian setting of Jesus' day; cf. *New Testament Theology: The Proclamation of Jesus* (New York: Scribners, 1971), pp. 108–21. A more popular treatment of this question can be found in D. Senior, *Jesus: A Gospel Portrait* (Dayton: Pflaum, 1975), pp. 69–82.

16. Cf. J. Dupont, "The Poor and Poverty in the Gospels and Acts," in *Gospel Poverty* (Chicago: Franciscan Herald Press, 1977); M. Hengel, *Property and Riches in the Early Church* (Philadelphia: Fortress Press, 1974), pp. 23–30, and above chap. 3.

17. There is a rapidly growing literature on the subject of Jesus' attitude toward women in the context of the patriarchal society of first-century Palestinian Judaism; cf., e.g., E. and F. Stagg, *Woman in the World of Jesus* (Philadelphia: Westminster Press, 1978); E. Tetlow, *Women and Ministry in the New Testament* (New York: Paulist Press, 1980); R. Karris, "The Role of Women according to Jesus and the Early Church," in *Women and Priesthood*, ed. C. Stuhlmueller (Collegeville, Minn: Liturgical Press, 1978), pp. 47–57.

18. Speaking of one aspect of this association with outcasts, that of table fellowship, Schillebeeckx makes the following comment: ". . . meal-sharing in fellowship, whether with notorious 'tax collectors and sinners' or with his friends, casual or close, is a fundamental trait of this historical Jesus. In that way Jesus shows himself to be God's eschatological messenger, conveying the news of God's invitation to all—including especially those officially regarded at the time as outcasts—to attend the peaceful occasion of God's rule; this fellowship at table is itself, as an eating together with Jesus, an offer here and now of eschatological salvation or 'final good' " (*Jesus*, p. 218).

19. Cf. A. Hultgren, *Jesus and His Adversaries* (Minneapolis: Augsburg Publishing Co., 1979); G. Bornkamm, *Jesus of Nazareth* (London: Hodder and Stoughton, 1960), pp. 96–100.

20. G. Bornkamm, *Jesus*, p. 114.

21. The entire discourse of chapter 18 has the earmarks of Matthew's style and theology. Some have suggested that the parable of the merciless official (18:23–35), which is unique to Matthew's Gospel, is, in fact, a composition of the evangelist and presents in story form the petition of the Lord's Prayer on forgiveness (cf. Mt. 6:12, 14–15). Cf., e.g., M. Goulder, *Midrash and Lection in Matthew* (London: SPCK, 1974), pp. 402–4. On chapter 18 as a whole, cf. W. Pesch, *Matthäus der Seelsorger*, Stuttgarter Bibelstudien 2 (Stuttgart: Verlag Katholisches Bibelwerk, 1966).

22. On the miracle tradition in the Gospels, cf. E. Schillebeeckx, *Jesus*, pp. 179–200; W. Kasper, *Jesus the Christ*, pp. 89–99.

23. E. Schillebeeckx, *Jesus*, p. 189.

24. L. Boff, *Jesus Christ Liberator* (Maryknoll, N.Y.: Orbis Books, 1978), p. 55; cf. also, F. Hahn, *Mission*, p. 33.

25. On this metaphor and the whole issue of a patriarchal image for God, cf. R. Hamerton-Kelly, *God the Father*, Overtures to Biblical Theology series (Philadelphia: Fortress Press, 1979). Hamerton-Kelly suggests that Jesus' way of using this metaphor liberates it from cultural constraints.

26. Cf. E. Schillebeeckx, *Jesus*, pp. 144–45; F. Hahn, *Mission*, p. 30; J. Jeremias, *Jesus' Promise*, pp. 40–54.

27. On these groups, cf. S. Freyne, *The World of the New Testament*, New Testament Message 2 (Wilmington, Del.: Michael Glazier, 1980), pp. 105–18.

28. Cf. F. Hahn, *Mission*, pp. 29–30; on the concept of the Twelve, cf. S. Freyne, *The Twelve Disciples and Apostles* (London: Sheed and Ward, 1968).

29. Cf. J. Jeremias, *Jesus' Promise*, pp. 41–46.

30. The prophetic character of Jesus' ministry is discussed in F. Gils, *Jésus Prophète d'après les Évangiles Synoptiques* (Louvain: Publications Universitaires, 1957); and D. Hill, *New Testament Prophecy* (Atlanta: John Knox Press, 1979), pp. 48–69.

31. The precise reasons that led to Jesus' execution and the involvements of Roman officials and Jewish leaders in his condemnation are diffiuclt to assess and intensely debated, especially because of the ecumenical implications of this issue. These issues are judiciously treated in W. Wilson, *The Execution of Jesus* (New York: Scribners, 1970), E. Lohse, *History of the Suffering and Death of Jesus Christ* (Philadelphia: Fortress Press, 1967), and G. Sloyan, *Jesus on Trial* (Philadelphia: Fortress Press, 1973).

32. H. Conzelmann, *Jesus* (Philadelphia: Fortress Press, 1973), pp. 74–81.

33. Cf. E. Schillebeeckx, *Jesus,* pp. 306–12; R. Pesch, *Das Abendmahl und Jesu Todesveständnis* (Freiburg: Herder, 1978).

34. Cf., e.g., Hos. 6:2. On this phrase, see the discussion in C. Evans (Naperville: Allenson, 1970), pp. 47–50, and K. Lehmann, *Auferweckt Am Dritten Tag Nach Der Schrift* (Freiburg: Herder, 1968), pp. 159–91.

35. Crucifixion was intended as a public humiliation and rejection of its victim and therefore as a deterrent. On this point, cf. M. Hengel, *Crucifixion* (Philadelphia: Fortress Press, 1977).

7

The Mission Theology of Paul

We are ambassadors of Christ, God making his appeal through us
[1 Cor. 5:20].

The importance of Paul for the biblical foundations of mission can hardly be exaggerated. Paul was not the only or the first to proclaim the gospel to non-Jews. Christian missionary activity had already spread across the empire (at least as far as Rome) before Paul. As we shall note, he was not the creator of the missionary preaching of the early church, being indebted for this both to early Christian tradition and to Judaism itself. But through accident or providence it is Paul's thought that fills almost a third of the New Testament writings. Alone among New Testament writers, Paul gives the most profound and most systematic presentation of a universal Christian vision. The force of Paul's word and personality and the energy of his missionary commitment continue to make the Pauline letters a powerful challenge to the church's self-understanding.

POSING THE QUESTIONS

Asking the mission question of Paul may be the most arduous task of this book. Not because mission theology is alien or rare in Paul's thought—obviously it is not—but because the theology of mission is practically synonymous with the totality of Paul's awesome reflections on Christian life. It is not our intention to attempt yet another introduction to Paul or a synthesis of his theology, although it is inevitable that major elements of his thought need to be reviewed. Rather, we want to ask of Paul, as specifically as possible, only those questions that guide this study. As a result of this narrower focus some important Pauline concerns may be pushed to the periphery (for example, some of Paul's ethical concerns, the chronology of his life, aspects of his ecclesiology, etc.).

The questions we want to pose of Paul can be reduced to two:

1. What are the theological foundations for Paul's mission, that is, what convictions led a "Pharisee of the Pharisees" (Phil. 3:4–5; Gal. 1:4) to become the "apostle to the Gentiles"? Note that in speaking of "theological foundations" or

161

"convictions" we do not mean to imply that Paul developed his mission on purely dogmatic grounds. Bound up with Paul's reflections are experiences and dynamics that were formative of his theology. These cannot be overlooked in attempting to articulate his theology.

2. What can we learn about the content and style of Paul's mission activity? The point is not to draw hasty conclusions about contemporary evangelization. Rather, analysis of Paul's mission strategy—on the basis of the partial evidence that we have—can give further insight into his theology. If further spinoffs come by way of instruction or insight for contemporary missionary work, so much the better.

THE SOURCES

Before bringing these two questions to the Pauline writings it is necessary to clear away a few preliminaries.

First of all we should acknowledge the nature of our sources and their potential to answer the questions we have posed. There is general consensus among Pauline scholars that the following are authentic correspondence of Paul: Romans, 1 Corinthians, 2 Corinthians, Galatians, 1 Thessalonians, Philemon.[1] A few have debated the authenticity of Philippians but reasons for excluding this letter seem very slim. 2 Thessalonians and Colossians may be more questionable but we shall consider them authentic Pauline material. In our view the Pastoral letters and Ephesians contain authentic Pauline tradition but it is likely they were composed subsequent to Paul, drawing on Paul's thought but reinterpreting it for a new time and a new situation. Therefore the mission theology of these letters will be taken up in separate chapters (chaps. 8 and 12, below).

It should be noted that in dealing with Paul we can make only passing reference to Luke's portrayal of him in Acts. Although much of the material on Paul in Acts is unquestionably based on reliable tradition, Luke reinterprets these traditions in the service of his own theology. Therefore, like the deutero-Pauline letters, Acts deserves separate treatment in the context of Lucan theology (cf. chap. 10, below).

Once we have settled on which letters to consider, our list of preliminary cautions is still not complete. It is important to keep in mind the nature of Paul's correspondence.[2] These letters are epistles and are not missionary texts in the strict sense. That is, they are not transcripts of Paul's initial preaching to non-Christian communities, nor do they directly address the questions about the foundation of Paul's mission that we have posed above. Neither are they theological treatises scanning the totality of Paul's view of the gospel. Romans comes closest to a comprehensive exposition but it, too, is ultimately an occasional letter and does not offer a systematic presentation of Paul's total theology.

Paul's correspondence is pastoral, responding to particular pastoral problems in a specific Christian community. Except in the case of Romans, a community that Paul had not evangelized, nor yet visited, the letters are written to churches Paul had established and with whom he had deep ties.[3] Thus there is much that is presumed and unsaid in the correspondence. As Leander Keck notes, "Reading these letters is somewhat like overhearing a telephone conversation: one must always infer what is being said at the other end of the line, as well as the context of the conversation."[4]

Fortunately for us there is also a public and universal character to Paul's correspondence. Even though written for a specific audience, the letters seem intended for public reading and perhaps even for circulation to other communities. Combined with Paul's soaring mind this makes the letters more than occasional and gives us access to much of the broader theological framework in which Paul works out specific pastoral conclusions. This tantalizing blend of the specific and the universal, of the pastoral and the dogmatic makes Pauline interpretation regarding the question of mission or any other topic both exciting and delicate.

Even though Paul's letters are not missionary documents in the strictest sense, it should not be forgotten that the major epistles were all written during the period of Paul's most energetic missionary activity, and all except Romans to communities that were the direct result of his mission. Even in the case of Romans it is likely that part of his reason for writing was the mission question, and the topic of salvation for Jews and Gentiles that dominates the letter is intimately tied up with Paul's entire mission theology.[5] Although the specific context of the Pauline letters must be respected, approaching them with the viewpoint of mission is not to introduce an alien or anachronistic subject.

INFLUENCES ON PAUL

Contemporary Pauline interpretation has expended much effort to determine the formative influences on the apostle's theology. Because Paul was a Greek-speaking Jew, trained in Palestinian tradition and active in the Gentile milieu of Greece and Asia Minor, he had access to diverse thought worlds whose own inter-relationship in the first-century world was diffuse and complex. No combination of "influences" or backgrounds determines Paul's theology. For example, Paul may derive some of his concepts and language for his understanding of the Christian community as the "body of Christ" from Stoic philosophy, but this "influence" does not produce or determine Paul's ecclesiology.[6]

In discussing Paul's mission theology, there are certain important influences that play a significant if not ultimately determinative role in the formation of Paul's thought.

Judaism

Even though Paul's view of the Christian mission ultimately placed him at odds with some aspects of Judaism, he still shared many convictions in common with this formative matrix, even on specifics of the mission question itself.[7] We may make a short list here: *(a)* Paul accepted the Hebrew Scriptures as the revealed Word of God and consistently worked out his theology in dialogue with Scripture, using rabbinic techniques acquired from Judaism; *(b)* in formulating his own ecclesiology, Paul retained a special role for Israel even though he firmly maintained the access of Gentiles to salvation; *(c)* in his estimation of the Gentile world and in certain basic themes of his missionary preaching, Paul employed stock themes of Jewish missionary preaching.[8]

Early Christian Tradition

Although few could deny Paul's creativity and the original cast of much of his theology, he was not the "second founder" of Christianity. Nor was he independent from the rest of the early community—even though Paul himself could give this impression (as in discussing his conversion experience in Gal. 1:11–17). At key points Paul explicitly identified his own preaching as received tradition (1 Cor. 11:23; 15:3) and he stoutly defended the authenticity of his mission and his gospel by noting his approbation by community authorities (cf., for example, Gal. 2:2–10). In a study of Paul's missionary preaching, Bussmann concludes: "[Paul] . . . was not in opposition to the rest of early Christian proclamation, rather he was conscious of totally identifying with it and did not propagate an alternate or opposing formulation of the kerygma."[9] Bussmann's assessment may exaggerate the homogeneity of Paul with other early Christian traditions (there is, after all, the bitter controversy in Galatians) but the emphasis on continuity is more accurate than posing Paul as a pure maverick.

Hellenism

Certainly Paul as a Roman citizen and as a diaspora Jew could not escape the influence of Greco-Roman culture. As recent studies have emphasized, even a strict Palestinian Jew would not remain unaffected, since Hellenistic culture had made deep inroads in Israel from the beginning of the fourth century B.C.[10] As a result, scholars are no longer so sure of a stark cleavage between Palestinian and diaspora Judaism on this point; but determining specific Hellenistic influences on Paul is difficult. For example, attempts to find a strong link between the mystery cults and Paul's views on baptism and Eucharist have met with increasing skepticism.[11] Another frequently alleged influence is that a Gnostic "redeemer myth" lies at the basis of Pauline soteriology. But the reconstruction of such a supposed myth depends on sources much later than Paul and in no extant source does such an elaborate myth exist.[12] While problems of Gentile and therefore Hellenistic communities triggered many of Paul's reflections (for example, mixed marriages, in 1 Corinthians 7; eating meat offered to idols, 1 Corinthians 8, Romans 14), and concepts and language from Hellenism are used in his correspondence (for example, the body, stock list of vices and virtues, etc.), it seems that the most determinative influences on Paul's theology are from early Christianity and Judaism (themselves influenced by a degree of Hellenistic culture) rather than directly from the Greco-Roman world itself.

The nature of Paul's correspondence and the complex matrix of his own thought world and that of the communities with which he communicated must be kept in mind in attempting to reconstuct his mission theology. It is to this task that we now turn.

THE STARTING POINT: PAUL'S CONVERSION

Determining the logical starting point for Paul's theology has been a perennial problem. Since Paul's mission theology is practically coextensive with his entire Christian vision, the same interpretive problem faces us. The question of starting point is not merely academic. Deciding on Paul's initial insight usually leads to a decision about the central theme of Paul's theology and therefore to the shape of his overall synthesis.[13] The challenge, as E. Sanders notes, is "to begin where Paul began."[14] Fortunately there is a concrete and chronological starting point for Paul's Christian vision, namely, his own conversion. Because Paul himself explicitly identifies his own missionary vocation with this inaugural Christian experience, we can be justified in our construction of his mission theology from this point. J. Fitzmyer notes, "Paul's theology was influenced most of all by his experience on the road to Damascus and by faith in the risen Christ as the Son of God which developed from his experience."[15]

Paul himself refers to his inaugural Christian experience in a few decisive texts. In contrast with the narratives in Acts, Paul does not give us a description of the event itself. Rather, there is an emphasis on the fact of the experience and its consequences for Paul's belief in Jesus and, especially, his role as apostle.

Galatians 1:11–17

> For I would have you know, brethren, that the gospel which was preached by me is not a human gospel. For I did not receive it from man, nor was I taught it, but it comes through a revelation of Jesus Christ. For you have heard of my former life in Judaism, how I persecuted the church of God violently and tried to destroy it; and I advanced in Judaism beyond many of my own age among my people, so extremely zealous was I for the traditions of my fathers. But when he who had set me apart before I was born, and had called me through his grace, was pleased to reveal his Son to me, in order that I might preach him among the Gentiles, I did not confer with flesh and blood, nor did I go up to Jerusalem to those who were apostles before me, but I went away into Arabia; and again I returned to Damascus.

Paul's immediate purpose in this passage was to convince the Galatian community that his gospel was authentic because it could be traced to "a revelation of Jesus Christ" (1:12). Thus any gospel alien to Paul's (such as the "gospel" that seemed to be influencing the Galatians) was counterfeit. Paul does not offer any details but he locates the revelation of that gospel in the decisive event that transformed him from "his former life in Judaism" and his "zeal for the traditions of [his] fathers" (1:14) to a "preacher of the faith" (1:23).

He describes this experience as a "revelation of [God's] Son to [or in] me." The word "revelation" seems to indicate a visionary experience that convinced Paul that Jesus of Nazareth was the risen Christ.[16] Paul also considered this inaugural experience as a call to preach Jesus (cf. 1:16) among the Gentiles, a vocation in the model of the prophetic calls of Isaiah and Jeremiah. Paul's words in 1:15–16, "when he who had set me apart before I was born" and the commission to preach to the Gentiles echo Jer. 1:4–5 and Isa. 49:6. Whenever Paul speaks about his conversion experience and his vocation he makes it clear that they originated in a decisive act of God.

1 Corinthians 15:8–11

Last of all, as to one untimely born, he appeared also to me. For I am the least of the apostles, unfit to be called an apostle, because I persecuted the church of God. But by the grace of God I am what I am, and his grace toward me was not in vain. On the contrary, I worked harder than any of them, though it was not I, but the grace of God which is with me.

In another context where Paul's apostolic authority and the reliability of his gospel are in question, we have further reference to his conversion. Here the question arises from confusion among the Corinthians about the meaning of resurrection (cf. 1 Cor. 15:12–58). Paul's defense is to recall the basic content of the tradition he handed on (15:1–3) and to locate the authority to preach that gospel in an experience of the risen Christ which, though later in time, was as valid as those of Peter and the Twelve.

Here the term used is "appear to" (*ōphthē*, 1 Cor. 15:8), which stresses more than Galatians 2 the visionary nature of the experience. Although his transformation from persecutor of the church to preacher of the gospel is not emphasized as much as in Galatians (where the controversy with Judaizers makes the point much more relevant), Paul still identifies his call to apostleship with this moment (15:9–10).

1 Corinthians 9:1–2

Am I not free? Am I not an apostle? Have I not seen Jesus our Lord? Are you not my workmanship in the Lord? If to others I am not an apostle, at least I am to you; for you are the seal of my apostleship in the Lord.

Here the reference to his conversion is fleeting but still significant. Once again a challenge to Paul's authority is implicit, in this case his discernment concerning the eating of meat offered to idols (cf. 1 Cor. 9:3). His defense recalls both his "seeing Jesus the Lord," the same root word used in 1 Corinthians 15, and his designation as apostle (9:1). In Paul's mind the two elements—encounter with Jesus as the risen Christ and vocation to apostleship—were intimately linked.

From these key texts (and other related ones in the Pauline corpus) let us attempt to summarize what can be known about Paul's conversion:

1. It is clear that prior to his conversion Paul was a committed and zealous Jew. In Gal. 1:13–14, Paul refers explicitly to his religious state prior to conversion: "I advanced in Judaism beyond many of my own age among my people so extremely zealous was I for the traditions of my fathers." This fact was not a cause of embarrassment for Paul. In Phil. 3:4–6 he boldly lists his Jewish pedigree: "circumcised on the eighth day, of the people of Israel, of the tribe of Benjamin, a Hebrew born of Hebrews; as to the law a Pharisee, as to zeal a persecutor of the church, as to righteousness under the law blameless." Similar texts where Paul proudly cites his Jewish heritage are found in 2 Cor. 2:22, and in Rom. 3:1–2; 9:1–5.

Paul's fidelity to Judaism drove him to the point of persecuting the Christian community. Paul's own statements (Gal. 1:13; Phil. 3:6, and probably 1 Cor. 15:8 where Paul's reference to being "monstrously born" presumably refers to the abrupt turnabout experienced at his conversion) and the descriptions in Acts (8:1–3; 9:1–30) indicate this.

It is not clear why Paul was so opposed to the Christian movement. Although its messianic claims may have been an irritant to other Jewish groups, there seems to have been relative tolerance on this point in pre-70 Judaism. Likewise the mere fact of dealing with Gentile proselytes could not have been startling to first-century Jews even if not fully endorsed. W. D. Davies plausibly suggests that Paul's extreme zeal for the law and his hostility to the Christian community may be symptomatic of his own personal struggle to resolve the sharp debate in Judaism about the fate of the Gentiles. As a Hellenistic Jew he could not be indifferent to the masses of his Gentile fellow citizens. As a Pharisaic Jew he maintained a strong conviction of Israel's elect status. Early Christianity's apparent relativizing of the law and its blunting of the sharp distinction between Jew and Gentile may have struck Paul as a dangerous slicing of the Gordian knot. As Davies notes, "his very extreme devotion to the Law may have been a shadow of the agony he felt for those without the Law; his human sympathies would be in conflict with his creed."[17]

2. Paul's inaugural experience was such that it caused a radical revision in his way of life and his world-view. From being a persecutor of the early Christian movement, Paul becomes one of its chief protagonists. From one "zealous for the traditions of our fathers," Paul becomes the "apostle to the Gentiles." From a blameless keeper of the law, he becomes one who completely discounts the law's value for the Gentiles.

Despite the radical nature of these changes, Krister Stendahl and other recent interpreters have objected to labeling Paul's experience as a "conversion." "Conversion," Stendahl contends, implies that Paul "changed his religion: the Jew became a Christian." Paul's own terminology is deemed preferable: "the persecutor was *called* and chosen to be apostle with a very special mission which focused on how the gospel should reach the Gentiles."[18]

Stendahl guards some important points under the banner of "call." Certainly Paul did not change from a "Jewish religion" to a "Christian religion." The organic relationship of early Christianity to Judaism makes such a discontinuity model anachronistic. Stendahl also is concerned not to impose on Paul the kind of religious experience typified in Lutheran tradition—that of the guilt-ridden sinner converting to a gracious God.[19]

These cautions aside it still seems preferable to use the term "conversion" to describe what happened to Paul. "Call" refers to Paul's commission to be an apostle, a commission received at the moment of his inaugural encounter. But this "call"—as substantial as it was for Paul's life—was not the only change that happened to Paul. He obviously experienced a radical revision in his perception of Jesus of Nazareth. And this in turn caused radical changes in Paul's understanding of God's plan of salvation, of the role of law, of the place of Israel and the Gentiles in salvation history—all issues we shall discuss below. "Call" seems too mild a word and too vocationally oriented to embrace all this. As a dominant image for Paul's inaugural experience it is, in fact, found only in Galatians and by implication in Rom. 1:5. "Conversion," despite the danger of misinterpretation, seems more adequate for describing the powerful turning point experienced by Paul in his encounter with the risen Christ.

3. The precise nature of Paul's experience is difficult to determine. In Gal. 1:12, 16 Paul uses the term *apocalupsai* ("revelation"), which allows room for a purely internal experience. But when we take into account 1 Cor. 9:1 and 15:8, where Paul uses the active and passive voices of the verb *horao* ("to see" and "to appear"), it seems that the apostle refers to a visionary experience similar in nature to the other resurrection-appearance stories related in 1 Cor. 15:5–7. As H. D. Betz suggests, we should not suppose that Paul saw any contradiction between the three references to his conversion experience cited above. "This would mean that Paul's experience was ecstatic in nature and that in the course of this ecstasy he had a vision."[20] The experience was of such a nature that it instructed Paul and "revealed" to him a new world-view. This we shall consider below.

4. The basic content of the revelation Paul received, or at least the immediate insight the experience provoked, can be stated as follows:

a. Paul realized that Jesus of Nazareth, who had been condemned to crucifixion, was, in fact, the Christ and had been raised from the dead and exalted as Son of God. His visionary experience drove home this astounding realization because the very subject of Paul's experience was Jesus himself: "Have I not seen Jesus our Lord?" (1 Cor. 9:1); "[God] was pleased to reveal his Son to me" (Gal. 1:16); the gospel Paul received "came through a revelation of Jesus Christ" (Gal. 1:12).

b. Paul also became convinced that through this Jesus, crucified and risen, God was offering salvation to all, both Jew and Gentile. This is the centerpoint of the "gospel" Paul defends in Galatians and which he attributes to his inaugural experience (Gal. 1:11-12). The same implication is found in 1 Cor. 15:8–11. Paul roots his apostolic authority and the success of his ministry to the

Gentiles in his inaugural experience. This apostolic role, in turn, confirms the authority of his gospel of salvation summarized in 1 Cor. 15:3-4.

c. Both of these previous points must have radically altered Paul's understanding of the course of history, even though no explicit link is made in the conversion texts themselves. That Jesus was the Christ and that salvation is offered to the Gentile world could only mean for a Jew that the final age had indeed begun.

d. Paul also became convinced that he himself was called, in the manner of the prophets of old, to be the herald of God's Word of salvation to the Gentiles. All three of the conversion texts cited above, but especially Galatians 1, show Paul directly links his call to preach to the Gentiles with his inaugural experience. For Paul's own lifestyle and self-image this conviction would have major repercussions. Most of the major epistles begin with Paul's self-identification as an "apostle" (cf. Rom. 1:1; 1 Cor. 1:1; 2 Cor 1:1; Col. 1:1; Gal. 1:1). Even though Paul insists on linking his conversion and his missionary call, it is not certain how clearly and how quickly he grasped all this at the moment of his conversion. The most energetic part of his missionary effort did not begin until several years after his Damascus experience. And, if the accounts in Acts are to be accepted, Jewish rebuffs to Paul's synagogue preaching also played a part in his decision to turn exclusively to the Gentile mission (Acts 13:46).[21] Nevertheless, Paul's repeated assertions that his call to preach to the Gentiles was part of his inaugural Christian experience leave little doubt that this was indeed the center of his revelation.

Having reflected on Paul's inaugural experience as "conversion," we are in a better position to trace the theological basis of his universal mission. What we know of Paul's conversion suggests at least what may *not* be the starting point even for his theological synthesis as a whole or his mission theology in particular (the two are practically synonymous, as we have indicated above).

First of all Paul did not embrace the Christian message and subsequently turn to the Gentiles because of dissatisfaction with Judaism and its law. This is one of the most significant advances in recent Pauline interpretation. It is anachronistic to portray Paul as tormented and guilt-ridden in his supposedly futile attempts to be faithful to the law. Krister Stendahl in a now classic essay, "Paul and the Introspective Conscience of the West," suggests that such an image is to impose on Paul the struggle of the individual conscience with guilt that became a focus of Western theology after Augustine, Luther, and the Reformation. As he notes: "the famous formula '*simul justus et pecatur*'—at the same time righteous and sinner—as a description of the status of the Christian may have some foundation in the Pauline writings, but this formula cannot be substantiated as the center of Paul's conscious attitude towards his personal sins. Apparently, Paul did not have the type of introspective conscience which such a formula seems to presuppose."[22]

Stendahl points out that texts such as Phil. 3:6 ("as to righteousness under the law blameless") reflect Paul's own assessment of his life in Judaism, and there is no hint of the law as a burden of guilt. The fact that Paul remained a zealous defender of the law up to the moment of his conversion also belies such an interpretation. The chief stumbling block to this new look at Paul is the apparently introspective text of Rom. 7:8: "I do not understand my own actions. For I do not do what I want, but I do the very thing I hate. . . . Wretched man that I am! Who will deliver me from this body of death?" Those who see Luther's struggle reflected in Paul consider this text as clinching proof that Paul found the burden of the law intolerable and found release only in the gift of salvation based on faith alone.

But such an autobiographical interpretation of Romans 7 seems in doubt. As Sanders notes: "The attempts to argue that Romans 7 shows the frustration which Paul felt during his lifetime as a practicing Jew have now mostly been given up; and one may rightly and safely maintain that the chapter cannot be understood in this way."[23] The larger context of Romans 7 indicates that Paul was not indicting the law but actually making a defense of its innate goodness (cf. Rom. 7:7,13). Paul goes on to show that the culprit is neither the law nor the self but sin, another type of "law," which makes the salvific potential of the law void. As Stendahl notes, the purpose of Paul's argument was not to accuse the law or the self but to acquit both by laying blame on the cosmic force of sin.[24]

The broader context of the epistle further suggests that Paul was not giving details of his own personal experience but describing the plight of non-Christian or pre-Christian humanity seen in retrospect from a conviction of salvation in Christ. In other words Paul was constructing a theological analysis of why the law was ultimately inadequate from the vantage point of now seeing that Christ is the only way. He was not describing the actual personal dynamic that led him to shed a tortured existence under the law to find relief in Christian faith.

Thus Paul does not seem to have been propelled to the point of conversion by an anguished analysis of the human condition. His life in Judaism seemed to have been successful and fully committed. We do not know exactly what Paul thought about the situation of the Gentiles. As we shall note later, his references to pagan culpability in not knowing God and the "idolatry" and other vices resulting from this ignorance were stock themes of Jewish reflections on the Gentiles. There is little indication, however, that Paul's concern for the fate of the Gentiles nudged him in the direction of Christianity. Paul, after all, persecuted the Christians and we can presume that he did not agree with their openness to non-Jews. For Paul, as for many Jews of his day, conversion to Judaism would have seemed an adequate solution to the Gentile problem. We have no evidence that Paul abandoned his traditional faith in a tortured pursuit of a more universalist perspective.

In other words, the starting point and catalyst for Paul's mission theology was not his pre-Christian experience—neither a supposed guilt about the law nor perplexity with the fate of non-Jews. Paul's own account of his conversion suggests that the catalyst came from "outside," from a religious experience that gave a startling insight into the nature of the God of Israel and his Christ. This experience convinced Paul that the God of Israel was indeed a God intent on the salvation of all humanity through the person of Jesus Christ and *therefore* apart from the law. Consequently, God was "impartial" or, better, *gracious* to Jews and Gentiles alike.

Thus, in Sanders's phrase, Paul works out his mission theology not from plight to solution but from solution to plight.[25] As Leander Keck states: "[Paul's] . . . encounter with Christ compelled him to rethink everything from the ground up. . . . Paul did not work out his theology as a solution to a set of problems with which he had been wrestling unsuccessfully; rather, it was in light of the universal salvation wrought by cross/resurrection that he discerned the real character of the human problem."[26]

We should note in advance that this does not mean that Paul's starting point is purely dogmatic. Discounting subjective guilt or an existential assessment of the human condition as catalysts for Paul's theology does not mean that Paul should be reduced to a theological mathematician who dispassionately glimpses a universal principle and goes on to make a series of corollaries from this abstract starting point. His initial insight about the universal character of salvation in Christ flows from a religious experience, an encounter with Christ that Paul considered an act of God ("revealed his Son to me"). As we shall note below, Paul's further conclusions about the limits of the law (especially in regard to Gentiles) and the transforming power of salvation in Christ were all grounded in experience—his own and those of his Gentile converts.

Thus Paul's mission theology was not an abstract construct dangling from a universal principle, but an analysis of reality triggered by an initial experience that gave Paul a new world-view. We may say, therefore, that the proper starting point and dominant motif of Pauline theology is soteriological. God offers salvation to all through the death-resurrection of Jesus Christ. Most of Paul's theological reflection dealt with the dynamics of that redemptive process and its implications for human existence in Christ.

THE THEOLOGICAL FOUNDATIONS OF PAUL'S MISSION

From this soteriological starting point let us now trace the main points in Paul's mission theology. From his conversion experience Paul was convinced that the God of Israel exercises his sovereignty over all creation and all people in freely choosing to call all to salvation through Jesus Christ. This was the cornerstone of his mission theology.

"Or is God the God of Jews only? Is he not the God of Gentiles also? Yes, of Gentiles also since God is one" (Rom. 3:29–30). This dramatic declaration of God's Lordship or sovereignty over *all* peoples was not an invention of the Christian Paul. Such themes as the pilgrimage of the nations to Zion and the culpability of the Gentiles for not knowing God show that a major assumption of developed Jewish thought was the universal sovereignty of God, even though, as we have seen in our study of the Old Testament, the extent and the means by which the nations would relate to that sovereignty were controverted. What does become new, and ultimately revolutionary, for Paul is the conviction that the God of

Israel exercises his sovereignty by directly choosing and calling all—Jew and Gentile—to salvation *in Jesus Christ*. The immediacy, scope, and means of that call became the new elements in Paul's religious vision.

This insight glows in numerous Pauline passages. Let us consider a few. Since salvation of both Jew and Gentile is a major concern of the letter to the Romans, it is not surprising that some of Paul's most penetrating statements on this issue are found here. In Rom. 1:16–17 Paul succinctly defines his gospel (a gospel ultimately revealed in his conversion experience): "For I am not ashamed of the gospel; it is the power of God for salvation for everyone who has faith, to the Jew first and also to the Greek." The qualifier "the Jew *first*" reflects Paul's struggle with the Israel question, which will erupt in chapters 9 to 11. It is not a dilution of his basic conviction about the disclosure of God's power to save for all who believe. Rather, the "first" shows that Paul could not fully integrate his basic insight into God's sovereignty with his Jewish heritage.[27]

Rom. 3:21–30 is another key text. Having reviewed the sinful plight of both Jew and Gentile in chapters 1–3 (again in the light of his conviction about the solution, cf. above) Paul states his central conviction: "But now the righteousness of God has been manifested apart from law, although the law and the prophets bear witness to it, the righteousness of God through faith in Jesus Christ for all who believe. For there is no distinction; since all have sinned and fall short of the glory of God, they are justified by his grace as a gift, through the redemption which is in Christ Jesus" (3:21–24).

This highly concentrated passage caps Paul's discussion in the first two and one-half chapters of his letter. Both Gentile and Jew are under the power of sin (3:9), an insight that Paul arrives at after his conversion experience. Release from this plight is a gift, a free manifestation of God's "righteousness." Few Pauline terms have triggered such enormous discussion as that of "righteousness" (*dikaiosune*), due in large part to the importance of the formula "justified by faith alone" in the Reformation controversies. For our purposes we can simply note that in this instance Paul uses the term "righteousness" to describe a quality of God, revealed in the very act of saving sinful humanity. As Fitzmyer states, "this term refers to his [God's] salvific uprightness, a quality by which he manifests his bounty and fidelity in acquitting and vindicating his people."[28]

The "justice" of God, or his "righteousness," is not an abstract or juridic term but describes God in relationship to humanity, a relationship that draws forth his compassion on behalf of all. Keck affirms this key Pauline insight by noting Rom. 4:5 where God is called the one "who justifies the ungodly," or in 4:17 the God "who gives life to the dead and calls into existence the things that do not exist."[29]

In Rom. 3:21–24, then, Paul states that the God who "justifies the ungodly" has chosen to do so for Jew and Gentile alike—*all*, in fact, are ungodly and *all* are called to experience God's compassionate justice in Christ Jesus. This is what Paul means by saying God is "impartial" (Rom. 3:11). It is striking how, despite differences in style and context, this image of God is close to the image of God at the heart of Jesus' own experience and teaching—an image that ultimately vindicates Jesus' own boundary-breaking ministry.

Paul repeatedly uses phrases that reveal that his image of God is a God who calls to salvation. In 1 Thessalonians he notes: "This is the will of God, your sanctification" (4:3). The destiny of Christians is not for wrath but for salvation (1 Thess. 5:9). The Christians are "called to be saints together with all those who in every place call on the name of our Lord Jesus Christ, both their Lord and ours" (1 Cor. 1:2).

The theme of "recognizing God," which Paul borrows from Jewish missionary preaching, conveys to a Gentile audience the same sense of God's initiative and call.[30] Gal. 4:8–9 is a clear example: "Formerly, when you did not know God, you were in bondage to beings that by nature are no gods; but now that you have come to know God, or rather *to be known by God*, how can you turn back again to the weak and beggarly elemental spirits, whose slaves you want to be once more?" "Knowledge" in this instance has the sense of total commitment to God in distinction to the use of the term in Rom. 1:21, where the Gentiles are said to have "known" God but not to honor him. "To be known by God," conversely, implies the kind of saving manifestation we are suggesting is the basis of Pauline missionary theology.

Undoubtedly Paul's conversion experience gave him a startling insight into God's urgent will to save. God as savior was, of course, not a strange notion for an exodus people. What would be startling for Paul was the fact that this saving attempt was not concentrated on Israel alone (even including Gentiles who would join Israel) but on *all*, Jew and Greek alike. Perhaps even more challenging for Paul, the persecutor of the Christians, was the disclosure that this salvific will was being exercised *through Jesus*.

This brings us to another foundation stone in Paul's mission theology: his perception of Christ. His conversion experience radically revised his understanding of Jesus. Paul had presumably dismissed Jesus as an impostor. He perceived the movement begun by Jesus and his followers as a threat to Judaism. Now this impostor, "this enemy," was revealed to him as God's Son, as the Messiah, as the instrument through which God's salvation would be offered to all people! No wonder Paul speaks of being "seized" by Jesus (Phil. 3:12).

The impact of Christ is a massive element of Paul's mission theology. We touch a conviction so basic to Paul's thought and so multiple in its expression that it is perceptible in practically every paragraph of his correspondence. Our purpose here cannot be to attempt a comprehensive statement of Pauline Christology. We can, however, state some basic notions that have particular significance for Paul's mission theology.

a. Key to Paul's entire vision was his conviction about the identity of Jesus as the exalted Messiah. As some have suggested, one of the reasons Paul was relatively uninterested in details of Jesus' life is the fact that for Paul the most important thing was not what Jesus did but who he was.[31] Paul, who shared in Israel's expectation of a coming Messiah, became convinced that Jesus was the one. As the leading sentences of Romans trumpet: ". . . the gospel concerning his Son, who was descended from David according to the flesh and designated Son of God in power according to the Spirit of holiness by his resurrection from the dead, Jesus Christ our Lord" (Rom.1:3-4). Thus Jesus of Nazareth was the historic personage through whom God's definitive plan of salvation would be effected. This conviction held enormous consequences for Paul's view of history and the Gentile's role within it.

b. Equally fundamental and equally shattering for Paul's world-view was the conviction that Jesus the Christ exercised his messianic function preeminently through his death and resurrection. Nothing in Jewish tradition had prepared Paul for this paradoxical fact. Only subsequently could Christian reflection coax harmony between the sufferings of Jesus and the Hebrew Scriptures. The center of Paul's entire theological synthesis—an explosive center that challenged all assumptions—was that through the crucified death of Jesus the Jew and in his subsequent exaltation through resurrection, all humanity was offered the possibility of moving from death to life, from sin to God.

Paul unequivocally states that this is the central theme of his "gospel": "For the word of the cross is folly to those who are perishing, but to us who are being saved it is the power of God. . . . we preach Christ crucified, a stumbling block to Jews and folly to Gentiles, but to those who are called, both Jews and Greeks, Christ the power of God and the wisdom of God" (cf. 1 Cor. 1:18, 23-24). Therefore the death-resurrection is the most intense act of Jesus' messianic misssion; it is the ultimate revelation of God's free gift of salvation to all.

Paul employs a variety of sacrificial and atonement language to describe the salvific effect of Jesus' death. In another definition of his "gospel" Paul appeals to traditional material (clearly showing that even the central theme of his message was not created by him):

> Now I would remind you, brethren, in what terms I preached to you the gospel, which you received, in which you stand, by which you are saved, if you hold it fast—unless you believed in vain. For I have delivered to you as of first importance what I also received, that Christ died for our sins in accordance with the scriptures, that he was buried, that he was raised on the third day in accordance with the scriptures, and that he appeared to Cephas and then to the twelve [1 Cor. 15:1-5].

A raft of designations such as "for us," "for sin," "for our justification," "to make us free" (from law and sin) are applied to Jesus' death throughout the Pauline letters.[32]

Paul was also convinced that Jesus' redemptive mission was coextensive with God's free gift of salvation; the saving death of Jesus is for *all*, Jews and Gentiles alike. This is Paul's point in Rom. 3:21-24—there is "no distinction," all are justified, made right with God, "through the redemption which is in Christ Jesus." The universality of Jesus' mission was the foundation of Paul's most sweeping "no distinction" texts: "For there is no distinction between Jew and

Greek; the same Lord is Lord of all and bestows his riches upon all who call upon him" (Rom. 10:12); "For in Christ Jesus you are all sons of God through faith. For as many of you as were baptized into Christ have put on Christ. There is neither Jew nor Greek, there is neither slave nor free, there is neither male nor female; for you are all one in Christ Jesus" (Gal. 3:16-18).[33]

Thus God's nature as "rectifier of the ungodly" (Rom. 4:5) was first demonstrated in his transformation of Jesus from one who died on the cross—and thereby was declared "cursed," totally weak, under the law (cf. Deut. 21:23; Gal. 3:13)—into a source of "blessing," a means of salvation to all who believe in him. Keck's conclusion on this point deserves to be quoted in full:

> Because Jesus was executed as one accursed by the law, the resurrection of precisely this Jesus reveals that God's verdict on him cannot be inferred from the Cross. Were that the case, God would indeed rectify the godly who put him there in the name of the law, and in the name of law and order. But Jesus' resurrection reveals God's freedom and otherness. Moreover, unless God's resurrecting Jesus was arbitrary (unthinkable to Paul), the resurrection must reveal God's fidelity to Jesus and to himself; that is, it revealed God's integrity over against what was presumed to be his integrity. The fact that the Christ-event occurred in a sinful world shows Paul that God is free to rectify the world and persons in it, that this rectification does not depend on human readiness, achieved goodness, or self wrought rectitude but solely on God's grace. Whoever trusts this God is therefore not only rightly related to God (rectified) but must realign every conception of God and of the human condition according to this event.[34]

A tantalizing parallel to the Jesus tradition can again be noted. Jesus' own sense of God's compassion and mercy pushed his ministry of salvation beyond the boundaries expected by his contemporaries. He ministered to outcast Jews and responded favorably to individual Gentiles. Paul senses this same universal scope to Jesus' mission, but for Paul this activity is best illustrated not by Jesus' historical ministry but by the ultimate expression of his ministry in death-resurrection. In a sense, Paul uses death-resurrection as the operative symbol of Jesus' entire existence. That existence—for both the Jesus tradition and Paul—was God's act of salvation for *all*.

c. In Paul's theology (and in all New Testament tradition), the salvation offered by God through Jesus was not "universal" in the sense that it makes human response inconsequential. Paul fuses "qualifiers" onto his statements about salvation such as to those "who believe," those "who are in Christ," those "called." Therefore we must consider another dimension of Paul's soteriology in order to do justice to his mission theology. This is what Sanders calls "participatory soteriology."[35]

To appreciate this aspect of Paul we must keep in mind the world-view that Paul seems to have had, a world-view quite different from our own. As a number of recent interpreters of Paul have stressed, the apostle conceived human existence "wholistically" or in terms of "structures," "spheres of influence." This is especially true in Paul's evaluation of moral existence. A person is either ruled by the "flesh" or "by the Spirit"; one is either under the "Lordship of Christ" or "a slave to sin," the believer is "in Christ," "belonging to him," "a member of his body."

As Keck notes: "Each of these polarities is a structure of existence in which one participates, in which one's existence is defined because the participant is, by definition, 'open' to and governed by the structure.'"[36] The redemptive process consists in being freed to move from one sphere or structure of existence to another. The redeemed person is given the power to move from the sphere of "sin" or "law" or "flesh" to the sphere of "life," "Christ," "Spirit." Paul uses a variety of such "transfer terms," as Sanders calls them. Paul conceives of this change of structure or spheres quite realistically. They effect the very nature of a person's existence.

The way Paul deals with the problem of fornication in 1 Corinthians 6 is a revealing example. Paul's argument against frequenting a prostitute is not on the basis of abstract principles. Rather, he reminds the Corinthians of their new existence under the Lordship of Christ: "Do you not know that your bodies are members of Christ?" (1 Cor. 6:15). His point is not simply that therefore such behavior is inappropriate. Rather, the new structure of their existence was so real that joining their own bodies (now "in Christ") to that of a prostitute would be tantamount to joining Christ's own body to that of the prostitute.

> Shall I therefore take the members of Christ and make them members of a prostitute? Never! Do you know that he who joins himself to a prostitute becomes one body with her? For, as it is written, "The two shall become one." But he who is united to the Lord becomes one spirit with him [1Cor. 6:15–18].

The important point of all this for the mission question is that Paul believed that those who experience the universal gift of salvation offered through Christ are the ones who respond to the gospel with faith. This conviction, which in a sense "limits" the scope of salvation, had significant consequences for Paul's reassessment of both Jew and Gentile. Because he was convinced—through his own conversion experience and subsequent reflection—that salvation was being definitively offered by God to everyone who responded by faith in Christ, then Paul realized it was *not* definitively offered through the *law*. By the same token, the Gentiles who, from a Jewish perspective, had evidently not experienced salvation could achieve salvation only through faith in Jesus and not by any other means (including the law).

Here again is Paul's "solution-plight" process. His conviction that Christ—and Christ alone—is God's means for salvation of all led Paul to the insight that prior to and apart from Christ everyone was basically in the same situation. He was convinced of a special role for Israel and its law, as we shall note, but not on this basic level. To put it in Paul's "participation" language: before Christ made it possible for all who respond to be under his Lordship (that is, to be saved, to be "in Christ," to live by the Spirit, etc.), *everyone*—Jew and Greek—was under a different "lordship" (of sin, of the law, of the flesh, of false gods, etc.). This is the deeper logic of Paul's fundamental argument in Romans 1–3 and practically the whole of Galatians. As Paul firmly states to the Jewish members of the Roman community: "What then? Are we Jews any better off? No, not at all; for I have already charged that all men, both Jews and Greeks, are under the power of sin" (Rom. 3:9). Conversely all—Jew and Greek—are justified through faith in Jesus Christ (cf. Rom. 3:21–26; Gal. 2:15–16; 3:15–19).

PAUL'S VIEW OF HISTORY, OF LAW, AND OF ISRAEL

The basic convictions of Paul that we have sketched above form the foundation of his mission theology. Paul was convinced that (1) God had freely chosen to offer his gift of salvation to all; (2) that gift was offered through Jesus of Nazareth, God's Messiah; (3) Jesus' messianic work was accomplished essentially through his death and resurrection for all; (4) access to salvation was open to those who respond in faith to Christ, thus effecting with him the transfer from death to life. These profound and wide-ranging convictions had enormous consequences for the rest of Paul's theological synthesis. We can note here some that have special significance for the mission question.

History

First, Paul's conviction that Jesus was the Messiah would inevitably cause a reshaping of Paul's view of history. The awaited messianic age had already begun. Paul's awed realization of this breaks out in many passages, as, for example, 2 Cor. 6:2: "Behold, now is the acceptable time; behold, now is the day of salvation." And 2 Cor. 5:17: "If anyone is in Christ, he is a new creation; the old has passed away, behold, the new has come." God's plan of salvation was a "mystery" kept hidden until this moment of grace but now broken open in the arena of human history (cf. Rom. 16:25–26; 1 Cor. 2:7). As we noted above, Paul's scheme of history leaves room for a definitive moment of salvation still in the future. The alien powers of the universe are being dissolved as Christ establishes his Lordship. At the appointed future moment, God will be "everything to everyone" (cf. 1 Cor. 15:20–28).

This revelation of Paul's historical consciousness had direct impact on his mission theology. It must have triggered for Paul the Jewish tradition that expected the fate of the Gentiles to be decided in the messianic age. As we discussed in an earlier chapter, the Gentiles were expected to come in pilgrimage to Zion at the end-time (cf. chap. 6, above.) Although Paul's insight into the universal scope of the gospel radicalized his notion of how the Gentiles fit into the messianic age (that is, on their own right, not by coming to Zion), his belief that the messianic age had dawned could only have fortified his call to be apostle to the Gentiles. And, as we shall consider below, the eschatological theme of the pilgrimage of the

Gentiles may also have influenced Paul's strategy in dealing with Israel. A partial motivation (but not the ultimate justification) for Paul's zeal among the Gentiles was to win over enough of them to convince Israel that the messianic era had indeed dawned, and so to win them (Israel) for Christ.

Second, this historical consciousness was coupled with another significant element in Paul's experience: his awareness that the Gentile Christians were participating in the gifts of the Spirit. Jewish tradition expected the final age to be an age of the Spirit; and the conviction that the community possessed the power and authority of the Spirit was a hallmark of early Christianity. What makes this phenomenon important is that not only would Paul be led to expect the eschatological gift of the Spirit to be present among his Christian communities (an expectation nourished by his Jewish heritage and by his contact with early Christian tradition) but his actual witness of this experience among the Gentile converts must have been a powerful affirmation of Paul's entire theological construct.

There are abundant texts in Paul where he speaks either of his own experience of the Spirit or of such experiences among his Christians.[37] This evidence of the Spirit's active presence guaranteed for Paul that the messianic age had dawned. God indeed was working out the salvation of the Gentiles and, therefore, Paul's own call to preach to the Gentiles was not an illusion. This confirmatory role of Christian experience is evident in Gal. 3:1–5:

> O foolish Galatians! Who has bewitched you, before whose eyes Jesus Christ was publicly portrayed as crucified? Let me ask you only this: did you receive the Spirit by works of the Law or by hearing with faith? Are you foolish? Having begun with the Spirit, are you now ending with the flesh? Did you experience so many things in vain?—if it really is in vain. Does he who supplies the Spirit to you and works miracles among you do so by works of the law, or by hearing with faith?

Paul, it should be said again, was not a speculative theologian but a pastoral theologian, drawing the convictions of his theology from incisive thought and genuine religious experience. Paul's belief in Jesus Christ formed his historical consciousness and gave him an overall vision of humanity's destiny. That vision, in turn, nourished his understanding of his own ministry as apostle to the Gentiles.

The Law

A second great consequence of Paul's Christian faith was his reassessment of the function of the Jewish law. This, in turn, modified his view of the place of Jew and Gentile in salvation history, a view that had direct impact on his missionary vocation. Because Paul was convinced that God's salvation came only and definitively through faith in Jesus Christ, it could not come through the law. The law was not worthless in Paul's view (Rom. 7:12,16). It was instructive; it served as a "custodian," or "tutor," keeping the child Israel in line until the real source of life came along (Gal. 3:23–29). Even the Gentiles had access to the informative power of the law if they would have followed the good instincts of their conscience (cf. Rom. 2:12–14). But, in any case, the law was not a means of salvation for anyone.

This insight ultimately made Paul's approach to the Gentiles substantially different from that of Jewish proselytizing. Salvation for a Gentile did not mean entry into Israel. It could not mean this because, for Paul, that would be an effective denial of the real way of salvation, faith in Jesus Christ apart from the law. This is why he so vehemently fights for his "gospel" against the Galatians, who were enticed by the law. Presumably Paul would have no objection to Jewish Christians maintaining practices of the law (as he himself did). But Paul seemed to fear that for a Gentile to take up the practice of the law would cloud an absolutely central point of the gospel: salvation comes to all through Christ alone. Therefore Paul was intransigent on this issue.

Once again it should be stressed that Paul's convictions about this were not forged by purely abstract principles. Neither in his own case nor for his converts had a decisive encounter with God's saving action taken place through the law. It was a "revelation of God's Son" that "seized" Paul. And he can remind his Gentile converts of their own experience: "Let me ask you only this: Did you receive the Spirit by works of the law, or by hearing with faith?" (Gal. 3:2).

One of Paul's principal theoretical supports for this devaluation of the law's salvific function was the figure of Abraham. As he argues in Gal. 3:7–29 and in Rom. 4:1–25, Abraham was a prototype of the Christian because Abraham was saved prior to and apart from the law on the basis of his faith. In this way Abraham earned his title "Father of many nations" (cf. Rom. 4:18, citing Genesis 12 and 15). The Christians were his promised descendants because, like Abraham, they too were saved by faith apart from the law.

Israel

A third major consequence of Paul's theological vision—and one with significant impact on his mission—was the question of Israel. Perhaps this more than any other question reveals the dynamic and passionate nature of Paul's theology. This question above all could not be a cool topic for Paul (cf. Rom. 9:1–5). His love for his Jewish traditions and his absolute commitment to the gospel seemed, on certain levels, to hit head-on.

Paul, for example, had to revise his notion of "election." Election could no longer mean simply the designation of a specific people (although Israel's special election was not erased). Now "election" referred to the dialectic between God's free offer of grace and a person's active response to that offer in faith. It is the "children of the promise" rather than the "children of the flesh" who are blessed by God's call (Rom. 9:8). It is those who are "justified by faith in Christ" who are the chosen ones (Rom. 8:28–30). As Ferdinand Hahn notes, Paul once again opts for the "sovereign freedom of God" (cf. Rom. 9:15-16). Election is manifested not by membership in a chosen people but "in the believing acceptance of the Christ event."[38]

The Christian community made up of Jew and Gentile was now a community of "elect" people. This left an opening for Paul to redefine the very notion of "Israel," symbolizing it as he seems to do in Gal. 6:16 by calling the Christians, "Israel of God." Such a concept allowed the Gentiles to be equal partners with Jews in the eschatological people of God and opened the way for appropriating the promises of the Hebrew Scriptures to the church.

However, it is typical of Paul that he did not in fact press this idea to its logical limits. Such logic would ultimately conclude that the historical Israel, the Jews as a people, would have no special role in salvation history. This Paul could not bring himself to say. Although he clearly believed that the Gentile mission was valid and that Gentile access to salvation apart from the law was central to the very meaning of the gospel, he still maintained that Israel itself had a unique place in God's plan.

Paul wrestles with this question in Romans 9-11. These chapters have an integral place in the epistle and reflect the dialectical nature of Paul's thought, as throughout the letter he views the question of salvation in relationship to both Jews and Gentiles. In chapters 9-11 that dialectic becomes more intense. Paul cannot block out the fact that the Gentiles are not only called but are, in fact, responding to the gospel. An equally compelling fact was that the people who had received God's promises of salvation—the Jews—were on the whole not responding.

Paul's struggle with this dilemma was complex and never entirely resolved. But from a mission standpoint some things are clear. Israel's rejection of the gospel had provided the opportunity (but not the justification) for the mission to be opened to the Gentiles (Rom. 11:11). But Israel itself is not out of the picture. Paul remained convinced that God's initial call to his people remained in force (cf. Rom. 9:4-5; 11:1,29). They may appear as "enemies of God" (11:28), as "hard of heart" (11:25), in their refusal to believe but, Paul insists, this is part of God's great plan, which manages to leave room for the Gentile mission (11:25) *and* to prepare for the grand finale when all—both Gentile and Jew—would be saved. Therefore Paul concludes: "the gifts and the call of God (on behalf of Israel) are irrevocable" (Rom. 11:29).

This promise itself gives additional scope to the Gentile mission. By accepting the gift of salvation in faith, the Gentiles might convince Israel that the final age of salvation has begun and lead them, too, to respond to the gospel. Provoking this holy "jealousy" was one of Paul's wider goals in his missionary zeal: "Inasmuch then as I am an apostle to the Gentiles, I magnify my ministry in order to make my fellow Jews jealous, and thus save some of them. For if their rejection means the reconciliation of the world, what will their acceptance mean but life from the dead?" (Rom. 11:13-15; cf. also 11:25-26, 30-31).

Paul's collection efforts may have been connected to this grand strategy.[39] The donation to the "poor" of Jerusalem became a concrete manifestation of Paul's service in God's plan. The success of the Gentile mission—symbolized in the collection—was an acceptable offering to God of Paul's "priestly service" (cf. Rom. 15:16). This "service" ultimately contributes to the grand drama of Jew and Gentile both experiencing God's mercy (Rom. 11:30-32).

Paul's struggle with the Israel question reveals again that his missionary efforts flow from the very center of his Christian vision. The mission is not mere recruitment. It expresses the very meaning of the gospel as God's precious call to salvation. And its strategy is bound up with the mysterious providence of God's work in history.

PAUL'S COMPULSION TO PREACH

All the elements of Paul's theology fused together to produce the explosive energy of his missionary apostolate. Once Paul became convinced that God was offering salvation to all people through the death and resurrection of Jesus, and that this message was his to proclaim, then the apostle felt a driving compulsion to preach.

This is apparent in those texts where Paul speaks most directly about his missionary commission. In 2 Cor. 5:16-20, for example, he alludes to the transformation his own estimation of Christ had undergone. That conversion experience had transformed his view of history and made him aware of his vocation to be an "ambassador for Christ" and a minister of "reconciliation":

From now on, therefore, we regard no one from a human point of view; even though we once regarded Christ from a human point of view, we regard him thus no longer. Therefore, if any one is in Christ, he is a new creation; the old has passed away, behold the new has come. All this is from God, who through Christ reconciled us to himself and gave us the ministry of reconciliation; that is, God was in Christ reconciling the world to himself, not counting their trespasses against them, and entrusting to us the message of reconciliation. So we are ambassadors for Christ, God making his appeal through us.

The awareness of God's unlimited graciousness broke down the boundaries between Jew and Greek. But now this message had to be announced so that all people could "call upon the name of the Lord" and experience the good news:

For there is no distinction between Jew and Greek. The same Lord is Lord of all and bestows his riches upon all who call upon him. For, "every one who calls upon the name of the Lord will be saved." But how are men to call upon him in whom they have not believed? And how are they to believe in him of whom they have never heard? And how are they to hear without a preacher? And how can men preach unless they are sent? As it is written, "How beautiful are the feet of those who preach good news!" [Rom. 10:12-15].

In Rom. 15:15–21, one of Paul's most extensive reflections on his mission strategy, the convergence of elements is again evident:

> But on some points I have written to you very boldly by way of reminder because of the grace given me by God to be a minister of Christ Jesus to the Gentiles in the priestly service of the gospel of God, so that the offering of the Gentiles may be acceptable, sanctified by the Holy Spirit. In Christ Jesus, then, I have reason to be proud of my work for God. For I will not venture to speak of anything except what Christ has wrought through me to win obedience from the Gentiles, by word and deed, by the power of signs and wonders, by the power of the Holy Spirit, so that from Jerusalem and as far round as Illyricum I have fully preached the gospel of Christ, thus making it my ambition to preach the gospel, not where Christ has already been named, lest I build on another man's foundation, but as it is written, "They shall see who have never been told of him, and they shall understand who have never heard of him."

Paul's ministry is a "grace" and a "priestly service." His mission to the Gentiles is an offering to God, one that will ultimately bring around Israel itself and so complete the mystery of salvation. His work will carry him around the rim of the Mediterranean world, not building on the foundations of another because the time is short and the task urgent.

The combination of experience and conviction expressed so forcefully in these passages left Paul with no real choice. He was compelled to preach: "Necessity is laid upon me. Woe to me if I do not preach the gospel! For if I do this of my own will, I have a reward; but if not of my own will, I am entrusted with a commission" (1 Cor. 9:16–17). From the moment of his encounter with the risen Christ, Paul of Tarsus' sense of mission was nothing less than the expression of his image of God, his sense of history, and his vision of human destiny.

THE STRATEGY AND CONTENT OF PAUL'S MISSION

Some further light might be shed on Paul's mission theology by considering briefly the scope of his mission activity. Once again our primary source must be the fragmentary references in Paul's own epistles rather than the full narrative of Luke in Acts. Our purpose is not to reconstruct a life of Paul but to examine aspects of his missionary career that further illustrate his theology.

Paul's Strategy

There is no doubt that Paul's conversion experience ultimately set the course for the remainder of his life. His mission shaped the aspirations and the very style of his life (cf. 1 Cor. 9:16–23). Although it may have taken Paul himself several years fully to comprehend the scope of his call, by the time of his major missionary work he seemed to be driven by a missionary goal as bold as his convictions. As we have discussed above, Paul was intent on "bringing in" the Gentiles, thereby to provoke Israel itself to repentance and so to precipitate the final act in the drama of salvation.

That awesome goal is reflected in the identifying labels Paul did not hesitate to apply to his person and his ministry. He relates his own call to the prophetic call of Isaiah (Gal. 1:15; Rom. 1:1; cf. Isa. 49:1) and Jeremiah (Jer. 1:5; cf. Gal. 1:15). He identifies his ministry as a "priestly act," offering the Gentiles to God as "an acceptable sacrifice sanctified by the Holy Spirit" (Rom. 15:16).[40] In another bold liturgical image, Paul conceived of his preaching as a means whereby God used him to "spread the fragrance of the knowledge of him everywhere." He is "the aroma of Christ to God among those who are being saved . . ." (2 Cor. 2:14–15). The apostle claims to be an "ambassador for Christ," "God making his appeal through us" (1 Cor. 5:20). His is the "ministry of a new covenant," appointed such by God (2 Cor. 3:6). He is God's "servant" through whom people come to believe (1 Cor. 3:5); he is God's "fellow worker" (1 Cor. 1:9). Above all, he clings to his most frequent identifying label as "apostle," or more specifically "apostle to the Gentiles" (Rom. 11:13)

These ambitious titles coexist with Paul's frank admission of weaknesses, weaknesses that became apparent in the carrying out of his apostolic vocation. But at no moment in his writing did Paul hesitate about the nature of the world-wide and definitive ministry to which his apostolic call had brought him.

The range of that ministry is implicitly plotted in Romans 15, a text that may have been among the last from Paul's hand. Paul sums up his entire ministry in Rom. 15:15–33. He reveals his inaugural call "to be a minister of Christ Jesus to the Gentiles" (15:16), "my work for God" (15:17). This mission Paul had pursued single-mindedly "by word and deed, by the power of signs and wonders, by the power of the Holy Spirit" (15:18–19). Therefore by Paul's own testimony his proclamation was not limited to preaching but included "healings and other signs." By the time he writes to the Romans, this ministry had already taken him "from Jerusalem and as far around as Illyricum." Thus Paul was conscious of having evangelized "from Jerusalem," the heart of Judaism and the base of the Jewish Christian community, to the western shore of Greece deep into Gentile territory.

Given the context of his letter, it seems probable that Paul intended to do more than review his itinerary. He writes to the *Roman* Christians, a community he himself had not evangelized but one that Paul is anxious to visit anyway, contrary to his usual custom (cf. Rom. 15:20–21). Paul wanted to visit them now that he had completed his work in the region of Asia Minor and Greece (15:23). After his visit to Jerusalem with the collection, Paul would pass through Rome on his way to Spain (15:24,28). All of this suggests that Paul considered his visit to Rome a significant milestone in his eschatological mission. The grand themes of Romans—salvation for both Jew and Gentile—provided the theological backdrop for the very scope of Paul's missionary apostolate. His own call thrust him toward the Gentiles—from Greece through the Roman capital and on to Spain. As he tells the Corinthians, "our hope is that as your faith increases, our field among you may be greatly enlarged, so that we may preach the gospel in lands beyond you . . ." (2 Cor. 10:15-16). The Gentile mission had eschatological implications for Israel itself. Therefore Paul must first take his collection from the Gentile churches to Jerusalem. He was always aware that his starting point to the Gentiles remained "from Jerusalem"(cf. Rom. 15:22-29).

The pace of Paul's ministry reflected this "big picture." As Haas notes, Paul did not attempt to Christianize the Gentile world totally.[41] He apparently focused on provincial centers that had not yet been evangelized, leaving to the communities themselves and perhaps to other apostolic workers the task of dealing with their non-Christian neighbors. He himself pressed on with his urgent task of preaching the gospel to those who had not yet heard it (Rom. 10:14).

Thus the scope and pace of Paul's mission matched his theological vision. Because Paul was convinced that God was offering salvation to all *now* and because he was called to proclaim that message of salvation to the Gentiles, he devoted his life's energy to a mobile ministry of preaching that swept across the Gentile world, which, for Paul the Hellenistic Jew, meant the Greco-Roman world. Thus he hoped to move from Jerusalem around to Illyricum, on to Rome, and beyond to Spain. Because that mission to the Gentiles had the added movitation of "provoking the Jews to jealousy," and thus initiating the final chapter of salvation history, Paul's mission took on a note of urgency. He did not want to duplicate what other missionaries had already done, as he moved on a broad scale through provincial centers. And that mission was never pursued in isolation from its roots in Judaism. Paul's collection and his efforts to validate his ministry with the Jerusalem community were symptoms of this concern.

The scale and urgency of his goal also seemed to contribute to the "apostolic anxiety" Paul experienced on behalf of his convert communities. These communities were for Paul concrete evidence of fidelity to his missionary call. "Are you not my workmanship in the Lord? If to others I am not an apostle, at least I am to you; for you are the seal of my apostleship in the Lord" (1 Cor. 9:1-2). They were the gifts he would bring forward at the final moment of salvation, when the risen Lord would appear in glory. "For what is our hope or joy or crown of boasting before our Lord Jesus at his coming? Is it not you?" (1 Thess. 2:19). Paul repeatedly prayed for his communities' fidelity and perseverance until the final day "so that . . . I may be proud that I did not run in vain or labor in vain" (Phil. 2:14).[42] This "anxiety" for the perseverance of the local church seemed to head the list of sufferings Paul endured as an apostle: "And, apart from other things, there is the daily pressure upon me of my anxiety for all the churches" (2 Cor. 11:28).

Paul's concern for the health of the local churches was not a matter of merely keeping his "catch" intact until the final weigh-in. Rather, the formation of these communities among the Gentiles was itself a dimension of the end-time. The "church," as gatherings of elect believers, demonstrated that *"now* is the day of salvation" (2 Cor. 6:2). Their life in Christ was unassailable evidence that God was offering salvation to all through the death and resurrection of Jesus Christ.

For Paul, therefore, the continued fidelity of his Gentile communities was a living witness to the eschatological vision he had discovered in Christ. Paul hoped that this "testimony" would penetrate the blindness of Israel and thus pull aside the veil shrouding the glorious finale of God's salvation plan.

For this reason, despite his protest against duplicating others' missionary efforts and his urge to press on to new territory (Rom. 15:20), Paul still spent considerable efforts in "pastoral care." The letters we have show that Paul was not content to "plant" and move on, despite some of his comments in this direction. He felt personal responsibility for the communities he had inaugurated and had no hesitation in sending specific directives to them. The fact that communities such as Corinth and elsewhere would address questions to Paul about particular pastoral problems indicated that Paul did not present himself as a mere evangelizer but as one who retained authority over these communities and who intended to help shepherd them toward the day of final salvation. Paul's frequent pastoral visits to his communities (and the expectations of his churches on this point) indicate a similar concern.[43]

We can conclude, then, that the broad lines of Paul's missionary strategy and style directly related to the mission theology we have outlined above. The focus on the Gentile world was a direct consequence of Paul's call to be apostle to the Gentiles. His drive rapidly to cover the entire "world" through Asia Minor, Greece, Rome, and beyond was fueled by Paul's commission to preach to the Gentiles and his conviction about eschatological implications of the mission. The fate of Israel—and therefore the final act in God's plan—hinged on the completion of the Gentile mission. Therefore Paul was anxious to move rapidly and with constant reference (by means of the collection as well as by his own theological reflection) to Jerusalem. And, finally, because the ultimate goal of the gospel was a community of God's people bonded in Christ, Paul's aim was to develop churches, communities of believers. Therefore he had to devote energy to "building up the churches" and was anxious that they remain in good health until the "coming of the Lord Jesus."

The Content of Paul's Preaching

Determining the content of Paul's missionary preaching on the basis of his authentic letters is no easy task. The letters, as we have noted, are not missionary texts as such. We have no direct sources for the content and style of preaching Paul may have used in his initial evangelization of Gentile communities. However, it seems reasonable that Paul's letters would reflect some of the basic themes he had employed in his missionary preaching to these communities and, in fact, certain fragments or echoes of this proclamation do seem detectable.[44] We do not want to repeat our discussion of Paul's theology, but merely to point out some texts that seem to reflect his initial missionary preaching and to note their relationship to the basic mission theology sketched above.

A number of such texts can be isolated because of their similarity to major themes of *Jewish* missionary preaching. In other words, Paul borrowed motifs from his own heritage, adapting them to his new Christian message. Following the treatment of C. Bussmann, we can briefly note some of these themes:

1. Paul appealed to the Gentiles to "turn from idols to serve a living and true God" (1 Thess. 1:9; Rom. 1:18-32). The accusation of idolatry was a strong motif of Judaism in its dialogue with the Gentiles, and it finds a place in Paul. The "conversion" from idols Paul referred to was not, of course, merely cultic. The stock theme of Gentile "idolatry" was not limited to their worship of idols but included a broader sense of allegiance to anything that was false.[45] Thus conversion from "idols" to the "true and living God" described the total transformation that was the goal of Paul's preaching, deliverance of all humanity from bondage to sin and death and acceptance of the Lordship of Christ. This conversion rescued the Gentiles from the "coming wrath," a traditional eschatological motif of Judaism and an important motivating point in Jewish missionary preaching. In Paul this release from bondage and deliverance from wrath were attributed to Jesus (cf. 1 Thess. 1:10). Central to Paul's entire theology was his conviction that God effected his salvation through the agency of Christ. Thus Paul brings a substantial Christian modification to this traditional Jewish motif.

2. "Knowing God" or being "known by him" as a description of conversion was another Pauline motif shared with Jewish missionary preaching. A key text is Gal. 4:8-9: "Formerly, when you did not know God, you were in bondage to beings that by nature are no gods; but now that you have come to know God, or rather to be known by God, how can you turn back again to the weak and beggarly elemental spirits whose slaves you want to be once more?"

In Jewish literature "knowing God" could refer either to knowledge of God through nature (the sense in which Paul uses the term in Rom. 1:18-23) or to a broader sense of "knowing" as total relationship and commitment to God.[46] Paul used "knowing" in this deeper sense in Galatians where he seems to evoke a theme of his missionary preaching. Coming to "know God" meant deliverance from the "ignorance" of being bound to false gods (cf. Gal. 4:8). This motif, like the previous one, reflects the emphasis on salvation that stands at the center of Paul's mission theology. Paul adds a new dimension when he speaks of our being "known by God." "Being known" was equivalent to God's choice or election of the believer and has no parallel in Jewish literature.

The apostle rooted both aspects—"knowing" and "being known," deliverance and election—in the redemptive act of Christ: "But when the time had fully come, God sent forth his son, born of a woman, born under the law, to redeem those who were under the law, so that we might receive adoption as sons" (Gal. 4:4-5). As with the idolatry motif, Paul thoroughly Christianizes themes borrowed from Judaism.

3. Although Paul apparently utilized traditional Jewish missionary themes as part of his initial evangelization, there is strong evidence that a major part of his approach was a direct proclamation of the death and resurrection of Jesus as God's act of salvation. A capital text is 1 Cor. 15:4. Here Paul seems to remind the Christians explicitly of the basic content of his initial preaching ("in what

terms I preached to you the gospel"). He utilizes a traditional formulation, which summarized the basic gospel message of Jesus' death, burial, and resurrection (1 Cor. 15:3-4). Paul's declarations in 1 Corinthians 23, "We preach Christ crucified" and 2:2, "For I decided to know nothing among you except Jesus Christ and him crucified," point in the same direction.

As Bussmann and others have suggested, it is likely that Paul did not have a rigidly fixed method of initial preaching. Like any good preacher, Paul's approach would depend on the particular circumstances of his audience. But no matter what particular slant the circumstances would dictate, the fragmentary evidence we have suggests that Paul's preaching was deeply etched by his basic mission theology even when he exploited traditional Jewish themes. Thus the convictions forged in Paul's own inaugural experience—that Jesus was the Christ and that God was now offering salvation to all through the death and resurrection of his son—formed the basic platform of his mission message.

CONCLUSION

Despite the richness and complexity of Paul's thought and the limitations of our sources, there remains a large degree of consistency running from the nature of his conversion and call through the main lines of his theology and into the style and content of his apostolic ministry. There are many trailing edges we have not pursued. Paul himself left many important questions unanswered. For example, the major Pauline epistles do not give adequate treatment to the non-Christian religions, nor does Paul seem to agonize over the fate of those Gentiles who will not hear the gospel (and thus perhaps will not be saved, in Paul's vision) with any of the intensity which he brings to the question of Israel.

But Paul does provide a central Christological focus for the mission question. The taproot of his universal mission was a personal belief in Jesus Christ as Savior of the world, a belief based on his own conversion experience and ratified by early Christian tradition and the experience and reflections triggered by his ministry. The intensity of Paul's convictions and his ability to articulate them in such a rich profusion of symbols and concepts forge his unparalleled contribution to the biblical foundations of mission.

NOTES

1. By "authenticity" is meant Pauline authorship; it is not a judgment about the value or canonicity of the letters in question. For a thorough review of the arguments pro and con on this issue, cf. W. Kümmel, *Introduction to the New Testament*, rev. English ed. (Nashville: Abingdon, 1975).

2. Cf. further, W. Doty, *Letters in Primitive Christianity*, Guides to Biblical Scholarship Series (Philadelphia: Fortress Press, 1973).

3. Paul had apparently not visited Colossae, but the community had been evangelized through his close associate, Epaphras (Col. 1:7); cf. further, below, pp. 192-93.

4. L. Keck, *Paul and His Letters*, Proclamation Commentaries (Philadelphia: Fortress Press, 1979), p. viii.

5. Cf. K. Stendahl, *Paul among Jews and Gentiles* (Philadelphia: Fortress Press, 1976), pp. 3–4. For further discussion on the situation at Rome, which prompted Paul's letters, cf. K. Donfried, *The Romans Debate* (Minneapolis: Augsburg Publishing Co., 1977).

6. Cf. L. Keck, *Paul and His Letters*, pp. 8–11.

7. On the Jewish background of Paul, cf. W. D. Davies, *Paul and Rabbinic Judaism*, 4th ed. (Philadelphia: Fortress Press, 1980); H. Schoeps, *Paul: The Theology of the Apostle in the Light of Jewish Religious History* (Philadelphia: Westminster Press, 1961); E. Sanders, *Paul and Palestinian Judaism* (Philadelphia: Fortress Press, 1977).

8. Cf. C. Bussmann, *Themen der paulinischen Missionspredigt auf dem Hintergrund der spätjüdischhellenistischen Missionsliteratur* (Bern: Herbert Lang, 1971), and above, pp. 185–87.

9. C. Bussmann, *Themen der paulinischen Missionspredigt*, p. 191. We should also note that Paul did not carry out his missionary work in isolation but had an extensive network of co-workers and support groups among the communities; on this cf. W.H. Ollrog, *Paulus und seine Mitarbeiter*; Wissenschaftliche Monographien zum Alten und Neuen Testament 50 (Neukirchen–Vluyn: Neukirchener, 1979).

10. For a detailed study of the impact of Hellenism on Palestinian Judaism, cf. M. Hengel, *Judaism and Hellenism*, 2 vols. (Philadelphia: Fortress Press, 1974); on Paul's attitude to non-Jews, cf. R. Dobelstein, *Die Beurteilung der 'Heiden' bei Paulus*, Beitrage Zur biblischen Exegese und Theologie 14 (Frankfurt am Main/ Bern/Cirensester: Lang, 1981).

11. Cf. the discussion in L. Keck, *Paul and His Letters*, pp. 8–10.

12. Ibid., p. 9.

13. R. Bultmann, for example (*Theology of the New Testament* [London: SCM Press, 1952], vol. 1) places that initial point in Paul's assessment of humanity's plight, that is, his anthropology. Paul's realization of the human person's inability to lead a responsible and authentic existence led to an emphasis on the individual's justification by faith alone as the cornerstone of Pauline theology. E. Käsemann (*Perspectives on Paul* [Philadelphia: Fortress Press, 1971], especially pp. 1–31, 60–78), who has become a central figure in European interpretation of Paul, agrees with Bultmann's focus on justification by faith but decries the existentialist and individualistic emphasis of Bultmann's anthropological starting point. K. Stendahl (*Paul among Jews and Gentiles*) has added fuel to the debate by challenging the centrality of the justification-by-faith issue in Paul. For Stendahl the key issue for Paul was the access of both Jew and Gentile to salvation and the interrelationship of the two to salvation history. On the whole question of "starting point," cf. the thorough discussion of E. Sanders, *Paul*, pp. 434–42.

14. E. Sanders, *Paul*, p. 434.

15. J. Fitzmyer, "Pauline Theology," *Jerome Biblical Commentary* (Englewood Cliffs, N.J.: Prentice-Hall, 1968), 2:803.

16. H. D. Betz, *Galatians* (Philadelphia: Fortress Press, 1979), p. 70.

17. W. D. Davies, *Paul and Rabbinic Judaism*, p. 67. H. Schoeps, on the other hand, emphasizes Jewish Christian disregard of the law as the reason for Paul's reaction prior to his conversion (*Paul*, p. 219). As with most human reactions, a convergence of several, even conflicting, motivations might be possible.

18. K. Stendahl, *Paul among Jews and Gentiles*, p. 12; cf. also similar remarks in H. D. Betz, *Galatians*, p. 64; a fine balance between the notions of "call" and "conversion" as descriptions of Paul's inaugural experience can be found in J. Beker, *Paul the Apostle* (Philadelphia: Fortress Press, 1980), pp. 3–10.

19. Cf. his famous essay, "The Apostle Paul and the Introspective Conscience of the West," *Harvard Theological Review* 56 (1963):199–215 (reprinted in *Paul among Jews and Gentiles*, pp. 78–96).

20. H. D. Betz, *Galatians*, p.71.

21. Cf. Acts 13:5,14,56; 14:1; 17:1,17; 18:4,24. Note, however, that continuity with Judaism is a major concern of Luke and this may have colored Luke's presentation of Paul's strategy, particularly the programmatic statement of 13:46.

22. K. Stendahl, *Paul among Jews and Gentiles*, p. 82. A prime example of this approach is found in R. Rubenstein's *My Brother Paul* (New York: Harper & Row, 1972). Rubenstein does not work from the classical Christian stance but from the perspective of one who had been a strict Orthodox Jew and found release from guilt and legalism through psychoanalysis. Stendahl's point is that such personal guilt does *not* seem to have been part of Paul's experience in Judaism.

23. E. Sanders, *Paul*, p. 443.

24. K. Stendahl, *Paul among Jews and Gentiles*, pp. 92–93.

25. E. Sanders *Paul*, pp. 442–47.

26. L. Keck, *Paul and His Letters*, p. 117.

27. Cf. W. D. Davies's discussion of Paul's conflict in *Paul and Rabbinic Judaism*, pp. 58–59.

28. J. Fitzmyer, "Pauline Theology," p. 808.

29. L. Keck, *Paul and His Letters*, pp. 118–23.

30. On this theme of Jewish missionary preaching, cf. C. Bussmann, *Themen der paulinischen missionspredigt*, pp. 57–74.

31. On this point, cf. J. Dunn, "Paul's Understanding of the Death of Jesus," in *Reconciliation and Hope*, ed. R. Banks (Grand Rapids, Mich.: Wm. B. Eerdmans, 1974), p. 126.

32. Cf. P. Stuhlmacher, "Achtzehn Thesen zur Paulinischen Kreuzestheologie," *Rechtfertigung: Festschrift für Ernst Käsemann*, ed. J. Friedrich, W. Pöhlmann, P. Stuhlmacher (Tübingen: Mohr, 1976), pp. 509–25, especially pp. 512–13; also J. Dunn, "Paul's Understanding," pp. 131–37.

33. Cf. also, Phil. 2:9–11; Col. 3:9–11 and Eph. 2:11–22 (this deutero-Pauline work builds on the seminal insight of the earlier Pauline texts; on this point, cf. below, chap. 8).

34. L. Keck, *Paul and His Letters*, p. 123.

35. E. Sanders, *Paul*, p. 508.

36. L. Keck, *Paul and His Letters*, p. 79.

37. For Paul's own experience, cf. 1 Thess. 1:5; 1 Cor. 2:4; 7:40; 2 Cor. 12:12; Rom. 15:18–19; in references to Christians, cf. 1 Cor. 1:7; 2:12; 3:16; 6:19; 7:7; 2 Cor. 1:22; 4:13; 5:5;Gal. 3:2,5; 4:6; Rom. 5:5; 8:9,11,23. On the importance of the experience of the Spirit in Paul, cf. E. Sanders, *Paul*, pp. 447–53, and H. Betz, "In Defense of the Spirit: Paul's Letter to the Galatians as a Document of Early Christian Apologetics," in *Aspects of Religious Propaganda*, ed. E. Fiorenza (South Bend, Ind.: University of Notre Dame Press, 1976). pp. 99–114.

38. F. Hahn, *Mission in the New Testament* (Naperville: Allenson, 1965), p. 104.

39. On the theological implications of Paul's collection, cf. K. Nickle, *The Collec-*

tion: A Study in Paul's Strategy, Studies in Biblical Theology 48 (Naperville: Allenson, 1966), and D. Georgi, *Die Geschichte der Kollekte des Paulus für Jerusalem* (Hamburg: Reich, 1965).

40. On Paul's use of sacrificial language to describe his ministry, cf. O. Haas, *Paulus der Missionar*, Münsterschwarzacher Studien 11 (Münsterschwarzach: Vier-Türme, 1971), pp. 30–34.

41. On Paul's mission strategy, cf. O. Haas, *Paulus der Missionar*, pp. 82–87; also, R. Allen, *Missionary Methods: St. Paul's or Ours?* (Grand Rapids, Mich.: Wm. B. Eerdmans, 1962); R. Hock, *The Social Context of Paul's Ministry* (Philadelphia: Fortress Press, 1980). Hock explores the ramifications of Paul's trade as tentmaker and suggests that the workshop and market place provided an important forum for the exchange of ideas in the Greco-Roman world. However, because Paul addresses the question of his "strategy" only indirectly, we have to be cautious in attempting to spell out any overall plan he may have had.

42. Cf., also, 1 Thess. 3:5,8,12–13; 5:23–24; similar motifs are found in the prayers of thanksgiving at the beginning of some of Paul's epistles: cf. 1 Cor. 1:4–9; Phil. 1:3–11; for further discussion of these prayers see D. Stanley, *Boasting in the Lord* (New York: Paulist Press, 1973).

43. On the whole question of Paul's authority in his communities, cf. B. Holmberg, *Paul and Power* (Philadelphia: Fortress Press, 1978), especially pp. 70–93.

44. Cf. the thorough discussion of this question in C. Bussmann, *Themen der paulinischen Missionspredigt*; also, H. Schoeps, *Paul*, p. 6.

45. C. Bussmann, *Themen der paulinischen Missionspredigt*, p. 41.

46. Ibid., p. 173.

8

The Cosmic Scope of the Church's Mission in Colossians and Ephesians

A plan for the fullness of time . . . [Eph. 1:10].

Colossians and Ephesians reflect a significant development in the mission theology of the New Testament and therefore deserve special attention. With these two letters the horizons of the Christian mission are pushed beyond the ethnic boundaries of Jew and Gentile to embrace the entire universe.

Not all would agree with this evaluation. Some scholars believe that the theologies of Colossians and especially Ephesians blunt the outer-directed missionary thrust found in Paul. Ferdinand Hahn, for example, sees the momentum of these letters turning from a worldwide mission toward a world-dominating church. A subtle cleavage begins between genuine mission to the world and the more absorbing pastoral needs of building up the church.[1]

But another assessment is possible, and that is the view we shall suggest in this chapter. Colossians and Ephesians do not represent the victory of a triumphant ecclesiology at the expense of a world-serving missiology. The church in these letters is not the final goal but only a means and a sign of Christ's own cosmic mission of salvation.

THE RELATION OF COLOSSIANS AND EPHESIANS TO PAUL

Before exploring the mission theology of these two letters, it is necessary to consider their relationship to each other and to the rest of the Pauline correspondence.

Even a casual reading of the two works shows their marked similarity (but not identity) in thought. Most scholars today explain this in terms of Ephesians' dependency on Colossians rather than Colossians being a truncated version of Ephesians, as had been suggested by earlier scholarship.[2] The cosmic scope of their Christology, the use of such terms as "head" (of the body), "fullness," and "mystery" are all important links between the letters and significant elements of their mission theology. Yet the two works are decidedly different in style and structure, and have distinctive theological viewpoints. Colossians follows the basic format of a Pauline letter, interacting with concrete problems in the community (for example, 2:16,20–23) and concluding with personal greetings to individuals (cf. 4:7–17). Many of the terms and concepts are familiarly Pauline.

However, a significant number of commentators question the authenticity of Colossians.[3] They point to a large amount of vocabulary (thirty-six words) never found in Paul's other letters, some noticeable differences in style, and the absence of such key Pauline issues as justification and concern over law. More substantial arguments can be raised concerning the central themes of Colossians. The letter emphasizes spatial categories more than temporal ones when speaking eschatologically. It uses cosmic categories to reflect on Christ, especially in the famous hymnlike passage of 1:15–20. In contrast to the other Pauline letters, Christ is declared "head" of the body (1:18; 2:19).

Scholars who defend the Pauline authorship of the letter point out that even though these themes are more emphatically developed in Colossians, they are not entirely absent from the major Pauline letters. The differences in style are hardly that probative and could be explained not only by some sort of secretarial hypothesis (cf. Col. 4:18) but simply by Paul's use of traditional material and by the ordinary degree of uniqueness given to any letter by the particular circumstances of time, place, and occasion that triggered its writing. The more pronounced spatial categories of the letter's eschatology and its cosmic Christology may be explained by Paul's interaction with a Hellenistic community that was dabbling in such matters. Hence, under close examination many of the arguments against Pauline authorship tend to be blunted or even to evaporate. In this study we shall side with those who consider Colossians to be a genuine letter of Paul's.

Ephesians, on the other hand, does not seem like a letter at all. The address "to the Ephesians" (1:1) is quite likely a later addition. There are no references to the concrete problems of the community and none of the personal greetings typical of Paul's letters. Ephesians may be best described as "treatise" or general theological presentation.

Because of its literary style and its theology, a majority of New Testament scholars believe that Ephesians was written some time after Paul's death.[4] This is the viewpoint adopted here. Ephesians represents a theological vision in touch with Pauline tradition, and in particular with the letter to the Colossians, but it is a new statement in a different time and place. As we shall note below, its concern with unity between Jews and Gentiles and its ease with Greek cosmic and ethical categories suggest a Hellenistic Jewish author addressing a predominately Gentile audience.

We might reconstruct the origin of Colossians and Ephesians as follows. Paul wrote to the Colossians from prison. Of Paul's three imprisonments, Rome or Caesarea seem preferable to Ephesus, but one cannot be sure. The Colossians were a Gentile community, which Paul himself had not evangelized personally but apparently had been instrumental in forming through the work of his "fellow servant," Epaphras (cf. 1:7-8; 4:12-13).

This community had been experiencing some difficulties with false teachers (Col. 2:8,16,18). Although the identity of these teachers and the precise nature of their errors cannot be determined, it seems to have been some form of syncretism, a religious stew combining elements of Jewish ritual, angel worship, Greek speculation about the powers of the cosmos, and rigorous world-denying asceticism.

To offset this potent mixture Paul reminded his Christians of the authentic gospel they had received (1:5-7, 23)—a typical strategy in all his letters. He then attempted to dampen their superstitious cosmic speculation by reflecting on Christ's relationship to the universe. Christ is not only the head of the church, but the triumphant Lord of the universe (cf. 1:15-20; 2:15). Paul also offered some practical exhortations for faithful Christian living in an attempt to offset the misguided asceticism of the false teachers (cf. 2:16-23).

This pastoral response of Paul to the situation at Colossae sets the stage for the development of mission theology, as we have asserted at the outset of this chapter. A threat to Paul's "gospel" at Colossae and the cosmic scope of the opponents' aberrant teaching provoked a defense of Paul's message on an equally cosmic scale. The Christ who is head of the church is also the "fullness" of God and the Lord of the universe. Church and universe have been joined in the body of Christ.

It is this insight that the author of Ephesians will later amplify and develop. In Ephesians the gospel will be seen against the backdrop of God's plan of salvation, the "mystery" hidden for all eternity but now revealed in the church's mission. The union of Jew and Gentile in the church becomes sign and even instrument of the cosmic triumph and reconciliation being effected by God through Jesus Christ. Ephesians broadens the church's vision of Christ, and therefore its understanding of itself and its mission.

Ephesians was not written by Paul, but the dimensions of its theological vision were staked out by Colossians, an authentic Pauline letter. The author of Ephesians was a creative yet faithful interpreter of the Pauline tradition.[5] Therefore the more cosmic scope injected into Pauline theology by the situation at Colossae and the development of that horizon by the deutero-Pauline author of Ephesians justify our separate consideration of their works.

NEW DIMENSIONS: PREPARATION FOR COSMIC MISSIOLOGY IN THE LETTER TO THE COLOSSIANS

Our purpose here is to isolate some of the concepts in Colossians that led to the more developed mission theology of Ephesians.

Paul's Mission to the Gentiles

Even though Colossians does not wrestle with questions as immediate to Paul's missionary preaching as the issue of Jew and Gentile (as in Romans) or the law question (as in Galatians), consciousness of Paul's missionary call is not absent.

He firmly introduces himself as "an apostle of Christ Jesus by the will of God" in the opening of the letter. And consciousness of his "divine office" breaks out in other sections as well (cf. especially Col. 1:25-29). He also reflects on his special call to preach to the Gentiles. In Col. 1:5 he refers to "the word of truth, the gospel," which through the instigation of Paul and the mediation of Epaphras (1:7) had come to the Colossians. There is a sense of accomplishment evident in Colossians that is not apparent in the major letters. The gospel that has come to the Colossians is "bearing fruit in the whole world and growing" (1:6). It has been heard not only in this local church but "been preached to every creature under heaven" (1:23). Paul has been the minister of this universal proclamation (1:23,28).

This mood of "completion," of "looking back" on a successful proclamation of the gospel, is taken by some interpreters as further evidence of the post-Pauline character of Colossians. But the conclusion is not necessary. If Paul is writing from prison, especially from Rome or Caesarea somewhat late in his missionary career, then his words may reflect a genuine sense of accomplishment. The gospel had been preached through Asia Minor and Greece under Paul's auspices. Other missionaries had already carried the good news to Rome, not to mention the success of the Jewish Christian mission from Jerusalem to Syria and other regions. Paul's statement in Colossians is simply the follow-through on his confident assessment in Romans 15 where he had noted the completion of his proposed circuit "from Jerusalem and as far round as Illyricum" (Rom. 15:19). In this text, too, Paul speaks of "having completed" his preaching task.

We have to keep in mind Paul's strategy, which called for the implantation of the gospel in major cities rather than total conversion of the populace. Thus the hyperbole present in Col. 1:6 ("the whole world"), 1:23 ("every creature under heaven"), and 1:28 ("every person") was not any impossibility for the historical Paul. This reflective juncture in Paul's ministry will be one of the elements taken up by the author of Ephesians in his theologizing on the role of the Gentile mission in the cosmic plan of God.

As in his other epistles, Paul is here personally concerned with the vitality of his community. Their faith is the cause of his prayer of thanksgiving (Col 1:3-5a) and the object of his anxious prayer for perseverance (Col. 1:9-14). He recalls the hardships he had endured in his apostolate and affirms that these sufferings have a redemptive value (Col. 1:24). Twice he reminds the Colossians of his imprisonment (4:3; 4:18). Even though he is absent from them and may never have visited them (this is implied in the statements of 1:4,8,9 and especially 2:1), Paul considers himself as "present" with them and sees his ministry as a "struggle" or "contest" on their behalf (Col. 1:29-2:1). This theme of redemptive apostolic suffering will be struck in Ephesians, too, and makes Paul a model of the cosmic mission of the church itself.

The object of Paul's mission, the inclusion of the Gentiles, is also referred to. In typical language he reminds his readers that they (and Paul himself) have been "delivered from the dominion of darkness and transferred . . . to the kingdom of his beloved son" (1:13). They, the Gentiles, who were once "estranged and hostile in mind, doing evil deeds" have now been "reconciled in his [Christ's] body of flesh by his death" (Col. 1:21–22). The Colossian community have been the "recipients of the Word of God, . . . the mystery hidden for ages and generations but now made manifest to his saints" (1:25–26). "To them [presumably the Colossian Christians, although this is not certain; Paul could be referring to the Jewish Christians] God chose to make known how great among the Gentiles are the riches of the glory of this mystery, which is Christ in you, the hope of glory" (Col. 1:27).

We shall take up the notion of "mystery" below; it is sufficient to note here that Paul reflects on the overall meaning of the Gentile mission (not unlike Romans 9–11), relating it to God's cosmic plan of salvation, the "mystery" now manifest. The cosmic and eschatological significance of the Gentile mission will be a major motif in the theology of Ephesians.

These typical reflections of Paul—his apostolic authority, his care and suffering for the church, and the implications of the Gentile mission—are all elements used by the author of Ephesians to forge a new vision of the Christian mission.

Cosmic Christology

What may be the major contribution of Colossians is found in the much discussed passage, 1:15–20. This exalted description of Christ's role in creation and in the reconciliation of the cosmos lays the foundation for the advance in the New Testament mission theology we are attempting to describe in this chapter. We shall quote the passage in full and then make some comments on its meaning:

> He is the image of the invisible God, the first-born of all creation; for in him all things were created, in heaven and on earth, visible and invisible, whether thrones or dominions or principalities or authorities—all things were created through him and for him. He is before all things, and in him all things hold together. He is the head of the body, the church; he is the beginning, the first-born from the dead, that in everything he might be preeminent. For in him all the fullness of God was pleased to dwell, and through him to reconcile to himself all things, whether on earth or in heaven, making peace by the blood of his cross.

There has been an enormous amount of speculation about the origin and nature of this passage.[6] Many authors detect an early pre-Pauline Christological hymn underneath the present "edited" version of the text. Paul may have adapted the hymn to his own vision, especially by adding the phrases "the church" in verse 15 and "the blood of the cross" in verse 20. Both of these phrases bind the cosmic reconciling role of Christ to the historical realities of the crucifixion and the Christian community. This helps to prevent the letter's Christology from drifting off into metaphysical speculation about Christ as "head" of the cosmos (= the body) and achieving reconciliation through some physical infusion of the universe rather than through the historically grounded act of crucifixion.[7]

Four aspects of the cosmic Christology found in the hymn deserve comment:

1. The hymn gives the risen Christ a central role in all creation. Christ is declared one in whom the "fullness" dwells (Col. 1:19). The Revised Standard Version adds the explanatory phrase "of God," which is not in the Greek but accurately defines the meaning of the term "fullness" as God's divine being.[8] In Col. 2:9 Paul states this unequivocally: "For in him the whole fullness of deity dwells bodily." These statements affirm that Jesus is the definitive revelation of God, a basic assertion of New Testament Christology.

The hymn uses "wisdom" categories to describe the exalted Christ's relationship to creation. The Old Testament speaks of "wisdom" as God's self-manifestation through the beauty and order of the created world. Early Christianity applied such reflections to the exalted Christ. Christ is "the image of the invisible God," a similar attribute is applied to wisdom (cf. Wis. 7:26, "the image of his goodness"). Wisdom personifies God's presence in the world (cf. Prov. 8:4, 31; Sirach 24:8; Wis. 7:27), just as Christ's power and beauty image God. He is "the first-born of all creation." By this phrase Christ's sovereignty is stressed (cf. Rom. 8:29). Through his resurrection and exaltation Jesus' preeminent role over all creation is clearly evident (in Col. 1:18 he is called "the first-born from the dead"). Jesus personifies that which all of the creative power of God tends to bring into being; he is the pattern of all creation or, as the hymn puts it, "in him all things were created . . . all things were created through him and for him." Here, too, Jewish wisdom speculation is used to enrich reflection on Christ. Wisdom was the pattern for all creation (Prov. 8:22–31). So Jesus, as the ultimate personification of God's creative presence, becomes not only the pattern but the very goal toward which creation tends.[9]

As the hymn goes on to state (cf. Col. 1:16), because Christ is the source, pattern, and goal of all creation, there is no created being superior to him. "All things in heaven and on earth, visible and invisible, whether thrones or dominions or principalities or authorities"—*all* are subordinate to Christ. This list of "powers" probably refers to angelic beings who ruled over the fate of humanity.

Whatever their identity and potential power, Paul firmly subordinates these supernatural beings to Christ. They are *created* beings and they must fall in step behind the firstborn. This subordination is reemphasized in Col. 2:10 where the risen Christ is declared "head of all rule and authority," and again in Col. 2:15 where it is stated that Christ's death has "disarmed the principalities and powers and made a public example of them, triumphing over them in him."

Paul uses these passages to meet head-on the anxieties of the Colossians. As Schweizer notes:

> For centuries they [the Hellenists] thought of the world as of a living and divine body, and of God as of its ruler, governing it as its head or permeating it as its soul, or surrounding it like the air in which it lives, or like the

womb of a mother. Man in this Hellenistic area was not so much worried with his personal problems, his sin and his righteousness, as with the problems of this world, the meaninglessness of life, the threat of an unavoidable fate, the tyranny of the heavenly rulers, that is the star that determines every move of earthly life. . . . The author to the Colossians takes up such an interpretation. Indeed, Christ is not only Savior of the individual redeeming from sin and leading him to a pious life. He is Lord of the whole world. He is not only the answer to specifically religious problems, for consciences tortured by sinfulness and longing for forgiveness. He is also the answer to modern Hellenistic problems in a world that had lost God and therefore its aim, its meaning, that is bound to meet its fate, that was full of fear and yet not able to evade it.[10]

2. A second crucial aspect of this letter's cosmic Christology is the connection between Christ's lordship over the cosmos and his lordship over the church. In Col. 1:18 Christ is declared "head of the body, the church." Scholars who hold that Col. 1:15-20 is built on a pre-Pauline hymn detect a significant addition to the original version with the phrase "the church." The affirmation of Christ as "head of the body" might originally have referred to his lordship over the cosmos. Hellenistic speculation conceived of the universe itself as a "body," with the deity such as Zeus or Ether as its "head."[11] By the "addition" of the word "church" the author of Colossians gives a new interpretation to this cosmic speculation.

Although Christ is Lord of the created universe, his lordship is not to be confused with mythical "physical" power of the Greek gods over the world. The tenor of Christ's lordship is manifested historically and concretely in that community bound to him by love, the church. Paul's image of the church as body of Christ (cf. 1 Cor. 12; Romans 12; Col. 1:24; 2:19) now serves as a definition of Christ's cosmic lordship. In the community's struggle to be faithful to God's love can be seen the ultimate nature of God's relationship to the world, his "lordship." This illustrative function of the church will be amplified by Ephesians when it singles out the reconciliation of Jew and Gentile in the one church as an example of what Christ's lordship can effect in the world.

3. A third dimension of the cosmic Christology of Colossians is its emphasis on universal reconciliation through the death and resurrection of Jesus. In his earlier letters Paul had spoken of reconciliation between God and humanity (cf. Rom. 5:10–11; 11:15; 2 Cor. 5:18–20). But in Colossians this reconciling work of Christ is pushed to a cosmic scope. Not only humanity but "all things, whether on earth or in heaven" are reconciled "by the blood of his cross" (Col. 1:18). The explicit tie-in to "the blood of his cross" is another place where scholars detect evidence of a Pauline "correction" in what may have been a pre-existing hymn.

The cosmic reconciling work of Christ is not achieved through some physical disarming of hostile powers but through the life-giving death and resurrection of Jesus Christ. As Schweizer notes: "Into a theology focusing exclusively on resurrection and exaltation, probably understood as the physical event that connected earth and heaven anew, he [the author of Colossians] introduces the Pauline stress upon the cross as the redeeming act of Christ."[12]

Although Col. 1:18 speaks of redemption as a "reconciliation," in 2:14–15 Christ's relationship to the cosmic powers is proclaimed a victory. As a victorious general he "disarmed the principalities and powers and made a public example of them, triumphing over them." In both sets of language the cosmic preeminence of Christ is stressed without reservation. Both these dimensions of Christ's work—reconciliation and victory—will be absorbed into the mission synthesis of Ephesians, becoming the language of its reflection not only on the redemptive work of Jesus, but on the missionary goal of the church.

4. A final dimension of the letter's cosmic Christology is that the cosmic lordship of Christ leads not simply or primarily to a renewed nature but to a renewed humanity. Hellenistic speculation concentrated on the structure of the cosmos itself. Although Pauline thought was also concerned with the renewal of nature (cf. Romans 8), its primary focus is on the world of humanity. The verses following the key passage of Colossians 1:15–20 illustrate that the same Pauline priority is at work here. The cosmic reconciling work of Jesus transforms people: "And you, the ones who are estranged and hostile in mind, doing evil deeds, he has now reconciled to his body of flesh by his death, in order to present you holy and blameless and irreproachable for him" (Col. 1:21–22).

The text goes on to make a critical link-up between the redemptive work of Jesus and the missionary preaching of the community. It is through the preaching of the gospel that the redemptive power of the cosmic Christ has flooded into the lives of the Colossians. The "hope of the gospel" that they heard is the same as that "which has been preached to every creature under heaven" (Col. 1:23). Paul himself (even though he had not preached at Colossae) is the "minister" of that gospel (1:23,25). This gospel is the "Word of God fully known"; it is "the mystery hidden for ages and generations but now made manifest to his saints" (1:25–26).

The concept of the gospel as "mystery" ushers in the final concept, which will be fully exploited in the theological synthesis of Ephesians. In Col. 1:25 "mystery" is equivalent to "gospel": God's work of salvation now fully manifest in Christ's redemptive work. In Col. 1:27 the term is more narrowly conceived of as "this mystery, which is Christ in you, the hope of glory." In both cases "mystery" is used to refer to something long hidden, which is now revealed. Ephesians will use this term to speak of the cosmic mission of Christ and his people. God's universal plan of salvation is a "mystery" now revealed in Christ and in the community who lives in his name.

A consistent trait of the theology of Colossians is to relate wide-ranging cosmic speculation to the historical base of Christian experience: the humanity of Jesus (that is, his death and resurrection), the church, and the church's mission. These are the very elements that the author of Ephesians will weave into a full-blown mission theology. Thus it was the Pauline theology of Colossians that ultimately gave the language, the spirit, and the scope to the vision of the deutero-Pauline epistle to the Ephesians.

COSMIC LORD AND COSMIC MISSION:
THE MESSAGE OF EPHESIANS

In a study of Ephesians, R. P. Meyer notes that the purpose of this epistle is not only "to describe the mystery of the Church, but also its capacity for world service."[13] Anyone who has read Ephesians is aware of its exalted ecclesiology. Perhaps less apparent is the connection between its ecclesiology and its description of the church's mission. Agreeing with Meyer, we contend that the ultimate purpose of Ephesians is not to narrow the church's vision to itself but to stretch that vision to embrace the world. Let us scan the epistle (especially the first four chapters, which are crucial for its mission theology) and isolate its fundamental message.

God's Universal Plan of Salvation (Eph. 1:3–23)

The breathtaking opening section of the epistle to the Ephesians—including the blessing of 1:3–15 and the thanksgiving passage of 1:16–23—sketches the cosmic scope of God's plan of salvation and its implications for the church. Here is clear evidence of how the author of Ephesians has absorbed the Pauline theology of Colossians, synthesizing it and casting it into a fully developed framework.

The blessing section (Eph. 1:3–15) portrays God's plan of universal salvation in broad strokes. God is praised for having blessed and chosen the Christians "before the foundation of the world" and called them to holiness and to union with him as "sons" through Jesus Christ (Eph. 1:3–6). That redemptive call is carried out by means of the death of Jesus (Eph. 1:7), an emphasis characteristic of Pauline tradition. The church's experience of redemption gives it profound insight into God's salvific plan. God has made known to the church "the mystery of his will, according to his purpose which he set forth in Christ as a plan for the fullness of time, to unite all things in him, things in heaven and things on earth" (Eph. 1:9–10).

These latter verses are especially significant because they fix the horizon for the entire reflection on ecclesiology and mission that follows. As Meyer notes, the author states right from the beginning the key items on his agenda: God's universal plan of salvation and the church's place in this cosmic plan.[14] The church has insight into this plan, or "mystery" (Eph. 1:9), only by gift. It is only by God's choice, through the experience of salvation in the community, that Christians have glimpsed the mystery. This will be an important insight into the epistle as a whole: the thrust of Christian experience is not inward but outward, not toward the church's privilege but toward its universal mission.

The scope of that mission is coextensive with the universalism of God's plan. That awesome frontier is boldly stated in Eph. 1:10: "In the fulness of time, to unite all things in him, things in heaven and things on earth." The Revised Standard Version's "unite," which we quote here, masks the richness and the ambiguity of the verb *anakephalaiō* used by the author of Ephesians. M. Barth suggests the translation "to be comprehended under one head."[15] This admittedly awkward phrase has the merit of catching the connotation of the root word *kephale*, or "head," which implies that the "union" spoken of involves the cosmic proportions of Christ's headship over the universe and the church. "Comprehend," in addition, catches the basic meaning of "summing up" or "uniting" that is associated with the composite verb *anakephalaiō* in some Hellenistic writings and in Rom. 13:9.[16]

The span of this "unity," this "summing up," is across the chasm of heaven and earth; it is cosmic in scope. As the following verses and the entire context of the chapter will make clear, this cosmic reconciliation is concretized in *people* (particularly Jews and Gentiles in the church), but it also embraces the alienated elements of the universe itself. Thus as much or more than Colossians, Ephesians takes soundings from the full dimension of God's universal plan and relates it to the church and its mission.

The tie-in to ecclesiology is emphasized in the remaining verses of the blessing section (Eph. 1:11–15), where another major theme of the entire epistle is announced. Those who "first hoped in Christ"—that is, the Jewish Christians— were destined to "live for the praises of his glory." Through Christ's redemptive work now the Gentiles too have come into contact with the "gospel of salvation" and are also destined for such a glorious inheritance (Eph. 1:13–14). This joining of Jew and Gentile in the church and its connection to the universal plan will be spelled out in chapter 2 of the epistle.

The thanksgiving section (Eph. 1:16–23) intensifies the reflections already stated in the blessing section.

> I do not cease to give thanks for you, remembering you in my prayers, that the God of our Lord Jesus Christ, the Father of glory, may give you a spirit of wisdom and of revelation in the knowledge of him, having the eyes of your hearts enlightened, that you may know what is the hope to which he has called you, what are the riches of his glorious inheritance in the saints, and what is the immeasurable greatness of his power in us who believe, according to the working of his great might which he accomplished in Christ when he raised him from the dead and made him sit at his right hand in the heavenly places, far above all rule and authority and power and dominion, and above every name that is named, not only in this age but also in that which is to come; and he has put all things under his feet and has made him the head over all things for the church, which is his body, the fullness of him who fills all in all.

The theme of "knowledge" introduces the section. The author prays that the recipients may comprehend the richness of the destiny to which God calls them (Eph. 1:17–20). Once again the initiative of God in the work of salvation is stressed. God's immeasurably great power achieved salvation through Christ's death and resurrection and this same power places the exalted Christ "far above all rule and authority and power and dominion, and above every name that is named, not only in this age but also in that which is to come" (Eph. 1:20–21).

As Meyer notes, this description of Christ's exaltation and cosmic lordship is preparatory to the author's description of the church and its responsibility.[17] The level of discourse is the *cosmic* level: the relationship of the church to the world. This cosmic level of the discourse is another point where a debt to the thought of Colossians is apparent, but the explicit application of this cosmic Christology to the church is a particular contribution of Ephesians.

Without doubt the most critical verses in this first chapter are the final two: "and he has put all things under his feet and has made him the head over all things for the church, which is his body, the fullness of him who fills all in all" (Eph.1:22–23). Here the tie-in between the cosmic Lord and the worldwide mission is made. The passage serves as the climax and conclusion of the segment begun in verse 20. The subject is God, who raised Christ from the dead and placed him above all creatures, including the heavenly powers. A snatch of Ps. 110:1 ("and made him sit at his right hand")—a favorite early Christian exaltation text—helps to make the point. This cosmic rule of Christ spans the present age and "the age to come," that is, it not only encompasses all levels of being but the whole range of history.

This stress on Christ's cosmic rule prepares for the ecclesial application which follows in verses 22–23. Another fragment of psalm—"he has put all things under his feet" (Ps. 8:7)—leads into the ecclesial statement: "He has made him [or literally "given him"] as head over all things for the church." The coupling of headship and church recalls Col. 1:15–20. There, too, Paul had interpreted what could be seen as Christ's headship over the material universe in a concrete, ecclesial sense. The "body" over which Christ is "head" is the church (cf. Col. 1:18).

But Eph. 1:22–23 does not merely repeat what was stated in Colossians: namely, Christ is Lord of the universe and head of the church. Instead it emphasizes that Christ, whom God had exalted above all things, has also been *given* as "head over all things" *to* the church. Verse 23a goes on to state that this church is also the *body* of this head, as Col. 1:15 had done. But a new nuance of thought seems to have been introduced. The stress is on Christ's cosmic lordship in and of itself, apart from any connection with the church. By gift this cosmic Lord is also made or "given" as head of a historical community of people. This nuance should not be lost. Here, as we shall discuss, is the margin that separates the thought of Ephesians from any triumphant ecclesiology. The church does not bottle up the cosmic rule of Christ: the Lord who continues to serve all things is also "given" to the church, which is his body.

The concluding phrase of verse 23 adds to the richness and the complexity of this much discussed verse. Through God's donation of the cosmic Christ to the church, the community is now described as partaking of the "fullness of him who fills all in all." "Fullness" is also part of the Colossian heritage of Ephesians. But here, for the only time in the New Testament, the term "fullness" is applied not simply to Christ but also to the church. The church itself experiences, "contains," the divine fullness of him who fills all in all: the very divine richness that impregnates the exalted Christ.

In what sense is this fullness as applied to the church to be understood? The word *pleroma* can have an active or passive sense, that is, something that fills or that is filled up (= "full"). If the active sense were intended here it would imply that the church completes or fills up something lacking in Christ. But the context of the epistle, particularly 1:20–22, makes clear that there is nothing lacking in Christ's lordship. He has been exalted above all things by the power of the Father. Therefore the passive sense is preferable. The church is suffused with Christ's own fullness, with that same world-embracing love with which Christ "fills all in all" (cf. also Eph. 3:19).

This latter phrase "all in all" also involves complicated translation: what is the sense of the two uses of *pas* ("all") here? The first *pas* ("fills *all*") is probably to be defined by the other two uses of the word in verse 22. Thus it would be equivalent to "everything," the total cosmos. The concluding phrase "in all" could either be a shortened form of "all the saints," in other words a personification of the "all" as in 1 Cor. 15:28, or might be equivalent to the adverb *pantapasin* and mean "wholly" or "completely." In view of the movement back and forth in this text between the cosmic and human perspective, I prefer to see both "alls" in a similar vein. In other words the entire phrase could be translated: "the fulness of him who fills all things in all people." The final *pasin* would refer primarily to those in the church, "the saints," since this is the immediate concern of Eph. 1:23, but would also carry a second level of meaning referring to all of humanity.[18] This is especially true if Eph. 1:23 is linked with the sweeping vision of Eph. 1:9–10 where the divine plan catches up *panta* in its most absolute sense—every thing and person in heaven and earth. The deeper side of this vision is brought out even more explicitly in the majestic text of Eph. 4:4–5: "There is one body and one spirit, just as you were called to the one hope that belongs to your call, one Lord, one faith, one baptism, one God and Father of us all, who is above all, through all and in all." Here, too, the context of the epistle allows no narrow ecclesiastical boundaries to define the "all." All humanity is to be swept up into "the one body and the one spirit."

This crucial passage, Eph. 1:1–23, sets the proper tone for the entire mission theology of the letter. As we shall say again at the conclusion of the chapter, this epistle is not concerned solely or even primarily with inflating the church's glory. The opening statement of the epistle dwells first on God's decisive, all-embracing saving action in the world and only secondarily does it turn to the impact of this on the church. The church is obviously in view here. The epistle is, after all, not a declaration for unbelievers but an exhortation to the church. Thus the church's role in all this is a major interest for the author, but this does not mean that he considers the church the ultimate goal of God's work. By linking the cosmic lordship of Christ with the church, the author has defined the *responsibilities* of the community. Because it is filled with the fullness of the one who fills the universe with his lordship, then the universe—everything in heaven and earth, every thing present and future—becomes the concern of the church. The church is swept up into the cosmic concern of its Lord.

Barth puts it well in his commentary on Ephesians:

In Ephesians and Colossians fullness and filling denote a dynamic unilateral relationship: the revelation of God's glory to the world through Jesus Christ; the power exerted by God in Christ and in the church for the subjection of the powers and the salvation of all mankind; the life, growth, and salvation given by Christ to his body; or, in brief, the presence of the living God and his Messiah among his chosen people for the benefit of all creation. If there is a cosmic role ascribed to the church in Ephesians then it is as servant (cf. 2:7; 3:10; 6:10-20; 4:12). She is to manifest the presence of the loving and powerful God. Not God, Christ, or the Head, but solely the body of Christ, that is, the house of God, the church, is "to grow" (2:21-22; 4:15-16; 4:13). Any notion of world dominion by the church is missing, but the church is equipped to do a "work of service" and to "stand against," and "resist," the attacks of evil powers (4:12; 6:13-14). The idea is lacking that one day the church will fill or replace the world. Assurance is given that Christ is filling all things (1.23, 4.10) and that the saints will attain or will be filled with, all of God's and the Messiah's fullness (3:19; 4:13).[19]

From this God-given horizon of concern springs the nature of the church's mission.

The Reconciliation of Jew and Gentile
as Sign of God's Redemptive Work (Eph. 2:11-22; 3:3-6)

Even though the author of Ephesians reflects on a cosmic level, he does not fall victim to pure abstraction. The unity toward which God's redemptive plan moves all being is already being experienced historically and concretely in that fallible community of human persons, the church. This church is touched with the "fullness" of Christ (Eph. 1:22-23). It is the "body" of him who is head of the cosmos (Eph. 1:23). It is the sign and instrument of what God intends to do for all humanity and all history. To illustrate this concrete experience of redemption, the author singles out a key issue of Paul's own ministry and, as we have been stating throughout, a major concern of early Christianity: the union of Jew and Gentile in the church.

The main texts for this are found in chapter two of the epistle. Having laid down the foundation for the cosmic-mission perspective of the church in chapter 1, the author now appeals to the mission experience of the church to confirm its world-reconciling responsibility. Verses 1-10 review the futility of life without salvation and contrast this with the gift of God's merciful love in Christ (Eph. 2:4). Through baptism and faith we are saved (Eph. 2:4-9). Verse 10 captures the spirit that animates the entire epistle: "For we are his [God's] workmanship, created in Christ Jesus for good works, which God prepared beforehand, that we should walk in him."

Beginning in verse 11, the author addresses the Gentiles directly, recalling their dismal status prior to their conversion: "separated from Christ, alienated from the commonwealth of Israel, and stranger to the covenants of promise, having no hope and without God in the world."[20] But now through Christ this alienation and isolation have been dissolved (Eph. 2:13). The author cites Isa. 57:19, "You who were once far off have been brought near," a text originally referring to exiled Jews but used by both later Judaism and early Christianity to refer to the plight of pagans.[21]

Verses 14–22 concentrate on the reconciliation theme. The central reconciling act that breaks down the walls of division and thereby carries out God's cosmic plan of salvation is the death of Jesus. This point is stressed again and again. Those far off are brought near "in the blood of Christ" (v.13). The breaking down of the law and the creation of "one new man in place of the two," peace-making, is done "in his flesh" (a code phrase for the death of Jesus, cf. v. 15). The reconciling of both Jew and Gentile to God in one body is "through the cross" (v.16; cf. Eph. 5:2, 25).

As Meyer notes, there are two dimensions to the term "body" as used in Ephesians: the *body of the church* finds its origin and meaning in the crucified *body of Jesus*.[22] This twofold use of "body" seems present in the profound yet illusive words of Eph. 2:16: "Christ reconciles both Jew and Gentile to God in one body through the cross, thereby bringing hostility to an end." As Schnackenburg and others have suggested, this text seems to build on the thought of Rom. 7:4, "You have died to the law through the body of Christ."[23] In his "body," that is, his historical person, Christ atones for all humanity. Therefore united to him in faith the believer "dies" and is "risen." Eph. 2:16 develops this same thought. Through Christ, the representative human being, the wall of hostility between all peoples (concretely here between Jew and Gentile) is broken down.

On one level, then, the term "body" in Eph. 2:16 refers to the body of the crucified and risen Jesus. But the other dimension of "body" is also present: the church united to the risen Lord. This is clear from the context, especially Eph. 2:18, where the parallel phrase "in one spirit" shows that the intention of the writer is to speak of the post-Easter experience of the church. In the body of the church, which is filled with Christ's world-embracing "fullness" and over which he who is Lord of the universe is "head" (cf. Eph. 1:22–23), the redemptive work of the cross is actualized and concretely experienced. The building up of this one community (Eph. 2:19–22) from diverse and formerly alienated people is a sign of the ultimate goal of God's plan. This understanding of the nature of the church further defines its missionary responsibility: its own experience of reconciliation is to be communicated to the world.

Responsibility of a Missioned Church (Eph. 3:10, 14–20; chaps. 4–6)

The exhortation sections of Ephesians should not be cut off from the cosmic-mission perspective of the first two chapters. Interpreters who consider Ephesians to be wholly absorbed in ecclesiology tend to make this mistake. The exhortations to awareness, to unity, to right conduct that dominate chapters 4–6 are all in function of the church's world-serving mission.

The first sign of this breaks out in chapter 3, a section in which "Paul" describes his own ministry. His personal mission is to make known God's awesome plan of salvation (Eph. 3:8–9). This ministry "creates" the church, a community whose reconciled life concretizes the nature of God's redemptive work and helps to reveal it to the world. Thus, as the author states, "through the church the manifold wisdom of God might now be made known to the principalities and powers of heavenly places." Thus one of the first things Paul prays for on behalf of the church is "knowledge," an experiential awareness of the scope of its life and mission (Eph. 3:14–21). As 3:19 eloquently states, this "knowledge" is equivalent to the experience of salvation itself—the world-embracing love of Christ, the "fullness" of God, which is destined to suffuse all reality: "To know the love of Christ which surpasses knowledge, that you may be filled with all the fullness of God."

The main exhortation section begins in chapter 4. The opening verses moor the exhortation to the cosmic-mission perspective we have been delineating: "lead a life worthy of the calling to which you have been called . . . " (Eph. 4:1). The reconciliation dimension of the cosmic plan is once again invoked: "There is one body and one Spirit, just as you were called to the one hope that belongs to your call, one Lord, one faith, one baptism, one God and Father of us all, who is above all and through all and in all" (Eph. 4:4–6). Given the context of the first three chapters, there can be little doubt that the fourfold use of "all" (*pas*) in verse 6, though beginning with the unity of the church, edges out beyond the borders of the community to involve the cosmic "all" of such key texts as 1:10 and 1:23. In other words, the church's call to unity is always in function of the *world's* call to unity.

The author's instructions on the right use of gifts and roles within the community are in view of this cosmic vision. In verse 7 he begins a discussion of the "gifts" given to the community by the exalted Christ. The curious verses 8–10, which apparently are a midrashic development of Psalm 68, seem to make the same point.[24] The victorious Lord now "ascended on high" (vv. 9–10) is he who "gave gifts to men" (v.10). The gifts to the church, in other words, are a part of the world-embracing mission attached to the "fullness" of Christ.

The variety of gifts and offices mentioned (cf. Eph. 4:11 and the codes of chap. 5–6) are for the purpose of "building up the body of Christ" (cf. Eph. 4:12–16). The context for this ecclesial ministry must again be emphasized. "Building up of the body" does not mean absorption with the domestic needs of the church. The "body is built up" so that the church can be an effective sign and expression of the cosmic mission of Christ. As Caird notes: "The building up of the body of Christ is not achieved by pastoral concentration on the interior life of the Church, but by training every member for his part in the Church's mission to the world."[25]

The missionary thrust of this exhortation section comes to term in Eph. 4:15–16. As in many passages of Ephesians, abstracting from the cosmic perspective of the first two chapters can distort the meaning of subsequent passages. The translation difficulties of 4:15 bear this out. Many interpreters translate the Greek words *ta panta* ("the all") in 4:15 as an adverbial phrase, as, for example, in the Revised Standard Version: "Rather, speaking the truth in love, we are to grow up *in every way* into him who is the head, into Christ." But such a translation overlooks the fact that the phrase "the all" has been consistently used by the author of Ephesians as a quasi-technical term for the entire cosmos, which is the missionary object of Christ and his church. In her recent study of this passage, R. Meyer opts for the following translation: "We should say the truth in love and so allow 'the all' to grow toward him who is the head.''[26] Translating "the all" as an object rather than an adverb helps Eph. 4:15–16 to fit neatly into the preceding context, which discussed the place of various gifts and roles in the church's mission. The same object is in mind here—the union of all in Christ. But now the missionary activity singled out is "speaking the truth in love." "Speaking the truth in love" refers to proclamation: in Eph. 1:13 the author describes the gospel as "the word of truth." But, as Meyer notes, "speaking the truth in love" in the context of Eph. 4:15 does not have to mean exclusively verbal proclamation. Rather, in the light of 4:1–14, the entire life of the church—its gifts, its service roles, its missionary work, its very life and unity—all of these become "the word of truth."[27]

This comprehensive sense of mission is ratified in verse 16. Through its mission of speaking the truth, the church unites all its efforts with Christ, "from whom the whole body, joined and knit together by every joint with which it is supplied, when each part is working properly, makes bodily growth and upbuilds itself in love." This, Meyer points out, has been the central insight of the missionary theology of Ephesians: it has joined together the cosmic mission of Christ for the all with the total life of the church as a community of God's redeemed people. Thus the "total apostolate of the church . . . implies a missionary service of proclamation.''[28]

Paul: Model of the Missionary Apostolate of the Church

One final aspect of the missionary theology of Ephesians to be considered is the epistle's image of Paul. As Meyer suggests, the author of the epistle presents the apostle as a model for the church by drawing on Paul's own statements in Colossians (cf. especially 1:24–27) and general Pauline tradition.[29]

The key texts are found mainly in chapter 3. Paul's "knowledge" of the "mystery" is stressed (cf. Eph. 2:3–5). What has been hidden has been made known to him as one of the "holy apostles and prophets." As is characteristic of Paul's own letters, his vocation as an apostle is also highlighted. He has been given the "stewardship of God's grace" (Eph. 3:2), made "a minister of the gospel" (3:7), and offered the "grace to preach to the Gentiles" (3:8).

The contents of the mystery entrusted to Paul are revealed in the very nature of his ministry. His preaching to the Gentiles that they are "fellow heirs, members of the same body, and partakers of the promises in Christ Jesus" (Eph. 3:6) unveils the cosmic reconciliation of "all in all," which God intends. As chapter 2 had already disclosed, the inclusion of the Gentiles is both concrete experience and sign of this cosmic reconciliation: "To make all men see what is the plan of the mystery hidden for ages in God who created all things; that through the church the manifold wisdom of God might now be made known to the principalities and powers in heavenly places" (Eph. 3:9–10).

Not only is Paul's ministry a disclosure and a model for the church's own mission, but so, too, is his personal experience. He prays on the church's behalf (cf. especially Eph. 3:14-21) and exhorts the church to unity and fidelity (Eph. 4:1-32). He suffered on behalf of the Gentiles and the church (Eph. 3:1,13; 4:1,20). In his imprisonments and other hardships Paul mirrors the salvific suffering of Jesus who "died in the flesh" that all might be reconciled (cf. especially Eph. 2:13-18). Thus the entire church—those who labor in a missionary apostolate like Paul and those who work for the interior unity of a world-serving church—can experience the redemptive power of Christ's suffering when, like Paul, they suffer on behalf of a cosmic reconciliation.[30]

CONCLUSION

The missionary theology that was triggered with the Christology of Paul's letter to the Colossians reached fuller development in the deutero-Pauline epistle to the Ephesians. This development was not a defeat for the outward-directed mission of the earlier generations but a triumph of universalism. Now the very nature of the church is seen as universal, world-serving, missionary. The rather pessimistic conclusion of Hahn and others seems unjustified. He laments that in the post-Pauline theology of these letters, "The Church's main task lies in its right existence as a Church, and its main service to the world lies in its existence and growth towards its head."[31] This leads to what Hahn calls "the very characteristic and distinctive mark of the post-Pauline period," that is, "the separation of mission and Church and the concentration of theological utterances on the ecclesiological problem."[32]

But such a view does not seem to catch the major concern of these letters, which is not the aggrandizement of the church but the cosmic scope of Christ's lordship. The church's existence is entirely subordinated to this awesome rule of Christ. As Markus Barth concludes:

> When Christ is the subject of any statement seeking to define the church, and when the world is included in her definition as both the field and the necessary beneficiary of the blessing bestowed upon her, then justice is done to "Christ" the "head": now Christ's headship over the world no longer stands in tension with his being head of his body, the church (1:22-23). The servant function of the body is brought to light and an ontology of the church will never be sought apart from, or at the cost of, the description of the church's activity in the world. The church will seek to live "for the world," rather than segregate herself from the world, at its expense, or for its subjugation. Now she cannot consider herself as an end in herself, and will desist from claiming identity with Christ. Christ is "in" the church and the church is "in" him and "with" him (Rom. 8). But her greatest honor is to be his covenant partner, that is, a distinct person who is loved by him, and who serves the demonstration of his love to the world.[33]

The missionary theology of Colossians and Ephesians forms therefore one of the most powerful statements in the New Testament concerning the universal missionary nature of the church. No longer can the church's horizons be narrow, its agenda timid. It serves a cosmic Lord: therefore its field of service is as wide as the world.

NOTES

1. F. Hahn, *Mission in the New Testament* (Naperville: Allenson, 1965), p. 147.

2. Cf. the discussion in W. Kümmel, *Introduction to the New Testament*, rev. English ed. (Nashville: Abingdon, 1975), pp. 358-60.

3. Cf. the state of the question in W. Kümmel, *Introduction to the New Testament*, pp. 340-46. Kümmel himself holds for the Pauline authorship of the letter.

4. Cf. the full state of the question in M. Barth, *Ephesians* (Garden City, N.Y.: Doubleday, Anchor Bible, 1974), 1:36-41. For a recent author who argues in the opposite direction, cf. L. Johnson, *Invitation to the New Testament Epistles III* (Garden City, N.Y.: Doubleday, 1980), pp. 73-77.

5. H. Merklein, *Christus und die kirche*, Stuttgarter Bibelstudien 66 (Stuttgart: KBW, 1973), pp. 101-2.

6. Cf. the extensive discussion in E. Lohse, *Colossians and Philemon* (Philadelphia: Fortress Press, 1971), pp. 41-61; J. Sanders, *The New Testament Christological Hymns*, Society for New Testament Studies Monograph Series 15 (Cambridge, England: University Press, 1971); and a popular yet thorough treatment in R. Martin, *Colossians: The Church's Lord and the Christian's Liberty* (Grand Rapids, Mich.: Zondervan, 1973), pp. 34-55.

7. Although the possibility that Col. 1:15-20 does incorporate an early hymn is attractive, it is impossible to be conclusive on this question. G. Caird (*Paul's Letters from Prison*, New Clarendon Bible [Oxford: University Press, 1976], pp. 174-75), for example, argues that the passage looks like a hymn only *after* removing material from the text, a procedure that begs the question. Solving the issue is not crucial for our purposes. What is crucial, as E. Schweizer points out, is that in this passage Paul gives full attention to the cosmic dimensions of his Christology and thereby provides another basis for the universal mission of the church and its preaching (cf. "The Church as the Missionary Body of Christ," in *Neotestamentica* [Zurich-Stuttgart: Zwingli Verlag, 1963], pp. 323-24).

8. On the meaning of the term *pleroma,* or "fullness," cf. the discussion in M. Barth, *Ephesians*, 1:200-205. He notes that the term takes on more specific and technical meaning in later Gnostic literature, but for Paul's use of the term the biblical notion of God's manifest presence in the world, his *Shechinah*, is a more likely background.

9. For the importance of Wisdom speculation in Judaism as a preparation and background for early Christology, cf. M. Hengel, *The Son of God* (Philadelphia: Westminster Press, 1980), pp. 163-212; and J. Dunn, *Christology in the Making* (Philadelphia: Westminster Press, 1980), pp. 163-212.

10. E. Schweizer, *Neotestamentica*, p. 325. Cf. also the comments of S. Freyne: "In a word, the first impact of the Greek influence on the New Testament world was to create an atmosphere of universal anxiety and fear in the face of the impersonal

force that dominated men's lives, namely Fate. This created a situation in which the search for ways of coping religiously with life was very active, even when it often gave rise to practices and beliefs that could only be described as superstitious and bizarre. In the end, astrology, magic, sorcery and the like did not solve the problem of Fate, but merely offered possibilities of escaping its clutches" (*The World of the New Testament*, New Testament Message 2 [Wilmington, Del.: Michael Glazier, Inc., 1980] p. 28).

11. On this, cf. E. Schweizer, *Neotestamentica*, pp. 324-25.

12. Ibid., pp. 326-27.

13. R. Meyer, *Kirche und Mission im Epheserbrief*, Stuttgarter Bibelstudien 86 (Stuttgart: KBW, 1977), p. 11. We are indebted to Meyer's study for much of our own treatment of Ephesians and the mission question.

14. Ibid., p. 21.

15. M. Barth, *Ephesians*, 1:89-90.

16. M. Barth refers to the epistle of Barnabas II, and to 4 Ezra 12:25; cf. *Ephesians*, 1:90.

17. R. Meyer, *Kirche und Mission*, p.25.

18. Cf. the discussion in R. Meyer, *Kirche und Mission*, pp. 45-48.

19. M. Barth, *Ephesians*, 1:209; cf. similar remarks in R. Meyer, *Kirche und Mission*, p. 33.

20. This was a typical assessment of the plight of the pagans on the part of Judaism; cf. C. Bussmann, *Themen der paulinischen Missionspredigt* (Bern: Herbert Lang, 1971), pp. 132-35.

21. Cf. M. Barth, *Ephesians*, 1:260, 276-79.

22. R. Meyer, *Kirche und Mission*, p. 39.

23. Cf. R. Schnackenburg, "Todes-und Lebensgemeinschaft mit Christus. Neue Studien zu Röm 6,1-11," *Schriften zum Neuen Testament* (Munich:Kösel, 1971), pp. 361-91.

24. Cf. Ps. 68:18: "Thou didst ascend the high mount, leading captives in thy train, and receiving gifts among men, even among the rebellious, that the Lord God may dwell there." Cf. the discussion of the use of this psalm in Judaism, in G. Caird, *Paul's Letters*, pp. 73-75.

25. Caird, *Paul's Letters*, p. 76.

26. R. Meyer, *Kirche und Mission*, p. 73.

27. Ibid., pp. 76-77.

28. Ibid., p. 77.

29. On Paul as "model" in the deutero-Pauline letter of Ephesians, cf. M. de Boer, "Images of Paul in the Post-Apostolic Period," *Catholic Biblical Quarterly* 42 (1980): 359-80; R. Meyer, *Kirche und Mission*, pp. 58-60.

30. On the exemplary value of Paul's suffering in the deutero-Pauline writings, cf. M. de Boer, "Images of Paul," pp. 366-69.

31. F. Hahn, *Mission in the New Testament*, p. 147.

32. Ibid, p. 151. Underlying Hahn's perspective is, I believe, a broader assumption about the development of the early community and the New Testament itself. Hahn seems to accept the position of E. Käsemann and others, which concludes that after the Pauline period, institutionalization began to transform substantially the early community and its theology. This "early Catholicism," as it is sometimes called, is reflected in such symptoms as a concern for authority and tradition, the development of order, and the diminution or transformation of eschatology. The problem with this hypothesis, however, is that the data are more complex than the hypothesis; many of

the signs of "early Catholicism" considered characteristic of post-Pauline writings are also found in Paul's letters. On this issue, cf. the discussion in J. Elliott, "A Catholic Gospel: Reflection on 'Early Catholicism' in the New Testament," *Catholic Biblical Quarterly* 31 (1969): 213–23; and D. Harrington, "The 'Early Christian' Writings of the New Testament: The Church Adjusting to World History," in *The Word in the World*, ed. R. Clifford and G. MacRae (Weston, Mass.: Weston College Press, 1973).

33. M. Barth, *Ephesians*, 1:198–99.

9

The Mission Theology of Mark

The gospel must first be preached to all nations [Mk.13:10].

INTRODUCTION: THE GOSPELS AND THE MISSION QUESTION

The mission question that so dominates the Pauline tradition is still very much alive in the Gospel literature. The Gospels, of course, are not theological treatises or pastoral letters directly grappling with such issues as the Gentile mission or cosmic salvation. The Gospels are narratives, telling a story out of the past. But modern exegesis has emphasized the theological and pastoral nature of these narratives.[1] The Gospels summon up the past in order to proclaim the meaning of Christian faith in the present.

The communities from which and for which the Gospels originated were communities freshly formed by the missionary efforts of the church. There is every reason to believe that all of these communities were "mixed," that is, composed of both Jewish Christians and a swelling majority of Gentile Christians. Such a mix was bound to cause some problems of adjustment. It seems likely that the Gospels were meant to give these same communities fresh perspective in difficult times as they struggled with basic questions about Christian responsibility to the world.

For these reasons, as we shall see, the Gospels are mission literature in the fullest sense of the term. They are not propaganda, not equipment designed for proclamation to nonbelievers. They are mission documents for the church itself, meant to justify, renew, and motivate the church's claim on the heritage of Jesus' own boundary-breaking ministry.

From the Pauline literature and from the rest of the New Testament evidence, one can safely deduce that Christianity underwent an explosive expansion in the latter half of the first century. The gospel moved rapidly beyond its Palestinian base and practically encircled the Mediterranean basin, not to mention deep incursions into Syria, Asia Minor, and Greece. The dynamism of this mission outreach, as well as the inevitable problems it must have caused, are apparent in the letters of Paul. Probing between the lines of the Gospels, too, reveals the glories and the bruises of this vigorous early Christian history.

The point of our study is not to attempt a detailed review of the complex and largely irretrievable history of the evolution of the Gospels. Instead we want to concentrate on the new synthesis achieved by the evangelists in the latter half of the first century. The evangelists drew their material from the traditions of their communities, traditions forged in the dynamic missionary era of the church. At the same time they wanted to respond to the pastoral needs of their communities. Many of the needs were the result of the mission of the church. In this process the evangelists shaped a reinterpretation of the Christian message. The gospel was preached again, in a new time, a new place, and, we might add, in a new way, by means of narrative.

THE BACKGROUND OF MARK

Most New Testament scholars consider Mark to be the first Gospel written. Mark was the creative genius who reinterpreted the tradition and effectively communicated it by means of a fully developed narrative, thereby becoming the inspiration and source for the work of Matthew and Luke.

The identity of the evangelist, the precise dating of the Gospel's composition, and its place of origin are much debated in the cascade of literature on this Gospel in recent years.[2] Although Mark has been traditionally identified with the John Mark mentioned in Acts (12:12, 25; 15:37, 39), Paul (Col. 4:10; 2 Tim. 4:11; Philemon, v. 24) and 1 Peter (5:13), many scholars question the validity of this traditional information and prefer to leave the evangelist in his anonymity.

Most scholars date the Gospel either shortly before or shortly after the fall of Jerusalem in 70 C.E.* Mark's ambiguous reference to the fate of the holy city and the temple (cf. Mk. 13:2) makes it difficult to decide whether these sayings are harbingers of future doom or subtle illusions to a past tragedy.

The place of origin is also illusive. The statement of Papias associates Mark with Peter and Rome, but other scholars think that internal evidence (i.e., Mark's concentration on Galilee, cf. below) suggests a Palestinian or Syrian location. There is even more cacophany among scholars concerning the particular community situation that produced Mark's Gospel.[3]

These broader issues cannot be decided here. For the record, I tend to side with those who see Mark as written from Rome, probably shortly after the destruction of the temple or at least the beginnings of the Jewish revolt (66–70 C.E.). Its purpose was not so much to quell a single group or single doctrinal aberration as to rearticulate the Christian message for a frightened and bewildered Christian community desperately in need of a fresh perspective.

It should be noted that isolating Mark's mission theology is related to but not absolutely dependent upon the decisions the interpreter makes about date, place, and context. Whatever the particular circumstances of the Gospel, we can be confident about the basic contours of its message.

*Common Era.

HANDING ON THE TRADITION:
THE KINGDOM MINISTRY OF JESUS IN THE GOSPEL OF MARK

One of the first things to be noted about the Gospel of Mark is that it faithfully transmits the basic content and thrust of the kingdom ministry of Jesus. Given the mission implications of this motif, we should not overlook this fundamental datum before turning to Mark's particular emphases.

Mark clearly presents the kingdom motif as the keynote of Jesus' ministry. This is explicitly announced in the summary of 1:14-15: "Now after John was arrested, Jesus came into Galilee, preaching the gospel of God, and saying, 'The time is fulfilled, and the kingdom of God is at hand; repent, and believe in the gospel.'" The evangelist follows through on this programmatic announcement by presenting the full range of Jesus' activity, which defines the meaning of the kingdom.

Signs of Jesus' extraordinary piety break out in the *abba* prayer of 14:36 and in the scattered yet intense moments of prayer throughout the Gospel (1:35; 6:46; 14:32). Jesus' sense of God's compassion is communicated through his way of interpreting the law, whereby forgiveness (2:1-12) and compassion (3:1-6) take precedence over any other commandment.

A special feature of Mark's account is his emphasis on the powerful acts of Jesus, especially his exorcisms. Although no text explicitly links this activity with the kingdom motif (as there is in Mt. 12:28 and Lk. 11:20), there is no question that the healing activity, undertaken by the Marcan Jesus immediately after his keynote statement of 1:14-15 (cf. 1:21-45), is a direct illustration of the kingdom's presence. In this *exousia* of Jesus, one encounters the saving power of the kingdom, the very "gospel of God" (1:14).

The compassionate face of Yahweh the King and his saving intent is also revealed by Jesus' provocative association with outcasts and marginal people. This theme is not as developed as it will be in Luke, but it is firmly present in Mark's stories of Jesus' table fellowship with tax collectors and sinners (2:14-17); his association with women (1:30-31; 5:25-34,35-43; 12:41-44; 14:3-9; 15:40-41, 47; 16:1-8), children (10:13-16), and lepers (1:40-45); his statements on behalf of the poor and the marginal people ("the little ones," cf. 9:42; 10:17-31); the implications of his encounter with the rich young man, and his openness to Gentiles (7:24-30).

The prophetic dimensions of Jesus' kingdom ministry are also not ignored in Mark's account. Conflict begins almost immediately in the Gospel story (cf. 2:1-3:6) as Jesus directly challenges the scribes and Pharisees over Sabbath law and fasting. This kind of confrontation erupts again (7:1-23) over the dietary laws and the custom of Corban, and over questions of divorce (10:2-12) and taxation (12:13-17). Jesus' prophetic challenge to wrong priorities and insincere piety comes to a dramatic climax in the cleansing of the temple (11:15-18).

The eschatological demands of Jesus' kingdom ministry are also in evidence. The Marcan Jesus proclaims an urgent message: the kingdom "is at hand" (1:14-15; 9:1; 13:30). He restlessly plunges into his mission (1:21,38, etc.), conscious that "the time is fulfilled" (1:15), the wedding feast prepared (2:19), the seed already planted (4:3–9,26,30), the awaited Elijah already come (9:13). He calls disciples (cf. 1:16–20), sharing with them his eschatological mission and sending them to proclaim and to heal (3:13–19; cf. 6:7–13). The choice of the Twelve (3:14) announces his intention to restore Israel to its hoped for future. To these disciples has been revealed the mystery of the kingdom (4:11), and they are earnestly invited to repent (1:15) and to devote themselves totally to the mission of the kingdom (cf. 1:17; 8:34; 10:29–31, 42–45). About the future of this kingdom there is no doubt. The Marcan Jesus exudes a sense of ultimate victory, a supreme confidence about the final triumph of God's rule (a major theme of the parables: cf. 4:8, 26–29, 30–32; cf. also 9:1; 13:27–31; 14:62).

When one adds the final and central ingredient of Jesus' death and resurrection, the Christological base on which the authority of Jesus and the truly universal dimension of his mission rests, we can conclude that Mark has faithfully transmitted to his community the full scope of Jesus' ministry. The raw materials for undergirding the church's universal mission are all in place. Now we can examine how the evangelist constructs his own theology of mission from this Jesus material.

INTERPRETING THE TRADITION: THE MESSAGE OF MARK AND THE MISSION OF THE CHURCH

Recent Gospel exegesis has continuously emphasized that the evangelists are not mere transmitters of tradition, handing on messages from the past like the members of a bucket brigade. The Gospel writers creatively interpret tradition for the sake of their own communities. The following factors of Mark's interpretation of the tradition are of special significance for the question of mission.

The Choice of a Story Genre

The power of narrative to communicate human and religious truth effectively and creatively is a special interest of contemporary theology. Mark must be given credit for adopting this genre in order to communicate the meaning of the gospel. This narrative genre itself has several important mission implications.

First of all, the tenor of the gospel is communicated by the very nature of the narrative genre. Jesus and his message are *dynamic,* not static. The story Mark tells is ongoing. It is a *communication,* involving invitation and response. The basic story Mark offers his readers is the account of a man driven to communicate a message to others and exercising power on their behalf, even in and through his death. The "feel" of Christian reality as presented by Mark's narrative is not that of detached analysis. The gospel is an explosive revelation, a compelling invitation.[4] Essential to any mission theology is a conviction of the inherent communicability of the person and message of Jesus. By the very choice of a dynamic story form for his message, Mark signals the missionary character of the gospel.

But Mark does more than simply choose a story format to convey the dynamic meaning of Christ. The manner in which he constructs that story enhances its essentially dynamic (and therefore potentially missionary) character. Even though scholars do not agree on the precise structure of Mark's account, certain broad features of the Gospel's layout are clear.

A series of opening scenes (1:2-13) serve as prologue. Jesus' mission is connected with the eschatological mission of John (vv. 2-8). Jesus is endowed with the Spirit and declared to be God's son (vv. 9-11). His ministry is previewed as an epic and definitive victory over evil (vv. 12-13).

Following this, the keynote text of 1:14-15 introduces the first major portion of the Gospel: the kingdom ministry of Jesus in Galilee. This section can be seen as stretching all the way to 8:21, immediately prior to the crucial scene of Peter's confession at Caesarea Philippi. This major section embraces almost the whole of Jesus' powerful ministry of healing, teaching, and prophetic conflict.

With the Caesarea scene (8:27-9:1) the mood and orientation of the Gospel changes considerably. The motif of Jesus' suffering is introduced (cf. 8:31, and the subsequent passion prediction of 9:31 and 10:32) and the stage is almost wholly occupied by Jesus and his disciples, the crowds and opponents pushed to the periphery of attention. Although Jesus does not actually leave Galilean territory until 10:1, the whole section (8:22-10:52) is cast as a journey from the northernmost reaches of Caesarea Philippi south to Judea and Jerusalem (cf. 9:30,33; 10:1, 17, 32, 46, 52).

A final major section of the Gospel is initiated in 11:1 with the entrance into Jerusalem. From this point until the concluding scene at the tomb (16:1-8) the locus of action is the Holy City. Here Jesus will perform his dramatic prophetic sign at the temple (11:11-25), engage in a last series of sharp clashes with his opponents (11:27-44), and give his apocalyptic discourse (13:1-37). The remainder of the section is taken up with the passion narrative (chaps. 14-15) and the empty tomb story (16:1-8).

By means of this taut structure, the evangelist is able to give a special character to his narrative proclamation of Christ. The Christological view and the theme of the way are two basic aspects that are essentially tied into the broad narrative framework and that directly relate to Mark's mission theology.

The Theme of the "Way." As R. Pesch and others have noted, a "way" or "journey" motif seems to permeate the entire span of Mark's Gospel.[5] The "journey" is announced in the opening quotation from Isaiah (Mk. 1:2-3), heralding the "way of the Lord." John's ministry (Mk. 1:4-8) is the advent of the "way" and Jesus is its embodiment. He is clearly designated as God's beloved Son (1:11; 9:7; 12:6), as the last messenger to be sent (12:6), as the one animated with the Spirit (1:10). His way takes him into Galilee, into a forceful and almost breathless ministry of healing, exorcism, teaching, and conflict. The hostility that mounts early in Jesus' ministry (cf. 2:1-3:6) signals the direction that the journey of God's Son must take. The Son of man must go to Jerusalem and give his life for the sake of the many (cf. 10:33; also 8:31; 9:31; 14:21). Just as the disciples are called to follow Jesus' way at the beginning of the Gospel story (cf. 1:16-21; 2:13-15), so that call is intensified as the direction shifts toward Jerusalem. Now discipleship is defined as sharing in Jesus' own life-giving death and resurrection (8:34). Mark highlights this motif by contrasting Jesus' fixed determination to go to Jerusalem and the cross with the bewilderment and even the resistance of Peter and the disciples (cf. below, under Discipleship).

The conclusion of the Gospel reaffirms the basic journey motif. That "way of the Lord," which began in Galilee and moved through opposition, ignorance, and even death in Jerusalem, will be taken up again by Jesus and the disciples. This is the promise of the Marcan Jesus at the supper (14:28) and is the final message communicated to the women at the tomb: "Go, tell his disciples and Peter that he is going before you into Galilee; there you will see him, as he told you" (16:7).[6] The risen Jesus gathers his community in Galilee for the triumphant continuation of the "way." As Pesch observes, "His way has flowed into their way. . . . their way has become the way of discipleship."[7]

The "title" that heads Mark's Gospel seems to fit this "journey" character. Mark's work as a whole is entitled "the beginning of the gospel . . ." (1:1). Although the precise meaning of the evangelist's words are open to speculation, it seems probable that this opening verse is meant as a characterization of the entire narrative of Mark. His whole story—from Galilee to Jerusalem and back again—is the "beginning" of proclamation, the beginning of the church's "way," which is begun and shaped by the way of Jesus.[8]

This entire journey motif gives an inherently missionary character to Mark's Gospel. The Christian message is described as a way, as a mobile, dynamic transmission of God's Word that sweeps through the heart of Judaism, overcoming opposition and death, and moves out into the world. It is just a beginning. Thus the overall shape Mark gives his narrative suggests that the nature of Jesus' personal message will necessarily propel the community beyond traditional confines.

The Christological Character of Mark's Narrative. The second basic aspect of Mark's narrative that has missionary implications is its essential concentration on Jesus (a point so obvious as to be overlooked). The issue here is not the specific notes of Mark's Christology but the very *fact* of it. If we can presume that Mark is, in effect, "preaching" to his church and thereby offering perspective and instruction to an early community attempting to define its role in the world, then it is noteworthy that the evangelist attempts to define his community's mission by appealing to (and at the same time interpreting) features of the life and mission of the historical Jesus. Here is a distinctive feature of the Gospels in contrast to Paul. The evangelists and Paul share a fundamental starting point—the most revelatory aspect of Jesus' history and the basis of his authority as the Christ, the Son of God, rest on the central issue of death and resurrection. This concentration is evident in Paul's letters and is equally evident in the narrative framework of all four Gospels. For the Synoptics and John the momentum of Jesus' entire life runs in the direction of Jerusalem and the cross. For each Gospel the cross is essentially linked to resurrection. All other materials of the Gospel are interpreted, narrated, and placed in the overall framework of the Gospel from the vantage point of the resurrection of Jesus.

But the Gospel tradition parts company with Paul in that it "defines" the fuller implications of death and resurrection—and thus of Jesus' salvific mission—in the light of Jesus' *entire* ministry. Each Gospel writer does this in a unique fashion, but each does it. Mark, presumably the first Gospel writer, gets the credit for this bold feature of early Christian proclamation. He is convinced that Jesus' character as Son of God, as the Christ, as Son of Man—although fully revealed only in the events of death, resurrection, and final exaltation—is already present and operative in his *pre*-Easter humanity.⁹ Thus the "style" of Jesus' preaching, his relationships, his interpretation of law, his healing activity are, at once, the actions of the authoritative Son of Man and therefore definitive for the mission of the community formed in his name. For this reason, too, the concentration of Mark (and the other Gospels in turn) remains fixed on the person of Jesus. He and his mission are the magnetic center of the Gospel. All other characters (for example, the crowds, the family, the opponents, even the disciples) are subordinate to this focus. In effect Mark's definition of the church's mission becomes a recital of Jesus' life. For Mark that mission can be understood only by means of Jesus' kingdom proclamation and in the context of his death and resurrection.

Signs of a Universal Mission

Geography: Galilee and Jerusalem. One of the devices Mark uses to affirm the universal horizon of the community is the geographical deployment of his story. Mark centers the beginning of his narrative in Galilee (1:2–8:21), its conclusion in Jerusalem (11:1 16:8), and uses the central section as a transition from one area to another (8:22–10:52). The result is that most of Jesus' kingdom ministry takes place in Galilee, while opposition, suffering, and death are located in Jerusalem.

Much of this framework is undoubtedly rooted in solid historical traditions. Jesus was a Galilean and apparently carried out most of his public ministry in this northern region. He was crucified in Jerusalem, the religious and cultural center of Judaism. But Mark highlights this geographical polarity in order to exploit the symbolism inherent in both regions.

Galilee was a region of mixed population.¹⁰ Portions of the Jewish population were interspersed with Greek and other foreign elements due to colonization in the period after Alexander's conquest of the Middle East (333–323 B.C.E.). Therefore the Jewish orthodoxy of the population was somewhat suspect in the eyes of the more pronounced Jewish centers in Judea. This had been true long before Jesus' day. Even as far back as the time of the exile (587 B.C.E.), the northern region of Israel was viewed with suspicion by those in the south.

The political arrangement of the country had shifted considerably in the three decades that separated Jesus' lifetime from the probable date when Mark wrote his Gospel. The area was no longer under the rule of the Herodians but was administered directly by the Romans as part of a larger expanse of territory called "Syria-Palestine." From Mark's vantage point, "Galilee" was the whole northern region of Palestine. It was the place where Jesus had begun his ministry and also the place where the mission of the church had been inaugurated. Here the great opening to the Gentiles had achieved its first great success, as the early church moved eastward into Syria. Thus Mark's favorable attitude to Galilee and his hostility to Jerusalem reflect later Christian experience as much as it does the historical period of Jesus' own lifetime.

Mark's vantage point becomes clearer when we look at the Gospel itself. The term "Galilee" or "Galilean" is used thirteen times in Mark, all but four confined to the first nine chapters of the Gospel. As we have already seen, it is in this region that the full scope of Jesus' kingdom ministry of healing and teaching is carried out. J. Van Canghe points out that the proclamation of the good news is exclusively reserved to Galilee (cf. 1:14,38–39,45; 3:14; 5:20; 6:12; 7:36).[11] The only two references found in the "Jerusalem" section of the Gospel (13:10; 14:9) refer to *future* preaching to Gentiles. It is in Galilee that all of Israel gathers around Jesus (cf. the great Marcan summary of 3:7–12). Jesus himself comes from Galilee (cf. 1:9). "Galilean" is an identifying mark of Peter's discipleship (14:70) and "coming up from Galilee" typifies the faithful women at the cross (15:41).

Jerusalem, by contrast, is almost exclusively painted as a place of opposition and death. Even during his Galilean mission Jesus' adversaries are identified as being "from Jerusalem" (cf. 3:22; 7:1). Jerusalem is the place toward which Jesus must go to meet his fate as the suffering Son of Man who gives his life in ransom for the many. This theme is implicit in the journey motif of 8:21–10:52 and is explicitly stated in the passion prediction of 10:32–33. In the holy city itself Jesus is engaged in direct confrontation with his opponents (cf. chaps. 11–12) and is ultimately condemned by the Jerusalem leaders and Pilate (cf. chaps. 14–15). It is here that he is crucified and buried.

Mark amplifies this geographical symbolism by directing the reader's attention back to Galilee at the conclusion of his story. At the Last Supper, Jesus promises his disciples, "After I am raised up, I will go before you into Galilee" (14:28). The word *proagein* ("go before") duplicates the term used in 10:32, where Jesus was depicted walking out ahead of his disciples on the way to Jerusalem. Now, after the shattering experience of Jesus' death and the scattering of the community (cf. the prediction of 14:27), the risen Jesus will lead his disciples back to Galilee, the place of his kingdom ministry. This hint of a renewed mission is repeated at the very conclusion of Mark's Gospel in the message given to the women by the young man at the tomb: "But go, tell his disciples and Peter that he is going before you into Galilee; there you will see him, as he told you" (16:7).

The return to the place of Jesus' mission is the effective message of resurrection in Mark's Gospel. The community is to be regathered in the very territory where Jesus had first collected them and given them a share in his boundary-breaking kingdom ministry. The community is not to remain in Jerusalem, but to move with renewed awareness and power back to Galilee where the universal mission of the church beckons.[12]

The universal symbolism of Galilee is reinforced when we take a closer look at how Mark casts Jesus' ministry within this region. W. Kelber has drawn attention to the significance of Jesus' journeys around and across the Sea of Galilee.[13] His kingdom ministry on both sides of the lake—one predominantly Jewish and the other Gentile—is Mark's way of depicting the church's mission as inclusive of both Jew and Gentile.

This aspect of Mark's story begins in 4:35 and will dominate the rest of the Galilean section until 8:21. Up until 4:35 Jesus' ministry is located exclusively in a Jewish setting, albeit in Galilee. But in 4:35 Jesus orders the disciples to accompany him across the lake "to the other side." The journey is dominated by the storm story (4:35-41), which demonstrates Jesus' awesome power and leaves the disciples in bewildered amazement. Throughout this "lake section" of the Gospel, the disciples' failure to grasp the scope or significance of Jesus' mission is a constant subplot.

Upon reaching the other side of the lake, Jesus uses his power to free the Gerasene demoniac from his enslavement (cf. 5:1-20). There is little doubt that Mark deliberately places this long exorcism story in a Gentile setting. There is a herd of swine (5:11) nearby and at the conclusion of the story a liberated man is sent on mission to his own people in the Decapolis (that is, Gentile) region (cf. 5:19-20). As Kelber concludes with only slight exaggeration:

> Mark adopts this massive miracle because it underscores the extraordinary nature of what has happened. But for him the point of the miraculous happening does not lie in Jesus' breaking of the demonic power, but in his breaking of the Gentile barrier. He has subordinated the epiphanic miracle to his more comprehensive scheme of the expansion of the Kingdom. Similar to the conversion of Cornelius in Acts 10, the Gerasene exorcism in Mark 5:1-20 constitutes the crucial watershed of the mission to the Gentiles.[14]

From this point in the Gospel (cf. 5:21) begins a series of journeys by Jesus and his disciples back and forth across the lake and into outlying Gentile regions. Although Mark apparently had scant traditions about Jesus' direct dealings with Gentiles (only the story of the Syro-Phoenician woman in 7:24-30), use of the geographical setting enables him to underscore the universalism of Jesus' ministry to both Jew and Gentile. After returning to the western side of the lake in 5:21 there is a renewal of his mission in an evidently Jewish setting (the woman with the hemorrhage and Jairus' daughter, cf. 5:22-43). The rejection of Jesus by his own people in Nazareth (6:1-6), the death of John the Baptist (6:14-29) as well as the commissioning of the Twelve and their first efforts at ministry (6:7-13, 30) are clear overtures to the later missionary experience of the church. The feeding miracle of 6:33-44 begins another chain of miracles illustrating the binding of Jew and Gentile in the kingdom. The feeding of the "lost sheep" in Mark, chapter 6, is in Jewish territory and will be paralleled by one in presumably Gentile territory in 8:1-10. The inclusion of the disciples in both feeding stories and their failure to grasp the significance of the two bread miracles (cf. 8:15-21) shows that Mark is keeping the later mission of the church firmly in mind.

After the feeding story of chapter 6 there is another sea story (6:45-52; cf.

4:35–41). Once again Jesus' divine power of rescue is displayed but the community has not yet grasped its significance (cf. 6:51–52, where the disciples' failure to understand is explicitly linked to the feeding stories). As Kelber notes, the disciples' ignorance is not simply about the nature of Jesus' action but about the scope of his mission.[15] The issue of "scope," of the inclusion of both Jew and Gentile, is taken up again in the scene following the lake story. In 7:1–23 Jesus argues about ritual purity with Pharisees and scribes who, significantly, come "from Jerusalem" (cf. 7:1) . The outcome of the debate is Jesus' declaration that all food is clean (7:19). The criterion of inner purity allows access on the part of all who respond and thus breaks down an arbitrary boundary between Jew and Gentile. That point is reinforced by the wide-ranging missionary journey Jesus now launches into Gentile territory (cf. 5:24, 31). Here is where Mark places the key story of the Syro-Phoenician woman (5:24–30; cf. below under Salvation History), illustrating Jesus' ultimate acceptance of the Gentile woman on the basis of her great faith. The section concludes with a second feeding story (8:1–10), now for the sake of Gentiles, and with continued opposition to Jesus by his opponents (8:11–13) and continued bewilderment by his disciples (8:14–21).

Jesus' life-giving mission among Jews and Gentiles shows that Mark defines the "Galilean" ministry of Jesus in truly universal dimensions. His concern is to unite both Jew and Gentile in one community. Kelber concludes:

> The boat trips are designed to dramatize, not a centrifugal course of action, spinning out from the Galilean center to ever more distant lands, but a unitive movement, alternating between the two sides of the sea. The lake, losing its force as a barrier, is transposed into a symbol of unity, bridging the gulf between Jewish and Gentile Christians. The two are the one. Galilee is no longer ethnically confined to either a Jewish or a Gentile Christian identity, rather "all of Galilee" is where Jewish Christians and Gentile Christians live together in the newness of the Kingdom.[16]

Kelber's insistence on inclusiveness is good but his hesitation about this being a "centrifugal" action is unfounded. The point is not only the unity of Jew and Gentile *within* the church. The Marcan Jesus, after all, does travel *out* to these regions and in turn *sends out* the apostles and even the cured demoniac of Gerasa. When we fit the Galilee symbolism into the whole dynamic of Mark's story, we see that the unifying work of Jesus is offered as a pattern for the ongoing mission of the church. The community is asked to consider Jesus' embrace of Jew and Gentile—even through rejection and death—as the pattern of the proclamation of the Gospel that now "begins" (1:1).[17]

Salvation History. Another device that Mark uses to reflect on the universal mission of the community is "salvation history." History viewed from the perspective of faith enables the evangelist to link in meaningful continuity the promise of the Old Testament, the life of Jesus, his rejection by Israel, and the church's mission experience. The saving intent of God is discernible even in this paradoxical and turbulent series of events. This salvation-history perspective is merely a by-product of the strong eschatological bent of Mark's Gospel (and of early

Christianity in general). Mark's entire Gospel is drenched with the expectation of the coming triumph of the Son of man (cf. 14:62 and the whole of chapter 13). That triumphant return and the gathering of the elect (13:26–27) form the final moment of salvation toward which all of the history of Israel and the mission of Jesus and the church lead. Therefore this perspective loops around all the elements of Mark's story.

The Gospel opens with a composite quotation from the Old Testament, assuring the reader that the events of John's ministry and the appearance of Jesus are, in fact, the promised "way of the Lord" (cf. 1:2–3). He moves inexorably to the heart of Judaism, the holy city of Jerusalem. There Jesus will be rejected by the leaders, capping a pattern of blindness and hostility initiated even in Galilee (cf. 2:1–3:6). But instead of being a defeat for God's salvific plan, this becomes a paradoxical opportunity (cf. 12:9–13); now salvation is experienced by those who are open to perceive it. A Gentile centurion will be the first human being to confess openly that Jesus is the Son of God (15:39). This pattern, too, was already discernible in Jesus' ministry. The outcasts (2:13–17), the disciples (4:10), and the Syro-Phoenician woman (a double outcast—woman and Gentile, cf. 7:24–30) are to respond better than the self-righteous who cannot see.

For Mark this paradoxical history is sacred history; it bears the imprint of God's intent. "The children of the household first" (7:27) not only describes an actual sequence in the historical past of Mark's now Gentile community, but a sequence that reveals the stages in the ever widening circle of salvation that characterizes the final days. Thus, as Hahn notes, the "Jews first" text of 7:29a gives way to the universal commission of 13:10: "The gospel must first be preached to all nations."[18] Once more the pattern of Jesus' own life—his transcending of opposition and narrow boundaries to reach out to those who see—becomes authority for the church's own life.

This authority, as we have already noted, is the foundation of the community's appeal to Jesus. The Gospel clearly states this personal authority of Jesus. He is designated Spirit-filled Son (1:11; 8:7), the eschatological Son of man (2:10; and passim), the transcendent Son of God (1:1; 5:7; 14:61; 15:39), the Christ (8:9; 14:61; 15:2), Lord of the Sabbath (2:27), and so on. This brace of titles is backed up by Jesus' powerful words and deeds, including the awesome displays of divine power over the sea (cf. 4:35–41; 6:47–52). This unique person acts in God's name and through his life, death, and resurrection reveals the intent and scope of the community's mission. It is ultimately the God of Israel, the God of history, who sends Jesus into Galilee, who hands him over to death and raises him to new life.

Some of the major passages in Mark that illustrate this pattern of salvation history deserve closer attention.

The Rejection of Jesus and the Opening to the Gentiles. Hahn correctly notes that much of the first major section of the Gospel (1:14–8:21) is taken up with the consequences of Jesus' mission to Israel.[19] His powerful ministry of words and deeds meets with rejection on the part of the leaders and his Israel "family," but with varying degrees of openness and faith on the part of the disciples and Gentiles.

The rejection motif is quickly introduced in the collection of controversy stories in 2:1–3:6, which concludes with the ominous threat: "The Pharisees went out, and immediately held council with the Herodians against him, how to destroy him." The theme is taken up again in 3:20–35. Here Jesus' uncomprehending family (3:20, 31ff.) and "scribes from Jerusalem" are placed together in their attempt either to limit or to reject Jesus' mission. The intransigence of the scribes climaxes in their blasphemous evaluation of Jesus (3:22). The whole episode is counterbalanced by Jesus' disassociation from his blood relatives and his affirmation of a new form of kinship ("Whoever does the will of God, is my brother, my sister, and mother") in 3:31–35. This principle—access on the basis of response to God's will rather than by blood membership in the family of Israel—is a crucial theological support for the early church's mission. The parable discourse of 4:1–34 is also essentially linked to the rejection motif. To those associated with Jesus "has been given the mystery of the kingdom of God" but to those destined to reject his good news, those "outside," "everything happens" in baffling parable or riddle (4:11–12, 33–34).[20]

It is not by accident that at this juncture in the Gospel, Mark begins to describe Jesus' journey across the lake and into Gentile territory (4:35). In such persons as the Gerasene demoniac (5:1–20) and the deaf-mute of the Decapolis (7:31–37), Jesus encounters openness to his ministry.

The premier example, however, is that of the Syro-Phoenecian woman of 7:24–30: here the issue of the universal mission is explicitly joined. As Hahn and others have pointed out, this paradigmatic encounter with a Gentile is prepared for by the conflict story of 7:1–23.[21] The Pharisees and scribes (once more significantly labeled "from Jerusalem," 7:1) challenge Jesus because he and his disciples do not live "according to the tradition of the elders" concerning ritual purity (7:5). Jesus' response is a strong condemnation of his opponents' lack of integrity and their faulty interpretation of the law (cf. 7:6–13). In 7:14–23 he goes further, teaching his disciples in private that the principle of internal purity even negates the dietary laws altogether (cf. 7:19). This radical statement undoubtedly reflects a pastoral solution of the early Gentile mission as much as it does the prophetic critique of Jesus. This removal of a cultural and religious boundary obviously prepared for Jesus' encounter with the Gentile woman in 7:24–30. Jesus' sharp rebuff to her initial approach reaffirms the salvation-history perspective already implied in Jesus' ministry in Galilee: "Let the children [i.e., Israel] first be fed . . ." (7:27). But her persistent faith causes Jesus' admiration and the use of his healing power, thus illustrating in story the principle that membership in God's family is determined by obedient faith rather than bloodline (cf. above, comments on 3:35).

The theme of rejection and response continues throughout the Gospel but reaches its climax in the Jerusalem section (11:1–16:8). Jesus' opponents categorically reject his teaching (cf. especially Mark, chap. 11–12) and ultimately plot his death. The Gentile centurion (15:39), the outcast women (15:40–41), and ultimately, after failure, the disciples are the inheritors of the vineyard. This rejection-acceptance theme is played out in a slightly different mode in the Jerusalem segment of the Gospel and it is to this that we now turn.

A New Temple "Not Made by Hands." Recent scholarship has highlighted the "temple" motif in chapters 11–15 of Mark and the connection of this motif with the question of Israel and the church.[22] By means of this theme, Mark follows through on the geographical and salvation-historical motifs of his narrative. Because the story now moves to Jerusalem, the appropriate symbol for speaking of Israel and its paradoxical response to Christ becomes the temple. Chapters 11–13 all take place in the setting of the temple, and some key episodes in the passion narrative (cf. especially 14:58 and 15:38–39) complete the temple motif.

A detailed exegesis of these important chapters would expand our study beyond its limits. We have to be content with a cursory reading of the most significant elements. As J. Donahue has insisted, chapters 11–12 (and to an extent chapter 13), must be seen as a single unit.[23] The entry into Jerusalem, the prophetic condemnation of the temple, and the disputes over Jesus' teaching are intimately linked together around the issue of Jesus' authority and the rejection of that authority by the leaders of Israel.

The mood is set in the opening scene (11:1–11). With an air of sovereign authority Jesus commands his disciples to prepare for a solemn entry into the holy city. The messianic identity of Jesus is openly hailed by the crowds that accompany him (11:9–10). He enters Jerusalem and immediately goes to the temple, the seat of Jewish worship and teaching authority.

Mark's embellishment of the next scene causes an interruption in the action; the action parable of the cursing and withering of the fig tree (11:12–14, 20–25) serves as a rueful commentary on the temple's future. Because it bears no fruit, it is condemned. Mark's narration of Jesus' action in the temple is particularly significant. The original story Mark used may have had a prophetic meaning: the Christ *purifying* the temple. But in Mark's rendition, Jesus' actions and words are a prophetic *condemnation* of the temple and a signal of a new locus of worship open to Gentiles. In 11:16 Mark notes that Jesus "would not allow anyone to carry anything through the temple." This cryptic text may refer to the vessels necessary for the cult and would suggest that Jesus is bringing the sacrifice to a halt. The teaching of 11:17 becomes a commentary on the ultimate significance of his action: " 'My house shall be called a house of prayer for all the nations . . .' but you have made it a den of robbers." The first line is a quotation from Isa. 56:7, and it relates Jesus' actions in the temple to the theme of universalism. As Donahue notes, this text announces that "the eschatological 'house of prayer for all nations' will replace the temple."[24] The sharp quotation from Jer. 7:11—"but you have made it a den of thieves"—provides the counterpoint: the opening to the Gentiles is paradoxically tied to the rejection of Jesus by Israel. This rejection motif is driven home in 11:18 where, in words reminiscent of 3:6, Mark observes that "the chief priests and the scribes . . . sought a way to destroy him."

The motif of the rejection of Jesus provides a link between Jesus' action in the temple and the subsequent parts of chapters 11 through 13. The theme is immediately taken up in Mark 11:27–33, where the leaders challenge Jesus' authority "to do these things" (11:28) and even more strongly in the parable of the vineyard in 12:1–12. This parable is of major concern for our study because here themes of

Jesus' mission, his rejection, and the opening to the Gentiles are clearly stitched together in a salvation-history perspective. The heavily allegorical story describes God's efforts on behalf of Israel, his vineyard (cf. Isaiah 5). A series of messengers (most likely the prophets) are sent to the vineyard but are rejected by the tenants. Finally the son is sent but he too is rejected and even killed. This rejection provoked God's judgment on the tenants (12:9) and the transfer of the vineyard's care "to others." The implication is clear: these "others" will be open to God's messengers and will respond (the very point Matthew will emphasize in his version of the parable: cf. Mt. 21:43).

A citation from Ps. 118:22–23 ties the parable's meaning to the temple theme: "The very stone which the builders rejected has become the head of the corner." The rejection of Jesus and the opening to the Gentiles are symbolized in the condemnation of the temple and the erection of a "spiritual" edifice, a new worshiping community. All of this falls within the purview of God's mysterious working in history: "This was the Lord's doing, and it is marvelous in our eyes" (12:11).

The subsequent scenes continue the motif so firmly sounded in Mk. 11:1–12:12. The conflict stories and the teaching of 12:13–44 simultaneously emphasize Jesus' authority and the rebuff of the leaders. An explicit link between the fate of the temple and the universal mission is reintroduced in chapter 13. Jesus' prediction of the destruction of the temple (13:2) leads off the discussion of the travails to be experienced by the community as it awaits the end-time. These experiences have a "missionary" flavor; the disciples will endure imprisonment, trial, persecution, and hardship in the carrying out of their witness on Jesus' behalf (cf. 13:9–13). But these trials must be endured while the gospel is "preached to all nations" (13:10). Mark in effect identifies the community's activity between Jesus'own ministry and the cataclysmic end of the world as a time of universal proclamation and witness. Only after this is completed will the Son of Man come and the community be gathered "from the four winds, from the ends of the earth" (13:27).

The salvation-history theme of paradoxical rejection and acceptance, of transfer from old to new, of death and new life breaks through in its final form in Mark's passion narrative. Here again the temple motif provides the backdrop. In 14:58 false witnesses testify against Jesus: "We heard him say, 'I will destroy this temple that is made with hands, and in three days I will build another, not made with hands.' " The "fallacy" of their witness (Mk. 14:56, 59) is due more to their hostile intent and their confusion (in contrast to the majesty of Jesus in the trial scene) than to the inaccuracy of their statement, for the threat against the temple and the promise of a new spiritual temple seem to coincide with the entire message of chapters 11–13.

The connection of this implicit prophecy regarding the fate of the temple with the rejection motif is made in the next verses. In one of the capital Christological moments of the Gospel, the high priest demands of Jesus: "Are you the Christ, the Son of the Blessed One?" (14:61). Jesus accepts those titles without reservation and goes on to add a third: "You will see the Son of Man seated on the right hand of power, and coming with the clouds of heaven" (14:62). Here the key confessional titles—Son of God, Christ, Son of Man—are brought together in the setting of the passion. For Mark's whole Christology this passion context is essential. Only when Jesus is recognized as the suffering Son of Man can the meaning of "Son of God" and "Christ" be properly understood. While Jesus fully discloses his identity, the high priest and the rest of the leaders formally reject his claim (cf. 14:64-65). Thus they will experience Jesus in the context of the coming judgment ("you will see the Son of Man").

The finale is reached in 15:37-39. At the moment of Jesus' death, the veil of the temple is torn in half and the Gentile centurion confesses Jesus as Son of God. The connection of these verses with the salvation-history material we have been considering cannot be denied. The precise meaning of Jesus' wordless death-shout is disputed; it may connote a cry of victory and be related to the theophany motif Mark has developed earlier in his Gospel.[25] At any rate, it is Jesus' life-giving death (cf. 10:45) that triggers the two significant events that follow. The temple veil, symbolic of the divine presence in the temple, is destroyed. The end of the temple predicted by Jesus takes place at the very moment of his death and resurrection. The rejection of Jesus and his mission means the end of the old way; now the vineyard is being handed on to others (cf. 12:14).

Thus in Mark the tearing of the veil is primarily a negative sign, a sign of judgment. The response of the centurion, on the other hand, is essentially positive. He becomes the first member of the new temple "not made by hands," the worshiping community that is able to recognize in the suffering and death of Jesus God's work of salvation. The centurion "sees" and confesses his faith in Christ (15:39) while the leaders of Israel mock him and demand he come down from the cross (15:30-32).

It cannot be accidental that the evangelist has a *Gentile* centurion be the first person in the Gospel to acclaim Jesus as Son of God and to have that take place by the Centurion witnessing Jesus' life-giving death.[26] At this denouement of his story Mark dramatically signals the direction that the community itself must go. The message of the young man at the tomb, "Go to Galilee" (16:7), amplifies the mission message already depicted in the centurion's response at the cross. The Marcan community is now to go to Galilee and take up the task of proclaiming the gospel to the ends of the earth until the coming of the Son of man and the gathering of his elect (13:9-10,26-27). The death of Jesus—as was his life—is a death on behalf of the many (10:45; 14:24).

Discipleship: Following a Crucified Jesus

Approaching the Gospel from the vantage point of mission puts in relief the evangelist's concern with response to Jesus. The very format of the story is a dynamic communication of the person and message of Jesus that begs reaction. The tragedy of Israel's rejection and the fresh surprise of the Gentiles' acceptance play on the same theme. It is not unexpected, therefore, that Mark's portrayal of the disciples should have an integral part in his theology of mission.[27] They more than any other set of characters in the Gospel story exemplify the meaning of response to Jesus.

Mark in effect "defines" genuine discipleship in Christological terms. How one perceives and responds to the identity of Jesus ultimately distinguishes the blind leaders (for whom all is riddle; cf. 4:10–13) from the chosen disciples (those to whom the mystery of the kingdom is revealed; cf. 4:10). For Mark the true identity of Jesus is revealed in his life-giving death. Recognition of Jesus as the suffering Son of Man who gives his life in ransom for the many (10:45) is the touchstone for all genuine faith. The powerful acts of Jesus, his teaching, his messianic identity, his claim to be God's Son—all of these must be seen in the light of the passion and resurrection. The life-giving service of Jesus sets the pattern for the church's own existence, including the style and intent of its mission. Thus the degree to which the disciples are able to comprehend the cross is the degree to which they comprehend the meaning of the kingdom of God.

This basic message of the kerygma underwrites Mark's entire portrayal of the disciples. From the start it is apparent that they represent the Christian community itself. They receive a call to follow Jesus and to share in his eschatological mission as "fishers of human beings" (1:16–20; 2:14). They are the constant companions of Jesus and the privileged observers of his powerful acts. From the disciples Jesus selects the Twelve, a sign of the promised restoration of Israel (3:13–19). They are sent out as missionaries to do as Jesus does (3:14; 6:7–13, 30). The disciples are the privileged recipients of Jesus' private instruction.[28] They are promised a full share in the rewards of the kingdom (10:28–31). This whole spectrum of experiences—call, fellowship with Jesus, sharing in his ministry, promise of reward—obviously reflects Christian experience itself.

However, Mark also portrays a dark side of the disciples and uses this motif to throw into relief the full meaning of genuine discipleship. The key issue remains one's response to Jesus. Mark employs the metaphor of perception or understanding—not understanding in a purely academic sense but understanding as a personal commitment to Jesus' person and mission. The disciples' perception of Jesus seems to deteriorate as the Gospel progresses. The closer the narrative draws to Jerusalem and the cross, the more evident is the disciples' failure.

In the first major section of the Gospel (Mk. 1:2–8:21) the disciples fail to understand Jesus and the nature of their relationship to him, in spite of the privileges enjoyed by them (cf. above). Thus, for example, they do not understand the parables (4:10–13), they question Jesus' ability to rescue them (4:38–41), and they are baffled by his power over the sea (6:51–52). Of particular significance is their confusion about the meaning of the loaves. On the occasion of each feeding story (cf. 6:35–44; 8:1–9) the disciples seem reluctant to take responsibility for the multitudes. Their lack of perception is underlined in the climactic scene where Jesus challenges them on their failure to understand about the loaves (8:14–21). As we have already noted, the two stories of the loaves demonstrate not only the messianic nature of Jesus' mission but also its universal scope, embracing both Jew and Gentile. By failing to recognize Jesus, the disciples fail to recognize their mission.

In the second major section (Mk. 8:21–10:52) the failure of the disciples and its connection to the passion story become more evident. The pattern is set with Peter's confession (8:27–30). To the key question of the Gospel—"Who do you say that I am?"—Peter responds, "You are the Christ." In the next segment (8:31–33) it becomes clear that Peter's conception of messiahship is faulty, for it does not include the essential link to the passion (cf. 8:31–32). Peter protests against the prospect of a suffering Son of Man (8:32). Jesus' sharp rebuke of Peter (8:33) and a series of discipleship sayings emphasizing the necessity of the cross (8:34–9:1) round out this first block of explicit passion theology in the Gospel. A similar pattern occurs after each of the passion predictions, which serve as the backbone of this central section (9:30–37; 10:32–45). While Jesus speaks of giving his life for the many, the disciples argue about who is the greatest (9:34) or seek places of honor (10:37). In his responses, the Marcan Jesus consistently makes the cross the paradigm for all genuine discipleship. The disciples' failure is ultimately a failure to perceive Jesus' identity (and therefore the pattern for the church's life) as the "Son of Man who gives his life in ransom for the many" (10:45).

Here again a link can be made to the mission question. As we have already seen, Mark considers the cross the paradoxical turning point in salvation history (cf. 15:39). The death of Jesus is a death "for the many" (10:45; 14:24) and the Gentile centurion is a sign of these "many" who will recognize the death and resurrection of Jesus as God's act of salvation for the world. Thus not to accept the cross, and to interpret Jesus wholly within nationalistic messianic terms—as the Marcan disciples seem to do—is to miss the nature of the church's worldwide mission.

The final section of the Gospel (Mk. 11:1–16:8) illustrates this thesis in dramatic terms. The disciples' failure to accept the cross is demonstrated by their "sleep" (a sleep that has symbolic overtones of an eschatological nature; cf. 13:32–37) in Gethsemane and their precipitous flight at the moment of the arrest (14:50–52). Two of the Twelve are singled out for an even more painful failure: Judas betrays Jesus (14:10–11, 44–45) and Peter publicly disavows knowing Jesus (14:66–72). In Mark's passion story, no disciple witnesses the death of Jesus; only the Gentile centurion and the faithful women are present (15:39–40). The latter will, in effect, be designated as disciples because they "came up from Galilee to Jerusalem" (15:40–41) and are the first to proclaim the message of resurrection (16:7).

For some interpreters of Mark's Gospel, the story of the disciples ends in total failure.[29] The disciples are scattered and the women even fail to bring the resurrection message to them (cf. 16:8). Through this definitive failure, the evangelist discredits those groups in his community exemplified by the characters of the disciples in the Gospel story.

But this stark conclusion cannot hold up in the face of other crucial evidence in the latter part of Mark's Gospel. At the Last Supper (cf. especially Mk. 14:17–21, 27–31) the Marcan Jesus prophetically envisions his betrayal and the flight of the disciples. Their failure is explicitly accounted for. Equally accounted for is the ultimate gathering of the disciples in Galilee after the resurrection: "But after I

am raised up, I will go before you into Galilee" (14:28). The prediction of reconciliation is on a par with the prediction of failure.

This text should be decisive for interpreting the ambiguous reference to the
women's silence in the closing verse of the Gospel (16:8). The women's fear and
silence after the encounter with the young man at the empty tomb is not another
instance of failure, but a typical response to an act of divine power. They are
struck with awe. The thrust of the entire Gospel story—in fact the telling of the
story at all—presumes the readers' understanding that ultimately the women did
communicate their Easter message and the gospel did begin to be proclaimed in
Galilee (cf. 1:1). For Mark, too, the church's continuation of the universal
kingdom ministry of Jesus can only begin under the power of the risen Christ's
initiative and only after disciples who had fled from the cross are reconciled to it
by the crucified Son of Man himself. Thus, once again, we discover a basic affirmation of New Testament theology: the authority, the style, and the scope of the
church's mission are determined by the death and resurrection of Jesus for all of
humanity.[30]

Jesus as Revelation of God

One final feature of Mark's theology that relates to mission can be briefly
noted—"briefly," not because this feature is unimportant but because it is implicit in most of the other aspects of the Gospel that we have already discussed.

Commentators have long noted the "numinous" character of the Marcan
Jesus.[31] Despite his efforts to conceal his transcendent identity, Jesus' divine
power is always on the brink of announcement. He is declared God's Son at
baptism (1:11) and transfiguration (9:7). He manifests divine power through his
exorcisms and healings (cf. the reaction of the demons in 1:24 and 5:7) and
through his control of nature (4:35-41; 6:45-52). Throughout the Gospel, the
reactions to Jesus follow the pattern of the theophany texts of the Old Testament:
he provokes awe (cf., for example, 1:27), fear (9:32), silence (16:8). The reaction
of the women (fear, awe, silence) to the announcement of Jesus' resurrection
(16:5-8) typifies the kind of reactions that pervade the Gospel. As John Donahue
points out, Mark uses such numinous qualities and theophanic reactions as a
means of declaring that Jesus is the revelation of God, God's parabolic presence
in the very person and mission of Jesus.[32]

Here is a parallel, however subtle it may seem, to the cosmic Christology of the
Pauline and deutero-Pauline literature. The Jesus proclaimed by the Gospel of
Mark is the transcendent Jesus whose words and actions—particularly the capital
action of death and resurrection—disclose the saving power of the God of Israel.
The universal, cosmic scope to God's saving intent thus makes of Jesus a figure
who breaks the bonds of the narrow and the particular. Belief in such a transcendent Jesus should inevitably lead to a worldwide horizon of concern.

Donahue's conclusion lays bare some of the mission implications:

In Mark, Jesus is the parable of God who is present in privileged time
(*kairos*) and who summons those who hear him to radical faith and radical

conversion (1:14). This Jesus is a figure of power in conflict with the powers of the cosmos and the powers of hardness of heart (3:5; 6:52; 8:17). Yet broken, and abandoned by the source of all power, he dies as the radically powerless one. During his life his power is manifest yet hidden. His disciples and followers are also to be empowered with his spirit (1:10; 13:11). They will confront evil powers and spread the gospel (13:10), but will also die, broken by betrayal and suffering (13:11–13). Their power, too, is hidden. . . . To share in his power is not to possess power of prestige and playing lord over others, but is to practice the self-emptying service which becomes the source of liberation to the many (10:41–45).[33]

CONCLUSION

The inherently dynamic force of Mark's narrative, its portrayal of Jesus, his opponents, and his disciples, and its fundamental message of cosmic salvation earn for this Gospel the title "A Mission Book."[34] Not only does mission have a firm place in Mark's Gospel, but it comes to the fore in precisely those texts and themes that are at the center of the evangelist's concern. Mark invites the church to take up the powerful redemptive mission of Jesus, a mission that embraced Jew and Gentile. But this mission will be genuine only when the community has been transformed by a servant Jesus and his cross.

NOTES

1. On this point, cf. the essays of C. Talbert, "The Gospel and the Gospels," and J. Kingsbury, "The Gospel in Four Editions," in *Interpreting the Gospels*, ed. J. Mays (Philadelphia: Fortress Press, 1981), pp. 14–40. For a clear presentation of modern exegetical methodology and its implications for interpreting the Gospels, cf. D. Harrington, *Interpreting the New Testament: A Practical Guide*, New Testament Message 1 (Wilmington, Del.: Michael Glazier, 1979).

2. For reviews of recent Marcan scholarship, cf. H. Kee, "Mark's Gospel in Recent Research," in *Interpreting the Gospels*, pp. 130–47; J. Kingsbury, "The Gospel of Mark in Current Research," *Religious Studies Review* 5 (1979): 101–7; and D. Senior, "The Gospel of Mark," *The Bible Today* 103 (1979): 2096–2104.

3. Some currents of recent scholarship, typified in the study of T. Weeden (*Mark: Traditions in Conflict* [Philadelphia: Fortress Press, 1971]), view Mark as having a polemical purpose. He writes his Gospel to indict a faction in the community that holds unorthodox or deviant views. Mark's negative portrayal of the disciples is, therefore, a device by which the evangelist is able to discredit heretical or erroneous "disciples" in the Marcan community. The precise nature of the error is debated: for some, such as Weeden, the disciples represent a group who maintain a "divine man" Christology; others see Mark's target as an apocalyptic group (W. Kelber, *The Kingdom in Mark* [Philadelphia: Fortress Press, 1974]), or the Jewish side of the Jew/Gentile polarity in the early community (J. Tyson, "The Blindness of the Disciples in Mark," *Journal of Biblical Literature* 80 [1961]:261–68), while other interpreters maintain that Mark is not attacking a particular faction in the community but

attitudes typical of a large percentage of the community, such as the failure to embrace the cross and the necessity of service (R. Martin, *Mark: Evangelist and Theologian* [Grand Rapids, Mich.: Zondervan, 1973]). More recent commentators (cf. e.g., the monumental commentary of R. Pesch, *Das Markusevangelium*, 2 vols., Herders Theologischer Kommentar zum Neuen Testament [Freiburg: Herder, 1980]) have reacted to this polemical interpretation, pointing out that evidence for Mark's critique of the disciples must be balanced with other positive statements about the disciples (e.g., their call, mission commission, etc.) in the Gospel. Pesch, in particular, stresses that the evangelist is not free to shape his Gospel at will (e.g., for polemical purposes) but must be responsive to tradition, handing it on to his community. On this latter point, cf. also the remarks of C. Kazmierski, *Jesus, the Son of God*, Forschung zur Bibel 33 (Würzburg: Echter, 1979), p. 10.

4. R. Pesch notes how the opening scene of Jesus' ministry in Mark (cf. 1:21–27) involves a revealing action of Jesus (a powerful exorcism) and the responding acclamation of the crowd; this scene typifies Mark's presentation. Cf. R. Pesch, *Das Markusevangelium*, 1:48–53.

5. Cf. R. Pesch, *Das Markusevangelium*, 1:59–60; W. Kelber, *The Kingdom in Mark*, pp. 67–85.

6. With most recent commentators, I judge that the original ending of Mark's Gospel is 16:8; later editors added "more complete" endings to bring Mark into line with the other evangelists. But the story of the discovery of the empty tomb and the awed response of the women to this divine manifestation fits well into Mark's style and no further ending is needed to complete the Gospel. On this, cf. N. Petersen, "When Is the End Not the End?" *Interpretation* 34 (1980): 151–66, and R. Meye, "Mark 16:8-The Ending of Mark's Gospel," *Biblical Research* 14 (1969): 33–43.

7. R. Pesch, *Das Markusevangelium* I:60.

8. For a fuller discussion of this title, cf. R. Martin, *Mark*: *Evangelist and Theologian*, pp. 27–28; R. Meye, *Jesus and the Twelve* (Grand Rapids, Mich.: Wm. B. Eerdmans, 1968), pp. 211–13.

9. Mark explicitly links the body of the Gospel story with the central events of death and resurrection by such devices as the fate of John the Baptist (1:14; 6:14–29), the plotting of Jesus' opponents (3:6; 11:18), and the predictions of the passion (8:31; 9:31; 10:33–34).

10. On the historical background of Galilee, cf. S. Freyne, *Galilee: From Alexander the Great to Hadrian, 323 B.C.E. to 135 C.E.* (Wilmington, Del.: Michael Glazier, 1980), and E. Meyers and J. Strange, *Archaeology: The Rabbis and Early Christianity* (Nashville: Abingdon, 1981), pp. 31–47; a fine discussion of Mark's use of the Galilee motif can be found in J. Van Canghe, "La Galilée dans l'évangile de Marc: un lieu theologique?" *Revue Biblique* 79 (1972): 59–75.

11. J. Van Canghe, "La Galilée dans l'évangile de Marc."

12. Some interpreters of the Gospel assert that Mark ends his Gospel on a polemical note: the women's silence (16:8) means that the disciples are not given the resurrection message, and hence their Galilean mission is never taken up (cf., e.g., N. Perrin, *The Resurrection according to Matthew, Mark, and Luke* [Philadelphia: Fortress Press, 1977], pp. 14–38). But such a polemical interpretation seems unwarranted: the women's silence is a typical reaction to an epiphany and the fact that the Marcan Jesus predicts his eventual encounter with the disciples in Galilee (14:27–28) must be decisive for interpreting 16:7–8. On this point, cf. R. Meye, "The Ending of Mark's Gospel."

13. W. Kelber, *The Kingdom in Mark*, pp. 45–65. This motif was also noted by F. Hahn, *Mission in the New Testament* (Naperville: Allenson, 1965), pp. 112–14.

14. W. Kelber, *The Kingdom in Mark*, pp. 51–52.

15. Ibid., pp. 62–65. While accepting Kelber's analysis of Mark's overall literary work in this section, I do not agree with his final interpretation that Mark, through his portrayal of the disciples, is attempting to discredit an apocalyptically oriented Jerusalem faction. As our discussion of Mark indicates, I would prefer to locate Mark's intention in the broader issue of the universal mission.

16. W. Kelber, *The Kingdom in Mark*, pp. 62–63.

17. ". . . as with the story of Jesus as a whole, it is merely the beginning of what has been happening ever since, and so it is the basis of the disciples' task after Easter. As Jesus already in his lifetime went out beyond Israel, so with his death every restriction disappears the more completely, and the gospel is preached to all the nations in the world, with no need of any further missionary command to do so" (F. Hahn, *Mission in the New Testament* [Naperville: Allenson, 1965], p. 119).

18. Ibid.

19. Ibid, pp. 112–14.

20. Mark seems to view the parables as baffling or veiled communications for those "outside" who are opposed to Jesus and his mission; on the parables in Mark, cf. C. Carlston, *The Parables of the Triple Tradition* (Philadelphia: Fortress Press, 1975), pp. 97–109; P. Achtemeier, *Mark*, Proclamation Commentaries (Philadelphia: Fortress Press, 1975), pp. 65–70.

21. F. Hahn, *Mission in the New Testament*, pp. 113–14.

22. Cf. J. Donahue, *Are You the Christ?* Society of Biblical Literature Dissertation Series 10 (Missoula, Mont.: Society of Biblical Literature, 1973), p. 137; D. Juel, *Messiah and Temple*, Society of Biblical Literature Dissertation Series 31 (Missoula, Mont.: Society of Biblical Literature, 1977), p. 212.

23. J. Donahue, *Are You the Christ?* pp. 113–35.

24. Ibid., p. 114.

25. Cf. the discussion of this text in K. Stock, "Das Bekenntnis des Centurion. Mk 15,39 im Rahmen des Markusevangeliums," *Zeitschrift für Katholische Theologie* 100 (1978): 289–301.

26. Cf. M. Kiddle, "The Death of Jesus and the Admission of the Gentiles in St. Mark," *Journal of Theological Studies* 35 (1934): 45–50; F. Hahn, *Mission in the New Testament*, pp. 117–18.

27. Recent exegesis has given considerable attention to Mark's portrayal of the disciples. For many interpreters, the Marcan disciples are representative of factions in the Marcan community, and the evangelist's essentially negative portrayal of the disciples enables him subtly to refute these factions (cf. the aforementioned works of T. Weeden, J. Tyson, W. Kelber, N. Perrin). But such a purely polemical purpose can be maintained only if other, more positive data on the Marcan disciples are over looked. In our discussion of Mark we have tried to present the full range of material on the disciples; this tends to make them more representative figures, symbolic of both positive and negative attitudes in the Marcan community. On this, cf. E. Best, "The Role of the Disciples in Mark," *New Testament Studies* 23 (1977): 377–401.

28. Cf., e.g., Mk. 4:10–11; 7:17; 9:28; 10:10, 23, 32, 42; 12:43; 13:1–2.

29. Cf., e.g., J. Crossan, "Empty Tomb and Absent Lord (Mark 16:1–8)," in *The Passion in Mark*, ed. W. Kelber (Philadelphia: Fortress Press, 1976), pp. 135–52; N. Perrin, *The Resurrection*, pp. 14–38.

30. Cf. P. Achtemeier, "Mark as Interpreter of the Jesus Tradition," in *Interpreting the Gospels*, pp. 127–29.

31. M. Dibelius's characterization of the Gospel as one of "secret epiphanies" captures its spirit; cf. the discussion in J. Donahue, "Jesus as the Parable of God in the Gospel of Mark, " in *Interpreting the Gospels*, pp. 148–67; R. Pesch, *Das Markus evangelium*, 1:61.

32. J. Donahue, "Jesus as Parable of God," p. 381.

33. Ibid., pp. 385–86.

34. R. Pesch, *Das Markusevangelium*, 1:48–69.

10

The Mission Theology of Matthew

Make disciples of all nations [Mt. 28:19].

The question of the universal mission of the church is clearly central to Matthew's Gospel. The bold commission to "make disciples of all nations" that concludes the Gospel (28:16–20) is sufficient evidence in itself. The presence of an explicit mission discourse (chap. 10) further demonstrates that the mission question is a prime issue in the evangelist's theology. Our limited goal, once more, is not to review all of Matthew's rich message but to isolate those aspects of the Gospel that directly relate to the universal horizon of Christian proclamation.

THE CONTEXT OF MATTHEW'S COMMUNITY

There is probably more scholarly consensus about the situation that shaped Matthew's Gospel than there is about any of the other Gospels. The evangelist seems to have constructed his message in conscious response to the transitional period following the Jewish revolt of 66–73 C.E. and the resulting transformation in both Judaism and Christianity. Although precision is impossible, it is likely that Matthew writes his Gospel sometime in the decades of the 80s and 90s, probably to an urban church in the area of Syria.[1]

For Judaism the shattering experience of the revolt, including the destruction of Jerusalem and the temple in 70 C.E., meant a radical shift in the texture of its religious life. The variety that characterized pre-70 Judaism had to give way to a more homogenized expression in order to survive. The temple-based Sadducee party was no longer viable. Radical groups such as the Essenes and the Zealots were either destroyed or crippled. The Pharisees were the only ones with sufficient moral stamina and political astuteness to coordinate Jewish survival. Under their leadership, centered at Jamnia, the Pharisees reconstructed Judaism on the basis of strict fidelity to the law (as interpreted by the Pharisees). Their efforts would set the tone for subsequent rabbinic Judaism.

This post-70 consolidation meant less tolerance for fringe groups than had been the case in the period prior to the revolution. Apocalyptic movements and Christians were now seen as a dangerous dilution of Jewish orthodoxy and, consequently, as a threat to survival. As a result, such groups were expelled from the synagogues during the last quarter of the first century and relationships between church and synagogue became increasingly hostile.

The Jewish revolt also caused fundamental shifts in Christianity. Prior to the revolt, Jewish Christians remained in close contact with Judaism, undoubtedly adhering to the Jewish law and participating in the religious life of temple and synagogue. The seeds of future separation were already in place: claims regarding the person of Jesus, interpretation of some points of the law, attention to the Gentiles. But chronic tensions and even sporadic outbursts of hostility (for example, the case of Stephen in Acts 7) could be tolerated under the overarching umbrella of diversity. But the destruction of Jerusalem and the emergence of a stricter orthodoxy under the leadership of the Pharisees deeply affected not only Christian relations to Judaism but the internal consciousness of Christianity itself. The growing rift and eventual expulsion from the synagogue must have created a crisis of identity for Jewish Christians whose faith in Jesus had been seen as an act of fidelity to their heritage rather than as a betrayal. At the same time, the destruction of Jerusalem also meant an acceleration in the shift of power and identity away from Judaism and in the direction of Gentile Christianity. Jewish Christians in the decades of the 70s and 80s may well have wondered how fidelity to their heritage could be maintained in a church that was rapidly becoming Gentile in membership and culture.

Matthew seems to have written his Gospel for a Christian community astride such a transitional period. We cannot be certain that the evangelist himself was Jewish in origin,[2] but his Gospel is sensitive to Jewish issues such as interpretation of law, the teaching authority of the rabbis, the promises of the Old Testament, and the dietary and ritual obligations of Jewish life. The hostile tone of some of Matthew's material (for example, chap. 23) suggests that the atmosphere of his community was strongly influenced by the friction between the Christians and the Pharisees in the post-70 period.

Matthew's audience, however, was not Judaism itself but the mixed population of his own Christian community. For the Jewish Christians, in particular, Matthew wanted to affirm that Jesus' mission was "not to destroy the law and the prophets but to bring them to fulfillment" (Mt. 5:17). Christianity, in other words, was not antithetical to Judaism but its God-intended outcome. At the same time, for both Jewish and Gentile Christians, the evangelist sought to put the universal mission of the church in perspective. That, too, was part of God's plan and was in accord with the pattern of salvation detectable in the Old Testament and in the history of Jesus himself. Despite the tension such a mission had brought to the community, the very nature of the gospel demanded that the teaching of Jesus be brought to "all the nations." Precisely because Matthew was exercising such a "ministry of continuity" in a time of transition and because the catalyst for that transition was the movement of the gospel from Israel to the nations, the mission question is central to the Gospel of Matthew.

Since the identity of Jesus and the implications of his message were the basic points of tension between the synagogue and the church and the ultimate catalyst for the church's move to the Gentiles, it is not surprising that Matthew's perspective is radically Christological. The person and message of Jesus as interpreted by the evangelist becomes the focal point through which Matthew rescues continuity with the heritage of Judaism and, at the same time, opens up new vistas for the future. Jesus is both the preeminent Son of Israel and the inaugurator of a new age of salvation extending to all nations. The centrality of the mission question and Matthew's Christological concentration also explain this Gospel's emphasis on the Jewish rejection of Jesus. As we shall note below, the question of response to Jesus and his message becomes paradigmatic for all salvation history.

Matthew's attempt to bridge two moments of religious consciousness may also explain the presence of apparently conflicting traditions within the Gospel. The law is declared to have enduring validity, but important prescriptions are contradicted or eliminated (5:17–48). The Jewish authorities are the targets of scathing criticism but are given deep respect (23:2–3). The apostles are told to restrict their mission to Israel at one stage in the Gospel, and are sent to the nations in another (10:5; 28:19). In these and other examples Matthew attempts to mediate an evolution from a particularist to a universalist perspective. Because this evolution is so central to the purpose of our study, Matthew's theology is fundamental in the New Testament perspective on mission.

ELEMENTS OF MATTHEW'S MISSION THEOLOGY

Matthew's Debt to Mark

The question of what sources Matthew used to construct his Gospel is still debated. A majority of contemporary scholars, however, contend that Matthew used the Gospel of Mark as the principal source for his own retelling of the story of Jesus.[3] This, of course, does not mean that the evangelist is a passive transmitter of previously formed materials. Matthew proves to be a faithful yet creative interpreter of the gospel tradition that comes to him via his Marcan source. Almost all of Mark's material is incorporated into Matthew's account, but much of it is edited and absorbed in a way that adjusts its meaning to the broader perspective of the evangelist and his community situation.

Not all of Matthew's Gospel is reinterpreted Marcan material. The evangelist also seems to have had access to a written or oral collection of Jesus' sayings, commonly referred to as "Q" in modern scholarship (from the German *Quelle*, "source"). The inclusion of this material (to which the Gospel of Luke had independent access) gives a special tone to Matthew's Gospel by developing the image of Jesus as teacher (cf. below). In addition, there are a number of passages in Matthew that cannot be attributed either to Mark or to a sayings collection. Some of these may be independent traditions handed on in Matthew's community. Other passages may represent the creative work of the evangelist himself, drawing on motifs in his sources. In every case these sources and traditions are thoroughly digested by Matthew and worked into the Gospel through the filter of the evangelist's own style and theology. Before considering Matthew's special emphases, however, let us recall those aspects of his Gospel that resonate with the mission theology of Mark. Because these have been treated at length in the chapters on Jesus and on Mark, we shall not go into great detail here.

First, it should not be overlooked that Matthew, like his Marcan source, had adopted the gospel genre as a means of communicating his message. As we have already suggested, the inherent dynamism and communication force of this story form is linked to the very nature of the Christian message, as presented by Mark and now endorsed by Matthew. The Christian story is one that must be communicated; it is an ongoing, inherently infectious message of salvation moving across frontiers of time and culture.

Matthew's access to additional sayings material and his shaping of it into a series of "discourses" (cf. chaps. 5-7,10,13,18,24-25) does tend to blunt the energy of Mark's narration. But the basic story form remains intact. The Matthean Jesus moves into Galilee (4:12-17) to inaugurate his kingdom ministry and presses his message home by proclamation, teaching, and healing. Then—parallel to Mark's account—the story begins to tilt toward Jerusalem and crucifixion with Peter's confession at Caesarea Philippi and Jesus' first passion prediction (cf. 16:13-28). The story comes to its climactic point with the entry into Jerusalem (21:1ff.), final teaching and confrontation in the temple area (chaps. 21-25) and the passion-resurrection account (26-28:15).

Matthew has, in fact, expanded the scope of Mark's story. By means of his infancy narrative (chaps. 1-2) he has pushed the origins of Jesus more firmly into Israel's past and traced the significance of Jesus from the beginning of his human history. The conclusion of the story is also stretched. Where Mark ends abruptly with a promise of reunion in Galilee (Mk. 16:7-8), Matthew supplies the resurrection appearances both in Jerusalem (Mt. 28:9-10) and in Galilee (28:16-20). This final pericope manages to push the leading edge of the Jesus story out into the community's own history by the mission command and promise of abiding presence (Mt. 28:20). Thus the sense of the Christian message as inherently dynamic and destined for ongoing communication is firmly retained by Matthew.

Second, Matthew's fidelity to basic aspects of Mark's mission theology extends to content as well as to form. Of fundamental importance for our mission perspective is the fact that Matthew, following Mark, interprets the ministry of Jesus under the general rubric of the "kingdom of God" (or in Matthew's typical formulation, "kingdom of heaven," "heaven" being a reverential euphemism for God, reflecting the evangelist's Jewish sensitivity). As we have already suggested, this overarching symbol was used by Jesus himself and is retained by the Synoptic tradition as a comprehensive way of understanding the scope and meaning of Jesus' mission. The community's post-Easter faith recognized that Jesus embodied the coming rule of God: by his piety, preaching, teaching, his acts of healing, his liberating challenge, his relationships, his very person. Here was the decisive act of salvation promised in the Old Testament and longed for by the people of Israel.

The kingdom of God motif in Matthew's Gospel is every bit as comprehensive as it is in Mark. In fact, Matthew seems to exploit the image more than his source.[4] The raw statistics are indicative of this: Matthew uses the term "kingdom of God" or its equivalent some fifty-one times, compared to eighteen times in Mark. As in Mark, the approach of the kingdom and the consequential call for repentance are the keynotes of Jesus' Galilean ministry (Mt. 4:17). It is the dominant subject of his proclamation (cf. 4:23; 9:35), his parables (cf. passim, in the parable discourse of chap. 13), and his healings and exorcisms (cf. Mt. 12:28). The Twelve are explicitly commissioned to continue the kingdom proclamation of Jesus in their own ministry (cf. 10:7).

In concert with Mark and the general perspective of the New Testament, Matthew maintains a fragile balance concerning the temporal nature of the kingdom. The full expression of God's rule is still future (cf. the connotation of the term "approaches" in 3:2; 4:17; 10:7; and the references to the future consummation of the kingdom in the parables and the eschatological discourse of chaps. 24–25). Yet Matthew is so convinced that Jesus Christ embodies and precipitates God's rule that the anticipated experience of the kingdom strains this future perspective. Hence Matthew can also describe the kingdom as a present reality. Through the miraculous healing power of Jesus the rule of Satan is defeated and the kingdom "has come upon you" (12:28). Israel's rejection of Jesus and the Gentiles' faith in him will cause the kingdom "to be taken away" from one and "given" to another. In the enigmatic Mt. 11:12 ("From the days of John the Baptist until now the kingdom of heaven has suffered violence and violent ones plunder it"), the kingdom is again spoken of as a present reality although the meaning of "violence" and "violent ones" is not clear.[5]

These fluid dimensions of the kingdom concept make sense when we keep in mind that in Matthew (as in Mark), the kingdom of God has become a cipher for the entire Christ-event. The ministry of the historical Jesus, the decisive event of death-resurrection, and the post-Easter proclamation of the risen Christ in the community have been collapsed into the symbol of "the kingdom of heaven." In Jesus Christ one encounters God's rule. Although this is a present reality for the believer, it still retains future dimensions. The full consummation of Christ's redemptive work—the full experience of God's rule through him—awaits the Parousia.

This equivalence between the full scope of the Christ-event and the metaphor of the kingdom supports a uniquely Matthean expression that is particularly suggestive for the mission dimension. In three texts Matthew refers to "the [or "this"] *gospel* of the kingdom" (cf. 4:23; 9:35; 24:14; 13:19 uses a similar phrase, "the *word* of the kingdom"). Each of these occurrences is significant: the first two (4:23 and 9:35) are found in important summaries of Jesus' ministry, and 24:14 is a key statement in the eschatological discourse referring to the mission proclamation of the community. By "gospel," then, Matthew does not refer simply to Jesus' preaching or teaching but to the whole "event" of his ministry, not only in the time of Jesus but as proclaimed by the community. "Gospel" is good news because it is an announcement, an experience of salvation.[6]

From Matthew's perspective, to encounter the kingdom is to encounter Jesus

Christ as proclaimed by the community's preaching, teaching, and ministry. As Kingsbury notes, " 'The Gospel of the Kingdom' is the news, which saves or condemns, that is revealed in and through Jesus Messiah, the Son of God, and is proclaimed to Israel and to the nations alike to the effect that in him the rule of God has drawn near to humankind.'" Matthew's unique phrase underlines the inherent universal and missionary character of the kingdom ministry of Jesus. This universal horizon of the kingdom metaphor is implicit in Mark but comes much closer to the surface in the mission theology of Matthew.

Other facets of Marcan theology are either more fully developed by Matthew (cf. the salvation-history theme, below) or move in a different direction (for example, Matthew's consideration of discipleship and some nuances of his Christology). Still others are left dormant. The temple motif, for example, which in Mark helps to illustrate the historic passage from Israel to the Christian community, is not exploited by Matthew. The references in the trial to a temple "not made by hands" (cf. Mk. 14:58) are eliminated by Matthew. For Matthew the charge becomes one of Jesus' alleged messianic *power* over the Jerusalem temple (26:61), thus a Christological issue rather than a salvation-historical one.⁸ One also senses that the Galilee-Jerusalem polarity, which Mark utilizes as part of his mission perspective, while vaguely present in Matthew, is not at the center of his focus. This geographical device gives way to an emphasis on the rejection of Jesus by the leaders and people.

As we noted above, Matthew is a faithful yet creative interpreter of the tradition received from his sources. While Matthew will retain and even develop some aspects of his sources (for example, the gospel genre, the kingdom motif), others will be left unattended or given a fresh interpretation. It is to particular dimensions of the mission question in Matthew that we now turn.

Salvation History in Matthew

One of the crucial elements in Matthew's mission perspective is his view of salvation history. Major dimensions of the evangelist's religious traditions are fitted into a framework of ongoing history: the heritage of Judaism, the Jesus-event, the experiences of the church. This historical framework takes on theological significance or is "salvific" because, from the perspective of faith, the evangelist and his tradition are able to detect the ongoing action of God in the sometimes disparate and even conflicting events that make up the flow of history. For a buffeted community like Matthew's, such discernment was essential.

As we have seen, Mark had crafted a salvation history in his Gospel, too. Reflection on the sacred and salvific patterns of history was, in fact, an art well developed in Judaism and one easily adapted by the Christian community. Thus Mark put such things as the rejection of Jesus, the destruction of the temple, and the Gentile mission into an overarching salvation-history perspective. Matthew, as we shall see, gives even more attention to this question, as would be expected from his more intense interaction with Judaism and with the transitional situation of his own community.

Recent scholarship has been torn over the precise contours of the historical framework Matthew seems to construct.[9] Some authors, for example, define three major periods in Matthew's schematization: (1) a period of Israel stretching from Abraham to John the Baptist; (2) the unique time of Jesus' own life; and (3) a period of the church stretching from the resurrection of Jesus until the end of the world. Others contend there are merely two periods in Matthew's viewpoint: (1) the sacred past of Israel, stretching from Abraham to John the Baptist, and (2) the sacred present inaugurated by Jesus and moving through the church until the end of time. Even within these broad schemata various nuances or subdivisions are suggested.

As in the discussion of the structure of the Gospel, it may well be that the evangelist's historical framework is not reducible to a sharply defined and comprehensively lucid outline. Like history itself, Matthew's perspective moves in broad and sometimes diffuse patterns. However, we can trace some of the main characteristics of Matthew's historical framework.

It is obvious, first of all, that, for Matthew, Jesus is the crucial turning point in all history. (Whether the Jesus-event begins with the ministry of John or whether John is the climax of Old Testament history is ultimately of minor significance.) Jesus is the inaugurator of a new period of history, which not only seals and climaxes the sacred history of Israel but, through Christ's risen presence (Mt. 28:20), will be sustained until the consummation of the world. But for the evangelist this Jesus-event is not a uniform moment. There is an inner dynamic within the Gospel story that places even the elements of Jesus' own history into a developing framework. Thus the death and resurrection of Jesus are the climax of his personal history; it is the paradigmatic event that symbolizes the meaning of his mission and signals the new age he inaugurates. The transition from the old period of history—Israel—remains apparent until the event of death-resurrection; from that key moment the inauguration of the new age is overwhelmingly evident.

A number of special Matthean passages bolster this viewpoint. His description of the moment of Jesus' death (27: 51–53) emphasizes that indeed this is the opening of the awaited eschatological age. Utilizing the account of Mark and drawing upon Jewish apocalyptic tradition, Matthew presents the death of Jesus as an explosive trigger that tears open the temple veil (27:51), signaling judgment upon Judaism and the old way as well as the opening of new access to God. This much is found in Mark. But Matthew strikingly develops the texts by adding a chain of cosmic events: an earthquake, the splitting of rocks, and the opening of tombs. All these cosmic signs culminate in the resurrection of the "holy ones" and their entry into the holy city (27:51–53). This awesome display—these "happenings" as the text expresses it (27:54)—provokes the faith confession from the centurion and his companions who stand guard at the cross: "Truly this was the Son of God" (27:54). The rumblings of nature and the resurrection of the elect are typical signs of the end-time anticipated in Jewish apocalyptic literature. The evangelist patently interprets Jesus' death (and its inevitable connection to resurrection) as the decisive event that inaugurates the end-time.[10]

Matthew's embellishment of the empty-tomb story moves in the same direction. The earthquake, the "angel of the Lord" and his brilliant raiment, and the trembling and fear of the guards (cf. Mt. 28:2-3) are elements added to Mark's account by Matthew. The net effect is an enrichment of the inherently eschatological significance of the resurrection proclamation. The empty tomb is another sign that the awaited age of resurrection has dawned.

For Matthew, then, Jesus inaugurates a new and decisive stage of salvation history. But Jesus' life is not homogeneous. What began with his human origins (chaps. 1-2) and picked up momentum with his public ministry (chaps. 3-4) comes to its full impact and expression in his death and resurrection. Here is the Jesus-event par excellence and on this fulcrum the world turns.

This fulcrum, or pivot, helps to explain many of the conflicting elements of the Gospel. Prior to Jesus' death and resurrection the old order has validity (although even in the history of Israel and certainly in the events of Jesus' life prior to his crucifixion, the signs of the new age are appearing). Thus the law is not destroyed (Mt. 5:17) and its least prescriptions are to be obeyed (5:18-19). The focal point of God's prophetic emissaries, including Jesus and his disciples, is the people of Israel, God's people. This helps to explain, in part, the baffling restrictive mission statements in the discourse of chapter 10 ("Go nowhere among the Gentiles and enter no town of the Samaritans, but go rather to the lost sheep of the house of Israel," Mt. 10:5) and in the story of Jesus' encounter with the Canaanite Woman ("I was sent only to the lost sheep of the house of Israel," Mt. 15:24). These texts, unique to Matthew, may have stemmed from the historical Jesus or, more probably, reflected the narrow viewpoint of the early Jewish-Christian community.[11] In any case they reflect the historical reality of the scope and intent of Jesus' mission: his work was for all practical purposes confined to Israel.

But the death and resurrection of Jesus signal a new and final age where the old restrictions no longer hold. Here again the evangelist follows through in his narration of the Gospel story. The law holds only "until heaven and earth pass away," or "until all is accomplished" (Mt. 5:17). That terminal point is signaled by the climax of Jesus' death and resurrection. Therefore what the church is instructed to obey and teach in the postresurrection period is not the Jewish law but *Jesus'* commands (cf. Mt. 28:16-20). This "fulfilled law" (cf. 5:17) is the law of the new age.[12]

A similar pattern explains the shift from the restricted mission statements of Mt. 10:4 and 15:24. Prior to Jesus—or more precisely, prior to his climactic work of death and resurrection—God's mission of salvation was directed primarily to Israel. Now, after the beginning of the new age, God's grace is offered to all, and so the Gospel concludes with the ringing directive to the post-Easter community to preach to "all nations" in 28:19 (and 24:14, which also envisages the post-Easter community). For Matthew, then, the church's mission to the Gentiles is not an accident of history but a consequence of history: an intended act of God appropriate for the final age when the frontiers of salvation were expected to be pushed open to all nations.

Ultimately it is Matthew's Christology that undergirds this view of salvation history. His conviction that Jesus of Nazareth was, in fact, the Christ, the Son of God, enables him to depict Jesus as the fulfillment of Jewish hopes embodied in the Scriptures. Through this fulfillment Jesus brings to completion the old age of anticipation. By the same token, because Jesus of Nazareth, crucified and risen, is proclaimed as exalted Son of God, as the awaited Son of Man, Matthew can depict him as the inaugurator of the new age, as one whose abiding presence will propel the community and its worldwide mission to the end of time and the final triumph of the kingdom. Past, present, and future are viewed through the lens of Matthew's Christian faith.

A number of characteristic Matthean themes directly relate to this Christological view of history. We here consider three principal themes.

Jesus as the Fulfillment of the Promises to Israel. It has long been recognized that Matthew emphasizes the basic Christian conviction that Jesus fulfilled the prophetic hopes of the Scriptures. This is stated programmatically in 5:17: "Think not that I have come to abolish the law and the prophets; I have come not to abolish them but to fulfill them." The word "fulfill" ($\rho l\bar{e}r\bar{o}sai$) used here is best understood in the promise-fulfillment mode. Jesus fulfills the law not simply by obeying it but by bringing it to the end for which it was intended. His teaching, eloquently stated in the sermon that follows, is not a synthesis of the old law but a new revelation for a new age.

Matthew casts the aura of fulfillment over his entire portrait of Jesus. The chief means is his studied use of Scripture. Through his so-called fulfillment texts, the evangelist applies the label of fulfillment to practically every dimension of Jesus' life: his origins (cf. Mt. 1:22; 2:23), the initiation of his mission in Galilee (4:14–16), his ministry of healing (8:17; 12:17–21), his entry into Jerusalem (21:4–5), his deliverance to death (26:54–56). Even hostility to Jesus falls under the spell of fulfillment in the threats of Herod (2:17), the rejection of his teaching (13:14–15), and the fate of his betrayer (27:9–10). These texts are only a fraction of the scriptural citations and allusions in the Gospel story but they stand out because the evangelist introduces each of them with a standardized formula, which explicitly states that Jesus' life "fulfills" the promises and hopes of the Scriptures.

There are many other ways in which the evangelist casts the mantle of the Old Testament around Jesus. The genealogy that opens the Gospel (Mt. 1:1–7) plants Jesus deep within the heritage of Judaism. Jesus is subtly cast as a new Moses in the way that Matthew describes the dramatic circumstances of his birth and his teaching from the mountain top. Throughout the Gospel, titles forged in the Hebrew Scriptures are applied to Jesus: Emmanuel, Christ, Son of God, Son of David, Son of Man, Servant—to name some of the major ones. By drawing on this fund of Old Testament materials, the evangelist proclaims that Jesus indeed fulfills the promises of the covenant to Israel and brings its history to its intended climax.

Jesus as Present and Future Hope. Just as Matthew is convinced that Jesus fulfills Israel's hopes and thereby ties his community to its past, so too the evangelist affirms that the risen Jesus is the animator of the community's life in the present and the hope of its future. Here again the evidence suffuses the entire Gospel.

The Matthean Jesus is evidently present in the community. He is the "Emmanuel, . . . God with us" (1:23) who fulfills the covenant promise of God's ongoing loyalty to his people. He is present where the community gathers in faith (18:20) and will remain with the community as it begins its mission in the world (28:20). He is the exalted Son of Man to whom all authority has been given (28:16). The entire Gospel story is a proclamation of this abiding presence. The miracle stories affirm that the risen Jesus continues to effect healing, liberation, and forgiveness within the community. Thus the leper is cleansed from his illness (8:2). The centurion successfully intercedes on behalf of his servant (8:6). The floundering disciples (8:21) and the drowning Peter (14:30) all cry out for rescue to the "Lord" (*kyrie*), a title that in Matthew's Gospel clearly designates the power and divine authority of the risen Jesus.[13] The Jesus who effects forgiveness of sins for the paralytic is in fact "the Son of Man on earth" (cf. 9:6).

What is true of the healing stories is true of virtually all of the Gospel. The Jesus who preaches and teaches (cf. particularly chaps. 5–7) is no longer simply Jesus of Nazareth but the risen Christ proclaiming the will of God for the new age. The priority of the love command (cf. 7:12; 5:43–48; 22:34–40) is a revelation to the community in the present, not simply a prophetic statement from the past. In chapter 18 the parable of the lost sheep, which originally dealt with Jesus' ministry to the marginal people of Israel (cf. Lk. 15:1–7), is now a proclamation of community responsibility to its own faltering members. In its exercise of reconciliation and compassion, the community activates the teaching and ministry of the risen Lord in its midst (cf. 18:15–35).

The Lord is also present in the community's mission. The call to the Twelve remains the marching orders for Matthew's own community (10:1ff.). The rebuffs and persecution the missionaries experience are a share in Jesus' own ministry and experience (cf. 10:24). Conversely, hospitality shown to one of these "little ones" is hospitality shown to the risen Christ who sends them and abides with them (cf.10:40–42). This same abiding Lord and glorified Son of Man is the one who sends the community out on mission at the end of the Gospel and promises to remain with the missionary church (28:16–20).

The same Lord present in the community and its mission will "come" as Son of Man at the end of time to gather the elect and to effect judgment on all peoples. The force of that conviction can be felt in Mt. 26:64, where Jesus declares to the high priest: " . . . I tell you, hereafter you will see the Son of Man seated at the right hand of power, and coming on the clouds of heaven." The word "hereafter" (or more literally, "from now on") implies that in the triumph of resurrection, the exaltation of the Son of Man and his coming have already begun. In the destruction of the temple veil (27:51) and the raising of the holy ones from death, signs of the future judgment are now visible. But the Gospel clearly expects the full consummation of the end and the victorious judgment of Jesus as Son of Man to be a future event. It is then that the Son of Man will separate the wheat from the weeds (cf. 13:36–43). Matthew's amplification of judgment material in chapters

24-25 shows this was an important part of his theological perspective (cf. especially 24:30-31, 37-44; 25:31-46). The judgment that has already been felt in Israel's experience will be shared by all the nations of the earth (25:31-32).[14]

Matthew, then, views "Jesus" in the full spectrum of his existence: rooted in the history of Israel, carrying out his messianic mission in Galilee and Judea, present with the community as risen Lord and Son of God, coming to the world as Son of Man and judge at the end of time. And it is this faith perspective that enables the evangelist to link together the historical periods that coincide with each dimension of the Christ-event: the history of Israel and its law, the period of Jesus' earthly existence, the past and present experience of the Christian community, and its unknown future.

The Rejection of Jesus. Because Jesus Christ is considered the embodiment of God's saving acts and, therefore, *the* turning point in salvation history, response to Jesus and his message is also crucial. Salvation history is formed not simply on the pattern of God's initiatives toward Israel and the church but on the related pattern of human response to those initiatives. That is why Matthew gives such attention to the theme of "response" in his Gospel, including the negative response of outright rejection. Throughout his story Matthew illustrates how disciples, outcasts, and occasional Gentiles responded to Jesus with faith and conversion, while the Jewish leaders—and ultimately the people themselves—rejected him.

The evangelist's reflections on the rejection of Jesus is multidimensional. On one level Matthew's Gospel reflects the historical fact of Jesus' interaction with his opponents in the course of his ministry. Although the actual text of the Gospel has been influenced by subsequent development, there is little doubt that Jesus, like the prophets before him, engaged in some vigorous critical interaction with his contemporaries. It is also obvious that Jesus' mission ended in death by crucifixion. Here, too, the historical facts may have been blurred by later reflection and interpretation, yet it is likely that Jesus' death at the hands of Roman officials also involved some complicity on the part of Jewish leadership in Jerusalem (cf. chap. 6, n. 31, above).

This basic tradition of polemic, rejection, and death is the starting point—but not the finish—for the theological theme of rejection in Matthew. To this first level must be added the subsequent history of the early community leading up to the time of Matthew. It seems that by the time Matthew writes, the failure of the church's mission to Israel had become evident.[15] Although some Jews had obviously accepted Jesus as Messiah and formed the nucleus of the early community, the vast majority of Jews had not and the church was becoming more Gentile in orientation. This "rejection" of the gospel and the turn to the Gentiles are, therefore, another layer of experience that works its way into the Gospel story. Therefore rejection of the historical Jesus is matched by the rejection of the risen Jesus in the form of his presence in the community and its mission.

One final dimension of the rejection theme should be noted. This dimension does not involve the relationship of Jew and Christian but is fully within the Christian community itself. Matthew is also concerned with the divisions existing in his own church, divisions triggered in part by the tensions of the mission to the Gentiles. Here the polarity is between those maintaining a particularist view of history versus those who are open to a universalist perspective. On this level the "scribes and Pharisees" who oppose Jesus and his mission are no longer the opponents of the historical Jesus or the contemporary leaders of the synagogue but *Christians* in the community who impede the church's outreach. For them, too, the story of the gospel's movement from Israel to the nations is retold.

In all three of these levels or dimensions, Matthew discerns a pattern of sacred history. Just as God's offer of grace was encountered in the person of Jesus, in the community's mission to Israel, and in the internal commitment of the church to the Gentiles, so, too, does *rejection* of Jesus on each level become part of the pattern of sacred history. In each instance the act of rejection becomes a para- doxical impulse to a new life-giving stage in God's plan of history. From the death of Jesus comes the birth of a resurrection community; from the failure of the mission to Israel comes the opening to the Gentiles.

We shall return to the theme of response, but for the moment let us concentrate on a few key Matthean texts that illustrate the salvation-history implications of this motif. The theme is orchestrated throughout the Gospel. As early as the infancy narrative the pattern emerges: Herod and the leaders of Jerusalem are hostile to Jesus and plot his death while the Gentile Magi offer the infant Messiah their homage (2:1-18). In 3:7-10 (a passage unique to Matthew) John the Baptist, a forerunner of Jesus' own kingdom ministry, challenges the Pharisees and Sad- ducees on the authenticity of their repentance, and discounts their claims to be sons of Abraham.

Jesus' own mission picks up the same impulses. Challenges to inauthentic re- sponse rumble through the Sermon on the Mount (cf. Mt. 5:20; 6:1-6) and the miracle section of chapters 8-9. The faith of the Gentile centurion is contrasted with that of Israel (8:10-12). Forgiveness offered to the paralytic scandalizes the scribes (9:3). Jesus' mission to outcasts (9:10-13), his compassion for his disciples (9:14-17), and his exorcisms (9:32-34) are all viewed with skepticism by the leaders. The rumblings break out into open polemic beginning in chapter 11. The rejection of both John and Jesus leads to the words of judgment over the Jewish towns and they are unfavorably contrasted with Tyre, Sidon, and Sodom (11:1-24). The hostilities continue throughout chapter 12 (cf. especially the plot to destroy Jesus, in 12:14), into the parable discourse of chapter 13 (cf. especially 13:10-15), and remain a constant undercurrent carrying the drama forward to Jerusalem and the cross.

Thus it is this comprehensive rejection of Jesus and his message that leads to the cross. Two texts, in particular, illustrate how Matthew interprets this rejection in accordance with his salvation-history perspective. The first is Mt. 21:33-46, the parable of the vineyard. Matthew has drawn this parable from Mark (12:1-12) and he retains its basic allegorization of salvation history. The arrival of the son climaxes a series of prophetic messengers who have been mistreated and rejected by Israel. The son, too, is rejected and killed "outside of the vineyard" (Mt. 21:40), an allegorization based on Jesus' crucifixion outside the walls of the city, a detail added by Matthew (cf. Mk. 12:8). In Mark this parable was already used to interpret Jesus' rejection by Israel and his vindication through resurrection (cf. the use of Ps. 118 in Mk. 12:10–11). But Matthew adds verse 43: "Therefore I tell you, the kingdom of God will be taken away from you and given to a nation producing fruits of it." The verse makes explicit the salvation-history perspective already contained in the Marcan parable (cf. Mt. 21:41, parallel Mk. 12:9). Matthew highlights this aspect because it is central to his theological reflection on the meaning of Israel's failure and the influx of the Gentiles. The rejection of Jesus by Israel becomes the paradoxical opening to the nations.[16]

The parable of the vineyard also shows that Matthew considers the death-resurrection of Jesus to be the decisive turning point in history. The evangelist follows through on his conviction in the passion story. Throughout the narrative Matthew emphasizes the involvement of the Jewish leaders in the betrayal, arrest, and condemnation of Jesus.[17] The climax is reached in Matthew's presentation of the trial before Pilate (27:11–26). The evangelist reshapes the Marcan narrative to stress the decisive *choice* of leaders and people: "Whom do you want me to release for you, Barabbas or Jesus who is called Christ?"(Mt. 27:17; cf. also 27:21). In a tradition reported only by Matthew, the Gentile wife of Pilate pleads on behalf of this "just man" (Mt. 27:19) while the leaders sway the crowd.

The forceful conclusion of the scene comes in verses 24–25, again material unique to Matthew:

> So when Pilate saw that he was gaining nothing, but rather that a riot was beginning, he took water and washed his hands before the crowd, saying, "I am innocent of this man's blood; see to it yourselves." And all the people answered, "His blood be on us and on our children!"

Pilate's decision to release Barabbas and to deliver Jesus to death (Mt. 27:26) is prefaced by a dramatic declaration on the part of the Gentile procurator and the Jewish leaders and people. Matthew uses Old Testament traditions to create the contrasting response. Pilate affirms his innocence by using a Jewish ritual of handwashing (cf. Deut. 21:1–9; Ps. 26:6). Until this point Matthew had distinguished between "crowds" and "leaders" in the passion story. Now, however, they are joined in one collective designation, *laos*, or "people," and together they use an Old Testament formula for declaring one's responsibility (cf. 1 Sam. 2:33; Jer. 26:15). The people accept Jesus' blood on themselves and their children. The link between the two actions is that of Jesus' "blood," or his death. The evangelist had already spoken of Jesus' death in these terms in the sharp prophetic critique of 23:25 and in the story of Judas' return of the "blood money" (27:3–10). At the decisive moment of the trial, Matthew presents Israel as rejecting Jesus, a rejection vividly symbolized in his death.

Before proceeding it is important to note the anti-Semitic potential of these texts.[18] As the tragic history of Christian anti-Semitism has repeatedly demonstrated, this potential cannot be brushed aside. However, it should be pointed out that the evangelist's purpose is not to indict the Jewish people (Matthew himself is probably a Jew and so was a large percentage of his community). Matthew the evangelist is trying to fit a series of baffling, even tragic, events into his conviction that God acts in and through history. These tragic facts, from Matthew's viewpoint, included the death of Jesus, the failure of the Christian mission to Israel, and the intransigence of Christians in his own church who were opposed to accepting Gentiles. Matthew sees all of these events as involving a refusal of grace; but at the same time, as a paradoxical moment of resurrection, Jesus' death becomes the threshold for new life. The "death" of the mission of Israel and the resulting suffering within the community become the overture to a new moment of opportunity in the church's own destiny.

These considerations do not completely remove the dark potential of Matthew's formulations in 27:24–25. But they do show that the evangelist was not engaged in simply tagging Jews with responsibility for the death of Jesus and thereby declaring Christians innocent. Such a twisted religious excuse for anti-Semitism is anachronistic to the Gospel's own perspective.

Matthew's reflections on history, particularly the history of Jesus, enabled him to provide a theological basis for the universal mission of his church. Jesus was the Messiah promised to Israel and therefore his life and mission—climaxing in death and resurrection—were at once the fulfillment of the age of Israel and the beginning of the new and final age of revelation. Now all the nations of the earth would participate in the drama of redemption that had been hitherto reserved to Israel.

But there was more. The pattern of Jesus' destiny enabled the evangelist to detect a deeper pattern in sacred history itself. During the lifetime of Jesus it was the outsiders, Gentiles and sinful Jews, who responded to the Christ, while the leaders of God's people seemed blind. The outcasts whose life appeared to be a No were, in fact, the ones who said a genuine Yes, and therefore they were entering the kingdom first (cf. the provocative Matthean parable of the two sons in 20:28–32). It was the Jewish leaders and eventually the people as a whole who would reject Jesus (27:24–25), yet from this rejection would ultimately spring the Gentile mission.

This recovery of new and unexpected life from seemingly bankrupt death is the deep pattern of history revealed by Jesus. In it Matthew seems to detect a pattern that is present prior to Jesus' own fate. As Matthew's artful genealogy plays back Jewish history from Abraham to Jesus, here too the reader of the Gospel discovers that in the rebound from exile, in the moment of grace through unexpected outsiders like Tamar, Rahab, Ruth, Bathsheba, and Mary herself, God carries forward the history of his people from death to life. And in the public ministry of Jesus the pattern continued: outcasts, tax collectors, sinners, Gentiles respond in faith, thereby illustrating the paradoxical pattern of God's way. The death and resurrection of Jesus himself is the final triumphant revelation of God's paradoxical power in forming his people.

For a Christian community concerned about its Jewish roots, brokenhearted over the failure of its mission to Israel and yet anxious about the consequences of a full-blown Gentile mission, such a Christological review of history must have been good news.

Response as a Universal Principle

There is another contributing element in Matthew's mission theology that we need to consider. Here again we turn to the motif of "response"—this time, however, not under the rubric of salvation history but as a self-standing principle derived from that history. The massive emphasis on right response in Matthew's Gospel makes of this motif not only a pattern of history but a criterion of salvation itself. Regardless of social or religious background, whoever responds with faith and obedience to the gospel of Jesus becomes thereby a member of God's people. As we shall note, there is a sweeping universalism inherent in this principle.

Much of the evidence for this motif has already been mentioned in our discussion of salvation history. We can quickly draw together some examples. *Proper* response to Jesus and his message includes an active faith in Jesus' person and the transformation of life derived from this faith. The evangelist uses a variety of expressions to describe the response of faith and action.

In the miracle stories Matthew describes faith as a firm trust in Jesus' power to save (cf., for example, 8:1-4, 5-13; 9:18-31; 15:21-28).[19] Implicit here is a recognition of Jesus' true identity and the consequent entrusting of one's life to him. The disciples represent those who lay aside other preoccupations and "follow" Jesus, a form of faith in action (cf. Mt. 4:18-22; 9:5). The faith of the disciples is much more evident in Matthew than in Mark; in Mt. 14:33, for example, they unhesitatingly acclaim Jesus as "Son of God," a confession lacking in Mark's account (cf. Mk. 6:52). However, Matthew also uses the disciples as models of "little faith" (cf. Mt. 6:30; 8:26; 14:31; 16:8), thereby making them representative of the ambiguity of Christian existence.

A term similar but not identical to "faith" is "understanding." Again in contrast to Mark, who repeatedly depicts the disciples as lacking understanding, Matthew insists that they *do* understand (cf., for example, Mk. 8:21; Mt. 16:12).[20] As the explanation of the parable of the sower suggests (cf. Mt. 13:23), "understanding" is part of the process of faith. The theme of "understanding" in Matthew harmonizes with his emphasis on Jesus as teacher. The genuine disciple "understands" Jesus because he or she absorbs the meaning of his teaching and moves to act on it. The opponents of Jesus, by contrast, are depicted as having closed minds and hearts and thus "never understanding" (cf. Mt. 13:14-15).

These and other expressions of proper response to the gospel betray Matthew's concern for action. To "believe," to "follow," to "understand" all contain an element of active commitment that flows into deeds. This dimension of proper response to Jesus is a major theme of Matthew's Gospel. Jesus himself is billed as the one who comes to "fulfill all righteousness" (3:15). The term "righteousness," or "justice" connotes Jesus' active obedience to the will of his Father.[21] This "righteousness," or obedience to God's will, must also characterize the disciple (5:20). Therefore the disciple is exhorted to "hear" Jesus' words and to "do" them (cf. 7:24–27), as well as to teach and to do them (5:19). Obedience to the will of the Father revealed in Jesus' own teaching will be the criterion for the final judgment (notice the emphasis on good deeds in the Judgment parables: 24:45–51; 25:14–30, 31–46). And the command "to do all that I have commanded" is the centerpiece in the missionary message of the church (cf. 28:20).

By contrast the Matthean Jesus depicts sin or failure as the lack of good deeds, even if one might have the right words. Herod and the leaders of Jerusalem have access to the Scriptures concerning the Messiah's origin, but they have failed to respond (2:1–5). The Pharisees and Sadducees who come for baptism from John are blistered for failing to show the fruits of repentance (3:7–10). The "hypocrisy" of the leaders (a favorite Matthean characterization) is a result either of inauthentic actions (for example, "done for people to see," cf. 6:1, 23:5) or, even more typically, a result of "bold words but no deeds" (cf. 23:3). At the conclusion of the Sermon on the Mount the testing of "false prophets" is to be on the basis of their actions (7:16). It will not be those who cry out ecstatically "Lord, Lord" who will enter the Kingdom but the one "who *does* the will of my heavenly Father" (7:21). The judgment falls on the leaders because, unlike "the tax collectors and the harlots" who believe in Jesus and ultimately go to work in the vineyard, they say Yes but do not go to work (cf. the parable of the two sons in Mt. 21:28–32). The scorching tone of chapter 23 continues this mood of judgment; the "scribes and Pharisees" are condemned for their hypocrisy, which consists in inauthentic deeds or words without action. And the failures in the remaining judgment parables—the wicked servant who violates the love command (25:45–48), the foolish virgins who have no oil (possibly a symbol of good deeds, 25:1–13),[22] the one who buried his talents (25:14–30), and most evidently, those who fail to offer deeds of mercy to the unrecognized Jesus (25:31–46)—all experience judgment for their failure to *act*.

This emphasis on action as the expression of faith is something Matthew derives from the whole spirit of Judaism, a spirit the evangelist finds strongly ratified in the teaching and ministry of Jesus. As we have already discussed, it is also part of Matthew's reflection on history. True membership in God's people from Abraham to the Messiah was finally decided on the basis of "righteousness," active obedience to God's Word, the commitment to doing his will. Joseph, who serves as an example of Israelite faith in Matthew's infancy narrative, is characterized almost wholly by his obedience: the will of God comes to him in the revelatory medium of dreams and he instantly acts on that word (cf. Mt. 1:24; 2:13–14, 20–21). And the same criterion becomes the saving factor for the "outsiders": the centurion at Capernaum (8:5–13), the Canaanite woman (15:21–28), the tax collectors and outcasts (9:9–13; 11:18–19; 21:28–32). They are saved because they are animated by an authentic faith that leads to action. Under the impact of the same criterion, in Matthew's view, Israel loses its prerogative: the kingdom is taken away from those who reject Jesus and given to the nations that *produce fruit* from the vineyard (21:43).

As R. Pregeant has pointed out, Matthew so emphasizes this criterion that it becomes a universal principle threatening to move beyond the bounds of Christian confession.[23] Certainly the whole context of the Gospel presumes that the saving human response includes not only good deeds but the confession of Jesus as Christ and Son of God. The missionary command of Mt. 28:16–20 verifies this: those who are told to "observe all I have commanded" are those who have first been baptized in Jesus' name (28:19). But, as Pregeant points out, there are some texts in Matthew where this confessional element seems to take second place to the criterion of action that conforms to the will of God. In 7:21, for example, proper confession—"Lord, Lord"—is not sufficient; doing the will of the Father is. And in the intriguing judgment scene of 25:31–46, the "just" are those who carry out the love command, even though they do not recognize Jesus in the "least brethren." Here the "nations" (25:32) fall under the same criterion of judgment as Israel itself.[24]

The universal scope of the judgment is expressed in other passages of Matthew as well. In 13:36–43, for example, all of the "world" is the impact point of God's Word, and all, world and church, will be judged on the basis of deeds at the end of time (cf. 13:41–43). Here Matthew seems to open up the arena of salvation to the world, with all humanity judged on the basis of action. We might also note the evangelist's significant addition to the banquet parable (22:1–14). The first portion of the parable (parallel to Lk. 14:16–24) allegorizes the failure of Israel and the inclusion of the Gentiles. The invited guests fail to respond and therefore experience judgment, including, in Matthew's version, the burning of their city, probably an allusion to the destruction of Jerusalem in 70 C.E. (cf. 22:7). Therefore the guest list is expanded to include "all," both bad and good (cf. 22:1–10). But invitation to the banquet is not sufficient for salvation, either for Israel or for the nations: all are judged on an equal basis. Thus Matthew adds verses 11–14 where one of the newly invited guests is condemned for not wearing his wedding garment, a symbol of a transformed life.

Although the evangelist remains in a thoroughly confessional framework, his emphasis on good deeds as the criterion for inclusion in the kingdom is stressed to such a degree that it seems to take on validity independent of explicit recognition or confession of Jesus. Here is a principle of universality that is inherent in the gospel message, even if unconscious to the evangelist. Although not exploited in biblical thought, this represents an opening in the New Testament tradition for assessing the validity of religious traditions and human life outside a Christian context.[25]

In any case, the Gentiles' willingness to respond to Jesus, and thereby transform their lives on the basis of his teaching, becomes for Matthew a fundamental theological datum that justifies their membership in the kingdom of God and, therefore, justifies the Gentile mission. By so emphasizing good deeds the evangelist fingers a sinew that binds his church's experience with the spirit of Jesus' own ministry and with his Jewish heritage.

THE MISSIONARY AND MATTHEW'S CHURCH

From this discussion of the basic elements of Matthew's mission theology, let us turn to the two "mission texts" of 10:1–47 and 28:16–20. The basic supports for Matthew's universal-mission perspective are found throughout his Gospel in such motifs as the kingdom of God, salvation history, and emphasis on action. The two mission texts do not add substantially to this more diffuse theological basis, but they do give a dynamic thrust to the Gospel and enable us to build a composite portrait of the motivation and style of missionary activity in Matthew's church.

The Mission Discourse of Matthew 10

The missionary discourse really begins in Mt. 9:36. After a summary of Jesus' own ministry of preaching, healing, and teaching (9:35; cf. 4:23), the evangelist goes on to note Jesus' compassion for the crowds and the need for laborers to reap the plentiful harvest (9:36–38). The compassion of Jesus and his exhortation to pray for "laborers to be sent out into the harvest" (9:38) form the immediate introduction to the discourse, which opens with 10:1.

The section that follows includes the whole of the chapter (10:1–42), closing with Matthew's typical transitional formula in 11:1. The intervening material is a combination of Mark's commissioning of the Twelve (Mk. 3:13–19; 6:7–11), a missionary "discourse" found in Q (cf. Lk. 10:1–23), and a section of Mark's apocalyptic discourse, which Matthew transplants from Mark 13 (cf. Mk. 13:9–13) in order to place it here in his Gospel.

Besides the Marcan and Q materials, Matthew also adds his own elements to the text (cf. 10:5–6). The very fact that Matthew uses Mark's apocalyptic material (which refers to the community's history *after* the death of Jesus) shows that the evangelist conceives of this discourse not simply as a moment in the past story of Jesus but as an exhortation to the ongoing mission of his community. As we discussed earlier in this chapter, the restrictive instruction of 10:5 ("Go nowhere among the Gentiles") fits into Matthew's salvation-history perspective. Prior to the new age inaugurated by Jesus' death and resurrection, the arena of salvation is limited to Israel. But with the dawn of the new age it will be thrown open to "all nations" (Mt. 28:16–20). To this extent, the discourse of chapter 10 is confined to the "past." But on another level—as part of the gospel proclaimed to the post-Easter community—the contents of chapter 10 are current instruction for the church's mission.

Our goal is not to analyze the composition or structure of this passage. Instead, we shall survey the content of the discourse as a way of synthesizing Matthew's mission theology.

a. The missionary effort of the church, like Christian existence itself, is rooted in God's power and call. This is the importance of the introduction and opening section of the discourse. The disciples need to pray that God will send laborers for the harvest (9:38). And Jesus, as God's agent, is the one who calls the Twelve and sends them out as "apostles" (10:1–5).

b. The scope and content of the community's mission are the same as that of Jesus. This includes announcement of the coming of the kingdom and the performance of the powerful acts of healing and liberation, as Jesus himself had done (10:7-8). In the discourse of chapter 10, the important element of "teaching" is not mentioned. Matthew seems to reserve this key function until the final commission (28:20), since in the Gospel story the disciples have not yet been exposed to all of Jesus' great discourses.[26]

c. The mission of the community shares in the eschatological urgency of Jesus' work. The missionary is to travel light (10:9-15); the time before the end is short (10:23). This element fits Matthew's theme of salvation history. The age inaugurated by Jesus and shared in by the church is the final age. Because it is the decisive time, it is also a time of crisis and division (cf. 10:34-39).

d. Like his or her master, the missionary can expect opposition and persecution (cf. 10:24-25). Matthew uses material from the apocalyptic discourse to illustrate this (cf. especially 10:16-23). Persecution will be inflicted by both Jews (10:17) and Gentiles (10:18). But, as in the case of Jesus, such hostility is ultimately impotent (10:22).

e. The missionary can count on the empowerment of the Spirit (10:19-20) and the life-giving providence of the Father (10:28-33). Hence their proclamation is to be bold and fearless (10:26-27).

f. An underlying theme of the whole discourse is the identity of the risen Jesus with his missionaries. This is implied in the programmatic verses 24-25: "A disciple is not above his teacher, nor a servant above his master; it is enough for the disciple to be like his teacher, and the servant like his master." And even more explicitly in the sayings on hospitality due the itinerant missionary, in 10:40-42: "He who receives you receives me. . . ." The identity of the sender with the one sent was a theme of Jewish literature, and it is used by the evangelist to stress the abiding presence of the risen Christ even with the apparently insignificant "little ones" who proclaim the gospel.

The Final Commission, Matthew 28:16-20

Many commentators have labeled this concluding segment of Matthew's Gospel a synthesis of the evangelist's entire message. From our perspective it should not be forgotten that this final synthesis is a *mission* charge, highlighting the dynamic thrust of the entire Gospel. The passage takes the form of a commissioning, reminiscent of the prophetic commissions of the Old Testament.[27] The hand of the evangelist is clearly evident in the composition of the text, as he draws together major themes of his Gospel. Again let us concentrate on the major components of his message.

a. The mission of the community is rooted in the authority of the risen Jesus who reigns as the Son of God and Son of Man within the community. This foundation is asserted in the opening verses of the pericope (Mt. 28:16-18). The Eleven (Judas' failure is conspicuously noted by Matthew, cf. 27:3-10) return to Galilee as Jesus had directed them (cf. 26:32; 28:7, 10). The place of encounter is a mountaintop, a setting for revelation in Matthew's Gospel. The powerful appearance of Jesus melts the hesitations of the disciples and provokes their awed worship (28:17). Jesus' own declaration, reminiscent of the Son of Man text in Dan. 7:14, emphasizes his authority which undergirds the universal mission of the community: "All authority in heaven and on earth has been given to me. Go therefore . . ." (28:18). This Christological basis of mission has been transparent in every dimension of Matthew's mission theology.

b. The first instruction for those sent is that they "make disciples." The community is to precipitate the same type of conversion experience that touched the disciples of Jesus: belief in Jesus and transformation of life on that basis.

c. The mission is to be universal: to "all nations" (Mt. 28:19). The restriction of 10:5 ("Do not go to the Gentiles") falls away because the community is now firmly within the final age of history. The exact scope of the word "nations" has been debated. Does it include Israel? Or does Matthew envisage a termination of any missionary effort among the Jews and exclusive concentration on the Gentiles? Although the term *ethnos* ("nation") is used almost exclusively of Gentiles in the Gospel and in biblical literature in general, it is unlikely that Matthew excludes Jews altogether. Israel as an entity is no longer the place of the mission: now the boundaries have fallen back and "all nations" have access to the gospel of the kingdom. In Matthew's theology no single group has any privileged status as God's people. Now both Jew and Gentile come as *ethnois* before the gospel to be judged on the basis of their response to God's gracious offer of life.[28]

d. Missionary proclamation includes the formation of a community, or "church." This is the implication of Matthew's use of the baptismal formula in 28:19. Such ecclesial interest harmonizes with the whole tone of Matthew's Gospel. The *ekklesia* (or "church") that gathers in Jesus' name (cf. 16:18; 18:17, 20) is the place where the values of the kingdom are to be manifest: mercy, compassion, reconciliation.

e. The missionary responsibility of the community centers on teaching (28:20). As we noted above, this central theme of Matthew's Gospel was conspicuously absent from the first mission discourse of chapter 10. Now that the disciples have been thoroughly schooled in Jesus' teaching, including the primary experience of his death and resurrection, they are ready to teach others. *What* they teach is also typical of Matthew's perspective: they are to teach others "to observe all that I have commanded." The action thrust of the Gospel is carried through into the content of its missionary proclamation.

f. The final injunction is the risen Christ's promise of abiding presence until the end of the age (Mt. 28:20). The death and resurrection of Jesus carry the people of God into the new and final age of salvation history. The abiding presence of the risen Lord in his missionary church will sustain it and animate it until the close of the age and the complete triumph of God's Kingdom.

CONCLUSION

Taken together the discourse of chapter 10 and the final commission of chapter 28 do indeed synthesize the mission theology of Matthew. The wrenching separation between church and synagogue and the anxiety bred by the influx of Gentiles into a Jewish-Christian community were soothed by the evangelist's recall of salvation history and by his vigorous Christology. The risen Christ on whom both Jewish and Gentile Christians had banked their hopes was the key to reconciliation within the community and the source of the ongoing mission of the church. That community of reconciled people was called to transcend its tensions and to move out to the nations who awaited the good news.

NOTES

1. On the background of Matthew, cf. the discussion in J. Meier, *The Vision of Matthew*, Theological Inquiries Series (New York: Paulist Press, 1978), pp. 6–25; D. Senior, *Invitation to Matthew* (Garden City, N.Y.: Doubleday, 1977), pp. 11–19.

2. Meier, for example, argues that in spite of the evident Jewish material in Matthew, there are certain things apparently incompatible with a Jewish author, such as his lack of precision about the differences between Pharisee and Sadducee that seems to occur in Mt. 16:12, where he lumps the two groups together. Nevertheless most modern interpreters of Matthew believe that the evangelist was a Hellenistic Jew.

3. Cf. the state of the question provided by D. Harrington, "Matthean Studies since Joachim Rhode," *The Heythrop Journal* 16 (1975):375–88.

4. On Matthew's presentation of the kingdom of God, cf. J. Kingsbury, *Matthew: Structure, Christology, Kingdom* (Philadelphia: Fortress Press, 1975), pp. 128–66.

5. Cf. J. Kingsbury, *Matthew: Structure, Christology, Kingdom*, pp. 142–43, who suggests that the reference is to Satan and his followers. The kingdom would be the reality made present by John and especially by Jesus, and the "violent ones" are those who attack the kingdom, in the setting of Jesus' ministry the Pharisees and the other opponents of Jesus; cf. a similar interpretation in J. Meier, *Matthew*, New Testament Message 3 (Wilmington, Del.: Michael Glazier, 1980), p. 122.

6. This is clear from 26:13, where the Matthean Jesus blesses the woman who had accomplished his burial anointing. Her good deed will be told "wherever *this gospel* is preached in the whole world."

7. Cf. J. Kingsbury, *Matthew*, p. 137.

8. Matthew changes the text of Mark to read, ". . . I am *able* to destroy the Temple of God . . ." (26:61). On this passage, cf. D. Senior, *The Passion Narrative according to Matthew;* Bibliotheca ephemeridum theologicarum lovaniensium 39 (Louvain: Louvain University Press, 1975), pp. 168–71.

9. On this issue, cf. the discussion of J. Meier, "Salvation History in Matthew: In Search of a Starting Point," *Catholic Biblical Quarterly* 37 (1975):203–15, and *The Vision of Matthew*, pp. 26–39.

10. Cf. D. Senior, "The Death of Jesus and the Resurrection of the Holy Ones," *Catholic Biblical Quarterly* 38 (1976):312–29; and J. Meier, "Salvation History in Matthew."

11. Cf. the discussion in J. Meier, "Salvation History in Matthew."

12. This is the main thesis of J. Meier's work, *Law and History in Matthew's Gospel*, 71 (Rome: Biblical Institute Press, 1976).

13. On Matthew's use of this title, cf. D. Senior, *The Passion Narrative*, pp. 70–71, and G. Bornkamm, "End-Experience and the Church in Matthew," *Tradition and Interpretation in Matthew* (Philadelphia: Westminster Press, 1963), pp. 41–43.

14. For a thorough discussion of the judgment texts in Matthew, cf. J. Lambrecht, "The Parousia Discourse. Composition and Content in Mt., XXIV–XXV," in

L'Évangile selon Matthieu: Rédaction et Théologie, ed. M. Didier; Bibliotheca ephemeridum theologicarum lovaniensium 29 (Gembloux: Duculot, 1972), pp. 309–42.

15. Cf. a discussion of this issue in W. Thompson, "An Historical Perspective in the Gospel of Matthew," *Journal of Biblical Literature* 93 (1974):243–62, and D. Hare, *The Theme of Jewish Persecution of Christians in the Gospel according to St. Matthew,* Society for New Testament Studies Monograph Series 6 (Cambridge, England: University Press, 1967).

16. The important study of W. Trilling (*Das Wahre Israel,* Studien zum Alten und Neuen Testament 10; 3rd rev. ed. [Munich: Kösel, 1964]) focuses on this parable and Matthew's editing of it as a key to the evangelist's theology of history.

17. Cf. D. Senior, *The Passion Narrative,* p. 338.

18. Cf. the discussion in G. Sloyan, *Jesus on Trial,* pp. 74–88, and the article of J. Fitzmyer, "Anti-Semitism and the Cry of 'All the People' (Mt. 27:26)," *Theological Studies* 26 (1965):667–71.

19. On this point, cf. H. Held, "Matthew as Interpreter of the Miracle Stories," *Tradition and Interpretation in Matthew,* pp. 275–91.

20. On the theme of "understanding" as a symptom of genuine discipleship in Matthew, cf. Markus Barth, "Matthew's Understanding of the Law," *Tradition and Interpretation in Matthew,* pp. 105–12.

21. Cf. the discussion of this key Matthean concept in J. Kingsbury, *Matthew,* Proclamation Commentaries Series (Philadelphia: Fortress Press, 1977), pp. 86–90.

22. Oil is suggested as a symbol of good deeds in the article by K. Donfried, "The Allegory of the Ten Virgins (Matt. 25:1–13) as a Summary of Matthean Theology," *Journal of Biblical Literature* 93 (1974):415–28. Evidence for this is relatively scarce, however.

23. Cf. R. Pregeant, *Christology beyond Dogma* (Philadelphia: Fortress Press, 1978), pp. 115–20.

24. One of the problems in the interpretation of Mt. 25:31–46 is the identity of the "least brethren." Some link the allegory of 25:31–46 with the "little ones" of the mission discourse, where themes of hospitality are also present (Mt. 10:41–42). If this be the case, then the Gentiles are being judged on their response to the missionaries of the Christian community. For this interpretation, cf. L. Cope, "Matthew XXV, 31–46. "The Sheep and the Goats' Reinterpreted," *Novum Testamentum* 11 (1969):37–41, and the thorough discussion in J. Lambrecht, "The Parousia Discourse," pp. 329–40.

25. Cf. a discussion of this issue in part III, below.

26. Cf. J. Meier, *Matthew,* p. 107.

27. On the form of this text, cf. B. Hubbard, *The Matthean Redaction of a Primitive Apostolic Commissioning: An Exegesis of Matthew 28:16–20,* Society of Biblical Literature Dissertation Series 19 (Missoula, Mont.: Society of Biblical Literature, 1974). On the overall meaning of the scene, cf. J. Meier, *The Vision of Matthew,* pp. 210–19, and J. Matthey, "The Great Commission According to Matthew," *International Review of Missions* 69 (1980):161–73.

28. For a debate on the precise meaning of *ethnoi* ("nations") in Matthew, cf. D. Hare and D. Harrington, "Make Disciples of All the Gentiles (Matt. 28:19)," *Catholic Biblical Quarterly* 37 (1975):359–69, who argue that the term refers exclusively to Gentiles, and the reply of J. Meier, "Gentiles or Nations in Matt. 28:19?" *Catholic Biblical Quarterly* 39 (1977):94–102, who opts for a broader meaning for the term, that is, that the Jews are now one among many nations in Matthew's perspective.

11

The Mission Perspective of Luke-Acts

And you shall be my witnesses in Jerusalem and in all Judea and Samaria and to the end of the earth [Acts 1:8].

Luke's two-volume work, the Gospel and the Acts of the Apostles, may be the clearest presentation of the church's universal mission in all of the New Testament.[1] The very fact that Luke binds together the story of the early community with the story of Jesus' life indicates that one of his major purposes was to show the relationship between the mission of Jesus and the mission of the church.

Luke's theology has become a central focus of contemporary biblical scholarship.[2] Some of this interest is generated by the third world churches. Luke's stress on the prophetic character of Jesus' ministry as well as his confrontation with issues of justice fit the powerful concerns of liberation theology. New Testament historians are aware that Luke's presentation of the early community's development, despite its evident theological interpretation, still offers the best data available on the history of the primitive church. Therefore interpreters interested in history and in pastoral issues have been drawn to Luke's books.

Luke's prologue (Lk. 1:1–4; cf. Acts 1:1) suggests that the evangelist may have wished to accommodate both kinds of questions. Theophilus, the real or fictitious beneficiary of Luke's work, is given a review of the events that form the foundation of his Christian existence. In putting together the Gospel part of this "review," Luke uses Mark's account and a collection of Jesus' sayings—a combination of sources equivalent to that used by Matthew. He orders and shapes this traditional material to form his own unique portrayal of Jesus. Luke also adds significant amounts of material found only in his Gospel. Therefore when Luke tells Theophilus he is writing an "orderly" account he cannot mean he is writing a strictly literal history. The "order" Luke imposes on the material reflects his own understanding of the *significance* of Jesus' history, not just a dispassionate recital of events. The same is true for Acts, although here the source question is much more difficult, since we have no other work with which to compare Luke. Here again it is likely that the evangelist draws his material from a variety of sources and traditions in his community and gives this material a shape and focus that illustrate his understanding of what this history meant.

255

Luke, therefore, is interested in history but not in history for its own sake. This long view of how the community began is meant to give perspective and strength to his readers. They can see Jesus' relationship to Israel, the character of his mission and the essential link between Jesus' purpose and that of the community. Here is where the mission question comes to the fore. As we shall discuss in detail, Luke's reflections on the dynamic kingdom ministry of Jesus and on the expanding mission of the church show that one of the evangelist's prime purposes was to fortify the ongoing universal mission of his community. It is difficult to pinpoint the situation of Luke's church. The Gospel and Acts were probably written sometime after 80 C.E. and probably for a largely Gentile church.[3] The community seems to be undergoing some sort of persecution, perhaps experiencing hostility from both Jews and pagans as it carries out its ministry. Therefore Luke wants to demonstrate that the mission of the community is neither contrary to God's work in the history of Israel nor incompatible with responsible citizenship in the empire. But Luke ultimately does not write from a defensive posture. His goal is positive and bold: he urges his fellow Christians to move out into the world with the same vigorous spirit that animated Jesus and the first generations of the church.

THE LINK BETWEEN THE STORY OF JESUS AND THE STORY OF THE CHURCH: THE KEYNOTE OF LUKE'S MISSION THEOLOGY

The fact that Luke provides a theology of mission by presenting the story of Jesus and the story of the church suggests that we start by examining the link between these two essential pieces of Luke's work. In the climactic resurrection appearance story of Lk. 24:44–49 (and its echo in Acts 1:3–8) we have a passage that synthesizes Luke's theology of the gospel and propels the reader into the follow-up account of Acts.[4]

The passage is the last in a series of three incidents that close the Gospel story: the discovery of the empty tomb (Lk. 24:13–35), the appearance to the disciples on the way to Emmaus (Lk. 24:1–12), the appearance to the community gathered in Jerusalem (Lk. 24:36–49). All three incidents take place on the "first day of the week" (Lk. 24:1), all are oriented to Jerusalem, and all lead up to the final statement in Lk. 24:44–49 and the triumphant ascension, which concludes the history of Jesus. The text we are considering, then, is what the risen Jesus leaves with his church: its net effect is to instruct the community on the nature and scope of its mission.

Let us cite the full passage and then enumerate its major themes:

> Then he said to them, "These are my words which I spoke to you, while I was still with you, that everything written about me in the Law of Moses and the prophets and the psalms must be fulfilled." Then he opened their minds to understand the scriptures, and said to them, "Thus it is written, that the Christ should suffer and on the third day rise from the dead, and that repentance and forgiveness of sins should be preached in his name to

all nations, beginning from Jerusalem. You are witnesses of these things. And behold, I send the promise of my Father upon you; but stay in the city, until you are clothed with power from on high" [Lk. 24:44–49].

1. The first thing to note is that this is a statement of the *risen* Christ and it speaks of a ministry that the community will carry out only *after* Jesus returns to his Father. Luke shows that he is conscious of the evolution of the Christian mission. As this study of the question has suggested, Jesus of Nazareth did not inaugurate a full-blown universal mission. The nature of the church's universal mission became clear only in the post-Easter experience of the community. In Acts, Luke reveals that this was not an instantaneous conviction of the community. Only gradually, even painfully, and only through the power of the Spirit would the apostles come to perceive and accept that call to go to "the end of the earth."

But equally important, Luke wants to ground that eventual universal mission in the history of Jesus. Luke emphasizes that the risen Christ *is* the vindicated Jesus of the Gospel story. He comes in triumph to renew table fellowship with the very ones he had chosen at the beginning of his ministry. As in Mt. 28:16–20 the marching orders for the community's mission come from the authority of Christ and will be carried out "in his name" (Lk. 24:47; cf. Mt. 28:19). This is why the gospel serves as a paradigm for the community's mission. The vigor of Jesus' prophetic ministry, his call for repentance and conversion, his powerful acts of healing and exorcism, his boundary-breaking compassion, and his efforts to form community—all of these give shape to the community's own mission. The parallels that Luke constructs between the events of Jesus' life and the life of the early community express on a literary level what is presupposed on a theological level.

2. The opening statement of the passage reveals another foundation for Luke's theological perspective: fulfillment of Scripture. The risen Christ makes explicit the conviction that flows beneath the surface of the entire Gospel: ". . . everything written about me in the law of Moses and the prophets and the psalms must be fulfilled" (Lk. 24:44; cf. Lk. 24:27). A similar viewpoint is an important part of Matthew's theology. Luke, in company with the rest of the New Testament, believed that the person and ministry of Jesus fulfills God's plan of salvation prophetically expressed in the Old Testament. By this means continuity is found with the heritage of Israel. Though the leaders of Israel reject Jesus and the mission of his church, a bridge to the past is maintained. Even the scandalous events of the rejection and death of Jesus fit this pattern of God's mysterious plan. The prophets, too, had been rejected.

It is significant that Luke sees the fulfillment of the Scriptures not only in the history of Jesus but in the history of the community as well. All the elements of verses 46–48 fall under the spell of the lead, "thus it is written": the death and resurrection of Jesus, the worldwide proclamation of conversion and forgiveness, the gift of the Spirit to the witnessing community. God's plan enunciated in the Scriptures will not be completed until "all flesh has seen the salvation of

God'' (cf. Lk. 3:6). Luke also implies that this correspondence between the promise of the Scriptures and the universal mission is not easily grasped. Only the power of the risen Christ and the direction of the Spirit enabled the apostolic leaders finally to understand.

3. Placing the call for a universal mission in the context of the resurrection appearance also shows that Luke, in concert with all of the New Testament, sees the death and resurrection as the climactic event of Jesus' history. The journey narrative begun with such deliberation in Lk. 9:51 and carried through to the entry into Jerusalem (Lk. 19:41) turns the momentum of the story in this direction. So, too, does the resistance hurled at the prophetic Jesus at the very start of his ministry (cf., for example, Lk. 4:28-29; 13:31-35; etc.). The suffering endured by Jesus and his ultimate vindication by God in resurrection forged a pattern that Luke sees as a trademark of God's work in history.[5] The prophetic messengers to Israel had suffered the same fate (Lk. 13:34). So, too, had the lowly ones of Israel borne the yoke of suffering (cf. the canticles of the infancy narratives). But God's power would reverse this legacy of pain and bring new life. "Thus," Luke writes, "it was necessary that the Christ should suffer these things and enter his glory" (Lk. 24:26). In Acts, Luke will etch a similar pattern for the community itself. Its message of salvation will be brought to the nations in and through suffering: the imprisonment of the apostles is an opportunity for preaching (Acts 5:40-42), the death of Stephen brings the message to Samaria (Acts 8:4-5) and the Greeks (Acts 11:19-21), Paul's apostolic hardships leave the Spirit unhindered (Acts 28:30-31).

The rest of the keynote passage we are considering moves beyond foundation statements to describe the style and content of the community's mission (cf. verses 47-49).

4. The brunt of the message is a call for conversion and a promise of forgiveness. This emphasis on the transforming power of the gospel is typical of the Lucan Jesus and of the apostles' preaching in Acts.[6] Through his words and powerful acts, the Lucan Jesus takes away pain, forgives sins, and transforms human life. There is a relentless call for full commitment in Luke's Gospel: response to the gospel must be deliberate and open-eyed (cf. the parables of Lk. 14:28-33). When the Pentecost crowd in Jerusalem cries out to the apostle, "Brethren, what shall we do?" Peter's response echoes the commissioning statement of Jesus: "Repent, and be baptized every one of you in the name of Jesus Christ for the forgiveness of your sins . . ." (Acts 2:37-38).[7] Thus salvation and its consequences are a dominant motif of both the Gospel and Acts. By implication, Luke reminds his own community that salvation remains the goal of its mission to the world.

5. The mission is to be universal, "beginning at Jerusalem" and moving out to "all nations" (Lk. 24:47). Both ends of Luke's vision are significant for his theology: the origin in the heart of Judaism and the worldwide goal. The importance of Jerusalem for Luke has long been recognized.[8] The infancy narrative begins and ends in the Jerusalem temple (cf. Lk. 1:9; 2:41-52). Jesus' dramatic journey to Jerusalem dominates the structure of the Gospel (cf. Lk. 9:51-19:40).

Luke, in distinction to Mark and Matthew, confines all the post-Easter activity of Jesus and the disciples to Jerusalem (cf. Lk. 24:49,52; Acts 1:4). There is little doubt that the capital city of Israel takes on symbolic meaning for the evangelist. Jesus, who fulfills the promise of the Old Testament, climaxes his messianic work in Jerusalem (cf. Lk. 13:33); and from Jerusalem flows the Christian community and its mission. Jerusalem symbolizes, therefore, the central role of Israel in the history of Jesus and the church. Throughout his Gospel and Acts, Luke takes pains to show the inner connection between these moments of sacred history.

6. While Luke gives full homage to the Jewish roots of the church, he also affirms the boundary-breaking nature of the church's universal mission. Even though Jesus' mission is confined mainly to the borders of Israel, signs of this universality break out in the Gospel story. And the whole structure of Acts will chart the breakout of the mission as it moves from "Judea and Samaria and to the end of the earth" (Acts 1:8). Luke will ultimately base this universality on God's will: Jesus is driven by the Spirit to inaugurate his mission of salvation (Lk. 4:14,18) and it is this "impartial" God who draws Peter the Jew and Cornelius the Gentile together (cf. Acts 10:34)

7. Luke's programmatic mission text designates the apostles as "witnesses of these things" (Lk. 24:48). Here, too, is a characteristic element of the evangelist's theology. The "twelve apostles" have a unique role in Luke-Acts because they form the living link between the history of Jesus and the history of the community.[9] As in the other two Synoptics, the chosen disciples/apostles are the constant companions of Jesus and privileged observers of his ministry. Perseverance in this association is crucial for Luke's perspective (cf. the requirements outlined in Acts 1:21–22) because this fragile group will become instruments of the mission once they have received the power of the Spirit. As we shall see, Luke does not have enough traditions about the missionary activity of the Twelve to follow through on this schema, but, especially in the early chapters of Acts, Peter and the Twelve play an essential role in the launching of the universal mission. It is Paul who will pick up the witness role in the second half of Acts. Even though he does not fulfill Luke's strict requirements for an "apostle," this chosen instrument (Acts 9:15) will dominate the stage of Acts after chapter 15 by being the one who brings the gospel from Jerusalem to the "end of the earth."

8. Finally, Luke's keynote text refers to the source that will sustain and direct the church's mission: the spirit (Lk. 24:49). Here again is another characteristic Lucan motif.[10] Jesus's own prophetic ministry inaugurated the age of the Spirit. The gift of the Spirit to the community is the true result of Jesus' redemptive work (cf. Lk. 24:49; Acts 1:4–5). Beginning with the dynamic event of Pentecost and throughout the story of Acts, Luke will consistently link the ever widening scope of the church's mission with the work of the Spirit.

The fibers of Luke's mission theology visible in this key passage of 24:44–49 run throughout the Gospel and Acts, binding this two-volume work together. Our task now is to trace these vital fibers through each of the two segments of Luke's story.

THE GOSPEL OF LUKE: JESUS AND THE UNIVERSAL MISSION

As we noted above, Luke is aware that a full-blown universal mission did not begin with Jesus himself; his ministry of forgiveness was generally restricted to the territories of Galilee, Samaria, and Judea. But, at the same time, Luke is convinced that the church's own mission finds its source and inspiration in the history of Jesus. When Luke reviews that history through the eyes of faith, the inner connection between the life of Jesus and the life of the community becomes clear. Each of the elements we have noted in the commission text of Lk. 24:44–49 is amplified in Luke's story of Jesus.

The Universal Scope of the Mission

Despite the geographical restrictions of Jesus' ministry, the evangelist clearly signals the universal potential of the Jesus-event. Simeon's canticle sounds the theme in the infancy narrative: "a light for revelation to the Gentiles and for glory to thy people Israel" (Lk. 2:32).[11] The entire atmosphere of these opening chapters of the Gospel moves in the same direction. The apparently insignificant birth of this Jewish boy is checked off against the chronology of the world ruler, Augustus, and Quirinius, his governor (Lk. 2:1), and the beginning of Jesus' ministry is related to the rule of Tiberius (Lk. 3:1). Luke suggests that these circumscribed events will have worldwide repercussions.

The universal theme is trumpeted again in the Isaiah quotation that introduces the preaching of John: ". . . all flesh shall see the salvation of God" (Lk. 3:6). God's "salvation" is what Simeon recognized in Jesus as the infant Messiah was brought to the temple (cf. Lk. 2:30). And Paul will echo Isa. 40:5 again at the conclusion of Acts when he turns from the Jews to the Gentiles: "Let it be known to you then that this salvation of God has been sent to the Gentiles; they will listen" (Acts 28:28). God's salvation embodied in Jesus will be brought to the end of the earth in the mission of the community.

This announcement of salvation for all finds its ratification in the boundary-breaking proportions of Jesus' ministry as presented by Luke.

The centrifugal force of Jesus' mission can be felt in the dramatic inaugural scene at Nazareth in Lk. 4:16–30.[12] The quotation is from Isa. 60:1–2a:

The Spirit of the Lord is upon me, because he has anointed me to preach the good news to the poor. He has sent me to proclaim release to the captives and recovering of sight to the blind, to set at liberty those who are oppressed, to proclaim the acceptable year of the Lord.

It designates those on the periphery—the poor, the captives, the blind, the oppressed—as the recipients of Jesus' Spirit-filled ministry. This centrifugal dimension is highlighted even more by the somewhat puzzling exchange in verses 22–29.

The Lucan Jesus seems to provoke his townspeople deliberately by challenging their provincialism ("Physician heal yourself; what we have heard you did in Capernaum, do here also in your own country") with reminders of the prophets Elijah and Elisha, who ministered not to Israel but to the Gentile widow of Zarephath and Namaan the Syrian. In this inaugural scene, Luke manages to preview the ultimate consequences of Jesus' own ministry.

Although Jesus the prophet does minister within Israel, the style of his ministry retains the limitless potential announced at Nazareth. He befriends and shares table fellowship with tax collectors and sinners (cf. Lk. 5:27-32; 15:1-2; etc.). More than any other evangelist Luke emphasizes Jesus' association with women—a stunning crossing of a social and religious barrier in the patriarchal society of his day. The Lucan Jesus is open to "official" outsiders such as the Gentile centurion (7:1-10) and Samaritans. The latter outcast group is a special concern of Jesus in Luke's story Jesus planned to exercise his mission there (cf. Lk. 9:52), and despite their rebuff he will not allow his disciples to take vengeance on Samaritan villages (Lk. 9:53-55). Twice in the Gospel, Samaritans are used as examples of virtue (cf. Lk. 10:30-37; 17:11-19). Jesus reaches out to lepers (Lk. 5:12-15), and care for the poor is a constant theme of his preaching (for example, Lk. 16:19-31; 18:18-27).[13]

There can be little doubt that Luke sees the connection between this expansive dimension of Jesus and the efforts of the church to move beyond its own frontiers. In Acts 10:38, as Peter is on the brink of accepting the Gentile Cornelius into the community, he recalls how Jesus "went about doing good and healing all that were oppressed by the devil, for God was with him." Luke gently urges his own community to make the same connection by placing the story of Jesus' ministry in tandem with the story of the community's missionary efforts.

Continuity with the History of Israel

Even though Luke begins to point the community to its future in the way he describes the provocative ministry of Jesus, the evangelist does not neglect continuity with the past. In fact one of the central concerns of Luke-Acts is the relationship between Israel and the church.[14]

The Gospel clearly states that Jesus is the Messiah, the Davidic Son of God, who carries out the promises to Israel. The infancy narrative is particularly important in this regard. Gabriel's message to Mary announces that Jesus will inherit "the throne of his father David" (Lk. 1:32) and the fruit of her womb "will be called holy, the Son of God" (Lk. 1:35). Zechariah's canticle picks up the same theme (cf. Lk. 1:68-79). The angels declared to the shepherds that "to you is born this day in the city of David a Savior, who is Christ the Lord" (Lk. 2:11), and Simeon gives thanks for having seen the salvation of Israel "prepared in the presence of all people" (Lk. 2:30). In fact the whole atmosphere of the infancy narrative roots Jesus' origin in the hopes of Israel. Zechariah, Elizabeth, Mary, Joseph, Simeon, Anna, the shepherds form a gallery of Old Testament figures, steeped in the longing of God's people for salvation. Their Spirit-filled expectations of salvation demonstrate that the birth of Jesus is the climax of the promises to Israel.[15]

The rest of the Gospel carries through this sense of continuity with the past. The Jesus who comes for baptism is designated as God's beloved Son (Lk. 3:22) and the genealogy (Lk. 3:23–38) traces his lineage back through the Davidic line to Abraham, Adam, and God himself. The whole history of salvation is preface to Jesus. Jesus rightly declares that the messianic promise of Isaiah 61 is fulfilled in the inauguration of his mission (Lk. 4:17–22). The story that follows is a vivid display of his salvific work.

Even the rejection and death of Jesus is seen as fulfillment of God's plan; on this score, too, Luke is similar to Mark and Matthew. Luke gives special emphasis to the prophetic cast of Jesus' ministry. Yahweh's messengers to Israel had been repeatedly rejected by a stubborn people.[16] The pattern continues in the last and greatest of God's envoys (cf. the allegory of Lk. 20:9–18). Because humanity resists God's Word, it is inevitable that the Christ "must" suffer. "Behold I cast out demons and perform cures today and tomorrow, and the third day I finish my course. Nevertheless I must go on my way today and tomorrow and the day following; for it cannot be that a prophet should perish away from Jerusalem" (Lk. 13:32–33). That necessity is stated by Luke more than once not only in explicit declarations (cf. Lk. 17:24; 18:31–34; 24:7, 26, 44; cf. also Acts 17:3; 26:22–23) but in the deliberateness with which the Lucan Jesus moves toward his death in Jerusalem (cf., for example, Lk. 9:51; 13:33).

Therefore Jesus' ministry is the climax of God's salvific work with his people Israel. Like the prophets in the past Jesus suffers rejection and death. But Luke does not conceive of Jesus as strictly one more in the ongoing stream of messengers. He is the Son (cf. Lk. 20:12), God's definitive Word. Jesus the prophet moves through suffering and death to glory. He completes his messianic work in spite of trial and therefore initiates the promised age of salvation. The community formed in Jesus' name is therefore *the* messianic people (cf. Lk. 22:28–30), heirs to the promises of Israel and continuing God's work of redemption in the world through the power of the Spirit. The salvation-history framework forged by Luke (and other New Testament writers) allows continuity to run from Israel to Jesus to the church. This framework finds a codified expression in Luke's phrase "beginning at Jerusalem" (cf. Lk. 24:49).

A Mission of Salvation

The *content* of Jesus' ministry has important consequences for the community's mission. The keynote text of Lk. 24:47 had summarized the community's proclamation as that of "repentance and forgiveness of sins," a message that will reverberate throughout the sermons in Acts (cf. 2:38; 3:19, 26; 8:22; 10:43; 13:38; 17:30; 20:21; 26:18,20). The same theme is announced by Zechariah in his canticle on John's preparatory ministry: ". . . for you will go before the Lord to prepare his ways, to give knowledge of salvation to his people in the forgiveness of their sins" (Lk. 1:77). This is exactly how John is depicted in Lk. 3:3: ". . . he went into all the region about the Jordan, preaching a baptism of repentance for the forgiveness of sins" (cf. also John's own words in Lk. 3:7-14, which spell out the meaning of genuine repentance).

Jesus' ministry, too, is one of transformation and forgiveness.[17] The inaugural scene at Nazareth again provides the lead to Luke's presentation: Jesus' mission is to preach good news to the poor, liberation for the captives and oppressed, healing for the blind. This is precisely what Jesus does as his dynamic ministry begins to unfold after the Nazareth incident (cf. Lk. 4:31ff.). The Greek term for forgiveness, *aphesis,* has the connotation of "release," a freedom from the bondage of sin. The Lucan Jesus not only directly forgives sins, as in the cases of the paralytic (Lk. 5:20), the "woman of the city" (Lk. 7:47-48), and his own executioners (Lk. 23:34), but he "releases" those bound with the physical burdens of pain and illness, which the biblical mind recognized as part of the legacy of sin. The case of the woman bent double—found only in Luke (13:10-17)—is typical of this liberating dimension of forgiveness. When Jesus is challenged by the ruler of the synagogue for curing on the Sabbath, he openly declares the priority of his mission: "Ought not this woman, a daughter of Abraham whom Satan bound for eighteen years, be loosed from this bond on the Sabbath day?" (Lk. 13:16).

The reference to Satan in this text points to another dimension of Jesus' ministry of liberation that Luke shares in common with the other synoptics but to which he gives special emphasis.[18] Jesus' struggle with sin and illness brings him face to face with ultimate evil, Satan. This personification of evil enters the story for a direct encounter with the Messiah in the wilderness. Having failed to subvert Jesus' mission, Satan leaves him "until an opportune time" (Lk. 4:13). That opportune time seems to come in the passion story when Luke notes that "Satan entered into Judas called Iscariot" (Lk. 22:23). The "test" (Lk. 22:28) of the suffering and death of Jesus are thus attributed to the agency of Satan, even though on a deeper level they are part of God's own life-giving plan. Jesus the Christ will faithfully endure his sufferings and enter his glory despite the threats of evil.

Between the time of the wilderness temptation and the passion trial Satan is still active, though in a more subtle way. Here the marks of evil are found embedded in human life: the possessed, the sick, the blind, the lame, the oppressed. Like Mark and Matthew, Luke recognizes a transcendent dimension to the burdens of human pain. Lurking behind these symptoms is the mystery of evil itself. Therefore the healings and exorcisms of Jesus' kingdom mission have a cosmic significance and fit the universal potential of his mission: "If it is by the finger of God that I cast out demons, then the kingdom of God has come upon you" (Lk. 11:20).

The call for conversion is also an essential part of Jesus' mission of salvation. Not only are broken bodies and broken spirits made whole, but lives without purpose are invited to make a full commitment to the kingdom of God. The metanoia that is to characterize the community's preaching (Lk. 24:47) and which had been a hallmark of John's message (Lk. 3:3), is also the purpose of Jesus' mission: "I have not come to call the righteous but sinners to repentance" (Lk. 5:32). The breathtaking mercy parables of Luke 15—the lost sheep, the lost coin, and the lost son—all revolve around the theme of God's overwhelming graciousness and the invitation to metanoia (cf. Lk. 15:7,9,32). This is the good news that Jesus offers (notice that these parables are told by Jesus precisely to defend his ministry to outcasts, cf. Lk. 15:1-2). The demands of discipleship are an intensive form of this call to metanoia. The would-be followers of Jesus should calculate the cost and realize the need to renounce every obstacle to complete commitment before setting out on the way of discipleship (cf. Lk. 14:25-33).

The liberating and transforming mission of Jesus in the Gospel story defines what the community's message of "conversion and forgiveness of sin" is about. The tone of the sermons and the healing power of the apostles and missionaries in Acts will be Luke's way of showing that the commission of the risen Jesus is faithfully carried out by the community formed in his name.

The Formation of Community

The disciples gathered in Jerusalem at the end of the Gospel (cf. Lk. 24:33) not only continue Jesus' mission in the post-Easter period but are, in one sense, the final result of that mission. The purpose of Jesus' mission is to restore Israel (Lk. 1:68-79), to fashion God's people. The Pentecost story will climax in the formation of a community that prays and breaks bread together (cf. Acts 2:43-47). Throughout his two-volume work, Luke shows that the plan of God is to incorporate "all flesh" within the people of God; no arbitrary boundary can be used to exclude from his household those "who fear God and act uprightly," (Acts 10:34). Therefore one of the central roles of mission as envisaged by Luke is the formation of community among diverse peoples bound together in faith and love.

This motif will be evident in the community's struggles in Acts over the issue of the Gentiles. In the Gospel the formation of community is more subtle but no less present. Luke gives particular attention to Jesus' gracious table fellowship with sinners and outcasts. The meal becomes a provocative theater in which the Lucan Jesus discloses God's embrace of all peoples. The guest list in the Gospel stories invariably includes the "unwanted." Jesus dines with Levi the tax collector and his unsavory friends and earns the disapproving murmurs of Pharisees and scribes (Lk. 5:29-32). Jesus is characterized as "a glutton and a drunkard, a friend of tax collectors and sinners" (Lk. 7:34; cf. 15:1-2). A woman of the streets breaks into Simon the Pharisee's banquet and offers Jesus extraordinary gestures of affection, winning his approval but scandalizing his hosts (Lk. 7:36-50). Jesus deliberately chooses to be a house guest of the tax collector Zacchaeus (Lk. 19:1-18). His death and resurrection are marked by meals with his baffled disciples (cf. Lk. 22:19-20; 24:13-35, 41-43).

These meals and their outcast guests preview the mission experience of the community in Acts: the Jewish-Christian community will struggle to accept table fellowship with Gentiles, and the outcome of that struggle becomes decisive for the universal mission.[19] The parable of the banquet in Lk. 14:15-24 seems to use the table-fellowship theme as an object lesson on salvation history. The invited guests balk and offer contrived excuses so the host opens the banquet to "the poor and maimed and blind and lame" (Lk. 14:21). When places still remain open, the servants are sent out to the "highways and hedges" (Lk. 14:23) until the hall is full. The saying of Lk. 13:29 uses the meal motif in a similar way to speak of the eventual mission to the Gentiles: "And many will come from east and west, and from north and south, and sit at the table in the kingdom of God."

Thus Luke joins hands with both Matthew and Mark (and the rest of the New Testament) in asserting that the outcasts are as capable of a genuine response to God's offer of salvation as the "invited guests" of Israel. In Acts this will be referred to as God's "impartiality" (cf. Acts 10:34). In the Gospel story this important conviction is illustrated not only by the meal theme where, in effect, God's great guest list includes the outsider, but by a number of sayings, parables, and incidents in which outcasts, even Gentiles, respond better than "insiders." So the faith of the centurion (Lk. 7:1-10) is greater than that found in Israel. The sinful woman "loves much," far more than the Pharisee Simon (Lk. 7:42-50). The towns of Tyre and Sidon are declared more likely to reform than the cities of Galilee (Lk. 19:13-15). The queen of the south and the citizens of Nineveh responded better to the wisdom of Solomon and the preaching of Jonah than "this generation" does to the "something greater" proclaimed by Jesus (Lk. 11:29-32). The Samaritan leper knows how to give thanks (Lk. 17:11-19) and a Samaritan turns out to be a faithful keeper of the love command, the essence of the law (Lk. 19:29-37). The poor man Lazarus (Lk. 16:19-31) and the repentant publican (Lk. 18:9-14) are heard by God, while the rich man and the proud Pharisee fail. The offering of the poor widow is worth more than the weighty gifts of the rich (Lk. 21:1-4).

By means of these examples another taut line is tied between the universal mission of the church and the boundary-breaking ministry of Jesus. The right to be included in the community of God's people is not defined by one's heritage or status but only by response to God's universal invitation.

Persevering Witnesses

As we have already noted in the cases of Mark and Matthew, the Gospels are built on the expectation of response. Those who encounter Jesus and his mission must react. Although these reactions cross the spectrum from hostility to complete faith, the Gospels focus most of their interest on the response of those called to be disciples. Here is the core group that mirrors the experience of the Christian community itself.

This axiom is certainly true in Luke's case. In Lk. 24:47 we saw that the risen Lord declares to the "eleven and those with them" (Lk. 24:33), "You are witnesses of these things." As the story of Acts unfolds it will be the apostles (now restored to "twelve," cf. Acts 1:15-26) and other leading disciples such as Barnabas and Paul who will witness to Jesus in their missionary preaching from Judea to the end of the earth. Thus missionary proclamation is one of the expressions of genuine discipleship in Luke's view.

This function, too, has its roots in the history of Jesus, even though its full expression must await the mission consciousness of the post-Easter community. One of the requirements for apostleship, according to Peter's words in Acts 1:21–22, is to have walked with Jesus from the beginning, from the baptism of John to the ascension. Only those who have deeply absorbed the experience of Jesus are able to lead the community in its mission to the world. The Gospel drama fully supports this. One of the ideal discipleship types in Luke's account is the figure of Mary.[20] As Luke protrays her, she embodies the description of the genuine disciple outlined in the sower parable: "Those who, hearing the word, hold it fast in an honest and good heart, and bring forth fruit with patience" (Lk. 8:15). This is precisely how Mary performs in the annunciation drama, as she hears the Word, ponders it, and gives it birth (cf. Lk. 1:26–38). Three times in the Gospel, Mary is acclaimed for this kind of persevering faith (cf. Lk. 1:45; 8:19–21; 11:27–28).

This notion of genuine discipleship as attentive hearing of the Word and faithful, persevering response to it carries over in Luke's portrayal of the group whom Jesus chooses as his witnesses in the community's mission. The mission aura of discipleship is present in Luke's unique story of calling at the beginning of Jesus' public ministry (Lk. 5:1–11). The evangelist seems to combine a resurrection-appearance story of the disciples' frustrated fishing expedition (similar to that of Jn. 21:1–14) with the story of calling found in Mk. 1:16–20. The result is a typically Lucan scene in which the willingness of Simon and his companions to obey the word of Jesus (Lk. 5:5) leads to an abundant catch and to their commission as disciples destined to "catch human beings" (Lk. 5:10).

The special function of the Twelve in Luke begins to emerge with 6:12–16 where Jesus selects from the general body of disciples a group of twelve whom he names "apostles." This designation, the "twelve apostles," takes on special meaning in Luke-Acts, since it refers to that nucleus of witnesses who will provide continuity between the history of Jesus and that of the early church.[21] In Lk. 9:1–6 these same twelve are "sent" (the meaning of the word *apostolos*) to "preach the kingdom of God and to heal," the exact mission of Jesus himself and the mission that will eventually characterize the community of Acts. There remains a wider circle of followers, for example, the "disciples" from whom the Twelve are selected and the Seventy who are also sent out on mission, combating the power of evil just as Jesus does (cf. Lk. 10:1–20). The distinctive role of the twelve apostles, however, remains that of an authoritative link between Jesus and the community.

Luke reinforces this role for the twelve apostles in his passion story. They join Jesus for a final fellowship meal (Lk. 22:14). Their weakness is painfully evident in the dispute that erupts even during this sacred moment: they argue among themselves about "which of them was to be regarded as the greatest" (Lk. 22:24–27), a dispute quelled only by Jesus' own example of humble service. Despite the apostles' frailty they will persevere with Jesus through the great test of suffering and become the leaders of God's renewed people. Into the tragedy of death Luke presses a special reflection about the apostles' role: "You are those who have continued with me in my trial; and I assign to you, as my Father assigned to me, a kingdom, that you may eat and drink at my table in my kingdom, and sit on thrones judging the twelve tribes of Israel" (Lk. 22:28-30). Even Simon, whose failure is painfully reviewed in Mark and Matthew, will ultimately persevere and exercise his apostleship: "Simon, Simon, behold Satan demanded to have you, that he might sift you like wheat, but I have prayed for you that your faith may not fail; and when you have turned again, strengthen your brethren" (Lk. 22:31-32).

To maintain this motif of perseverance Luke has to downplay some of the abject failure of the apostles related in the traditional passion story. Thus he makes no mention of the disciples' flight at the moment of arrest and seems to suggest the hesitant presence of Jesus' followers at the crucifixion itself (cf. Lk. 23:49, "and all his acquaintances and the women who had followed him from Galilee stood at a distance and saw these things"). Luke does not omit the story of Peter's denial, but this breakdown of apostleship appears to be healed by the face-to-face encounter between Jesus and his errant apostle during the trial (cf. 22:61-62, a detail found only in Luke).

The bent but not broken fidelity of the followers of Jesus prepares for the special atmosphere of Luke's Easter stories. All three incidents build up to the reassembly of the community around the eleven disciples in Jerusalem and the commission they will receive from Jesus as he completes the journey to the Father. The women who discover the empty tomb will report back "to the eleven and all the rest" (Lk. 24:8), a report accepted with disbelief by the "apostles" (24:9). The two disciples on the road have left Jerusalem in discouragement (a sign that their perseverance is faltering) but after the encounter with the risen Jesus at a meal, they too report back to the eleven and the rest of the community in the holy city (Lk. 24:33). The climax of the story comes in Lk. 24:36-49 when the risen Jesus appears to the whole community and lays before them the mission that will carry the good news of the kingdom to the end of the earth. They will be the "witnesses of these things" not only by announcing the good news of healing, as Jesus did, but also by experiencing, like him, rejection, suffering, death. But together with their risen Lord the disciples will also enter into glory and will see the message of forgiveness brought to the end of the earth.[22]

For Luke, then, one of the most important ingredients in the missionary program of the community is those leaders who ensure the authenticity of the community's message by linking its mission to that of Jesus. The story in Acts shows that much of the actual mission work is done by people other than the twelve apostles. But this nuclear group authorizes the Gentile mission and monitors it.

The Power of the Spirit

The final words of the risen Jesus to his disciples guarantee the gift of the Spirit: "And behold, I send the promise of my Father upon you; but stay in the city, until you are clothed with power from on high" (Lk. 24:49; cf. Acts 1:4-5, 8). Of all the evangelists, Luke has the most elaborate treatment of the Spirit. This motif expresses a number of convictions about the Christ-event and the Christian experience, including the universal scope of the church's mission. Acts shows how the power of the Spirit propels the community into the Gentile world and guides its pastoral strategy.

Because the Spirit becomes in a sense the "replacement" of the person of Jesus in the community, it is not surprising that the Spirit plays a more prominent role in Acts (42 times) than in the Gospel (13 times). But, as is the case with all the elements of Luke's mission theology, the experiences of the church are thoroughly rooted in the history of Jesus. Thus before the risen Christ sends the gift of the Spirit to the community, he himself has tasted the "promise of the Father."

Not all of the significance of the Spirit is directly related to mission. The "storm of the Spirit" that seems to accompany the birth of Jesus signals the coming of the age of salvation, a time when Judaism expected an increase of God's charismatic activity.[23] The great characters of the infancy narrative—Zechariah (Lk. 1:67), Elizabeth (Lk. 1:41), John (Lk. 1:15), Simeon (Lk. 2:25), Anna (a "prophetess," Lk. 2:36)—are all filled with the Spirit of God and speak prophetically. Luke's annunciation account seems to describe the gift of the Spirit in creation tones: "The Holy Spirit will come upon you and the power of the Most High will overshadow you" (Lk. 1:35). This burst of the Spirit demarcates the beginning of a new age, the age of Jesus the Messiah, an age of Spirit and of fire (Lk. 3:16), just as the Pentecost experience in Acts 2 will signal a new phase in the age of salvation with the birth of the church.

Luke also uses the Spirit motif to underline Jesus' identity as Messiah, the Son of God. Jesus' ultimate origin is from the Spirit of God (Lk. 1:35), and the descent of the Spirit on Jesus at the moment of baptism is a dramatic moment for his messianic designation as the Father's "Beloved Son" (Lk. 3:22). This communion between Father and Son is celebrated by Jesus with joy "in the Holy Spirit" (Lk. 10:21).

But, in addition, the power of the Spirit is connected with the dynamism of Jesus' mission. Luke links Jesus' desert test—where the authenticity of his messianic mission is subjected to trial—with his baptism; the phrase "full of the Holy Spirit" (Lk. 4:1) bridges the intervening genealogy (Lk. 3:23-38) and recalls the descent of the Spirit on Jesus at the Jordan (Lk. 3:22). It is this Spirit that "leads" Jesus into his confrontation with the power of evil (a preview of Jesus' struggle with Satan in his healing ministry, cf. above). And it is the "power of the Spirit" that accompanies Jesus to Galilee as he begins his mission (Lk. 4:14).

This mission orientation stands out clearly in the keynote passage of 4:16-30. Jesus' entire ministry starts off with the ringing words of Isa. 61:1, "The Spirit of the Lord is upon me, because he has anointed me . . ." (Lk. 4:18). This is the divine power that molds Jesus the prophet and gives force and direction to his ministry of liberation. The radiation of that mission beyond the confines of Palestine is already signaled in the Nazareth incident (4:23-30). This universal promise will come to fulfillment when Jesus' work is completed and the gift of the Spirit has been lavished upon the church.

Thus for Luke the concept of Spirit seals the kinship between God's universal will to save, the liberating ministry of Jesus, and the worldwide mission of the church. During the history of Israel that universal potential is hidden in promise: God would one day redeem his people and reverse the oppression suffered by the lowly (cf. the canticles of Zechariah and Mary). During the lifetime of Jesus, God's Spirit begins to fulfill the promise: those in pain are liberated, the poor are cared for, the outcasts and rejected are brought home. With the completion of the work of Jesus, God's full embrace of humanity can now become apparent, as the community formed by Jesus carries his message of forgiveness to the end of the earth. By the way he tells the Gospel story, Luke is able to base the scope and character of the church's mission in the person and ministry of Jesus. We can now turn to the second volume of Luke's work, where he shows the continuation of Jesus' mission in the development of the early church.

TIIE ACTS OF THE APOSTLES:
THE COMMUNITY'S UNIVERSAL MISSION

The mission program enunciated in the commission text of Lk. 24:44–49 and previewed in the Gospel's portrayal of Jesus' ministry is now carried out by the apostles and the community in the book of Acts.[24] The scope, the structure, and the content of Acts are dominated by the question of the universal mission. The kingdom ministry of Jesus, which reached a climax in Jerusalem with his death, resurrection, and triumphant return to the Father, will be continued through the guidance of the risen Christ and the power of the Spirit in the community's own history.

This perspective, already spelled out in the Gospel (cf. especially Lk. 24:44–49) is recapitulated in the opening verses of Acts. The community gathered in Jerusalem is instructed by the risen Jesus about the "kingdom of God" and the advent of the Spirit (cf. Acts 1:3–5). They are told to remain in the city until they receive the Spirit. The power of the Spirit will inaugurate a mission stretching from Jerusalem through all Judea and Samaria to the "end of the earth" (cf. Acts 1:8). While obediently awaiting this new dawn, the community reconstitutes the number of the twelve apostles so that all is in readiness for the beginning of the mission (Acts 1:15–26). Thus the opening chapter of Acts confirms what the final chapter of the Gospel had already made clear: the preoccupying concern of the evangelist is the universal mission of salvation announced by Simeon (Lk. 2:32) and the Baptist (Lk. 3:6), begun by Jesus' ministry and now to be carried out by his church. The apostolic leadership of the church, Peter and the Twelve, and Paul will take the mission to the end of the earth.

The Structure of Acts

As Ferdinand Hahn and others have suggested, the structure of the book of Acts takes its cue from this mission perspective.[25] The sequence of "Jerusalem-Judea-Samaria-end of the earth" guides the basic movement of the story. The decisive action for opening up the mission will be the conversion of Cornelius in chapter 10 and the acceptance of the consequences of this step by the Jerusalem church in chapters 11 and 15. But Luke already begins to illustrate the expansive nature of the mission in chapters 2 through 9. If Paul will be the "chosen instrument" (Acts 9:15) who carries the message of salvation to the "end of the earth," it is Peter and other leaders of the Jerusalem church who are the agents of the mission in Jerusalem, Judea, and Samaria.

Peter is the dominant figure in the Jerusalem mission. The phenomenon of the Spirit and Peter's subsequent Pentecost sermon touch Jews in Jerusalem who have gathered "from every nation under heaven" (Acts 2:5-11). Even though the concentration is still on Jew and not Gentile, Luke's emphasis on the diaspora in this text confirms that the saving event begun here will, as Peter's citation of Joel suggests, bring God's Spirit to "all flesh" (Acts 2:17). A similar universal dimension is implied in Peter's speech at Solomon's Portico, where he reminds the Jerusalemites that "you are sons of the prophets and of the covenant which God gave to your fathers, saying to Abraham, 'And in your posterity shall all the families of the earth be blessed' " (Acts 3:25). The healing ministry of Peter and John and the other apostles (cf. Acts 2:43; 3:1-10; 5:12-26) and the marvelous growth of the Jerusalem community (Acts 2:41-47; 4:4, 32-35; 5:14; 6:7) confirm the fulfillment of the first stage of the Lord's promise—the community has effectively witnessed to the mission of the risen Jesus in Jerusalem.

The death of Stephen and the persecution that follows (chap. 6-8) are the events that paradoxically widen the scope of the mission to "Judea and Samaria" (8:1). As with Jesus, the community arrives at life through death. Those scattered by the persecution "went about preaching the word" (Acts 8:4). Philip evangelizes Samaria (8:5-8), a step confirmed by the Jerusalem apostles and continued in the ministry of Peter and John themselves (8:25). Luke continues to assert the centrality of the Jerusalem church even as the mission pushes beyond its boundaries. Few details of the Judean mission are given, but in 9:31 we have a summation of its great success. Also in this section we are told of the conversion of the Ethiopian eunuch by Philip (8:26-39). The mission has not yet broken beyond the borders of Israel and this foreigner is most likely a proselyte to Judaism, but the miraculous nature of this encounter is a preview of God's universal salvation.

The introduction of Paul (cf. Acts 7:58; 8:3, 9:1ff.) brings us to the third stage. He will be an instrument carrying the word of salvation to the end of the earth— the dominant motif of the second half of Acts. But Paul's mission cannot get underway until Peter and the Jerusalem church have formally ratified the mission to the Gentiles. This is the crucial significance of Acts 10:1-11:18: Peter's vision at Joppa and his encounter with the devout Gentile Cornelius, who is noted for virtues dear to Luke, prayer and almsgiving (10:2). Luke artfully makes this story a micro-drama of the early church's entire struggle with the mission question. Peter and, ultimately, the Jewish Christians at Jerusalem are asked to absorb the staggering reality that their sacred customs are to give way before the "impartiality" of God (cf. Acts 10:15, 28, 34, 47; 11:9, 17, 18). The God who sent Jesus chooses to give to the people of "any nation" the same gifts of the Spirit he lavished on the Jerusalem Jews. Thus the awesome good news already promised by the risen Jesus in Lk. 24:47 finally strikes home: "Then to the Gentiles also God has granted repentance unto life" (Acts 11:18).

Even though Luke presents Peter and the Jerusalem church as grasping only gradually the full scope of the mission (an assertion that undoubtedly is historically true), he still insists on the central role of Jerusalem. Just as the mission to Samaria had to be "authenticated" by the Twelve (Acts 8:14–17), so too the full-blown Gentile mission of Paul and others cannot really get underway until the Jerusalem church has accepted it. Only now (Acts 11:19–20) are we told of the spread of the word in Antioch by the Hellenists—and only now are we prepared for the full presentation of Paul's mission (cf. 13:2–3). Acts 13 sets up a pattern repeated through the second half of Acts: Paul preaches first to the synagogues, but when rejected turns to the Gentiles (cf. 13:44–52). Thus the Lucan insistence on a salvation-history perspective of "Jews first" is apparent in the very structure of Acts. A corollary of this is the central role of the Jewish Christians themselves. All important initiatives of the universal mission (including Paul's work among the Gentiles) must ultimately be ratified by the apostles, who remain the authentic link to the mission of Jesus, a mission that "began in Jerusalem."

In the last half of Acts, Paul moves boldly on his mission to Asia, Greece, and finally Rome, thereby fulfilling the promise of God's universal salvation (cf. especially 28:29). The twelve apostles seem to fade from view, their essential work done. Now the mission is entrusted to a "second generation," ministers of the Word (cf. Lk. 1:2) such as Paul and Barnabas, a generation with whom the author of Acts seems to identify. This postapostolic generation is entrusted with the work of carrying God's message of salvation "to the end of the earth."

The Mission Message of Acts

Just as the universal mission shapes the structure of Acts, so too does the mission question dominate the content of the book. The major themes we isolated in the commission text of Lk. 24:44–49 and traced throughout the Gospel are vitally present in Acts as well.

Two of these motifs have already been considered in our examination of structure, namely, the mission's universal scope and its continuity with the history of Israel. In the very way Luke shapes the sequence of the community's early history, he confirms the statement of the risen Jesus that "repentance and forgiveness of sins should be preached in his name to all nations, beginning at Jerusalem" (Lk. 24:47; Acts 1:8).

The narrative equally confirms the salvation-history perspective implied in the phrase "beginning at Jerusalem." As we have already noted, Luke presents Jesus' own mission as climaxing in Jerusalem, the city that symbolized not only opposition to Jesus' prophetic ministry but also the role of Israel in God's plan of salvation announced in the Scriptures. Scripture is fulfilled by having the community receive its endowment of the Spirit in Jerusalem and by having its mission begin from this sacred center. As the early chapters of Acts make clear, the apostles and the Jerusalem church are a constant reference point as the mission radiates out to Judea, Samaria, and beyond. The anchor of the Christian mission in the sacred history of Israel is further confirmed by the experience of the early missionaries. Diaspora Jews are the first to hear and accept the preaching of Peter (Acts 2:5–12); God-fearing Gentiles who come to Israel, such as the Ethiopian eunuch and Cornelius, are the pioneers of the Gentile church. Paul consistently takes his mission to the synagogues of the Greco-Roman world, and only in the face of their refusal does he turn to the Gentiles (cf. Acts 13:46; 28:28). A recital of the history of Israel with particular emphasis on God's saving initiatives and the failure of Israel to respond forms a major part of the sermons of Acts (cf. especially 2:22–36; 3:12–26; 7:2–53; 13:16–41).

This insistence on the priority of Israel not only reflects the actual historical development of the early Christian mission but enables Luke to establish continuity with the Old Testament and thereby confirm that the church's work among Gentiles "fulfills" what was written "in the law of Moses and the prophets and the psalms" (Acts 24:44). Jesus himself is the first instance of this eschatological fulfillment. His inclusive mission, his death and victory had shaped and inspired the early community's vision. Now the Spirit-prompted work of the church carries out this fulfilling task begun by Jesus himself.

It should be noted that Luke's attention to continuity with Israel does not dilute the inherent universalism of the gospel or rob the Gentile mission of its own validity. The turn to the Gentiles follows upon the rejection by Israel but is not wholly explained by this. As the Gospel makes clear, the "salvation of all flesh" is intended by God from the beginning. The baptism of the Ethiopian, the conversion of Cornelius, and the mandate of Paul to go to the Gentiles are clearly the result of an explicit divine initiative, regardless of the response of the Jews. Paul's speeches in Acts 14:15–17 and 17:23–31 affirm that the offer of salvation to the Gentiles is not a mere crust from the table of Israel but is part of God's saving care for all peoples already expressed in creation.[26] Thus the movement from Israel to the Gentiles is not the cause of the universal mission, in Luke's view, but the God-ordained moment that clearly reveals God's saving intent for all.

The content of Acts clearly reveals that the purpose of the community's mission is salvation, the major theme of the summary commission of Lk. 24:44–49 and of the entire gospel. The work of Jesus in the Synoptic Gospels is presented as a ministry of salvation, proclaiming and actualizing God's saving deeds and calling on people to accept the results of that transformation in their lives. At its most fundamental level, this is what defines the "coming of the kingdom of God." Thus the Gospels are full of Jesus' acts of healing and exorcism, his fresh teaching, and his insistent call for conversion and repentance.

The same mission of salvation is entrusted to the community: "repentance and forgiveness of sins should be preached in his name. . . . You are the witnesses of these things" (Lk. 24:47–48). Luke presents the apostles, Paul, and the early missionaries as faithfully carrying out this mandate. The risen Jesus instructs the apostles on the meaning of the kingdom of God (Acts 1:3) and this key symbol is used to characterize the missionary preaching of Philip (Acts 8:12) and Paul (Acts 19:8; 20:25; 28:23, 31). More importantly, the *content* of the kingdom ministry of

Jesus is carried through in the various components of the community's mission. The sermons of Acts consistently speak of God's tireless graciousness and the need to respond by conversion of heart (2:38; 3:19; 5:31; 10:43; 11:18; 13:38-39; 16:30-31; 20:21; 26:18-20). This message of salvation is also proclaimed in the powerful healing ministry of the community, just as it was by Jesus' works of compassion. Therefore Luke gives full attention to the miracles performed by Peter, John, Paul, and others (cf., for example, Acts 2:43; 3:1-10; 5:12-16; 9:32-35, 36-42; 14:3, 8-10; 16:16-19). The sick, the lame, the disfranchised receive new life, fulfilling the prophecy of Isaiah 61 announced by Jesus in the synagogue of Nazareth. The first great miracle in Acts spells this out (3:1-16). The healing of the lame beggar at the gate of the temple is not meant to be a glorification of the apostles themselves but is evidence of the salvation brought about through the risen Christ and now effectively proclaimed by the mission of the church: "To this we are witnesses. And his name, by faith in his name, has made this man strong whom you see and know; and the faith which is through Jesus has given the man this perfect health in the presence of you all" (Acts 3:15-16). Unquestionably the mission of the community is a mission of salvation, as was the work of Jesus.

Related to the salvation theme is that of community. Luke highlights the motif of table fellowship with Jesus in the course of the Gospel and uses the metaphor of the banquet as a way of describing the nature of God's salvific work. This has a strong follow-through in Acts. The important summaries of Acts 2:42-47 and 4:32-35 illustrate that the formation of community is a direct result of the gift of the Spirit and, therefore, a symptom of conversion. The emphasis in these idealized descriptions of the Jerusalem church is on the sharing of goods and the absence of need, signs of the eschatological Israel.[27]

Other important events in Acts echo this motif. The key issue in the Cornelius story of Acts 10-11 is that of table fellowship with a Gentile (cf. especially 10:9-16, 28; 11:1-18). Peter's hesitation on this score is directly challenged by divine revelation. Luke artfully describes the dawning consciousness of Peter and eventually the rest of the Jerusalem church as they see this arbitrary boundary to community dissolved.[28] It is crucial to the whole theology of Luke that Peter's decision is ratified by his reflection in Acts 10:34-43, which relates his fellowship with Cornelius to the ministry of Jesus who "anointed . . . with the Holy Spirit and with power . . . went about doing good and healing all that were oppressed by the devil, for God was with him" (10:38). Jesus' own boundary-breaking ministry and his offer of forgiveness to "every one who believes in him" (10:43) are now being fulfilled in the momentous decision of the church to accept table fellowship with this Gentile centurion. The Jerusalem Council in chapter 15 concentrates on the issue of circumcision, but since the whole question of association with Gentiles is at stake, this key chapter, too, confirms the momentous step of sharing community with those considered "outcasts" in the particularist viewpoint of the Judaizers.

Thus it is not an exaggeration to say that the daring acts of table fellowship exercised by Jesus in the Gospel have, as their final consequences, the church's embrace of the Gentile world. Not only does the eschatological banquet of Israel now indeed include the "poor and maimed and blind and lame" of the city streets, but the invitation has gone out to the distant guests of "the highways and hedges" (cf. Lk. 14:15-24).

Another important component of Luke's mission theology is the role he assigns to the twelve apostles as persevering witnesses to the risen Jesus and as the nucleus of the community formed in his name (Lk. 24:44). Our discussion of Acts has already made this point. Following the restoration of the Twelve (Acts 1:15-26) and the reception of the promised Spirit, it is Peter and the Jerusalem apostles who become the spearhead of the mission. When the opening to the Gentiles is fully legitimized, the apostles' founding role appears to be completed and a "second generation" of witnesses typified by Paul dominates the stage of Acts.

Even though the mission statement of the Gospel had assigned to the Twelve a ministry of preaching the kingdom (Lk. 24:48), the evangelist is able to give specific illustrations of this only in the case of Peter and to a lesser extent John. Peter plays a prominent role, delivering the inaugural mission sermon at Pentecost (Acts 2:14-36), exercising (along with John) his power to heal (Acts 3:1-16; 5:15-16), fearlessly confronting hostile powers (Acts 4:8-12, 19-20; 5:29-32), enduring imprisonment and flogging (Acts 5:17, 40-41; 12:3)—all hallmarks of those sent on mission in the name of Jesus. Equally important, Peter plays a decisive role in the establishment of the community and its policies: the choice of Matthias as Judas' replacement (Acts 1:15), spokesperson for the community to the Jerusalem crowds (Acts 2:14), confronting the errant Ananias and Sapphira (Acts 5:1-11), bearing the gospel to Cornelius and persuading the Jerusalem church to accept him (Acts 10-11), leading the discussion at the Jerusalem Council (Acts 15:7). The activity of the rest of the Twelve is stated only in general terms (cf., for example, Acts 2:37, 42, 43; 4:33, 35; 5:2, 12, 18, 40; 6:2, 6; 8:1, 14; 9:27; 11:1; 14:4; 15:2, 6, 22, 23; 16:4). These references include the whole range of activities assigned to Peter, including the monitoring and validation of the expanding mission (for example, Acts 8:14; 11:22). Thus Luke follows through on the human link he has established between the Gospel and Acts; the twelve who walked with Jesus, witnessed his resurrection, and imbibed his Spirit are the ones who establish the universal mission of the church.

Paul shares the spotlight with Peter as witness to the risen Christ. As a second-generation "apostle" (cf. Acts 14:14) he is not a member of the Twelve, yet he commands the second half of the book because of his unique role among the Gentiles. Paul, too, experiences the whole spectrum of apostolic tasks and sufferings and eventually fulfills the universal promise of the mission by bringing it from Jerusalem to Rome, "the end of the earth." In the successive ministries of Peter and Paul, the evangelist is able to sketch the entire development of the community's mission.

In addition to these dominant personalities, Luke includes the whole cast of other witnesses who continue the mission of the risen Christ. The early chapters refer to John, and to Philip and Stephen, neither of whom are apostles but whose work pushes back the frontiers of the mission (cf. Acts 6:8; 8:5). Associated with

Paul is Barnabas (Acts 13:2), and with less prominence Silas (15:22), Judas (15:22), John Mark (12:25), Priscilla and Aquila (18:2). These "minor" characters, including women and men, demonstrate that the ministry of witness is not confined to the apostles. Luke had expanded the entourage of Jesus to include "outcast" disciples such as tax collectors and women. So, too, in Acts those poised to receive the power of the Spirit are not only the Twelve but the whole company of Jesus, including "the women and Mary, the mother of Jesus" (Acts 1:14-15). In the remainder of the story Luke shows that the witnessing power of the Spirit energizes all sorts of men and women in the community and mobilizes them for the universal mission of salvation.

The account in Acts, then, confirms a simple yet profound fact of early Christian experience: God's work of salvation promised in the Scriptures, proclaimed by Jesus, and effected by the Spirit is ultimately entrusted to very fallible human beings. Their "witness" is the agency of the universal mission.

The final component of Luke's mission theology in Acts is that of the Spirit. As we have already stated in considering this motif in the Gospel, not all of Luke's Spirit theology is directly related to universalism. Yet in Acts the evangelist consistently identifies the Spirit as both the catalyst and the guiding force for the community's expanding mission. Since the Spirit is the fulfillment of the Father's promise and is sent by the risen Christ as the completion of his messianic work (cf. Lk. 24:49; Acts 1:4-5, 8; 2:33), this motif forms the strongest of bonds between Acts and the Gospel, between the history of Jesus and the history of the community. The Spirit, in effect, maintains the presence and directives of the risen Christ in the church.

It remains for us to illustrate this theme in some detail. Two aspects of the Spirit's activity as described in Acts have particular relevance for the question of mission: the impulse to universalism and the power given to embolden the missionary preaching. In the first instance, Luke clearly shows that the Spirit guides the community in its dawning consciousness as it carries the work of salvation from Jerusalem to the "end of the earth." The starting point is, of course, the Pentecost experience (Acts 2:1-4) where the apostles and the community are lavished with the gift of the eschatological Spirit. The universal proportions of this empowerment are indicated by the gift of tongues, which enables the various populations of the diaspora to understand the message in their own language (Acts 2:4-12). Peter's speech explains to the crowds that what they "see and hear" is "the promise of the Holy Spirit" given to the community by the risen Christ (Acts 2:33).

The Spirit's role in widening the horizon of the mission is carried through in the rest of Acts. Philip's encounter with the Ethiopian eunuch is through the agency of the Spirit (Acts 8:29, 39). Peter's acceptance of Cornelius is confirmed when the Spirit is poured out "even" on this Gentile and his family (Acts 10:44-48; 11:12-18). And in his report to the Jerusalem community, Peter explains that it was the Spirit who told him to go to Cornelius, "making no distinctions" (Acts 11:12). The ratification of this decision by the Jerusalem Council is also under the impulse of the Spirit (Acts 15:28; cf. 15:8).

Paul's mission, too, is guided by the Spirit. He and Barnabas are "set apart . . . for the work to which I have called them" (Acts 13:2, 4). The Spirit even guides the geographical direction of Paul's work. He is prevented from going to Asia in order that he might take the momentous step of entering Macedonia (Acts 16:6-10). The fateful decision to go to Jerusalem is also Spirit-inspired (Acts 19:21; 20:22). This journey is charged with symbolism for Luke. By it Paul not only duplicates the fateful journey of his master to imprisonment and ultimately death, but, paradoxically, by means of his chains Paul will bring his mission to Rome and thus fulfill the risen Lord's promise (Acts 19:21; 21:11). The fact that the Spirit continues the work of the risen Jesus in the community is apparent when Luke can, in effect, substitute Spirit language for the direct words of the risen Christ. In the account of Paul's conversion, it is the risen Lord himself who proclaims Paul's universal mission (9:15-16; 22:21; 26:16-18). The Spirit's work in guiding the mission to the Gentiles also affects other less prominent workers, such as Barnabas (Acts 11:24; 13:2-4) and Apollos (Acts 19:6).

Luke also attributes the boldness of the community's witness to the power of the Spirit. Not only does the Spirit break open the horizon of the community's vision but it enables the missionaries to give fearless testimony even under the threat of imprisonment or death, thereby fulfilling the promise of Jesus in the mission discourse of the Gospel (Lk. 12:11-12). Peter confronts the Sanhedrin "filled with the Spirit" (Acts 4:8), the Jerusalem community is enabled to speak the Word of God "boldly" even under threat of persecution (Acts 4:31) and Stephen's prophetic speech is under the impulse of the Spirit (Acts 6:5, 10, 55).

For Luke, then, the same Spirit that animated Jesus in his prophetic mission of salvation has now been given to the community. Not only does this motif ensure continuity between Jesus and the church but it claims that all of that history—of Jesus and of the community who witness in his name—is an act of God.

CONCLUSION

A survey of Luke-Acts demonstrates that the church's universal mission is central to the evangelist's concern. The bringing of the message of salvation from its starting point in Israel to its full flowering among the Gentiles is key to the theology of both the Gospel and Acts. For Luke this work of salvation is the final outcome of Jesus' own ministry as through rejection, death, and resurrection he completes his work by ascending to the Father and sending the Spirit. The Spirit lavished on the community will propel it beyond Jerusalem to the end of the earth. This worldwide mission therefore "fulfills" the Scriptures.

While Luke triumphantly asserts the scope of the community's mission and, to an extent, its great success, he does not lapse into complete idealization. The reluctance of the Jerusalem church to share table fellowship with the uncircumcised, the dawning consciousness of Peter and the Twelve about the acceptance of the Gentiles, the conversion of Saul from persecutor to apostle are all signs that the universal mission of the community was to a degree carried out "against the grain" of its more narrow inclinations. Luke also shows that the community's mission bears a price: the missionaries, especially Peter and Paul, suffer persecution, imprisonment, hardship, and rejection as they carry out their apostolic roles. Both of these darker sides of the church's mission experience—a reluctant universalism and the cost of discipleship—were already demonstrated in the history of Jesus, the figure who remains the dominant paradigm for Luke's idea of the missionary. Jesus, too, had to press his mission to the outcasts against the grain of the established order. And Jesus, too, had suffered rejection and death, as the prophets had before him, in the pursuit of his Spirit-anointed mission.

Thus Luke-Acts provides a theological basis for the community's mission, and wise instruction for those involved in witnessing to it.

NOTES

1. F. Hahn, *Mission in the New Testament* (Naperville: Allenson, 1965), p. 128; cf. also the discussions of F. Danker, *Luke,* Proclamation Commentaries series (Philadelphia: Fortress Press, 1976), pp. 89–90, and R. Karris, "Missionary Communities: A New Paradigm for the Study of Luke-Acts," *Catholic Biblical Quarterly* 41 (1979). 80–97.

2. Cf. C. Talbert, "Shifting Sands. The Recent Study of the Gospel of Luke," *Interpreting the Gospels,* ed. J. L. Mays (Philadelphia: Fortress Press, 1981), pp. 197–213; R. Karris, *What Are They Saying about Luke and Acts?* (New York: Paulist Press, 1979) Despite the focus on Luke in current exegesis, there is considerable debate among scholars over the precise contours of Luke's theology.

3. Cf. E. LaVerdiere and W. Thompson, "New Testament Communities in Transition: A Study of Matthew and Luke," *Theological Studies* 37 (1976): 567–97.

4. Cf. R. Dillon, "Easter Revelation and Mission Program in Luke 24:46–48," *Sin, Salvation, and the Spirit,* ed. D. Durken (Collegeville: Liturgical Press, 1979), pp. 240–70; and his full-length study, *From Eyewitnesses to Ministers of the Word: Tradition and Composition in Luke 24,* Analecta Biblica 82 (Rome: Biblical Institute Press, 1978); J. Dupont, *The Salvation of the Gentiles: Studies in the Acts of the Apostles* (New York: Paulist Press, 1979), pp. 17–19.

5. On this overall motif, cf. D. Tiede, *Prophecy and History in Luke-Acts* (Philadelphia: Fortress Press, 1980); pertinent texts in the Gospel will be discussed below.

6. Cf., e.g., the keynote of the Baptist's mission in Lk. 3:3; for texts referring to Jesus, cf. Lk. 5:32; 7:48, and the constant theme in the sermons of Acts: 2:38; 5:31; 11:17, 18; 17:30–31; 20:21; 26:18, 20. Cf. further, F. Hahn, *Mission in the New Testament,* p. 131.

7. Cf. R. Zehnle, *Peter's Pentecost Discourse,* Society of Biblical Literature Dissertation Series 15 (Nashville: Abingdon, 1971), pp. 61–66.

8. As in one of the first redactional studies of Luke, H. Conzelmann, *The Theology of Saint Luke* (London: Faber and Faber, 1960), pp. 73–94.

9. Cf. S. Brown, *Apostasy and Perseverance in the Theology of Luke,* Analecta Biblica 36 (Rome: Biblical Institute Press, 1969), pp. 53–145; also S. Freyne, *The Twelve Disciples and Apostles* (London: Sheed and Ward, 1968), pp. 207–55.

10. Cf. G. Montague, *The Holy Spirit: Growth of a Biblical Tradition* (New York: Paulist Press, 1976), pp. 253–301. Montague accurately notes: ". . . surely if we had to single out any one evangelist as the 'Theologian of the Holy Spirit,' it would be

Luke. While the word 'spirit' occurs four times in Mark and five times in Matthew, the expression 'Holy Spirit' occurs thirteen times in Luke's gospel and forty-one times in Acts'' (p. 253).

11. The words echo Isa. 40:4 and 52:10 and perhaps other Isaian passages as well; the entire canticle of Simeon draws heavily on Isaiah and the theme of universal salvation: on this, cf. R. Brown, *The Birth of the Messiah* (Garden City, N.Y.: Doubleday, 1977), p. 458.

12. Cf. the thorough discussion of this scene in D. Tiede, *Prophecy and History,* pp. 19-64; and J. Yoder, *The Politics of Jesus* (Grand Rapids, Mich.: Wm. B. Eerdmans, 1972), pp. 34-40.

13. On this theme in Luke, cf. J. Dupont, "Les pauvres et la pauvreté dans les évangiles et les Actes," in *La Pauvreté évangélique,* Lire la Bible 27 (Paris: Éditions du Cerf, 1971), pp. 37-63 (an English translation, but without notes, is found in *Gospel Poverty* [Chicago: Franciscan Herald Press, 1977], pp. 25-52); R. Karris, *What Are They Saying about Luke and Acts?,* pp. 84-104.

14. This point is emphasized in two recent studies of Luke: cf. J. Jervell, *Luke and the People of God* (Minneapolis: Augsburg Publishing Co., 1972), especially pp. 41-74; E. Franklin, *Christ the Lord* (Philadelphia: Westminster Press, 1975), pp. 77-115.

15. Cf. E. LaVerdiere, *Luke,* New Testament Message 5 (Wilmington, Del.: Michael Glazier, 1980), p. 17.

16. Cf. 2 Kings 17:13-18; Jer. 44:4-6; 2 Chron. 36:15-16; Ezra 9:10; Neh. 9:26; on the theme of Jesus as the rejected prophet in Luke, cf. R. Dillon, "Easter Revelation and Mission Program in Luke 24:46-48," pp. 248-51 (he cites extensive literature), and D. Tiede, *Prophecy and History in Luke-Acts.*

17. On this major theme of Luke, cf. R. Martin, "Salvation and Discipleship in Luke's Gospel," *Interpreting the Gospels,* pp. 214-30; P. Achtemeier, "The Lucan Perspective on the Miracles of Jesus: A Preliminary Sketch," *Journal of Biblical Literature* 94 (1975): 547-62.

18. Cf. S. Brown, *Apostasy and Perseverance,* pp. 6-9.

19. Cf. above, pp. 273-74; the pivotal Cornelius story and the Jerusalem Council both have to do with diet and table fellowship.

20. Cf. R. Brown et al., eds., *Mary in the New Testament* (New York: Paulist Press, 1978), pp. 105-77.

21. This is the major thesis of S. Brown, *Apostasy and Perseverance.*

22. "The Christian *martyrium* before an obstinate and vindictive people could thus be shown to be the continuation of a classic trend of salvation-history. Our conclusion is that, for Luke, Easter witness meant the transmission of the risen Lord's 'opening up' of all the Scriptures by a total reenactment of his 'journey' on the part of the witnesses (see Acts 10:39)" (R. Dillon, "Easter Revelation and Mission Program in Luke 24:46-48," p. 255).

23. Cf., e.g., J. Jeremias, *New Testament Theology: The Proclamation of Jesus* (New York: Scribners, 1971), pp. 80-82; E. Franklin, *Christ the Lord,* pp. 132-34.

24. I am indebted especially to F. Hahn, *Mission in the New Testament,* pp. 128-36; cf. also, J. Dupont, *The Salvation of the Gentiles,* who consistently notes the connection between the Gospel and Acts on the question of the universal mission.

25. F. Hahn, *Mission in the New Testament,* pp. 131-34.

26. Ibid. p. 135.

27. Cf. the discussion of these texts in J. Dupont, "Les pauvres et la pauvreté dans les évangiles et les Actes," pp. 41–45.

28. Some commentators even suggest that Peter's sharing of table fellowship with Simon the Tanner (cf. Acts 9:43), a banned occupation and therefore making Simon an outcast, is a subtle indication that the leader of the Twelve is already acting in the spirit of the boundary-breaking Jesus but will now be asked to move even further; but see the comments in E. Haenchen, *The Acts of the Apostles* (Philadelphia: Westminster Press, 1971), p. 340, who is skeptical that Luke intended such a connection.

12

The Johannine Theology of Mission

As the Father has sent me, even so I send you [Jn. 20:21].

The distinctiveness of the Gospel of John in contrast to the Synoptic Gospels is plain for all to see. Its literary style and its portrayal of Jesus and the Christian message make it a singular contribution to the New Testament. The magnetism of the Fourth Gospel has gripped contemplatives and commentators throughout the history of the church and today is no exception. The explosion of studies in Johannine theology in recent years is staggering testimony to this.[1]

The question of mission in John has not played a major role in this flood of recent studies.[2] However, many of the questions that dominate contemporary Johannine research have a direct bearing on the subject. John's theology of mission, like every other aspect of his message, is unique and enticing. To pull together the elements of a Johannine theology of mission we shall turn first to the Gospel itself. Although there has been much speculation about the various stages of the composition and editing of the Gospel, we shall accept the text as it stands, trying to be aware of the variety of influences that may have shaped the final product but considering the final product as the fullest expression of the Johannine community's theology. We shall also take a brief look at the Johannine letters, although only a minimum of mission material is found there. The letters were probably written after the Gospel to "protect" it from what the author of the letters considered unwarranted interpretation.

THE ENVIRONMENT OF THE GOSPEL AND THE MISSION PERSPECTIVE OF THE JOHANNINE CHURCH

One of the most important convictions of recent scholarships is that the Johannine community was in dialogue or contention with a wide spectrum of groups and ideologies in the first century.[3] The Gospel is not only the end product of a succession of encounters with other groups and viewpoints that have influenced John's theology, but the Gospel in its finished form may represent an attempt to communicate with a variety of dialogue partners.

R. Brown, for example, has suggested that the Johannine community went through a series of stages as it developed its own unique Christology and community identity.[4] The community would have originated in Palestine with a group of Jews (including some followers of John the Baptist) who came to accept Jesus as the Davidic Messiah. This rather standard Christology would begin to experience significant evolution with the acceptance of Jewish believers in Jesus who had an "anti-temple" bias, similar to that of the Essenes and other maverick groups in first-century Judaism. This group would also be joined by an influx of Samaritan converts. Together these additions to the community became a catalyst for developing its Christology. Jesus was now interpreted in a Mosaic model, as one who has seen God and revealed him, rather than simply in Davidic messianic categories. This opened the way to John's characteristic preexistence theology: Jesus was the Word, the "Son of Man" who had come to reveal the Father.

These Christological convictions led to a severe rift with Pharisaic Judaism and to tension or even open break with other Jewish-Christian groups who held to a lower Christology. In the post-70 period, as we noted above, the Christians were expelled from the synagogue, a rupture that leaves its scar in chapter 9 of John's Gospel.[5] But the Johannine community is at odds with more than Pharisees. Brown sees evidence of a parting of the ways with Jewish Christians who do not agree with preexistence Christology (as in Jn. 6:60–66) and at least a strong critique of those Jewish Christians who accept the Johannine Jesus but do so only in secret because they fear expulsion from the synagogue (Jn. 9:22). There may also have been tension with the mainline apostolic church, represented by Peter and the apostles. The important position of Peter in the Fourth Gospel and his faithful allegiance to Jesus (cf. 6:68–69; 21:15–19) indicate that John's church was in communion with this apostolic group. But the privileged position of the Beloved Disciple as the source of Johannine tradition and the clear efforts of the evangelist to show the equality and, at times, superiority of the faith and insight of the Beloved Disciple over Peter (cf., for example, Jn. 20:1–10) suggest that some tension existed between these groups. John may have considered the Christology of the apostolic church adequate but not so profound as that of his own community.

The influx of Gentiles added another factor. Texts such as Jn. 7:35; 11:52; and 12:20–22 suggest that at some point in its evolving history the Johannine community experienced a significant shift in membership from a purely Jewish and Palestinian composition to that of a mixed membership, including Hellenistic Jews, Samaritans, and ultimately Gentiles. This, too, will become a factor for a more universalist viewpoint. It should be noted that there is very little evidence in John of the Jewish-Gentile tension found in Matthew or Luke-Acts. The acceptance of the Greeks seems to have been accomplished without trauma, a sign perhaps that the Johannine community had already burned its bridges with Judaism and, equally significant, that its theology was fully universal in scope. As we shall point out, several features of John's theology seem calculated to appeal to the Hellenistic mind.

The identification of the various factions encountered by the Johannine community in the course of its evolution remains speculative. But the evidence does seem to suggest that the church of the Fourth Gospel developed a unique theology and that its unyielding witness to this vision brought it into confrontation not only with Pharisaic Judaism but with Christian groups as well.

The polemical factor in John should not, however, screen out the more positive relationships of the Johannine community to its environment. Even though the Gospel is not content with mere traditional appreciations of Jesus, it does not reject these formulations out of hand but absorbs and transforms them in the service of a higher synthesis.[6] At times the Gospel will seem to place older and newer formulations, even ones that appear contradictory, side by side, with the old being retained in the richer perspective offered by the new.

G. MacRae has pointed to many features of the Gospel where this type of synthesis and reinterpretation have taken place.[7] The very literary form of John's Gospel is one such example. Many scholars believe that John utilized a "Signs Gospel" as a major source.[8] This Signs Gospel would have included a series of miracle stories demonstrating Jesus' messianic power and a passion narrative proclaiming that Jesus' death was in accordance with the Scriptures. John adopted this Gospel form and much of its basic content, but completely reinterpreted it in the light of his own unique Christology. Now the "signs" reveal both Jesus' power to heal and his identity as revealer of God. The passion story not only shows that Jesus' death is in accord with Scripture but becomes a triumphant exaltation of the Son of Man who reveals God's saving love for the world. By accepting the basic form of the Gospel narrative, John accepts the thoroughly messianic character of Jesus' history and its messianic meaning, both key points of traditional Christology. But these elements are fitted into a higher synthesis that sees Jesus as the eternal Word made flesh and the revealer of God's glory.

The same conserving and transforming tendency is detectable in other features of the Gospel. John accepts traditional titles for Jesus (cf. the string of titles in 1:19–51) but gives special importance to the "Son of Man" title, which the evangelist uses to describe Jesus' role as preexistent and heavenly revealer. This title becomes the touchstone for properly understanding the others.[9] Even what might be considered successive editions of the Gospel result in the conservation and adaptation of previous formulations rather than their abandonment. Thus sacramental experience is used to illustrate and concretize the Christological symbols in the bread of life discourse; references to a future eschatology are put alongside those of a realized eschatology; startling claims for the divinity of Jesus are placed alongside straightforward emphases on his subordination to the Father; the love command of chapters 13–15 seems to absorb all other demands of the gospel.[10]

As MacRae suggests, this reinterpretation of traditional categories seems to be directly related to the convictions of the Johannine community about the *universality* of Christ. The Fourth Gospel uses a wealth of symbols that are capable of touching a wide spectrum of religious experience. It uses language calculated to provoke reaction in a number of religious traditions. And, as we have suggested, it pushed traditional Christian categories to their ultimate scope. This tendency to move from the more particular to the more universal was itself a phenomenon detectable in the development of several religious systems as they fell under the influence of Greek culture. But for John's community it is not due simply to the impact of a more cosmopolitan culture. The universalism of the message flowed from the universal significance of Christ himself. Jesus revealed God, and only faith in this Jesus, a faith expressed in love, was adequate. As MacRae concludes:

> . . . the diversity of materials and backgrounds he uses may not only be in the eye of the beholder but in the eye of the Evangelist too. He wishes to imply that as long as one tries to grasp Jesus as a Jew or a Greek as a Gnostic or a traditional Christian would, he both succeeds and fails, for Jesus is the fulfillment of all these expectations, but he is caught up in none of them.[11]

Thus the bold Christology of John's community and its vigorous interaction with other viewpoints brought the Fourth Gospel into creative dialogue with its environment. The Gospel's conviction about the ultimate significance of Jesus as revealer of God led it courageously to reinterpret traditional formulations and to proclaim the gospel in potent, cosmic language and symbols. All of this makes the Fourth Gospel significant for the universal mission of the church.

CHRISTOLOGY AND MISSION

The Christological focus of the Fourth Gospel is the key to understanding its theology of mission, as it is for every other aspect of John's message. As we have already suggested, that Christology is universal, even cosmic in its scope, not only because the evangelist dealt with a cosmopolitan milieu but because of his conviction about Christ's cosmic significance. The core of John's Christology is the affirmation that Jesus Christ is the unique revealer of the living God (1:18). This central conviction is the key to the presentation of Jesus in the Fourth Gospel.[12]

The prologue (Jn. 1:1–18) sets the tone for the rest of the Gospel. As Joseph Cahill has suggested, these opening verses might be more accurately described as the conceptual "center" of the Gospel from which all of its other dimensions radiate.[13] With a poetic genius perhaps unparalleled in New Testament literature, this hymn to the Logos states the origin, purpose, and cosmic proportions of Jesus' mission from the Father. He is the Word with God from the beginning, and so intimately bonded with God and revelatory of him that the Word can be called "God" (1:1–2). This revealing Word begins a progressive penetration of the human sphere. All created reality is made in and through him; all created reality finds "life" and "light" in him (1:3–5). The Word penetrates even into the "world," the arena of human history which itself is made in and through the Word and whose inhabitants, if they accept him, will find their true identity in him (1:10–13). Finally, this Word is so firmly embedded in the human sphere that it becomes "flesh" and lives in the midst of the community (1:14). It is the believing community that is braced to recognize the "glory" of God revealed in the Word made flesh and thus to receive an unparalleled abundance of grace, to know truly the unknowable God (1:16–18).

Some aspects of this hymn are enticingly Hellenistic in tone, such as the pattern of spatial descent and ascent, the use of terms such as "Logos," "world," "flesh." But the momentum of recent Johannine scholarship moves more confidently to Jewish and biblical sources for John's presentation. The Old Testament had a developed notion of the "Word of God" as revealing his creative will and purpose. In prophetic texts such as Isa. 55:10–11 the dynamism of God's Word is spoken of in personified terms. Wisdom motifs are especially crucial for appreciating John's thought.[14] Wisdom as the manifestation of God's presence to the world shapes the pattern of creation (Wis. 9:1–2, 9; Prov. 8:22–31), comes to dwell in the world (Wis. 9:10; 18:14–15; Sir. 24:8–12), meets acceptance or rejection (Sir. 24:19–22; Prov. 8:32–36). John boldly identifies Jesus as the revealing Word of God, as Wisdom incarnate. This Logos preexists with God and then fully embraces a human history, becomes "flesh." In Jesus Christ, the Word-made-flesh, the believer encounters the glory of God and thus achieves the ultimate destiny of God's creation, eternal life.

Thus right from the start the Johannine canvas is cosmic and universal in proportion. Although the focus is specific and historical—the earthly Jesus announced by John the Baptist and the community who believes in Jesus—the issues are all ultimates: the origin and meaning of the creation, the attainment of authentic life, the search for God. These are the elements common to all religious systems. Even though John's Gospel is intensely Christocentric, these broader human and theological questions underlie his Christological language.

The bond between Father and Son and the unique revelatory role of the Son touch almost every facet of John's Christological language. Texts abound that state the intimate relationship between Father and Son. Of particular significance is John's use of the title "Son of Man." In the array of titles given to Jesus in the opening chapter of the Gospel (cf. Jn. 1:19–51) the most significant one is "Son of Man" (1:51) because John uses it to describe the mysterious heavenly origin of Christ in his mission to reveal God. For John the most intense moment of Jesus' mission to reveal God comes at the moment of death.[15] This death is a triumphant return to the Father at the completion of Jesus' mission. Therefore John can use such terms as "to be lifted up" (3:14; 8:28; 12:32, 34), or the "hour" in which the "glory" of God is manifested (12:27–28; 13:1; 17:1, 4–5; etc.). It is also the most vivid moment in that mission because Jesus' death "for his friends" (15:13) reveals God's compassionate love for the world (3:16–17). John is consistent, then, in connecting the Son of Man title, which depicts Jesus' mysterious heavenly origin and his descent to reveal God, with the moment of death (3:14; 8:28). When the Son of Man is lifted up on the cross he completes his mission of revealing God's saving love for the world (8:28).

The "I am" sayings are another intriguing component of John's revelation Christology.[16] Throughout the Gospel the Johannine Jesus uses the name of God revealed to Moses as a self-designation. The "I am" sayings are found either in absolute form or with predicates such as "bread," "life," "resurrection," "light," and so forth. In Jesus one encounters the presence of God, a salvific presence implied in the very name Jesus can dare to accept as his own. By linking the divine name to such predicates as "bread," "truth," "life," or "way," John ingeniously moves his revelation theology to an even more profound level. These predicates are symbols of the human quest for God. The hungers and longings signify the long search for the face of God, a search depicted in Wisdom literature precisely in such terms. Thus John implies by such declarations as "I am the bread of life" (6:35, 51) and "I am the light of the world" (8:12, 9:5) that, in Jesus, God's manifest presence and the groping of humanity for God meet.[17] Jesus' mission is to make God's name known (17:4).

Because John's Christology has this inherently "mission" character, that is, to reveal God to the world, it is not surprising that one of the most important designations of Jesus is the "one sent."[18] "To be sent" in Jewish thought is to be considered the "agent" of the sender.[19] The sender identifies with the one he sends and thereby invests him with authority. The capital text of Jn. 3:17 must be cited again because it so clearly states the goal of Jesus' mission: "For God sent the Son into the world, not to condemn the world, but that the world might be saved through him" (cf. Jn. 6:38–39; 12:49–50). This is Jesus' "work," his "food" (4:34). Since God is the one who "sends" Jesus on this mission of cosmic salvation, those who accept the Son and believe in him come in contact with God. Through the medium of the agent they encounter the sender. "Truly, truly, I say to you, he who hears my word and believes him who sent me, has eternal life" (5:24). Precisely because John puts such cosmic weight upon the mission of the Son, response to the one sent is crucial. Throughout the Gospel, John stresses that belief in the Son is the means for achieving eternal life (cf. 3:15, one of many such texts) and the only access to intimate fellowship with Father and Son (17:20–21).

One final category to be considered in John's Christology is that of "testimony." A. Harvey has suggested that the entire Gospel uses a "trial" format, with Jesus (and the Father, cf. 5:37) offering testimony on his behalf, certifying that his mission is indeed from God (cf. 5:30–47; 8:17–19).[20] Other characters in the Gospel, such as John the Baptist (1:6–8), the Beloved Disciple (19:35), and the community itself, are also called upon to bear witness to Jesus' mission to the world. Bearing witness is also a function of the Paraclete (15:26).

Therefore John portrays the entire history of Jesus as a cosmic mission. The Synoptic tradition utilizes the metaphor of the kingdom, or rule, of God as the keynote of Jesus' mission. But John has pushed aside the historical and nationalistic boundaries that might limit the scope of this Jewish symbol. Now the arena is no longer confined to Israel: the Johannine Jesus begins with God and steps into the whole world, the "cosmos." His mission is not only to fulfill the hope of Israel for God's rule but to reveal the face of the unseen God to all humanity (1:18). Thus he can be rightly acclaimed on this universal level as "savior of the world" (4:42), as "light of the world" (8:12; 9:5) and the lamb who takes away the "sins of the world" (1:29), as "bread for the life of the world" (6:51). We cannot forget that John still embeds this cosmic mission in the historical ministry of Jesus. The evangelist, after all, leaves aside the cosmic poetry of the prologue and adopts the Gospel genre, a narrative of a human life circumscribed by Judea,

Galilee, and the Transjordan (even though this Gospel format is thoroughly reinterpreted in a Johannine fashion). But while retaining this link with the earthly
history of Jesus, John consistently describes the meaning of Jesus' person and
mission on the universal plane. The basic reason for this level of discourse, I
believe, is not to be found merely in the influence of John's environment but in
the underlying goal of the Gospel. While John focuses intently on the figure of
Jesus, it is ultimately the *God* question that haunts the Gospel. The unseen God
who utters the "word" (1:2) is the one sought out by humanity. Because John's
community is convinced that Jesus Christ is the authoritative revealer of God and
the only sure access to him, the Christology and theology of the Gospel become
inseparable (cf. 14:8–11). The scope of this basic question makes John's Gospel
truly universal.

THE PARACLETE AND THE MISSION

John's Gospel gives an important role to the Spirit in the life of the community
and, as was the case with Paul and Luke-Acts, the Spirit is crucial for mission.

In this instance, as in almost every other, John's presentation is unique.[21] The
Fourth Gospel does share some of the conventional Spirit imagery of the synoptic
tradition. Thus at the first encounter between the Baptist and Jesus at the Jordan,
John testifies to the descent of the Spirit on Jesus and his "abiding" with him
(1:33), a scene not unlike Jesus' messianic investiture with the Spirit in the baptismal scenes of the Synoptic Gospels. Likewise Jesus' own messianic mission is
described as baptism in water and the Spirit (in contrast to the water baptism of
John; cf. 1:33; also 3:5, 8). As the awaited Messiah, Jesus' ministry inaugurates
the age of the Spirit. In the discourse with Nicodemus, however, the evangelist
will move beyond the traditional conception. There, "to be born from above" or
"to be born of water and Spirit" (3:5) is linked to Jesus' mission as Son of Man
who is sent into the world to save it (cf. 3:18ff.) By implication, belief in Jesus as
revealer of God's love is the authentic access to the life of the Spirit.

Another "conventional" element of New Testament pneumatology in John is
the insistence on the risen Christ as the giver of the Spirit. In the resurrection
appearance to the disciples in Jn. 20:22, the risen Christ "breathed" on the disciples and gave them the gift of the Spirit. Other texts of the Gospel make this link
between the death and resurrection of Jesus and the community's reception of the
Spirit, as in 3:34–35 and in the water symbolism of 7:38–39 (cf. also 4:10; 19:37).
This is similar to Luke's conception in the concluding chapter of his Gospel and
the opening chapters of Acts.

But typically John is not content with these traditional categories. A more
specific Johannine theology of the Spirit is found in the last discourse of chapters
14–16 where the term "Paraclete" is used and where the evangelist focuses on the
function of the Spirit in the community. The entire last discourse is critically
important for the theology of John. Here the themes of Jesus' unique relationship to the Father, his role as revealer, the necessity of faith in him, and vital
instructions to the believing community on love and service are presented in vivid
Johannine terms.

By its very nature the discourse focuses on the life of the community in the postresurrection period. It is a "farewell discourse," speaking of Jesus' impending departure and its consequences for the community's life in the world. It is not surprising then, that, the motif of "Spirit" and the community's mission should have a place here.

The term John uses for the Spirit in chapters 14–16 is "Paraclete." This is a Greek term with no exact Hebrew equivalent and can have legal connotations such as "advocate" and "mediator" or such meanings as "comforter" and "encourager."[22] The term's range of meanings may be the precise reason the evangelist uses it to name the community's experience of Spirit. From its use in chapters 14–16 we find that in Jesus' absence the Paraclete sustains the same life-giving relationship that the disciples had enjoyed with their Lord during his earthly ministry. This is the crucial function that enables the Johannine Jesus to speak of the Father's sending "another Paraclete" to be with the community (14:16). The Spirit sent by the Father does for the post-Easter community what Jesus did for his disciples. Thus the Paraclete is "with" the disciples (14:16), "teaches" and "guides" them (14:26; 16:13), reveals the Father's message to them (16:13), and enters into a prophetic confrontation with the nonbelieving world (16:8–11).

But in John's vision, the Paraclete performs more than a mere holding action in Jesus' absence. The presence of the Spirit so enriches the post-Easter community that its state is better than that of Jesus' own disciples; those "who do not see yet believe" are indeed blessed (Jn. 20:29). During Jesus' lifetime the disciples were not able to grasp fully the meaning of his message (cf. 2:22). But the Paraclete would teach them all things and help them "remember" everything Jesus said (14:26). Jesus' great works, his "signs," filled the Gospel, but through the power of the Spirit the community would be able to do "greater works than these" (14:12). The Paraclete, therefore, does not simply replace the presence of the risen Christ in the community but *intensifies* it.[23]

There is little doubt that this intensification of the power and presence of the risen Christ in the community through the presence of the Spirit-Paraclete is linked to the church's missionary experience. In the climatic resurrection appearance in John, chapter 20, the action of missioning the disciples ("As the Father has sent me, even so I send you," 20:21) is immediately ratified by the infusion of the Spirit (20:22). This same mission context is a backdrop to the sending of the Paraclete in the last discourse. The Paraclete sent from the Father by Jesus will "bear witness" to Jesus just as the disciples, too, will "bear witness" (15:26–27). The Paraclete confronts the power of evil in the world, just as Jesus had done and just as the community must do (16:8–11; 17:14–18).

Although the evangelist does not explicitly say so, it may be that the "greater works" (14:12) done by the community and its more penetrating understanding of Jesus' teaching (14:26)—both results of the presence of the Paraclete—are also tied to the community's mission experience. Taking the Gospel from Palestine to the "end of the earth" and reinterpreting the teaching of Jesus for the Hellenistic world were bold steps of the post-Easter missionary church. Luke sees this creative development—a development far beyond the horizons of Jesus' own ministry—as guided throughout by the power of the Holy Spirit. All three Synoptics and Paul attribute the power of missionary preaching and testimony before hostile powers to the Spirit's presence in the community. Could it not be that John works out of a similar conviction? The Christian generations after that of the apostolic eyewitnesses are more blessed precisely because they enjoy the full benefits of Jesus' redemptive work, the lavishing of the power of the Spirit of God on those who believe. The Spirit-Paraclete makes Christ more present, more comprehensible, more transforming. In its Spirit-prompted mission to the world, the church discovers the true meaning of the Word made flesh.

THE COMMUNITY AND ITS MISSION

Some recent interpreters of John speculate that the church of the Fourth Gospel was "sectarian" in nature.[24] In this view the Gospel comes from a closed and embattled community, entrenched in its own beliefs, pitted against a number of hostile groups and ideologies. There are aspects of the Gospel that seem to verify this interpretation. The Gospel of John, after all, is shot through with dualistic language emphasizing the chasm between light and darkness, truth and falsehood, believers and nonbelievers (the latter often designated as the "Jews"). The "world has hated" Jesus and will certainly "hate" the church (17:14). The community is "in the world" and "not of the world" (17:15-16). As we have already discussed, the Johannine church was engaged in conflict with both Jewish and Christian groups on several fronts, pivoting on its strict norm for properly understanding the person of Jesus. The stress on "loving one another" seems to add further evidence of a siege mentality, a tightly knit sect that seeks its own survival and shrugs off the rest of humanity as being lost in darkness. In such a picture, "mission" can have, at best, only a limited meaning. There is no positive thrust toward the world, no responsibility to go out to the world to communicate with it in word and action. The burden is on the world; it must leave the darkness and join the narrow circle of light on Johannine terms.

But this sectarian interpretation of John does not hold up. It can be maintained only if one overlooks substantial positive estimations of the "world" in the Gospel and only if one ignores the crucial place of mission in the evangelist's message. By reviewing the charges given to the disciples in the Gospel these essential positive aspects become clear.

John's portrayal of the disciples roughly coincides with that found in the Synoptic Gospels, although here too the creative distinctiveness of the Fourth Gospel is at work. Rather than being "called," as in the Synoptics, the disciples are drawn by the magnetism of Jesus and gradually deepen in their knowledge of him (cf., for example, 1:15-19). The same fundamental criterion holds for the disciples as it does for all invited by the Gospel message: to believe in Jesus as the unique revealer of the Father. A brand of faith less intense and penetrating than this is considered inadequate. Thus some disciples fall away because Jesus declares himself to be the "bread from heaven" (6:60-66), while Peter and the

Twelve manifest authentic faith (and therefore authentic discipleship) in declaring Jesus as the "Holy One of God" (6:69). Nicodemus offers another example of inadequate discipleship. He comes in darkness, recognising Jesus as a "teacher from God" (3:2), but fails to grasp the spiritual message about being born "from above" and about the Son of Man (3:4–15). As the Gospel progresses, however, Nicodemus' faith seems to mature as he defends Jesus before the chief priests and Pharisees (7:50–52) and provides for the burial anointing of Jesus' body (19:39). Other characters in the Gospel, such as the Samaritan woman of chapter 4 and the blind man of chapter 9, illustrate a similar progressive coming to faith, recognizing Jesus at a level far deeper than the traditional titles of prophet or messiah, as ultimately the light of the world and true giver of life-giving water. The Beloved Disciple clearly stands in the Gospel as one who is in close union with Jesus (13:23; 21:20–23), becomes a member of Jesus' family (cf. 19:26–27), and gives the testimony that serves as the basis of the Gospel itself (19:35; 21:24).

But "believing in Jesus" as revealer of God, crucial as this is, is not the only dimension of Christian existence foreseen by the Fourth Gospel. In resonance with the entire New Testament, John sees love and service as the necessary symptoms of authentic belief (cf. 13:15). The disciple who truly believes in Jesus, who is a "friend" of Jesus (15:14–15) and "abides in him" (15:1–11), shares in the very quality of life that unites Father and Son (15:10, 17:21, 23, 26). Therefore the disciples, too, must manifest caring love among themselves (13:12–16, 34–35; 15:12–17). Faith and love are the foundations of Christian existence that identifies the disciples as followers of Jesus.

An equally important mark of identification is that the disciples take on the mission of Jesus in the world. It is here, ultimately, that Christology and mission meet. The Fourth Gospel squarely bases the mission of the community on the mission of Jesus. The mission text of Jn. 20:21 states this in a concise formula: "As the Father has sent me, even so I send you." The formula also appears in the climactic prayer of chapter 17: "As thou didst send me into the world, so I have sent them into the world" (17:18). In fact, the whole atmosphere of this prayer is charged with awareness of the impending mission of the disciples.[25] An assumption of "being sent" also appears in Jn. 13:16, 20, which emphasizes the correspondence between the mission of Jesus ("the one who sends") and that of the disciple ("the one sent").

At the conclusion of the Samaritan woman's story, another strong mission text appears and again the correspondence between the mission of Jesus and the mission of the disciples is clear. In Jn. 4:34 Jesus declares that his "food is to do the will of him who sent me, and to accomplish his work." The attention shifts immediately to the disciples' mission: "I sent you to reap that for which you did not labor . . ." (4:38; cf. 4:35–38). As we have already noted, the triggering of this mission awaits the coming of the Spirit (20:21–22; 15:26–27).

If this mission of the community is modeled on that of Jesus, then it is crucial to review exactly how the mission of Jesus is portrayed in the Gospel. At this point John's entire Christology can come back into play, but we can limit ourselves to explicit "sending" passages. The prologue previews what other texts in the Gospel will enunciate: the Word breaks into creation, into the "world," to be "life" (1:4) and "light" (1:4–5) to humanity, to give the power of becoming "children of God" (1:12), to make the unseen God known (1:18). Some crucial "sending" passages ratify this awesome salvific thrust of Jesus' God-given mission. The keynote text of Jn. 3:16–17 must take its place here: "For God so loved the world that he gave his only Son, that whoever believes in him should not perish but have eternal life. For God sent the Son into the world, not to condemn the world, but that the world might be saved through him." This text stands out in the Gospel because of its bold and positive statement of Jesus' mission. But it is not an isolated text in the Gospel, nor is it incompatible with the overall vision of John. A similar view of the Son's mission is found in 6:38–40: "For I have come down from heaven, not to do my own will, but the will of him who sent me; and this is the will of him who sent me, that I should lose nothing of all that he has given me, but raise him up at the last day." The account of Jesus' ministry, the so-called Book of Signs, concludes on a similar note: "He who believes in me, believes not in me but in him who sent me. And he who sees me sees him who sent me. I have come as light into the world, that whoever believes in me may not remain in darkness. If anyone hears my sayings and does not keep them, I do not judge him; for I did not come to judge the world but to save the world" (12:44–47).

These texts (and other aspects of the Gospel that emphasize the salvific intent of Jesus' mission) are decisive for understanding how Jesus "is sent," or in other words, for determining *the* mission on which the community's mission is grounded and modeled. The Gospel's fundamental stance toward the "world," then, is emphatically positive. This positive bearing must be related to the other admittedly negative uses of the term "world" in John. Such negative estimations abound in John. The world "hates" Jesus, and "hates" the disciples (14:18–19). The world rejoices while the community sorrows (16:20). The community is in the world but must not belong to it, just as Jesus was not "of the world" (17:14–16). Behind the evil of the world lurks Satan himself, who is the "Prince of this world" (14:30).

These and other negative statements about the world do not directly contradict or neutralize the positive mission thrust we have detected in John. In fact, these negative statements are a consequence of the mission context of the Fourth Gospel. The prologue once again serves as a poetic vision of what the Gospel drama unfolds. Despite the fact that the world is created by and through the Logos, it is capable of not receiving that Word (1:10–11). This is because "world" in John is a metaphor for humanity itself; it is the arena where human life and interaction occur. Human beings remain free to accept the Word or reject it; they can be open to the light or prefer the cover of darkness (cf. 3:19–20). John's language about the world flows from this core meaning. Neither positive nor negative statements about the world are to be taken in a metaphysical sense: the evangelist is not reflecting on the inherent goodness or fallibility of the created order. Rather, he speaks *existentially*. From God's point of view the world is an object of love: the Son is sent not to condemn humanity but to save it. But from the human standpoint, this vital initiative of God can be either accepted or rejected. It is the act of acceptance or rejection, belief or nonbelief that determines the positive and negative characterizations of "world" in John.

That is why we can say that the negative statements about the world are a consequence of the community's mission experience. The Johannine community knew that Jesus' own mission had mixed results; some people found life in him, others rejected him and even destroyed him. The early church's mission to Israel followed a similar pattern: some acceptance, but also the bitter experience of rejection and alienation. By the time the Gospel was finally formulated, it is likely that similar patterns were occurring in the church's mission to the Gentile world. R. Brown's comments succinctly capture this connection between world and mission in John:

> On the one hand, texts reflecting alienation from a hostile world have comforted inward-looking Christians, inclined to leave outsiders to their own devices if they are not attracted by God toward Christian truth. This has often produced a fortress mentality. On the other hand, these texts have annoyed Christians very conscious of a mission to the world, whether that mission be to infiltrate and change it, or to enable it to develop its own spiritual potentialities, or to win it for Christ. Certainly it is some facet of the latter mood that dominates in Christianity today, and especially in my own Roman Catholic community after Vatican II. Nevertheless, the Fourth Gospel remains a warning against naïveté. The world is not simply unplowed ground waiting to be sown with the Gospel; it is not simply neutral terrain. There is a Prince of this world that is actively hostile to Jesus, so that the maxim *Christus contra mundum* ("Christ against the world") is not without truth. Presumably it was with an initial conviction of God's love for the world that the Johannine community had turned to Gentiles from "the Jews," and the feeling that men of all sorts preferred darkness to light must have come after bitter experience. By all means Christians must keep trying in various ways to bear a testimony about Christ to the world, but they should not be astounded if they relive in part the Johannine experience.[26]

From this sadder but wiser experience of "world" in the history of Jesus and of the community's mission came the insistence in John's Gospel on a prophetic cast to the community's mission. Jesus himself boldly confronted his opponents, challenging their unbelief, their closed-heartedness, their false priorities (cf. the Sabbath controversy in chaps. 5 and 9). In spite of the world's hostility, he overcame the world (16:33). The Paraclete, too, stands up to the world, indicting its errors and giving testimony to the truth (14:17; 15:26; 16:8-11, 12-15). And therefore the disciples' mission, modeled on that of Jesus and energized by the Paraclete, must not be seduced by the world. This is what explains the tone of Jesus' prayer in chapter 17. The world and the "evil one" hate them (17:14-15) because the disciples do not belong to the world that is hostile to the Word. Yet even in this alienated world the disciples must remain (17:14) because they share Jesus' mission to save it (17:18–21).

For John, then, the mission of Jesus, the mission of the Paraclete, and the mission of the community are tightly stitched together. In fact, they are one. James McPolin has provided a helpful schematization of four types of "sending" that occur in the Fourth Gospel.[27] John the Baptist is "sent" by God to testify about Jesus (1:6–8; 3:28). Jesus himself is sent by the Father to testify about the father and to do his work. The Paraclete is sent by both Father and Son to give testimony about Jesus. And, finally, the disicples are sent by Jesus to do as he did.

These missions are interrelated. All four are accomplished in the arena of the "world" and, ultimately, have the salvation of the world as their goal. All involve a personal relationship between the sender and the sent, between the agent and the one who invests the agent with authority. This is true in all cases, even for the Son (8:28–29) and the Paraclete (16:13). They do not speak on their own behalf but on behalf of the one who sends them. All of these missions revolve around Jesus: John announces his coming, the Paraclete reinforces his presence, the disciples declare his Word to the world. But this constellation of mission around Jesus does not end here. Just as John's Christology is not the final word of the Gospel but is ultimately related to the deeper quest for the face of God, so too, the endpoint of this Gospel's missiology is not Jesus but the Father. The Father, alone, is *not* sent. He is the origin and the goal of all the testimony of the Gospel. The final paragraph of Jesus' prayer raises the community's mission to this zenith:

> I do not pray for these only, but also for those who believe in me through their word, that they may all be one; even as thou, Father, art in me, and I in thee, that they also may be in us, so that the world may believe that thou hast sent me. The glory which thou hast given me I have given to them, that they may be one even as we are one, I in them and thou in me, that they may become perfectly one, so that the world may know that thou hast sent me and hast loved them even as thou hast loved me [Jn. 17:20–23].

CONCLUSION

Our study of John suggests that this Gospel, distinctive as it is, shares with the rest of the Gospels a universal outlook and a missionary orientation.

The Fourth Gospel is "universal" in character because it stands shoulder to shoulder with humanity's perennial and pervasive quest for God. The longing for truth, for life, for the way, for light are among many symbols of the Gospel that are truly expressive of the universal human search for the transcendent. As we have seen, the evangelist's Christology moves on this same universal plane: the mission of Jesus is to reveal God's saving love for all the world and to give it eternal life. From start to finish the Johannine Jesus remains in the high frequency of ultimates. The Gospel is "mission" in orientation because its final word to the community is that authentic disciples of Jesus are "sent," as he was sent, to the whole world, to bring it life. Despite John's dualistic language, which speaks of the sharp cleavage between belief and nonbelief, between the world that is open to the light or is disposed to darkness, and despite his warnings to the community to remain prophetically vigilant before the false values of the "world," the Gospel does not urge retreat from the world but commitment to it.

These dynamic casts to John's Gospel are not neutralized by its unabashedly confessional character. No writing in the New Testament is "universal" to the extent that absolute claims for Christ drop out of the picture. There is no version of Christian proclamation in John or anywhere else in the New Testament that would offer "a religious system of thought and practice which every person of every age can embrace in detail,"[28] if the price of such "universalism" means draining from the Gospel its convictions about the unique identity and mission of Jesus.

In a similar vein, John's community should not be branded as purely "sectarian" and questionably missionary simply because the Gospel is an "internal" document written for believers rather than for outsiders. No New Testament document is "missionary" in that sense; we have no New Testament texts written to persuade the nonbeliever. Rather, the Gospel is designed as a manifesto or statement of faith for a believing community. John writes to freshen his own Christians' faith in Jesus (cf. 20:30–31) and to give them perspective on the cosmic tasks they must accomplish in Jesus' name. Given this orientation, it is not surprising that John can emphasize the absolute necessity of faith for salvation and delineate the distinctiveness of the believer over against the nonbelieving world. Despite these domestic concerns, however, John couches his exhortations in categories and language that have the potential for bridging the gap between his community and the Hellenistic world. We can only speculate what John's Gospel might have looked like if, indeed, it had been written as an apologetic to nonbelievers.

The Fourth Gospel, then, keeps alive the powerful missionary impulse found in Mark, Matthew, and Luke-Acts. Whether the Johannine *letters* maintain this sense of mission is disputed. As we suggested above, these brief letters most probably come from a later stage of the Johannine community and have as their purpose the defense of a proper interpretation of the Gospel's message.[29] F. Hahn sees the epistle as a prime example of how later New Testament tradition moved away from outward-directed missionary interest toward more narrow and internal church interest.[30] He notes that some allusions to a universal outlook are still present, as in 1 Jn. 2:2: "and he is the expiation for our sins, and not for ours only but also for the sins of the whole world," or the reference to Jesus as "Savior of the world" in 1 Jn. 4:14 and the world-redeeming mission from the Father in 1 Jn. 4:9. But these appear in "standard christological turns of speech" and, in Hahn's view, do not represent the major concern of the letter. Hahn also interprets the mention of hospitality to the "brethren" in the third letter as referring to missionaries (cf. 3 Jn. vv. 3–8, 10). Here, too, the mission task has taken on the role of combating heresy within the church in addition to the traditional call to proclaim the Gospel to outsiders. The focus in these letters is maintenance of the tradition and the stifling of erroneous doctrine in the churches. Language such as "light and darkness," "world," and so forth are no longer used to describe the differences between the church and the nonbelievers but to categorize opposing factions *within* the church.

Hahn is surely right in noting the domestic concerns of the Johannine letters in contrast to the Gospel. As Raymond Brown states: "The Gospel reflects the Johannine community's dealings with outsiders, the epistles are concerned with insiders."[31] But it is less clear how the epistles support Hahn's thesis that the later New Testament writings gave up the missionary task in favor of narrow church concerns. The Johannine epistles are so limited in scope and purpose in comparison to the Gospel that it seems risky to deduce from these brief letters what exactly the state of its mission enterprise was. Even to take the concern for hospitality in 3 John, which Hahn and others see as referring to "missionaries," as indicative of a changing role for the community's emissaries seems tenuous. These texts might refer to the communication among the Johannine churches rather than to missionaries as such, and thus give us no information at all on whether "missionaries" were now employed in combating heresy.[32] It seems more prudent simply to say that the Johannine letters, like some other New Testament writings, yield very little concerning the mission question. The letters' Christology still has universal dimensions, but the problems that evoked the letters were internal ones. To have responded to these does not necessarily mean that the Johannine churches had lost their missionary perspective. The writings of Paul surely tell us that even churches with a decisive missionary character could be racked with internal disputes.

For the Johannine theology of mission, then, we must depend on the Gospel, where the literary genre enabled the evangelist to give us a full vision of the Christian message and the community's call to proclaim it to the world.

NOTES

1. Cf. the state of the question in R. Kysar, *The Fourth Evangelist and His Gospel: An Examination of Contemporary Scholarship* (Minneapolis: Augsburg Publishing Co., 1975).

2. Few monographs have been devoted to this question in John: cf. J. Kuhl, *Die Sundung Jesu und der Kirche nach dem Johannes-Evangelium* (St. Augustin: Steyler, 1967) and the popular work of J. Comblin, *Sent from the Father* (Maryknoll, N.Y.: Orbis Books, 1979). A few articles have been devoted exclusively to the topic: cf. the pertinent chapter in F. Hahn, *Mission in the New Testament* (Naperville: Allenson, 1965), pp. 152–63; J. McPolin, "Mission in the Fourth Gospel," *Irish Theological Quarterly* 36 (1969):113–22; J. Radermakers, "Mission et apostolat dans l' Evangile johannique," *Studia Evangelica,* Texte und Untersuchungen zur Geschichte der altchristlichen Literatur 87, 2 volumes (Berlin: Akademie-Verlag, 1964), 2:100–21.

3. R. Brown provides a convenient review of recent studies in this line in his own analysis of the ethos of the Johannine community: cf. *The Community of the Beloved Disciple* (New York: Paulist Press, 1979), appendix I.

4. Cf. R. Brown, *Community of the Beloved Disciple.*

5. On this, cf. especially J. Martyn, *History and Theology in the Fourth Gospel*, rev. ed. (Nashville: Abingdon, 1979), pp. 24–62.

6. Cf. R. Brown, *Community of the Beloved Disciple*, pp. 28–30, 51–54.

7. Cf. G. MacRae, "The Fourth Gospel and *Religionsgeschichte*," *Catholic Biblical Quarterly* 32 (1970): 13–24.

8. Cf. especially R. Fortna, *The Gospel of Signs*, Society for New Testament Study Monograph Series 11 (Cambridge, England: University Press, 1970), and his later article, "Christology in the Fourth Gospel: Redaction-Critical Perspectives," *New Testament Studies* 21 (1974–75):489–504. Source analysis of John's Gospel remains highly speculative, however.

9. On this title in John, cf. F. Moloney, *The Johannine Son of Man*, 2nd ed., Biblioteca di Scienze Religiose 14 (Rome: Las, 1978).

10. Cf. a fuller discussion of these examples in G. MacRae, "The Fourth Gospel," pp. 17–20.

11. Ibid., p. 12.

12. Cf. the study of J. Forestell, *The Word of the Cross*, Analecta Biblica 57 (Rome: Biblical Institute Press, 1974), especially pp. 17–57, and H. Schneider, " 'The Word Was Made Flesh': An Analysis of the Theology of Revelation in the Fourth Gospel," *Catholic Biblical Quarterly* 31 (1969): 344–56.

13. P. Cahill, "The Johannine *Logos* as Center," *Catholic Biblical Quarterly* 38 (1976): 54–72, and D. Senior, "God's Creative Word at Work in Our Midst," *The Sacraments: God's Love and Mercy Actualized*, ed. F. Eigo (Villanova, Pa.: University Press, 1979), pp. 1–28. It would be beyond the purpose of our study to discuss the structure and origin of the prologue itself; on this point, cf. R. Brown, *The Gospel according to John I–XII*, Anchor Bible 29 (Garden City, N.Y.: Doubleday, 1966), pp. 3–37.

14. Cf. the discussion in R. Brown, *The Gospel According to John I–XII*, pp. lix–lxiv.

15. C. A. Lacomara, "The Death of Jesus as Revelation in John's Gospel," in *The Language of the Cross*, ed. A. Lacomara (Chicago: Franciscan Herald Press, 1977), pp. 105–25, and J. Forestell, *The Word of the Cross*, p. 19.

16. On the background and use of the "I am" sayings in John, cf. the discussion in R. Brown, *The Gospel according to John I–XII*, pp. 533–38.

17. "All these figures of speech—that of bread and the light, the door and the way, the shepherd and the vine—mean what John, without using a figure, calls life and truth. That is, they all mean that which man must have and longs to have in order to be able truly to exist. With his 'It is I' Jesus therefore presents himself as the one for whom the world is waiting, the one who satisfies all longing" (R. Bultmann, *Theology of the New Testament*, 2 vols. [London: SCM Press, 1955], 2:65).

18. Cf., e.g., 3:17; 7:28; 20:21; 4:34; 5:23–24,30,36,37,38; 6:29,38–39,44,57; 7:16,19,28–29,33; 8:16,18,26,29,42; 9:4; 10:36; 11:42; 12:44–45,49; 13:20; 14:24; 15:21; 16:5; 17:3,8,18,21,23,25; 20:21. For further reflection on this theme in John, cf. J. Comblin, *Sent from the Father*, pp. 1–19.

19. On the Jewish notion of "agency," cf. P. Borgen, "God's Agent in the Fourth Gospel," in *Religions in Antiquity*, ed. J. Neusner (Leiden: E. J. Brill, 1968), pp. 137–48, and J. Miranda, *Die Sendung Jesu im Vierten Evangelium*, Stuttgarten Bibel Studien 87 (Stuttgart: Katholisches Bibelwerk, 1977).

20. A. Harvey, *Jesus on Trial: A Study in the Fourth Gospel* (Atlanta: John Knox Press, 1976).

21. On the Paraclete in John, cf. R. Brown, "The Paraclete in the Fourth Gospel," *New Testament Studies* 13 (1966-67): 113-32, and a similar treatment in *The Gospel According to John XIII-XXI*, Anchor Bible 29A (Garden City, N.Y.: Doubleday, 1970), pp. 1135-44.

22. Cf. R. Brown, *The Gospel According to John XIII-XXI*, pp. 1135-37.

23. Cf. J. Miranda, *Being and the Messiah: The Message of St. John* (Maryknoll, N.Y.: Orbis Books, 1977), p. 204.

24. Cf., e.g., W. Meeks, "The Man from Heaven in Johannine Sectarianism," *Journal of Biblical Literature* 91 (1972):44-72. Meeks considers John's use of the Son of Man title from a sociological perspective and judges that the community's access to privileged knowledge of the Son of Man was a device by which it distinguished itself from its surrounding environment.

25. Cf. P. Perkins, "The Missionary Character of Church in the New Testament," in *Evangelization in the World Today*, ed. N. Greinacher and A. Muller (New York: Seabury Press, 1979), pp. 1-7.

26. R. Brown, *Community of the Beloved Disciple*, pp. 65-66.

27. Cf., J. McPolin, "Mission in the Fourth Gospel."

28. Cf. R. Kysar, *John, the Maverick Gospel* (Atlanta: John Knox Press, 1976), p. 117. Such a definition of "universalism" is too vague and implies too much homogeneity to be practical.

29. On this, cf. R. Brown, *Community of the Beloved Disciple*, pp. 93-144.

30. This is a major thesis of Hahn's entire analysis of mission in the New Testament. As we discussed in the chapter on Colossians and Ephesians, and will state in the subsequent chapter on the remaining New Testament books, we take exception to this viewpoint. For Hahn's remarks on the Johannine epistles, cf. *Mission in the New Testament*, pp. 160-63.

31. R. Brown, *Community of the Beloved Disciple*, p. 97.

32. Brown labels those sent between churches "emissaries" sometimes, and in other places "missionaries," but the two roles would seem to be quite different; cf. *Community of the Beloved Disciple*, pp. 93, 98.

13

Witness and Mission: The Remaining Books of the New Testament

Maintain good conduct among the Gentiles, so that . . . they may see your good deeds and glorify God in the day of visitation [1 Pet. 2:12].

This final chapter of Part II collects several New Testament books whose contribution to the question of mission is less intense yet still significant. Some of the remaining books have almost no reference to the issue of the church's universal mission. This is the case with James, Jude, 2 Peter, and the letter to the Hebrews. Others, however, do add important dimensions to our understanding of how the early church envisioned its responsibility to the world: 1 Peter, Revelation, the Pastorals. Our attention will concentrate on this latter group.

1 PETER: THE WITNESS OF HOPE

The first letter of Peter is one of the New Testament's richest books.[1] Its radiant theology of baptism and its call for hope-filled Christian witness make a notable contribution to the question of mission.

Certainty about the precise circumstances that produced the letter is impossible, but some educated guesses can be made. It apparently originated from Rome; the author sends greetings from the church "at Babylon" (1 Pet. 5:13), a wry designation for the capital city found in Jewish literature and in Revelation (Rev. 14:8; 17:5, 18; 18:2). The addressees are a cluster of churches in northern Asia Minor (cf. 1 Pet. 1:1), indicating that the letter was meant to be circulated among these Christian groups. A tantalizing hint of the situation of these churches is given when the author addresses them as "sojourners" or "exiles" (1 Pet. 1:1; 1:11; 2:11) and members of the "diaspora" (1:1). The fact that he calls his own city of Rome "Babylon" (1 Pet. 5:13) suggests that the author, too, lives in a church of "exile."

This alien status apparently was social as well as spiritual.[2] Because of their

297

values and lifestyle the Christians were out of step with the dominant society around them (1 Pet. 4:3). This fact, rather than any systematic persecution, was the root cause of the suffering the Christians had to bear as the cost of being faithful to the gospel. The Christians were being ridiculed for the change in lifestyle that had accompanied their conversion (1 Pet. 4:4). Some Christians who lived in much more vulnerable situations, such as slaves and wives of non-Christians, were faced with more dire kinds of suffering as they walked the tightrope between societal duties and fidelity to the gospel. The Christians, then, were small groups scattered across a massive and sometimes hostile environment. Because of their minority status and their different world-view, they were "strangers" and a dispersed people in their own land.

The date and authorship of this letter are hard to pinpoint. The letter is attributed to Peter, "an apostle of Jesus Christ" (1 Pet. 1:1; cf. 5:1), but its polished Greek style and its contents (for example, familiarity with Pauline tradition and evidence of developed church structure) suggest that it dates from sometime after the death of the apostle. The fact that the letter comes from Rome and is attributed to Peter cannot be brushed aside, however. Some recent scholarship has suggested that a "Petrine group" may have been formed at Rome in the 60s.[3] It is very probable that Peter came to Rome near the end of his life, and suffered martyrdom there, thus connecting the name of the apostle with this church. References in the letter to Silvanus (1 Pet. 5:12) and Mark (1 Pet. 5:13) may provide clues to other influences on the letter. Both Mark and Silvanus (or "Silas") are identified by Luke as members of the Jerusalem church and as early associates in Paul's Gentile mission (Acts 12:25; 15:22). Paul himself refers to his missionary work with Silvanus (cf. 2 Cor. 1:19; 1 Thess. 1:1; 2 Thess. 1:1).

These associations might explain the make-up and concerns of the "Petrine group" behind the origin of this letter. Silvanus, and to a lesser extent John Mark, were acquainted with Paul's preaching. And, of course, the Roman church had the heritage of Paul's instruction through his letter to them and his visit and martyrdom there. This would explain the presence of important Pauline influences on 1 Peter. At the same time, Silvanus and John Mark, like Peter, had roots in the Jewish-Christian community of Jerusalem. And all the principals— the apostles Peter and Paul, and the missionaries Mark and Silvanus—were vitally involved in the development of the church's universal mission.

Influences such as these may have determined the theology of 1 Peter. It is unlikely that the letter was written during the lifetime of Peter, but he and his fellow missionary leaders had set the tone for the next generation. A leader of this succeeding generation would have written the letter from the capital city of Rome to outpost communities in Asia Minor, drawing on the authoritative tradition of the founding apostles and reflecting their concern for the wider community of the church. The Christians addressed seem to be newly baptized (cf. references to their recent conversion, 1 Pet. 3:21; 4:4), so the author traces an expansive vision of what baptism means for Christian life in the world. In doing this he develops some rich ideas on suffering, resurrection, and hope, ideas akin to those of Paul.

This hypothetical origin of 1 Peter might also explain the value of this letter for a theology of mission. Even though its readers confronted a hostile environment, the letter does not encourage a siege mentality. Its attitude to the pagan world, while discriminating, is refreshingly positive. Here would be continuity with the spirit of such important apostolic leaders as Peter, John Mark, Silvanus, and, of course, Paul—all of whom played significant roles in the defense and implementation of the church's decision to go to the Gentiles.

One of the striking things about this letter is that its sense of mission does not derive from the kind of reflections characteristic of the rest of the New Testament. For example, the Jew-Gentile question is not mentioned at all, and only a minimal salvation-history perspective is advanced (cf. the reference to the prophets in 1 Pet. 1:10–12). Instead, 1 Peter directly links Christian responsibility to the world with a theology of baptism and vocation.

The letter stresses from the outset that the Christian is "chosen" by God and "consecrated" for a life of obedience and holiness (1 Pet. 1:1–2). This saving call comes through the power of Christ's death and resurrection (1 Pet. 1:2). The Christian encounters this moment of grace in the missionary preaching of the church (1 Pet. 1:12, 25) and in the saving waters of baptism (3:21). These acts of salvation have transformed the lives of the Christians from the despair and meaninglessness of their former way of life to lives of good deeds, of love and hope (cf. 1 Pet. 1:14; 1:18; 4:3). The transformation that grace effects leads the author to speak of the saving encounter of baptism and conversion in boldly optimistic imagery: it is a "new birth" (1 Pet. 1:3), "a birth unto hope" (1:3), the gaining of an imperishable inheritance (1:4), a ransom from futility (1:18–21), a new awareness of God (3:21).

God's act of salvation becomes the basis of the community's identity and its responsibility. Throughout the letter, the author reminds the Christians that they are "God's people" (1 Pet. 2:10), "chosen" (1:2) and "called" by him (1:5). In 1 Pet. 2:4–10, what might be considered the doctrinal centerpiece of the letter, the author makes a collage of biblical images depicting the Christian community as God's people.[4] The community is the new spiritual "temple" where a holy priesthood exercises its ministry by offering "acceptable spiritual sacrifices" to God. The believers are God's "holy and kingly people," the object of his mercy and his covenant partners.

These powerful biblical images for the community set the stage for the letter's description of Christian responsibility. One of the amazing things about 1 Peter is that the community's minority status and its consciousness of conversion and election do not lead to a defensive attitude. Instead of closing the wagons in a circle and railing at a corrupt pagan world, the author encourages a positive attitude to the pagan world that may be unparalleled in the New Testament. The responsibility of the Christian, according to 1 Peter, is not to withdraw from the world, nor to condemn it. The Christian community must offer a living witness of hope that eventually may lead the world to give glory to its God. The threat of ultimate judgment against those who reject the gospel and persecute the church is present (1 Pet 2:8; 4:4,17), but it is a minor note in the overall tone of the letter.

The basic principles for this mission of witness are laid down in 1 Pet. 2:11–12.

Having completed a major section of the letter in which he focused on the identity of Christians chosen by God and born to hope (1:1–2:10), the author now concentrates on the practical consequences of this identity. Two basic guidelines are offered: on the one hand, the Christian must not give way to the "fleshly desires" that can destroy the human spirit (2:11). This sense of critical distance from the surrounding pagan culture is a direct result of conversion. The Christians have put aside the "futile ways" of their ancestors and no longer indulge in sensuality and excess (4:3–4). This change in lifestyle leads to conflict with the majority culture, since refusal to go along with current standards is viewed with bewilderment, suspicion, and even outright hostility (4:4). To offset this pressure to conform, the Christian must be "sober," "alert," and ready to resist actively the seductions of evil (5:8–9).

The second guideline receives more attention. Despite the threat posed by the majority culture, the Christians must be actively involved in society and offer it witness. The substance of this witness is the good deeds of the Christians and their sense of hope. The author repeatedly calls for "doing good" (for example, 1 Pet. 2:12,14; 4:19) and for a beautiful "way of life" (2:12). Since this witness must be visible, the Christian should "submit" or become involved in the created institutions of human society (1 Pet. 2:13).[5] This active involvement and the witness it offers might eventually "silence" the slanders brought against the Christians (1 Pet. 2:15). The Christians are exhorted to thread a narrow passageway between their free involvement in society and their unswerving reverence for God (1 Pet. 2:16–17).[6]

Two situations are singled out for detailed comment: household slaves and wives of nonbelieving husbands. These community members were likely to pay a special price for their mission of witness and they are held up to the whole community as an example of redemptive suffering.

The instructions for household slaves are found in 1 Pet. 2:18–25. They are exhorted to "submit" to their masters, that is, to continue in their position in society. It is precisely here that the testimony of their lives is to be given. Therefore they are to carry out their service in a spirit of "reverence" (1 Pet. 2:18), a word that 1 Peter restricts to one's attitude to God. This attempt to be a good servant and a good Christian may lead to suffering. The author sees no value in suffering that comes as a just punishment for evil deeds, but there is redemptive power and the potential for effective witness when a person suffers "in doing right" (1 Pet. 2:20). At this point the suffering of the slave and the suffering of Christ are joined (1 Pet. 2:21–24). Christ, too, suffered even though innocent, and his death was redemptive.

The author then considers a second repressed group, the wives of non-Christian husbands (1 Pet. 3:1–6). Since in Roman society a woman was usually expected to adopt the religious convictions of her husband, Christian wives in mixed marriages were in a vulnerable position.[7] This would especially be the case if the husband was hostile to Christianity, as seems to be the case the author had in mind (cf. "though they do not obey the word," 3:1). Even in this potentially intolerable position the author advises the Christian wife to "submit" (1 Pet.

3:1). An accurate sense of the word "submit" is particularly important in this context. The author is not counseling passive submission of wife to husband, since the issue is precisely one of courageous resistance to such "submission"! Rather, the author encourages the woman to continue in her role as wife *and* as committed Christian, just as he had told slaves to continue in or "submit" to their role. Prudence suggests that the woman resort not to direct verbal confrontation with her unbelieving husband but allow the "silent word" (1 Pet. 3:1) of her character as a good wife to give testimony to her husband. The example of Sarah is invoked, reminding the Christian woman to "do right and let nothing terrify you" (1 Pet. 3:6), hardly an exhortation to meek submission.[8]

The vivid example of household slaves and wives sets a pattern of courageous witness and redemptive suffering that is the responsibility of all Christians. Despite the likelihood of ridicule and suspicion, the Christian must continue to lead a life of integrity, not returning "evil for evil or reviling for reviling" (1 Pet. 3:9). Their call is "to bless," not to respond with hostility (1 Pet. 3:9). They are to live without fear (1 Pet. 3:13–14) because no one can truly harm someone who does what is right. In one of the most memorable witness texts of the New Testament the author calls on the Christians to "in your hearts reverence Christ as Lord" and "always be prepared to make defense to anyone who calls you to account for the hope that is in you, yet do it with gentleness and reverence" (1 Pet. 3:15).

The author consistently bases this testimony of hope on the example of the crucified Jesus. More than any other New Testament book, 1 Peter appeals to the sufferings of Jesus. Those sufferings are seen as an active ministry on Jesus' part. He died "for sinners . . . the righteous for the unrighteous that he might bring us to God" (1 Pet. 3:18). Even Christ's descent into the nether world as part of his death experience is seen as a redemptive opportunity. He is pictured as "preaching to the spirits in prison" (1 Pet. 3:19), a ministry that was meant to free them to "live in the spirit like God" (4:6).[9]

A significant point about the witness theology of 1 Peter is its eschatological tone. The ultimate objective of the community's witness is not described as a recruiting program for the church. Rather, the author hopes that eventually, seeing the good deeds of the community, the pagan world might be prompted "to give glory to God on the day of visitation" (1 Pet. 2:12). The community's role, then, is to prepare for the final day when nonbelievers are able to acclaim their God. This viewpoint harmonizes with the tone of the whole letter. The end-time hovers in the near future; the community need suffer only "for a little while" (1 Pet. 1:6; 5:10), "the end of all things is at hand" (4:7), the "time has come for judgment to begin" (4:17).

This emphasis on the consummation of human history is accompanied by a cosmic, "liturgical" tone in the letter as a whole. The final day will be a day of salvation in which God's power will be fully revealed and all humanity will be prompted to glorify him (cf. 1 Pet. 1:7, 13; 2:12; 4:11, 13; 5:10). The term "glory" echoes throughout the letter; it connotes a sense of God's triumphant presence made visible in created reality. This final revelation and humanity's response to it is the deepest motivation for the letter's theology of witness. The

Christians themselves are to be caught up in acclaiming God's glory (1 Pet. 4:11) and the testimony of their "good lives" might prompt the nonbelievers finally to do the same (2:12). This broad and positive vision of world history may be the secret to the expansive attitude 1 Peter takes toward the pagan world.

The theology of witness developed in this letter is an important contribution to the notion of mission in the New Testament. The author does not speak of itinerant mission preaching, but he does insist that the community members turn their interests and involvement *outside* the community.[10] They are not to withdraw into a defensive cocoon but are to participate in the created institutions of their society, and precisely there to offer a fearless testimony of good deeds. The purpose of this testimony is participation in the redemptive activity of the crucified Jesus whose suffering had brought the Christians themselves "to God" (1 Pet. 3:18). The climax of that redemptive mission of Jesus and of the community will come on the "day of visitation" when all the world can glorify God (1 Pet. 2:12; 4:11).

This kind of Christian vision shows no evidence of a narrow ecclesiastical concern. If our suggested dating of this letter is correct (that is, sometime after the death of Peter and Paul, probably in the 70s), then 1 Peter affirms that the mission spirit of the community had not abated. The increasingly delicate position of the local churches in Roman society, however, put the focus on one aspect of mission: the individual and corporate witness of the Christian in an alien society.

THE BOOK OF REVELATION: PROPHETIC WITNESS

It is interesting to compare the book of Revelation with 1 Peter on the issue of mission. These two works are radically different in form and tone, but both share a concern with witness in face of the Greco-Roman world.

In contrast to the exuberant homiletical tone of 1 Peter, Revelation has a biting prophetic and apocalyptic flavor. The author adopts a "letter" format (cf. especially 1:4–3:22), perhaps following the lead of the Pauline letters, which may have already established this type of pastoral literature in the early church. The main body of the work, however, draws on apocalyptic imagery as it constructs its dramatic vision of world history. But perhaps of greater importance for understanding the purpose of the book is the author's own description of his work as a "prophecy" (cf. Rev. 1:3). He writes to give his communities sharp and fearless teaching in a moment of crisis.

There can be no complete certainty about the dating of this book. Many scholars suggest a date during the reign of Domitian (81–96 C.E.) when emperor worship became a serious problem for the Christians and an occasion for systematic, if sporadic, persecution by the Roman state.[11] The situation facing the churches of Asia Minor, to whom the book is addressed, was not merely the problem caused by their being a small minority with a different set of values from the surrounding majority. A refusal to participate in such an important civic function as cultic honors to the emperor could and did have serious economic, political, and social consequences.

The problem addressed by the book of Revelation is not limited to encounters with Roman civil religion, however. There also seems to have been problems from those whom the author labels "so-called Jews" (Rev. 2:9; 3:9). These may be members of the synagogue who were in conflict with the Christians in the period following the destruction of the temple, when both groups were seeking a sense of self-identity. Even more serious were *internal* conflicts. Whereas 1 Peter offers no hint at all of any division or conflicts within the Christian community, John has harsh words for false teachers who, in his view, threaten the life of the church. The messages to the seven churches, which inaugurate the book, allude to these internal conflicts. Some have "abandoned the love [they] . . . had at first" (Rev. 2:4), others are "on the point of death" because their works are not "perfect" in the sight of God, and still others have become rich and smug (3:15–17).

But most troublesome of all are certain factions whose teaching and influence violently disturb John. These include the Nicolaitan party (cf. Rev. 2:6,15), a Jezebel-like woman prophetess (2:20), and those who hold "the teaching of Balaam" (2:14). We cannot be sure who these groups were or even if they were distinct factions in the community. We do, however, get some idea of their stance, as John interprets it. These teachers permit the eating of meat offered to idols (Rev. 2:14, 20) and practice "immorality" (2:14, 20). The eating of meats used in pagan cults was a difficult conscience problem for the early church. Only a portion of the animals were actually consumed in the cult itself; the remainder was sold in the public marketplace or served in the guild halls of the various trades. Particularly in the latter case, to abstain could cause economic and social difficulties for Christians. Paul had faced this issue in 1 Corinthians and in Romans, concluding that in itself eating this meat was not wrong but urging caution lest the conscience of the weak members of the community be scandalized.

For the author of Revelation, however, such a solution was not acceptable. John's reaction to this issue helps to capture his basic theological stance, including his sense of Christian witness. In his view, eating these meats was a symbol of solidarity with the whole specter of the Roman state and its emperor's blasphemous claims to divine prerogatives. The real issue was not the eating of religiously tainted meat but the cosmic struggle between the kingdom of God and the forces of sin and death personified in the Roman state and its idolatrous cult. When the author speaks of the "immorality" of the false teachers, he is probably not referring to sexual improprieties (the literal meaning of the Greek word *porneusai* used in Rev. 2:14,20) but is using the term metaphorically to refer to idolatry, as was often done in Jewish literature.[12] The Christian who has been redeemed by the blood of Christ cannot in any way compromise his or her allegiance to the kingdom of God. A heroic and prophetic witness of nonparticipation is absolutely necessary. The defeat of the forces of death is assured; until that final triumph, however, the Christians must lead lives of vigorous integrity.

The theological foundations of this call to heroic witness are found in the dramatic apocalyptic vision that John portrays in his book. The scenario is a cosmic one, encompassing the full span of future history. At stake is the resolution of the struggle between good and evil and the ultimate destiny of the created world. The immediate arena is the dehumanizing power of the Roman state, but lurking behind this struggle is the cosmic combat of God and Satan. The dramatic potential of apocalyptic imagery allows the author to engage the issues without the restraint of more conventional types of literature.

The span of the author's canvas enables him to affirm clearly the universal salvation intended by God and effected by the death and resurrection of Christ. Thus a key piece of mission theology found in Paul and the Gospel literature and other New Testament works is vigorously reaffirmed here. The "Lamb that was slain" is acclaimed as the one whose blood ransomed for God those "from every tribe and tongue and people and nations, and hast made them a kingdom and priests to our God and they shall reign on earth" (Rev. 5:9–10). Praise is offered to the Lamb from "every creature in heaven and on earth and under the earth and in the sea, and all therein" (Rev. 5:13). The gospel of this salvation is to be proclaimed to everyone: "to those who dwell on earth, to every nation and tribe and tongue and people" (Rev. 14:6).

This cosmic Christology is fundamental to the message of Revelation. Because the risen Christ has become the instrument of God's salvation to all the world, his "Lordship" has no peer. He is the "ruler of kings on earth" (Rev. 1:5) and his coming in judgment will cause "every eye [to] see him, every one who pierced him, and all tribes of the earth will wail on account of him" (1:7). In John's theological stance, here is the root of the conflict between the church and the Roman empire. Because Rome attempted to grasp a prerogative belonging only to Christ, it puts itself against God and thereby demonstrates that it is an agent of Satan. This inherent evil of the "Beast" is not a mere theological deduction for John. He cites its attacks on the community (Rev. 6:9; 13:7), its injustice (13:16–17; 18:3,11–19), and its sensuality (17:2–5; 18:1–3) as symptoms of its essentially corrupt nature.

The outcome of this cosmic confrontation between the followers of the Lamb and the forces of the empire, between the kingdom of God and the kingdom of Satan cannot be in doubt. Beginning in chapter 19 and extending through the concluding chapters of the book, the author gives an explosive portrayal of the triumph of Christ. Rome is defeated, Satan is cast out, and a new world free from sin, injustice, and death is created. Those who had persevered in their witness to the gospel are caught up in this triumphant moment: those "who had been beheaded for their testimony to Jesus and for the word of God, and who had not worshipped the beast or its image or had not received the beast or its image on their forehead or their hands" (Rev. 20:4).

It is important to note that John's vision of final redemption is thoroughly creation-centered.[13] Although apocalyptic language speaks of a "new heaven and a new earth" (Rev. 21:1) and supposes a thorough transformation of the "present age" ("the old heaven and the former earth will pass away," cf. 21:1), the author sees the redemptive drama as "coming down" to *this* world. Here will be the New Jerusalem and here will be the removal of pain and injustice (cf. Rev. 21:1–8). Even though John's apocalyptic language may give a first impression of world denial, that is not in fact the case. His deepest concern is with *this* world and its ultimate destiny. That is why he reacts so powerfully to the injustice and blasphemies of the Roman state: it is destructive of the God-intended nature of creation.

John's cosmic Christology and his concern for the redemption of the world lead him to his uncompromising witness theology. His work is literally "a call for the endurance of the saints" (Rev. 14:12). The Christians are asked to bear persecution, even martyrdom, rather than compromise their allegiance to Christ and his redemptive work. Because John sees the struggle betweeen the community and the Roman state on the ultimate terms of good and evil, Christ and Satan, there can be no room for compromise on such pivotal questions as the eating of meat offered to idols. The consequences of such a stance might entail effective withdrawal from the social and political spheres of Greco-Roman society—a stance completely different from that of 1 Peter. But this does not leave the book of Revelation in a totally aworldly posture. The Christians' withdrawal from society is a prophetic act of witness to and on behalf of society. The Christians are to proclaim the good news of universal salvation to the world, and their pulpit is a heroic refusal to compromise with a system they see as aligned with the forces of sin and death. They are to believe tenaciously in a vision of hope for the world, a transformation from pain and injustice to the good earth of peace and beauty. On a profound level the book of Revelation is one of the New Testament's most "worldly" books.

This emphasis on "witness"—by active participation in the case of 1 Peter, by active withdrawal in Revelation—is an expression of the community's mission. The call for witness flows from its convictions about the universal salvific will of God and from its sense of responsibility to all people because of the ministry of the risen Christ.

THE PASTORAL LETTERS: 1 AND 2 TIMOTHY, TITUS

The vigorous interaction with the surrounding environment that is a hallmark of 1 Peter and Revelation is not so evident in these three letters. Here concerns with the internal order and tone of the churches are dominant. Although these domestic preoccupations may blunt the missionary edge, they do not buff it away altogether.

The significance of the Pastorals for detecting the mission temperature of the early church is partially related to the question of their dating and authorship. Most contemporary scholars consider these to be post-Pauline writings dating from the end of the first century.[14] Some notable differences in style from the earlier Pauline writings, and especially a concern for church structure and for maintaining the tradition in the face of internal errors, are seen as evidence for placing these letters at a time considerably after Paul, when the church focused more on domestic issues. This concentration on internal affairs is considered symptomatic of a dampening of the missionary spirit in the latter part of the first century as the church became more institutionalized.[15]

While this view has some merit, we should be cautious not to draw more conclusions than the evidence permits. First of all, there is no intrinsic reason why a concern for the consolidation of church structures could not have coexisted with a sense of mission to the outside. The Gospels, too, show a concern for church order but are able to maintain a vigorous theology of mission. It is quite possible that the Pastoral letters were written at roughly the same time as some of the Gospels.[16] We should also keep in mind the specific purpose of these letters. They are directed to church leaders, reminding them of their responsibilities for the internal care of the churches and exhorting them to perform their duties in a manner worthy of their faith. This holds true whether these are authentic letters of Paul to Timothy and Titus or whether they are pseudonymous writings, evoking the memory of Paul as an instruction to a later generation of church leaders. Since the internal health of the community and its leadership is the focus, we can draw only limited significance from the absence of a strong mission thrust to the outside. In literature of a broader scope, such as the baptismal exhortation of 1 Peter or the Gospels, the full dimension of Christian responsibility can more easily come into play.

Even with their domestic concerns, the Pastorals are not silent on the mission issue. Several aspects of the letters' message are worth noting and contribute, at least indirectly, to an overall New Testament theology of mission.

First of all, the universal scope of salvation—a hallmark of New Testament mission theology—is clearly stated. One of the most vivid examples of this is found in 1 Tim. 3:16:

> He was manifested in the flesh,
> vindicated in the Spirit,
>   seen by angels,
> preached among the nations,
> believed on in the world,
>   taken up in glory.

This appears to be part of a hymn quoted by the author to reinforce an appeal for good behavior made in the preceding verse (3:15).[17] A series of interlocking statements charts the earthly and heavenly experience of Christ. The cosmic exaltation of Christ ("vindicated in the spirit, seen by angels . . . taken up in glory") is linked with the worldwide preaching of the gospel and its universal impact ("preached among the nations, believed on in the world"). This is not unlike the broad vision of Colossians and Ephesians. There is certainly an assumption in the hymn (and, presumably, in the author of the letter who quotes the hymn) that the scope of the community's mission is universal because the death and exaltation of Jesus is a universal, even cosmic event. The past tense of the verb ("preached," "believed") puts a certain distance between the author and the mission, as if the preaching to the nations were an accomplished fact.

Other passages in 1 Timothy reflect this universal horizon and have a greater sense of immediacy. In 1 Tim. 1:15 Paul reviews his own conversion experience and quotes a "saying" that confirms his experience: "Christ Jesus came into the world to save sinners." This statement of Jesus' salvific mission is reminiscent of Jn. 3:15–16, a key text in that Gospel's mission theology.

The will of God to save all people and the corresponding universal mission of Christ are strongly affirmed again in 1 Tim. 2:3-6:

> This is good and it is acceptable in the sight of God our Savior, who desires all . . . to be saved and to come to the knowledge of the truth. For there is one God, and there is one mediator between God and [humanity] the man Christ Jesus, who gave himself as a ransom for all, the testimony to which was borne at the proper time.

The context is once again Paul's reflection on his own missionary vocation. The scope of the salvation event sets the horizon of the mission: "For this I was appointed a preacher and apostle (I am telling the truth, I am not lying), a teacher of the Gentiles in faith and truth" (1 Tim. 2:7). Paul repeats this universal goal of his mission in 1 Tim. 4:10: "For to this end we toil and strive, because we have our hope set on the living God, who is the Savior of all people, especially of those who believe."

Such affirmations are less forceful in Titus and 2 Timothy, but still present. Tit. 2.11 proclaims that "the grace of God has appeared for the salvation of all people." The second letter to Timothy speaks more diffusely of "our Savior Christ Jesus, who abolished death and brought life and immortality to light through the gospel" (1:10). This gospel is the "word" that Paul was commissioned to proclaim, "fully, that all the Gentiles might have it" (2 Tim. 4:17).

Even though the Pastorals may bend these statements of universalism to inspire fidelity and good behavior *within* the community (cf. 1 Tim. 3:15; 1:18-19; 2:2,8ff.; Tit. 2:12; 2 Tim. 1:1,13; 4:15) the presence of such texts in the letters shows that the lynchpin of New Testament mission theology has not been removed.

Another feature of the Pastorals' mission theology is the example of Paul himself.[18] If the surmise is correct that these letters were not written by Paul, then the author used the example of the martyred apostle to instruct and inspire the community. It is important to note that the primary image of Paul in these letters is precisely that of missionary apostle.

The characteristics singled out are meant to be a source of inspiration for the recipients of the letters, moving them to guard faithfully the tradition Paul handed on and to remain vigilant and untainted in the exercise of their duties. Thus Paul is *the* apostle (1 Tim. 1:1; 2 Tim. 1:1; Tit. 1:1) appointed to God's service of preaching the gospel in spite of his former persecution of the church (1 Tim. 1:12-17; 2:7; 2 Tim. 1:11; 4:17; Tit. 1:3). Paul is the one who has brought that gospel to the whole world (2 Tim. 4:17; cf. also 1 Tim. 3:16).

Of special importance is the suffering Paul had to endure in carrying out his mission.[19] The most eloquent expression of this is found in 2 Timothy, wherein Timothy is exhorted to take on his "share of suffering for the gospel in the power of God" (1:8). This was Paul's own experience; he was appointed "a preacher and apostle and teacher" and "therefore I suffer as I do" (2 Tim. 1:11-12). Paul's chains, signs of his apostolic suffering, are a badge of honor (2 Tim. 1:16;

2:9). Like the crucified Jesus, Paul suffers for the good news of salvation (2 Tim. 2:8), bearing pain for the sake of the elect that they also may obtain the salvation that in Christ Jesus goes with eternal glory (2:10). Even though he is persecuted and buffeted, he will endure to the end; his suffering a worthy sacrifice to God (cf. 2 Tim. 3:10–11; 4:6–8, 17–18). The point of all this is that Timothy himself should fearlessly preach the Word and teach. Paul's own history should be remembered: "Now you have observed my teaching, my conduct, my aim in life, my faith, my patience, my love, my steadfastness, my persecution, my sufferings . . ." (2 Tim. 2:3–10). Unlike the opponents who promote false doctrine, Timothy must "always be steady, endure suffering, do the work of an evangelist, fulfill your ministry" (2 Tim. 4:5; cf. 1:8).

The domestic concerns of the Pastorals remain dominant. Even though Paul is portrayed as the great missionary to the Gentile world, his example is directed to Timothy's role as a leader concerned with the health of the church. Paul's fidelity to the gospel is a bulwark against false teaching; his apostolic suffering should inspire Timothy to persevere in his ministry of leadership. This puts a certain distance between the letters' concern and the missionary enterprise. Paul, in effect, looks *back* to a missionary career now completed. The success of that mission and the virtues it exemplified are now to inspire the church's internal life.

Despite this "distance," it is still significant that Paul the missionary has such an impact on the churches of the Pastorals. Again we can suggest that the latent assumptions of these books are that the gospel is universal and that it is to be proclaimed to all.

Although most of the exhortation materials in the Pastorals are directed to internal questions and thus trained on "Timothy" and "Titus" in their role as leaders of the community, the author still gives some attention to the positive witness that "good conduct" can give to the outside world.

For example, when the author speaks of good citzenship (cf. 1 Tim. 2:1–7) he immediately links this to universal salvation and to the vocation of preaching the gospel. Various members of the community should live with integrity so as not to give scandal to unbelievers. A woman, therefore, should be "modest" and perform "good deeds" (1 Tim. 2:9–10). Candidates for bishop are to have the kind of virtues accepted in society and must be "well thought of by outsiders" (1 Tim. 3:1–7).[20] Slaves are to be obedient "so that the name of God and the teaching may not be defamed" (1 Tim. 6:1).[21]

This call for good conduct does not have the dynamic tone of 1 Peter or the prophetic ring of the book of Revelation. Good conduct is to be maintained so that the community will be well thought of and can live in peace, an essentially defensive posture. But one should not push this too far. The Pastorals clearly affirm God's will to save all people, and these letters preserve a vivid memory of Paul as the fearless apostle to the Gentiles. The presence of these two components should caution us not to despair of a mission consciousness in the church of the Pastorals, even though in these letters such a viewpoint does not come to full expression.

HEBREWS, JAMES, JUDE, 2 PETER

The remaining books of the New Testament offer little material that bears directly on the issue of mission. James urges the Christians to lead lives of integrity, translating their faith into active good deeds of justice and mutual respect. Although it could be inferred from the material, the author does not reflect explicitly on the witness value of such good deeds.[22]

Jude concentrates solely on internal problems, castigating the errors and immorality of "ungodly persons" (Jude, v. 4) in the community. The second letter of Peter draws much of its content and its polemical spirit from Jude. It too targets problem Christians in the community. In contrast to Jude's situation, the "errors" attacked by 2 Peter seem to be mainly doctrinal. However, the letter is conscious of the community's wider environment. The author adapts the Jewish–Christian materials of Jude to a thoroughly Gentile context, and refers both to the missionary preaching of the apostles (2 Pet. 3:2) and the conversion experience of the Gentiles (2:20).[23] But these are passing references; the question of the universal mission is not on the author's agenda.

The letter to the Hebrews offers more potential for the question of mission. By means of an elaborate metaphor it compares the redemptive work of Jesus and his power as exalted Lord with the now overshadowed and passing cult of the Jerusalem temple and its priesthood. The range of theology in Hebrews, therefore, is cosmic and universal. The exalted Christ is the "Son," God's final Word to humanity, the climax in a long line of patriarchs and prophets who bore the message of salvation. Christ is the "heir of all things" and the agent of creation. "He reflects the glory of God and bears the very stamp of his nature, upholding the universe by his word of power" (Heb. 1:1–3). This awesome poetry portrays a cosmic role for Christ similar to the prologue of John. Without question, the letter conceives of Jesus' redemptive work as having universal significance. His compassion and intercessory role as priest are exercised on behalf of all humanity (cf. 2:9–10, 14–18; 5:7–9).

The image of Jesus as the final prophetic Word and as the singular high priest also gives a salvation-history perspective to Hebrews, another key element in the New Testament theology of mission. The temple priesthood was only a shadow of Christ's definitive role as priest (Hebrews 7–11); the faith of the patriarchs and Old Testament witness was only a hint of the glory to come in the experience of the Christians (cf. Heb. 11:39–40).

The author is also conscious of the missionary preaching of the community. The good news of "such a great salvation" was transmitted to the believers "by those who heard him" (Heb. 2:1–4). The author is also aware of the price that has been paid by those who are committed to the gospel; conversion often brought abuse and hostility from outsiders (Heb. 10:32–34).

Despite these elements of a mission perspective, however, Hebrews does not move in this direction. The bulk of the letter's message deals with the redemptive work of the exalted Jesus and its implication for Christian perseverance. There is no real attention given to such issues as the fate of the Gentiles or the responsibility of Christians toward the outside world.

CONCLUSION

Scanning these remaining books of the canon has produced some significant results. Because we know so little about the precise origin and date of many books of the New Testament, it is prudent not to draw airtight conclusions about "trends" in the missionary consciousness of the early church. The concentration on such domestic issues as church order, doctrine, and ethical conflicts may mean that a mission perspective waned as the church became more institutionalized. But many of these writers may be contemporary with the Gospels or even Paul, whose sense of mission is undisputed. And, in the case of 1 Peter and Revelation, there is no question that these communities were alert to the responsibilities of Christians to the world beyond their doorstep. From these writings in particular, we learn that the missionary effort of the early community was not seen as purely *verbal*. The testimony of citizenship lived with integrity (1 Peter) or even of prophetic refusal to compromise by withdrawing from certain societal functions (Revelation) were considered genuine testimony to the good news of universal salvation.

NOTES

1. There seems to be a revival of interest in the Petrine letters; cf. the brief but excellent study of J. Elliott, *I Peter: Estrangement and Community*, Herald Biblical Booklets (Chicago: Franciscan Herald Press, 1979), and D. Senior, *1 & 2 Peter*, New Testament Message 20 (Wilmington, Del.: Michael Glazier, 1980).

2. Elliott maintains that the recipients of the letter were "resident aliens" (the literal meaning of *paraikos* the term used in 1 Pet. 2:11), that is, people who had migrated to northern Asia Minor to work in large estates and as household servants. As such they enjoyed only partial legal protection. Cf. P. Ellis, *A Home for the Homeless,* esp. pp. 21–100.

3. Cf. J. Elliott, *I Peter*, pp. 32–36.

4. On this cf. J. Elliott, *The Elect and the Holy* (Leiden: E. J. Brill, 1966).

5. The connotation of the word "submit" *(hypotasso)* in this context is extremely important. The meaning of the word stands out more clearly when one considers the alternative course of action against which the author argues. That alternative is not rebellion (whose opposite would be "submit") but noninvolvement (whose opposite would be "participate"). The question before the community was whether or not to participate in the societal institutions of the surrounding culture; 1 Pet. 2:13 counsels them to "submit," that is, to "participate." On this point, cf. the excellent commentary of L. Goppelt, *Der erste Petrusbrief* (Göttingen: Vandenhoeck & Ruprecht, 1978), and the discussion in D. Senior, *1 & 2 Peter,* pp. 42–47.

6. 1 Peter consistently uses the term "fear" *(phobos)* to describe the reverence one owes to God alone; thus in 2:17 the author pointedly asks the community to fear only

God—the emperor is to be "honored," as is everyone else! Cf. further, D. Senior, *1 & 2 Peter*, pp. 46–47.

7. On this point, cf. D. L. Balch, *Let Wives be Submissive: The Domestic Code in 1 Peter*, Society of Biblical Literature Monograph Series 26 (Chico, Ca.: Scholars Press, 1981).

8. Unfortunately, this passage (1 Pet. 3:1–6) is consistently used to defend a subordinate role for women when, in fact, the author singles out women who are the wives of non-Christians as exemplars to the community because of their difficult witness role. The text cannot be properly used as an illustration of a biblical model for marriage.

9. On this enigmatic text, cf. W. Dalton, *Christ's Proclamation to the Spirits*, Analecta Biblica 23 (Rome: Biblical Institute Press, 1965).

10. Cf. the remarks of F. Hahn, *Mission in the New Testament* (Naperville: Allenson, 1965), p. 142, who on this basis considers 1 Peter to have only a "modified" sense of mission. But mission should not be defined exclusively in terms of verbal proclamation; cf. below, part III.

11. Cf. the state of the question by U. Vanni, "L'Apocalypse johannique, Etat de la question," in *L'Apocalypse Johannique et l'Apocalyptique dans le Nouveau Testament*, ed. J. Lambrecht, Bibliotheca ephemeridum theologicarum lovaniensium 53 (Gembloux: Louvain University Press, 1980), pp. 29–30.

12. Cf. J. Sweet, *Revelation*, Pelican Commentaries (Philadelphia: Westminster Press, 1979), p. 89, who refers to G. Vermes, *Scripture and Tradition in Judaism* (Leiden: E. J. Brill, 1961), pp. 127–77.

13. This more politico-social approach to Revelation is stressed by E. Fiorenza; cf. *Invitation to the Book of Revelation* (Garden City, N.Y.: Doubleday, 1981), and a succinct essay in *Hebrews, James, 1 and 2 Peter, Jude, Revelation*, Proclamation Commentaries, ed. G. Krodel (Philadelphia: Fortress Press, 1977), pp. 99–120. A more technical discussion can be found in "Redemption as Liberation: Apoc.1,5f. and 5,9f.," *Catholic Biblical Quarterly* 36 (1974): 220–32.

14. Cf. the thorough discussion in W. Kümmel, *Introduction to the New Testament*, pp. 370–87, and a more popular treatment in R. Karris, *The Pastoral Epistles*, New Testament Message 17 (Wilmington, Del.: Michael Glazier, 1979), pp. xi–xvi.

15. "The concentration on the life and strengthening of the churches is so strong [in the Pastorals] that it is now largely impossible to speak of an understanding of the mission, in the sense in which the phrase has so far been used and was characteristic of the oldest Christianity" (F. Hahn, *Mission in the New Testament*, p. 140). As we have remarked above, this kind of assessment takes on the character of dogma for Hahn.

16. A point conceded by Hahn and one that seems to baffle him; cf. his comments on pp. 162–63 of *Mission in the New Testament*.

17. Cf. M. Dibelius, H. Conzelmann, *The Pastoral Epistles* (Philadelphia: Fortress Press, 1972), pp. 61–63.

18. On this motif, cf. M. de Boer, "Images of Paul in the Post-Apostolic Period," *Catholic Biblical Quarterly* 42 (1980): 359–80.

19. Ibid., p. 366.

20. The lists of virtues in 1 Timothy are very similar to the lists of virtues sought for in the general good: cf. M. Dibelius, H. Conzelmann, *The Pastoral Epistles*, pp. 50–57, who provide interesting parallels in Hellenistic literature.

21. Cf. a similar exhortation in Tit. 3:1–6.

22. Note that in 1:1 James addresses the letter to "the twelve tribes in the dispersion," perhaps reflecting the same kind of minority status for the Christians as that in 1 Pet. 1:1. James, however, does not develop the implications of this for Christian witness.

23. On this aspect of 2 Peter, cf. T. Fornberg, *An Early Church in a Pluralistic Society: A Study of 2 Peter*, Coniectanea neotestamentica 9 (Lund, Sweden: Gleerup, 1977).

PART III

CONCLUSION

Donald Senior, C.P.
Carroll Stuhlmueller, C.P.

14

The Biblical Foundations for Mission

I have seen the affliction of my people who are in Egypt, and have heard their cry because of their taskmasters; I know their sufferings, and I have come down to deliver them out of the hand of the Egyptians, and to bring them up out of that land to a good and broad land, a land flowing with milk and honey [Exod. 3:7-8].

When he saw the crowds, he had compassion for them, because they were harassed and helpless, like sheep without a shepherd. Then he said to his disciples, "The harvest is plentiful, but the laborers are few; pray therefore the Lord of the harvest to send out laborers into his harvest" [Mt. 9:36-38].

This survey of Old and New Testament traditions relating to the universal mission of the church is now completed. In this final part we offer a reflective essay on the results of the search and their significance for the contemporary church.

SYNTHESIS

The working hypothesis affirmed throughout this book is that the entire Bible, not just the New Testament, lays the foundations for mission. Before enumerating our conclusions it may be useful to synthesize quickly the biblical data we have considered.

The Old Testament

Our study of the Old Testament began with the admission that, at first glance, the movement of Israel's history and its Scriptures appears to be centripetal, or inward. But a careful analysis of biblical tradition uncovers powerful currents that swirl in the opposite direction. Even though Israel treasured its identity as God's elect people, at its best moments it recognized other signs of deep solidarity with the nonelect nations and with the dynamics of secular history outside the annals of its covenant.

Israel's own origin is in the family of nations, and in the arena of secular history its own story of salvation was to be hammered out. Israel's religious thinkers knew that eventually the relationship of Israel to the nations would have to be faced, at least in the final age.

Secular events such as the exodus from Egypt and the settlement in the land, and non-Israelite celebrations such as the harvest feasts became absorbed and transformed into Israel's pattern of life and liturgy, becoming part of its self-understanding as God's people. The secular origins of these now explicitly sacred events and rituals left seeds of solidarity with the nations, links still present even if they had been generally forgotten or even denied.

When Israel's concern for self-identity became excessive and its sacred institutions of monarchy and temple became corrupt, the challenge of the prophets brought renewed attention to the fringes of Israel's life: the poor, the oppressed, the defenseless. Even the threat of foreign invasion could be interpreted as the purifying instrument of God's justice on behalf of his people. These thrusts to the outside were sober reminders of God's wider horizons, intuitions of salvation at work beyond the narrow borders of Israel.

The shattering experience of the exile illustrated once more the ambiguity of Israel's apparent exclusivity. In reaction to the exile, part of Israel's soul would turn more deeply inward, as illustrated in the prophetic voice of Ezekiel and the reforms of Ezra and Nehemiah. But an alternate vision also could be glimpsed in the soaring rhetoric of Deutero-Isaiah: the salvific role for Cyrus, the rumble of the distant coastlands, the light cast to the nations.

Thus a scan of Jewish history in the Old Testament reveals a dialectic between centripetal and centrifugal forces, between flight from the secular and absorption of the secular, between a concern for self-identity and responsible interaction with one's environment, between elect status as God's chosen people and humble awareness of one's solidarity with the entire human family.

From this larger framework, our study of Old Testament traditions moved to a closer examination of the themes and literature that illustrate the dialectic. The fundamental intuition of the Bible is that God is Savior before he is Creator. God did not begin with the construction of a perfect world, which then unfortunately ran down. Life, in the biblical perspective, begins with rescue; the fullness of salvation beckons in the future. Therefore the salvific experience of Israel can be conceived of as a process of "humanization," whereby Israel deepened its life as a people within its cultural and political setting, yet was drawn forward on a sacred journey to the fulfillment of a divinely inspired dream. Different moments of that process are detectable: (a) the eruption of new ideas and events that do violence to the status quo and create a new synthesis; the exodus, the conquest and settlement, the exile—these and other disruptive moments are seen as salvific by the Scriptures; (b) interludes in which new ideas, structures, and insights are absorbed by the people; this is a period of indigenization; (c) the cycle comes full term but yet advances with a new synthesis under the prophetic challenge that shatters Israel's complacency, purifying its politics and social structures and opening up new vistas.

Such a process, discernible in the long history of Israel, has not ceased with the Old Testament; it also helps illumine the experience of the New Testament and church history. The testimony of the Bible is that even in this constantly shifting pattern of history, the values of biblical religion are protected and enhanced.

Because the prophetic movement is a key element, our microscope moved in closer to examine this aspect of the biblical data, so important to understanding the mission theology of Jesus and the early church. The prophetic movement was seen as the third part of the cycle described above, challenging and purifying Israel's too complacent "indigenization," its uncritical and at times unfaithful absorption of secular values. The probing critique of the prophetic movement would, time and again, precipitate a comprehensive realignment of Israel's identity through such climactic experiences as the dispersal of the northern tribes in 721 and the ravaging of the south in 587. But from these ashes would come new impulses to life. Throughout the various prophetic challenges what remains key is the covenant love between Yahweh and Israel, a relationship that ultimately makes infidelity intolerable and pushes Israel to a new awareness and new experience of Yahweh's concern for the poor and the defenseless. This same probing experience of God's overwhelming compassion, and its purifying results, will be paramount in the prophetic career of Jesus himself, as we shall see. Jesus finds his predecessors in the scorching ministries of Hosea and Isaiah.

Because the prophets used the medium of secular events and because they brought into the consciousness of Israel the boundary-breaking sovereignty of God and his covenant, they have important consequences for the missionary dynamic of the Scriptures.

Of all the dimensions of biblical religion, that which seems to be most problematic for theology of mission is Israel's absorbing concern with its identity as an elect people, and so this became a peculiar focus of our study. The notion of election has, paradoxically, buried within it the doctrine of an *un*elect people. The elements of Israel's privileged status—land, security, peace, resources—were never absolute privileges but "always demanded an attitude of humble sharing." God chose Israel, the Scriptures affirm, not because of its prowess or status or achievements but as a demonstration of God's gratuitous love for those who have nothing. This fundamental affirmation of the Scriptures remains a constant check on the exclusiveness potentially present in the concept of election.

This inherent ambiguity in Israel's concept of itself as an elect people has echoes in its evolving view of the foreigner. During the patriarchal period, as far as one can tell, relations to the foreigners were relatively cordial. But the later shifting political fortunes of Israel dampened this cordiality. The enslavement in Egypt, and the exile, for example, created a deep aversion to the outsider. After the exile different strands of tradition emerged. The Jerusalem enclave, echoed in the writings of Joel and Ezra, looked harshly at all outsiders, and the apocalyptic tradition savored the certainty of future judgment against the enemies of Israel. Yet, Isaiah spoke benignly of the eschatological gathering of the nations in joy and prayer at Zion.

Paradoxically, Israel's notion of "election" also provided an opening to universalism. God's "choice" (*bahar*) of Israel was an act of gratuitous love. That love was the basis of Israel's identity as God's people. Yet that love, too, would strain at the narrow boundaries of Israel and reach out to the *goyim*. Deutero-Isaiah, particularly in the Songs of the Suffering Servant, illustrates that move to a universal perspective.

Bringing the mission question to the Bible reveals an evolving dialectic between identity and outreach, between absorption of secular events and values, and prophetic challenge to those secular elements. This brings us to the final dimensions of the Old Testament that have particular significance for mission: its prayer and liturgical life. Particularly in Psalms one senses the experiential basis of Israel's religious tradition. Secular events were absorbed and interpreted and celebrated in the light of Jewish faith. The intuitive power of prayer and celebration also enabled Israel to kindle and preserve intuitions of God's universal sovereignty—and therefore of the universal scope of his salvation—insights lost in the more discursive and polemical aspects of other Old Testament traditions.

In the Old Testament, therefore, one finds a number of significant elements crucial for mission: the universal sovereignty of God over all peoples and all history, a strong interaction between the community of Israel and secular culture and events, and a projection of future history in which the nations would form one elect people with Israel in acclaiming God. Yet these elements did not coalesce into an active missionary stance. Intuitions of a collegial role for the nations remained on the periphery, especially in the postexilic period. Although some proselytizing activity took place during the intertestamental period, this was always in an ethnocentric perspective: Gentiles could become Jews and thus share in Israel's privileged status. Israel was not called to go to the nations; the nations were permitted to come to Israel.

The New Testament

From a screening of Old Testament traditions we moved to the New Testament. Without question, the person and ministry of Jesus was the catalyst that triggered the Christian impulse for mission. Intuitions latent in the consciousness of Israel were now brought to a central position.

Yet the relationship of Jesus and the church's mission to the Gentiles is complex. The Gospel evidence suggests that Jesus did not engage in a full-scale mission to non-Jews; instead he confined his ministry to challenging and restoring the community of Israel. However, fundamental aspects of Jesus' mission became an inspiration and source for the post-Easter universal mission of the community.

Jesus' announcement of the coming rule of God—the keynote of his ministry as presented in the Synoptic Gospels—is of fundamental importance here. This traditional Jewish metaphor gives coherence to various aspects of Jesus' mission. His preaching, his parables, and his sayings speak of God's coming rule and the need for conversion in order to respond to his gracious love. Jesus' exorcisms and healing are vivid signs and proleptic experiences of God's compassion—a compassion that will characterize the coming kingdom. A central conviction of Jesus is that the God of the kingdom is characterized by gratuitous mercy, a theme that echoes through Jesus' parables and is confirmed in the compassion demonstrated in his own actions and his interpretations of law. Jesus reaches beyond the boundaries set up by his contemporaries and provocatively offers God's mercy to the poor, to outcasts and sinners, and even to occasional Gentiles.

This potential of Jesus' kingdom ministry is of capital importance for the New Testament sense of mission. Jesus, in effect, exercised a prophetic role, continuing the dynamics we noted in the Old Testament. His intuitive experience of God as a God of universal power and absolute graciousness led him to challenge the narrow particularism of his contemporaries. Although his ministry was for the most part confined to Palestine, the post-Easter churches saw these aspects of Jesus' mission as relevant for the scope of their own mission. The resurrection of Christ demonstrated that the new age of salvation had dawned, an age in which the fate of all humanity would be decided. And through the power of the risen Christ and his Spirit, the disciples were commissioned to bring his kingdom ministry to the world.

In the subsequent chapters we explored the diverse way in which the authors of the New Testament reflected on this universal mission. For all of this, the person of Christ remained central.

The starting point for Paul was his conversion experience. His encounter with the risen Christ transformed his view of humanity, of history, and of his own personal call. As a believing Jew, Paul had never doubted that God's power was sovereign over all peoples. But through his encounter with the risen Christ and, presumably, through his formation in the Christian community, Paul became convinced that God was exercising that sovereign power through Jesus Christ and, through Jesus Christ, that he was at that moment offering salvation to all peoples, Jew and Gentiles alike. Paul believed that he himself was called—in the model of the Old Testament prophets—to be the proclaimer of this grace to the Gentiles. From this seminal experience flows the extraordinary richness of Pauline mission theology.

Colossians and Ephesians expand the mission horizon of the community even further. The situation at Colossae stimulated Paul to affirm the Lordship of Christ over the entire universe. Through Christ, God's saving power surpasses any of the threatening fates of the cosmos. This cosmic Christology, in turn, enables the deutero-Pauline letter of Ephesians to open up the mission perspective of the church. The cosmic Christ is given as "head" over the body of the church, filling it with Christ's universal dimensions. Thus the church itself is called to be an instrument and model of universal reconciliation among all peoples. Paul's own mission of uniting Jew and Gentile in the one church is reflected upon as a symbol of the final moment of salvation where all peoples will be united under the power of the one God.

The Synoptic Gospels use a narrative of the person and life of Jesus to give direction to the church's mission. Mark, for example, recounts the Galilean ministry of Jesus in such a way that both sides of the lake—Jewish and Gentile—feel the impact of the kingdom proclamation. Through the experience of Jesus' death and resurrection the disciples are finally led to comprehend the scope of their mission and to proclaim the gospel to all nations (Mk. 13:10), as the community awaits the return of its Lord and the consummation of history.

Matthew offers guidance to his Jewish-Christian community in its struggle with the question of universalism. Once again the boundary-breaking potential of Jesus' own kingdom mission is recalled to provide authority for the disciples' mission to the Gentiles. Jesus' interpretation of law, as presented by Matthew, puts prophetic emphasis on compassion and justice. His healing touch reaches out to sinners and outcasts. He blesses the faith of Gentiles. These signs become normative as the new age is inaugurated by the death and resurrection of Jesus, and the community is sent out by the risen Christ to make disciples of "all nations."

Luke-Acts provides one of the most comprehensive reflections on the universal mission in all of the New Testament. The prophetic ministry of Jesus is again the model. His Spirit-anointed mission of mercy and justice is replicated in the expanding ministry of the post-Easter church. In Acts, Luke shows the struggle of the Jewish-Christian church at Jerusalem as it was propelled by the example of Jesus and the power of the Spirit to move beyond its narrow boundaries and to include Gentiles in its membership. The community's mission to go to "the end of the earth" is the final outcome of the work of salvation promised by the Scriptures and inaugurated by Jesus.

The Gospel of John brings a new literary and theological style, but the mission question remains central. The use of Wisdom traditions and an apparent sensitivity to Hellenistic culture give a cosmic perspective to Jesus' own mission as presented by John. He is the Word made flesh, the preexistent Son sent to redeem the world. Jesus' mission revealed the saving intent of God and reached its climax in the self-sacrificing act of laying down his life for his friends. Through death and resurrection Jesus returns triumphant to the Father and sends the gift of the Paraclete upon the community. The Spirit/Paraclete enables the community to continue Jesus' own mission in the world.

In a final chapter we considered the remaining books. Here the missionary nature of the community may be less dominant but it is still present. The first letter of Peter and the book of Revelation call for a mission of heroic witness. For John, the author of Revelation, this witness is a prophetic confrontation with the ungodly and dehumanizing features of the Roman state. For 1 Peter, by contrast, witness means a person's active participation in society as a good citizen while maintaining the integrity of one's commitment to the gospel. The call to witness lingers in other works such as James, Hebrews, and the Pastorals. But the concerns of these letters are not directed to mission. The Pastorals recall the missionary career of Paul, but his apostolic suffering and his zeal are used as a model for faithful leadership *within* the church rather than as a model for the church's responsibility to the world outside.

Thus throughout the Old and New Testaments the question of "mission" is far from peripheral. In the Old Testament this motif must be sought in the complex and evolving dialectic between Israel and its sovereign God and between Israel and its secular environment. With the figure of Jesus the centrifugal forces surging within the Scriptures break out into the non-Jewish world. The New Testament writings represent the multiple ways in which the members of the Christian community reflected on their mission experience and its relationship to the person of Jesus and the history of Israel.

BIBLICAL FOUNDATIONS

What can we learn about the foundations for universal mission from our review of the biblical literature? What were the convictions and dynamics that ultimately turned Israel and the early Christian community away from too exclusive a concern with self-identity and toward an active responsibility for the world outside? These dynamics present themselves as four key themes.

1. The Sovereignty of God and His Will to Save Humanity

The conviction that the God of Israel was sovereign over all peoples and that he was a saving God is absolutely fundamental to the Scriptures.

This conviction is readily apparent in the Old Testament. The God who rescues Israel from Egypt had absolute power over pharaoh. The God who shapes the world and makes the human person in his image is the Lord of all creation. Even when Israel concentrated on its own special privilege as an elect people, it never lost sight of the fact that this election was a gratuitous choice on God's part. Yahweh chose an insignificant people to be his own, but his Lordship and authority extended over all peoples, particularly as they were involved in Israel's history. That sovereignty only underlines the graciousness of his choice of Israel.

The power and authority of God are experienced as salvific. God's rescue of Israel from slavery is a revelation of the way this sovereign God can act on behalf of all nations—as Amos pointed out in a flashing insight: the same God who brought Israel out of Egypt brought "the Philistines from Caphtor and the Syrians from Kir" (Amos 9:7). Israel's election, too, is an act of salvation, calling the people to holiness and life. Even when Israel focused on its elect status it was never able to maintain consistently that God's saving power was *exclusively* trained on Israel. The deeper instincts of the Scriptures sense that God's saving will is as extensive as his compassionate concern for suffering people and as powerful as his sovereign authority. The fate of the nations is not a major focus, nor is any systematic answer hammered out; yet Israel glimpsed that the nations, too, would somehow encounter the Savior God.

This sovereign and saving nature of the biblical God underwrites the centrifugal impulses we have detected in several biblical motifs. Secular events and secular values are not discarded but are absorbed into Israel's culture, worship, and language. The prophets challenged the misuse of divine authority by the kings because their injustice seemed to push the poor and the defenseless outside the boundaries of God's kingdom. The shattering of Israel's peace by outside peoples could be seen, ultimately, as God's own saving initiative, purifying Israel and opening it up to new perspectives of grace. Convictions about God's universal, saving will convince Isaiah that a ministry concentrated exclusively on Israel was "too light a thing" and Yahweh must become a "light to the nations."

This profound image of God—universal and saving—is at the heart of the New Testament as well, and ultimately becomes the driving force of the church's mission. As such it is one of the strongest links between the Old and the New Testaments, between the experience of Israel and the experience of the Christian community. Here, too, the catalytic force is Jesus. The driving force of his prophetic ministry originates from his piety. A sovereign and gracious God is the ultimate actor in Jesus' parables of the kingdom and in his stories of mercy. The saving power of God that sweeps beyond the arbitrary boundaries of Sabbath laws and ritual purity undergirds Jesus' provocative association with sinners and his interpretation of law in the light of the love command. This liberating thrust of Jesus' own mission—a thrust powered by his experience of God as sovereign and saving—is, as we have repeatedly stated, a fundamental cause of the church's own mission.

The Gospels faithfully transmit this aspect of Jesus' message. The God of the coming kingdom as proclaimed by Jesus in the Synoptic Gospels is a saving God revealed in Jesus' acts of teaching and healing. The approach of God's rule demands the response of conversion. It also assures transformation and salvation for those who are open to it. Even though the appearance of that rule breaks first into Israel, each Gospel makes clear that its scope is worldwide, even cosmic. Outcasts, women, Gentiles are signs of this future eruption of God's saving power. Each evangelist sees this outbreak in the perspective of history: the same God who is the focus of Israel's hope is now making himself known through Jesus and his community to the world. Luke-Acts states this most clearly in its programmatic citation of Isaiah: "All flesh shall see the salvation of our God." John's Gospel, too, is filled with this sense of God's sovereignty and his saving will. The very purpose of the Son's mission is to reveal this loving power to all the world (Jn. 3:15–16) and this mission is the pattern for the community's own responsibility in the world.

The same case can be made for all of the New Testament writings. Through his conversion experience Paul becomes convinced that both Jew and Gentile are now offered salvation. That inaugural vision is confirmed by his reflection on God's universal authority and his saving intent: "Or is God the God of Jews only? Is he not the God of Gentiles also? Yes, of Gentiles also, since God is one" (Rom. 3:29). The wisdom of God is revealed in the cross because Paul understands that this paradoxical instrument of salvation allows the absolute power of God to be revealed without any restraint of human ingenuity or prowess. God wills to save—and not even death can blunt such power. Colossians and Ephesians advance this theme even further. Christ's own lordship is itself an expression of God's own "fullness," his sovereign authority. That lordship is salvific and it extends over every layer of the universe.

The reference to universal salvation in Timothy, the elaborate cultic metaphor of Hebrews, the liturgical sweep of 1 Peter, the apocalyptic triumph of salvation in the vision of Revelation—all flow from this fundamental conviction about the absolute sovereignty of the God revealed by Jesus. The mission implications of this should be evident. For Israel this God image meant that the fate of the Gentiles could never be brushed aside. Israel itself could not risk treating Yahweh as a purely private God. His transcendent power and his outreach to the nations were a constant reminder of the limits of Israel's claim on God, even though it was convinced of its elect status.

The early Christians were likewise convinced that in Jesus the God who ruled all peoples was calling them to bring word of his salvation beyond the confines of Israel. This was the ultimate significance of the mission of Jesus and this was the impulse given to the community by his death and resurrection and the consequent gift of the Spirit. But the tendencies to underestimate the scope of God's authority and to overestimate the elect privileges of the church were faults that the early Christians shared with their Jewish forebears. As we have repeatedly seen in our analysis of the New Testament, the universal mission was taken up by the early Christians with some degree of reluctance and confusion. The tendency to remain exclusive and to close off the "outsiders" as beyond the scope of God's saving intent, or at least to qualify God's approval of them, was a constant temptation. One of the most powerful antidotes to this exclusiveness was the recall by Jesus and by the New Testament writers of the Bible's most constant and profound belief: the God of Israel was the God of the nations and nothing could stand in the way of his saving rule.

2. History as Sacred and Revealing

A belief that God acts in and through history is a basic conviction pulsating throughout the Scriptures and one that has fundamental importance for the mission question. This has been noted time and again in the biblical texts we have examined. The God of Israel is not an architectural God who creates his world and pushes it out into the universe unattended. The biblical God is discovered in historical events and human institutions. The migration from Egypt, the incursion into Canaan, the development of legal codes, the evolution of monarchical government, the trauma of exile, the life of Jesus, the struggles and victories of the early church—all these form an arena where the Bible detects God's presence. From reflection on these peak moments in their history, the biblical traditions and writers present the vision of God and human destiny that forms the scriptural heritage.

An important feature of this revelation in history is that it is not confined to explicitly *religious* events and structures. So-called secular events well beyond the bounds of what was termed sacred or religious also become the arena of salvation. The original exodus event itself can be seen as a purely political and social phenomenon. The evolution of monarchical government under David was, in the main, a result of converging historical and political forces. The invasions of Assyria and Babylonia, the dominant personalities of Cyrus and Alexander and

Epiphanes were secular events of world history. Yet these and many other secular events were interpreted as, in fact, sacred—as events in and through which the God of Israel shaped the destiny of his people.

The institutions of Israel also followed this pattern. Purely secular phenomena such as language, celebration, legal codes, and other cultural institutions were absorbed into Israel and ultimately recognized as "sacred," as structures and values in which the God of Israel made his presence felt.

A list of examples could also be drawn from the New Testament, although a more compressed time frame did not provide as much scope for reflection on secular history. Nonetheless, events such as the census of Augustus, the vagaries of Pilate, the destruction of the temple by the Romans, the reflection of Stoic philosophers on human virtue are a few examples of these same tendencies to absorb what would be considered purely secular events and institutions into the circle of the sacred and the revealing.[1] Writers of the New Testament did not hesitate to use the language and thought categories of Hellenistic culture in their reflection on the person of Jesus.

The discovery of the sacred in the secular tends to rupture the wall between them. This may be the most important consequence for the theology of mission. If God's presence can be detected in secular events and in the history of peoples outside of the zone of the sacred or the confines of Israel and the church, then the horizon of God's people must be broadened. The Gospel literature points in this direction by means of the "good" outsiders who occasionally break into the story or into the zone of the explicitly sacred. The pagan Magi follow the stars and come seeking the Messiah, offering homage to him while a Jewish king and his court remain hostile and suspicious (Matthew 2). A Roman centurion displays more faith in Jesus than an Israelite does (Mt. 8:10). A Samaritan woman becomes a proclaimer of the Word to her people (John 4). A Syro-Phoenecian woman by her dogged faith wins from Jesus a cure for her daughter (Mk. 7:29). The Ethiopian eunuch and Cornelius—upright Gentiles—take the initiative and seek baptism (Acts 8:36; 10:8). Lists of virtues found in pagan Hellenistic society are absorbed and adapted to describe the ideal Christian leader (1 Tim. 3:2-7).

These and many other examples keep pushing back the boundaries of the "sacred." God and his Spirit are at work in the lives of people who are not yet incorporated into the zone of the explicitly sacred. Therefore the Bible sees *all* human history—inside Israel and beyond—as the canvas on which God paints. The Scriptures do not draw out the final consequences of this belief, but the belief is there.

Detecting fixed patterns in the complex history of Israel and the early church is a delicate art. Recent theology has become cautious about the constraints of a salvation-history perspective that would impose a neat evolutionary schema on what were the often broken and recurring patterns of history.[2] But our review of the biblical data suggests that at least some tentative patterns do emerge and that these patterns had a significance for the early Christian mission.

A basic and pervasive pattern of history as sacred is its *forward* momentum.

Israel and the early church share an eschatological perspective. Humanity moves forward to definition, fulfillment, judgment, salvation.

In the Old Testament some limited patterns break the surface of this deeper current. In reflecting on the process of humanization and prophetic challenge, we noted at several periods of Jewish history a sequence in which the eruption of new ideas or events is followed by a time of absorption or indigenization and then in turn by a renewed time of challenge and judgment, which brings fresh perspective and new life (cf. pp. 38–39, above). This surface movement of Jewish history continually purified Israel and allowed the questions of universalism and of new relationships to outside peoples to be continually reopened. Jesus' own prophetic ministry becomes part of this recurring cycle as he shatters the exclusive boundaries laid down by his contemporaries. Paul's own tenacious support of the Gentile mission may be another instance where a fresh perspective explodes the complacency of a moment of indigenization. From the biblical point of view, such junctures are not the arbitrary dynamics of historical forces but bear the imprint of God's own Spirit.

The deeper flow underneath these riptides remains a constant. The eschatological vision of the prophetic literature and of Jewish messianism depicts a climax of salvation in which evil and death are defeated, creation is renewed, and the just united in peace and security with their God. Thus the pattern of history is projected as a movement from fragmentation to wholeness, from chaos to creation, from promise to fulfillment, from the particular and the partial to the universal and the total. Even though the fate of the Gentiles in the eschatological climax was confused and debated, there was a conviction in Israel that "on that day" Yahweh would have to deal with them. No loose ends could dangle beyond that moment when wholeness was to be achieved. Thus the Gentiles (and unfaithful Jews) might experience God's purging wrath or they might be brought as captives to Zion finally to offer homage to the God of Israel.

The New Testament shares in the eschatological perspective of Israel even though the death and resurrection of Jesus bring deep transformation of the Jewish expectations. The New Testament, too, sees the momentum of history moving rapidly and inexorably to a climactic day of salvation when the scattered will be gathered and the broken made whole. But this view of history is reinterpreted in the light of the death and resurrection of Jesus. This means that the climax of history has been foreshortened. The resurrection of Christ begins the final period of history; the day of the Lord is already breaking into the present. The community lives in a time of expectancy when the vision of a redeemed and unified humanity makes ethical demands on the present life of the believer.

Viewing history through the lens of the person and mission of Jesus also means that the eschaton is not viewed primarily as judgment upon the nations but as an opportunity for grace and reconciliation. Judgment motifs are certainly not absent from the New Testament. The final day will be a time for sorting wheat from chaff (Mt. 13:24–30), for separating sheep from goats (Mt. 25:31–46), for the destruction of the beast (Revelation 20), and so on. But the criterion of judgment no longer falls along ethnic lines. Humanity is judged by the way it has responded to God's offer of grace in Jesus. Those who have responded—Jew or Gentile—are united in God's embrace. In Peter's phrase, God is "impartial" (Acts 10:24).

Thus the momentum of sacred history is viewed by most New Testament traditions as one of unity and reconciliation. Ephesians sees the unity of Jew and Gentile in the church as a sign of this eschatological hope. There is little doubt that the early community's conviction about living in the final age paved the way for its universal mission. *Now* was the period of history when God's will to save all people and to catch them up in the final moment of his creation was apparent. Here again we have an example of how an important theological foundation for New Testament mission finds its origin deep within the vision of Israel. Because Israel had learned to detect God's presence in history and had deduced that through historical experiences God was inching his people toward ultimate salvation, the New Testament traditions were prepared to extend that reading of history to Jesus and to the life of the church. Through Jesus' mission of mercy and through the climactic event of death and resurrection, the community perceived the ultimate message of history: "The person of any nation is acceptable to him." And in its own dawning awareness and by its encounters with the Gentile world, the community learned that its responsibility in the final age of humanity was to bring this message of salvation to the end of the earth.

3. The Created World: Arena of Revelation and Salvation

This biblical current runs alongside the theology of history we have just considered. In major traditions of the Scriptures, the material universe itself is revelatory of God and shares in his universal plan of salvation. Not only human beings and their history are found to be sacred but the earth and the cosmos they inhabit belong to God. This conviction is not as pervasive in the Bible as the theology of history. But it is present and has consequences for the biblical foundations of mission.

The primal intuition of the Old Testament does not disclose a creator, architectural God but a saving God. Even though the placement of the creation account at the beginning of the canon inaugurates the story of humanity with the sculpturing of a beautiful universe and the tranquil control of the human person over the garden, the deeper impulse of the Scriptures is to see the creative process as ongoing and future-oriented. Paradise beckons in the future; it is not a lost dream in the past. God propels humanity from chaos to order, from sterility and loneliness to fruitfulness and family.

The creation myths of Genesis assert fundamental convictions of the Bible concerning material reality. Creation comes from God as an expression of his redemptive love for humanity. It is ordered to the completion and fulfillment of God's saving plan for the world. Despite the brooding presence of chaos and the entry of sin and death into the garden, creation remains intrinsically good as a product of God's compassionate love for his people.

The Wisdom traditions give special importance to a theology of the created world. It is firmly asserted that God is the author of life and, as such, did not intend the evil and death that threaten creation. Such ills are attributed to Satan and to human perversion (Wis. 1:12–16). Creation, in fact, reveals God. His wisdom and law were present at the beginning of the created process and ensure that the world is made according to the pattern of God's self-manifestation in the Hebrew Torah. The ordered beauty of the material universe reveals God to those who are attuned to this wisdom. The psalms hymn the beauty of the world and praise the God whose creative hand shaped the earth and the history of Israel.

It is not surprising that some of Israel's most lyrical descriptions of human redemption include not only the resolution of human conflict and suffering but the renewal and fulfillment of the material world itself. On the day of the Lord, Israel will taste the choice wines and rich foods of the eschatological banquet (Isa. 25:6–9). Isaiah 65 describes a re-creation of the land, a "new heavens and a new earth," where the vineyards are fruitful and death is absent. This hope in the transformation and renewal of the earth is a strong theme of later apocalyptic literature. From such concrete hopes (and the influence of Greek and Persian thought) eventually developed the Jewish conviction of resurrection. Salvation, at least for the just, involved not only the restoration of the human spirit but the transformation and renewal of the human body.

The New Testament tightly embraces this biblical view of the material world. In a limited but still significant number of texts, the capacity of the material universe to reveal God is confidently asserted. A few instances are found in the Gospel literature. The Magi are drawn to a discovery of the Messiah by their consultation of the stars (Mt. 2:2). The prologue of John utilizes Wisdom motifs to affirm that creation is made in the pattern of God's Word. Luke, in Acts, has Paul, in his speech at Lystra (Acts 14:15–17), present a strong apology for the revealing of God through creation. The motif returns in his speech to the Athenians (Acts 17:22–31). The unknown God acknowledged by the Athenians was, in fact, "the God who made the world and everything in it, being Lord of heaven and earth" (Acts 17:24).

Paul himself picks up this traditional Jewish motif in Romans. The Gentiles have no excuse for their "ungodliness . . . for what can be known about God is plain to them because God has shown it to them. Ever since the creation of the world his invisible nature, namely, his eternal power and deity, has been clearly perceived in the things which have been made" (Rom. 1:19–20).

Creation as revelatory also augments New Testament Christology. God's sovereignty is now displayed by the risen Christ's exaltation over the hostile forces of the universe. In Col. 1:15–20 and in Ephesians 2, Pauline tradition counteracts Hellenistic speculation about the blind fates that lurk in the created world and reaffirms that the material universe itself is under the sway of God's rule in and through Christ. Optimism about the revelatory power of the material world is tempered. The Gentiles failed to find God in the beauty of nature. The Magi still needed to consult with Israel and its sacred writings before completing the journey to Bethlehem. But conviction about the inherent sacredness of the material universe remains fixed despite the power of sin and weakness to blind humans to this revelation.

The New Testament also shares Israel's convictions that the material world is the proving ground of salvation. The healings and exorcisms of Jesus in the Gospels bring the power of God's rule not only to the human spirit but to human bodies, to the chaotic sea, to empty wine vats, and to poor rations. These narratives affirm that the redemptive power of Jesus transforms the material world. The eschatological vision of a new earth is beginning to unfold under the impact of the messianic mission of Jesus.

Other New Testament traditions make similar assertions. Paul's lyrical review of the power of the Spirit in Romans 8 moves from reflection on the liberation of humanity from fear (8:14–17) to the liberation of creation itself (8:19–23). Creation was "subject to futility just as humanity was." But through the power of the Spirit creation, too, will be set free and will participate in the "glorious liberty of the children of God." Pauline intuitions about the redemption of creation will be more fully developed in the cosmic Christology of Colossians and Ephesians. In these texts a victory metaphor is used. Christ's exaltation means defeat for the hostile powers of the world and leads to an experience of redemption for the entire cosmos. The witness theologies of Revelation and 1 Peter are also predicated on a positive attitude to creation as the arena of redemption. For John the dehumanizing and satanic system of the Roman empire has polluted the earth and threatened it with ultimate death. Therefore he demands of his community a witness of prophetic noninvolvement until the final moment when the victorious Christ will complete his redemptive role by transforming and renewing the created world. 1 Peter also sees creation as bound up with redemption. In contrast to the theology of Revelation, however, this book counsels Christians to exercise their witness by actively participating in the "creative structures" (1 Pet. 2:13) of the world. Such testimony might lead the world to give glory to God on the final day.

An absolutely central symbol for all of the New Testament is, of course, resurrection. What was a single tradition among many in Jewish theologies of redemption becomes normative for Christianity because of the resurrection of Jesus Christ. Resurrection, by its very nature, implies a positive attitude to matter.[3] God's redemptive power is seen as transforming the corporeal human entity and, therefore, must involve the whole network of corporality to which the human body belongs. Here, again, the New Testament joins hands with the Old. The redemptive drama envisioned by Israel and the early Christian communities was never abstract or partial. All reality—spiritual and physical—would be purified, judged, transformed, redeemed.

Several implications for a theology of mission flow from this aspect of the biblical data. Just as the biblical theology of history tended to blur the distinctions between the sacred and the profane, so, too, does the biblical theology of creation. If creation manifests God and is a participant in the redemptive drama, then the zone of the sacred has moved far beyond the borders of Israel and of the church. The very cosmos becomes the frontier of God's redemptive work. This awesome perspective should stake out the boundaries for the church's mission. This, of course, is the very step taken in the theology of Ephesians, which recognized that the cosmic Lord who is suffused with the "fullness" of God and who rules the created universe is also the Lord of the church and "head" of its body. The body must take its lead from the head.

This biblical perspective also opens up potential avenues to the non-Christian world. Non-Christians, too, are in contact with creation as a sacrament of God's presence. Paul was not optimistic about this kind of sacramental encounter between non-Christians and their creator God, and other New Testament traditions do not draw out the implications of their creation theology for nonbelievers. The biblical texts are directed solely to the communities of Israel and the early church and never seek, sympathetically or adequately, to engage the nonbeliever except as someone in need of salvation. However, the biblical foundations for respectful dialogue with the religious experience of non-Christians (and non-Jews) are in place.

The biblical perspective on creation also suggests that mission, in a biblical sense, is not confined to survival of the human spirit or, in the traditional slogan, to "saving souls" or "making converts." Redemption is total: body, spirit, structure, world, cosmos. Therefore a mission that participates in the redemptive drama must have the same breadth. The prophetic call to justice that rumbles through the Old Testament certainly conceived of the "mission" of Israel in this holistic sense. The Gospels portray Jesus not only as teacher but as challenger of institutions, healer of bodies, and calmer of seas. This is the exact mission shared with the disciples in the Synoptic mission discourses. Paul, too, carried out his mission not only in word but "by word and deed, by the power of signs and wonders" (Rom. 15:18–19), and the surest symptom of his success was the formation of Christian communities in which care and sensitivity to the poor were instinctive. A biblical sense of mission, in short, extends beyond the spiritual and the verbal to include humanity's vital and corporeal relationship to the material universe. That sacred creation both manifests God and, mysteriously, is called to participate in the process of redemption.

4. Religious Experience: Catalyst to Mission

One of the most important impulses to mission in the Bible is religious experience. This motif obviously differs from the previous three we have considered; here we are speaking of a locus or a dynamic that propels the biblical perspective to mission rather than a theological current with intrinsic universal consequences. But it is precisely in the crucible of religious experience that Israel and the early Christian community forged a theology of God's sovereignty, a theology of history, and a theology of creation. Here, too, biblical leaders from Moses to Paul found the energy to translate intuitions into action. Because of its vital significance to the mission question we must consider this dynamic of biblical religion as one of the foundations for mission.

This survey of the Old Testament has located several junctures where Israel's religious experience and the question of universalism intersected. The liturgical life of Israel functioned as a communal memory, drawing on past "secular" events such as liberation from Egypt or settlement in the land, and then amplified and celebrated these as moments of Israel's *sacred* history. This liturgy enabled Israel to express its experience of God's action in history: here the mysterious workings of providence beneath the flow of secular events could be sounded and brought to the surface. This process frayed the boundary between the sacred and the profane and gave Israel the potential to see God at work beyond the confines of its own national story.

At the same time liturgy offered Israel a moment of solidarity with non-Israelite religions. Many of the elements of Jewish worship, such as harvest feasts and sacrifice rituals, began as pagan cults drawn from the surrounding cultures. They were, of course, thoroughly reinterpreted and adapted by Judaism, but their origin in the common religious impulses of other cultures remained a fact. This bond with the religious experience of other cultures was not positively exploited by the Bible. The Jewish cult, more often than not, was seen as a source of identification for Israel and as a mark of sharp contrast with the idolatries of the pagans. However, there are isolated moments when the religious potential of the pagan is acknowledged. The story of the Ninevite's response to Jonah's preaching, for example, challenged Israel's own narrowness and showed remarkable respect for the religious experience of a detested enemy. The psalmist recognized people of Rahab and Babylon, of Philistia, Tyre, and Ethiopia as born in Jerusalem and registered there among the chosen ones (Psalm 87). This same dynamic will be at work in the New Testament writings.

The religious experience of Israel was not confined to official cultic acts. God could touch the heart of the Jew in almost every moment of life: a vocational choice, a defeat or suffering, an experience of poetic rapture, the triumph of victory or the ashes of frustration. The Bible is studded with texts that transmit the profound experiences of a believing people.

It is surely no accident that in such moments Israel exhibited its most expansive spirit. When the awesome transcendence of the God of Israel was most intensely felt, religious leaders could gaze at distant coastlands and see Israel in proper perspective. Almost all of the Old Testament texts that have a universal perspective flow from such intuitive religious moments: the call to the nations felt by Jeremiah (1:5) and by Deutero-Isaiah (49:1-7), the hymns to creation as revealing God in Wisdom, the ecstasy of the psalms.

The same dynamic courses through the New Testament. Intimate experiences of the awesome power, compassion, and saving intent of the God of Israel break open the horizon. The taproot of Jesus' own ministry sinks deep into his experience of God. Trust in a God who searches for the lost sheep or the lost coin or the lost son empowers Jesus to reach out to tax collectors and sinners (Lk. 15:1-2). His call to cross the ultimate boundary and to "love your enemy" is justified by the experience of a God who "makes the sun rise on the evil and the good, and sends rain on the just and the unjust" (Mt. 5:45). The religious experience of Jesus ultimately has staggering consequences for the mission theology of the New Testament. The Gospel literature uses the pattern of Jesus' ministry—a ministry that flowed from his concept of God—as the norm for the universal mission of the church.

The religious experience of Paul must also be singled out. Our study of Paul suggests that his conversion was the starting point and foundation for his own dynamic theology. The dramatic transformation that Paul experienced in his view of history,.of the Gentiles, and of his own call vividly illustrates the importance of religious experience for the biblical view of mission. Paul's encounter with the risen Christ effected a profound renewal in Paul's awareness of God's transcendent power. The God of Israel had chosen to save all people—Jew and Gentile alike—through the death and resurrection of Jesus. From that moment, according to Paul's own testimony, his view of how God was working in history was shattered, and a new universal perspective catapulted a Pharisee of the Pharisees into the unexpected role of apostle to the Gentiles.

Genuine encounters with the biblical God lead, then, to an expanded vision of humanity and of history. This expansiveness permeates the hymns of the New Testament, products of the liturgical experience of the early church. The fragments of hymns found in Jn. 1:1–18, Phil. 2:6–11, and Col. 1:15–20 use Wisdom motifs to sketch the story of Christ's redemptive mission on a cosmic scale. The preexistent redeemer was sent from the Father to establish his sovereignty over all the cosmos. The hymn fragment in 1 Tim. 3:16 couples such a cosmic vision directly to the universal mission of the church ("Preached among the nations, believed on in the world"). The book of Revelation presents the entire drama of universal salvation in a visionary and liturgical atmosphere, and 1 Peter employs the liturgical motif of "glory" to affirm the ultimate triumph of God's plan of salvation and the participation of believers and nonbelievers in the final acclamation on the day of the Lord.

We should note that such religious experiences also provide a basis for kinship with those outside the biblical community. Here we return to a theme we considered above under the rubric of "History as Sacred and Revealing." The New Testament, in particular, shows sympathy for the upright and God-fearing pagan who already seems to have encountered the same God of Israel revealed by the Old Testament and proclaimed by Jesus. The Magi have had a vision of the star, a religious experience that draws them to Israel. The centurion already has faith that puts God's people to shame. Even before baptism Cornelius was, as Luke emphasizes, "a devout man who feared God with all his household, gave alms liberally to the poor, and prayed constantly to God" (Acts 10:2). Luke also presents Paul as acknowledging with respect the Athenians' cult to the "unknown god" (Acts 17:22).

These remain intriguing echoes in the New Testament literature, but their presence should not be overlooked or underestimated. Luke may well have summed up the daring but tentative viewpoint of the New Testament concerning the genuine religious experience of a non-Christian: "Truly I perceive that God shows no partiality, but in every nation anyone who fears him and does what is right is acceptable to him" (Acts 10:34). The Gentiles' ability to respond to the gospel is linked to their "fear of God," the same God who compelled the community to go to the pagan world in the first place. The willingness of Gentiles to respond to the gospel (often in contrast to the resistance met in the mission to Israel) is one of the prime justifications for a universal mission in the New Testament. Matthew, for example, raises this to a basic theological principle: The vineyard is taken away from the tenants and given to others "who will produce its fruits" (21:43). The sheep enter the kingdom because they carry out the love command (Mt. 25:31-36). Other New Testament authors work from the same vantage point; the ultimate justification of the decision to preach to the Gentiles is the fact that the Gentiles *respond* to the gospel. The New Testament sees this not as a lucky accident but as the manifestation of God's plan, a plan already initiated in Jesus' openness to peripheral peoples. God in his Spirit had already been at work, touching the hearts of the Gentiles and making them open to the proclamation of the gospel. Peter's words brook no argument: "If then God gave the same gift to them as he gave to us when we believed in the Lord Jesus Christ, who was I that I could withstand God?" (Acts 11:17).

This seems to imply that religious experience is an equalizer. Peter senses that the Spirit encountered by Cornelius is the same Spirit encountered by the Christians. Paul (in Acts) states that the unknown god saluted by the Athenians is the God known through Jesus. In writing to the Romans, Paul is sure that the God who can be met in nature (but, in fact, was ignored) is the same God who gave the law, the God who sent Jesus. Contemplation is expansive and equalizing. And for that reason, in both the Old and New Testaments, personal encounters with the sovereign and compassionate God of Israel provide the most profound and daring glimpses into the universal mission of God's people.

These themes, the sovereignty of God, the sacredness of history, the revelatory and salvific character of creation, and the dynamics of religious experience are the major conduits for a biblical theology of mission. They provide the intimations of universalism in the Old Testament and from them flow the explicit theologies of universal mission found in the various New Testament traditions.

THE MODALITIES OF MISSION

The biblical message of salvation, which we reviewed in the previous section, did not hang in midair. It was transmitted by religious leaders in Israel and the early church through an array of means ranging from the spoken word to eloquent prophetic symbol. In this section we want to review these different modes of communication. We do not imply that the biblical style of mission is absolutely normative for mission today. There is no definitive biblical recipe for proclaiming the Word of God. Then as now, the choice of means or strategy for communicating with people inside or outside the community will depend on the circumstances of culture and the prudential judgment and creativity of the communicator. Nevertheless there is a value in reflecting on the biblical patterns of evangelization. Some modes of communication are perennial and transcend a peculiar culture.

The spectrum of biblical communication might, therefore, be a fruitful review for modern evangelizers.

Since only in the New Testament do we find explicit examples of evangelization, we shall begin there, although we shall discover that these mission methods have precedents in the Old Testament.

Direct Proclamation

The most important means of evangelization in the early church was direct proclamation. Missionary preachers announced the good news of salvation and taught its implications to those who would listen. We have to make this judgment about the importance of "preaching" (taken in the broadest sense, that is, of direct and explicit communication in a variety of possible settings) even though we have no direct evidence of this material. As we have already pointed out, none of the New Testament writings offers genuine transcripts of the missionary preaching of the early community. The texts themselves are meant for the believers. Acts provides examples of sermons by Peter and by Paul, but they are Lucan constructions. Paul's own letters give us only brief hints of his initial evangelization to his communities.

Despite the limited evidence, we can still be confident that direct verbal communication of the gospel was the most important instrument of evangelization in the early church. Paul's own career is a prime example. He clearly states his "compulsion" to preach the gospel wherever possible. Even though Paul stands as a colossus in the missionary landscape of the early church, we know that a host of other itinerant missionaries must have crisscrossed the Mediterranean world.[4] The gospel had reached Rome before Paul, and in his letters Paul readily acknowledges many other missionaries such as Epiphanus, Silvanus, Apollos, Phoebe, to name but a few. Although in his letters Paul does not insist on the point, we may presume he expected the communities themselves to spread the gospel in their own areas. He congratulates the Thessalonians on this very point (1 Thess. 1:7-8). Acts, too, alludes to the proclamation of the gospel in Antioch and other centers by traveling missionaries other than Paul and his companions. The Gospels also affirm this by including the charge to proclaim the message of the kingdom in the mission discourses (cf. Mk. 3:14; 6:12; Mt. 10:7; Lk. 9:2). These discourses, written after Paul's career, were undoubtedly meant to instruct the community and its leaders on the demands of discipleship. Nor should one overlook the "informal proclamation" that must have gone on in the interaction of Christians with their non-Christian families and neighbors. One important source for the spread of the gospel was probably diaspora Jews who may have come into contact with Christians in Jerusalem or in their local diaspora synagogue and then may have begun to spread their new faith in their own family circle. Aquila and Priscilla, the couple who fled Rome and befriended Paul at Corinth, may be such an example. The author of 1 Peter exhorts the wives of non-Christians to exploit their situation and to proclaim the gospel, even if it must be by a "silent word" because of a husband's hostility.

We do not know whether the early church used the *written* word for missionary purposes. It is difficult to imagine the kind of setting in which this would be possible or advantageous. The liturgical and catechetical assemblies of the Christian communities provided a natural forum for the written texts sent to them, but it is not likely that the earliest generations would have had many opportunities to write about the gospel to Jewish or non-Christian groups. We have pointed out, however, that many of the New Testament texts themselves have a missionary purpose, even though written for believers. Their goal is not, technically speaking, "propaganda," but the Gospels and most of the other New Testament writings were intended to give a mission perspective to the Christians themselves. Thus the written word becomes a special medium of mission.

Direct proclamation of messages of salvation has deep biblical roots. The Gospels portray Jesus as a communicator of the word. A major part of his ministry as presented by all four evangelists involved preaching and teaching. The parables, effective oral proclamation, are the hallmarks of the historical Jesus. The poetic characterization of Jesus by John's Gospel and by Hebrews as "Word" is ingenious and accurate.

The roots of this mode go back even deeper in biblical tradition. Judaism is a religion of the "Word," and announcement of the message of salvation characterizes biblical religion from the speeches of Moses to the apocalyptic vision of Daniel. The Old Testament, particularly the prophetic traditions, had developed a sophisticated theology of the Word. God's Word, as in the famous text of Isaiah 55:9-11, was experienced as creative and inevitably fruitful. The power of the Word is seen as a quasi-personal force, communicating to Israel the saving power of the God who is not silent and distant, but who speaks to his people. The instinctive Christian trust in the power of the spoken word as a means for communicating the message of salvation was part of the heritage received from Judaism.

Prophetic Challenge in Word and Sign

Another important medium for communicating the mission message of the early church was "prophetic" proclamation. "Prophets" had an important ministry in the early church.[5] They were divinely inspired teachers, interpreters of traditions, and leaders of community prayer. But the prophetic style of communication we are referring to was probably not limited to those who were explicitly designated "prophet" in the community. Prophetic ministry as classically expressed in Israel involved dramatic challenges, delivered in word or symbolic gesture, to attitudes or structures considered incompatible with the message of salvation. This dimension of the prophetic vocation is also found in the New Testament and has important mission consequences. Even though such prophetic proclamation includes direct verbal communication and is, therefore, similar to our first category (direct proclamation), its prominence in biblical literature justifies a separate treatment.

There is little doubt that prophetic proclamation had an important part in the mission of the early church. Although each of the Gospels wraps the prophetic mantle around Jesus, Luke makes this a dominant role. Jesus is the Spirit-filled prophet who challenges the exclusive attitude of his contemporaries and suffers the rejection that the prophets of Israel had endured before him. Not only does Jesus blister false attitudes and false values by his preaching and storytelling, but he also chooses the apt prophetic sign: table fellowship with outcasts, healings on the Sabbath, cleansing of the temple, and so forth. This Spirit-filled mission is now instruction for the church. And the apostolic missionaries—Peter, John, Paul, Barnabas, and others—take up the prophetic mantle in their own missionary careers, and also suffer the consequences. John's Gospel sees a prophetic challenge to the world as a function of the Paraclete, the very Spirit breathed into those sent on mission. Paul understands his own vocation against the background of the call of Isaiah and Jeremiah.

The prophetic mode is also central to the theology of the book of Revelation. The author sees his exhortation to the community as a word of prophecy, an inspired vision challenging the church. But, even more important, he exhorts his community to take a prophetic stance toward the dehumanizing and anti-God Roman empire. The stance of his Christian opponents is vigorously rejected. They apparently counseled a compromise solution on such questions as eating meats that had been offered to idols. John will permit no such solution. The communities are asked to proclaim the gospel by the symbolic gesture of noninvolvement, a provocative prophetic stance that challenged the absolute claims of the empire.

The debt owed to the Old Testament for this model of missionary communication should be obvious. The prophets represented a crucial and recurring phase in the biblical experience. When Israel tended to become narrow or rigid or deadened to its responsibilities under the covenant, the voice of the prophets exploded such complacency and brought new life and vision—often at the cost of suffering and rejection to the prophet. The message of salvation for Israel came with the biting challenge of the prophetic word and the prophetic sign. It was a message Israel repeatedly rejected but whose savor it would never forget. Through Jesus that same prophetic mode of proclamation worked its way into the missionary consciousness of the early church. In the light of this tradition the early preachers found the backbone to confront the world, and they found meaning in their own experience of suffering on behalf of the gospel.

"Witness" on behalf of the Gospel

The early Christian community recognized that the message of salvation would be brought to the "end of the earth" not only by what the church preached to the Gentile world but by the way it lived and what actions it took. Therefore the "witnesss" or testimony given by Christian living was another important mode of mission in the early church.

Several features of this witness are highlighted in the New Testament. One of the most important was the bond of unity and love that was to characterize the life of the community itself. Practically every New Testament writing stresses this essential aspect of Christian life but, in some instances, its witness value was explicitly noted. We saw that Paul, for example, considered the establishment of community to be the ultimate goal of his mission. These centers of fellowship became signs of the final redemption. Paul was also conscious that the life of the community had a potential witness value for outsiders. Therefore Paul was embarrassed when the Corinthians washed the community's linen in public by taking disputes into civil courts (1 Cor. 6:1-6). He was also aware that the liturgical assemblies of the community could attract outsiders and should, therefore, be sensitive to them (1 Cor. 14:16, 23).

Ephesians lifts the notion of community to a universal principle of mission. The bond of reconciliation and unity between the once mutually hostile Jews and Gentiles is a sign and model of the cosmic reconciliation effected by Christ. Therefore the author pleads that the Christians be "eager to maintain the unity of the Spirit in the bond of peace" (Eph. 4:3).

The motif is not absent in the Gospel literature. The Synoptics describe Jesus' ministry as one of forming community. The disciples are drawn together around him in faith and love. Jesus celebrates meals of fellowship with outcasts and sinners. Mark emphasizes Jesus' mission of unity between Jewish and Gentile sides of the lake of Galilee. Matthew, too, signals the eventual unity of the Gentiles with God's people and emphasizes the need for reconciliation within the community itself. Luke presents the establishment of community as one of the primary results of the missionary preaching of the apostles (Acts 2:43-47; 4:32-35). This sign of the renewed Israel finds "favor with all the people" (Acts 2:47). More than any other evangelist, John makes the communal life of the church a means of witness: "By this all people will know that you are my disciples, if you have love for one another" (Jn. 13:35).

The early church understood an equation so simple that it could be overlooked: the love and compassion the Christians were able to give each other was a compelling testimony on behalf of the God who called them together. The Greco-Roman world of the first century was starved for meaning and strongly inclined to religious and civic support groups.[6] It is probable that the strong and refreshing community life of the early church was one of its most important missionary activities.

Another mode of "witness" highlighted in some New Testament traditions is "good conduct" or "good citizenship." Christians were exhorted to be obedient to legitimate civil authority and to be upright citizens. To some extent this was a prudential stance; in order to ensure its survival, the early church had to offset the suspicion of the Roman state and demonstrate that Christianity was not a subversive group. Some of this apologetic motivation may be behind Paul's exhortation to good citizenship in Romans 13. But in the case of 1 Peter, as we have seen, good conduct or citizenship goes far beyond the goal of keeping peace with Roman authorities. For the author of the letter, good conduct was a powerful means of witness to the gospel. Active participation in "created institutions" (1 Pet. 2:11), while maintaining one's fear of God and commitment to the gospel, would help to silence the abuse heaped on the community and, eventually, would help to prompt the nonbeliever to glorify God. The wives of non-Christians were asked to assume the same demanding role: by their integrity and gentleness of spirit they could give witness to their husbands.

A motif that runs through almost all of the New Testament mission texts might be introduced here: apostolic suffering. The mission discourses of the Synoptic Gospels affirm that the fate of those sent to proclaim the gospel will be the same as that of their master: persecution, rejection, even death. Paul takes inventory of the suffering he has endured in carrying out his missionary vocation. The model of the suffering Jesus is used in 1 Peter to tell the newly baptized Christians about their call to mission in the world. Revelation speaks openly of endurance and martyrdom in the call of the gospel.

Such missionary suffering is not simply the price that must be paid for authentic and fearless proclamation of the gospel to a hostile world. The suffering itself becomes part of the mission. This atonement motif becomes clear in the Pauline and deutero-Pauline traditions. Paul senses that his imprisonment and other sufferings "serve to advance the gospel" (Phil. 1:12). This happens not only because it gives witness to Christian and non-Christian alike (as Paul notes in Phil. 1:12–18), but mysteriously, through his sufferings, Paul participates in the redemptive death and resurrection of Jesus. The weakness and hardships he endures mean "death . . . at work" in Paul but "life" in his Christians. The same motif emerges in the deutero-Pauline letters. Ephesians portrays Paul as a "prisoner of Christ" (Eph. 3:1; 4:1), who as an apostle suffers for the community (Eph. 3:13). The theme is strong in 2 Timothy. Paul exhorts Timothy to be willing to "testify to our Lord" and to "share in suffering for the gospel in the power of God" (2 Tim. 1:18). Paul's vocation as "preacher and apostle and teacher" necessarily involves suffering (2 Tim. 1:11–12). Such sufferings are redemptive and share in the salvific work of God (2 Tim. 2:8–13). As we noted in our discussion of the Pastorals, Paul's missionary example is now being turned into a model of church *leadership*. But the notion of suffering as having a witness value in the mission itself still lingers.

The basis for this belief is the experience of Jesus. The ultimate exercise of his life-giving mission was his redemptive death. Crucifixion "on behalf of others," "the just for the unjust," becomes in early Christian thought the fundamental paradigm of the mission of the church. The theology of atonement strikes deep roots into the Bible.[7] The Servant figure in the writings of Deutero-Isaiah exercises his God-given mission by suffering on behalf of the community of Israel. This haunting paradigm had a powerful impact on New Testament soteriology and, ultimately, on its perception of the meaning of suffering endured in the cause of the gospel.

The quality of the community's life was recognized as part of its mission. The bond of love and unity among Christians, the commitment to good citizenship, and the suffering endured for others were part of their testimony to the gospel and, as such, proclaimed the good news as effectively as any word. This dimension of the mission was not unrelated to Israel's own destiny. God's people were expected to be a "light to the nations." The peoples of the earth were to gaze on Israel and to break out in wonder and praise at the greatness of Israel's God. This witness was not clearly understood as an active mission on behalf of the Gentiles, but in the service of Israel and its sovereign God. Nevertheless the exemplary role of God's people among the nations was a vocation that the church received from Judaism and one that would be thoroughly transformed by the missionary consciousness of the New Testament.

Mission as Personal and Social Transformation

The mission mandate of the early church was not limited to proclamation and witness. The good news of salvation was also transmitted by direct transforming action on the part of Christians. The Bible understood that salvation was not an abstract idea. The salvation promised by God meant the end of death, tears, and injustice; it meant good wine, many children, genuine peace. Action taken to effect this renewal of life was salvific action. Obviously the goal of all Christian mission, whether by word, witness, or direct action, is the transformation of human life under the impact of the gospel. Paul, for example, fully expected that conversion would involve a radical change of heart and be expressed in a different set of values and modes of behavior. Therefore he chides his Christians for immorality, or for failing to live a genuine communal existence (1 Cor. 11:17–22). But the modality we are referring to here is not simply the action expected to flow from conversion. We are referring to communication of the gospel itself by undertaking direct redemptive action on behalf of others.

This type of mission permeates the portrayal of Jesus' ministry in the gospel. He not only speaks about salvation; he accomplishes it through his healings and his exorcisms. Jesus' provocative befriending of the outcasts was not only a prophetic witness to God's compassion but actually broke down arbitrary boundaries and gave to the alienated a genuine experience of salvation. These acts of Jesus anticipated the full experience of salvation expected by Israel in the end-time. The mission discourses of the Synoptics are careful to include such acts of transforming power in their lists of the missionary responsibilities of apostles and disciples. They, too, were sent to cure and to cast out evil, to proclaim good news to the poor. In Acts the missionary work of the apostles includes transforming cures in the style of Jesus' own powerful redemptive mission. In the Johannine tradition, the miracles of Jesus are used primarily for Christological purposes; the signs disclose Jesus' identity as revealer of the Father. But the healings *are* narrated and never become fully abstract. John portrays a Jesus who heals paralysis (Jn. 5:1–18) and blindness (John 9), who overcomes death (John 11) and provides the messianic wine (Jn. 2:1–12), a vivid sign of the expected salvation. For the disciples, then, "to be sent" as this Jesus was sent (Jn. 17:19; 20:21) must also include direct acts of redemption.

Luke portrays Paul not only as preacher but also as miracle worker (Acts 19:11–12; 20:7–12). This might seem to clash with Paul's own emphasis on preaching in the description of his ministry that seeps through his letters. But, in fact, Paul too refers to *acts* of power that he has accomplished as part of his missionary work: "For I will not venture to speak of anything except what Christ has wrought through me to win obedience from the Gentiles, by word and deed, by the power of signs and wonders, by the power of the Holy Spirit" (Rom. 15:18-19).

Such texts demonstrate that the early Christians were conscious of exercising their mission not only by oral proclamation or by the exemplary value of their lives but also by direct action on behalf of humanity. The good news of salvation was communicated in the very experience of liberating a human body or a human institution from the grip of death and injustice.

THE BIBLE AND CONTEMPORARY MISSION

The fact that we have entitled this study *"Biblical* Foundations for Mission" clearly implies that other shafts need to be driven deep into our spiritual and intellectual heritage in order to support a vigorous contemporary theology of mission. Not just exegesis, but systematic theology, church history, sociology, and political science—to name a few—must be heard from. We have been reflecting on the biblical side of the equation.

However limited in the construction of a comprehensive theology, the biblical data remain unique and crucial. The biblical witness has been and will be the ultimate catalyst for the universal mission of the church. The biblical call to "go to the end of the earth" will ring in the ears of heroic Christians even if our communal reflection on why we should do so may cause hesitation.

What, then, are the spurs to mission that the biblical evidence leaves to the church? What are some of the questions, hopes, and problems that contemporary theologians and church leaders might take away from a close reading of the Bible on the question of mission? We offer the following as some of the major issues the church needs to address.

A Universal God

The Bible gives awesome witness to the universal sovereignty of God. His lordship and provident care transcend every human boundary—even those of Israel and the church. His compassionate embrace of humanity cannot be circumscribed by our careful moral calculations. The biblical story constantly shatters the efforts of religious people to bottle up God.

Thus the biblical God is the ultimate source of mission and the ultimate catalyst to the church's instinct to move beyond the boundaries of a particular culture or national group. The universal saving rule of God stands as the final seal on our common humanity. No human being or social group can be considered as absolutely alien when, in fact, the deepest impulse of biblical religion is that the God of Israel and the God of Jesus is the God of everyone. The biblical God remained "catholic" even when his people were not. This fundamental biblical conviction about the nature of God remains the most provocative challenge to the contemporary church. Any claim to exclusivity or religious triumphalism will eventually run aground on the expansive vision of the biblical God.

A Progressive Eschatology

The Scriptures communicate a dynamic and developmental view of world history. God moves humanity forward toward fulfillment and destiny, not backward or in circles. The thrust of history, of biblical eschatology, is, in fact, progressively *inclusive* in nature. Not just Israel or the church but the nations and even the cosmic powers will be caught up in the promised end-time. The various biblical traditions on judgment involve a final assessment of human responsibility, a sorting out of just and unjust, with rewards for the elect and punishment for the reprobate. But no one can be a mere spectator in the final drama. The nations may have been on the periphery of Israel's consciousness for most of its history. But Israel knew that as history progressed to its termination, the nations would be caught up in God's salvific plan. This view of history is a critical component of the early church's mission theology. The early Christian communities were convinced that, through the resurrection of Jesus, God had declared, *"Now* is the acceptable time, *now* is the day of salvation."

Thus the biblical view of history is, in the final analysis, decisively optimistic. The final word is life, not death. The final action is gathering and fulfillment, not dispersal and frustration. This view of history, as apocalyptic literature made clear, is not naive. The march to the end-time involves bitter suffering and cataclysmic transformation. But the end is without doubt salvific, because God will have the last Word.

From a biblical perspective, therefore, the church can have no meaningful mission to humanity unless it offers a positive vision of human destiny. If the church and its leaders become moral hand-wringers and prophets only of doom, then Christian mission is reduced to a salvage operation for a select few rather than a cause on behalf of the many. A theology of history is one of the church's prime mission responsibilities.

A Dialectic between Outreach and Identity

The biblical witness also alerts us to a continual and inevitable dialectic between the call to mission and the pastoral needs of the already gathered community. Israel itself veered from absorbing reflection on its own elect status to occasional realizations of Yahweh at work beyond its own border. The apostolic church, too, had no easy task in balancing its thrust toward the Gentile world with a need for its own stability and religious identity. This issue, in fact, dominates Jesus' historical ministry: the concern of his contemporaries for identity was punctured by Jesus' moves to the outcasts and sinners.

The Bible does more than take note of this inevitable balancing act between identity and mission. From the Christian perspective, at least, God's scale tilts in favor of outreach over identity. Even in the Old Testament the scars of a too narrow concern with identity, with possession of the land, with suspicion of the outsider can be clearly seen.[8] Jesus stands as the disturber of the status quo, as one who shatters the canons of propriety in the cause of an unexpectedly compassionate God. The most dynamic and vivifying impulses of the New Testament come from the missionary energy of Paul, the universal vision of the Gospels, the energetic prophetic challenge of Revelation, the cosmic hopes of Ephesians, to name but a few sources. The watchword is outreach over identity, even though the latter has obvious importance.

No church that affirms a universal mission responsibility should forget that such a mission cuts both ways. A Christian community that feels compelled to share the good news of salvation across a cultural or social boundary must be prepared to have its own hegemony challenged. If the gospel is universal, it cannot be expressed exclusively in European or Latin American or Asian or male or middle-class categories. Ultimately the affirmation of the universal mission will cause a revolution in the very categories in which we reflect on the gospel itself; that is a sure lesson of the biblical story. The same holds true for ecclesiology. The church will not be able to affirm true universalism and yet maintain (or at least yearn for) absolute uniformity and highly centralized structures. This is a sobering lesson of the biblical story, especially that of Jesus and the early church. It is no accident that the most powerful currents of reform in the church today come from mission countries rather than from the established churches of the West.

The Role of Religious Leadership

Commitment to a universal mission has consequences not only for the church's self-consciousness and its structures, but also for religious leadership. This too is a chapter of the biblical story. Models of leadership were learned from secular culture. The king, the prophet, the teacher, the overseer or *episkopos* were not the products of direct revelation but were roles that had analogies outside Israel and the church. Yet time and again the impulses that quickened the life of the biblical community and widened its horizons came from the intuitions and courageous visions of its leaders. Moses, David, the classical prophets, Jesus, Paul, the evangelists: on the lives of these and other great characters of the biblical history, the universal mission was built.

At times within the biblical stories of Israel and the church, religious leadership exercises a legitimate *conserving* function. David and Solomon consolidate the unity of Israel under a monarchic structure. Ezra and Nehemiah rebuild after the shattering experience of exile. Peter and the Twelve are presented by Luke as the rallying point for the Jerusalem community. But one senses that the heart of the biblical story is not here. The spirit of biblical religion that lingers long after the structures have been shattered is found in the expansive voices of Amos, Isaiah, Jeremiah. Even when Israel rejected the intuition of its prophets, it cherished their dreams. The same is true of the New Testament. The Jesus of the Gospels is not portrayed as an agent of stability but as an explosive prophetic presence who calls his people to new visions of God and humanity. In Acts, Luke wants to present an orderly account of the community's history, but even in his construction the most vital moments come when Peter sheds his caution and accepts Cornelius and when the stage is dominated by the revolutionary mission of Paul.

In conserving the Pauline letters, the early church retained not only the richness of Paul's mission theology but the object lesson of his ministry. His letters show evidence that Paul had to fight a constant rearguard action in which he defended the universalism of the gospel against factions who wanted, cautiously, to constrict that vision.

In short, the biblical saga reveals that the struggle to be universal was carried out by the convictions and courage of inspired religious leaders, leaders often rejected and harassed by their own contemporaries. Therefore the biblical call to mission is, at the same time, a summons to courageous leadership. The cross-cultural missionary will often have to play that role: a distant voice in his or her home church and a peripheral voice in the culture to which the missionary is called. But those whose Christian lives are driven by a profound intuition of the authentically universal scope of the gospel will inevitably be thrust into this prophetic role. By the same token the biblical call to mission stands as a word of warning to church authorities whose overanxiety to preserve the church's identity could stifle the church's openness to the outside.

The Value of Religious Experience

The vital function of the religious leader who is able to sustain intuitions of universalism and move them to expression in the church's life recalls another facet of the biblical heritage. Some of the most vivid moments of universalism in the Scriptures occur in connection with religious experience. It was in the prayers, hymns, and poetry of Israel and the early church that the awesome sweep of God's saving love and the mystery of Jesus' person were glimpsed. Here, too, a mysterious communion was felt with those "in the coastlands," with the people "of any nation who fear God" (Acts 10:35). The creative imagination of the biblical people was able to transcend the narrow confines of its official theology and structures.

This communion between religious experience and universal mission needs further exploration in systematic and pastoral theology. A case might be made that the church became more certain of its boundaries in direct proportion to the elaboration and systematization of its belief. The instinctive experiences of solidarity many Christians have felt with the religious sense of other traditions and cultures far outstrip regulations on ecumenical activity. Obviously it is no solution for the church to shed either its intellectual heritage or the prudent regulation of contact with other religions. But the biblical heritage does spur us to give more pastoral and theological weight to pastoral intuitions of solidarity with those beyond our boundaries.

The Scriptures as Source of Vision and Strategy

One of the most vital functions of the Scriptures is to suffuse the mind and heart of the church with a vision. The biblical stories and metaphors become the language of Christian hope.⁹ We long for "the new Jerusalem," a home "without tears," a people who are "neither Jew nor Greek, male or female, slave or free but all one in Christ Jesus." These and a multitude of other biblical metaphors continually nourish a world-view of faith that sees unity and peace as the God-given destiny of humankind. Even when the evidence of history seems to shatter that dream brutally, the biblical witness is clung to. This function of the Scriptures is seldom if ever replaced by other church documents or by the writings of individual Christians. The wisdom and authority of the Scriptures make its language of hope the common coin of Christianity.

A similar kind of authority seems to touch the missionary strategies found in the Bible. Such roles as prophet, apostle, atoning servant, teacher, healer, martyr have become classical categories used to interpret and authenticate contemporary forms of ministry.

More than once in this study we have insisted that hard-and-fast solutions to pastoral issues cannot be found by the imposition of biblical texts or biblical categories onto a modern situation. But properly understood and interpreted, the biblical models of mission can prove a valuable stimulus for contemporary ministry. These models evolved from the recurring impact of God's transforming Word on a community of belief. In Israel and in the early church, cycles occur of explosive intervention, leisurely indigenization, and prophetic critique. The firm belief in God's presence in history and his compassionate will to commune with his people led to repeated emphasis on the power of communication, of "word," and thus the roles of prophet, apostle, and evangelist are born. The biblical hope of salvation and the reality of evil and sin led to the ministry of servant, of healer, of enduring witness.

Many of these styles of missionary leadership emerge in dialogue between the biblical traditions and the particular social and political fabric of a given period in biblical history. Thus prophets arose when the process of humanization or absorption of pagan cultures had become too fixed or complacent. The martyr or witness arose when the biblical people found themselves a minority in a hostile environment. In the Bible there is no fixed pattern for mission but a plurality of responses to different circumstances.

This is an aspect of the Bible that the church needs to be attentive to when it uses the Scriptures as inspiration for its mission. The Bible reminds us that pastoral responses call for sensitivity to the contours of culture and time. The long span of the biblical drama compressed into the narrow arena of Palestine is now played out on a world stage. Some areas of the church's mission in East Africa or Papua New Guinea may be analogous to the patriarchal period of the biblical history, while the complexities of urban culture in Japan or the United States exceed that of any scenario in the Bible. The biblical models offer stimulating possibilities and instructive patterns but no sure guarantees. What remains constant is the presence of a sovereign and compassionate God moving his people toward the fulfillment of their dreams.

Pluralism as a Value

In a time when, at least in Roman Catholic tradition, centralization and orthodoxy seem to have become a concern of church leadership, it is important to underscore the pluralism inherent in the biblical theology of mission. Pluralism is understood here as legitimate diversity in the context of fundamental unity. Such pluralism is, of course, found on a descriptive level in the sheer variety of traditions and roles that make up the scriptural data on mission. There is no one cohesive "theology" of mission in the Bible, but a series of traditions, often though not always interrelated, which ultimately converge around the figure of Jesus and the church's impulse to proclaim the good news of salvation to the world.

Pluralism is not limited to this variety of theological motifs. On a deeper level pluralism is part of the basic vision of the Christian mission itself. It is a part of the destiny of humanity. The biblical story in its broadest sense moves from the single to the multiple, from the uniform to the plural. It is a story of humanity's pilgrimage toward God that begins as a saga of one people and one land. From a Christian perspective that journey takes a dramatic turn, and the ranks of the pilgrims are swelled by all the nations of the earth. At its deepest level, the vision is not one of uniformity: Christianity is not an ethnocentric religion. Gentiles need not become Jews; Chinese need not become Italian or Polish. The universalism of the gospel means that in faith one can find solidarity in and through the plurality of nations and bloodstreams. The salvation-history perspective of the New Testament sees the momentum of God's plan as inclusive and pluralistic.[10]

The lesson to the church is clear. No church leader can afford to be unaware of the often bitter experiences of mission countries where proclamation of the gospel meant suppression and even destruction of a local culture. Common sense and human respect for the rights of others are adequate reasons for maintaining pluralism in a global community; the biblical vision raises it to a sacred trust.

The Unanswered Questions

For all its richness, the Bible leaves several mission questions unanswered and even unasked. We review them briefly below.

Israel. It is not within the scope of this study to deal adequately with this vast question, but no discussion of mission in a biblical context can afford to omit it altogether.[11] Our approach to the mission question has spanned both testaments; the issues of world salvation are not an exclusively Christian concern. Nevertheless the church's conviction that it is called by God actively to share the good news of salvation across ethnic and cultural boundaries clearly separates Christianity from Judaism. But a more important issue is how Israel itself fits into the Christian sense of mission. Any solution on the part of Christians that can only see the church as the complete fulfillment of the promises to Israel and therefore considers Judaism to be an anachronistic and discarded prototype is incompatible with the Bible and with the facts of history.

The authors of the New Testament struggled for an answer. Paul's agony is seen in chapters 9–11 of Romans. For Paul the final chapter of salvation cannot come until God's fidelity to Israel has been worked out. The mission to the Gentiles does not replace the unique role of the Jews. Other New Testament traditions such as Matthew and perhaps John seem to take a harsher stance: the failure of Israel to respond to the gospel means loss of its privileged role as God's people or, at best, a sharing of that prerogative with the nations who respond. All of the New Testament testifies to the absolute dependence of Christianity on its Jewish roots.

Therefore the Scriptures leave hanging the question of how the worldwide mission of the church relates to the unique role of Israel. To treat Jews as one more non-Christian religion and to embark on a strategy of individual conversion is not in the spirit of the Bible and is to be too sure of a question that the biblical people hesitated to answer.

The Non-Christian Religions. A staggering question for the contemporary church is that of Christianity's relationship to non-Christian religions other than Judaism.[12] No comprehensive solution to this issue can be found in the Bible, but it does offer some leads.

We have noted how the roots of biblical religion were deeply implanted in the religions of the cultures surrounding Israel. Judaism did not begin as a fixed and autonomous religious system but adopted much of its religious concepts and practices from "pagan" religions. Eventually, as Israel's self-consciousness sharpened, other religious systems would be judged as worthless idolatry and potential seducers of Israel's religious purity.

There is a different story in the New Testament. Here a powerful sense of identity and authority (based in part on the early church's dependence on Judaism) is present from the beginning. Religious traditions other than Judaism are not explicitly addressed. In the view of some scholars, Greco-Roman religions such as the mystery cults and some early forms of Gnosticism left their imprint on Christian thought and practice. Paul was certainly influenced by some popular forms of Stoicism, and John's Gospel may have been in dialogue with certain proto-Gnostic motifs. But, as was the case with Judaism, explicit evaluations of other religions tended to be negative. The Gentiles suffered from "ignorance" and were considered to be caught in a life of idolatry and futility.

The Bible's attitude to individual Gentiles or non-Christians ran the spectrum from hostility to admiration. The New Testament saw the Gentiles as the object of the community's mission, peoples "far off" who were "brought near" by the death and resurrection of Jesus. Some biblical writers did recognize genuine religious experience in individual pagans, people capable of "fearing God and acting uprightly" (Acts 10:34). But in no instance was a religious "system" other than Judaism or Christianity considered to have any validity.[13] Paul and other biblical writers acknowledged the possibility of "natural religion" whereby the true God could be detected in the order and beauty of his creation. Luke presented Paul as making a passing, respectful reference to a pagan altar dedicated to the "unknown God" (Acts 17:22–23). But it was inconceivable for a biblical writer to express admiration for a full-blown cult or nonbiblical religion.

Two thousand years of history have left many modern Christians with a radically different perspective. That history has not resulted in the worldwide conversion of all of humanity. In fact, the religious boundaries of the world seem to be relatively fixed, with millions of human beings finding their cultural and spiritual roots in long-standing religious traditions other than that of Judeo-Christianity. The rise of national and cultural consciousness throughout the world in the twentieth century has also made Christians painfully aware of the darker side of their mission history. Too often missionary expansion was allied with imperialism and resulted in the destruction or suppression of the cultural identity of those converted. Church renewal has tempered some of our inclination to triumphalism and has enabled Christians to recognize beauty and goodness in those "outside" our tradition.

These and other experiences have resulted in a profound evolution in Christian attitudes to non-Christian religions. Instead of seeing "pagan" religions as aberrations, many Christians now acknowledge that for millions of people these systems provide genuine experiences of salvation. Instead of dismissing them as temporary obstructions to the triumph of the gospel, Christians may have to consider the proper role of other religions in the global salvation history of humanity. Instead of seeing mission as ultimately geared to proselytizing and conversion, Christians may also have to think of a dialectic between the good news of the gospel and the good news of another religious story.

Such an evolving stance is no easy task. The problem is not simply an adjustment in attitudes. Finding positive values in non-Christian religions also seems to put Christians on a collision course with their own deeply held beliefs. How can the story of Israel and the church be uniquely revealing if another genuinely sacred story can be found in the parallel history of other religions? How can Jesus Christ be claimed as cosmic Lord and sole Redeemer if people find salvation in a religious tradition that has not even heard of Jesus?

The challenge of the non-Christian religions was never felt with the same intensity by the biblical peoples. Even so, this study of the mission question suggests that the biblical heritage does offer some guidance on this issue. The biblical heritage ultimately began and continued to be influenced by other religions. Many of its deepest insights and most powerful symbols were adapted from and shared with supposedly "pagan" peoples. Many of the biblical themes we have discussed, such as the expansive nature of religious experience, the revelation of God in creation, the recognition of the Gentiles' capacity to respond to the gospel, and the awed awareness that God and his Spirit range far beyond the boundaries of human expectations, are some aspects of the biblical data that suggest positive links with non-Christian religions.

Equally important for this and other pastoral issues facing the church is the Bible's courageous, inquisitive spirit. Nothing is ruled out: from the exodus to the conquest by Romans, from the migration of Abraham to the travels of Paul, from the heavenly powers to the depths of Sheol, from God's Son to Balaam's donkey. Every historical event, every layer of the universe, and every human being that shaped the experience of Israel and the early church are part of the biblical story. All were absorbed, scrutinized, interpreted. The biblical writers were not afraid of ultimates, for the God of the Bible is a God who can never be threatened or impoverished by fearless reflection on human experience. The very spirit of the Bible encourages Christians not to cringe before questions posed by the reality of non-Christian religions. Facing such issues is, in fact, fidelity to the Christian mission. It is, after all, the God of the Bible who sends his people out to reveal and to discover his love in places beyond sectarian borders.

NOTES

1. Luke, for example, makes a point of relating the events of Jesus' origin and the inauguration of his ministry to the secular political time frame (cf. 1:1; 2:1; 3:1); all four Gospels present a major role for Pilate in the events that lead to the salvific death of Jesus; the apocalyptic discourses might be triggered in part by early Christian reflection on the destruction of Jerusalem and the temple; Paul consistently reflects the common moral wisdom of his day in the lists of virtues, as does 1 Timothy in its lists of qualifications for the office of bishop (cf. p. 308, above).

2. Cf., e.g., the cautions of M. Boys, *Biblical Interpretation in Religious Education* (Birmingham, Ala.: Religious Education Press, 1980), who studies the amazing impact of this concept on religious education in the late 1960s and early 1970s and its rapid demise. A judicious definition of what is meant by "salvation history" in our discussion is the following by J. Meier: "By salvation-history we mean a schematic understanding of God's dealings with men that emphasizes continuity-yet-difference. Insofar as the theologian, reflecting on saving events, sees the one and the same God acting faithfully and consistently within the flow of time, he perceives continuity, a basic horizontal line (though not always a straight one). Insofar as the theologian sees the different ways in which God acts at different times and the different ways in which man responds, he perceives the lines of demarcation which delimit the distinct periods of history—the vertical lines of division, as it were. Difference within continuity, the various stages within the one divine economy: this is the basic insight on which any outline or pattern of salvation-history is built" (*The Vision of Matthew* [New York: Paulist Press, 1978], p. 30).

3. Cf. G. O'Collins, *What Are They Saying about the Resurrection*? (New York: Paulist Press, 1978), pp. 68–86. He challenges theologians to be more imaginative in reflecting on the potential of matter and its connection to Christian belief in resurrection.

4. Cf. P. Bowers, "Paul and Religious Propaganda in the First Century," *Novum Testamentum* 22 (1980): 316–23. Bowers claims that, while there were many propagandists in the first-century world, Paul is unique because of his notion of the geographical spread of belief through his preaching ministry.

5. Cf. D. Hill, *New Testament Prophecy* (Atlanta: John Knox Press, 1979). Hill, however, seems to overemphasize the ecstatic and liturgical aspects of prophecy in his description of the New Testament phenomenon; as we have discussed at various

places in this study of the text, the early community also conceived of the prophetic role in continuity with the classic prophets of the Old Testament and, therefore, as one who functioned as a community conscience, ready to suffer rejection and persecution for the sake of the gospel.

6. Cf. H. Kee, *Christian Origins in Sociological Perspective* (Philadelphia: Westminster Press, 1980), pp. 74–76.

7. Cf., e.g., the discussion in E. Schillebeeckx, *Christ: The Experience of Jesus as Lord* (New York: Seabury Press, 1980), pp. 485–88.

8. Cf. the insightful study of W. Brueggeman, *The Land*, Overtures to Biblical Theology series (Philadelphia: Fortress Press, 1977).

9. In their study of the role of the Bible in ethics, B. Birch and L. Rasmussen make a similar point in speaking of the Bible as a "shaper of Christian identity"; cf. *Bible and Ethics in the Christian Life* (Minneapolis: Augsburg Publishing Co., 1976), pp. 184–86.

10. On this point, cf. the papers in *Christ's Lordship and Religious Pluralism*, ed. G. Anderson and T. Stransky (Maryknoll, N.Y.: Orbis Books, 1981); and D. Senior, "Religious Pluralism and Our Biblical Heritage," in *Toward a North American Theology*, ed. D. Flaherty (a collection of working papers published in a limited edition by the Center for Pastoral Ministry, Chicago, Ill., in 1981).

11. On this issue, cf. J. Pawlikowski, *What Are They Saying about Christian-Jewish Religions?* (New York: Paulist Press, 1981); E. Schillebeeckx, *Christ*, pp. 601–27; D. Harrington, *God's People in Christ*, Overtures to Biblical Theology series (Philadelphia: Fortress Press, 1980).

12. Cf. the discussion in Hans Küng, *On Being a Christian* (Garden City, N.Y.: Doubleday, 1976), pp. 89–116.

13. The term "system" is, of course, anachronistic from a biblical perspective; it is unlikely that biblical writers would think of their own or another person's religion in systematic terms. But they would be aware of an identifiable religious community to which they belonged and whose traditions and way of life had validity and authority.

Index of Scriptural References

OLD TESTAMENT

Genesis

1-3	100
1-11	84
1:4	37
1:10	37
1:12	37
1:18	37
1:21	37
1:25	37
1:31	37
2:2	121
2:4	36
2:7	84
4:4	84, 95
4:8	41
4:25-26	84, 95
6:8	95
9-10	10, 11
9-11	18
9:25-27	10, 84, 95
10-50	33
10:22-27	11
11:27	84
11:31	39
12	179
12-50	18
12:1	17, 84
12:1-2	17
12:1-3	18, 84, 95
12:1-4	33
12:3	83
12:6	17, 39, 45
12:8	17, 39
12:10-20	59
12:13	41
12:13-15	18
13:4	17
13:11	95
13:18	17
14:18-20	17
15	179
15:13	39, 89
16:1-6	39
16:1-4	89
19:24	74
20	39, 59
20:7	59
21:1-21	95
21:33	17
22	39
22:2	41
23	39, 89
23:4	39, 89
25:1	89
25:23	95
31:21	45
32:30	72
34	33
35:1-15	137
38	33, 50
38:12-19	90
38:27-30	90
45:5	33
49:5-7	33, 95
50:20	33

Exodus

3-6	16
3:8	95
6:1b	14
10:27-29	14
11:1	14
12:38	14, 33, 57
12:39	14
14	14
14:5a	14
14:21-22	64
14:31	19
15	18, 114
15:1-8	15
15:22-17:7	14
15:24	14
18	47, 48
18:13-21	48
18:17-22	19
19	47
19:3-6	9
19:4-6	84
20:2	66, 84
25-31	20
25:1-31:18	18
25:13-14	20, 86
33:7-10	18
33:11	19
33:20	72
34:6	23, 24, 56, 75, 79, 130, 136
34:6-7	20
34:7	97
34:29-35	19
35:1-40:38	18

Leviticus

1:1	18
1:39	125
6:26	18
6:30	18
8	18
16	118
16:21-22	137
20:14	41
21:11	41, 112
25	25
25:22	73
25:23	86

Numbers

1:47-54	18
3-4	18
5:6-8	125
6:1-21	58
11	48, 59, 60
11:4	134
11:4-6	14
11:16-17	48
11:25	48, 59
12	60
12:8	19
13:26	137
18:20	58
20:2-13	22
20:6-13	126
22-24	59
22:4	48

22:5	59	31:9	18	1:11	123
22:7	48	31:24-28	18	1:17	95
25:6-9	48	33:8-11	95	1:17-20	21
35:9-29	50	34	21, 44	2:33	245
		34:4-5	126	4:4	123
Deuteronomy		34:9	21	7:6	124
		34:10	19	7:16	137
1:2	137	34:11	48	8:5	22
1:19	14			8:6-7	49
1:37	126	**Joshua**		8:7	72
3:16	126			8:15	49
4:21-22	126	1-6	33	10:1	60
4:34	52	1:1-9	21	10:6	22
4:37	96, 97	3:7	34	13:13-14	22
4:37-28:5	96, 97, 98	4:14	34	15	22, 41, 42, 53
4:40	96	5:13-15	34	16:11-13	95
5:3	96	6:43-70	33	16:13	22, 60
6:3	112	7:6-9	124	17:40	95
6:4-9	35, 96	8:3	95		
6:6	96	8:30-35	45	**2 Samuel**	
6:10-12	52	10:28-11:23	45		
6:10-15	120	24	18, 90	2:8	34
7:1	89	24:27	33	4:4	34
7:1-2	10	24:28-29	21	5:11	90
7:1-5	96			6-21	22
7:6	83, 96	**Judges**		7	57
7:6-7	96			7:1-7	20
7:6-8	10	2:6-9	21	7:5-7	47
7:6-9	96, 97	2:6-3:6	91	7:8	34
7:6-15	96	2:7	21	7:8-17	71
7:7	97	2:10-23	22	7:12	88
7:7-8	86, 87	2:18	95	7:15-16	88
7:8a	97	3:10	21, 22	7:16	70
7:8b	97	3:12-20	22	8	70
7:9	97	4:4	60	8:2	90
7:11	96, 97	4:5	60	21-22	43
7:12-14	97	5	114		
7:16-26	96	5:2-31	15	**1 Kings**	
9:18	126	6:22-23	72		
10:14-15	96	6:34	21, 22	1-2	22
10:15	97	8:33	17	1:33-34	76
10:17	53	9	49	1:38-40	76
13:15	41	9:4	17	1:45	138
14:1-2	97	9:46	17	5:26	90
14:2	84, 85, 96, 105	11:29	45	6:7	20
16:18-18:22	60	13:22	72	8:6-8	47
17:5	41	13:25	22	8:8	86
18:1-8	27	20:18-28	137	8:13	70
18:15	60	20:23-26	124	8:33-36	124
18:15-18	64	21:2	124	9:20-21	89
21:1-9	245	21:25	22	11:29-39	24
21:10-14	98			12:14	24
21:23	175	**Ruth**		18:40	42
22:22	67			21	25, 42, 57, 60
23:8	98	1-4	29, 40	22	60
24:1	67	4:18-22	90	22:17	72
25:19	53				
26:5	89	**1 Samuel**		**2 Kings**	
26:5-10	18				
26:18-19	97	1:1-25:1	80	1:34	107
28:5	97	1:3	123	9	42, 55

9:1-3	60	**Psalms**		89:4	98
9:6-7	42			89:5-10	121
9-10	63	6:5	113	89:9	98
15:5	72	8:7	201	89:9-18	113
15:8-12	63	18	15	89:10	42
17	91	19a	113	89:11	98
17:13-18	278	19:6	53	89:13	98
18-19	71	22	127, 130, 132,	89:24	23
18-20	60, 96		133, 135, 136	89:25	98
21:16	71	22:1-26	133	89:28-29	88
22:1-23:30	96	22:22-26	133	89:36	88
		22:24	133	89:38	88
1 Chronicles		22:26	136	89:46	88
		22:27-31	133	89:49	88
6:31	113	24:8	53	94:17	113
8:33	33	26:6	245	95	111, 118, 119, 120,
8:34	33	29	98, 99, 101, 111,		121, 122, 137
9:39	33		113, 114, 116, 117,	95:1	119
9:40	33		118, 135, 137	95:1-5	119, 120
32:8	41	29:8	115	95:2	119
		29:9	115, 116	95:3-5	119
2 Chronicles		44	126, 127, 128,	95:6	119
			129, 130, 136	95:6-7c	119, 120
29-32	71, 96	44:1	129	95:7a,b,c	119
34-35	96	44:1-8	129	95:7c	119
36:15-16	278	44:2	128	95:7d-11	119, 120
		44:3	129	95:10-11	121
Ezra		44:4	128	96-97	28
		44:6	128	110:1	201
4	39	44:15	128	117	93, 94
4:1-3	27	44:16	129	118	245
9-10	92, 278	44:17-19	128	118:22-23	224
10	28, 29	44:20-21	128	137:9	91
		44:22	128	143:3	113
Nehemiah		44:23	128, 130	146:150	111
		44:27	129		
3:33-4:16	39	46	122, 123, 124	**Proverbs**	
6	39	46:1-3	123		
9:26	278	46:4-6	123	8:4	196
9:32	53	46:8	123	8:22-31	196, 284
		46-48	113	8:31	196
Tobit		48	57	8:32-36	284
		51	110		
8:3	137	51:1	132	**Ecclesiastes**	
		51:11	132		
1 Maccabees		51:16	110, 111	1:9, 11	12
		51:19	111, 132		
1-2	92, 93	51:21	132	**Wisdom**	
2:57	30	68	16, 205		
4:46	35	69:8	91	7:26	196
9:27	35	74:9	35	7:27	196
14:41	35	78:65	53	9:1-2	284
		79	91	9:9	284
2 Maccabees		79:11-12	91	9:10	284
		81:1-2	120	18:14-15	284
15:35	41	87	77, 90, 93, 98, 330		
		88:4-7	113	**Sirach**	
Job		89	23, 88, 98, 108		
		89:1	23	24:8	196
16:14	53	89:2	98	24:8-12	284
		89:3	23	24:19-22	284

Isaiah

1	72
1-39	69, 70, 71, 72, 73, 74,
	75, 76, 77, 78, 79, 123
1:1-17	154
1:2-3	73, 74
1:4-9	74, 75
1:9-10	74
1:10	74, 149
1:10-20	73
1:11-12	74
1:11-15b	74
1:13-15b	74
1:15c	74
1:16-20	74
1:17	74
1:19	73
1:21	56, 74
1:21-26	74, 75
1:23	56, 74
1:27-31	74
2:1-4	123
2:1-5	92
2:3	123
2:5	123
2:6	123
5	224
6	72
6:1	70
6:3	78
6:9-10	71
6:9-11	73
6:10	73
7	69
7-11	75
7-12	75
7:3	70, 75
7:4	70, 123
7:9b	70
7:11-12	71
8:1	75, 78
8:3	61
8:6-7	138
8:6-8	76
8:9-10	77
8:17	123
9:1	76
9:5	53
9:6-7	76
9:8	123
10:5-6	78
10:5-7a	77
10:5-15	77
10:5-27	77
10:6	78
10:7-15	78
10:13-14	91
10:13b-15a	77
10:20	123
10:20-21	78, 135

10:20-22	77
10:21	53
11:1	57, 71
11:4	82
14:1	123
16:4	57
22:1-4	123
27:6	123
27:9	123
30:15-17	123
40	109
40-55	27, 28, 94, 100,
	101, 109, 110
40-66	108
40:3-5	101
40:4	278
40:5	260
41-48	102, 104
41:8-10	102
41:17-20	102
41:21-29	104
41:25-49	27
41:29	102, 104
42:1	94
42:1-4	103, 104
42:1-5	101
42:5-7	103, 104
42:8	104
42:8-9	104
43:1-7	32, 50, 102
43:8-13	102
43:16-21	102
43:19-21	102
43:22-28	27
44:1-5	102
44:24-45:7	103
44:28b	27
45:1	27, 101
45:1-7	27
45:4	83, 101, 107
45:9-13	107
46	101
48:1-13	102
48:22	103, 104
49-55	103
49:1	183
49:1-4	103, 104
49:1-7	330
45:5a,b,c	103, 104
49:5-13	103
49:6	27, 100, 103, 105,
	107, 135, 166
49:7	103, 104
49:8	103, 104
49:9a	103, 104
49:9b-12	104
49:14	103
49:19	103
49:20	103
49:20-21	104
50:1	103

50:1-3	104
50:3	104
50:4-9a	103, 104
50:9b	104
50:10-11	103, 104
51:1-3	101
51:2-3	16
51:4-6	103, 104
51:6b	104
51:8d	104
51:17	103
52:10	278
52:11-12	27
52:13-53:12	103, 104
52:15	105, 109
53	109
53:7	109
53:10-11	105
54:1-10	50
54:7-10	101
55:3-5	27, 101
55:6-11	37, 38
55:9-11	334
55:10-11	112, 284
56-66	29, 30, 35, 40, 92
56:3-4	30
56:6-8	92
56:7	223
56:7-8	30
57:19	204
57:21	103, 104
60:1-2a	260
61	273
61:1	260
65	327

Jeremiah

1:1	55
1:4-5	165
1:5	183, 330
1:7	24
1:10	43
2:1-3	58
4:19	91
6:4	53, 91
6:22-23	91
7:4	25
7:11	223
7:25	91
7:26	48
11:13	33
12:1-5	134
12:14-17	53
14:8	57
15:10-21	134
16:2	41
16:3	43
16:4	43
18:7-9	53
20:11	53

22:7	53	**Hosea**		13:5	63	
22:13-17	24			13:5-6	63	
23:5	82	1-15	63, 64, 65, 66,	13:6	67	
24	27		67, 68, 69	13:9	87	
24:6	53	1:3	81	13:10-11	63	
26:4	25	1:4-5	63	13:14	87	
26:6	25, 57	1:6	81	13:16	81	
26:11	134	1:8	81			
26:15	245	2:2	67	**Joel**		
26:16	134	2:2-15	65, 68			
31:26	53	2:3	63	3:9	53	
31:31-34	35	2:8	63	3:9-21	92	
31:40	53	2:14-15	63, 65	3:10	92	
32:18	53	2:15	63, 81	3:18	138	
37:15	134	2:16-17	33, 68			
38:11-12	62	2:16-23	68	**Amos**		
42:10	53	2:19-20	68			
43:1-7	27	3:1	66	1:3-2:16	91	
44:4-6	278	3:1a	67	2:11-12	58	
45:4	53	3:1b	67	3:2	99	
51:27-27	53	3:3	69	3:8	34, 55	
		4:15	81	4:4-13	108	
Lamentations		5:8	81	4:13	99	
		6:2	160	7:10-13	34	
2:6-11	26	6:6	147	7:10-17	34	
3:22	26	6:7	81	7:13	25	
3:31	26	6:8	81	7:14	61	
		7	81	7:14-15	34, 62	
Ezekiel		7:1	81	7:15	24, 55	
		7:16	66	7:17	101	
1:28	101	8:5-6	81	8:11-12	62	
4-24	27	8:13	66	9:7	57, 99, 321	
11:14-21	27	9:3	66			
14:4	61	9:6	66	**Jonah**		
16:3	11, 89	9:7f	61			
18:5-20	125	9:9	63	1-4	29, 40, 219, 230	
24:16-18	41	9:10	63, 67			
33-39	27	9:15	81	**Micah**		
33-48	27, 28	10:5	81			
36:16-38	27	10:9	63	2:2	57	
38-39	27, 92	10:9-12	63	3:5	53, 59	
40-48	27	11	63, 66	4:1-4	92	
40:46	27	11:1	6	6:8	136	
43:1-5	55	11:5	65, 66			
43:1-9	27	11:8	65, 66	**Zephaniah**		
43:19	27	11:8-9	67, 87			
44:15-31	27	11:9	67	3:12	136	
46:2	27	11:11	65-66	3:17	53	
47	138	12:2-4	63			
		12:4	81	**Haggai**		
Daniel		12:8	66			
		12:10	64	2:23	107	
7-12	30, 42, 93	12:11	81	**Zechariah**		
7:14	251	12:12	63			
9:27	30	12:13	64	14:8	138	
		13:4	66	14:16-21	117	

NEW TESTAMENT

Matthew

1-2	*236, 240*
1:1-7	*241*
1:3	*90*
1:22	*241, 251*
1:23	*242*
1:24	*248*
2	*324*
2:1-5	*248*
2:1-12	*152*
2:1-18	*244*
2:2	*327*
2:13-14	*248*
2:17	*241*
2:20-21	*248*
2:23	*241*
3-4	*240*
3:2	*237*
3:7-10	*244, 248*
3:15	*247*
4:1	*137*
4:12-17	*236*
4:14-16	*241*
4:17	*237*
4:18-22	*247*
4:23	*237, 250*
4:23-25	*149*
5-7	*236, 242*
5:8	*44*
5:17	*234, 240, 241*
5:17-48	*235*
5:18-19	*240*
5:19	*248*
5:20	*244, 248*
5:23-24	*149*
5:27	*43*
5:43-48	*146, 242*
5:44	*148*
5:45	*146, 330*
6:1	*154, 248*
6:1-6	*244*
6:1-18	*154*
6:12	*148, 152, 160, 253*
6:14-15	*152, 160*
6:26-30	*152*
6:30	*247*
7:12	*242*
7:15-27	*154*
7:16	*248*
7:21	*152, 248, 249*
7:24-27	*248*
8-9	*244*
8:1-4	*247*
8:2	*242*
8:5-13	*142, 147, 152, 153, 154, 247, 248*
8:6	*242*

8:10	*324*
8:10-12	*244*
8:11	*153, 156*
8:17	*241*
8:21	*242*
8:26	*247*
9:3	*244*
9:5	*247*
9:6	*242*
9:9-13	*248*
9:10	*147*
9:10-13	*147, 244*
9:14-17	*244*
9:18-31	*247*
9:32-34	*244*
9:35	*237, 250*
9:36-38	*250*
9:38	*250*
10	*233, 236, 240, 250*
10:1	*250*
10:1-5	*250*
10:1-42	*250*
10:1-47	*242, 249*
10:4	*240*
10:5	*142, 235, 240, 250, 252*
10:5-6	*250*
10:7	*237, 333*
10:7-8	*251*
10:9-15	*251*
10:15	*153, 154*
10:16-23	*251*
10:16-31	*156*
10:17	*251*
10:18	*251*
10:19-20	*251*
10:23	*251*
10:24	*251*
10:24-25	*242*
10:26-27	*251*
10:28-33	*251*
10:34-39	*251*
10:40-42	*242, 251, 254*
11	*244*
11:1	*250*
11:1-24	*244*
11:12	*237*
11:16-30	*147*
11:18-19	*248*
11:19	*147*
11:20-24	*147, 153*
11:22	*154*
12	*244*
12:7	*147*
12:14	*244*
12:17-21	*241*
12:22-30	*149*
12:28	*149, 213, 237*

12:29	*150*
13	*236, 237, 244*
13:10-15	*244*
13:14-15	*241, 247*
13:14-43	*156*
13:19	*237*
13:23	*247*
13:24-30	*155, 325*
13:36-43	*242, 249*
13:41-43	*249*
13:44	*146*
13:45	*146*
13:47	*146*
14:49-50	*156*
14:30	*242*
14:31	*247*
14:33	*247*
15:1-20	*148*
15:21-28	*152, 247, 248*
15:24	*142, 240*
16:8	*247*
16:12	*247*
16:13-28	*236*
16:18	*252*
18	*160, 236, 242*
18:15-35	*242*
18:17	*252*
18:20	*242, 252*
18:20-35	*149*
18:21	*149*
18:23-35	*149, 155, 160*
18:27	*149*
18:35	*149*
20:1-16	*146*
20:28-32	*246*
21-25	*236*
21:1ff	*236*
21:4-5	*241*
21:28-32	*154, 248*
21:33-46	*244*
21:40	*244*
21:41	*245*
21:43	*224, 332*
22:1-10	*249*
22:1-14	*153, 249*
22:7	*249*
22:11-14	*249*
22:34-40	*242*
22:40	*148*
23	*234, 248*
23:2-3	*235*
23:3	*248*
23:5	*248*
23:9	*152*
23:15	*141, 142*
23:23	*148*
23:25	*245*
24-25	*236, 237, 242, 243*

23:14	*142, 237, 240*	1:14	*213, 218, 229, 230*	5:21	*219*
24:37-44	*243*	1:15	*146, 214*	5:22-43	*219*
24:45-51	*248*	1:16-20	*214, 226, 266*	5:24-30	*220*
25:1-13	*153, 248, 254*	1:16-21	*215*	5:24	*220*
25:14-30	*248*	1:17	*214*	5:25-34	*213*
25:31-32	*243*	1:21	*213*	5:31	*220*
25:31-36	*332*	1:21-27	*230*	5:35-43	*213*
25:31-46	*152, 154, 156, 243,*	1:21-45	*213*	6	*219*
	248, 249, 254, 325	1:24	*228*	6:1-6	*219*
25:32	*249*	1:27	*228*	6:7-11	*250*
25:45-48	*248*	1:30-31	*149, 213*	6:7-13	*214, 226*
26:1-28:15	*236*	1:35	*213*	6:12	*218, 333*
26:13	*142, 253*	1:38	*213*	6:14-29	*219, 230*
26:18	*156*	1:38-39	*218*	6:30	*226*
26:32	*251*	1:40-45	*213*	6:33-44	*219*
26:39	*159*	1:45	*218*	6:35-44	*226*
26:54-56	*241*	1:48-53	*230*	6:45-52	*219, 228*
26:60	*238*	2:1-12	*213*	6:46	*213*
26:61	*253*	2:1-3:6	*213, 215, 221, 222*	6:47-52	*221*
26:64	*242*	2:10	*221*	6:51-52	*220, 226*
27:3-10	*245, 251*	2:13-15	*215*	6:52	*229, 247*
27:9-10	*241*	2:13-17	*221*	7:1	*218, 220*
27:11-26	*245*	2:14	*226*	7:1-23	*148, 213, 220, 222*
27:17	*245*	2:14-17	*213*	7:5	*222*
27:19	*245*	2:15-17	*147*	7:6-13	*222*
27:21	*243*	2:19	*214*	7:14-23	*222*
27:24-25	*245, 246*	2:23-28	*148*	7:17	*231*
27:26	*245, 254*	2:27	*221*	7:19	*220, 222*
27:51	*239, 242*	3:1-6	*148, 149, 213*	7:24-30	*142, 147, 154, 213,*
27:51-53	*239*	3:5	*229*		*219, 221, 222*
27:54	*239*	3:6	*223, 230*	7:27	*221, 222*
28:2-3	*240*	3:7-12	*218*	7:29	*324*
28:7	*251*	3:13-19	*214, 226, 230*	7;29a	*221*
28:9-10	*236*	3:14	*214, 218, 226, 333*	7:31-37	*222*
28:10	*251*	3:20	*222*	7:36	*210*
28:16-18	*251*	3:20-35	*222*	8:1-9	*226*
28:16-20	*142, 233, 236, 242,*	3:22	*218, 222*	8:1-10	*219, 220*
	249, 250, 254, 257	3:22-27	*149*	8:7	*221*
28:17	*251*	3:27	*150*	8:9	*221*
28:18	*252*	3:31-35	*222*	8:11-13	*220*
28:19	*142, 235, 240, 249,*	4:1-34	*222*	8:14-21	*220, 226*
	252, 254, 257	4:3-9	*156, 214*	8:15-21	*219*
28:20	*236, 239, 242, 248,*	4:8	*214*	8:17	*229*
	250, 252	4:10	*221, 226*	8:21	*215, 219, 247*
		4:10-11	*231*	8:21-10:52	*218, 227*
Mark		4:10-13	*226*	8:22-26	*149*
		4:11	*214*	8:22-10:52	*215, 217*
1:1	*216, 220, 221, 228*	4:11-12	*222*	8:27-30	*227*
1:2-3	*215, 221*	4:26	*146, 214*	8:27-9:1	*215*
1:2-8	*215*	4:26-29	*156, 214*	8:31	*215, 230*
1:2-8:21	*217, 226*	4:30	*146, 214*	8:31-32	*227*
1:2-13	*215*	4:30-32	*156, 214*	8:31-33	*227*
1:4-8	*215*	4:33-37	*222*	8:34	*214, 216*
1:9	*218*	4:35	*219, 222*	8:34-9:1	*227*
1:9-11	*215*	4:35-41	*219, 220, 221, 228*	9:1	*213, 214*
1:10	*215, 229*	4:38-41	*226*	9:7	*215, 228*
1:11	*215, 221, 228*	5:1-20	*219, 222*	9:13	*214*
1:12-13	*215*	5:7	*221, 228*	9:28	*231*
1:14-15	*144, 146, 155,*	5:11	*219*	9:30	*215*
	213, 215	5:19-20	*219*	9:30-37	*227*
1:14-8:21	*221*	5:20	*218*	9:31	*215, 230*

9:32	*228*	13:7-27	*156*	1:15	*268*
9:33	*215*	13:9-10	*225*	1:26-38	*266*
9:34	*227*	13:9-13	*224, 250*	1:32	*261*
9:42	*213*	13:10	*142, 218, 221, 224,*	1:35	*261, 268*
10:1	*215*		*229, 230*	1:41	*268*
10:2-12	*213*	13:11	*156, 229*	1:45	*266*
10:4-45	*229*	13:11-13	*229*	1:67	*268*
10:10	*231*	13:26-27	*221, 225*	1:68-79	*261, 264*
10:13	*156*	13:27	*224*	1:77	*263*
10:13-16	*213*	13:27-31	*214*	2:1	*260, 347*
10:17	*215*	13:30	*213*	2:11	*261*
10:17-31	*213*	13:32	*155*	2:25	*268*
10:23	*231*	13:32-37	*227*	2:30	*260, 261*
10:28-31	*152, 226*	13:33-37	*156*	2:32	*260, 269*
10:29-31	*214*	14-15	*215, 218*	2:36	*268*
10:32	*215, 218, 231*	14:3-9	*213*	2:41-52	*258*
10:32-33	*218*	14:9	*218*	3:1	*260, 347*
10:32-45	*227*	14:10-11	*227*	3:3	*263, 277*
10:33	*215*	14:17-21	*227*	3:6	*258, 260, 269*
10:33-34	*230*	14:21	*215*	3:7-14	*263*
10:37	*227*	14:24	*225, 227*	3:8	*11*
10:42	*231*	14:25	*156*	3:16	*268*
10:42-45	*214*	14:26	*156*	3:22	*262, 268*
10:45	*225, 226, 227*	14:27-28	*230*	3:23-38	*262, 268*
10:46	*215*	14:27-31	*227*	4:1	*268*
10:52	*215*	14:28	*216, 218, 228*	4:13	*263*
11-12	*218, 222, 223*	14:32	*213*	4:14	*259, 268*
11-13	*223, 224*	14:36	*146, 159, 213*	4:16-30	*260, 268*
11-15	*223*	14:44-45	*227*	4:17-22	*262*
11:1	*215*	14:50-52	*227*	4:18	*268*
11:1-11	*223*	14:56	*224*	4:22-29	*260*
11:1-12:12	*224*	14:58	*223, 224, 238*	4:23-30	*268*
11:1-16:8	*217, 222, 227*	14:59	*224*	4:28-29	*258*
11:9-10	*223*	14:61	*221, 224*	4:31ff	*263*
11:11-25	*215*	14:62	*214, 221, 225*	5:1-11	*266*
11:12-14	*223*	14:64-65	*225*	5:5	*266*
11:15-18	*213*	14:66-72	*227*	5:10	*266*
11:16	*223*	14:70	*218*	5:12-15	*261*
11:17	*223*	15:2	*221*	5:12-16	*149*
11:18	*223, 230*	15:30-32	*225*	5:20	*263*
11:20-25	*223*	15:37-39	*225*	5:27-32	*261*
11:27-33	*223*	15:38-39	*223*	5:29-32	*264*
11:27-44	*215*	15:39	*221, 222, 225,*	5:32	*264*
11:28	*223*		*227, 231*	6:12-16	*266*
12:1-12	*223, 224*	15:39-40	*227*	6:20-26	*147*
12:6	*215*	15:40-41	*213, 222, 227*	6:35	*148*
12:8	*245*	15:41	*218*	7:1-10	*261, 265*
12:9	*224, 245*	15:47	*213*	7:31-35	*147*
12:9-13	*221*	16:1-8	*213, 215*	7:34	*264*
12:10-11	*245*	16:5-8	*228*	7:36-50	*147, 264*
12:11	*224*	16:7	*216, 218, 225, 227*	7:42-50	*265*
12:13-17	*213*	16:7-8	*230, 236*	7:47-48	*263*
12:13-44	*224*	16:8	*227, 228, 230*	8:1-3	*147*
12:14	*225*	16:14-20	*142*	8:15	*266*
12:31	*148*			8:19-21	*266*
12:41-44	*213*			9:1-6	*266*
12:43	*231*	**Luke**		9:2	*333*
13:1-2	*231*			9:51	*258, 262*
13:1-37	*215, 221, 223, 224*	1:1	*255, 347*	9:51-19:40	*258*
13:2	*212, 224*	1:2	*271*	9:52	*261*
		1:9	*258*		

9:53-55	261	22:16	153, 156	3:15	285
9:55	154	22:18	156	3:15-16	306, 322
10:1-20	266	22:19-20	264	3:16-17	152, 284, 290
10:1-23	250	22:23	263	3:17	285, 295
10:10-37	147	22:24-27	166	3:18ff	286
10:17	156	22:28	263	3:19-20	290
10:21	268	22:28-30	262, 267	3:28	292
10:25-37	148	22:31-32	267	3:34-35	286
10:30-37	261	22:61-62	267	4	147, 289, 324
10:33	154	23:34	263	4:10	286
11:2	152	23:49	267	4:27	147
11:2-4	146	24:1	256	4:34	285, 289, 295
11:4	148	24:1-12	256	4:35-38	289
11:5-10	152	24:7	262	4:38	289
11:10-13	152	24:8	267	4:42	285
11:20	149, 213, 263	24:9	267	5	291
11:21-22	150	24:13-35	256, 264	5:1-18	338
11:27-28	266	24:26	258, 262	5:23-24	295
11:28	155	24:27	257	5:24	285
11:29 32	265	24:33	264, 265, 267	5:30	295
12:11-12	276	24:36-49	256, 267	5:30-47	285
12:14-23	149	24:41-43	264	5:36	295
13:10-17	263	24:44	257, 262, 274	5:37	285, 295
13:13	156, 259, 262	24:44-49	256, 257, 259,	5:38	295
13:16	263		260, 269, 271	6:29	295
13:28-29	153	24:46-48	257, 278	6:35	285
13:29	265	24:47	112, 257, 258, 262,	6:38-39	285, 295
13:31-35	258		263, 265, 271	6:38-40	290
13:32-33	262	24:47-48	272	6:44	295
13:34	258	24:47-49	258	6:51	285
14:15-24	153, 265, 274	24:48	259, 274	6:57	295
14:16-24	249	24:49	259, 262, 268, 275	6:60-66	281, 288
14:18	259	24:52	259	6:68-69	281
14:21	265			6:69	289
14:21-24	153			7:16	295
14:23	265	**John**		7:19	295
14:25-33	264			7:28	295
14:28-33	258	1:1-2	283, 286	7:28-29	295
15	146, 147, 264	1:1-18	283, 331	7:33	295
15:1-2	147, 330, 261, 264	1:3-5	283	7:35	281
15:1-7	242	1:4	290	7:38-39	286
15:6	153	1:4-5	290	7:50-52	294
15:7	264	1:6-8	285, 292	8:12	285
15:9	153, 264	1:10-11	290	8:16	295
15:22-24	153	1:10-13	283	8:17-19	285
15:32	264	1:12	290	8:18	295
16:19-31	261, 265	1:14	283	8:26	295
17:11-19	147, 261, 265	1:15-19	288	8:28	284
17:24	262	1:16-18	283	8:28-29	292
18:9-14	265	1:18	283, 285, 290	8:29	295
18:18-27	261	1:19-51	282, 284	8:42	295
18:31-34	262	1:29	285	9	289, 291, 338
19:1-18	264	1:33	286	9:4	295
19:13-15	265	1:51	284	9:5	285
19:29-37	265	2:1-12	338	9:22	281
19:41	258	2:22	287	10:36	295
20:9-18	262	3:2	289	11	338
20:12	262	3:4-15	294	11:42	295
21:1-4	265	3:5	286	11:52	281
22:14	266	3:8	286	12:20-22	281
		3:14	284		

12:27-28	284	19:35	285, 289	4:19-20	274
12:32	284	19:37	286	4:30	276
12:34	284	19:39	289	4:32-35	270, 273, 336
12:44-45	295	20	287	4:33	274
12:44-47	290	20:1-10	281	4:35	274
12:49	295	20:21	142, 287, 295, 338	5:1-11	274
12:49-50	285	20:21-22	289	5:2	274
13-15	282	20:22	286, 287	5:12	274
13:1	284	20:29	287	5:12-16	273
13:12-16	289	20:30-31	293	5:12-26	270
13:15	289	21:1-4	266	5:14	270
13:16	289	21:15-19	281	5:15-16	274
13:20	289, 295	21:20-23	289	5:17	274
13:23	289	21:24	289	5:18	274
13:34-35	289			5:29-32	274
13:35	336	**Acts of the Apostles**		5:31	273, 277
14-16	286. 287			5:40	274
14:8-11	286	1:1	255	5:40-41	274
14:12	287	1:3	272	5:40-42	258
14:16	287	1:3-5	256	6-8	270
14:17	291	1:3-8	256	6:2	274
14:18-19	290	1:4	259	6:5	276
14:24	295	1:4-5	275, 259, 268	6:6	274
14:26	287	1:8	259, 268, 269,	6:7	270
14:30	290		271, 275	6:8	274
15:1-11	289	1:14-15	275	6:10	276
15:10	289	1:15	274	6:55	276
15:12-17	289	1:15-26	265, 269, 274	7:2-53	272
15:13	284	1:21-22	259, 266	7:58	270
15:14-15	289	2	268	8:1	270, 274
15:21	295	2-9	270	8:1-3	167
15:26	285, 291	2:1-4	275	8:3	270
15:26-27	287, 289	2:4-12	275	8:4	270
16:5	295	2:5-11	270	8:4-5	258
16:8-11	287, 291	2:5-12	272	8:5	274
16:12-15	291	2:14	274	8:5-8	270
16:13	287, 292	2:14-36	274	8:12	272
16:20	290	2:17	270	8:14	274
16:33	291	2:22-36	272	8:14-17	271
17	289, 291	2:33	275	8:22	262
17:1	284	2:36	158	8:25	270
17:3	295	2:37	274	8:26-39	270
17:4	285	2:37-38	258	8:29	275
17:4-5	284	2:38	262, 273, 277	8:36	324
17:8	295	2:41-47	270	8:39	275
17:14	288, 292	2:42	274	9:1	270
17:14-15	291	2:42-47	273	9:1-30	167
17:14-16	290	2:43	270, 273, 274	9:15	259, 270
17:14-18	287	2:43-47	264, 336	9:15-16	276
17:15-16	288	2:47	336	9:27	274
17:18	289, 295	3:1-10	270, 273	9:31	270
17:18-21	292	3:1-16	273, 274	9:32-35	273
17:19	338	3:12-26	272	9:36-42	273
17:20-21	285	3:15-16	273	9:43	278
17:20-23	292	3:19	262, 273	10	219, 270
17:21	289, 295	3:25	270	10-11	273, 274
17:23	289, 295	3:26	263	10:1-11	270
17:25	295	4:4	270	10:2	270, 331
17:26	289	4:8	276	10:8	324
19:26-27	289	4:8-12	274	10:9-16	273

10:15	270	17:1	189	5:10-11	197
10:18	270	17:3	262	6:1-14	126
10:24	326	17:17	189	7	170
10:28	270, 273	17:22	331	7:4	204
10:34	259, 264, 265, 270,	17:22-23	346	7:7	170
	331, 345	17:22-31	327	7:8	170
10:34-43	273	17:23-31	272	7:12	178
10:35	342	17:24	327	7:13	170
10:38	261, 273	17:30	262	7:16	178
10:43	262, 273	17:30-31	277	8	198
10:44-48	275	18:2	275	8:9	189
10:47	270	18:4	189	8:11	189
11	270	18:24	189	8:14-17	328
11:1	274	19:6	276	8:15	159
11:1-18	273	19:8	272	8:19-20	328
11:9	270	19:11-12	338	8:23	189
11:12	275	19:21	276	8:28-30	179
11:12-18	275	20:7-12	338	8:29	196
11:17	270, 277, 332	20:21	262, 273, 277	9-11	172, 179, 180,
11:18	270, 271, 273, 277	20:22	276		181, 195
11:19-20	271	20:25	272	9:1-5	167, 179
11:19-21	258	21:11	276	9:8	179
11:22	274	22:21	270	9:15-16	180
11:24	276	24:44	272	9:45	180
12:3	274	26:16-18	276	10:12	175
12:12	212	26:18	262, 277	10:12-15	181
12:25	212, 275, 298	26:18-20	273	10:14	184
13	271	26:20	262, 277	11:1	180
13:2	275, 276	26:22-23	262	11:11	180
13:2-3	271	28:23	272	11:13-15	180
13:2-4	276	28:28	260, 272	11:13	183
13:4	276	28:29	271	11:15	197
13:5	189	28:30-31	250	11:25	180
13:14	189	28:31	272	11:25-26	180
13:16-41	272			11:28	180
13:38	262	**Romans**		11:29	180
13:38-39	273			11:30-31	180
13:44-52	271	1-3	172, 177	11:30-32	181
13:46	169, 272	1:1	169, 183	12	197
13:56	189	1:3-4	174	13	336
14:1	189	1:5	168	13:9	200
14:3	273	1:16-17	172	14	164
14:4	274	1:18-23	186	15	183, 194
14:8-10	273	1:18-32	186	15:15-21	182
14:14	274	1:19-20	327	15:15-33	183
14:15-17	272, 327	1:21	173	15:16	181, 183
15	259, 270, 273	2:12-14	179	15:17	183
15:2	274	3:1-2	167	15:18-19	183, 189, 329, 339
15:6	274	3:9	177	15:19	194
15:7	274	3:11	172	15:20	185
15:8	275	3:21-24	172, 174	15:20-21	183
15:22	274, 275, 298	3:21-26	177	15:22-29	184
15:23	274	3:21-30	172	15:23	183
15:28	275	3:29	322	15:24	183
15:37	212	3:29-30	171	15:28	183
15:39	212	4:1-25	179	16:25-26	177
16:4	274	4:5	172, 175		
16:6-10	276	4:17	172		
16:16-19	273	4:18	179		
16:30-31	273	5:5	189		

1 Corinthians

1:1	169
1:2	173
1:4-9	190
1:7	189
1:9	183
1:18	174
1:23	187
1:23-24	174
2:2	187
2:4	189
2:7	177
2:12	89
3:5	183
3:16	189
5:20	183
6	176
6:1-6	336
6:15	176
6:15-18	176
6:19	189
7	164
7:7	189
7:40	189
8	164
9:1	166, 168
9:1-2	166, 184
9:3	166
9:16-17	182
9:16-23	182
11:17-22	338
11:23	164
12	197
14:16	336
14:23	336
15	166
15:1-3	166
15:1-5	174
15:3	164
15:3-4	169, 187
15:4	186
15:5-7	168
15:8	166, 167, 168
15:8-11	166, 168
15:9-10	166
15:12-58	166
15:20-28	177
15:28	202

2 Corinthians

1:1	169
1:19	298
1:22	189
2:14-15	183
2:22	167
3:6	183
4:13	189
5:5	189
5:7	177

5:16-20	181
5:18-20	197
6:2	177, 184
10:15-16	184
11:28	184
12:12	189

Galatians

1	169
1:1	169
1:4	161
1:11-12	168
1:11-17	164, 165, 166
1:12	165, 168
1:13	167
1:13-14	167
1:14	165
1:15	183
1:15-16	166
1:16	166, 168
1:23	165
2	166
2:1-14	158
2:2-10	164
2:15-16	177
3:1-5	178
3:2	179, 189
3:5	189
3:7-29	179
3:13	175
3:15-19	177
3:16-18	175
3:23-29	179
4:4-5	186
4:6	159, 189
4:8	186
4:8-9	173, 186
6:16	180

Ephesians

1:1	192
1:1-23	202
1:3-6	199
1:3-15	199
1:3-6:14	199, 200, 201, 202, 203, 204, 205, 206, 207
1:7	199
1:7-8	193
1:9	199
1:9-10	199, 202
1:10	199, 205
1:11-15	200
1:13	206
1:13-15	200
1:16-23	199, 200
1:17-20	200
1:20-21	201
1:20-22	202

1:22-23	201, 203, 204, 207
1:23	202, 203, 205
1:23a	201
2	200, 206, 327
2:1-10	203
2:3-5	206
2:4	203
2:4-9	203
2:7	203
2:10	203
2:11	203
2:11-22	189
2:13	204
2:13-18	207
2:14-22	204
2:15	204
2:16	204
2:18	204
2:19-22	204
2:21-22	203
3	204
3:1	207, 337
3:2	206
3:6	206
3:7	206
3:8	206
3:8-9	205
3:9-10	206
3:10	203
3:13	207, 227
3:14-21	205, 207
3:18	37
3:19	202, 203, 205
4	204, 205
4:1	205, 207, 337
4:1-14	206
4:1-32	207
4:3	236
4:4-5	202
4:4-6	205
4:6	205
4:7	205
4:8-10	205
4:9-10	205
4:10	203, 205
4:11	205
4:12	203
4:12-13	193
4:12-16	205
4:13	203
4:15	205, 206
4:15-16	203, 205, 206
4:20	207
5-6	205
5:2	204
5:25	204
6	204
6:10-20	203
6:13-14	203

Philippians

1:3-11	190
1:12	337
1:12-18	337
2:6-11	331
2:9-11	189
2:14	184
3:4-5	161
3:4-6	167
3:6	167, 169
3:12	173
3:12-14	21

Colossians

1:1	169
1:1-19	196
1:3-4:18	193, 194, 195, 196, 197, 198
1:3-5a	194
1:5	191
1:5-7	193
1:6	194
1:7	187, 194
1:9-14	194
1:13	194
1:15	195, 201
1:15-20	192, 193, 195, 197, 198, 201, 327, 331
1:16	196
1:18	192, 196, 197, 198, 201
1:20	195
1:21-22	195, 198
1:23	193, 194, 198
1:24	194, 197
1:24-27	206
1:25	198
1:25-26	195, 198
1:25-29	194
1:27	195, 198
1:28	194
1:29-2:1	194
2:1	194
2:8	193
2:9	196
2:10	196
2:14-15	198
2:15	193, 196
2:16	192, 193
2:16-23	193
2:18	193
2:19	192, 197
2:20-23	192
3:9-11	189
4:3	194
4:7-17	192
4:10	212
4:18	192, 194

1 Thessalonians

1:1	298
1:5	189
1:7-8	333
1:9	186
1:10	186
2:19	184
3:5	190
3:8	190
3:12-13	190
4:3	173
5:9	173
5:23-24	190

2 Thessalonians

1:1	298

1 Timothy

1:1	307
1:12-17	307
1:15	306
1:18-19	307
2:1-7	308
2:3-6	307
2:7	307
2:8	307
2:9-10	308
3:1-7	308
3:15	306, 307
3:16	306, 307
6:1	307

2 Timothy

1:1	307
1:8	308
1:10	307
1:11	307
1:11-12	307, 337
1:13	307
1:16	307
1:18	337
2:3-10	308
2:8	308
2:8-13	337
2:9	308
3:10-11	308
4:5	308
4:6-8	308
4:11	212
4:15	307
4:17	307
4:17-18	308

Titus

1:1	307
1:3	307

2:11	307
2:12	307

Philemon

v.24	212

Hebrews

1:1-3	309
2:1-4	309
2:9-10	309
2:14-18	309
3-4	121
3:14	121
4:5	121
4:14	121
4:16	121
5:7-9	309
7:11	309
8:13	20
10:32-34	309
11:39-40	309
12:1-2	20, 21

James

1:1	311

1 Peter

1:1	297, 298, 311
1:1-2	299
1:1-2:10	300
1:2	299
1:3	299
1:4	299
1:5	299
1:6	301
1:7	301
1:10-12	299
1:12	299
1:13	301
1:14	299
1:18	299
1:18-21	299
1:25	299
2:4-10	299
2:5	32
2:8	299
2:9	32
2:10	299
2:11	297, 300, 310, 336
2:11-12	299
2:12	300, 301, 302
2:13	300, 310, 328
2:14	300
2:15	300
2:16-17	300
2:17	310
2:18	300

2:18-25	*300*	**2 Peter**		2:4	*303*
2:20	*300*			2:6	*303*
2:21-24	*300*	2:20	*309*	2:9	*303*
3:1	*300, 301*	3:2	*309*	2:14	*303*
3:1-6	*300, 311*			2:15	*303*
3:6	*301*	**1 John**		2:20	*303*
3:9	*301*			3:9	*303*
3:13-14	*301*	2:2	*293*	3:15-17	*303*
3:15	*301*	4:9	*293*	5:13	*304*
3:18	*301, 302*	4:14	*293*	6:9	*304*
3:19	*301*			13:7	*304*
3:20	*298*	**3 John**		13:16-17	*304*
3:21	*299*			14:6	*304*
4:3	*298, 299*	3-8	*293*	14:8	*297*
4:3-4	*300*	10	*293*	14:12	*305*
4:4	*298, 299, 300*			17:2-5	*304*
4:6	*301*	**Jude**		17:5	*297*
4:7	*301*			17:18	*297*
4:11	*301, 302*	4	*309*	18:1-3	*304*
4:13	*301*			18:2	*297*
4:17	*299, 301*	**Revelation**		18:3	*304*
4:19	*300*			18:11-19	*304*
5:1	*298*	1:3	*302*	20	*325*
5:8-9	*300*	1:4-3:22	*302*	20:4	*304*
5:10	*301*	1:5	*304*	21:1	*304*
5:12	*298*	1:7	*304*	21:1-8	*304*
5:13	*212, 297, 298*				

Index of Authors

Achtemeier, P., 231, 232, 278
Albrektson, B., 32
Allen, R., 190
Alt, A., 138
Anderson, A., 114, 137
Anderson, B., 52
Anderson, G., 348
Balch, D., 311
Baltzer, D., 35
Banks, R., 189
Barr, J., 32, 33
Barth, C., 53
Barth, M., 199, 208, 209, 210, 254
Barton, J., 81
Beker, J., 189
Bergman, J., 107
Best, E., 231
Betz, H., 168, 188, 189
Birch, B., 348
Boer, M., 209, 311
Boff, L., 150, 160
Bonnard, P., 138
Borgen, P., 295
Bornkamm, G., 148, 159
Boys, M., 347
Braude, W., 158
Bright, J., 35, 159
Brown, R., 278, 281, 291, 294, 295, 296
Brown, S., 277, 278
Brueggemann, W., 24, 33, 34, 35, 52, 56, 86, 107, 108, 348
Bultmann, R., 188, 295
Bussmann, C., 164, 186, 187, 188, 189, 190, 209
Cahill, J., 283, 295
Caird, G., 205, 208, 209
Campbell, E., 54
Carlston, C., 231
Carroll, R., 52-53
Cazelles, H., 137
Childs, B., 34, 110, 137
Clines, D., 109
Coats, G., 34, 81
Comblin, J., 294, 295
Conzelmann, H., 156, 160, 277, 311
Cope, L., 254
Craigie, P., 40, 41, 53
Crenshaw, J., 108

Cross, F., 33, 53
Crossan, D., 232
Dahood, M., 138
Dalton, W., 311
Daly, R., 138
Danker, F., 277
Davies, W., 167, 188, 189
Delitzsh, F., 137
DeVries, S., 80
Dibelius, M., 232, 311
Didier, M., 254
Dietrich, W., 52
Dillon, R., 277, 278
Dion, P., 84, 91, 107, 108
Dobelstein, R., 188
Donahue, J., 223, 228, 231, 232
Donfried, K., 188, 254
Doty, W., 187
Dumortier, J., 34, 108
Dunn, J., 159, 189, 208
Dupont, J., 158, 277, 278, 279
Durken, D., 277
Eichrodt, W., 79
Eigo, F., 108, 295
Eisman, M., 54
Elliott, J., 210, 310
Evans, C., 160
Fiorenza, E., 158, 311
Fitzmyer, J., 165, 188, 189, 254
Flaherty, D., 348
Foerster, W., 29, 35
Forestell, J., 295
Fornberg, T., 312
Fortna, R., 295
Franklin, E., 278
Freedman, D. N., 33
Freyne, S., 160, 208, 277
Frick, F., 54, 56
Friedrich, J., 189
Fuller, R., 159
Furnish, V., 159
Gelin, A., 133, 138
Georgi, D., 190
Gils, F., 160
Goppelt, L., 310
Gordis, R., 35
Gottwald, N., 44, 53, 54, 56
Goulder, M., 160

363

Gowan, D., 35
Greenberg, M., 53
Haas, O., 190
Haenchen, E., 279
Hahn, F., 143, 158, 160, 179, 180, 189, 191,
  207, 208, 209, 221, 222, 231, 269, 277, 278,
  293, 294, 296, 311
Hamerton-Kelly, R., 160
Hamlin, E., 107, 109
Hanson, P., 35, 52, 108
Hare, D., 254
Harnack, A., 143
Harrington, D., 210, 229, 253, 254
Harvey, A., 285, 295
Harvey, J., 81
Held, H., 254
Hengel, M., 159, 160, 188, 208
Hill, D., 160, 327
Hillers, D., 35
Hillman, E., 54
Hock, R., 190
Holladay, W., 77, 81, 82
Hollenberg, D., 108, 109
Holmgren, F., 54, 190
Hölscher, G., 75, 81
Hubbard, B., 254
Huber, F., 53
Hultgren, A., 159
Jacquet, L., 138
James, F., 81
Japhet, S., 35
Jeremias, J., 143, 158, 159, 160, 278
Jervell, J., 278
Johnson, L., 208
Karris, R., 54, 159, 277, 278, 311
Käsemann, E., 188, 209
Kasper, W., 145, 158, 159, 160
Kazmierski, C., 230
Keck, L., 163, 171, 172, 175, 176, 188, 189
Kee, H., 229, 348
Keel, O., 137
Kelber, W., 218, 219, 220, 231, 232
Kellermann, D., 52
Kiddle, M., 231
Kingsbury, J., 229, 238, 254
Kirwen, M., 54
Klein, G., 158, 253
Knierim, R., 73, 81
Kraus, H., 138
Krodel, G., 311
Kuhl, J., 294
Kümmell, W., 187, 208, 311
Küng, H., 348
Kysar, R., 249, 296
Lacomara, A., 295
Lambrecht, J., 253, 254, 311
LaVerdiere, E., 277, 278
Lehamann, K., 160
Lelièvre, A., 122, 138
Lipinski, E., 138

Lohse, E., 160, 208
Long, B., 81
Luther, M., 170
McCarter, P., 53
McCullough, W., 35
McPolin, J., 292, 294, 296
MacRae, G., 282, 295
Maillot, A., 122, 138
Martin, R., 208, 230, 278
Martyn, J., 295
Matczak, S., 108
Matthey, J., 254
Mays, J., 229, 277
Meeks, W., 43, 44, 53, 296
Meier, J., 253, 254, 347
Mendenhall, G., 44, 45, 54, 56, 93, 95-96, 97,
  108
Merklein, H., 208
Meye, R., 230
Meyer, R., 199, 201, 204, 206, 209
Meyers, E., 230
Milgrom, J., 125, 138
Miranda, J., 295, 296
Moloney, F., 295
Montague, G., 277
Mowinckel, S., 124, 138
Mulder, M., 17, 34
Neusner, J., 295
Nickle, K., 190
Noth, M., 81
O'Collins, G., 347
Ollrog, W., 188
Osiek, C., 54
Pawlikowski, J., 348
Perdue, L., 35
Perkins, P., 296
Perrin, N., 158, 159, 231, 232
Pesch, R., 160, 215, 216, 230, 232
Petersen, N., 230
Piper, J., 159
Pöhlmann, W., 189
Pregeant, R., 248, 249, 254
Rad, G. von, 11, 32
Radermakers, J., 294
Rasmussen, L., 348
Rendtorff, R., 61, 80
Reumann, J., 52
Ringgren, H., 54, 107
Roberts, J., 12
Robertson, D., 33
Rosenbloom, J., 32
Rubenstein, R., 189
Sanders, E., 165, 170, 171, 175, 176, 188, 189,
  208
Sandmel, S., 32, 84, 107
Scanlin, H., 80
Schillebeeckx, E., 150, 159, 160, 348
Schnackenburg, R., 204, 209
Schneider, H., 295
Schoeps, H., 188, 190

Schottroff, L., 159
Schweizer, E., 196, 198, 208
Seebass, H., 86, 94, 107, 108, 159
Senior, D., 108, 109, 159, 229, 253, 254, 295, 348
Seux, J., 107
Shafer, B., 108
Sloyan, G., 160, 254
Sobrino, J., 158
Staff, F., 159
Stagg, E., 159
Stanley, D., 190
Steinmann, J., 75, 82
Stendahl, K., 167, 168, 170, 188, 189
Stock, K., 231
Stone, M., 35
Strange, J., 230
Stransky, T., 348
Stuhlmacher, P., 189
Stuhlmueller, C., 32, 53, 54, 81, 82, 108, 109, 137, 138, 159
Sweet, J., 311
Swetnam, J., 35
Talbert, C., 229, 277

Tetlow, E., 159
Thompson, T., 13, 33, 53
Thompson, W., 254, 277
Tiede, D., 277, 278
Trilling, W., 254
Tyson, J., 231
Urbach, E., 35
Van Canghe, J., 218, 230
Vanni, U., 311
Vaux, R. de, 19, 33, 54
Vawter, B., 10, 17, 32, 33, 34, 81
Vermes, G., 311
Vogels, W., 108
Weeden, T., 229, 231
Westermann, C., 52, 124, 138
Whitelam, K., 54
Wijngaards, J., 33
Wilcoxen, J., 33
Wilson, R., 53, 59, 61, 63-64, 80, 81
Wilson, W., 160
Wolff, H., 33, 52, 64, 81, 108
Yeivin, S., 54
Yoder, J., 278
Zehnle, R., 277

Index of Subjects

Aaron, 22
Abel, 41, 84
Abba (Aramaic), 146, 159, 213
Abimelech, 49, 59
Abraham, 15, 17, 18, 39, 41, 46, 59, 79, 83, 95, 106, 134, 179, 239, 244, 248, 262, 347
Abram, 84
acculturation, 36, 44, 46, 49, 50, 51-52, 54, 65, 83, 85, 107, 114, 118, 122, 124, 125, 135, 141, 222, 283, 288, 316, 324, 330, 342
Achor, Valley of, 63, 65, 81
action, 247-50, 252, 300, 302, 309, 336
Adam, 29, 63, 84, 262
adultery, 66, 67, 68
Ahab, 42
Ahaz, King, 70, 71
Alexander, 217, 323
Alexandria, 31
aliens, 89, 90-96, 98, 101, 103, 106-9, 129, 133-35, 137, 141, 142, 144, 152, 154, 156, 157, 163, 166-68, 170-72, 175, 177-80, 184-85, 194-95, 204, 213, 218-24, 237, 240, 244-49, 252, 254, 260-65, 269, 273, 281, 293, 298, 316, 317, 320, 332
Amalekites, 53
Amarna Tablets, 45, 54
Amaziah, 34, 62
Amenophis III, 45
Amenophis IV (Akhenaten), 45
Amorites, 52
Amos, 29, 34, 42, 55, 57, 58, 61, 62, 64, 69, 91, 101, 108, 137, 321, 341
'anah (Hebrew), 132
Anakephalaio (Greek), 199, 200
Ananias, 274
Anath (female deity of Canaan), 68
anger, 9
'anîthanî (Hebrew) [afflicted soul, my], 132
'anawim (Hebrew) [poor, afflicted, outcasts], 133, 136, 153, 258
Anna, 261, 268
'ânniyyathî (Hebrew) [heard/answered], 132
Antioch, 271, 333
anti-Semitism, 245, 246
aphesis (Greek) [forgiveness], 263
'apiru, 23, 34, 39, 45, 49, 57, 79, 89, 101
apocalupsai (Greek) [revelation], 168

Apocalyptic literature, 42, 92, 150, 302
apostate, 103
apostleship, 266
Apollos, 276, 333
Aquila, 275, 333
Ark of the Covenant, 18, 20, 21, 46, 49, 73, 86, 122, 123, 135, 137
Arpachshad, 11
asceticism, 43
Asia Minor, 183, 185, 194, 211, 271, 297, 298, 302
Assyria, 31, 66, 70, 71, 76, 77, 78, 87, 323
Athens, 54
atonement, 125, 126-29, 130, 136, 337
Augustus, 260, 324
authenticity. *See* sincerity
authority, 48, 251, 252, 257, 285
Azazel, 118, 137
Baal, 17-18, 68, 114, 116, 117
Baal-berith, 17
Babylon, 30, 31, 62, 77, 85, 92, 101, 102, 103, 297, 323, 330
bahar (Hebrew) [election], 94, 95, 96, 102, 106, 107, 108, 318
Balaam, 59
banquet, 153, 264, 265, 273, 274
baptism, 262, 263, 268, 297, 298, 299, 324
Barabbas, 245
Barak, 60
Barnabas, 265, 271, 275, 276, 335
basileus (Greek) ["rule," "reign"], 145
Bathsheba, 246
Beersheba, 17
benê yiśra'el (Hebrew), 9
Betharbel, 63
Bethel, 17, 34, 35, 60, 63, 108, 118, 123, 124, 137
beth-mamlaka (Hebrew) [royal palace], 35
bishops, 308
bosheth (Hebrew) [shame], 17
bread, 285, 288
Caesarea, 192, 194, 215, 236
Cain, 84, 95
call, 168, 216, 243, 299, 305
Canaan, 17, 19, 23, 39, 44-46, 51, 57, 62, 64, 68, 79, 80, 89, 90, 97, 106, 112, 119, 120, 134, 135

Canaanites, 52, 64, 68, 89, 93, 113, 116, 117, 118, 240
Canaanite woman. *See* Syro-Phoenician woman
Canticle of Deborah. *See* Song of Deborah
capital punishment, 41
Catholic Church. *See* Roman Catholic Church
celibacy, 43
centurion, 142, 154, 222, 225, 227, 239, 244, 248, 261, 265, 331
charity, 148, 157, 242, 248, 249, 264, 282, 286, 288, 289, 299, 303, 332, 336
children, 64
Christian life, 161, 336
Christians, Gentile, 234, 271, 281
Christians, Jewish, 234, 270, 273, 281
Christology, 192, 195-97, 201, 207, 208, 216, 224-26, 235, 238, 240-41, 247, 252, 253, 281, 282-86, 289, 292-94, 304-5, 319, 328
church. *See* ecclesiology
circumcision, 273
city, 46, 49, 54, 56, 58, 135
clergy. *See* Levites; priesthood
Colossae, 193
communication, 214, 332, 333
community, 93, 97, 113, 128, 157, 163, 192, 201-3, 205, 224, 238, 242, 252, 253, 255-60, 262, 264, 267, 273, 276, 283, 285-90, 292, 298, 299, 301, 305, 209, 325, 336
community, Johannine, 281, 282, 283, 286, 287, 291, 293
compassion, 147, 156, 242, 250, 252, 257, 273, 320, 330, 336
conversion, 146, 186, 249, 251, 252, 257, 258, 263, 264, 272, 273, 278, 299, 300, 318, 331, 338, 340
Corinth, 333
Cornelius, 219, 259, 261, 269, 270, 272-75, 278, 324, 331, 332, 342
covenant, 25, 64, 67, 68, 79, 86, 87, 97-99, 101, 107, 108, 130, 134, 144, 207, 241, 242, 299, 317; of Abraham, 101, 106; of David, 70, 98, 101; of Moses, 20, 23, 29, 62, 68, 79, 80, 84, 86, 89, 96, 101, 112, 114, 134; of Noah, 101, 106
creation, 36, 100, 113, 114, 195, 196, 284, 305, 326, 327, 328, 329
cross, 44, 216, 218, 226, 227
crucifixion, 160, 195, 216
Cyrus, King, 83, 101, 102, 103, 106, 316, 323
da'at 'elohim (Hebrew) [knowledge of God], 62
Damascus, 169
Dan, 137
Daniel, 334
David, 16, 18, 22, 23, 28, 29, 31, 34, 35, 45, 60, 71, 72, 77, 79, 88-90, 93, 95, 89, 106, 134, 135, 323, 341
David, House of, 71, 72, 75, 79, 87, 88, 98, 100, 113, 124

death, 112, 124, 125, 145, 150, 156, 284, 304
Deborah, 60, 114
desert, 115
Deuteronomic Tradition (D), 33, 56, 59, 60, 61
Diaspora. *See* Jews—Diaspora
discipleship, 216, 222, 224, 226, 227, 231, 254, 264, 266, 277, 289, 292
divorce, 67
Domitian, 302
East Africa, 343
ecclesiology, 163, 164, 191, 197-207, 214, 216, 238, 252, 255, 256, 341
Egypt, 12, 14, 15, 18, 27, 30, 31 39, 44-46, 56, 57, 62, 64-66, 80, 84-86, 90, 93, 97, 101, 112-14, 120, 134, 135, 316, 317, 321, 323
Ehud, 22, 34
eklegomai (Greek) [choose], 96
EL, 17
El-berith, 17
elders, 59, 60
Elijah, 42, 60, 137, 214, 261
Elisha, 42, 53, 60, 63, 137, 261
Elizabeth, 261, 268
Elohist Tradition (E), 33, 56, 59, 60, 61
Emmaus, 256, 267
Epaphras, 187, 193, 194
Epiphanes, 324, 329
Epiphanus, 333
episkopos (Greek), [overseer], 341
'ereb rab (Hebrew) [mixed multitude], 33, 57
'eretz (Hebrew) [earth], 101, 109
Esau, 95
eschatology, 143, 325, 340
Essenes, 30, 141, 153, 233, 281
Esther, 197
ethics, 79
Ethiopia, 98, 270, 330
Ethiopian eunuch, 272, 275, 324
Ethnos (Greek) [nation], 252
Eucharist. *See* Lord's Supper
Exile, the, 92, 93, 100, 106, 129, 134, 217, 323
Exodus, the, 11-15, 28, 31, 46, 51, 63, 65, 66, 99, 102, 108, 114, 120, 122, 134, 137, 316, 323; New, 102, 103, 106
exorcism, 149, 150, 155, 156, 213
Exousia (Greek) [power], 213
Ezekiel, 27, 28, 29, 41, 62, 101, 125, 316
Ezra, 28, 29, 35, 92, 316, 317, 341
faith, 15, 23, 33, 37, 69, 70, 72, 75, 80, 91, 96, 104, 123-24, 129, 132-34, 137, 154, 156, 176, 179-80, 194, 203, 218, 221, 222, 226, 238, 242, 244, 246-48, 252, 256, 260, 264-66, 283, 285, 289, 293, 298, 330, 336, 343
fear, 65, 301
foreigners. *See* aliens
forgiveness, 148, 149, 160, 213, 242, 244, 257, 258, 260, 262-64, 267, 269, 271, 272
fornication, 176
freedom. *See* liberty
friendship, 147

Gabriel, Archangel, 261
Galilee, 215-19, 221, 227, 230, 231, 236, 241, 244, 251, 260, 265, 286
Galilee, Sea of, 218
Gentiles, *See* aliens
ger (Hebrew), 39, 52
Gerasa, 220
Gerasene demoniac, 219, 220, 222
gibbor (Hebrew), 41
Gibeah, 63
Gideon, 22, 49, 72
Gihon, 76, 121
Gilead, 63
Gilgal, 64, 137
glory, 301, 302, 331
go'el (Hebrew), 49, 50, 54, 102
Goliath, 95, 106
Gomer, 63, 65, 66, 67, 68
good and evil, 88, 116, 117, 137, 150, 156, 303, 305
good deeds. *See* action
gôyim (Hebrew), 89, 318
grace (theology), 146
Greece, 31, 183, 185, 194, 211, 271
grief, 41
gûr (Hebrew). *See ger*
Hagar, 89
Ham, 10, 84
Hammurabi, 85
hapeṣ (Hebrew) [to take delight], 111
ha'sapsus (Hebrew), 33, 57, 59
Hasmoneans, 29, 30
healing, 149, 263, 274, 323
Hebron, 17
Hellenism, 164, 198, 281
herem (Hebrew), 10, 41, 53, 89, 96, 98, 106, 108
heresy, 293
Herod, the Great, 30, 241, 244, 248
Herodians, 222
Hexateuch, 29
Hezekiah, King, 71, 96, 124
historiography, 12
history, 155-57, 177, 178, 182, 220, 239, 248, 254-56, 302, 323, 324, 329, 330, 332, 340
Hittites, 52, 89
holiness, 75, 299
home, 64
honesty. *See* sincerity
hope, 22, 31, 37, 68, 75, 109, 117, 130, 144, 145, 150, 156, 198, 241, 298, 300, 301, 305, 328, 343
horao (Greek) [to see, to appear], 168
Hosea, 27, 62, 64-69, 79, 81, 87, 100, 106, 137
hospitality, 293, 294
hypotasso (Greek) [submit], 310
idolatry, 64, 96, 166, 186, 302, 303, 305, 345
Illyricum, 183, 184, 194
Immanuel, 75, 76, 77, 79, 80, 82
immortality, 113, 298

indigenization, 39, 44, 47, 49, 51-52, 316, 317, 343
infidelity. *See* idolatry
integrity. *See* sincerity
intuition, 110, 111, 135
Isaac, 95
Isaiah, 29, 41, 42, 58, 60, 61, 69, 70-81, 92, 123, 124, 166, 183, 278, 317, 335, 341
Isaiah, Second, 16, 18, 27, 28, 29, 37, 40, 50, 94, 98, 100-112, 126, 129, 130, 134, 135, 216, 318, 330, 337
Isaiah, Third, 92
'ishî (Hebrew), 68
Ishmael, 95
Jacob, 29, 56, 63, 72, 73, 95, 101, 137
Jairus' daughter, 219
Jamnia, 233
Japan, 343
Japheth, 10, 84
Jehoiakim, King, 24
Jehoshaphat, Valley of, 92
Jehu, King, 42, 53, 63
Jeremiah, 24, 27, 29, 41, 43, 48, 53, 55, 58, 61, 62, 89, 91, 100, 104, 106, 125, 130, 132, 134, 135, 166, 183, 330, 335, 341
Jericho, 45
Jeroboam I, 137
Jeroboam II, 63
Jerusalem, 25, 27, 29, 30, 39, 41, 48, 54, 57, 72-79, 91-93, 98-100, 120, 129, 183, 185, 194, 215-18, 221-26, 233-36, 244, 249, 256, 258, 259, 262, 264, 269, 270-76, 298, 317, 320, 330, 333; Council of, 273, 275, 278
Jethro, 47, 48
Jewish Revolt, 233, 234
Jews: in Diaspora, 27, 30, 31, 141, 164, 270, 272, 333; election of, 9, 17, 28, 29, 43, 45, 83-90, 93-110, 129, 130, 134, 136, 179, 315, 317, 318; history of, 12, 15; political and social conditions of, 47, 49, 51
Jezebel, Queen, 42
Job, 40
Joel, 92, 108, 270, 317
John, the Apostle, 270, 273, 274, 281, 285, 289, 303, 335
John the Baptist, 215, 219, 230, 231, 239, 244, 248, 253, 260, 262, 263, 268, 269, 281, 284-86, 292
John Mark, 275, 298, 299
Joppa, 270
Jordan (River), 45, 65, 89, 113, 126, 286
Jordan, Valley, 95
Joseph, 248
Joshua, 17, 21, 25, 29, 39, 40, 44, 45, 56-59, 64, 65, 77, 89, 90, 93, 95, 97, 116, 134
Josiah, King, 24, 96, 124
Jotham, King, 70
journey, 121, 215
joy, 65, 112, 117

Judah, Kingdom of, 26, 53, 62, 70, 77, 78, 90, 92
Judas, Apostle, 227, 241, 251
Judas Aristobulus I, King, 88
Judea, 30, 215, 243, 265, 269, 270, 272, 285
Judges, 21, 39, 44, 60, 97
Judgment, 152, 153, 154, 249, 325
justice, 154, 255, 304, 309, 320
justification, 192
Kadesh, 115, 117
Kadesh-Barneh, 137
kairos (Greek) [time], 143, 145, 150, 157, 170, 177, 228, 239, 251, 301, 340
kephale (Greek) [head], 200
Keturah, 89
Kidron Valley, 119, 120
Kingdom of God, 90, 93, 117, 118, 144-46, 149, 150-56, 214, 219, 226, 236-37, 252-53, 263, 272, 303-5
Kingdom of Satan, 303, 304, 305
Kings, 60, 108, 341
knowledge, 186, 200, 205, 206
laity, 31, 69, 72, 79
Last Supper, 156
Law, Scroll of the. *See* Torah Scrolls
Lazarus, 265
leadership, 47, 48, 58, 258, 306, 308, 337, 341, 342, 344
Levi, 33
Levi, tax-collector, 264
Levirate, 50, 54
Levites, 57, 95, 113, 120, 125
liberation theology, 255, 330
liberty, 14, 44-46, 56, 120, 150, 255, 263 64, 268-69, 328, 339
liturgy and ritual, 13, 15, 20, 28, 31, 41-42, 47, 65, 73, 79, 108, 111, 113, 117-20, 123-25, 134, 318, 330
Lord's Prayer, 148, 149, 160
Lord's Supper, 164, 266
Lot, 84
loyalty, 147
Luke, Evangelist, 255, 298
Maccabees, 29, 88
Macedonia, 276
Magi, 244, 324, 328, 331
Maher-Shalal-hash-baz, 75, 78
Manasseh, King, 71
Manoah, 72
Mark, Evangelist, 212, 235
marriage, 43, 59, 63, 64, 79, 164, 300
Mary, Blessed Virgin, 246, 261, 266, 269
Mary, Magdalene, 253, 265
Massah, 120
Matthias, 274
Medes, 77
Melchizedek, 17
mercenary troops, 45, 49
mercy, 147, 248, 252, 264, 326
Mercy Seat. *See* Ark of the Covenant

Meribah, 120
Mesopotamia, 12, 27, 45, 85, 93, 135
Messiah, 173, 177, 226, 238, 241, 246, 248, 261, 268, 281, 328
metanoia. *See* conversion
Micah, 29, 58, 69, 92
Micaiah, 60, 72, 73
Middle Kingdom, 85
Miriam, 15
missionaries, 100, 136, 178, 242, 251, 254, 277, 293, 294, 307, 333, 339; lay, 69, 79
Mizpah, 137
Moabite, 90
morality. *See* ethics
Moriah, 41
Moses, 9, 12, 14, 15, 17-26, 28, 29, 31, 34, 44-49, 56-58, 60, 64, 65, 72, 73, 79, 84, 93, 97, 101, 106, 116-18, 126, 134, 284, 334, 341
"mystery," 195, 199, 206
mysticism, 110
mythology, Canaanite, 63-68, 79, 115, 118, 121-24
Nabi (Hebrew), 61, 62, 80
Naboth, 42
Nahor, 84
Namaan, the Syrian, 261
Nathan, 46, 57
nations. *See* aliens
Nazareth, 219, 260, 261, 263, 268, 273
Nazarites, 57, 58
Nebuchadnezzar, King of Babylon, 62
Nehemiah, 132, 316, 341
Nicanor, 41
Nicodemus, 286, 289
Nicolaitan Party, 303
Nineveh, 265, 330
obedience, 74, 97, 152, 247, 248, 249, 259, 299
Oracles against the Nations, 91
ophthe (Greek) [appear to], 166
pacificism, 43
pain, 43, 44, 145, 150, 258, 263, 308
Palestine, 109, 163, 268, 281, 319
ta panta (Greek) [the all], 205, 206
pantapasin (Greek) [wholly], 202
Papias, 212
Papua New Guinea, 343
"Paraclete." *See* Spirit
Parousia, 237
pas (Greek) [all], 202
Pastoral Letters, 305-8
pastoral theology, 255
patriarchs, 17, 18, 40, 56, 90, 93, 134
Paul, 18, 30, 107, 153, 156, 161, 165-68, 170, 182, 206, 207, 216, 258-60, 265, 269, 270-77, 286, 288, 299, 303-7, 319, 323, 325, 328-42, 347
peace, 65, 92, 102, 116, 123, 145, 156, 305
Pentateuch, 84
Pentecost, 258, 259, 264, 268, 274, 275
persecution, 251, 257, 298, 305

perseverance, 300, 301, 309
Peter, Apostle, 212, 215, 227, 236, 242, 258, 259, 267, 269-81, 288, 298, 299, 326, 333, 335, 341, 342
Pharisees, 30, 141, 142, 153, 213, 220, 222, 233, 234, 244, 248, 253, 264, 281, 282, 289, 331
Philip, Apostle, 270, 272, 274
Philistia, 330
Philistines, 49, 98
Philo, 141
phobos (Greek) [fear], 310
Phoebe, 333
Pilate, 218, 245, 324
pleroma (Greek) [full], 202, 208
pluralism, 344
politics and religion. *See* religion and politics
polygamy, 49-50, 54
polytheism, 111, 116, 135
power, 43, 45, 46
praise, 111, 112, 113, 118, 119, 122
prayer, 43, 59, 110, 111, 121, 124, 134, 152, 213, 250, 318
preaching, 164, 181-82, 184-87, 198, 206, 208, 217, 258, 263, 275, 288, 299, 306, 308, 309, 333-35, 338
presbyteros (Greek), 47
priest, chief, 289
priesthood, 28, 47, 54, 60, 95, 134, 309
Priestly Tradition (P), 33
Priscilla, 275, 333
Promised Land, the, 11, 14, 85, 87, 89, 120, 126, 129
prophecies, 56-62, 75
prophetic challenge, 85, 95, 100, 111, 118, 149, 155, 156, 211, 325
prophets, 25, 29, 47, 55, 56, 58-62, 69, 79, 80, 91, 108, 134, 147, 257, 258, 262, 321, 334, 335, 343
proselytes, 9, 30, 31, 32, 35, 83-86, 141, 142, 158, 163, 179, 186
"Q" Source, 235, 250, 255
Quirinus, 260
rabbis, 31, 35
Rahab, 246, 330
Ramah, 49, 60, 63
reconciliation, 146, 148, 149, 155, 157, 181, 198, 204, 207, 242, 252, 253, 336
Rehoboam, King, 24
rejection, 243, 244, 246, 257
religion and politics, 69, 71, 72, 79, 90, 111, 113, 122, 125, 145
Remaliah, 76
repentance, 251, 256, 257, 262, 263, 271, 272
retribution, 154
Rezin, 76
Roman Catholic Church, 40, 344
Romans, 30, 154, 158, 217, 324, 347
Rome, 31, 54, 84, 185, 192, 194, 212, 271, 276, 297, 298, 304, 333
Russia, 14

Ruth, 246
Sabbath, 148
sacrifice, 30, 111, 125, 223, 308
Sadducees, 30, 141, 233, 244, 248, 253
sages, 35
salvation, 36, 44, 106, 130, 163, 171, 173-76, 179, 180, 182, 185, 186, 195, 199, 205, 221, 235-37, 240, 247, 249, 258, 262, 265, 268, 272, 273, 275, 276, 285, 299, 301, 304, 305, 307, 308, 323, 327, 328, 338
salvation history, 13, 36-37, 44, 114, 120, 168, 182, 184, 220, 221, 222-24, 235, 238, 239, 243-47, 250-53, 265, 271, 299, 344
Samaria, 29, 63, 76, 91, 108, 258, 260, 269-72
Samaritans, 29, 147, 154, 261, 281
Samaritan woman, 289, 324
Samson, 22
Samuel, 21, 42, 49, 56, 60, 95, 132
Sanhedrin, 276
Sapphira, 274
Sarai (Sarah), 41, 59, 134, 137
Satan, 149, 150, 156, 237, 253, 263, 267, 290, 304, 328
Saul, King, 22, 45, 53, 60, 63, 72
Scribes, 31, 213, 220, 222, 244, 248, 264
Scroll of the Law. *See* Torah Scrolls
Sefer Torah. *See* Torah Scrools
Sennacherib, 74
Septuagint, 117
Servant, Suffering. *See* Songs of Suffering Servant
service, 286, 289
Seth, 84, 95
Seventy, the, 266
sexual ethics, 50
shalah (Hebrew) [sent], 76
Shearjashub, 69, 75, 78
Shechem, 17, 49, 118
Shelah, 11
Sheleph, 11
Shem, 84, 95
Shiloah, 76, 77
Shiloh, 21, 57, 95, 123, 124
shosu, 57, 101
Sidon, 153, 244, 265
Silvanus (Silas), 298, 299, 333
Simeon, 33, 260, 261, 269, 278
Simon, the Pharisee, 264, 265, 267
Simon, the Tanner, 279
sin, 66, 67, 68, 112, 124, 125, 126, 137, 170, 172, 263, 304
Sinai, 14, 18, 23, 44, 46, 47, 62, 63, 65-84, 89, 113-15, 120
sincerity, 154
slavery, 45, 89, 300, 308, 317, 321
social justice, 55, 70, 74, 79
Sodom and Gomorrah, 74, 153, 244
Solomon, King, 20, 22-25, 28, 36, 45, 47, 76, 77, 89, 90, 93, 134, 135, 138
Solomon, Wisdom of, and pagan philosophy, 93

Song of Deborah, 15, 114
Song of Moses, 15, 114
Songs of the Suffering Servant, 102, 103, 104, 107, 110, 126, 132, 318
Soviet Union, 12, 14
Spain, 183, 184
Spirit, the, 178, 251, 257-59, 262, 267-78, 285-92, 319, 320, 323, 328, 332, 335
spirituality, 108, 114, 118
Stephen, 234, 258, 274
stoning, 41
story, 32, 214
suffering, 43, 109, 112, 124, 125, 130, 132, 145, 150, 194, 207, 258, 266, 274, 298, 300, 307, 337, 340
Sukkoth, 117
Syria, 45, 70, 76, 99, 135, 194, 211, 218, 233
Syro-Phoenician woman (Mk. 7:24-30), 142, 154, 219, 220, 221, 222, 240, 248, 324
tabernacle, 18
Tabernacles, Feast of. *See* Sukkoth
Table of Nations, 10, 11, 100
Talmud (Babylonian), 39
Tamar, 89, 246
Teacher, 341
teaching, 248, 250, 251, 252, 308, 323, 334
Temple of God, 28-30, 46, 47, 49, 51, 56, 58, 70, 72, 73, 80, 86, 98, 100, 101, 113, 116-24, 213, 223-25, 233, 236, 238, 253, 260, 309
Terah, 33
testimony, 285, 288, 301, 302
theologians, 143
theology, 87, 88, 90, 94
Theophilas, 255
Thessalonians, 333
Tiberius, 260
Torah Scrolls, 10, 15, 36, 47, 96, 114, 118, 178, 179, 192, 240

tradition, 214
Transformation. *See* conversion
Transjordan, 286
truth, 285, 292
Twelve, the, 264, 266, 267, 269, 271, 274, 276, 289, 341
Tyre, 90, 98, 153, 244, 265, 330
Ugaritic literature, 114, 137
understanding, 247, 254
United States, 343
Uzziah, King, 70, 72, 264
Vatican II, Council of, 40
violence, 39, 40-43, 51, 77, 98
vocation, 166, 299
Vulgate, 41
war and religion, 40, 41-42, 117, 123, 124
water, 120, 286
way, 285, 292
wisdom, 30, 196, 284, 320, 326, 328, 331
witness, 275, 276, 300-303, 305, 337, 338
wives, Christian, 300, 337
woman and hemorrhage, 219, 263
women, 59, 146, 159, 213, 217, 220, 227, 228, 230, 231, 261, 267, 275, 308, 311
"Word of God" (Logos), 283, 284, 334
world, 290, 291, 292
worship, 58, 64, 73, 97, 106, 108, 110, 111, 114, 117, 122, 134, 135, 149
worth, 23, 40, 51, 63, 98, 347
Yahwist Tradition (J), 33, 59
Yom Kippur, 118
Zacchaeus, 264
Zadokites, 29, 31
Zaqen, 47
Zarephath's widow, 261
Zealots, 30, 233
Zechariah, 63, 261, 262, 268, 269
Zion, 31, 143-144, 152, 153, 171, 177, 317, 325
Zeus, 197